Georgia

WITHDRAWN

the Bradt Travel Guide

Tim Burford

edition
5

www.bradtguides.com

Bradt Travel Guides Ltd, UK
The Globe Pequot Press Inc, USA

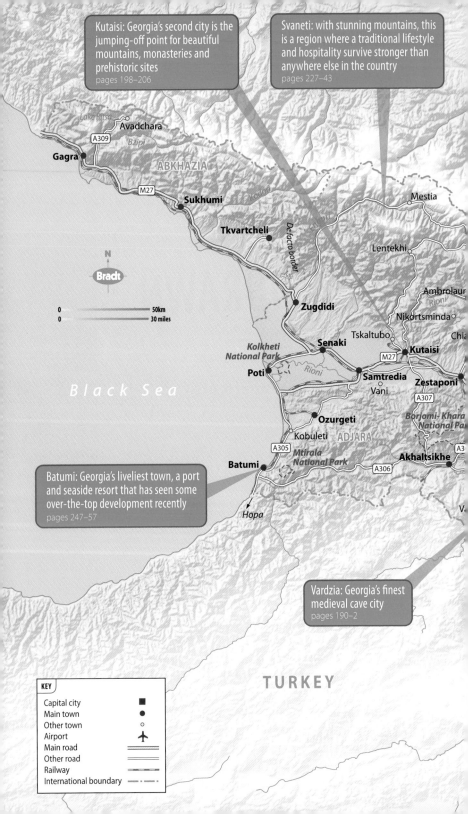

Kutaisi: Georgia's second city is the jumping-off point for beautiful mountains, monasteries and prehistoric sites
pages 198–206

Svaneti: with stunning mountains, this is a region where a traditional lifestyle and hospitality survive stronger than anywhere else in the country
pages 227–43

Lake Ritsa
Avadchara
Gagra
A309
Bzipi
ABKHAZIA
M27
Sukhumi
Tkvartcheli
Kodori
Mestia
De facto border
Lentekhi
N
Bradt
Ambrolaur
Rioni
Zugdidi
Nikortsminda
0   50km
0   30 miles
Kolkheti National Park
Senaki
Tskaltubo
Chia
Kutaisi
Poti
Rioni
M27
B l a c k   S e a
Samtredia
Zestaponi
Vani
A307
Borjomi- Khara National Pa
Ozurgeti
A3
Kobuleti
ADJARA
A305
Mtirala National Park
Akhaltsikhe
Batumi
A306

Batumi: Georgia's liveliest town, a port and seaside resort that has seen some over-the-top development recently
pages 247–57

Hopa

Vardzia: Georgia's finest medieval cave city
pages 190–2

T U R K E Y

KEY
Capital city   ■
Main town   ●
Other town   ○
Airport   ✈
Main road
Other road
Railway
International boundary

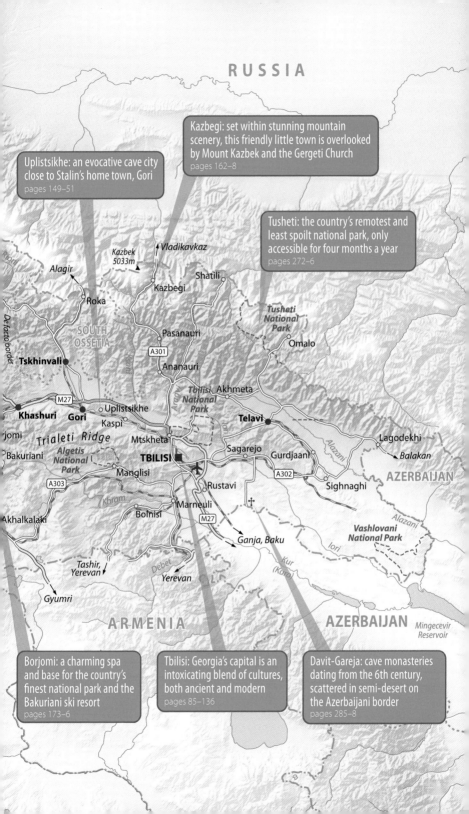

RUSSIA

Kazbegi: set within stunning mountain scenery, this friendly little town is overlooked by Mount Kazbek and the Gergeti Church
pages 162–8

Uplistsikhe: an evocative cave city close to Stalin's home town, Gori
pages 149–51

Tusheti: the country's remotest and least spoilt national park, only accessible for four months a year
pages 272–6

Kazbek 5033m ▲

↑ Vladikavkaz

Alagir

Shatili

Roka

Kazbegi

SOUTH OSSETIA

Tusheti National Park

Pasanauri

Omalo

De facto border

Tskhinvali

A301

Ananauri

Akhmeta

Tbilisi National Park

M27

Uplistsikhe

Telavi

Lagodekhi

Khashuri

Gori

Kaspi

Mtskheta

Sagarejo

Gurdjaani

↑ Balakan

jomi

Trialeti Ridge

Algetis National Park

TBILISI

Rustavi

A302

Sighnaghi

AZERBAIJAN

Bakuriani

Manglisi

Alazani

A303

Marneuli

M27

Vashlovani National Park

Akhalkalaki

Khram

Bolnisi

↘ Ganja, Baku

Kur (Kura)

Iori

Alazani

Debet

↓ Yerevan

Tashir, Yerevan ↙

Gyumri ↙

ARMENIA

AZERBAIJAN

Mingecevir Reservoir

Borjomi: a charming spa and base for the country's finest national park and the Bakuriani ski resort
pages 173–6

Tbilisi: Georgia's capital is an intoxicating blend of cultures, both ancient and modern
pages 85–136

Davit-Gareja: cave monasteries dating from the 6th century, scattered in semi-desert on the Azerbaijani border
pages 285–8

Georgia
Don't
miss...

Ancient churches
The monastery of Gelati, near Kutaisi, is decorated with fantastic frescoes of saints and Georgian kings
(WC/S) pages 206–8

Svaneti villages
Hidden in the remotest reaches of the High Caucasus and dotted with ancient towers and frescoed churches, the land of the Svans is seen by many as the spiritual heartland of Georgia
(KV/DT) pages 227–43

Georgian Military Highway

The Russo-Georgian Friendship Monument, by the Georgian Military Highway, is a unique viewpoint in the heart of the High Caucasus

(MP/S) pages 155–70

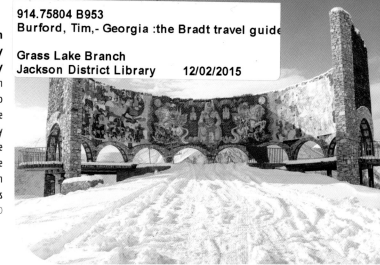

Tbilisi Old Town

Inhabited at various times by Persians, Tatars, Jews and Armenians, the heart of the Georgian capital is an intriguing array of architectural styles

(YG/S) pages 117–21

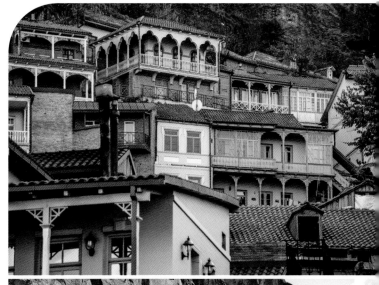

Cave cities

Once a working monastery with 3,000 chambers, Vardzia is the site of Georgia's most famous cave complex

(r/S) pages 190–2

Georgia in colour

above With its cypress trees, fine 18th- and 19th-century buildings and setting high on a ridge overlooking the Alazani Valley, Sighnaghi is reminiscent of a Tuscan hill town (LM) pages 280–4

right This fountain in Kutaisi's central square echoes the forms of ancient Colchian jewellery found at Vani (B/S) page 204

below Shenako is typical of the remote and tiny villages of Tusheti, where you'll virtually always find one or two welcoming guesthouses (MaP/S) pages 275–6

AUTHOR

Tim Burford studied languages at Oxford University. In 1991, after five years as a publisher, he began writing guidebooks for Bradt, firstly on hiking in east-central Europe and then on backpacking and ecotourism in Latin America. He has now written nine books for Bradt, as well as the Rough Guides to Romania, Alaska and Wales.

DEDICATION

For Chris and Natalie, to mark 35 years of friendship.

> Spending on feasting and wine is better than hoarding our substance; that which we give makes us richer, that which is hoarded is lost.
>
> Rustaveli

HOW TO USE THIS GUIDE

MAPS
Keys and symbols City maps (but not regional maps) include alphabetical keys covering the locations of those places to stay, eat or drink that are featured in the book.

Grids and grid references Some maps use grid lines to allow easy location of sites. Map grid references are listed in square brackets after the name of the place or sight of interest in the text, with page number followed by grid number, eg: [84 C3].

LISTINGS Accommodation and restaurants are marked with price codes and listed alphabetically in descending price code order (**$$$$$–$**); in the Tbilisi and Batumi sections they are also divided geographically.

HISTORIC SITES Prices and opening hours are included where they apply. Otherwise assume the site is free and always open.

PUBLISHER'S FOREWORD · *Hilary Bradt*

It's always a pleasure to welcome a new edition of one of Tim Burford's guides, and *Georgia* has been one of his stalwarts. I remember a meeting at the Frankfurt Book Fair a few years ago with an Englishman who runs a bookshop in, of all places, Tbilisi. His bookshop is called Prospero's Books, and he was quite misty-eyed with praise for Tim's guide. This is what I love about publishing guides to unusual destinations. When they hit the spot they dispel a bit of magic in all directions!

Fifth edition published October 2015
First published in 1998

Bradt Travel Guides Ltd, IDC House, The Vale, Chalfont St Peter, Bucks SL9 9RZ, England. www.bradtguides.com
Published in the USA by The Globe Pequot Press Inc, PO Box 480, Guilford, Connecticut 06437-0480

Text copyright © 2015 Tim Burford
Maps copyright © 2015 Bradt Travel Guides Ltd
Illustrations copyright © 2015 Individual photographers (see below)
Project manager: Laura Pidgley
Cover research: Pepi Bluck, Perfect Picture

ISBN: 978 1 84162 556 0 (print)
e-ISBN: 978 1 78477 134 8 (e-pub)
e-ISBN: 978 1 78477 234 5 (mobi)

British Library Cataloguing in Publication Data
A catalogue record for this book is available from the British Library

Photographs Adam Balogh (AB); Alamy: Aldo Castellani (AC/A), Ivan Vdovin (IV/A); AWL images: Ivan Vdovin (IV/AWL); Dreamstime: Actrisavesna (A/DT), Ilia Torlin (IT/DT), Joye Ardyn Durham (JAD/DT), Karolina Vyskociloya (KV/DT), Lukas Blazek (L/DT), Speculator27 (S/DT); Kote Gabrichidze (KG); Laurence Mitchell (LM); Shutterstock: Andrew Fletcher (AF/S), Baciu (B/S), Erni (E/S), Milosz_M (M/S), Magdalena Paluchowska (MaP/S), Michal Piec (MP/S), My Good Images (MGI/S), Prometheus72 (P/S), roibu (r/S), Roxana Bashyrova (RB/S), salajean (s/S), Sobol Igor (SI/S), thomas koch (tk/S), Vahan Abrahamyan (VA/S), Wiktor Bubniak (WB/S), Wojtek Chmielewski (WC/S), Yurcha (Y/S), Yulia Grigoryeva (YG/S); Tim Burford (TB)
Front cover Gelati Monastery (IV/A)
Back cover Mount Kazbek (s/S); local man outside Mtskheta Monastery (AB)
Title page Narikala Citadel MaP/S); white-winged redstart (L/DT); Adjaran dancers in Batumi (tk/S)

Maps David McCutcheon FBCart.S and Liezel Bohdanowicz; colour map base by Nick Rowland FRGS; regional maps based on ITMB Publishing Ltd (*www.itmb.com*), 2015; some town plan maps include data © OpenStreetMaps contributors (under Open Database License)

Typeset by Ian Spick, Bradt Travel Guides Ltd
Production managed by Jellyfish Print Solutions; printed in India
Digital conversion by www.dataworks.co.in

Acknowledgements

Thanks to: Dr Jonathan Aves, Rowan Stewart, Neil Taylor, Ed Manning, Eilidh Kennedy, Arthur Gerfers, Mark Elliott, Koba and Leila, Gela and Cristina, Ana Anganashvili, Vano Vashakmadze, Remaz Rekhiashvili, Mary Ellen Chatwin, Manana Kochladze, Aleko Motsonelidze, David Tarkhinishvili and Jesse Tsinadze in Tbilisi; Tamuna and Nugzar Kvaratskhedia in Kutaisi; Natia Khordiani in Mestia; Alek and Sophiko in Zugdidi; Ramaz Georgadze in Batumi; and above all to Boris and Tsira Arhdabevsky.

Further thanks for their assistance on the second edition to: Peter Nasmyth, Amy Spurling, Hugo Greenhalgh, Eleanor O'Hanlon, Rebecca Weaver and Andrew Barnard, Polly and Susan Amos, Maka Dvalishvili, Besik Lortkipanidze, Lars Nejsig and the Javakhishvili family, Raffi Kojian and Dave Mitchell.

Also Ben and Suki – I'm still waiting to get my Truso map back!

Thanks on the third edition to: Amy Spurling, Boris and Tsira, Laurie Dalton, Till Bruckner, Ed Raupp, Erekle Tavartkiladze, Natia Muladze, Knut Gerber, Ramaz Gokhelashvili, Rati Jabaridze, John Graham, Inga Gotsiridze, Molly Corso, Rob Ainsley and Ian Colvin.

For help with the fourth edition, Laurence Mitchell would like to thank Nino Ratiani, Giorgi Giorgadze, Eto Jajanidze, Dodo Kevlishvili, Meri Maxatelashvili, Martha Bakhtiari and Bob Thompson in Georgia; Nick Rowlands for comments on the last edition and Tim Burford for copious compiled notes.

Thanks for help on the fifth edition to Tony and Lali Hanmer, Roza and Vitaly Shukvani and Koka Chartolani (and Paata and Rusu) in Svaneti; Ia Tabagari, Giorgi Nebieridze, Mark Richmond, Rauf, Erekle, Eka Tchvritidze and as ever Boris and Tsira Arhdabevsky in Tbilisi; Ana Uturgaidze (Rooms, Kazbegi); Giorgi Giorgadze (Kutaisi); Gulnasi and Sophie (Batumi); Artur Stepanian (Borjomi); Inga Gotsiridze-Furley (Bakuriani); Gaga Mumladze (Borjomi-Kharagauli National Park); Nazy Dakishvili and Gurjeet Batth (Pankisi); Dima Bit-Suleiman (Kisiskhevi); Dato Luashvili (Telavi) and Nato and John Wurdemann and all at Pheasant's Tears (Sighnaghi); and Laura Pidgley and all at Bradt.

FEEDBACK REQUEST AND UPDATES WEBSITE

At Bradt Travel Guides we're aware that guidebooks start to go out of date on the day they're published – and that you, our readers, are out there in the field doing research of your own. You'll find out before us when a fine new family-run hotel opens or a favourite restaurant changes hands and goes downhill. So why not write and tell us about your experiences? Contact us on ☏ 01753 893444 or e info@bradtguides.com. We will forward emails to the author who may post updates on the Bradt website at www.bradtupdates.com/georgia. Alternatively you can add a review of the book to www.bradtguides.com or Amazon.

Contents

LIST OF MAPS

Introduction

Despite recent improvements, many things in Georgia are still run-down, yet it's one of the most heart-warming and exciting of all European destinations. This is above all due to its people, who are some of the most hospitable and generous you could meet anywhere. In addition you'll see fantastic scenery, including Europe's highest mountains, and lovely ancient churches and cave-cities.

This does in part raise the question of whether Georgia is in Europe, Asia, the Middle East, or some other region; travellers can easily spend half their trip debating this issue. If the Caucasus is the dividing line between Europe and Asia, it's unclear which side is European and which is Asian. Armenia and Russia have international phone codes in the European 003 series, yet they are separated by Georgia and Azerbaijan, which have chosen codes in the Asian 009 series. Despite this, since 2007 Georgia has competed in the Eurovision Song Contest (apart from 2009 when they withdrew as a protest against it being held in Moscow). Certainly, the Georgians seem to spend a lot of time squatting on their haunches in an Asian way waiting for the good times to come around, yet civil society (non-governmental organisations, pressure groups, a fair judicial system and so on) is stronger here than in the neighbouring countries.

To illustrate the joys and perils of travel in Georgia, here's an account of a cycle trip in 1995 when the country was still raw and newly independent:

> In a month we managed to cover 1,000km on our bikes; however, we could probably have completed it in half the time but for the Georgians taking Rustaveli to heart and insisting that we share their food with them all the time. There was the man walking by the side of the road who gave us the loaf of bread that he was carrying. There were the policemen who constantly stopped us and, when we expected to have to show our documentation, merely wished to give us a watermelon or figs. Old women would give us apples or walnuts, people driving past in cars would pass out bubble gum while on the move, the list goes on. We were constantly surprised and humbled by the generosity of everyone from the countryside to the cities. We were invited into many people's homes, by cow herders in the mountains, peasants in villages and sophisticates in towns. In every household the inevitable bottle was brought out and the toasting began … needless to say, on some days our cycling was seriously curtailed after such meetings.
>
> Ella Truscott

Twenty years on, Georgia is a little better known to the outside world and foreign visitors are not quite the rarity they once were. Nevertheless, any brave souls attempting to cycle across the country independently can still expect a royal welcome and some serious 'hospitality'. Don't be in too much of a hurry!

Part One

GENERAL INFORMATION

1

Background Information

GEOGRAPHY

With an area of 69,700km² (26,911 square miles), Georgia is slightly smaller than Austria or the Republic of Ireland, and under half the size of the American state of Georgia. More than half this area lies above 900m and almost 40% (2.69 million hectares) is wooded. The country's dominant feature is, of course, the High Caucasus range which forms its northern border. Although its highest peak, Elbruz (in fact Europe's highest peak at 5,642m, or 18,510ft), lies wholly within the Russian Federation, Georgia does have three peaks over 5,000m (Shkhara, 5,068m; Janga, 5,059m; and Mkinvartsveri (Kazbek), 5,033m) and ten more over 4,000m. The Caucasus is, like the Himalayas, a very young and dynamic range; it was formed just 25 million years ago, and linked about 15 million years ago to the Iranian Massif. It stretches for roughly 1,200km and contains over 2,000 glaciers, covering an area of 1,780km². The High Caucasus falls into three parts. The first of these is the Western Caucasus, stretching 440km from the Black Sea to Elbruz, its highest peak being Dombay (4,046m), on the border with the Russian Federation. It's composed of granite, gneiss and crystalline shales, with limestone and sandstone ridges parallel to the north and west, and is very beautiful with canyons and dense vegetation. The 100km west of Elbruz are higher and more alpine, with glaciers. The Central Caucasus covers the 180km from Elbruz, where the range is at its widest (180km), to Kazbek, where it's at its narrowest (60km), and includes all the peaks over 5,000m. Its western half is granite and shale, and its eastern half andesite and diabase, with a last small spot of granite near Kazbek. Elbruz and Kazbek are very ancient volcanoes, while the peaks between, such as Uzhba, Tetnuldi, Shkhara and Dykhtau, are younger upthrust peaks sculpted by glaciers, with gigantic north faces and lots of scree. Finally, the Eastern Caucasus, from Kazbek to the Caspian Sea, is a confused mass of argillaceous slate, with outcrops of diabase, porphyrite and sandstone; its climate is far drier than to the west, with very little glaciation.

The High Caucasus forms the border with the Russian Federation, but nowhere does Georgia directly adjoin Russia itself; the Muslim peoples of the northern Caucasus, who speak at least 30 different languages, live in half a dozen autonomous republics: from west to east Karachai-Cherkesbaijan (or Circassia), Kalbardino-Balkaria, North Ossetia, Ingushetia, Chechnya and Daghestan.

From almost anywhere in the central valleys you'll be able to see the High Caucasus as a long white wall to the north; in many places you'll also be able to see the Lesser Caucasus, to the southwest towards the Turkish border. This is a gentler, more rounded range, rising to 3,301m at Didi-Abuli; the Trialeti Ridge, covered in rich pastures and forests, stretches to the outskirts of the capital, Tbilisi. The two ranges of the Caucasus are linked by the very young Suran (or Likhi) range, which

3

forms the watershed between the Black and Caspian seas and separates eastern and western Georgia, Kartli and Kolkhida.

The country is dominated by one main river, the Mtkvari (Kura in Russian; 1,364km in total, including 435km in Georgia), which rises in Turkey, enters Georgia near Vardzia, then flows east through Kartli and Tbilisi and then through Azerbaijan to the Caspian Sea. The main river of western Georgia is the Rioni (327km), which flows from the foothills of Racha through Kutaisi to the Black Sea; others are the Enguri (213km), which flows from Svaneti to the Black Sea, the Iori (320km) and Alazani (351km, the longest wholly within Georgia), which flow through Kakheti and into the Mtkvari, and the headwaters of the Terek (623km in all), which flows north into Russia and eventually into the Caspian Sea.

The main centres of industry and population lie along an east–west axis, from Rustavi through Tbilisi, Gori, Zestaponi, Kutaisi, Samtredia and Senaki to Poti; the only other major cities are two Black Sea ports, Batumi, near the Turkish border, and Sukhumi, in the secessionist republic of Abkhazia.

Georgia has over 2,000 mineral springs producing 130 million litres a day, most of which are wasted. There are over 500 different waters (both hot and cold), of which most contain carbon dioxide, such as those from Borjomi, Sairme and Nabeghlavi; there are also sulphide, nitric and silicon waters (mostly hot), such as those from Tskaltubo, Tbilisi, Nunisi, Tkvartcheli and Makhinjauri, and Gagra, Sukhumi and Aspindza in Abkhazia.

At least 15% of Georgia is limestone, so it's not surprising that there are plenty of fine caves; few of them are set up properly for visitors, but there are great opportunities for exploring. The Gumistavi Cave, near Tskaltubo, is a particularly fine recent discovery, and the Pantiukhin Cave is claimed to be the second deepest in the world at 1,540m (5,050ft). The Tovliana Cave contains snow and ice far underground but has been badly polluted by cavers' rubbish, such as burnt carbide from their lamps. The people of the Tskaltubo area have unwittingly been polluting their own water supply by dumping garbage in caves; some have also been used for agricultural storage and even as hothouses.

GEORGIA'S REGIONS Georgia is much more regional and less centralised than the other Transcaucasian countries, and since independence there has been a marked increase in the power of the regions vis-à-vis the centre. The country includes the two autonomous republics of Abkhazia and Adjara, the formerly autonomous region of South Ossetia, and ten administrative regions (*mkhare*). From east to west these are: Kakheti, Kvemo (Lower) Kartli, Shida (Inner) Kartli (which includes the seceded region of South Ossetia), Mtskheta-Mtianeti, Samtskhe-Javakheti, Imereti, Samegrelo, Racha-Lechkhumi and Kvemo Svaneti, Zemo (Upper) Svaneti and Guria.

Kakheti is the easternmost region of Georgia, projecting into Azerbaijan; it's known almost entirely for its vine growing and winemaking. **Kvemo (Lower) Kartli** lies to the south of Tbilisi, across the routes to Armenia; it's largely inhabited by people of Azerbaijani origin who produce much of the food sold in the markets of Tbilisi. Although there are secessionist tendencies and in 1992–95 there was some sabotage of pipelines and railways, both the Georgian and Azerbaijani governments are keen to keep things calm. Further west, around Lake Tsalka, is a population of Greeks raising livestock and growing potatoes.

In general the people of Kvemo Kartli are reformist, wanting to be allowed to make money, while the Kakhetians are conservative, with plenty of old-style communists who want to be left alone with their wine.

Shida (Inner) Kartli is the heartland of eastern Georgia; with a population of 343,000 it produces 5–10% of Georgia's industrial output as well as most of its fruit. It now theoretically includes the autonomous region of **South Ossetia** (also known as Samachablo, with a population of about 51,000), which has now seceded.

Mtskheta-Mtianeti, to the north of Tbilisi, straddles the Georgian Military Highway, the main route to Russia; it's an agricultural area with vegetables grown in the lower region and sheep raised in the high mountains. Industry is growing in Mtskheta and Dusheti, and Georgia's main ski resort is at Gudauri.

Samtskhe-Javakheti covers the bleak, empty volcanic tablelands of the southwest of Georgia; 90% of the population is Armenian and in many ways the area is largely autonomous. Few speak Georgian and they are not conscripted into the Georgian army; however, the Russian army base near Akhalkalaki (which closed in 2006) took recruits for the Russian army. Javakheti, near the present border of Armenia and Turkey, was settled by Armenians in the 19th century, after the Russian conquest of the area; here and in **Meskheti**, to the west, there was also a heavily Islamised population of largely Georgian stock, the so-called Meskhetian Turks, who were deported to Central Asia in 1944 and have still not been permitted to return. There's little industry, apart from some low-grade coal and Swiss and French investment in sugar plants. There are now road crossings to Turkey at Vale and Çıldır, and a 98km extension of the railway from Akhalkalaki to Kars in Turkey will open soon (page 60), which will link Azerbaijan and Turkey, and thus Kazakhstan and China with Europe, moving freight faster than the Trans-Siberian.

Georgia's second city is Kutaisi, capital of **Imereti**; 10–25% of Georgian industrial production is based here, although this share is declining – it's largely dependent on the Chiatura mine (which used to produce a quarter of the Soviet Union's manganese) and the connected ferro-alloys plant at Zestaponi.

Samegrelo (or Mingrelia), in the northwest of Georgia, has historically had a considerable degree of autonomy, partly because the Mingrelian dialect is almost unintelligible to the people of Tbilisi. Politically the area is still strongly associated with Zviadism and opposition to the central government. The regional capital, Zugdidi, is now overloaded with refugees but benefits from illicit trade with Abkhazia. The subtropical climate makes tea and citrus fruits important crops, while traditionally Zugdidi has produced porcelain and Senaki carpets. Exports of tea have crashed since the end of the Soviet Union and many plantations are now being replanted with hazel trees.

To the north of Kutaisi, **Racha-Lechkhumi and Kvemo Svaneti** lie in the foothills of the Caucasus; the only roads here are minor and circuitous because of the hills. Winters are harsh, with much of the population decamping to the city, but nevertheless Racha manages to produce both tea and wine. The chief towns of Racha are Ambrolauri and Oni, both little more than villages. Lentekhi, capital of Kvemo Svaneti, is even smaller. Kvemo (Lower) Svaneti was historically part of the feudal system of western Georgia, while **Zemo (Upper) Svaneti** was always self-governing and has developed a far stronger cultural identity. With its stunning Caucasian landscape, its defensive towers, its haunting music and its superb and ancient icons, Zemo Svaneti is the area to which all the more enterprising tourists to Georgia are drawn like moths to the flame.

Guria, a small swampy region on the coast south of Poti, is known for its subtropical crops, stunningly complex polyphonic songs and the humour of its people. People usually come here *en route* to **Adjara**, which dominates Georgia's trade both across the Turkish border and through the port of Batumi. With this trade, subtropical agriculture, beach tourism and some copper and gold mining, Adjara is a prosperous republic.

Finally, the autonomous republic of **Abkhazia**, in the extreme northwest of Georgia, has effectively seceded (pages 30–2), making it difficult for foreign visitors to visit. In the past this was perhaps the most sought-after holiday area of the entire Soviet Union and Russian holidaymakers are starting to return in large numbers, entering by means of the western border near Sochi. Its exports are citrus fruits, hazelnuts and timber, so there is some tax revenue, and arrangements have been made to share the power produced by the Enguri hydro-electric station between Georgia and Abkhazia; but it'll be a long time before normality returns.

CLIMATE

There's quite a wide range of climates in Georgia, from the warm, humid, subtropical Black Sea Coast, via the colder, wet, alpine climate of the High Caucasus, to the arid steppes of the east.

Temperatures in the mountains range from an average –4.6°C in February to 16.4°C in July and August, with an annual average of 5.7°C. In Svaneti the winter lasts for up to eight months, with an average temperature of –15°C; it gets even colder on the high bare plateaux of Javakheti where temperatures drop to –30°C. On the coast of Adjara, temperatures range from 5.8°C in January to 23.8°C in August, with an annual average of 14.5°C; on the Abkhaz coast temperatures are slightly lower in winter, noticeably warmer in April and May, but virtually the same in high summer. In eastern Georgia temperatures range from 0.5°C in January to 23°C in August, with an annual average of 11.8°C, and in the south they range from –2.1°C in January to 20.1°C in August, with an average of 9.1°C.

The weather in the Caucasus is more stable than in the Alps. In June there may still be too much snow for high hikes; July and August have the best weather, but even then it can drop to –10°C at 3,000–3,500m. Lower altitudes can often be hot and humid at this time of year, and the inhabitants of Tbilisi and Kutaisi flee to the coast or the mountains.

Precipitation ranges from 2,800mm in Abkhazia and Adjara to 300–600mm in the east (with 462mm in Tbilisi), and about 1,800mm at the main Caucasian passes. There's an average of 1,350–2,520 hours of sunshine per year (4–7 hours per day) in Tbilisi.

CLIMATE IN TBILISI

Month	Temperature				Humidity %		Rain
	max °C	ave °C	min °C	max/min °F	max	min	mm
January	7	0.9	–1	44/30	79	60	17
February	9	2.6	0	48/32	75	53	15
March	13	6.6	3	55/37	69	50	27
April	17	11.9	8	62/46	66	49	61
May	24	17.3	12	75/53	61	47	75
June	28	21.1	16	82/60	57	42	54
July	31	24.4	19	87/66	57	40	46
August	30	24.2	19	86/66	60	42	46
September	26	19.6	15	78/59	66	49	45
October	20	13.8	10	68/50	71	53	30
November	14	7.6	5	57/41	78	60	27
December	9	2.8	1	48/33	80	65	19

Climate change is affecting Georgia, with temperatures rising, glaciers shrinking and snowfall decreasing. More extreme weather in the last decade has resulted in flooding, landslides, forest fires and coastal erosion. Rainfall has become far more irregular, with droughts and heavy downpours; in spring 2005 heavy rain, warm temperatures and the consequent sudden snowmelt caused flooding across much of Georgia, with landslides and mudflows in many mountain areas. In 2014 there was a wet spring and autumn, but a very hot and dry summer.

In the last couple of decades, the winter snowline has risen from 1,300–1,500m to 1,800–2,000m, and over the last century glacial volume in the Caucasus has declined by 50%. Georgia's glaciers are currently retreating by between 5m and 25m a year, and it's possible that hardly any glaciers will remain by the end of this century, with reduced water supply affecting both agriculture and hydro-electric generation in the longer term.

NATURAL HISTORY AND CONSERVATION

Despite its small size, Georgia is ecologically very interesting. Located between the forests of northern Eurasia and the tropical deserts of Iraq and Iran, and incorporating Europe's highest mountains and a subtropical coastline, it has Europe's highest level of biodiversity and is a route for many migratory bird species. It is characterised by its complex interaction of west Asian, east European and purely local communities. There's a wide variety of plant communities, with examples of almost all the main habitat types found in Europe and some of those in Asia; many are highly valuable in terms of biodiversity, including subalpine coniferous forests, meadows, wetlands, peat bogs and lakes; coniferous and beech forests; oak woodlands; caves and mountain gorges; unique Colchic forests with evergreen undergrowth; Mediterranean and sub-Mediterranean communities; steppe grasslands; arid light woodlands; and riparian shrub and forest vegetation along rivers such as the Alazani and Mtkvari.

Forest covers 2.7 million hectares (36.7% of Georgia's area), of which only 59,500ha is artificially planted; around 6% of the natural forest is virgin, and 40% has avoided serious human impact.

Overall, Georgia can be split into two main biogeographical regions: firstly the Colchic and Caucasian districts, forest landscapes with plenty of autochthonous animals and plants, and others related to middle and eastern European species; and secondly the uplands of the Lesser Caucasus and the Mtkvari district, with species related in some places to Anatolia and the Middle East, and in others to the arid and semi-arid Turanian region, beyond the Caspian. Between these two main regions are mixed zones, notably the Borjomi Gorge and the Trialeti Ridge, as well as the southern slopes of the High Caucasus in eastern Georgia.

The **Colchic (or Euxine) district** covers most of western Georgia, between the Black Sea, the Meskhetian Mountains, the Surami Ridge and the High Caucasus; the climate is mild and humid, rarely freezing and with a metre or more of precipitation each year, and the characteristic landscape is subtropical forest with well-developed evergreen underwood consisting of many Tertiary relicts (such as *Laurocerasus officinalis*, *Ilex aquifolium* and *Rhododendron ponticum*).

The **Caucasus district** lies to the north at 2,000m and higher, with a severe climate and over a metre of precipitation per year. It harbours some of the most diverse and distinctive temperate coniferous and deciduous forests in Eurasia, ranging with altitude from subalpine beechwoods (half of the country's forested area), dark coniferous forests and crook-stem woods to subalpine, alpine and subnival plant communities and, above these, bare nival (ie: dominated by snow) landscapes. Its borders are fluid, with many Colchic elements in the west, and Turanian elements in the east; on the northern slopes there are many eastern European and boreal species.

The plateaux of the **Lesser Caucasus** are largely treeless grassland, either subalpine meadows or mountain steppes, as well as forest and semi-arid steppes. There's a severe continental climate, with annual precipitation between just 400mm and 800mm. The **Mtkvari district** covers much of Kartli and Kakheti, and is largely arid and semi-arid steppe, with xerophytic Turanian (or Armeno-Iranian) species predominating, and forested only along the banks of the Mtkvari. There's a warm continental climate, rarely dropping below −5°C, with under 400mm of precipitation per year.

The 'mixed' zones, at the borders of these main zones, are the most biologically fascinating regions of Georgia. There are three main mixed zones: firstly the northern slopes of the **Trialeti Ridge**, from the northwestern side of Tbilisi to the Borjomi Gorge, mostly dry deciduous mountain forests with a temperate climate and 400–800mm of precipitation per year – the fauna and flora are mostly Caucasian, with some Turanian and Colchic elements, and no great diversity; secondly the **forests of eastern Georgia**, which are relatively similar to the Trialeti forests, but with more Turanian elements – the climate is subtropical/mild, with 400–600mm of precipitation; and thirdly the smallest but most interesting is the **Borjomi Gorge**, which has a well-balanced range of elements from all over Georgia (although Turanian elements are scarce) with a mild temperate climate and 800–1,200mm of precipitation per year. The gorge marks the divide between the humid west and the arid east, and between Mediterranean and Turanian fauna.

Endemic species comprise about 9% of Georgia's flora, a surprisingly high proportion for so small a country, with another 5% endemic to the Caucasus. The highest proportion (for instance 87% of western Georgian scree flora) is in certain mountain areas which were turned into islands when the seas rose around 15 million years ago, in the Miocene epoch; the surrounding areas have since dried out and gone their own way biologically, while the humid subtropical forests of the mountains have survived largely unchanged, and many species there now have their closest relatives in Anatolia and Europe. Indeed, the only relative of the Caucasian parsley frog (*Pelodytes caucasicus*) is *P. punctatus* in France and northern Spain, while the nearest relative of the Caucasian salamander (*Mertensiella caucasica*) and *M. luschani* (in Greece and southwest Turkey) is the gold-striped salamander (*Chioglossa lusitanica*) in Portugal and northwestern Spain.

FLORA Georgia boasts around 4,200 species of **vascular plants** (including 153 trees and 11 lianas), of which 380 are endemic to Georgia and about 600 to the Caucasus; and between 8,400 and 10,000 cryptogamous or spore-bearing plants (including between 7,000 and 21,000 fungi, 2,600 algae and seaweeds, 675 mosses, 738 lichen and 74 ferns). Ten species are extinct, notably the chickpea (*Cicer arietinum*), the Georgian elm (*Ulmus georgica*), the Transcaucasian poplar (*Populus transcaucasica*) and the Eldari pine (*Pinus eldarica*), which now exists only in Azerbaijan. Fifty species are in a critical state, including the royal fern (*Osmunda regalis*), the Mingrelian birch (*Betula megrelica*), the Colchic water chestnut (*Trapa colchica*) and the Caucasian yam (*Dioscorea caucasica*). Around 300 species are now rare, including the Pitsunda pine (*Pinus pithyusa*), the Saguramo camomile (*Anthemis saguramica*) and a type of brassica called *Pseudovesicaria digitata*; about 140 are seriously reduced, including the joint-pine (*Ephedra distachya*), a red-berried undershrub (*Pachyphragma macrophyllum*) and the Mediterranean caper

(*Capparis spinosa*). Others of interest include: *Campanula mirabilis*, found only in one gorge in Abkhazia; *Iris iberica*, only in the southeast of Georgia; *Hypericum thethrobicum*, only in Javakheti; *Senecio rhombifolius*, a Caucasian endemic found throughout Georgia; *Solidago turfosa*, in peat bogs; *Epigaea gaultherioides*, in the Colchic forests; *Heracleum sommieri*, in subalpine megaphorbias; *Rhododendron caucasicum*, in alpine habitats; and *Delphinium caucasicum*, in subnival habitats. Around 2,000 vascular species are of economic value (for timber, fruits, dyes, oils, fodder and medicinal properties) and at least 150 fungi are edible.

Lowland Colchic forests are dominated by oak (*Quercus pedunciflora, Q. hartwissiana, Q. imeretina*), chestnut (*Castanea sativa*) and lime (*Tilia sp*), while higher regions are covered by beech (*Fagus orientalis*), fir (*Abies nordmanniana*) and spruce (*Picea orientalis*), with an evergreen understorey. At subalpine levels there are crook-stem and dwarf forests of birch (*Betula litwinowii, B. raddeana, B. medwedewii, B. megrelica*) and oak (*Q. pontica*). Other trees and shrubs found in the Colchic district include hornbeam (*Carpinus caucasica*), pine (*Pinus kochiana, P. pithyusa*), juniper (*Juniperus foetidissima, J. polycarpus*), pistachio (or turpentine; *Pistacia mutica*), Colchic boxwood (*Buxus colchica*), cherry-laurel (*Laurocerasus officinalis*), holly (*Ilex colchica*), bladder-nut (*Staphylea colchica*), Colchic hazel (*Corylus colchica*), rhododendron (*Rhododendron ponticum, R. luteum, R. caucasicum, R. ungernii, R. smirnovi*), rowan (mountain ash; *Sorbus subfusca*), wing-nut (*Pterocarya pterocarpa*), Caucasian wing-nut (*P. fraxinifolia*), small-leaved elm (*Zelkova carpinifolia*) and the extremely rare strawberry tree (*Arbutus andrachne*).

The High Caucasus is also rich in endemics; on the southern slopes at lower to mid altitude there's thick deciduous forest, which on the southwestern slopes is described as 'temperate rainforest' (although it falls far short of Chilean or British Columbian standards). Then between 1,250m and about 2,300m there's mixed deciduous–coniferous forest of birch, dwarf rowan and rhododendron (the lilac-flowered *R. ponticum* below and the bright yellow *R. luteum* at the forest limit), with spectacular flowers in clearings and on the forest edges, such as the yellow Turk's cap lily (*Lilium monadelphum*), purple bellflower (*Campanula latifolia*), columbine (*Aquilegia olympica*), fragrant orchid (*Gymnadenia conopsea*), butterfly orchid (*Platanthera chlorantha*) and marsh orchid (*Dachylorhiza* spp). Around Mestia you'll also find red helleborine (*Cephalanthera rubra*), tall pink campion (*Silene* sp), large yellow loosestrife (*Lysimachia punctata*), henbane (*Hyoscyamus niger, Datura* sp), endemic giant hogweed (*Heracleum sommieri*), hollyhocks (*Alcea* sp), as well as white foxgloves, yellow cinquefoil, and wild strawberries and gooseberries.

Above the treeline (between 1,800m and 2,400m) are subalpine meadows that are very lush to the west: herbaceous plants include masterwort (*Astrantia* sp), maroon lousewort (*Pedicularis* sp), bistort (*Polygonum bistorta*), lilies, columbine, delphinium, ranunculus, bellflowers, orchids, campion, vetch, scabious, pansies and cornflowers. Above these you'll see the white-flowered *Rhododendron caucasicum* and alpine meadows (up to 3,000m), home to perennials, many in rosettes or cushions. These include spring gentians (*Gentiana verna pontica*), Pyrenean gentian (*G. septemfida, G. oschtenica*), purple oxlip (*Primula elatior meyeri, P. algida, P. auriculata* and *P. bayerni*), pink cinquefoil (*Potentilla oweriana*) and yellow cinquefoil (*P. ruprechtii*); sandwort (*Arenaria* sp), chickweed (*Cerastium undulatifolium*), fleabane (*Erigeron* sp) and dwarf forget-me-not (*Myosotis* sp), Snowdon lily (*Lloydia serotina*), rock-jasmine (*Androsace villosa* and *A. albana*), whitlow grass (*Draba bryoides*) and wild pansies (*Viola caucasica, Pulsatilla aurea*), fumitory (*Corydalis conorhiza, C. alpestris*), fritillaries (*Fritillaria latifolia*), the white *Anemone impexe* and yellow *A. speciosa*, prophet flower (*Arnebia pulchra*, *Trollius ranunculus*), and finally, saxifrages, bellflowers and buttercups.

Many **native plants** have suffered from an increase in trade: in 1994, 515,000 bulbs of the snowdrop (*Galanthus ikeriae*), a species listed in Appendix II of the Convention on Trade in Endangered Species of Wild Fauna and Flora (CITES), were illegally collected in Georgia and subsequently exported by Turkish traders to Western Europe. Other species have also been affected by this illicit trade, including wild cyclamen (*Cyclamen* spp) and snowflakes (*Leucojum* spp).

FAUNA There are 105–110 species of mammals (the most in any European country), over 350 species of birds (253 nesting), about 52 reptiles and 13 amphibians, around 160 fish and thousands of invertebrates (including 290 molluscs, 150 homoptera and eight lepidoptera). Nearly a quarter of the mammals, reptiles and amphibians are endemic to the Caucasus. Twenty-one species of mammals, 33 birds, and ten reptiles and amphibians are listed as rare, threatened or endangered; these include the goitered or Persian gazelle (*Gazella subgutturosa*), which probably became extinct in Georgia in the 1960s, although it is still found in Azerbaijan. The striped hyena (*Hyaena hyaena*) and Caucasian leopard (*Panthera pardus ciscaucasia*) were thought to have met the same fate, but it now appears that a few remain in the arid steppes of southeastern Georgia. Two species are listed as critically endangered: the Kazbegi birch mouse (*Sicista kazbegica*) and the Mediterranean monk seal (*Monachus monachus*). Large mammals such as red deer, bear, wolf, boar, lynx, golden jackal, ibex, chamois, wild goats and wild sheep (mouflon) are found almost exclusively in the High Caucasus. However, populations of many species have been halved in recent years, largely due to increased poaching; wildlife has fled from conflicts in the northern Caucasus (notably Chechnya) and from the south in Azerbaijan, then been shot in Georgia (partly by hunters from Russia).

Mammals There are four species of wild goat: the west Caucasian tur (*Capra caucasica*), the east Caucasian tur or Daghestanian goat (*C. cylindricornis*), bezoar or pasang (*C. aegragus*) and chamois (*Rupicapra rupicapra*), and all are suffering from being hunted. The bezoar has been in decline since the 19th century, and there's now a maximum of 100 on the northeastern slopes of the High Caucasus. The Daghestanian goat, endemic to the eastern Caucasus, is endangered, with its population falling from about 5,000 in 1985 to a current estimate of around 1,000; the west Caucasian tur, endemic to the western Caucasus, is listed as vulnerable, but its population has also been halved from around 5,000 in 1985, with perhaps 1,000 in Svaneti. The chamois is endangered, its population having fallen from around 6,000 in 1985 to perhaps 2,000 today; however, there are many more in the Carpathians and Alps.

The red deer (*Cervus elaphus maral*) is also endangered by the increase in hunting; in eastern Georgia numbers fell from 2,500 in 1985 to 880 in 1994, and there were an estimated total of 500 in the whole of Georgia (only in the Borjomi-Kharagauli, Lagodekhi and Tusheti parks) in 2014. Likewise lynx (*Felis lynx orientalis*) numbers have fallen from over 500 in 1990 to just 100 today. The Eurasian or common wolf (*Canis lupus lupus*) is also endangered, and the bear (*Ursus arctos syriacus*) is vulnerable, its numbers having fallen from over 3,000 in the 1980s to under 500. In fact the main hazard for hikers in the mountains is the nahgaaz or Caucasian sheepdog, used to guard sheep; this supposedly gentle giant (in medieval times visiting ambassadors would nervously ask for the lion next to the throne to be removed) is seen as a national treasure, and competitive shows (often won in the past by Aslan Abashidze! – see page 244) are very popular. Bear gall, as well as skins and horns, are smuggled into Turkey. Tougher legislation is under consideration and bounties are no longer paid for killing animals that attack flocks, while reintroduction programmes are under way for wolves and other large mammals.

Mid-sized mammals in the mountains include the badger (*Meles meles*), pine marten (*Martes martes*), stone marten (*M. foina*), marbled polecat (*Vormela peregusna*), wildcat (*Felis silvestris*), fox (*Vulpes vulpes*), hare (*Lepus europaeus*) and weasel (*Mustela nivalis*), which here fills the niche of the marmot, scavenging in campsites. Other endangered species include the jungle cat (*Felis chaus*) whose range stretches from here to Indochina, the European otter (*Lutra lutra*), the Caucasian mink (*Mustella lutreola caucasica*) and the golden jackal (*Canis aureus*). The Persian squirrel (*Sciurus anomalus*) is suffering from an invasion by the European squirrel (*S. vulgaris*).

Twelve species of small mammals are endangered or vulnerable, largely due to overgrazing or agricultural expansion; these include the red-backed vole (*Clethrionomys glareolus ponticus*), the Transcaucasian golden hamster (*Mesocricetus brandti*), the pygmy or grey hamster (*Cricetulus migratorius*), the shrew (*Sorex volnuchini*), the birch mice (*Sicista caucasica, S. kluchkorica, S. kazbegica*) and the Prometheus mole vole (*Prometheomys shaposhnikowi*), most of which have been split up into isolated groups. Many of these are endemic to the Caucasus: the Transcaucasian golden hamster; the black-chested hamster (*M. raddei*); the shrews (*Sorex volnuchini, S. raddei, S. caucasica*) and the water shrew (*Neomys schelkownikowi*); birch mice (*S. caucasica, S. kluchorica, S. kazbegica* and *S. armenica*); the Prometheus vole; the Caucasian moles (*Talpa caucasica, Terricola daghestanicus* and *T. nasarovi*); the yellow-breasted mouse (*Apodemus fulvipectus*), as well as the Black Sea field mouse (*A. ponticus*); and hybrids with the house mouse (*Mus musculus*).

Cetaceans There's been little research on the cetaceans of the Black Sea, but the harbour porpoise (*Phoecoena phoecoena*), bottlenose dolphin (*Tursiops truncatus*) and common dolphin (*Delphinus delphis*) are all present.

Reptiles There are around 52 species of reptiles in Georgia (the total keeps changing as lizards are reclassified), 25% of which are endemic to the Caucasus. The dominant lizard species is *Lacerta praticola*, while *L. rudis, L. derjugini, L. parvula, L. unisexualis, L. clarcorum, L. valentini* and *L. mixta* may or may not be separate species. Much the same applies to the *Vipera (pelias) kaznakovi* complex. Threatened species include Schneider's skink (*Eumeces schneideri*), the lidless skink (*Ablepharus pannonicus*), the leopard snake (*Elaphe situla*) – perhaps the most beautiful in Europe – and the Transcaucasian ratsnake (*E. hohenackeri*), the dwarf snake (*Eirenis collaris*), the boigine snake (*Malpolon monspesulanus*), the racerunner (*Eremias arguta*), the turtle (*Clemmys (Mauremis) caspica caspica*), the snake-eyed lizard (*Ophisops elegans*), the commonest lizard in the Anatolian steppes, the javelin sand boa (*Eryx jaculus*), the garter snake (*Natrix megalocephala*), the Caucasian viper (*Vipera kaznakovi*), the Transcaucasian long-nosed or sand viper (*V. ammodytes transcaucasiana*), the Levantine viper or *giurza* (*V. lebetina obtusa*, up to 1.8m in length) and Dinnik's viper (*V. Dinnicki*).

The population dynamics of the Caucasian salamander and rock lizards are particularly fascinating to scientists, with lots of more or less distinct species living together, some hybridising and some not. Some of the lizards also live in all-female colonies, reproducing by parthenogenesis (asexually). There's lots of interesting micro-evolutionary research to be done here, but the potential is almost unknown to foreign scientists.

Amphibians Georgia's amphibians consist of four species of Caudata: the Caucasian salamander (*Mertensiella caucasica*), the banded newt (*Triturus vittatus ophryticus*), the smooth newt (*T. vulgaris lantzi*) and the southern crested newt (*T. cristatus karelini*), and nine species of Anura – the frogs and toads (*Pelobates syriacus syriacus, Pelodytes caucasicus, Bufo viridis viridis, B. verrucosissimus, Hyla arborea shelkownikowi, H. savignyi, Rana macrocnemis, R. camerani* and *R. ridibunda*). A quarter of these are endemic to the Caucasus (*Mertensiella caucasica, Pelodytes caucasicus, Bufo verrucosissimus*, and hybrids of *Rana macrocnemis* and *Hyla arborea*). The Caucasian salamander is, in fact, found only in the Lesser Caucasus of Georgia and Turkey, not the High Caucasus. *Pelobates syriacus, Mertensiella caucasica* and probably *Hyla savignyi* are threatened, and *Pelodytes caucasicus, Bufo verrucosissimus* and *Rana macrocnemis* are in decline.

Fish A quarter of fish species are also endemic to Georgia: the ship sturgeon (*Accipenser nudiventris*) is probably extinct in Georgia, while *A. guldenstadti* and *A. sturio* are endangered. Eastern European fish have been introduced into the lakes of the Javakheti Plateau, virtually wiping out local fish species; the Crucian carp (*Carassius carassius*) is also harming newt populations.

Birds Georgia acts as a 'funnel' for birds migrating from their breeding grounds in Siberia and northern Europe to their winter homes, so it's hardly surprising that very few are endemic to the Caucasus, and even these are subspecies rather than distinct species. Twenty species are endangered: the lammergeyer or bearded vulture (*Gypaetus barbatus*), the black or cinereous vulture (*Aegypius monachus*), the griffon vulture (*Gyps fulvus*), the Egyptian vulture (*Neophron percnopterus*), the peregrine (*Falco peregrinus*), the lanner falcon (*F. biarmicus*), the short-toed eagle (*Circaetus gallicus*), the marsh harrier (*Circus aeruginosus*), the Imperial eagle (*Aquila heliaca*) and lesser-spotted eagle (*A. pomarina*) (the Georgian populations of both are under 85 pairs), the golden eagle (*A. chrysaetos*), the booted eagle (*Hieraaetus pennatus*), the Caucasian snowcock (*Tetraogallus caucasicus*), the black francolin (*Francolinus francolinus*), the grey partridge (*Perdix perdix*), the black stork (*Ciconia nigra*), the spoonbill (*Platalea leucordia*), the crane (*Grus grus*), the demoiselle crane (*Anthropoides virgo*) and the glossy ibis (*Plegadis falcinellus*), as well, probably, as some woodpeckers and passerines. Certainly the Syrian woodpecker (*Dendrocopus syriacus*) is vulnerable, as, amazingly, is the pheasant (*Phasianus colchicus*); having taken over the world it is suffering in its land of origin from loss of forest and increased hunting.

Many raptors migrate along the flyway down the Black Sea Coast; lammergeyer live year-round in the High Caucasus, but the population has dropped from 40 pairs to 20 pairs in the last 50 years. Others nest in the mountains but can often be seen hunting in the semi-desert of Davit-Gareja; other mountain species include the Caspian snowcock (*Tetraogallus caspius*) – from the Eastern Caucasus to Iran, the Caucasian snowcock (*T. caucasicus*) – more to the west, and the Caucasian black grouse (*Tetrao (Lyrurus) mlokosiewiczi*) – typically Caucasian, and probably a relict species. There's an isolated population of the alpine finch or great rosefinch (*Carpodacus rubicilla*), which otherwise lives in Central Asia; the scarlet grosbeak (*C. erythrinus*) breeds from Sweden to Japan and passes through to winter between Iran and China. An endemic subspecies of the rock partridge (*Alectoris graeca*) (which is kept as a domestic fowl in Armenia) can be seen near the snowline.

Other species found in the High Caucasus include Kruper's nuthatch (*Sitta kruperii*), the white-winged or Guldenstat's redstart (*Phoenicurus erythrogaster*),

Radde's accentor (*Prunella ocularis*), the red-fronted serin (*Serinus pusillus*), the grey-necked bunting (*Emberiza buchanani*) and rock bunting (*E. cia*), the alpine accentor (*Prunella collaris*), the redwing (*Turdus iliacus*) – only in winter – and a subspecies of jay (*Garrulus glandarius krynicki*).

In the deserts you may find the trumpeter bullfinch (*Rhodopechys sanguinea*), the rufous bush robin or tugai nightingale (*Cercotrichas galactotes*), the chukar (*Alectoris chukar*) and, in winter, great bustard (*Otis tarda*) and little bustard (*O. tetrax*).

Perhaps the most important bird habitats are the wetlands of the Black Sea Coast and the Javakheti Plateau, where you may see migratory birds such as white spoonbills (*Platalea leucorodia*), red-breasted geese (*Rufibrenta ruficollis*), red-necked grebe (*Podiceps grisigena*), white pelican (*Pelecanus onocrotalus*), Dalmatian pelican (*P. crispus*), squacco heron (*Ardeola ralloides*), great white egret (*Ardea alba*), little egret (*Egretta garzetta*), white stork (*Ciconia ciconia*), black stork (*C. nigra*), glossy ibis (*Plegadis falcinellus*), ruddy shelduck (*Tadorna ferruginea*), ferruginous duck (*Aythya nyroca*) and other ducks, herons, geese and cormorants.

CONSERVATION Royal **hunting reserves** known as *korugi* (similar to Britain's New Forest) are first mentioned in the *Law Book of Vakhtang VI* (1709). Georgia's first nature reserve in the modern sense was created in 1912 to protect the wolves of the Lagodekhi Gorge; by the end of the Soviet era there were 15 reserves, totalling 168,800ha (1,680km², or 2.4% of the country's area), in addition to forests and other protected zones, now covering a total of 4.4% of the country. The WWF (now the World Wide Fund for Nature) set up an office in 1989, and started to create a Western-style system of Protected Areas, with a hierarchy from Protected Landscapes through Nature Reserves to National Parks; in March 1996 parliament declared the law on Protected Areas, creating the first modern National Park, at Borjomi. This replaces the Soviet *zakaznik* system of totally closed reserves with a flexible system allowing sustainable use of many areas. The Kolkheti, Tusheti and Vashlovani national parks were established between 1998 and 2003. The Department of Protected Areas was created in 2004 within the Ministry of Natural Resources and became the independent Agency of Protected Areas (*www.apa.ge*) in 2008, since when the Mtirala, Javakheti, Machakhela, Algeti, Saguramo and Kazbegi national parks have been created. A National Park of Glaciers based on the Pshav-Khevsureti Protected Area is planned. There are now ten national parks spanning over a total area of 27,6723ha.

Georgia also signed the International Convention on Biodiversity in 1994 and the CITES agreement in 1996. Land privatisation began in 1992; by mid-1995, 38% of arable land (around 20% of all agricultural land) had been privatised, and in 1999 a land-registration programme made farmers the official owners of their land. Since 1996 hunters have required permits, but this has generally been ignored. In 2005, an Environmental Protection Inspectorate (or the ecological police) was set up, but initially had no budget except what was provided by international donors.

The WWF also set up an environmental education programme which involves teaching the teachers, making television programmes, and opening ecocentres for school groups.

There's an **active 'green' movement** in Georgia, which grew out of a 1989 campaign against a planned dam in Svaneti; the Georgian Greens are now affiliated with Friends of the Earth, and Zurab Zhvania, prime minister from 2003 to 2005, was first elected as a member of the Green Party. Since 1991 they have been campaigning against the truly dreadful pollution of the Black Sea and for a sustainable forestry industry; the government imposed a tax of US$46 per square metre of timber, but the International Monetary Fund (IMF) forced its withdrawal. Nuclear issues have a high profile, even though the research reactor in Mtskheta was closed in 1990, and plans for a second nuclear power station in Armenia were abandoned in 1996 after big protests. In 1997, 11 servicemen on the Red Army's former Lilo base near Tbilisi developed skin burns, which after three months (and no help from the Russians) were diagnosed as radiation burns; eventually nine radiation sources were found, including stores of depleted uranium bullets and capsules from Geiger counters. Around 300 radiation sources were found at the former nuclear missile base of Vaziani, 30km east of Tbilisi. Russia was unable or unwilling to provide any information, which led to large demonstrations at the Russian embassy in 1998. In addition, strontium fall-out from Chernobyl in Ukraine caused illness in western Georgia. The oil pipelines across Georgia have undergone surprisingly strict and detailed Environmental Impact Assessments, but there's scepticism about the standards in Azerbaijan and the Central Asian states.

Georgia inherited many **environmental problems**, largely due to Soviet industrialisation, with pollution by oil, heavy metals and fertilisers, disrupted water-catchment areas, and erosion due to uncontrolled logging and overgrazing. The numbers of sheep in the mountains are still 2.5 times optimum levels, and 30% of pastures are affected by erosion, silt from which covers spawning beds. Forests and wetlands continue to be converted to farmland, causing serious ecological damage.

What foreigners notice at once, however, is the amount of **litter** strewn around, especially along main roads; Georgians don't even notice it, but littering from cars became illegal in 2015. Nor is there any recycling at all; but a national tourism strategy to be drawn up by 2016 will have the litter problem as a top priority.

HISTORY

It can be said that the history of Georgia goes back to the dawn of time. Noah's son Thargamos settled in the land of Japhet, somewhere between the Ararat and Caucasus mountains; the Georgians claim descent from him via his great-grandson Karthlos (while the Armenians claim descent from his brother Haik), and therefore still call themselves Karthians, or Kartvelebi, and their country Sakartvelo. Protohuman remains about 1.7 million years old and human remains about 200,000 years old have been found (at Dmanisi) as well as Palaeolithic artefacts. By the 2nd millennium BC, tribes were on the verge of statehood, and Medea and her father King Aetes probably did live between the 14th and 13th centuries BC on the Black Sea Coast. Certainly the state of Colchis (Kolkhida or Egrisi) existed here by the 9th century BC, when tribute was demanded by Assyria, with Greek trading ports by the 6th century BC. The oldest (and somewhat lurid) account of Georgia is by Xenophon, who retreated from Persia at the end of the 5th century BC. In the east of the country the state of Kartli (known to the Greeks as Iveria) was created by one of Alexander the Great's generals, overthrown in 335BC by King Parnavaz I. In the 1st century BC it was an ally of Rome, ruled for a time by Mithridates IV Eupator, King of Pontus, who turned against Rome and also seized Colchis. He was finally beaten in the Third Mithridatic War (66–65BC) by Pompey, who incorporated Colchis into the Roman Empire, although few traces remain. Iveria continued as a Roman satellite state until AD298, when Rome signed a treaty with Persia, recognising the Persian-born Mirian III as king of Iveria; he founded the Chosroid dynasty which ruled for two centuries. In the 4th and 5th centuries Colchis (now known as Lazika) also came under Persian influence. In AD337 Mirian, following his wife Nana, was converted to Christianity by Nino, a slave from Cappadocia. Thus Georgia became the world's second Christian state, preceded only by Armenia. By the end of the 5th century the Chosroid king Vakhtang Gorgasali (AD442–502) ruled a feudal state which included Abkhazia, Ossetia and much of Armenia; he moved the capital of Kartli from Mtskheta to Tbilisi, and secured autocephalous (self-governing) status for the Church. However, from the mid 6th century the Persians took control again, followed by the Byzantine Empire, and then the Arabs who had conquered Georgia by the mid 7th century, leaving its kings in power as long as they acknowledged the supremacy of the caliphs: their dominance lasted until the 9th century. The Armenian family of the Bagratids (who claimed descent from David and Bathsheba via Bagrat or St Pancras) had moved to the Georgian borderlands by the late 8th century; Ashot Bagration became chamberlain to the Byzantine emperor and soon de facto ruler of Kartli and, in AD866, Adarnase IV took the title of king; their dynasty ruled until the Russians took over in the 19th century.

THE MYTH OF JASON AND THE *ARGO*

In Greek mythology, Jason was the son of Aeson, King of Iolcus, near Volos in Thessaly. After his uncle Pelias seized the throne Jason was reared by the centaur Chiron on Mount Pelion (the concept of the centaur has its origin on the steppes to the north of the Caucasus, where men were first seen riding horses). When Jason grew up, Pelias ordered him to bring him the legendary Golden Fleece from Colchis, expecting never to see him again. Jason built a ship called the *Argo*, and assembled a crew of 50, including such heroes as Hercules, Orpheus, Theseus, Castor and Pollux. After overcoming storms, monsters and seductive women, they at last reached Colchis, where the king, Aetes (son of Helios and brother of Circe and Phaethon), agreed to give Jason the fleece if he succeeded in further trials such as yoking two fire-breathing bulls to a plough and sowing the dragon's teeth of Cadmus (which sprouted as armed men). He won the love of Medea, daughter of Aetes and a sorceress who gave her name to the science of medicine; she secretly helped him win the fleece and escape from Colchis. They returned to Iolcus, supposedly sailing up the Danube and carrying the *Argo* overland to the Adriatic. Pelias was killed but his son drove Jason and Medea from the city; they took the fleece to Orchemenus in Boetia, and settled in Corinth, living there for many years. Jason abandoned Medea when he fell in love with King Creon's daughter Glauce; Medea took revenge by making a magic robe that burnt to death both father and daughter. For breaking his vow to Medea, Jason was condemned to be a wanderer until, as an old man, he at last returned to Corinth and was killed when the prow of the *Argo* fell over and crushed him.

The Jason myth dates from around 1400BC but the definitive compilation came only in the 4th century BC with the *Argonautica* of Apollonius of Rhodes, who worked out their actual route; it was a great success and Apollonius became director of the great Library of Alexandria, one of the Seven Wonders of the Ancient World.

The first voyage myth is in part a metaphor for the expansion of Greek trade, the fleece and Medea's gifts of magic oil and stone being exchanged for technology, represented by harnessing bulls and ploughing. The legend of the fleece itself arose from the use of sheep fleeces to trap particles of gold from mountain streams in the countries around the Black Sea, as witnessed by the writers Patrick Leigh Fermor in Romania and Tim Severin in Georgia.

MEDIEVAL GEORGIA Bagrat III became King of Kartli in AD975, and united east and west Georgia by 1008 (excluding Tbilisi); in 1068 the Seljuk Turks under Alp Arslan came out of Central Asia, creating havoc and finally defeating the Byzantine Empire at Manzikert in 1071. However, the kings were allowed to keep their thrones, although Georgia remained a backwater until it was again united under King Davit IV Agmashenebelis (David the Builder). Born in 1073, he took over from his father Giorgi II in 1089, annexed Kakheti in 1105 and, in 1121, drove the Seljuks out of Tbilisi, making it his capital the next year. He made Georgia the most powerful state in the Near East, and economic strength led to a cultural Golden Age in the 12th century. Davit died in 1125, and was succeeded by his son Demetre I (1125–56) and then Giorgi III (1156–84).

Georgia's favourite monarch remains Davit's great-granddaughter Queen Tamar (Tamar Mepe in Georgian – this is sometimes mis-translated as King Tamara, as *mepe* simply means monarch), who was born in 1154 and who ruled jointly with her father Giorgi III after crushing a revolt in 1178, and then alone from 1184 to 1213. In 1185 she married Prince Giorgi Bogoliubskoi of Suzdal, a vicious, drunken adventurer (a typical Russian in the eyes of many Georgians) who was soon divorced and expelled for sexual (perhaps homosexual) misconduct; after the fiasco of this political union she married the far more suitable David Soslan, an Ossetian prince, who led her armies and fathered Giorgi IV Lash and his sister and successor Queen Rusudan (said to have been 'fearless only in her lusts'). Tamar extended Georgian rule from the Black Sea to the Caspian, defeated the Turks at the battles of Shamkhori (1195) and Basiani (1202), and after the sack of Constantinople by the Fourth Crusade in 1204 she set up a new Byzantine Empire in Trebizond (now Trabzon) under her kinsman Alexius Comnenus, who had been brought up in Georgia. The Golden Age was brought to an abrupt end in 1220 by Chinghiz (Genghis) Khan and his Mongol hordes, followed by the Black Death from 1366, and by Temur Lang (Tamerlane) who invaded six times between 1386 and 1403. The last king of a united Georgia was Alexander I (1412–43); on his death the country was divided between his three sons, with the eldest taking Kartli (with his capital in Tbilisi), the second Imereti (based in Kutaisi) and the third Kakheti (based in Telavi). As the centralised state fell apart, other noble families took control of smaller areas, such as the Dadianis in Mingrelia, the Gurielis in Guria, and the Gelovanis in Svaneti. After the fall of Constantinople in 1453, Persia and the Ottoman Empire vied for control of the area in a protracted and destructive struggle – Georgia was split between them, although the kings were left on their thrones as long as they did what they were told. Shah Abbas (ruler of Persia from 1587 to 1629) established his rule over Kakheti and Kartli, punishing an uprising in 1615–16 by killing 60,000–70,000 and deporting 100,000.

RUSSIAN RULE The 18th century saw the rise of a third power in the region: Russia, which claimed to protect the Orthodox from Islamic oppression, and specifically Daghestanian raids. It began the process of conquering the northern Caucasus in 1722 under Peter the Great, who died three years later. The enlightened Vakhtang VI of Kartli fled into exile in Russia in 1723; fortunately he had constructed irrigation channels and other public works (and written the history of Georgia) before he left. In 1744 the Persians installed Erekle (or Heraclius) II as King of Kakheti, and his father (who had ruled Kakheti since 1733) as King of Kartli; Erekle (1720–98) also ruled Kartli from his father's death in 1762 until his own death, but despite heroic efforts to resist Persian dominance (fighting over 200 battles) finally had to call for Russian help. Nevertheless, Frederick the Great of Prussia saw him as an invincible equal due to his youthful exploits with Nadir Shah on his campaign in India. In 1768 the first Russo–Turkish war began, and in 1769 the Russian general Todleben crossed the Caucasus, taking Tbilisi and Kutaisi, but was recalled before he could capture Poti; in the Treaty of Kutchuk-Kainardji of 1774, the Turks gave up their claims to western Georgia, and agreed not to help the Muslim tribes of the Caucasus against Russia, though in fact they continued to do so.

In 1783 Persia's new shah, Ali Murad, tried to reimpose his sovereignty, and Erekle II was forced to ask for Russian aid; the Treaty of Protection was signed in Gurgievsk Castle on 24 July 1783, and Count Paul Potyomkin (cousin of the Russian empress Catherine the Great's lover, Grigori Potyomkin) reached Tbilisi later that year, becoming the first viceroy of the Caucasus in May 1785. Also in 1785 the Chechens of the north Caucasus rose in a revolt that lasted until 1791; to deal with this Russian troops were withdrawn from Tbilisi in 1787, and in 1795 the city was razed by Shah Aga Mohammed Khan of Persia, who killed 50,000 and took 20,000 slaves. Catherine refused to help, even though there had been plenty of warning (much like Stalin refusing to help the Warsaw uprising), but the Russians then attacked Persia, thus seizing Azerbaijan. However, Catherine died the next year and her successor, Paul I, withdrew to the River Terek. In December 1800 George XII died in Tbilisi, and in March 1801 Paul was assassinated; his successor, Alexander I, at once violated the Treaty of Gurgievsk and abolished the monarchy of eastern Georgia (Kartli and Kakheti), annexing it as the province of Tiflis. In 1802 Alexander installed a viceroy, Prince Paul Dmitrovich Tsitsianov (Georgian born and Russian educated), who deported the remnants of the royal family to Russia and in 1804 occupied Imereti.

Russia was at war with Persia from 1804 to 1813, and with Turkey from 1807 to 1812, and in 1812 Napoleon invaded Russia; amidst all this confusion Russia was still able to crush revolts in Kakheti (1802 and 1812–13) and Imereti (1819–20), the last Georgian king, Solomon II, fleeing in 1810. Tsitsianov was killed in Azerbaijan in 1806, but by 1813 Persia had been forced to give up its claims to Georgia and Daghestan. In 1825 Nicholas I became tsar and in 1827 appointed as Viceroy Prince Alexander Paskevich, who on the tsar's behalf captured Yerevan and Tabriz. In 1828 Russia made peace with Persia (retaining eastern Armenia) then began another war with Turkey; Paskevich captured Kars, Akhaltsikhe, Erzurum and Poti. The Treaty of Adrianople (now Edirne) in 1829 restored Erzurum and Kars to Turkey (prompting many Armenians to flee), but Guria was reunited with Georgia. In 1856 the Crimean War ended and Prince Alexander Baryatinski (a veteran of the never-ending campaigns against the Muslim tribes of the northern Caucasus) became viceroy; in 1857 he occupied Mingrelia and Svaneti, and by 1859 he had been able to defeat the Chechen leader Shamyl who had led a very effective guerrilla revolt since 1837. In 1864 the Circassians of the north Caucasus were crushed (and 600,000 fled to Turkey), and the next year Abkhazia was also incorporated into the Russian Empire. Another Russo–Turkish war followed in 1877–78, with Russia capturing Kars and Adjara (both reoccupied by Turkey in 1918).

Under Russian rule economic development proceeded apace, but the Georgian populace did not benefit greatly. By the late 19th century, 58% of Georgia's area was owned by Russians and by the government, and the merchant class was overwhelmingly Armenian. Ilia Chavchavadze (1837–1907) and Akaki Tsereteli (1840–1915) led the group of intellectuals known as 'the men of the '60s', or *Tergdaleulebi*, who began to infuse a sense of national consciousness in the Georgian people; in the 1890s another wave of Russian-educated men returned to their homeland, including Noe Zhordania (1868–1953). Political unrest grew in Georgia

Lavrenti Pavlovich Beria, born in 1899 near Sukhumi, was involved in undercover revolutionary activities in Baku and elsewhere before the revolution, and it's likely that he was an agent for the British as well. He only joined the Bolshevik Party in 1917; in 1921 he became head of the Cheka (secret police) in Transcaucasia, where he implemented Stalin's purges so effectively that in 1938 he became head of the secret police of the whole Soviet Union. He also became a politburo member and deputy chairman of the Council of Ministers in 1946; suspected of involvement in Stalin's death and of planning to take power himself, he was arrested and executed on 23 December 1953. He probably didn't kill Stalin but may have given him warfarin which brought on other complications.

Although he has a terrible reputation in the West, he was by no means the worst of the purgers (reaching the top only after the 1936–38 terror), and he began to empty the Gulag camps after Stalin's death. He was surprisingly pragmatic and might well have been a better leader than the more idealistic Khrushchev, leading a faster and more thorough process of de-Stalinisation. His downfall came because he had no party base and so was isolated after Stalin's death.

as elsewhere in the Russian Empire, with the various strands of Marxist thought as influential as elsewhere. On 28 October 1905, 60 people were killed when Cossacks broke up a Social Democrat meeting in Tbilisi, and in 1907 Ilia Chavchavadze was killed; this was long blamed on tsarist agents, but the feeling now is that in fact the Bolsheviks wished to remove his persuasive voice for moderation.

After the Russian revolutions of 1917 Georgia briefly regained independence, but found itself the pawn of larger countries competing for access to the Caspian oil fields. In April 1918, Transcaucasia (Georgia, Armenia and Azerbaijan) declared itself an independent federal state, but on 26 May 1918 Georgia broke away, having been persuaded by Germany that it would provide protection against the Bolshevik threat from north of the Caucasus. German troops helped to drive the Turks, supposedly their allies, out of Batumi; a week after the defeat of Germany and Turkey at the end of 1918, 15,000 British troops landed in Batumi to occupy Transcaucasia (stopping fighting between Georgians and Armenians in the Akhalkalaki area after Turkey's withdrawal). Britain and its chief commissioner, Oliver Wardrop, wanted to maintain Georgia as a buffer against Bolshevism, but the Social Democrat (Menshevik) government led by Zhordania from June 1918 refused to form an alliance with Denikin's White Russians, the last tsarists. Zhordania's government introduced universal suffrage, health insurance and some nationalisation and land redistribution; but this wasn't enough for the Bolsheviks in Russia who imposed a blockade, leading to food shortages. In May 1920, a Bolshevik coup attempt in Tbilisi and a revolt in South Ossetia failed; in January 1920 the Allies granted de facto recognition to all three Transcaucasian republics, and a year later Britain and France granted full *de jure* recognition. Zhordania felt protected by the League of Nations, but Prime Minister David Lloyd George was more interested in a deal with Moscow; the British troops left early in 1920, and on 16 February 1921 the Red Army invaded, occupying Tbilisi nine days later.

The takeover was engineered by the Soviet ambassador Sergei Kirov and Sergo Ordjonikidze (a Georgian Bolshevik, who in 1937 'committed suicide at Stalin's urgent suggestion, being granted in return a state funeral', as Fitzroy Maclean, then a diplomat in Moscow, put it) on Stalin's instructions and against Lenin's wishes; in Moscow it was denied that it was happening and Lenin was very unhappy with the brutality used. A Russo–Turkish treaty restored large areas of historically Georgian territory to Turkey (where they remain today), while Georgia retained Akhalkalaki, Akhaltsikhe and Batumi. Georgia became a Soviet socialist republic, but in December 1922 was absorbed into the Transcaucasian Soviet Federative Socialist Republic; this was dissolved in 1936 (with the adoption of the USSR's second constitution), and Georgia became a Union Republic. The Soviets closed around 1,500 churches and monasteries, leading to a revolt in 1921–22; in August 1924 there was another uprising and General Mogilevski was killed when his Georgian pilot deliberately crashed. This was brutally suppressed by Stalin and Ordjonikidze and 7,000–10,000 were killed, followed by widespread emigration. There were further purges in 1936–37 and 1953. Nevertheless, communism brought some social and material advances and the Georgians fought bravely in World War II (although some fought in the SS against the Soviet Union). Stalin died in 1953, and in 1956 Khrushchev's speech denouncing his crimes led to anti-Russian (and pro-Stalin) riots which were crushed on 9 March by tanks, with more than 100 being killed in Tbilisi.

THE END OF THE SOVIET UNION In 1972 Eduard Shevardnadze, then the republic's interior minister, was promoted to First Secretary of the Georgian Communist Party, and followed the Brezhnevite line of the time, although he took action against corruption. In 1985, Mikhail Gorbachev became leader of the Soviet Union and chose Shevardnadze as his foreign minister. Although there had already been some surreptitious glasnost pre-Gorbachev, from 1985 political agitation escalated (with 80% of Georgian men avoiding their military service). In February 1989 the Abkhazian campaign for secession (begun in the 1970s) was renewed, followed by counter-demonstrations in Tbilisi and then hunger strikes against Russian involvement. On 9 April 1989 (a date now commemorated by street names in many towns), tanks were sent on to the streets of Tbilisi and Russian troops attacked the demonstrators (using sharpened entrenching tools and gas), killing 21 of them (mostly young women), who at once became martyrs. Jumber Patiashvili, First Secretary of the Georgian Communist Party, resigned and Shevardnadze flew in from Moscow to calm things down. As the Soviet Union began to fall apart, the Georgian Supreme Soviet declared Georgian law superior over USSR law in November 1989, and then declared Georgia 'an annexed and occupied country' in February 1990; in March the Communist Party's monopoly on power was abolished.

In August, the statue of Lenin in Lenin Square (now Freedom Square) was removed (supposedly to permit 'repairs' to the square), and multi-party elections were held in October and November 1990. These were won by a coalition of nationalist parties known as the Round Table–Free Georgia, which was led by Zviad Gamsakhurdia, a university lecturer and translator of French and English poetry. The son of the writer Konstantin Gamsakhurdia (most of Georgia's Gamsakhurdia Streets are named after him, not Zviad), he had co-founded Georgia's Helsinki monitoring group in 1976, was jailed for five years but controversially was released after two after recanting on television. (Merab Kostava, who co-founded the Helsinki group and did not recant, stayed in prison from 1977 to 1987 and died in October 1989 when his car supposedly hit a cow.)

Georgia was the first Soviet republic to elect a non-communist government, Gamsakhurdia becoming chair of the new Supreme Soviet. He was a naïve and charismatic nationalist, working on the assumption that the Georgians had long been a persecuted minority in their own country and set out to rectify this injustice (proposing, for instance, to limit the franchise to Georgian speakers); this led to

STALIN

Josef Vissarionovich Djugashvili probably had more influence on people's lives than anyone else in the 20th century, bringing between 45 and 66 million of them to a premature end. Nazism killed around 25 million and Chinese communism about 65 million. Yet he did have charm and charisma, and 45 years after his death one Russian in six calls him their greatest leader (which admittedly is not saying much).

He was a Georgian, born in the Russian quarter of Gori. Although his birthdate was officially given, from around 1922, as 21 December 1879 (9 December by the Old Style calendar), it seems he was born a year earlier and may have changed it once he had absolute power in order to have a nationwide celebration of his 50th birthday. His mother did laundry, and his father was an alcoholic cobbler. He was born with a webbed left foot, was pockmarked by smallpox from the age of six, and acquired a crooked left arm when he was run over by a cart; it seems likely that these deformities in some way fuelled his ruthless ambition, together with his mother's obsessive desire for him to succeed as a priest and beatings from his father which made him hate authority.

He was a star pupil at the church school in Gori, and won a scholarship to study at the seminary in Tbilisi in 1894. In 1895 and 1896 seven of his poems were published in *Iveria* (edited by Ilia Chavchavadze), but he was soon involved in revolutionary politics. He was expelled from the seminary in 1899, and worked as an accountant and record-keeper at the Tbilisi Meteorological and Geophysical Observatory until March 1901.

After the violent demonstration of May Day 1901, he was expelled from Mesame Dasi (Social Democrats) and went underground in Batumi and Baku. He was arrested in 1902 after strikes in the Rothschild oil plants and sent to Siberia, escaping in 1904 and returning to Batumi and then Tbilisi. At this time he first met Nadezhda Alliluyeva, then aged three, whom he was to marry 16 years later, and who was to shoot herself in 1932. In 1903 the Social Democrats split into two groups, the Bolsheviks and Mensheviks; Koba, as he then called himself, supported the more radical Bolsheviks and their leader, Lenin, and took a new *nom de guerre*, Stalin, suggesting 'Man of Steel' in Russian. From this time on his loyalty was to Russia and to international communism, rather than to Georgia; although he had no oratorical skills or charisma, he had plenty of energy, organisational talent and a retentive memory. He roamed the Caucasus, fomenting strikes and spreading the message of socialism, as well as staging robberies to raise funds, together with Simon Ter-Petrossian (known as Kamo), who was also from Gori, although Armenian.

Between 1902 and 1913 he was frequently arrested and sent to Siberia, but he always escaped. In 1912 he founded the party newspaper *Pravda* ('Truth') and Lenin rewarded Stalin's loyalty by appointing him to the Bolshevik Central Committee; he began to gain influence in the party, but was arrested again in 1913 and this time had to stay in Siberia until the March revolution of 1917.

IN POWER In the Bolshevik government Stalin served as commissar of nationalities (fomenting trouble in Baku), and in 1920 as commissar of the army heading for Berlin, being blamed by Trotsky for its defeat in the Battle of Warsaw. In 1922 he the worst outbreak of messianic nationalism in any of the former Soviet republics. From the beginning, some political groups had refused to recognise the legitimacy of a legislature and government elected under the Soviet system; these groups

became general secretary of the party's Central Committee, and on Lenin's death in 1924 used all the levers of power to crush his rivals as he manoeuvred into a position of absolute power, despite Lenin having specifically instructed the party to beware of him.

Initially he advocated moderate economic policies and an end to world revolution, which aroused the opposition of the leftists led by Trotsky, Kamenev and Zinoviev; by 1928 he had driven them from any position of power, and then adopted leftist policies such as rapid industrialisation and agricultural collectivisation, arousing the opposition of the rightists. By the end of 1929 Stalin was the undisputed master of the Soviet Union, and communism died in any meaningful sense.

Having seized the land of the *kulaks* (bourgeois peasantry) in 1928, Stalin was able to fund industrialisation by exporting their grain stocks, and continued collectivisation despite dogged resistance from the peasants and a famine in 1932 which may have cost over 10 million lives. Sergei Kirov, the Leningrad party secretary, protested, and was murdered in 1934; Stalin used this as a pretext for his first purge, arresting virtually all his senior colleagues and staging the Moscow show trials between 1936 and 1938. Only 41 of the 139 deputies elected to the Central Committee in 1934 survived, and millions more died as he purged the party, the professions and intellectuals throughout the Soviet Union. By 1938 there was no doubt that this was a dictatorship.

By concluding a non-aggression pact with Nazi Germany in 1939 (including a secret clause agreeing to a joint attack on Poland) Stalin bought time for further industrialisation and rearmament before the Nazi attack in June 1941. The Soviet people made immense sacrifices in what they know as the Great Patriotic War, but its huge reserves of manpower (expended extravagantly by Stalin) and industrial power, coupled with ferocious winter weather and the contributions of the Allies, finally brought victory. Stalin (now a generalissimo) was far more of a hands-on commander than any of the other Allied leaders, while also out-manoeuvring them diplomatically.

There was no relaxation after the war; the imposition of communist rule on eastern and much of central Europe led to further waves of repression and the outbreak of the Cold War with his former allies. In 1953 his health failed but he claimed to have discovered a plot by his doctors to kill him; a massive new purge seemed imminent, but he died on 5 March 1953. In 1956 his successor Nikita Khrushchev denounced his crimes and in 1961 his body was moved out of the Red Square mausoleum. Under Brezhnev criticism of Stalin was muted, but again in 1987 Gorbachev told a party congress that his crimes were 'enormous and unforgivable'. The huge death toll of the purges and collectivisation was finally revealed, and with the opening of the Soviet and KGB archives more and more is becoming known.

Nevertheless he is widely seen, particularly in Georgia, as a 'strong man', the sort of leader who might pull the country out of the morass, and his crimes are widely overlooked as a price worth paying.

organised public demonstrations and hunger strikes, which Gamsakhurdia met with repression. He had no understanding of democracy, believing that winning an election gave him absolute power and the right to treat all criticism as an attack on the nation; it was soon clear that he was succumbing to clinical paranoia. He also nearly bankrupted Georgia by isolation both from Russia and the Commonwealth of Independent States (CIS), and from the West.

In January 1991 the National Guard was founded as a new army and Jaba Ioseliani, a playwright who had founded a paramilitary body known as the Mkhedrioni (Horsemen) after the 1989 massacre, was arrested with the help of Russian troops after failing to disarm. The referendum on the future of the Soviet Union in March 1991 was boycotted, except in South Ossetia, Abkhazia and Red Army barracks, which all turned out, unsurprisingly, to be strongly pro-Union. On 31 March, the Georgian government held its own referendum in which 93% (of a 95% turnout) voted for independence; on the anniversary of the 9 April 1989 killings the Soviet declared independence and in May Gamsakhurdia was elected president with 86% of the vote. Things went very wrong after the August 1991 Soviet coup attempt which he, at first, failed to condemn; Tengiz Kitovani (formerly a sculptor) was sacked as leader of the National Guard, before Gamsakhurdia declared a state of emergency in Tbilisi and clamped down on the media. Ioseliani was jailed, followed in September by Georgi Chanturia, leader of the opposition National Democratic Party. Demonstrations gathered momentum, turning in December to fighting. Gamsakhurdia was besieged in the parliament building by the National Guard and Mkhedrioni, who released Ioseliani and Chanturia and also about 8,000 common criminals whom they equipped with Kalashnikovs.

Between 113 and 200 people were killed in street fighting, which wrecked a few buildings near the parliament and Freedom Square; in January 1992 Gamsakhurdia fled to Armenia (soon reappearing in his home town of Zugdidi and being driven out again to Chechnya). A military council had little choice but to invite Eduard Shevardnadze to take charge again. He returned in March and was designated chair of the State Council, which replaced the Military Council; Ioseliani was deputy chair and Kitovani was minister of defence.

POLITICS

THE SHEVARDNADZE PRESIDENCY In October 1992 elections (boycotted in South Ossetia, Mingrelia and parts of Abkhazia) were held for the State Council (formerly the Supreme Soviet). The largest party won just 29 seats out of 235, giving free rein to Shevardnadze. However, he struggled to control the National Guard and Mkhedrioni, who by now were running the country as one massive protection racket, controlling petrol and cigarette distribution and setting up roadblocks to 'tax' motorists; for most of 1992–93 the interior minister (in charge of the police) was Temuraz Khachishvili, a convicted criminal put in place by the Mkhedrioni. Economic policy was chaotic, with a disastrously loose credit policy and pyramid investment scandals.

Throughout 1992 unrest continued in the west, stronghold of the Zviadists (supporters of Gamsakhurdia); in June they seized Tbilisi's TV Tower, recaptured only with the loss of 40 lives. In August, Kitovani precipitated fighting in Abkhazia by his recklessness when the interior minister was kidnapped; he was finally forced to resign in May 1993. In August the Council of Ministers resigned after parliament rejected the 1993 budget, and Shevardnadze also resigned when parliament refused to let him declare a state of emergency; crowds blockaded the government building and his resignation was rejected by the parliament. A state of emergency was declared in September, but already the country seemed ungovernable; in October Abkhazia was lost (see below), and Zviadist rebels captured Poti and Samtredia, and began advancing east. The only way out, as in the 18th century, was to call for Russian help; Georgia finally agreed to join the Commonwealth of Independent States, Russian troops arrived in late October and within weeks defeated the Zviadists. Gamsakhurdia himself was surrounded by government troops in January 1994 and committed suicide; he was buried (eventually) in Chechnya and moved to the Pantheon in Tbilisi in 2007. Russia was given permission to maintain four bases in Georgia (Vaziani near Tbilisi, Akhalkalaki, Batumi and Gudauta in Abkhazia) for 25 years, although they in fact closed in 2006.

The winter of 1993–94 saw the start of large-scale operations against organised crime, particularly the National Guard and Zviadist groups; the Mkhedrioni were largely left alone, being nominally incorporated into the army as the 'Rescue Corps' until they were finally disarmed in May 1995. By the summer of 1994 basic law and order had been re-established, but there then followed a wave of political assassinations, of which the most prominent victim was Giorgi Chanturia in December 1994. Some land and housing was sold in 1993, but economic reform really began with price liberalisation in 1994, with gas prices increasing five times, electricity ten times and bread up to 280 times.

In January 1995, Kitovani and his followers set out in an attempt to 'liberate' Abkhazia but were arrested (Kitovani was eventually jailed for eight years). A new constitution was approved by parliament in August, virtually as drafted by Shevardnadze; it established a presidential republic with a minister of state instead of a prime minister, acting as adviser to a president directly elected for a maximum of two five-year terms.

The militia leaders were unhappy at being marginalised, and on 29 August a car bomb exploded in the courtyard of parliament – the closest of the many attempts on Shevardnadze's life since 1992. However, Shevardnadze, the 'silver fox', managed to play the gangsters off against one another until all were in jail, gradually bringing reformers into government.

A new currency, the lari, was successfully introduced and elections were held under the new constitution in November 1995. The results were something of a surprise, with only three parties over the 5% barrier for party-list seats: the Citizens' Union of Georgia (CUG or SMK), set up by Shevardnadze as a personal vehicle, won almost half these seats with a quarter of the vote, and over 60% of the electorate voted for parties which polled under 5%. With further seats filled by a first-past-the-post system, the CUG won a total of 107 seats, followed by the National Democratic Party with 34 seats and the Union for Georgian Revival (led by the Adjaran strongman Aslan Abashidze) with 31 seats. Shevardnadze won the presidential election with 75% of the votes. Parliament elected the moderniser Zurab Zhvania to be its chair or speaker; trained as a biologist, he was leader of the Greens before joining the CUG. Real structural economic reforms began at last, with an IMF stabilisation programme, a Partnership and Co-operation Agreement with the European Union, and similar deals with neighbouring countries. The reformers won the election but this was not reflected in Shevardnadze's government, and the overlap continued of law enforcement and criminal gangs.

In October 1999, soon after the Russians launched their latest Chechen war, inadequately clean parliamentary elections were held: the CUG won 42% of the vote and 132 seats (56% of the total). In April 2000, the presidential election (again less than fully free and fair) was won by Shevardnadze with 80% of the vote (Stalin's grandson Evgeni Djugashvili was refused registration when it was decided that he was not a Georgian citizen). In January 1999, Georgia was admitted into the Council of Europe, and in June 2000 into the World Trade Organization (in both cases well ahead of Armenia and Azerbaijan).

THE STRUGGLE FOR THE SUCCESSION In August 2001, justice minister Mikheil Saakashvili proposed confiscating luxury houses built by ministers and senior officials, unless they could prove they were built with legitimate funds (many were worth US$200,000 or more, though even cabinet ministers earned only US$200 a month), but Shevardnadze refused to overturn the principle of the presumption of innocence. Saakashvili specifically accused three ministers of corruption and resigned on 19 September, two days after Shevardnadze had announced that he planned to relinquish the leadership of the CUG and wouldn't seek a third term as president in 2005. The showdown between the CUG's 'young reformers' – Saakashvili, Zhvania, finance minister Zurab Noghaideli, tax minister Mikhail Machavariani and Nino Burjanadze, head of the parliament's foreign relations committee – and the Soviet-era old guard, led by interior minister Kakha Targamadze, became increasingly bitter as it turned into a battle for the succession to Shevardnadze. Shevardnadze's perpetual balancing act worked when he was popular, but was less effective once he sank to just 6% in the polls. Suffering from diabetes, he was seen as ageing, tired and confused. The CUG halved in size, from 98 to 50 deputies, with at least two new factions forming; the opposition likewise realigned itself, with Aslan Abashidze's Union for Georgian Revival the dominant force.

Shevardnadze parroted his commitment to rooting out corruption but achieved little. Georgi Sanaia, an outspoken journalist on the Rustavi-2 television channel, was shot dead in July, presumably for attacking corruption, which led to protests on the streets. In October, Rustavi-2 was raided by tax inspectors; demonstrators again took to the streets, accusing Targamadze and also Shevardnadze of trying to suppress free speech and Shevardnadze was forced to sack the state security minister, but said he'd resign if deputies voted to force out Targamadze (generally supposed to know some dirty secret about Shevardnadze, perhaps dating from the Abkhaz war of 1993). Then Zhvania claimed Targamadze and associates were planning to stir up unrest as a pretext to arrest him and his supporters, and declared that he would resign to force Targamadze out; they both resigned on 1 November, and Shevardnadze, with his support now almost non-existent, had no choice but to dismiss the whole government. He was still unable to have a proper clean-out and the 'power' ministries and security apparatus remained entangled with organised crime.

Shevardnadze created a new alliance, For A New Georgia, out of his faction in the CUG plus the National Democratic Party, the Socialists and the Greens, as well as unions and business groups. Zhvania, now clearly opposed to Shevardnadze, left the CUG in early 2002 and formed his own party, the United Democrats; likewise, the more confrontational Saakashvili (elected Mayor of Tbilisi in November 2002) created the National Movement, allied with the Republicans and Conservatives. Shevardnadze claimed victory in parliamentary elections in November 2003, leading to demonstrations by up to 15,000 people calling for his resignation after exit polls and independent observers showed that he had in fact lost. Saakashvili and his associates insisted on peaceful protest, backed up by a sharp statement from the US ambassador complaining that many people had been 'denied their constitutional right to vote' – presumably not what Shevardnadze expected. After almost three weeks, official results gave Shevardnadze's For a New Georgia 21.3%

of the vote, Revival 18.8%, and Saakashvili's National Movement 18%. Busloads of protestors came to Tbilisi to prevent the new parliament from meeting, and the head of the Security Council admitted fraud and called for new elections (but not Shevardnadze's resignation); Aslan Abashidze sent his supporters to Tbilisi for pro-Shevardnadze counter-demonstrations. When the parliament met, protesters

EDUARD SHEVARDNADZE

The youngest of five children, Eduard Shevardnadze was born in Mamati, Guria, in 1928. His parents wanted him to become a doctor but he chose politics, joining the Communist Party at 20 and working his way up to be Georgia's Minister of Internal Affairs, ie: head of the secret police. In 1972, aged just 44, he was appointed Secretary-General of the Georgian Party, with a mission to cut corruption. At his first politburo meeting, it's said that he asked those present to raise their hands if they agreed that corruption should be eliminated; naturally they all agreed, and he asked them to keep their hands up while he went round the table; all those with foreign watches were sacked. In fact, he failed to make much impact in this area, but his reforming policies presaged perestroika, and when Gorbachev became Soviet leader in 1985 he appointed Shevardnadze foreign minister. He is still especially popular in Germany where he is seen as having brought about the fall of the Berlin Wall and German reunification more or less single-handedly. In 1989 he resigned in protest at Gorbachev's repressive attempts to slow the break-up of the Soviet Union, although he did serve again as foreign minister during the Soviet Union's final days, before returning to Georgia.

As chair of parliament from 1992 he had no formal powers but rapidly built up a semi-presidential apparatus while parliament was too fractured to play a real role; in 1995 he became president. Although his own party, the Citizens' Union of Georgia (CUG), dominated parliament, Shevardnadze ruled outside formal political structures, preferring an informal network of contacts and cronies, which is very much part of Georgian culture and a breeding-ground for corruption.

The CUG comprised both progressive 'greens' and reactionary 'reds', and its political identity was unclear; some reformers, such as Zurab Zhvania, established themselves in positions of power, but without being allowed to rival Shevardnadze. This helped him effectively to blackmail the electorate, saying 'it's me or it's chaos'. Shevardnadze was re-elected president in 2000; in September 2001 he announced that he was relinquishing the chair of the CUG, and began to plan the transition to post-Shevardnadze politics – rather than simply finding a successor (or allowing someone else to seize power), he seemed to prefer to hand over the business of the state slowly to a prime minister who would become an heir apparent, if successful. He followed a classic 'divide and rule' strategy, giving hope to both the 'young reformers' led by Zhvania and the conservatives led by Targamadze. Eventually the country tired of his fence-sitting and swept him from power; however, he stayed in his palace until his death in 2014 and often appeared on television to give his opinions.

Although most people accepted that Shevardnadze was clean of corruption himself, he was seriously tainted by the activities of his nephews, particularly Nugzar Shevardnadze who dominated the cigarette and kerosene trades; he may not have directly used access to the president, but he certainly assumed that his name made him untouchable.

1

stormed in as Shevardnadze was in the middle of a speech declaring a state of emergency; he was rushed away by bodyguards and Nino Burjanadze, reformist speaker of parliament, declared herself temporary president. The next day, 23 November 2003 (St George's Day), Shevardnadze resigned, having been abandoned by the army and the police. Due to the roses carried by the protesters, this became known as the Rose Revolution.

THE SAAKASHVILI ERA Zhvania became prime minister and in January 2004 Saakashvili, the only opposition candidate, won a presidential election with 88% of the vote. In parliamentary elections in March, the National Movement-Democrats (uniting Saakashvili's, Zhvania's and Burjanadze's supporters and the Republicans) took 67% of the vote and 135 of the 150 party-list seats; the Rightist Opposition alliance was the only opposition grouping over the threshold, with 7.6% and 15 seats. With the addition of constituency members elected in November 2003, the government had the support of at least 150 of 235 deputies.

Saakashvili soon fell out with the Republicans, then with Aslan Abashidze, who cut three bridges linking Adjara to the rest of Georgia in May 2004; Saakashvili gave him ten days to disarm and return to constitutional rule, sending the army on manoeuvres just across the border, while activists were smuggled in to lead protests and seduce Abashidze's guard away from him. Fortunately he was also persuaded to go peacefully and was flown to Russia, and Adjara returned to being a normal part of Georgia.

In February 2005 Zhvania was found dead, supposedly of carbon monoxide poisoning; many people assumed he'd been murdered, and investigations were reopened in 2014. He was replaced by finance minister Zurab Noghaideli, although he had less power than the interior and defence ministers. In May 2005, US President George W Bush visited Tbilisi and was greeted with great enthusiasm (although an Abashidze supporter did throw a grenade at him, which failed to explode).

The Rose Revolution was great PR, with corruption tackled vigorously and the entire police force replaced. Tariffs were cut from 16 bands (up to 30%) to just three: 0, 5 and 12%, and a flat 20% income tax was introduced, with collection rates rising sharply.

In January 2006, banker Sandro Girgvliani was murdered after an argument in the Sharden Bar, apparently on the orders of interior minister Vano Merabishvili's wife; four men were jailed but there were widespread accusations of a cover-up and calls for Merabishvili to resign. In March a prison riot, that the government claimed was part of a nationwide plot by the 'criminals-in-law' (the top dogs who controlled Georgia's prisons as well as much criminal activity outside), was put down with seven deaths; the opposition parties suspected a cover-up but demands for an investigation were voted down. Merabishvili remained in office, and was still Georgia's most powerful figure after Saakashvili, having widened the Interior Ministry's responsibilities.

Saakashvili began to lose much of his earlier popularity, due to the Zhvania and Girgvliani affairs and to his constant publicity-chasing – on the ski slopes, opening the new Rustavi prison several times, and similarly the tunnel to Batumi (first at one end, then the other ...). More substantially, he managed relations with Russia very badly, causing massive damage to Georgia's economy and compounding this when Georgia broke off all diplomatic relations with its powerful neighbour in late August 2008.

THE RUSSIAN CRISES Externally, despite efforts to move towards the West and specifically NATO and EU membership, Georgian politics is dominated by its poor relations with Russia, which has always sought to dominate the surrounding countries. After the outbreak of the latest Chechen war in 1999 Russia tried even harder to manipulate Georgia, wanting the country to allow Russian troops in to seal the border with Chechnya; this was refused (although Russian jets and helicopters did drop bombs on the Georgian side of the border), so from 2000 Russia required visas for Georgians (up to a million of whom work there), though not for Abkhazians or Armenians. Russia accused Georgia of harbouring Chechen terrorists (and even al-Qaeda guerrillas) in the Pankisi Gorge in Kakheti, an enclave populated by Kists or Islamic Chechens and 7,000 Chechen refugees. In 2001, various foreigners were kidnapped and held in Pankisi; this was linked to just about every possible political faction, but was simple criminality and in time they were freed. British banker Peter Shaw was kidnapped in June 2002 and held with a chain around his neck in a tiny cellar in the Pankisi Gorge until his release in November of that year. Less happily, the brother of the AC Milan footballer and Georgian captain Kakha Kaladze was kidnapped in 2001 and eventually murdered.

In mid-2002 Georgia (backed up by the US) twice accused Russia of bombing Pankisi, but Russia accused Georgia of staging it. In August, 1,000 Georgian Interior Ministry troops, trained by US Army Special Forces, went into Pankisi and arrested a few criminals, failing to find any al-Qaeda training camps. Even so, in September Russia accused the Georgian government of being 'fellow travellers' of international terrorism and threatened economic sanctions and even a Russian 'anti-terrorist' operation across the border.

After the Rose Revolution, Russia was determined to block Georgian entry to NATO by keeping the Abkhaz and South Ossetian conflicts active; Saakashvili retaliated by blocking Russian entry to the World Trade Organization. In January 2006, Russia doubled the price of gas supplied to Georgia and later that month, during a particularly cold spell, an explosion (presumably sabotage) cut the gas pipeline from Russia to Georgia, leaving most of the population without heat or power for a week (gas supplies had also been briefly cut off in the winter of 2000 due to 'Georgia's lack of co-operation on Chechnya'). In March Georgian wine was banned by Russia, supposedly due to impurities, soon followed by Georgian mineral water and fruit. The quantity of Georgian wine sold in Russia was always far greater than that actually produced, and any health risks were entirely due to the fake wine produced in Russia, a country in which 35,000 people a year die due to bad booze. In actual fact, the ban hurt Russian retailers and consumers as much as it did Georgia. Saakashvili reacted by blithely saying 'What doesn't kill you makes you stronger', and sought alternative markets for Georgian wine in Asia, but he was widely blamed for provoking the crisis.

In July 2006, Russia's only border crossing with Georgia was suddenly shut 'for repairs'. In September there was apparently a pathetic attempt at a coup by four Russian military intelligence officers, and 11 Georgians were arrested for spying; this was seen as very obvious grandstanding in the run-up to local elections, but the Russian response was furious, withdrawing the ambassador and staff and families from the embassy in Tbilisi and ceasing to issue visas to Georgians. The Russian officers were released after three days, but Russia stepped up the punishment, suspending transport and postal links, expelling at least 5,000 Georgians from Russia (with two dying in the process), raiding Georgian-owned businesses for 'tax irregularities' and encouraging a xenophobic hysteria in which some schools expelled children with Georgian names. It was estimated the crisis could cut Georgian economic growth by 1.5%, but in fact the economy continued to grow, and the government did indeed do very well in the local elections.

As Russia became sure of its stranglehold over European gas supplies, it became increasingly willing to offend the West and to take a harder line with Western-minded neighbours. In November 2006, Gazprom announced that the price of Georgia's gas would double again in January; a few days later it suggested it could leave the price unchanged if Georgia sold it the pipeline instead, a proposal greeted by the sound of Georgian jaws hitting the ground at the sheer brazenness of the blackmail attempt. In the end Georgia agreed to pay the higher price, but can now buy most of its gas from Azerbaijan.

In September 2007, former defence minister Erekle Okruashvili accused Saakashvili of corruption and was himself arrested two days later on corruption charges. For once, the opposition formed a united front and organised a mass protest; after demonstrators had blocked Rustaveli Avenue for four days they were brutally driven away by police, sparking international outrage, and a state of emergency was declared. The next day Saakashvili gambled by calling early elections for January 2008, in which the main opposition candidate was Conservative leader Levan Gachechiladze; Saakashvili won with 53% of the vote, sparking claims of vote-rigging. Almost at once Badri Patarkatsishvili, who had won 7% of the vote for president after his Imedi television station had been closed down in the state of emergency, was

MIKHEIL SAAKASHVILI

The idealistic young man who drove Shevardnadze from power was born in Tbilisi in 1967, his father a well-known doctor and his mother a historian at Tbilisi State University. He studied international law in Kiev, Strasbourg and Columbia Law School in New York, acquiring fluent English, French, Ukrainian and Russian along the way, as well as a Dutch wife, Sandra Saakashvili-Roelofs, with whom he has two sons.

In 1995 he was persuaded by his old friend Zurab Zhvania, who had been commissioned by Shevardnadze to recruit talented young Georgians, to return to Georgia and enter politics. Together with current Republican Party leader David Usupashvili and Conservative Party founder Koba Davitashvili, they were leading members of the Georgian Young Lawyers Association, which became a pro-reform pressure group.

Saakashvili and Zhvania both entered parliament in 1995 for Shevardnadze's CUG and were soon noticed. Saakasahvili was successful as chair of the parliament's judiciary committee and in January 2000 became vice-president of the Parliamentary Assembly of the Council of Europe. In October 2000 he became justice minister and implemented major reforms, but was unable to root out top-level corruption, despite producing documents at a cabinet meeting that showed some colleagues had built huge houses with illicitly gained cash.

He was finally ground down by the 'power' ministries (notably Kakha Targmadze's Interior Ministry), or else decided he had to provoke a showdown, and resigned in September 2001, founding his own party, the National Movement, in the social-democratic mould.

In June 2002, with the backing of the Labour Party, he became Mayor of Tbilisi, home to a third of Georgia's population, and, already one of the country's most popular politicians, he built a strong power base by delivering local services and fixing roofs and drains. As a crusader against corruption and poverty, he built a populist bandwagon that clearly won more votes than Shevardnadze's For a New Georgia in November 2003's elections, and harnessed the general indignation to bring up to 100,000 people on to the streets in non-violent protests for two weeks, until Shevardnadze was forced charged with plotting a coup; he died in England in February from what seems to have been a genuine heart attack. Further mass demonstrations took place against Saakashvili in 2009, following the August 2008 conflict with Russia (page 33).

At the end of 2009, controversial amendments were introduced to election laws, clearly intended to favour Saakashvili's United National Movement Party (UNM) in the May 2010 local elections, and the capital's roads and historic quarters were renovated at breakneck pace, with the Peace Bridge also being constructed. A media campaign attacked former ambassador to the UN Erekle Alasania, leader of the Free Democrats and a strong candidate to be mayor of Tbilisi and probably for the presidency, too, before long. The UNM won the local elections, but international observers registered 'deficiencies' in the process. Saakashvili also introduced a controversial new constitution to augment the prime minister's powers at the expense of the president, a clear sign that he wanted to become prime minister in 2013 after his presidential term just as Putin did in Russia; this was opposed by the Council of Europe, but was passed by parliament in October 2010.

In May 2011 the opposition again organised mass protests, which were cleared by riot police; four people were killed, two of them by the cars of the protest leaders as they fled. As the October 2012 parliamentary elections approached, the

to resign and was replaced by the speaker of parliament. Saakashvili had to wait until the elections of January 2004 to become Europe's youngest president. He was forgiving of his predecessor, saying: 'History will judge him kindly.'

He immediately replaced the country's flag with a new one, and set out vigorously to tackle corruption. These efforts and a new tax code had considerable effect in increasing government revenues and thus expenditures too; Georgia was named the world's leader in economic reform and one of the best to do business in, well ahead of its neighbours. However, Saakashvili's populism often tipped into demagoguery and authoritarianism, for instance in a media law in 2004 and the favouritism shown to some television stations (notably Rustavi-2) and pressure on others.

Saakashvili's fiercely pro-USA and pro-NATO stance earned him friends across the Atlantic but it created enemies elsewhere, most notably in Russia but also at home. Despite – or, perhaps, because of – his economic and political reforms he was increasingly criticised for authoritarianism. Critics pointed to the worsening in Georgia's human rights record during Saakashvili's presidency and he was accused of election rigging, as well as smearing opponents and crushing protest rallies. As it turned out, the slavish media (especially TV) support for him was undermined by opposition use of social media. He'll also be remembered for his taste in brash contemporary architecture (page 46) as part of his project to modernise Georgia in a hurry. It is hard to feel too sorry for him though; as is so often the case, initial reforming zeal led to a conviction that no-one else could do the job and thus an urge to keep power by any means, and Saakashvili's belief that he could take on Russia led to the disastrous war of 2008.

Bizarrely, since leaving the presidency and the country in November 2013, he has become an advisor to the Ukrainian government due to his experience in dealing with Vladimir Putin. Clearly, they should have listened to his advice and done the opposite. From 2014, various Georgians became ministers in the Ukrainian government and in May 2015 Saakashvili's bizarre trajectory continued with his appointment as governor of the Odessa region and giving up his Georgian citizenship.

reclusive billionaire Bidzina Ivanishvili (page 35) announced plans to form a party with the specific aim of removing Saakashvili from office, and at last the opposition began to pull together, forming the Georgian Dream coalition.

In September 2012 a video was released of systematic abuses (including sexual assault with a broom by senior officials) at Gldani Prison in Tbilisi and the prison and interior ministers resigned. In the parliamentary elections of 1 October 2012 both sides claimed victory, with Georgian Dream leading in the party lists and Saakashvili in the constituency seats; but Saakashvili admitted defeat before too long and promised to lead a peaceful opposition (while remaining as president). It was a polarising campaign but, in the end, a fair vote.

To show its democratic, pro-Western credentials, Georgia has deployed peace-keeping troops in Afghanistan since 2004 (and remains the largest non-NATO contributor of troops there), in Iraq since 2008 and in the Central African Republic since 2014.

ABKHAZIA Under Georgia's 1921 constitution Abkhazia was virtually autonomous; Stalin made Abkhazia an autonomous republic in 1930, but he also encouraged large numbers of Georgians to immigrate and by 1989 the population of 450,000 was 46% Georgian, 18% Abkhaz, 14% Armenian, 14% Russian and 3% Greek. Perestroika encouraged the growth of secessionism and in July 1989 demands for teaching at the University of Sukhumi to be in Georgian rather than Abkhazian led to fighting and 14 deaths. In August 1990 the Abkhaz Supreme Soviet voted for independence as a Union Republic within the Soviet Union, but was persuaded to reverse this; in the referendum of March 1991 virtually the whole non-Georgian population of Abkhazia voted in vain to stay in the Soviet Union, seeing it as less of a threat than being part of an independent and nationalist Georgia.

Although the 1921 constitution was restored in 1992, the Abkhaz were convinced that Tbilisi was bent on denying them autonomy and saw no choice but independence; therefore a Republic of Abkhazia was declared in July 1992 (though without the required two-thirds majority). The next month Shevardnadze's defence minister, Kitovani, sent the National Guard into Abkhazia, ostensibly to protect transport links with Russia, and full-scale conflict broke out. The Abkhaz leader, Vladislav Ardzinba (a historian in Moscow until 1987), retreated to the Russian army base at Gudauta; with help from Russia and Muslim paramilitaries from the northern Caucasus he had regained control of northern Abkhazia by October. By spring of 1993 the front line seemed stable along the River Gumista, north of Sukhumi, although the city was largely destroyed by Russian bombing. Shevardnadze flew to Moscow to urge Yeltsin to bring his generals under control, but he found that Russia was determined to dominate the former Soviet Republics. By July there was a ceasefire and UN observers arrived in August; however, the Abkhazians launched a surprise attack in September and soon 'liberated' Abkhazia (Shevardnadze went to Sukhumi vowing to defend it himself, but had to flee ignominiously by air). Around 8,000 people were killed between August 1992 and October 1993.

Between 200,000 and 350,000 Georgians and others fled, about 400 dying in the mountains on the border with Svaneti. In July 1994, 3,000 CIS (mainly Russian) peacekeepers moved in, and in August the first 5,000 refugees returned.

Gali, the ethnically Georgian district of Abkhazia bordering Mingrelia, was virtually unscathed in 1993–94 and became a demilitarised zone; but in May 1998 Georgian paramilitaries killed up to 20 Abkhaz militiamen before being driven out of Gali, with between 60 and 200 deaths, and at least 30,000 refugees took to the roads again. Over 2,000 buildings were burnt down by the Abkhaz in the buffer zone patrolled by the Russian peacekeepers (which even Russian officials later admitted was too close to turning a blind eye to ethnic cleansing). Many Georgian refugees began crossing by day to work the fields in Gali, returning to sleep in Zugdidi, and in 1999 they began to return to their homes. In 2011, over 46,000 ethnic Georgians were still living in Abkhazia, mostly in Gali and nearby districts. Between 40,000 and 60,000 refugees have returned to Gali, some commuting daily across the ceasefire line and others migrating seasonally following agricultural cycles.

The two sides continued to talk, with Abkhazia insisting on equal confederal status with Georgia, and Georgia insisting on an asymmetric arrangement with more power for Tbilisi. As discussed on pages 71–2, Russia was thought to be fomenting instability in Georgia to keep it out of NATO and boost its own Caspian–Black Sea pipeline. It is claimed that the Russian airfield at Vaziani (just east of Tbilisi) was the base for the 1995 attempt to assassinate Shevardnadze, and Moscow has failed to extradite Igor Giorgadze and Guram Absandze, both accused of involvement in the plot; Giorgadze appeared regularly on television but Russia's police responded to an Interpol warrant by denying it knew where he was, until he was granted asylum in 2006. In 1999, Russia opened its border with Abkhazia (although it had been very porous for a long while).

In October 1999, Abkhaz presidential elections produced a 99% vote for Ardzinba, the only candidate, and a referendum on independence was approved by 97%; a week later the Abkhaz parliament formally declared independence, and the new Abkhaz premier Anri Jergenia spoke of applying to join the Russian Federation, though this was still a step too far for Putin. In 2001, Russia failed to withdraw (as agreed in 1999) from Gudauta, the base for the CIS peacekeepers and also for dodgy Russian arms shipments worldwide.

The upper part of the Kodori Gorge, adjoining Svaneti, still in Georgian hands, became a flashpoint; in 1999 first Georgian government officials and then UN observers were kidnapped there, with armed clashes in July 2001. In October 2001 Georgian guerrillas, reportedly aided by Chechen fighters, launched raids there resulting in at least 30 deaths, and a few days later a UN helicopter was shot down near the Kodori Gorge, killing five UN military observers, three Ukrainian crew members and a Georgian interpreter – it seems likely that Russian missiles from Gudauta, and possibly Russian personnel, were involved. In July 2006, Georgian special police were sent to the gorge to arrest the renegade governor turned warlord, Emzar Kvitsiani, and disperse his paramilitary Hunter battalion. There was some skirmishing in the villages of Azhara and Omarishi, but order was soon established (with, apparently, some slaves being freed), and the Abkhazian government-in-exile was moved from Tbilisi to the Kodori (renamed Upper Abkhazia).

Saakashvili pledged to reunite Abkhazia and South Ossetia with the rest of Georgia by 2008, but despite some alarming signs that a military solution might be attempted this did not happen. Russia lifted its sanctions on Abkhazia and granted citizenship to most residents, while Saakashvili continued for Russian peacekeepers to be replaced by an international force. It might seem odd to the independent observer that the separation of Kosovo from Serbia, used by Russia as a precedent for separating Abkhazia and South Ossetia from Georgia, has not been taken up by Russia as a template for its own Chechnya region. The lifting of sanctions against South Ossetia and Abkhazia in March 2008 was seen as the first step towards recognition of their independent status by Russia. This raised concerns within the EU which had recognised Georgia's territorial integrity since the break-up of the Soviet Union. In April 2008, a Georgian unmanned drone was shot down over

Abkhazian territory; the Georgian government asserted that it possessed video footage showing that a Russian MiG-29 had been involved, an accusation denied by Russia and Abkhazia. This event would turn out to be a forerunner of the short but brutal Russian–Georgian war that unfolded in the summer of that year (page 33). Abkhazia was largely unaffected by that conflict, apart from accepting a Russian army base in 2010: its economy continues to do quite well, with a boom in tourism from Russia and lots of associated development.

Sergei Bagapsh died of lung cancer in May 2011, 18 months after being re-elected for a second presidential term; he was succeeded by his vice-president Aleksandr Ankvab, defeating Bagapsh's perennial rival Raul Khajimba, leader of the Forum of National Unity of Abkhazia. Russian-backed protests led to Ankvab fleeing to the Russian base in Gudauta in May 2014; elections in August were won, by just 559 votes, by Khajimba. In October 2014, a new draft treaty on relations and integration with Russia (clearly a quid pro quo for Russian support against Ankvab) triggered a storm of protest; in Tbilisi it was seen as a step towards Abkhazia's incorporation into the Russian Federation and in Abkhazia it was seen as curtailing the powers of the army (a pillar of national identity) and leading to the abolition of Russian–Abkhaz border controls. Surprisingly, Russia took into account virtually all the Abkhaz objections and also offered to invest US$260 million by the end of 2017; the treaty was signed in November.

SOUTH OSSETIA The Ossetians are ethnically totally distinct from all their neighbours and, as the majority population in South Ossetia (an autonomous region since 1922), felt entitled to protection from an independent and nationalist Georgia. Demands in 1989 for unification with North Ossetia, within the Russian Federation, were rejected heavy-handedly by Georgia, but in 1990 South Ossetia declared independence within the Soviet Union, confirmed by a referendum. In December the Georgian Supreme Soviet abolished the autonomous region and declared a state of emergency there.

The Shevardnadze government released the chair of the South Ossetian Supreme Soviet from prison, blaming Gamsakhurdia's runaway nationalism for all the preceding problems. However, another referendum called for integration with the Russian Federation and in 1992 Georgian troops attacked the capital, Tskhinvali; 400 Georgians and over 1,000 Ossetians were killed before a ceasefire was brokered in June. Monitors from the Organisation for Security and Co-operation in Europe (OSCE) and Russian peacekeeping troops managed to maintain this until 2008, and many refugees returned home. However, many South Ossetians were unable to forgive the brutality of the Georgian military. Lyudvig Chibirov was elected president in 1996 and South Ossetia seemed to have effectively seceded (with its budget entirely financed by Moscow) until North Ossetia rejected the idea of unification. In 1999, relations worsened after Chibirov's party lost elections (held illegally, according to Georgia) to Russian-oriented communists, who won more than 80% of the seats, and the Georgian government cut the electricity supply to just 30 minutes per day. In 2001 Chibirov himself lost a presidential election (also unrecognised by Georgia), to the more radical Eduard Kokoiti, a 37-year-old Moscow-based businessman, and in March 2002 the South Ossetian parliament asked the Russian Duma to recognise its independence. Saakashvili's rapid success in bringing Adjara back into the fold led him to try for the same result in South Ossetia, leading to rapid militarisation there. Saakashvili claimed Russia was using the illegal gun trade in Tskhinvali, a market claimed to be worth US$20 million a year, to undermine Georgia's economy, and in August 2004 sent in Interior Ministry troops to close it down, resulting in several dozen deaths. In 2005 he offered an autonomous parliament and government but this was dismissed by Kokoiti. In July 2006 Oleg Albarov, secretary of South Ossetia's National Security Council, was killed by a bomb, allegedly for being willing to talk to Georgia – but the attack was blamed by South Ossetia on Georgia. Five days later a bomb exploded in front of the home of a South Ossetian MP; he was unharmed, but two teenagers were killed and four passers-by were wounded. In September missiles were fired at two Georgian helicopters, one carrying Georgia's defence minister, and one Georgian and three South Ossetian policemen were killed in a clash outside Tskhinvali.

Kokoiti, running against token opponents, was re-elected president in November 2006, and another referendum called for independence – Georgian passport-holders were not allowed to vote and only South Ossetia and Russia took the results seriously. Georgia set up a parallel administration in a Georgian-majority village outside Tskhinvali.

The tensions between Georgia and Russia over the question of South Ossetian and Abkhazian sovereignty came to a head in the summer of 2008, both sides insisting that it was the other that had initiated the conflict. Georgia, accused of shelling South Ossetian villages, killing six civilians, claimed that it had merely responded to South Ossetian attacks on Georgian-controlled villages; Russia claimed it was 'unable to control the Ossetian militias'. Stupidly responding to provocation, Saakashvili launched a brutal military attack against Tskhinvali on the night of 7–8 August. Russian forces counter-attacked in South Ossetia and bombed targets deep within Georgian territory, and then Russian marines landed on the Black Sea Coast. A third front was opened at the Kodori Gorge adjoining Svaneti with the participation of Russian and Abkhaz forces. The Georgian army held off the invasion for a couple of days, as Russian forces shot down several of their own planes; a Russian general was wounded by shrapnel, and tank commanders resorted to using mobile phones and shop-bought GPS (ie: US satellites) instead of the faulty equipment they had been issued with (clearly the Russian army was re-equipped before getting involved in Ukraine). However, overwhelming force eventually told and after five days Russian troops had occupied the Georgian cities of Poti, Zenaki, Gori and Zugdidi, stopping outside Tbilisi only due to US pressure. This was also the first cyber war, with attacks on Georgian government servers. A ceasefire brokered by the French-led EU was agreed on 12 August although skirmishing continued for a while. Russia withdrew its forces to buffer zones around South Ossetia and Abkhazia by 8 October and has kept troops in South Ossetia under a bilateral agreement.

The war may have been short but it was costly: hundreds died, thousands were injured; Tskhinvali was left in ruins, many ethnic Georgian villages were razed to the ground, and an estimated 20,000 ethnic Georgians and 24,000 Ossetians were displaced. About 17,500 have been housed in new settlements around Gori and elsewhere. Late in August, militias were still looting Georgian villages in South Ossetia while Russian troops looked on. Despite Georgia's refusal to recognise its existence as a bona fide political entity, South Ossetia remains, de facto, an independent territory that is recognised, along with Abkhazia, by just four nations – Russia, Nicaragua, Venezuela and Nauru.

The war finally ended the Georgian belief in quick fixes to solve the Abkhazia and South Ossetia disputes; they now realise that they'll have to entice the secessionists back with prosperity and stability in the longer term. Likewise, Georgians have lost their unrealistic expectations of speedy integration into the West and particularly NATO. Meanwhile, the conflict convinced Putin that he could seize Crimea without Western interference. However, in July 2015, just as this book went to press, Russian troops moved the South Ossetian border fence 300m south, to within 500m of Georgia's east–west highway – and over a 1.6km section of BP's Baku–Supsa pipeline – leading to international outrage but predictably little action. For updates, see www.bradtupdates.com/georgia.

In December 2011, former South Ossetian Education Minister Alla Dzhioyeva won, according to unofficial results, the election for de facto leader as the population rejected the corrupt and authoritarian Kokoiti regime, defeating the Kremlin's nominee Anatoly Tibilov; the Supreme Court of South Ossetia annulled the election, accepting Tibilov's absurd charges that Dzhioyeva had bribed voters, and barred her from new elections in March 2012. She was hospitalised after a raid by around 200 masked security personnel on her headquarters, and Tibilov was elected to succeed Kokoiti. He appointed Dzhioyeva deputy premier and David Sanakoyev (defeated in the presidential runoff) foreign minister, and opened criminal investigations into how most of the 27.3 billion roubles allocated for reconstruction by the Kremlin in 2008–11 had simply vanished.

Following Abkhazia's 'friendship, cooperation and mutual help' treaty with Russia, South Ossetia was happy to accept a treaty with even less autonomy; Tibilov has said that he simply wants to join the Russian Federation. With a population of just 20,000, few natural resources apart from timber, and virtually all its food imported from Russia at inflated prices, he may have little choice.

AFTER SAAKASHVILI Bidzina Ivanishvili created an alliance to defeat Saakashvili and to make him prime minister for no more than two years, and used his immense wealth to achieve that. He appointed a government of calm pragmatic types, many with experience of life and business in the West. A number of members of the Saakashvili regime disappeared, although some have been jailed and had their ill-gotten gains confiscated; the Georgian Dream's determination to extradite others to face justice has been widely seen abroad as an unfair witch-hunt, and in December 2012 Saakashvili, still president, threatened to dismiss the government.

In October 2013 Giorgi Margvelashvili, a little-known academic who became the Georgian Dream government's Minister of Education and Science, was elected president. In November, Ivanishvili stepped down as prime minister after just over a year, installing his long-standing associate Erekle Garibashvili as his successor. Saakashvili left Georgia soon after stepping down as president in November 2013 (moving to the US) and has refused to return, but he's willing to testify by Skype (although this is yet to happen); he has since been charged with abuse of office in connection with a 2005 assault on opposition politician Valeri Gelashvili and the November 2007 protests, and also for spending almost GEL400,000 on cosmetic treatments; in November 2014 new charges were laid in the Girgvliani case (page 26). He's still leading the UNM and still appears on Rustavi-2, attacking the government for letting Russia annexe Abkhazia and for ignoring a 'crime wave'.

An EU Association Agreement and DCFTA (Deep and Comprehensive Free Trade Area) was signed in June 2014 (with visa-free travel to the EU expected in 2015), and a NATO–Georgia Substantive Package was agreed in October. Also in June, the fairly clean local elections resulted in the Georgian Dream's David Narmania (another academic who was Minister of Regional Development and Infrastructure) becoming mayor of Tbilisi. In November 2014, the coalition was hit by its first major crisis when Defence Minister Erekle Alasania was dismissed after criticising the arrests of some of his officials on corruption charges as 'an attack on Georgia's Euro-Atlantic choice'. The foreign minister also resigned and his Free Democrats left the ruling coalition; however, 12 independent MPs were recruited to keep it in office. The crisis appeared to be mainly about tensions within an amorphous coalition of unlike-minded parties (including liberals, socialists, and nationalists) with the godfather-like Ivanishvili pulling the strings;

Currently worth just over US$5 billion (almost a third of Georgia's GDP), according to *Forbes* magazine, Bidzina Ivanishvili made his fortune by importing computers to Russia in the 1980s, then co-founding a bank and branching out into metals, mining and real estate. He left Russia when Putin came to power in 2002, living in France before retiring to his native village of Chorvila (near Sachkhere), which was transformed by his donations into an oasis of prosperity; he also subsidised struggling artists and actors, renovated theatres and secretly paid for the construction of the grandiose Sameba Church in Tbilisi. In addition to his home in Chorvila and a huge seaside retreat (with a private zoo), he built his sci-fi glass 'business centre' on a ridge overlooking Tbilisi, hung with replicas of his collection of contemporary art (the originals are in a vault in London).

Having attempted to build a new society from behind the scenes, he finally decided to directly enter politics with the specific purpose of ousting President Saakashvili. Having announced in December 2011 that he was creating a new party and opposition coalition and intended to become prime minister himself, for a very limited period, he didn't appear in public for another ten days, leading to speculation about his reclusiveness and possible messiah complex. His aims were to eradicate corruption, create an independent judiciary and the conditions for restoring Georgia's jurisdiction over Abkhazia and South Ossetia, boost foreign investment and to improve relations with Russia, the US and the EU. He refused to foment street protests, insisting on coming to power only through the ballot box, although the fact remains that his wealth was the key. In fact, he functions perfectly well in public, but doesn't hedge his words like a true politician and is suspicious of colleagues, preferring power to be shared among small parties rather than held by one big one.

Having seen a new president elected in 2013, he left office as promised and continues to work for a civil society, boosting NGOs to continue Georgia's transformation into a 'typically European' society and country. He's planning to put on a daily programme of social and political analysis on his GDS TV channel (its name '2030' reflecting his 20-year strategy), with Ivanishvili himself summarising on Sundays. Having attacked the Saakashvili administration for its lack of transparency, he has, however, created something even more opaque, an elected government that he continues to direct from behind the scenes.

Alasania's dismissal pleased the Kremlin, which saw him as too pro-American, but there's little doubt that Georgia continues to lean to the west.

Despite this, there's a sense of stagnation in the current climate, which may be largely due to the contrast with Saakashvili's hyper-activity and to growing disunity within the ruling coalition. Parliamentary elections are due in the autumn of 2016, which might mark a UNM comeback or perhaps major gains by Alasania (Georgia's most popular politician, especially since his dismissal) and his Free Democrats.

ECONOMY

During the Soviet period, Georgia's industry was, of course, state-owned and directed from Moscow; it was a major supplier of electric locomotives and jet fighters to the Soviet Union, and the city of Rustavi was founded in 1948 to supply metallurgical products. Although there was more private production in agriculture, it was also excessively oriented to the production of tea, citrus fruit, grapes and wine for the rest of the Soviet Union, leaving Georgia dependent on imported grain and meat. Nevertheless Georgia had a higher standard of living than most other republics. Naturally there has been major restructuring since independence, and coupled with the energy crisis (see box below) and the collapse of the Russian market this meant that much of Georgia's industry simply closed down, with production virtually halving in 1992.

GEORGIA'S ENERGY CRISIS

In 1985, Georgia produced 14.4GW of energy (6.2GW of hydro-electric power and 8.2GW of thermal power); however, in 1996 total production was just 7.2GW (6.1GW hydro-electric and just 1.1GW thermal). This was largely due to Turkmenistan cutting off supplies of natural gas (due to unpaid bills of US$465 million) and to a lack of funds to buy fuel elsewhere, but it also illustrates the rottenness of the Georgian state as a whole. During the civil war and the period of chaos that followed, gas supplies and other utilities simply ceased to function. Gas was restored by 1995 in a few cities, such as Gori, where the administration could be bothered; in Tbilisi it began to be restored from 1996, but effectively was only restored in 2000. On New Year's Eve 2000 gas supplies from Russia were cut off, partly due to unpaid debt, but more as cynical political bullying. By 2003 energy production had grown to just 8.3GW (80% hydro-electric and 20% thermal).

There's a huge potential for reducing consumption with elementary energy efficiency measures. Georgia has reserves of 350 million tonnes of relatively poor coal (in the Tqibuli, Tkvartcheli and Akhaltsikhe areas), with a maximum annual output of three million tonnes; oil reserves of around 12 million tonnes are known, though there may be far more. Oil production peaked in 1980 at 3.3 million tonnes and is now just 50,000 tonnes per year, but exploration has restarted and there's now potential for 150,000–200,000 tonnes per year.

Georgia's hydro-electric potential is 100–160 billion kWh, but under a fifth of this has been developed; a new approach is needed, as the gigantism of the Soviet approach leads to dams that soon silt up and cause all kinds of erosion and other environmental problems. Two modern plants opened in 2014, the 6MW Kazbegi HPP (Hydro-electric Power Plant) and the 85MW Paravani HPP, and the government is planning a US$10 billion investment over the next ten years, with projects including the Khudoni (1800MW), Nenskra (280MW), Dariali (109MW), Mestia Chaladidi (30MW) HPPs, plus a Chinese plan for 16 HPPs on the Mtkvari River and more than US$400 million for new power lines. Georgia has emerged from its energy crisis and will actually export power to Turkey via the Black Sea Transmission Line, completed in 2014; it will also see a major reduction in carbon emissions, as well as requiring re-afforestation to make the dam projects carbon-neutral.

As for alternative energy sources, Georgia produces 200–250 million cubic metres per year of geothermal hot water, enough to provide heating for half a million people. Wind energy has huge potential, with a capacity of around 1000MW (4 billion KW per year) and the 20MW Kartli wind energy project near Gori to open in 2016.

In 1993 Georgia withdrew from the rouble zone, introducing a temporary coupon currency, and then in 1995 its own currency, the lari (meaning 'scales', as in *libra* or *lire*), at GEL1.3 to the US dollar. By the end of 1993 a combination of pyramid savings frauds, the Abkhazia war (which cost 50 million roubles a day) and a disastrous policy of printing money had caused hyperinflation. Consumer prices rose by 15,606% in 1994: savings were wiped out, industry shut down, half the economy went underground and the tax base fell from 40% of GDP to under 10% – the lowest in the former Soviet Union. This led to Georgia applying to the IMF for help, and committing itself to the required reforms. From September 1994 prices were freed, and privatisation began in 1995, although there was little progress in Adjara. The electrical supply industry was split up and privatised in 1998, and land, water supply, ports and telecommunications followed.

The economy turned around in 1995; in 1996 and 1997, Georgia had the fastest-growing economy in the Newly Independent States, with GDP growth over 11% for 1996 and 1997 (admittedly from a very low base), but 1998 was a bad year, with a poor harvest, and an appallingly low rate of tax collection; the lari had to be devalued in the wake of the Russian economic collapse. GDP grew by 3% in 1998 and 1999, and by just 1.9% in 2000 (to US$4.8 billion), after a drought hit agriculture again. Nevertheless manufacturing output rose by 10%, and mining by 75%, and services have grown steadily as a share of the economy. Average incomes crept above the subsistence level, but in fact expenditure was 36% above reported income on average, indicating that people were rather better off than they let on. In 2002, GDP grew by 5.4% to US$3.3 billion (US$674 per head), and inflation was 6%. Tax collection improved slightly, with some high-profile raids to spread the message, but customs was still corrupt and inefficient; in 1998 excise stamps, printed by the German company that is also printing the euro notes, were introduced on alcohol and tobacco, to reduce evasion. As a result of the shortfall in tax revenues, IMF loans were delayed and public spending was cut across the board, except for social spending.

The retirement age was raised by five years, to 65 for men and 60 for women; a State Social Allowance was introduced in 1998, intended mainly as a top-up for lone pensioners, of GEL9 a month, in addition to the basic GEL15.

In the years between the Rose Revolution and the South Ossetia war the Saakashvili government produced some remarkable economic achievements, an anti-corruption drive yielded big increases in tax revenue and privatisations also boosted the state coffers. The civil service was cut and the tax code simplified, persuading international lenders to restructure Georgia's debt and provide more aid. This allowed the government to pay, and increase, pensions, to refurbish infrastructure, and to strengthen the military. By 2007 many big construction projects (notably pipelines, worth US$195 million, the new terminal at Tbilisi Airport, worth US$65 million; the Khulevi oil terminal, worth US$45 million, and hotels in Adjara, worth US$100 million) were also complete.

The economy almost doubled in size in the first five years of the century, from GEL6.7 billion in 2001 to GEL11.5 billion (US$6.4 billion – US$1,424 per capita) in 2005. GDP grew by 9.3% in 2005, and probably would have grown by a bit more in 2006 until the Russian economic sanctions knocked it back to 8% (about GEL13 billion). Growth was predicted to be 8% for 2007, then 6–7% for 2008–10, but thanks to the 2008 South Ossetia war this would not be achieved and GDP fell by 5% in 2009.

Georgia struggled with high inflation in the 2004–08 period and agreed with the IMF to cut the fiscal deficit from 4% of GDP (GEL550 million) to 2% (GEL340 million), which kept inflation to around 9% at the start of 2007. By 2012 it was estimated at

3.3% and in Janury 2015 stood at 1.4%. High unemployment remains a perennial problem. In 2006 it was estimated that 12% of the labour force was unemployed (26% in Tbilisi), and in mid-2014 this had risen to 14%; however, it's estimated that 22% of the economy is in the untaxed shadow sector, down from 53% in 2003. Such figures may not be wholly accurate, however, as statistically anyone who owns half a hectare of farming land, even if it is not used, is classified as being employed, and many of the unemployed are actually working in the shadow economy.

Up until 2008 Russia had been Georgia's main trading partner, but trade with Turkey grew steadily throughout the first decade of the 21st century and by 2009 formed the largest share of Georgia's trade, accounting for almost 20% of its exports and 18% of its imports.

The 2008 South Ossetia war severely affected Georgia's economy: the IMF estimated Georgia's nominal GDP to be US$10.3 billion in 2007, but this fell by 3.9% in the following year. Similarly, foreign investment fell to a mere US$150 million in the third quarter of 2008 compared with US$430 million in the first and US$525 million in the second. Georgian currency came under pressure in the period following the war but financial stability was maintained thanks mainly to international aid; in 2014 there was a 25% drop in remittances from Georgians working in Russia (to US$116 million) due to the collapse of the Russian economy and the fall of the rouble, so that the lari's value also fell by 9% against the US dollar. GDP grew by 4.7% in 2014 (to US$16.1 billion, or US$2,157 per capita) and should be at least 5% in 2015. The current account deficit is high but is expected to decline from 2015, with tax revenues ahead of expectations, and expenditure often less than budgeted.

Georgia's foreign trade increased in 2014 to US$10.3 billion, with exports growing 0.5% to US$2.62 billion and imports by 9% to US$7.7 billion. Foreign trade with CIS countries fell 4% to 31% of the total and trade with EU countries grew by 4%. Georgia's main trading partners are Turkey (US$1.7bn), Azerbaijan (US$1.07bn) and Russia (US$752m). Surprisingly, Georgia's main export, worth US$492.5m, is cars (and minibuses) – imported, fettled up and sent onwards at a profit. Next come ferroalloys (US$260.8m), copper ores and concentrates (US$229m), wine (US$184m), nuts (US$161m) and mineral waters (US$130m). In 2013, Russia lifted its ban on Georgian wine and now takes 63% of Georgia's wine exports; however, Georgia has worked hard to find new markets and now sells wine to 46 countries. Wine exports grew 33% by volume and 36% in value on 2014, with brandy exports doing almost as well.

Foreign direct investment in the third quarter of 2014 was US$508 million, 99% higher (virtually double) that in the same period of 2013. US$149 million of this came from China, and US$181 million was invested in construction, followed by the transport and communication sector, real estate, manufacturing, finance, energy, hotels and restaurants, and agriculture.

In the future, one of the best sources of foreign exchange should be tourism; in the Soviet era four million tourists a year (and 47% of all foreign visitors to the Soviet Union) came to Georgia, almost all to the Abkhazian coast. The loss of Abkhazia, coupled with the occupation of Georgia's hotels by refugees from Abkhazia and the general economic crisis, almost wiped out the tourist industry. The 2008 South Ossetia war with Russia was another considerable setback as many countries like the UK and USA issued travel advisories against travel to Georgia. The top end of the business is over-regulated, but there's also a huge number of rooms available informally. Tourism is now increasing once again, from a very low base; in 2014 there were 5.5 million international arrivals (1.6 million of them from Turkey), 1.9% more than in 2013. The number of Israeli tourists to Georgia has doubled every year for the past three years, and many more Poles and Ukrainians are coming too.

GOD GAVE GEORGIA TO THE GEORGIANS – BUT CAN THEY HOLD ON TO IT?

Rowan Stewart

A lot of rhetoric flows about the beauty and hospitality of this fertile land. The tourist potential of Georgia is immense and it appeals to foreign investors, especially the tourism sector. However, business control and the majority of profits will remain firmly with the foreign investor, leaving minimal financial benefit for Georgia and, more particularly, the local community.

Tourism is a powerful and unpredictable beast, as other parts of the world can testify; its capacity to ravage communities and environments, distort local economies and prostitute cultures is frightening. Handled carefully, it can bring considerable benefits to local people as well as providing a friendlier, more authentic experience to visitors. The skills and training gained in the trade are easily transferable. If organised properly, local ownership of tourism facilities can provide much-needed income. Furthermore, it improves the chance of local cultures being presented to visitors in an accurate and respectful way. By placing control with local people, villagers are to some extent protected from outsider 'fat-cats' and from a dehumanising tourist invasion which reduces villages to zoos, and cultures to roadside spectacles. Throughout the world a new kind of tourism is coming to life which rejects multi-national ownership and control. With so many large elegant houses standing empty, so many skilled, well-educated people unemployed and its excellence at hospitality, Georgia is ideally placed to choose this new kind of tourism.

Today the elegantly carved balconies of Tbilisi gaze disdainfully down on Guinness bars and McDonald's. Will this small pristine land succumb to a new invasion of foreign investors bent only on exploitation?

AGRICULTURE Agriculture suffered as much as the rest of the economy, with production in 1995 half that of 1990; but the 1997 and 2001 harvests were good, thanks to privatisation, foreign technical aid and credit, and agriculture offers promise for the future. Although its share of GDP has fallen from 38% in 1995 to just 9% in 2013, it still employs half the workforce. This was the only Soviet Republic where farmers were able to keep some of their land, and privatisation of collectivised land began in 1992. Only 13.2% of agricultural land (although over half the better-quality land) had been privatised by 1998. In 2013 a law allowed the creation of agricultural co-operatives, but unfortunately people confuse them with collective farms.

PEOPLE

With 15 major ethnic groups (and up to 80 in Tbilisi), Georgia is the least homogeneous of the Transcaucasian states. The population is probably about 4.95 million, although statistics are unreliable, due to population movements since the 1989 Soviet census, when the population was 5.5 million, including Abkhazia and South Ossetia; many Russians, Armenians, Jews and Greeks have left the country, some Georgians have returned home but some still live and work in Russia. It is estimated that almost 84% of the population is Georgian, 6.5% Azeri, 5.7% Armenian, 2% Ossetian, 1.5% Russian and other groups, including 95,000 Kurds, 52,000 Ukrainians, 12,000 Jews, 8,600 Belarussians, 6,000 Assyrians and

4,000 Tatars. Germans, invited to come as colonists in the 1780s by Potyomkin, first viceroy of Caucasus, were deported to Central Asia in 1941 but then left for Germany. As of 2010 there are about 260,000 Internally Displaced Persons or refugees, mainly from Abkhazia. Life expectancy is 74 on average (70 for men and 78 for women), and the population is ageing, 16.4% now being over 65 years old. The birth rate is one of the highest in Europe (and rising), while the abortion rate is falling. The population density is 78 per square kilometre overall, and up to 300 per square kilometre in the fertile plains; 56% of the population is urban (one-third of them in Tbilisi).

Overall, the Georgians are marked by what the historian W E D Allen called 'aesthetic irresponsibility'; or as the writer Laurens van der Post put it, they and the Irish both 'realise the positive creative uses of irresponsibility'. They are impulsive and passionate people for whom hospitality and having a good time are the highest aims. Unlike the more serious Armenians, who have suffered from genocidal attacks more than once, the Georgians have managed to dance their way through history and come out laughing. The Georgians grew out of a blend of Neolithic and Bronze Age cultures, and the present-day nation is still a mix of very different types: the Megrels or Mingrelians in the west who are quick, smart, boastful and can't be stopped from feeding guests; the naïve and funny Svans; the extremely hospitable and talkative Imeretians; the slow and careful Rachvels; the political and humorous Gurians; the calm wine-loving Kakhetians; not to mention the Karts, Khevsurians, Pshavians, Mokhevians and Meskhians. As for the Adjarians, they are said to have all the above qualities; they are ethnically and linguistically Georgian but mostly Muslim in religion.

Some groups share ethnicity and religion with the majority population but are linguistically distinct: these include the million or so Megrels, the Svans, and the Laz, most of whom (around 200,000) live across the border in the Hopa region of Turkey. Related to the Megrels, the Laz are very extrovert and humorous, and tend to have reddish hair.

MINORITY COMMUNITIES The **Armenians** form the largest ethnic minority in Georgia and are found all over the country; however, the vast majority live either in Tbilisi (200,000) and in the Javakheti region (Javakhk in Armenian, around Akhalkalaki and Ninotsminda), where they form a majority of the population. Their ancestors settled here as refugees from western Anatolia during the 19th-century Russo–Turkish wars, and also just before and after World War I. It's a bleak area with poor infrastructure, and there is some discontent with the bad conditions here. Tbilisi, on the other hand, has always been a major centre of Armenian culture and continues to produce many leading figures in Armenian life. Their lingua franca has always been Russian, and few in the rural areas speak Georgian. The Armenian government is not particularly interested in changing its borders, but it takes an interest in the wellbeing of the Armenian population in Georgia.

Russians are scattered thinly across Georgia, apart from small groups of religious dissidents such as Molokans and Doukhobors, mainly in the centre and south. Some arrived in the 19th century, but the bulk came during the Soviet period, settling mainly in urban and industrial areas such as Tbilisi and Rustavi as well as in Abkhazia. These later arrivals tend not to speak Georgian and many have emigrated in recent years, mainly to Russia but also to Canada and elsewhere. This has drained away many of Georgia's skilled workers and technicians. However, Georgians see Russian men as drunks and the women as sexually easy ('sleep with Russians, marry a Georgian' is the Georgian male's credo).

The **Azeri** population occupied the southeastern corner of the country, around Marneuli, Bolnisi and Gardabani, in the early 17th century when it was de-populated by the Persian wars. This is an underdeveloped area and life is tougher than these hard-working farmers deserve, although they are relatively well off. They are mostly Shia Muslims, although not fervently so. Between 1926 and 1989, when the national population doubled, their population quadrupled. Not all are ethnically Azeri in the purest sense, but it's generally accepted that all the Turkophone Muslims in Georgia can be included in this category, and the government of Azerbaijan does take a certain degree of responsibility for them.

Until recently the majority of the 165,000 **Ossetians** in Georgia lived outside the then autonomous region – mainly in Tbilisi and Rustavi, and also in some rural areas. An Indo-European people, speaking an Iranian language, they are unrelated to the other peoples of the Caucasus. They are held to be the descendants of the Alans, one of the many nomadic peoples who came out of Asia and settled in the north Caucasus. During the last two centuries they have increasingly moved into the highlands on the south of the Caucasus, living peacefully for the most part (and inter-marrying) with the Georgians. Now many have moved to South Ossetia, and there's a tendency towards learning Russian rather than Georgian, especially now that cultural ties have been strengthened with the north Caucasus. Most are Orthodox Christians, although some of the later arrivals are Sunni Muslim, and paganism still plays a strong part in their religious lives.

The **Abkhaz** are considered to be one of the aboriginal peoples of the Caucasus, entitling them to an autonomous republic under Stalin's scheme for ethnic relations (while the South Ossetians, having arrived relatively recently, were entitled only to an autonomous region). Even before secession, they almost all lived in Abkhazia, but they formed just 18% of the republic's population; since secession they have formed a much higher proportion of its population, due to Georgians and other groups like Armenians and Russians leaving. Closely related to the Adigh peoples of the northern Caucasus, they have preserved their traditional culture and their highly prized oral literary heritage. The population is made up of both Christians and Sunni Muslims, although many Muslims emigrated to Turkey after the Russian conquest in the 19th century.

Greeks live in the Tsalka and Tetri-Tskaro areas of Lower Kartli (the so-called Anatolian Greeks, or Rums), and on the Black Sea Coast (the Pontian Greeks). Although it's tempting to assume that the latter have been there ever since the classical Greeks established trading ports, in fact they arrived from 1829, fleeing persecution in Turkey. Although most are Orthodox Christians, some have converted to Islam. There's a steady flow back to Greece, although some speak Pontian Ancient Greek rather than the modern language, and most of those in Lower Kartli (a poor isolated community) speak Turkish; many have also moved to Tbilisi.

Most of the **Kurds** in Georgia are Yezidi (Mithraist pagans), descended from refugees from Ottoman persecution. They live mainly in Tbilisi and Rustavi, but although fairly well integrated socially, they preserve their distinct ethnic identity, language and cultural traditions. There was also a small rural (Muslim and Turkish-speaking) population living in southern Georgia, which was deported to Central Asia in 1944.

It's a proud boast in Georgia, and largely true, that **Jews** have lived there for 2,600 years without suffering persecution (ironically, yet another way for Georgians to show their superiority to the Russians). It may have helped that they have the same appetite for wine as the Georgians. The population numbered about 80,000

1

in the 1970s but is now reduced to around 13,000, divided between Ashkenazim (European or Russian Jews) and Georgian Jews (Georgian-speaking, and considered as Sephardim due to their religious ritual); over half live in Tbilisi, with many of the rest in the west of the country. As a rule they feel very attached to Georgia, and although most have now emigrated to Israel and, to a lesser extent, the USA, they maintain close links with Georgia and preserve Georgian cultural traditions.

Georgia and Turkey are the only two countries that are home to all three families of **gypsies** – the Rom, Dom and Bosha– with just 4,400 or so in Georgia.

Finally, a group that currently is scarcely represented in Georgia are the so-called **Meskhetian Turks**. Under the Ottomans, Javakheti was heavily Islamicised from 1624, producing a population of mixed Georgian and Turkish ethnicity; in November 1944 all 70,000–120,000 of these people were deported to Central Asia, for supposedly pro-Turkish (and thus possibly pro-Axis) sentiments – even though most of their menfolk were serving in the Red Army. Unlike most other deported groups they were not allowed to return after the Stalinist era, and struggled to establish themselves in their new homes. After the break-up of the Soviet Union, and mob violence against them in Uzbekistan in 1989 (officially ascribed to a dispute over the price of strawberries), they began demanding to return home, moving to the northern Caucasus and Azerbaijan. Now they number around 300,000, of whom 100,000 live in camps in northern Azerbaijan. Georgia is reluctant to take them back, due to its lack of resources, but in 1996 agreed to a plan for 5,000 to return, subject to their learning the Georgian language and other conditions. Nothing happened, and in September 1998 a demonstration in their support in Tbilisi met with a heavy-handed response; due to international pressure an initial 5,000 should soon return. The government is still procrastinating, as it is already struggling to cope with the displaced people from Abkhazia and South Ossetia.

LANGUAGE

While the Turks and Azeris speak Turkic languages, and the Armenians, Ossetians and Russians speak Indo-European languages, **Georgian** is the most important of the Caucasian group of languages. This is divided into three families: the South Caucasian or Kartvelian – comprising Georgian (Kartuli), Megrelian, Laz and Svan, spoken by 3.5 million people in all – and the relatively similar northeastern and northwestern Caucasian families, spoken by about a million people each. These comprise about 40 languages in an area the size of France, although Strabo recorded that in the 1st century BC the Romans needed no fewer than 70 interpreters in the Dioscurias (Sukhumi) area alone. Just in Daghestan there are 14 ethnic groups and 29 languages, and it's no surprise that the name Caucasus derives from the Arabic for 'mountain of languages'.

Efforts have been made to place the Caucasian languages in a 'super-group' with the Indo-European, Turkic, Semitic, Finno-Ugric and even Chinese languages, but no links have been proved. Nor has it been possible to prove links with Basque, although some scholars speak of an Ibero-Caspian group.

The Caucasian languages are all grammatically complex; the northwestern languages have verbs with a huge variety of inflections, while the northeastern ones have simple verbs, but complex nouns, with up to eight grammatical classes (such as male, female, animal and mass noun), and up to 46 cases. The southern languages, ie: Georgian, have both a large case system for the noun and complex verbs. Likewise, they all have complex sound systems. The northwestern languages have only two distinct vowels, but highly complex consonant systems. The northeastern languages have fewer consonants, but large numbers of vowels. The southern languages are simpler but still have enormous clusters of consonants, 'back-of-the-throat death-rattles' that utterly baffle foreigners. Georgians love to test foreigners with tongue-twisters such as '*Baqaqi tskalshi kikinebs*' (the frog is croaking in the water), and a similar one about the duck (*ikhwi*) going quack (*khaadha*) in the water. Just to make things even harder, there are no capital letters.

Naturally, **Russian** is still used as the lingua franca of the area; virtually everyone over 30 in Georgia is bilingual, and few have any hang-ups about using the colonisers' language. However, Russian is being replaced by English as the second language in schools. **Turkish** may be useful in Batumi and also Kutaisi.

The Georgian alphabet has five vowels and 28 consonants, and looks like nothing else on earth, except the Armenian alphabet. An alphabet may have existed in the 3rd century BC but was supplanted by Greek and Aramaic; the present alphabet may have begun to evolve with the arrival of Christianity, and was certainly in use by AD450; after the 10th century a more cursive script was adopted that was smaller and easier to read. There are a variety of forms of many letters, but at least there's no upper or lower case. The Abkhaz language uses an extended Cyrillic (Russian) alphabet.

See *Appendix 1*, pages 294–5, for vocabulary and other practical information.

RELIGION

Christianity was introduced to Georgia in the 1st century by the apostle Andrew the First-Called, who travelled around the Black Sea before becoming the first Patriarch of Constantinople, and also by the apostles Simon and Matthew. Armenia was converted to **Christianity** in AD301 (or perhaps AD314); in AD313 the Roman emperor Constantine granted freedom of worship to Christians and it became the most favoured religion in the empire. However, it didn't become the sole official religion until AD380, while Georgia was converted in AD337, making it the world's second Christian nation. St Nino, a slave from Cappadocia, cured a child by placing her hair shirt on him and praying; Queen Nana heard of this and Nino cured her by prayer of some unknown malady, and converted her to Christianity. King Mirian followed his wife in converting when Nino was able to cause a thunderbolt to destroy the pagan idols, followed by an eclipse of the sun which she didn't lift until he agreed to convert. However, Christianity was not firmly established until the 6th century, when the Syrian Fathers came from Antioch; it's uncertain whether they were Georgians or Chalcedonians, but it's clear they could speak the language before they arrived. They founded several monasteries in Kartli and Kakheti, such as Shiom-ghvime, Zedazeni, Samtavisi, Alaverdi, Nekresi and Davit-Gareja, and spread the Gospel throughout the country. Between AD790 and 861 more monasteries were founded by St Gregory of Khantza. In the 10th century classical texts such as Zeno's *On Nature* and works by Porphyrius were preserved in Georgian monasteries, and the texts of Buddhism were first translated by St Euthymius in the Georgian monastery on Mount Athos, in Greece. Bachkovo, the second most important monastery in Bulgaria, was founded in 1083 by the Georgian Grigorii Bakuriani, who renounced the governorship of Smolyan and Edirne to be a monk, and his brother Abasius.

For centuries the **Orthodox Church** was split by theological disputes and heresies: firstly Arianism, which denied the full deity of Jesus claiming that he was created by God, and 'there was a time when he was not'; and then from the 4th century Monophysitism, the doctrine that Jesus had only one nature, rather than two, divine and human. Finally, in the 5th century, Nestorianism argued against the Virgin Mary being called 'mother of God', claiming she was mother of Christ only in his human aspect. Monophysitism was popular in the monasteries of Davit-Gareja and it survives as official doctrine of the Armenian Church; however, the Georgian Apostolic Autocephalous Church has followed the official Orthodox line. It was granted autocephaly or self-governing status in AD466; this was abolished in 1811, when authority was transferred to the Moscow patriarchate.

Stalin repressed religion here as elsewhere, but by 1943 he felt he'd broken its back and recognised autocephaly. In the post-Stalinist period there was a limited revival in the Church's fortunes, and from 1988 some churches were reopened. However, it never played the sort of role in the nationalist movement that the Roman Catholic Church did in Poland and Lithuania, partly due to its conservative hierarchical nature and its addiction to being allied with authority, and partly due to the Catholicos, Ilia II, having been selected by the KGB.

While the Orthodox Church may seem utterly conservative, many monks are extremely fundamentalist and regard the Catholicos and priests as dangerously liberal. In particular, the decision to join the World Council of Churches was seen as virtually heretical (Orthodox doctrine being that there are no other legitimate churches), and Ilia was forced to reverse this in 1997. Nevertheless, the next year he celebrated the 20th anniversary of the election of the Pope, who then visited Georgia in 1999. The True Orthodox sect, which also exists in Russia and Greece, is also active here, and has links with extreme nationalist groups such as the Zviadists. Fundamentalist groups such as Jvari (the Cross) and the Society of Saint David the Builder have been accused of orchestrating attacks on Baptists, Pentecostalists and Jehovah's Witnesses; but Saakashvili tackled harassment of those following non-traditional faiths, for instance by sending police to break into a church and arrest a priest blamed for attacks on Jehovah's Witnesses. The 14,000-odd **Jehovah's Witnesses** have seen widespread discrimination, due mainly to their pacificism, but are now highly visible on the streets handing out leaflets. The tiny **Roman Catholic** congregation is due largely to Turkish oppression of Orthodox believers in the 17th century, mainly in Meskheti.

As described above, there are various **Muslim** communities (mostly Shia) and a very long-established **Jewish** presence (pages 41–2), with synagogues in Tbilisi, Kutaisi and Batumi. Most of the Kurds are **Yezid** or openly **pagan** rather than Muslim, but in fact pagan influences can be found throughout Georgia, and above all in the remoter mountain areas. Decorative motifs are often derived from nature

THE LEGEND OF SAINT GEORGE

St George, the patron saint of Georgia and England, was a senior Roman army officer who was martyred in Palestine in about AD300. The legend that he saved a Libyan princess by killing a dragon arose in the 12th century, possibly from the myth of Perseus slaying a sea monster near the site of George's martyrdom. He had nothing to do with England but, also in the 12th century, Crusaders picked up the habit of praying for his help in battle and in 1347 England's Order of the Garter was founded in his name. Nor does he have anything to do with the name 'Georgia', which comes from *gurj*, the ancient Arabic and Persian name for the country, perhaps derived from *gorg* or wolf, a pagan idol. George is also patron of Portugal, Aragon, Catalonia and Lithuania, and of horsemen, landowners, herdsmen and travellers.

AINworship, and fertility rites and offerings can be found in many places, notably trees with pieces of cloth tied to the branches, as at a Cornish holy well. This is especially so in Svaneti – see *Chapter 8* for more details.

There are also many premature deaths in Svaneti, mainly due to traffic accidents, although inter-family feuds are not as prevalent as they once were – see page 229 for the elaborate funeral rites there. Georgian **cemeteries** are usually fenced plots on the edge of fields, rather than next to a village church; in the west of the country the graves can be very elaborate, often roofed and with benches, and sometimes a family plot will be more like a *dacha* or summer house. Easter in particular is a time for feasting at the graveside. **Weddings** are also big events in Georgia, traditionally lasting for two or three days, with brain-damaging quantities of alcohol consumed. On summer and autumn Saturdays (the Tbilisoba weekend seems particularly popular in Tbilisi) you'll see many convoys of over-excited people rushing to and from churches, hooting and yelling and driving even worse than usual. Women in particular should dress respectfully to enter churches, and cover their heads; in Tbilisi there is less need for this.

CULTURE

ARCHITECTURE Lovers of architecture will already be aware of Georgia's churches. On a compact ground plan they combine simple and efficient forms with attractive proportions and perfect harmony with their setting. The oldest, dating from the 4th to 6th centuries, are basilicas derived from the law courts of Rome and Byzantium, a tradition transmitted via Syria and Asia Minor. These are relatively long, straight buildings with a semi-circular apse at the east end for the altar and priest. In Georgia they take two forms: firstly triple-aisled with a common ceiling and no transepts, and then from the late 6th century a uniquely Georgian form known as the triple-naved basilica, which has longitudinal walls and doors rather than arches, and again no transepts. Bolnisi Sioni is the only survivor of the first type, with later and less pure forms at Anchiskhati and Urbnisi.

Domed churches derive from the form of eastern Georgian homes since the 3rd or 4th millennium BC; from the 6th century AD these developed into cruciform churches, with a central cupola at the centre of a cross. In a cruciform church the central area becomes the liturgical focus of the church, under a dome that symbolises the sphere of heaven. Again there are two types: firstly with a semi-circular apse at the east end and the other ends square (such as Samtsevrisi), and secondly the tetraconch form, with apses on all four arms of the cross. This developed fast around the turn of the 7th century, when the Jvari Church at Mtskheta, with smaller chambers filling the spaces between the arms, became the prototype for many others such as Ateni Sioni, Dzveli-Shuamta, Martvili and Dranda. This architectural flowering was stopped by the Arab invasion in the second half of the 7th century, although hybrid forms did appear in the 8th and 9th centuries, with a fusion of central domed church and triple-church basilica, such as at Kvelatsminda (Gurjaani) and Vachnadziani. The Georgian Renaissance brought a new climax in the 11th and 12th centuries, with much bigger churches such as Svetitskhoveli (Mtskheta), Bagrati (Kutaisi) and Alaverdi. In these churches, too, the interior seems unexpectedly large, since the compact proportions of the ground plan keep the volumes tightly packed.

RELIGIOUS ART Many of the churches are decorated with **frescoes**, which are also largely based on Byzantine traditions. Until the mid-9th century the church discouraged the painting of human images, and in the Great Iconoclasm of

AD726–843 all religious art other than images of the cross and symbolic birds and plants was destroyed. However, Byzantine art then entered a Golden Age, named after the ruling Macedonian dynasty, in which the development of the cruciform church was matched by the flowering of fresco and mosaic art. This was now organised thematically with Christ Pantocrater (Lord of All) in the central dome, the Virgin in the apse over the altar, and the Life of Christ and the saints painted elsewhere.

In the Greek tradition the figures portrayed in religious art were strongly modelled but unemotional, with a calm dignity and stern grandeur. However, Georgia was also marked by the much freer and more humanistic tradition of Antioch and Alexandria, in which figures were portrayed more naturalistically and with concern for their emotional impact. There are few ancient mosaics in Georgia, but fresco art reached its peak between the 11th century and the first half of the 13th. The best are those preserved in the churches of Ateni Sioni, Kintsvisi, Timotesubani and Ubisi; and in the cave monasteries of Bertubani and Udabno (at Davit-Gareja) and Vardzia, as well as in Svaneti. Others worth looking at are in the churches of Nekresi, Zemo Krikhi and Gelati.

SAAKASHVILI'S STATEMENTS

As president, Mikheil Saakashvili saw architecture as a key part of his campaign to modernise Georgia at speed; he commissioned foreign architects to produce iconic (and amazingly expensive) statements such as the new parliament in Kutaisi and his own presidential palace. In Tbilisi he also built the Peace Bridge, various buildings for the Justice and Interior ministries and the Bank of Georgia, as well as the new airport; he also fostered a capitalist free-for-all that allowed glitzy new towers to be shoehorned into very unsuitable areas of historic urban fabric. But it's worth noting that he spread the work evenly across the whole country, with almost every good-sized town getting new police stations and a Public Service Hall – and every one of them totally different to all the others – while a remote town like Mestia also received a new airport (and a striking bridge leading to it) and a commercial centre. Border posts were also given special attention.

Most of his modern projects have been interesting and not entirely tasteless, but his treatment of existing buildings and urban settings was less successful. The 'old quarters' of towns like Sighnaghi and Gori and the Rabati (fortress) area of Akhaltsikhe have been over-restored and turned into tacky settings for kitschy restaurants and tourist hotels; the old town of Tbilisi has quite simply been devastated, either left to collapse or dismantled and rebuilt using a concrete structure with nothing authentic about it. He also insisted, against the forceful advice of UNESCO and many experts, on rebuilding, but essentially ruining, the Bagrat Cathedral in Kutaisi. Why the great moderniser felt the need to get into bed with the reactionary church is unclear, but he was in good company, as Bidzina Ivanishvili paid for the construction of the new Sameba Cathedral in Tbilisi.

Saakashvili said in an interview that 'If I hadn't been a politician, I should have been an architect' – perhaps wanting to be remembered as Misha the Builder, echoing the great king Davit Agmashenebelis. Well, at least Georgia was spared that. And, it's worth remembering that far more damage is being done by the monks returning to ancient churches and making them fit for use again, as they have little interest in architecture or heritage conservation.

Icons (religious images) were also produced, of three types: silver, painted on wood, and combined (silver and painting), the silver surface of the icon being generally covered with gilt. The images, of Christ, the Virgin and saints, followed the same stylistic patterns as the frescoes. The standard of metalwork in Georgia is amazing – see pages 131–2.

The sack of Constantinople by the Fourth Crusade was closely followed in Georgia by the Mongol invasions, bringing an end to the high period of Georgian religious art. However, in the secular sphere (illuminated manuscripts, for instance), Persian influence later led to much fine work in Georgia.

PAINTING AND SCULPTURE Perhaps it's unfortunate that Georgia's best-known **paintings** are those of Pirosmani, as his charming naïf works have nearly hidden from foreign view the country's many other fine artists. Many of these worked in Paris in the 1920s and 1930s and were well known at the time. Perhaps the best known was Elena Akhvlediani (1901–75), who was born in Telavi. Her mother was a princess but her father was poor; however, they managed to send her to Tbilisi's Second Gymnasium in 1911 and then to the Tbilisi Art Academy. She spent two years in Italy, and three in Paris, where she exhibited in the Salon des Indépendents, before returning to Georgia in 1927, where she worked for Koté Marjanishvili as a stage designer. After a long and varied career, she was declared a People's Artist of Georgia in 1960, and awarded the Rustaveli Prize in 1971. She had a wide range of styles, none especially challenging, and was the most romantic of the Georgian painters, with a great interest in traditional rural life. She also produced designs for films, and many illustrations for books, by Longfellow and Mark Twain among others, and for some children's stories.

David Kakabadze was born to a peasant family near Kutaisi in 1889, studied science in St Petersburg until 1918, but was then able to change to an artistic career, going to study in Paris in 1920 before living in Tbilisi from 1927 until his death in 1952. Lado Gudiashvili was born in Tbilisi in 1896 and lived in Paris from 1920 to 1925 and then in Tbilisi until his death in 1980. He toed the party line during the Stalinist period (although for some reason his characters often have no ears), but also produced bitterly ironic graphics for private consumption, and played an important role in post-Stalin liberalisation. Niko Pirosmani (once known as Piroshmanvili) was born in 1862 and moved to Tbilisi when he was orphaned; he worked as a self-taught sign painter, earning drinks with his quirky portraits. He was 'discovered' in 1912 by three artists down from Moscow on their holidays, but despite increased earnings his lifestyle did not change. In 1918, he was found unconscious in a basement and taken as an unknown beggar to hospital, where he died. Only 200 of a possible 2,000 of his paintings survive; quite a few can be viewed at www.pirosmani.org/marias. A new website selling Georgian art is www.Georgian-Art.com. The contemporary art scene is surprisingly lively; two of my favourites are Gogi Lazarishvili and Erekle Sutidze.

There's also a strong tradition in Georgia of public art, most notably monumental **sculpture** and mosaics that somehow managed to avoid being totally derailed by communist dogma (there are a few surviving Stalin busts across the country). Iacob Nikoladze (1876–1951) was a student of Rodin and father of Georgian sculpture. The best-known sculptor is Elgudja Amashukeli (1928–2002), whose *Mother Georgia* (1958–63), *King Vakhtang Gorgasali* (1967) and *Pirosmani* (1975) in Tbilisi, and *King David the Builder* (1995) in Kutaisi, are all characterised by stylised monumentalism and muscularity. His contemporary Merab Merabishvili was responsible for the statues of Griboedev (1961) west of Saarbrücken Platz in

Tbilisi, and of Erekle II in Telavi. A possible successor is Merab Berdzenishvili who created the statues of the poets Galaction Tabidze and David Guramishvili (1966) near Chavchavadze Avenue 21, of Paliashvili (1973) outside the Opera House, and of King David the Builder (1997) outside the Hotel Iveria, all in Tbilisi. In Moscow the 'monstrous creations' of Zurab Tsereteli (b1934) are impossible to avoid (thanks to his schoolboy friendship with Mayor Luzhkov) – freakish iron reanimations of Russian folk tales and other high kitsch. A recent project was a 100m-high statue of Columbus to be erected in Puerto Rico to commemorate the 'discovery' of America in 1492. When he saw it the client cancelled the deal, but Tsereteli swiftly arranged for the city of Moscow to buy the statue, calling it 'Peter the Great' (as founder of the Russian navy); Dervla Murphy described it as 'monumental kitsch … a grotesque agglomeration of ships and sails and rigging seeming to rise out of the river, dwarfing every building in sight'. Although he has a house with a very strange and wonderful garden in the hills outside Tbilisi (just visible to the left of the Manglisi road soon after the Vake cemetery), there was very little of his work to be seen in the city, except for the psychedelic mosaic façade of the Israeli embassy (1977), another on the Ortachala bus station (1973), and the statue of St George and the Dragon now installed in Freedom Square, until he created his own museum, MOMA-Tbilisi (page 122).

THEATRE A uniquely Georgian style of theatre, stylised but emotionally powerful, has developed and is rightly seen as one of its national treasures. Under great directors like Robert Sturua (who runs the Rustaveli Theatre in Tbilisi), this style is turned loose on foreign classics as much as on Georgian texts. Shakespeare is a particular favourite, with very successful world tours of plays such as *Richard III*, which oddly is seen as his greatest work. ('It's magnificent, but it's not Shakespeare,' was the comment of the Royal Shakespeare Company's director Adrian Noble.) It's remarkable how many Shakespearean references Georgian journalists use.

GIFT, the Georgian International Festival of the Theatre, was founded in 1997 with a bravura publicity campaign and made a great impact, with many highly renowned international artists and companies appearing for next to nothing; the 1998 festival was smaller, due to funding problems. The festival, in or around October or November each year and based at Tbilisi's Marjanishvili Theatre, is well worth seeing, although there were accusations of political interference by the Saakashvili government when pro-opposition directors were sacked.

BALLET The Georgian National Ballet is usually abroad nowadays, thanks to a worldwide reputation for athleticism and spectacle, including sabre dances and knife-throwing. The State Ballet, now run by Nina Ananiashvili, ex-prima ballerina of the Bolshoi and the American Ballet Theatre, is undergoing a remarkable revival; the ballets of George Balanchine (page 206) are of course very important to them.

FILM Georgia had a highly successful cinema industry, based at the Gruzhia film studios in Tbilisi's Digomi suburb. Sandro Akhmetil worked with the Rustaveli Theatre from 1928 to 1935 before directing films to such effect that he now has a metro station named after him. Koté Marjanishvili also worked at the Rustaveli, and the main square on the left bank of the Mtkvari is named after him. Both men were shot in Stalin's reign of terror.

Sergei Paradjanov was born to an Armenian family in Tbilisi and lived in Kyiv until his death in 1990, so, although he filmed quintessentially Georgian subjects as in *The Surami Fortress*, he's not generally thought of as a Georgian director.

Misha Chaiureli, Stalin's favourite director and a personal friend, made historical and propaganda films, and his daughter Sophiko Chiaureli starred in Paradjanov's masterpiece *The Colour of Pomegranates*. The successful biopic *Pirosmani* was directed by Eldar Shengelaia, son of the director Nikoloz Shengelaia and the actress Nato Vachnadze, after whom the *Nato*, the Georgian equivalent of the Oscar, is named. One of the most successful Georgian films of recent years is *Repentance* (*Monanieba*; 1986, directed by Tenghiz Abuladze), about a dictator who was a thinly veiled composite of Stalin and Beria; it won six prizes. Temur Babluani's *The Sun of the Sleepless* (1991) won a Silver Bear at the Berlin Film Festival. The director Nana Jorjadze, meanwhile, earned an Oscar nomination for *Chef in Love* (with the French comic star Pierre Richard) in 1996 and was elected a member of the Academy of Motion Picture Arts and Sciences. Another success has been *13 Tzameti*, written and directed by Gela Babluani, which won two awards at the 62nd Venice Film Festival and the World Cinema Jury prize at the 2006 Sundance Film Festival. Fine directors such as Jorjadze, Otar Iosseliani, Mikheil Kobakhidze, Dino Tsintsadze and Erekle Kvirikadze are doing well abroad (especially in France), as well as actors such as Dato Bakhtadze, Nutsa Kukhianidze and Merab Ninidze. The mountainous Georgian landscape itself has also become a star: *The Loneliest Planet*, a German–US produced thriller directed by Julia Loktev and starring Mexico's Gael Garcia Bernal and Israeli actress Hani Furstenburg was shot entirely in Georgia in 2010. Both *Corn Island* and *Tangerines* (a Georgian-Estonian co-production) were nominated as Best Foreign Language Film in 2015's Academy Awards.

The Hollywood film *5 Days Of August*, directed by Renny Harlin of *Die Hard 2* fame and starring Andy Garcia as Mikheil Saakashvili, was shot in Tbilisi in 2009 and released in 2011, telling the story of the August 2008 South Ossetian conflict from a pro-Georgian perspective. Saakashvili allowed use of his residence and office for filming, and the Georgian army provided military uniforms, tanks and helicopters. In contrast, the Russian internet film *War 08.08.08: The Art of Betrayal* (*http://war080808. com*) portrays, in documentary form, how the same conflict is seen by the Russians.

LITERATURE The classic work of Georgian literature is *The Knight in the Panther's Skin*, by Shota Rustaveli, who was Queen Tamar's treasurer; the writer Fitzroy Maclean described it as 'a fine allegorical poem of great breadth of vision, harmoniously fusing the currents of Neoplatonist philosophy and eastern romance.' It foreshadows the literature of courtly (platonic) love of the European Renaissance, but was only translated into English after World War I by Marjory Wardrop, whose brother Oliver was then Britain's chief commissioner of Transcaucasia. In the 19th century there was a fine crop of romantic poets, led by Alexander Chavchavadze (1786–1846), a friend of the Russians Pushkin and Griboedov (who married his daughter); others included Nikoloz Baratashvili (1817–45) and Akaki Tsereteli (1840–1915), who is not to be confused with the radical journalist Georgi Tsereteli (1842–1900). Galaction Tabidze (1892–1959) is the most popular of Georgia's 20th-century poets, whose suicide is still bitterly regretted. His less famous cousin Titsian Tabidze (b1895) was shot in the purge of 1937 (he was a close friend of Boris Pasternak, who translated his work into English, and whose genuine love of Georgia probably helped save him in the purges; many of his translations of Georgian poetry were done in Tabidze's flat on Griboedov kucha in Tbilisi). Currently Russia's hottest novelist is Grigori Chkartishvili (under the un-Georgian pseudonym Boris Akunin) whose books about his fictional 19th-century detective Fandorin are aimed at the middle class and are not at all trashy. You'll find detailed information at http://rustaveli.tripod.com/lithistory.html.

GEORGIAN MUSIC Georgia has a wonderful and highly distinctive tradition of **polyphonic singing**, which developed several hundred years before it appeared in western Europe. Instrumental music and music for dancing are also quite common, but as later developments from the vocal tradition. Folk songs span many genres, with women singing traditional lullaby and healing songs, while men, often accompanied by large quantities of wine, sing war and feasting songs; some festival songs may have been sung by men and women together.

Igor Stravinsky said that Georgian polyphony was 'more important than all the discoveries of new music'. This was recognised when it was named part of humanity's intangible cultural heritage by UNESCO in 2001 and the Research Center for Traditional Polyphony of Georgia was founded at Tbilisi State Conservatoire. Its website (*www.polyphony.ge*) is a great source of information on Georgian song.

Georgians sing in a tuning all their own, which baffled the 19th-century musicologists who first tried to transcribe Georgian folk songs and church chants into Western notation. Georgian **folk music** is modal and often breaks out of simple 'major' or 'minor' classifications, being characterised more by the dissonance and resolution of close harmony. This produces a rich sonorous flow of sound stabbed from time to time by startling disharmonies, often repeated, before returning to the smooth flow. Parallel firsts, fifths and octaves, long 'banned' in the West, still predominate in Georgia; minor and major thirds are both considered dissonant, hence the frequent use of non-resolving fourths and sevenths.

Polyphony and harmony are both supposed to have existed in Georgia when both Orient and Occident were still monodic. It's easy to see the roots of polyphony in Georgian **choral song**, in which a single melody was supported by an organ-point or plain chant, to keep the lead singer in pitch; in Georgia the plain chant is usually sung by the middle part. This very strong drone may have evolved for the church acoustic. The 11th-century scholar Ioanne Petrisi explained the nature of the Trinity in terms of the harmonic and melodic functions of the three voices – the *mzehekri mazkhr* or top voice (in fact a mid tenor), *zhir*, a middle voice or low tenor, and *bam* or bass. The various genres of folk song include *mushuri* (working songs), *supruli* (table songs, including toasts), *satrpialo* (love songs) and *sagmiro* (epic songs – a long solo from the oral tradition or from a 19th-century writer such as Chavchavadze). Songs are mostly in the form of a strophic rondo, with or without a refrain, with syllabic setting as a rule. Rhythmically, there's often a swift alternation of 3/4 and 6/8 in the same phrase, accounting for the 'bouncy' nature of Georgian secular song.

The most complex polyphony is to be found in the western regions, above all in Guria, where the composer Honegger was defeated trying to notate a seven-part song; every voice is given a special degree of freedom, with even the bass improvising freely and taking solos. *Naduri* songs (from *nadi*, voluntary co-operative labour for harvesting or house-building) are unique to Guria, with two choruses of four voices alternating; the top voice (*gamkivani* or *krimanchuli*) simply indulges in yodel-like wordless cries, the tenor or *damtskebi* carries the poetic text, the third voice or *shemkmobari* carries the organ-point, and the bass or *bani* sings a wordless melodic counterpoint to the tenor. The Mingrelians also excel in weaving voices, with 'composed' *ritenuti* and *accelerandi*. Mingrelia is the only place where you may find mixed choruses of men and women. Wordless (glossolalic) phrases (like 'hey-nonny-no' in an English madrigal) are especially common in the west of Georgia.

Svaneti, high in the Caucasus, has kept alive a primeval and ethereal style of three-part singing, with pentatonic harmonies (unlike the rest of Georgia). This is often accompanied by the *changi*, the Svan harp, which looks as if it's come straight off a Greek vase, or the lute-like *chianuri* or *panduri* (which can only be played by men). Svaneti is also rich in round-dances called *perkhuli*, which gradually accelerate to end in fantastic male dance solos, and in female mourning songs. The funeral traditions here and in Racha combine pre-Christian wailing traditions with Christian singing, mainly by women though sometimes by men, but not together.

In eastern Georgian songs the bass often sings a long steady wordless drone, over which the heroic tenors sing ornamented tunes with words in close harmony; church chants show similarities to the region's secular music, although all parts sing words. Some of the richest, most sonorous and wine-soaked songs predictably come from Kakheti, while further south you find the long, lyrical *orovel*, a rare example of a solo song originally sung while ploughing or riding an oxcart. These are closely related in name and sound to the *horhovel* songs of Armenia.

Church music, which shows a direct line of descent from Byzantium, is slower and softer than secular music with harmonies and melodic patterns more interwoven, and a static rhythm. Hymns are sung with great intensity and voices overlapping to give continuous moving harmonies, as if the singers are not breathing. The unique Orthodox chant tradition of medieval Georgia survives in the form of manuscripts from the 10th century onwards and from handwritten transcriptions from the early 20th century into Western musical notation. Chant developed as Byzantine texts were translated in Palestine and Mount Athos in the 9th and 10th centuries by Georgian monk scholars such as Giorgi Mtatsmindeli and Grigol Khandzteli.

Three-part homophonic chant is believed to have begun during this period, as academies were founded to propagate church traditions such as chanting, centred on Gelati monastery near Kutaisi. Students spent up to seven years learning their craft from *sruligalobeli* (master chanters) before being initiated as chanters themselves.

The *neumas* (musical notation) was gradually lost from the 17th century, and only deciphered in the mid 20th century, although local styles were passed down verbally, while medieval neumatic notation is still undeciphered. A hymn to the Virgin by King Demetre I (1125–56), 'You are the Vine' (*Shen Khar Venakhi*), has also been sung at weddings for a century or more. The mixture of a strong secular singing tradition and the professional school of church chant yielded a genre of 'folk-sacred' songs such as *chona*, fertility songs performed just before Easter, and *alilo*, carols sung around the village on Christmas Eve (5 January). Though group singing is the dominant traditional form of music, **instruments** abound in Georgia, the oldest yet found being a 3,000-year-old bone shawm (*salamuri*) from near Mtskheta. The *doli*, a round skin-covered drum, beat out 5/4 rhythms to accompany ancient Georgians into battle (as attested by Xenophon, writing about the Mossynoeci tribe). There are two traditional bagpipes, the *chiboni* from Adjara and the *gudatsviri* from Racha. Introduced instruments include the clarinet-like *duduki* and the oboe-like *zurna*, both from Armenia.

Since the 19th century Western harmonies have combined with Georgian three-part singing to form a popular genre known as **'urban music'**, which can now be heard in every car and bar of Georgia. It has catchy tunes and sentimental lyrics, sung in simple harmony and sometimes accompanied by guitar or piano. The most famous example is 'Suliko', a song of homesickness by the poet Akaki Tsereteli, which as everyone will remind you was Stalin's favourite.

In the communist period, the Rustavi Choir was the best known of Georgia's professional ensembles, and produced some fine recordings, now on CD, which serve as a good introduction to Georgian song. Similarly the Tsinandali Choir produced an enjoyable collection, *Table Songs of Georgia*, in fact all from Kakheti. French companies such as Ocora have produced some good compilations of field recordings, including a fine collection from Svaneti. However, in post-communist Georgia it's the Anchiskhati Choir and a group called Mtiebi ('Morning Star'; *http:// mtiebi.com*) who have emerged as the leaders in rediscovering and preserving the most authentic examples of Georgian song. The Anchiskhati Choir's five CDs are available from Marika Lapauri-Burk, Max-Brauer-Allee 68, 22765 Hamburg, Germany (✆ +49 40 389 2222; e *info@lile.de; www.lile.de*). Their first CD, *Anchiskhati Choir – Sacred Music from the Medieval Ages – Georgian Polyphonic Singing*, is a great introduction. Others to look out for include Zedashe (*http:// zedashe.bandcamp.com*), Elesa and the women's choir Mzetamze; Georgian choirs have also appeared in the West, such as the London Georgian Singers, the Canadian groups Kavkasia and Darbazi, and in the USA Iveria (*www.iveria.org*), which has released a CD, *Songs from the Republic of Georgia*.

In addition, *99 Georgian Songs: A Work Book for Singers* by Mtiebi's founder, the late Edisher Garakanidze, is published by the Centre for Performance Research at the University of Wales, 6 Science Park, Aberystwyth SY23 3AH (*www.thecpr. org.uk*). Songbooks are available online from Northern Harmony in Vermont

KATIE MELUA

Katie (originally Ketevan) Melua has put Georgia on the map for a whole generation of Westerners. However, as a folk-jazz-bluesy singer-songwriter inspired by Eva Cassidy, Ella Fitzgerald, Freddie Mercury, Nick Drake, Joni Mitchell and Bob Dylan, she seems an unlikely candidate for chart success, even with her classically Georgian good looks and her lack of ego.

Born in Kutaisi in 1984, she came to Britain in 1992 when her surgeon father took a job in Belfast, moving to Surrey in 1997. As a student at the BRIT School for Performing Arts, she was discovered by producer Mike Batt; fortunately Melua was unaware of his earlier career as creator of *The Wombles*.

Her first album, *Call Off The Search*, was released in 2003, with songs by Melua, Batt, John Mayall and Randy Newman; it sold 1.7 million copies in the UK, making her the country's best-selling female artist two years running, and three million abroad. Her debut single, 'The Closest Thing to Crazy', written by Batt, was a top-ten hit in the UK. Her follow-up album *Piece by Piece*, released in 2005, was darker but just as successful.

In 2005 she became a British citizen, partly so as to be able to travel without needing visas almost everywhere, but she retains Georgian citizenship. She's never been seen as a turncoat in Georgia – probably because few over the age of 20 recognise the name, and those who do think of her as 'half-Georgian' – and returned in 2005 to record with a traditional male-voice choir. She gave her first concert there in November 2005 and says she'd like to do an album of Georgian folk songs. A year later she performed the world's deepest gig on a Norwegian oil rig, a record 303m underwater. Her 2010 album *The House*, produced by William Orbit, showed a move towards electronica.

Melua's sense of humour came to the fore after a tongue-in-cheek media debate about the scientific accuracy of some lyrics in her song 'Nine Million Bicycles'. She duly produced a spoof 'corrected' version which went: 'We are 13.7 billion light-years from the edge of the observable universe. That's a good estimate with well-defined error bars and with the available information, I predict that I will always be with you.'

For more information, see www.katiemelua.com.

(*www.northernharmony.pair.com/store/GEsongbooks.html*). If you read German, see also *Musik aus Georgien* by Thomas Houssermann (Erka Verlag, 1993). If addicted, you could join the **Georgian Harmony Association** (*c/o Michael Bloom, 5 Alder Lodge, 292 Bury St West, London N9 9LL;* \ *020 8360 9991;* e *info@ georgianharmony.org.uk; www.georgianharmony.org.uk*), or the Maspindzeli choir in London (*http://maspindzeli.org.uk*).

In the field of **classical music**, the great bass Paata Burchuladze (b1955) is Georgia's main claim to fame; he's very much in the Western operatic tradition rather than the Russian, and remains in great demand worldwide. Less well known are the conductors Jansugh Kakhidze and Evgeni Mikeladze, the pianists Eliso Virsaladze, Khatia Buniatishvili and Mariam Batsashvili, the sopranos Nino Surguladze and Anita Rachvelishvili, and the violinists Lisa Batiashvili and Marina Iashvili. The Tbilisi opera house is named after the composer Zakaria Paliashvili (1871–1933), who established classical music in Georgia with his operas *Abessalom and Eteri* (1918, a monumental tragedy), the lyric-dramatic *Daisi* (1923, prefiguring Khachaturian but with a 'Georgian' tone in its peasant crowd scenes) and the heroic-patriotic *Latavra* (1927). Mikhail Ippolitov-Ivanov (1859–1935), a student of Rimsky-Korsakov, was conductor of the Tbilisi Symphony Orchestra for a decade, and his *Caucasian Sketches* (1895) is based on Georgian folk tunes. It may be interesting to know that Stravinsky based *Les Noces* on Georgian harmonic and melodic patterns. The leading Georgian composer of the 20th century was Gia Kancheli (b1935), whose violent early symphonies have given way to increasingly subdued, wistful later works.

Armenia, by contrast, is known for lively instrumental music (derived from the Islamic world) with drums and the *duduk*, like a reedy clarinet (usually played in pairs, with the second instrument providing a drone). The other traditional style is that of the *ashugs* or troubadours, who were poets and storytellers as well as musicians. The most famous was Sayat Nova (1712–95) who was based in Tbilisi, at the court of Erekle II.

2

Practical Information

WHEN TO VISIT (AND WHY)

Georgia may not suffer as much from energy shortages these days, but winter is still not the smartest time to visit, unless you are just interested in Tbilisi and the ski resorts. High summer can be too hot and humid, but spring and autumn are ideal times to visit; in particular the golden autumn colours can be spectacular, and the wine harvest makes this a great time to visit Kakheti.

HIGHLIGHTS Given the difficulties and unpredictabilities of travel in Georgia, some visitors will confine themselves to Tbilisi, with brief excursions to places such as Mtskheta and Davit-Gareja. However, the rewards for venturing outside the capital are great for those prepared to make the effort. To the east, Kakheti is ideally placed for an outing of two to four days, sampling wines and churches, and to the north the Georgian Military Highway leads into the heart of the High Caucasus. The country's main axis is the highway from Tbilisi to Kutaisi and on to Poti or Batumi, or to Zugdidi and Abkhazia; this begins by following the Mtkvari and then crosses into the Rioni Basin in the west of the country. Batumi is one of the most pleasant and laid-back cities in Georgia, although the Black Sea's beaches are not really worth visiting. From Zugdidi it's also possible to head north into the heart of the Caucasus, to the region of Svaneti, where unique architecture and semi-pagan customs are preserved.

SUGGESTED ITINERARIES Almost all itineraries start in the capital, Tbilisi, although it's also common to arrive in Georgia at Kutaisi Airport or overland from Turkey in Batumi. From Tbilisi, it's easy to head east for a couple of days to Kakheti to enjoy a bit of wine tourism and visit the ancient monasteries of Davit-Gareja. Otherwise you'll head west on the country's main highway, either swinging north to Gudauri and Stepantsminda (Kazbegi) in the High Caucasus, or continuing to Gori and Kutaisi and then the coast at either Poti or Batumi. There are other options to turn north into the High Caucasus, notably from Kutaisi to Racha and from Zugdidi to Svaneti; equally, from Khashuri, between Gori and Kutaisi, you can head south to Borjomi in the Lesser Caucasus, continuing to the cave city of Vardzia and either looping east to Tbilisi or (in summer) west to Batumi. The itineraries suggested below are feasible by rental car, bus or *marshrutka* (minibus).

One week From Tbilisi head west to Mtskheta and Gori, detour south to Borjomi and Vardzia, then return to the main highway to visit Kutaisi and finish in Batumi on the Black Sea.

Two weeks From Tbilisi head west to Mtskheta and then north to Stepantsminda in the heart of the High Caucasus; then follow the one-week itinerary west to the

Black Sea and return to Tbilisi. Leave time to finish with some restorative wine tourism in Kakheti, east of the capital.

Three weeks This option gives plenty of time to explore the mountains; follow the one-week option west to Kutaisi for an optional side-trip north to Racha, then go via Zugdidi to Mestia and Ushguli in Svaneti. If you don't get enough hiking there you can also divert to Stepantsminda on the way back to Tbilisi, before finishing in Kakheti, east of the capital – in addition to wine, there's also the Tusheti National Park, perhaps Georgia's most remote wilderness.

TOURIST INFORMATION

There is a very useful website for advance planning – www.georgia.travel – and a number of helpful **tourist information centres** throughout the country that can provide maps, brochures, itinerary suggestions and practical help. The best of these is in Tbilisi at Freedom Square, but there are others at Batumi, Telavi, Borjomi and Sighnaghi (see individual towns for other locations). The **Department of Tourism and Resorts** (*Chanturia 12, 0108 Tbilisi;* \ *+995 32 436996;* e *georgia@ tourism.gov.ge, marketing@tourism.gov.ge; www.georgia.travel*) can be contacted to answer specific questions; they also have a 24-hour English-language helpline (\ *0800 800909*).

Using the internet for research you will find that searches for 'Georgia' inevitably produce vast amounts of material on the US state – try 'Tbilisi' or 'Caucasus' instead. See page 299 for useful websites.

MAPS If venturing anywhere outside Tbilisi, you should pick up the 1:500,000 map of Georgia published by GeoLand in Tbilisi (page 116) or the 1:610,000 map published by International Travel Maps and Books (*www.itmb.ca*), both available in major stores such as **Stanfords** (*12 Long Acre, London WC2E 9LP;* \ *020 7836 1321; www.stanfords.co.uk*). A 1:800,000 German map called *Georgien – Reisekarte* is produced by ERKA-Verlag (*www.erka-verlag.de*), also based in Tbilisi. Several 1:1,000,000 maps of the entire Caucasus are also available through Bartholomew's at Stanfords and other shops. Tourist offices in Georgia also give away a reasonable 1:950,000 map of Georgia for free in addition to quite detailed provincial maps (1:200,000 to 1:350,000).

TOUR OPERATORS

UK
Birdfinders Westbank, Cheselbourne, Dorset DT2 7NW; \ 01258 839066; m 07768 691997; www. birdfinders.co.uk. This specialist company runs 1-week birding tours for £1,695 inc flights.
Cox & Kings 30 Millbank, London SW1P 4EE; \ 020 7853 5000; www.coxandkings.co.uk. This company offers a 7-night 'Wonders of Georgia' tour (£1,075 group, £1,555 private), as well as tours combined with Armenia or Turkey.
Exodus Grange Mills, Weir Rd, London SW12 ONE; \ 020 8772 3936, 0845 287 7537; www.exodus. co.uk. This company operates a 14-day 'Highlights

of Georgia & Armenia' cultural tour (from £1,699).
Explore Nelson Hse, 55 Victoria Rd, Farnborough, Hants GU14 7PA; \ 0843 561 1721; www.explore. co.uk. They offer 'Adventures in Georgia' (9 days from £890), 'On Foot in the Caucasus' (16 days in Svaneti & Kazbegi from £1,490), 'Land of the Golden Fleece' (16 days in Georgia & Armenia from £1,425, or £2,150 as a private trip, or £2,079 with Azerbaijan extension); all prices exc flights. See ad, 1st colour section.
Naturetrek Mingledown Barn, Wolf's Lane, Hants GU34 3HJ; \ 01962 733051; www.naturetrek.co.uk. A 10-day birding trip from £2,100 plus flights.

2

Regent Holidays Colston Tower, Colston St, Bristol BS1 4XE; ☎ 020 3588 6120; www.regent-holidays.co.uk. Regent is the leading British operator, offering tailor-made tours to suit any budget or interest & can book accommodation, transport, guides or other services. Long w/ends cost from £715 in Tbilisi; their 9-day 'Essential Georgia' tour costs from £2,155pp, with a Svaneti add-on available from £450. A 16-day 'Caspian to Black Sea' tour costs £2,515. All prices inc flights. See ad, 2nd colour section.

Ride World Wide Staddon Farm, North Tawton, Devon EX20 2BX; ☎ 01837 82544; www.rideworldwide.co.uk. Offers a 10-day horseback trip for £1,620, exploring the little-touristed area south & southwest of Tbilisi inc the 12th-century monasteries of Gudarekhi & Pitareti.

Scott's Tours 141 Whitfield St, London W1T 5EW; ☎ 020 7383 5353; www.scottstours.co.uk. This small company, originally specialising in tours to Russia, can organise tailor-made tours of Georgia.

Steppes Travel 51 Castle St, Cirencester, Wilts GL7 1QD; ☎ 01285 601618; www.steppestravel.co.uk. Steppes East arranges tailor-made or group trips to Georgia as well as Armenia & Azerbaijan; a 7-day 'Highlights of Georgia' trip costs £1,785, an 8-day 'Food & Wine' tour costs £2,275, & a 13-day tour inc Svaneti, Kazbegi & Kakheti costs from £2,115.

Wild Frontiers Adventure Travel 78 Glentham Rd, London SW13 9JJ; ☎ 020 7736 3968; www.wildfrontiers.co.uk. Offers a range of adventurous trips such as the 'Wild Walk in the Caucasus' (9 days from £1,495), 'Wild Walk in Svaneti' (11 days from £1,595), or 'Land of Myths & Mountains' (9 days from £1395), visiting Kazbegi, Juta & Roshka. It also combines Georgia with Azerbaijan & Armenia, a 15-day trip costing £2,545 as well as horse treks (9 days from £1,525) – all without flights.

Cruises

Noble Caledonia 2 Chester Cl, London SW1X 7BE; ☎ 020 7752 0000; www.noble-caledonia.co.uk. Offers a 'Black Sea Odyssey' cruise inc a stop in Batumi from £3,995 for 11 nights.

USA

From the United States there are more expensive trips on offer.

Ker & Downey 6703 Highway Blvd, Katy, TX 77494; ☎ +1 281 371 2500, toll-free 1 800 423 4236; http://kerdowney.com. Luxury 'handcrafted holidays' lasting 8 or 10 days from US$8,995 or US$9,935, plus a 2-week tour of Georgia, Armenia & Azerbaijan.

MIR 85 South Washington St, Suite 210, Seattle, WA 98104; ☎ +1 800 424 7289, 206 624 7289; www.mircorp.com. MIR offers a variety of packages: among others, a 14-day 'Taste of Georgia' tour from US$5,495 & a 15-day 'South Caucasus' tour from US$7,195; private trips include the 8-day 'Essential Georgia' from US$3,095, the 10-day 'Essential Caucasus' from US$4,295 & the 12-day 'Essential Georgia & Armenia' trip from US$4,695.

Natural Habitat Adventures PO Box 3065, Boulder, CO 80307; ☎ +1 303 449 3711, toll-free 1 800 543 8917; www.nathab.com. Nine days of hiking (inc a helicopter flight into Tusheti) & wine-tasting from US$4,995.

Wilderness Travel 1102 9th St, Berkeley, CA 94710; ☎ +1 800 368 2794; www.wildernesstravel.com. This company offers 11-day trips for about US$4,095, inc strenuous hiking in Tusheti, & a 15-day cruise around the Black Sea, visiting Batumi, from US$12,980.

WORLDWIDE

Eastern Europe Travel Bureau 5th floor, 75 King St, Sydney, Australia; ☎ 02 9262 1144, 1300 668844; www.eetbtravel.com. Working with Visit Georgia (page 57), they offer the 'Wonders of Georgia' tour (8 nights for AU$2,205).

ERKA Reisen Postfach 4240, Robert Stolz Str 21, 76626 Bruchsal, Germany; ☎ +49 7257 930390; www.erkareisen.de. This German company offers tours for Germans, naturally, inc climbing, riding & farm stays.

GEORGIA

Adventure Club Jomardi Robakidze 7, 0159 Tbilisi; m 570 100244, 599 141160; www.adventure.ge. Adventure tours, especially rafting.

Argotour Paliashvili 28/8, Tbilisi; ☎ 32 229 2779; www.argotour.ge. This company's branches are open 7 days a week (⊙ 09.30–19.00 Mon–Sat, 10.00–18.00 Sun). Historical, skiing, rafting & spa tours, plus weekend breaks in Tbilisi.

Badagoni Tours Digomi 1/11/64, Tbilisi; ☎ 32 251 6701, m 593 937751; e zazamakharadze@yahoo.com, zazamakharadze@gmail.com; www.badagonitour.com. Specialising in wine tours but offering a range of other excursions.

Batumi Birding Melashvili 5, 6010 Batumi;

422 241777, 558 217706; www.birdlife.ge. New company based on the Batumi Raptor Count (page 259) but expanding to cover Georgia & neighbouring countries.

Caucasus Travel Peritsvaleba 22, Avlabari, 0103 Tbilisi; 32 298 7400; e online@caucasustravel. com; www.caucasustravel.com. Set up in 1991 by some of Georgia's leading climbers as Caucasian Travel, it was renamed when it was found that this could give offence; now it's the leading agency dealing with incoming tourists & has associated companies offering car hire, business consultancy & adventure tours. Service is superb & they're totally reliable regarding what is possible or safe; their website is an excellent reference tool. Their city tour costs US$50–95 depending on numbers; day trips to Davit-Gareja cost US$70–160.

Concord Travel Barnov 82, 0179 Tbilisi; 32 222 5151; www.concordtravel.ge. Concord has a wide variety of tours on offer, inc wine, adventure & archaeological.

Exotour Galaktion Tabidze 9, 0105 Tbilisi; 32 291 3191; www.exotour.ge. A company providing a good range of services – food & wine, hiking, horseriding & off-road jeep tours.

Explore Georgia Shevchenko 5, 0108 Tbilisi; 32 292 1911; www.exploregeorgia.com. A full range of hiking, climbing, horseriding, mountain-biking & caving trips.

Georgian Adventures (GATA) Barnov 42, 0171 Tbilisi; m 599 535589; e georgianadventures@ gmail.com; www.facebook.com/ georgianadventures. Trips to Lagodekhi & Khevsureti & 14 w/end tours for expats; also rafting.

Georgian Discovery Tours Chavchavadze Av 80, 0162 Tbilisi; 32 229 4953; www.gdt.ge. This Georgian–Swiss company offers tailor-made tours.

GeorgiCa Travel Erekle II St 5, 0105 Tbilisi; 32 225 2199; www.georgicatravel.ge. This company offers cultural tours, trekking, horseriding, cycling & climbing. They can book accommodation & car hire, & offer trips with other Caucasian & Silk Road countries. See ad, page 53.

Geotour Rustaveli Av 18, 0114 Tbilisi; 32 245 0110; m 599 156840; www.geotour.ge. A wide range of culture, adventure & wine tours, plus hiking, riding, rafting & skiing. Also offer tours to Armenia & Azerbaijan.

John Graham (US) +1 609 906 3665; m (Georgia) +995 599 365372; e jagraham@ wesleyan.edu; www.georgianchant.org/tours. John runs music courses in Sighnaghi, & also offers tours of medieval monasteries & Svaneti (as well as Tao-Klarjeti, now in Turkey), focusing on wine, food, culture & above all music, with 3 leaders who sing traditional polyphony in the churches – unforgettable.

Kaukasus Reisen Tumanianis 15, Tbilisi; +49 170 337 7228; m 599 570554; e kaukasus@ gmail.com, www.kaukasus-reisen.de. Adventure tours (German- & English-speaking), inc a 14-day introductory tour for €1,380 (land-only); trekking & riding in Tusheti from €1,340 for 11 days; or a 12-day trek in Khevsureti or Svaneti for €1,280.

Living Roots Baratashvili 18, 4200 Sighnaghi; www.travellivingroots.com. Excellent company specialising in finding the most authentic off-the-beaten-track cultural experiences, with emphasis on wine & music.

Omnestour Abesadze 4, 0105 Tbilisi; 32 293 3400; e info@omnestour.ge; www.omnestour. ge. Efficient, friendly company offering historic, adventure & cultural tours.

Sunny Travel Bakhtrioni 7, Tbilisi; 32 242 1618; e geo_sunnytravel@yahoo.com. Adventure & cultural tours, inc horseriding & day tours of Tbilisi & Davit-Gareja.

Tbilisi Tourist Centre Akhvlediani St 5, 0108 Tbilisi; 32 298 5075; e ttc@wanex.net; www.ttc. ge. General & cultural tours mainly for Germans, as well as cycling & hiking in the Borjomi-Kharagauli National Park.

Visit Georgia Ingorovka 4A, Tbilisi; 32 292 2246; www.visitgeorgia.ge. Large, well-established company offering a wide range of tours; prices vary with the standard of hotels. As well as individual & group tours they offer wildlife, hiking & archaeology.

Wild Georgia Tsinamdzgvrishvili Av 17, 0102 Tbilisi; m 599 941320; e eka@wildgeorgia.ge, inanycase23@yahoo.com; www.wildgeorgia.ge. Hiking & horseriding in Tusheti & from a vineyard in Kakheti, with excellent local guides.

INDEPENDENT TRAVEL Tariel Tabashidze (322 64 8928; m 899 648928; e tariel_ tabashidze@yahoo.com) is a good Tbilisi-based guide who speaks German and English, with a Subaru 4x4 car, for US$40 per day plus petrol (US$50 for a Niva jeep). You can find similar contacts on the noticeboard at **Prospero's Books** (page 116).

2

RED TAPE

Citizens of the European Union, USA, Canada, Australia, New Zealand, Japan, Israel and many other countries do not require visas for visits to Georgia of up to 90 days; you should have a full passport with 90 days validity remaining. Otherwise you'll need to buy a single-entry 30-day visa at an embassy or consulate, or online at www.evisa.gov.ge (queries to e contact@evisa.gov.ge or ☏ 322 94 5050). Visas are no longer issued at rail or sea entry points. Visa application forms can be downloaded from embassy websites (*www.geoemb.org.uk/docs/visa_application_GEO.pdf*); you'll also need to send your passport, a colour photo, US$50 and a paid self-addressed envelope.

For further information contact the Ministry of Foreign Affairs (*Chitadze 4, 0118 Tbilisi;* ☏ *322 94 5000, 240 1010;* e *inform@mfa.gov.ge; www.mfa.gov.ge;* ☉ *10.00–14.00 Mon–Fri*). It's better not to overstay – there's a penalty of GEL180 for up to three months beyond your visa's expiry or GEL360 beyond that.

It's easy enough to cross from Georgia to Abkhazia but you cannot travel from Russia to Georgia via Abkhazia; however, it's not possible to visit South Ossetia or Tskhinvali for the time being. British and US embassies advise against visiting both Abkhazia and South Ossetia.

There was a great deal of petty corruption and grafting at Georgia's borders in the past, with officials demanding a few dollars from travellers, but this has been cleaned up since the Rose Revolution.

GETTING THERE AND AWAY

BY PLANE Travelling directly from western Europe or North America, you have little choice but to fly; however, almost all the schedules are pretty inconvenient and there are no longer any direct flights from London.

The most obvious route is to go via Istanbul, and **Turkish Airlines** (*THY; www. thy.com*) give the most options: from Britain there are five flights a day from London (both Heathrow and Gatwick), two from Manchester and one each from Birmingham and Edinburgh, the latter connecting with a midnight flight from Istanbul (Ataturk) that reaches Tbilisi at 04.25 (there's also an 06.45 flight that arrives at 11.00); they also fly from Ataturk to Batumi.

THY is a Star Alliance member, offering worldwide connections. Others are **Lufthansa** (*www.lufthansa.com/uk*), which has flights six nights a week from Munich, arriving at 04.15 (with connections from Heathrow at 16.45 and 17.50); **LOT** (*www.lot.com*), which has five flights a week from Warsaw, arriving at 05.00 (with a connection from Heathrow at 17.50); and **Aegean** (*http://en.aegeanair.com*), which has a weekly connection from Heathrow via Athens, leaving at 16.20 on Sundays.

The only Oneworld member flying to Tbilisi is **Qatar Airways** (*www.qatarairways. com*), and the only Skyteam member is **Aeroflot** (*www.aeroflot.com*), which has reasonable (but not cheap) connections through Moscow (Sheremetyevo), leaving London Heathrow at 13.30 and reaching Tbilisi at 03.00. **Ukraine International Airlines** (*www.flyuia.com*) have flights from Kiev daily at 19.25, arriving Tbilisi at 00.10. The return flight is at the very inconvenient time of 07.20. However, there are decent connections to/from London Gatwick, Amsterdam, Berlin, Brussels, Munich, Paris and Zurich in both directions; they also fly four times a week from Kiev at 11.30 (too early for connections from western Europe), arriving at 16.15. It's also worth considering **Air Baltic** (*www.airbaltic.com*), with flights from Riga up to three nights a week, leaving at 23.30 and arriving in Tbilisi at 04.00. All the modern airlines use modern Airbus and Boeing planes, and fares are broadly competitive, starting from around £270 return in winter.

Turkish budget carriers also provide good connections via Istanbul: **Pegasus** (*www.flypgs.com*) has daily flights from London Stansted via Istanbul Sabiha Gökçen (SAW) that depart Stansted at 13.10 and arrive Tbilisi at 03.20. Return flights leave Tbilisi at 06.30 to arrive London Stansted at 12.30. This is relatively cheap, from around £200 return, but as well as highly inconvenient arrival and departure times at Tbilisi it requires lengthy stopovers in each direction at Istanbul's modern but uninteresting – and expensive – second airport. Pegasus also fly from SAW to Batumi and Kutaisi. **Atlasjet** (*www.atlasglb.com*) fly from London Luton daily at 12.15 via Istanbul's main Ataturk airport, arriving in Tbilisi at 03.40, with comparable fares.

Other low-cost airlines fly into the new Kutaisi Airport (linked by modern minibuses with Kutaisi, Tbilisi and Batumi), notably **Wizzair** (*www.wizzair.com*) from Budapest, Warsaw, Katowice, Vilnius and Kiev; it's possible to travel through from western Europe, but long waits are required.

From North America you'll usually have most options with Turkish Airlines, with return fares starting from around US$800 including taxes; leaving New York (JFK) at 13.15, you'll arrive at 11.00. They also fly from Chicago (US$1,000), San Francisco (US$1,900), Toronto (CDN$1,400) and Vancouver (CDN$1,500). Ukraine International Airlines fly from New York via Kiev four times a week (with code-shared connections from Los Angeles and San Francisco), costing from US$650.

From Asia and Africa it's easiest to fly via the Gulf, with low-cost airlines such as **Air Arabia** (*www.airarabia.com*) and **Fly Dubai** (*www.flydubai.com*) serving cities such as Mumbai, Delhi, Nairobi and Dar Es Salaam. Qatar Airways serves these and further-flung destinations such as Johannesburg, Auckland, Hong Kong, Tokyo and Perth via Doha. Turkish Airlines is also a possibility, with flights from Singapore via Istanbul from €1,200.

The main Georgian operator is **Georgian Airways** (*www.georgian-airways. com, www.airzena.com*), still sometimes referred to as Air Zena. In 1991, the Georgian division of Aeroflot became Orbi Georgian Airlines; it flew ancient Soviet planes and maintained them so badly that US embassy staff were not permitted to use the airline. In 1999, the charter line Airzena bought the bankrupt Georgian Airways, as it now is, and Air Georgia, and the state now holds just 20% of the company. In 2000, it leased two Boeing 737s which fly to Amsterdam, Paris, Vienna (code-sharing with Austrian Airlines) and Tel Aviv; it also has four Canadair Regional Jets, which fly to Batumi and Kutaisi.

Ticket agencies

Levon Travel 408 East Broadway, Glendale, CA 91205, USA; ☎+1 818 552 7700, 800 445 3866; www.levontravel.com

Regent Holidays 6th floor, Colston Tower, Colston St, Bristol BS1 4XE, UK; ☎020 7666 1244; www.regent-holidays.co.uk

STA Across the UK; ☎0333 321 0099; www.statravel.co.uk; across the USA; ☎+1 800 781 4040; www.statravel.com

TravelCUTS c/o Merit Travel, 408 King St, Toronto ON, M5V 1K2, Canada; ☎+1 800 667 2887; www.travelcuts.com

BY RAIL It's no longer feasible to travel all the way to Georgia by train: services from Moscow ran via Baku (Azerbaijan) to Tbilisi (3,214km, taking 3 days) until the opening in the late 1930s of a line along the Black Sea Coast. This became the main route (2,509km, taking 41hrs), but is now closed due to the secession of Abkhazia. There have been various attempts at building a direct route through and under the Caucasus, but all were abandoned and it seems unlikely to be tried again.

(The writer Fitzroy Maclean records how it used to be announced in Tbilisi that 'the train to the Soviet Union will leave from platform such-and-such ...')

There are overnight trains from Baku and Yerevan to Tbilisi; both are run in the Russian style (although the carriages have been modernised), with *kupé* (KP) four-berth second-class compartments and *spalny vagon* (SV) two-berth first-class compartments; the Yerevan train also has *platskartny* third-class open couchettes. Travelling towards Tbilisi, you will be woken twice for lengthy passport checks; coming from Tbilisi you can get this out of the way earlier and get a decent night's sleep.

The train from **Baku (Azerbaijan) to Tbilisi** is liable to serious delays, with perhaps a couple of hours at the Georgian border post and the same at the Azeri border. Leaving Baku every night at 20.45, it takes around 15 hours for 549km, and fares start at about US$37. You can book online via http://railway.gov.az, but only for the train from Baku – click 'Onlayn Bilet Satisi', then 'EN' for English. You'll have to register ('series' means your nationality), then select the Baki–Tiflis train and either a 'SV' (first class) or 'KP' (second class) carriage. Collect the ticket at the station by 19.45 – go to counter 22 with your passport and a printout of the booking confirmation email. From Tbilisi, you'll have to buy your ticket at the station; the train leaves at 16.30 daily and reaches Baku at 10.20.

The train from **Yerevan (Armenia) to Tbilisi** takes about 10½ hours to cover 374km, but allow a bit more time for delays. From late September to mid-June it leaves Yerevan for Tbilisi at 22.00 on even dates, returning at 20.20 on odd dates. In summer it runs nightly and is extended to Batumi (Makhinjauri) – it leaves Yerevan at 15.15 and arrives in Tbilisi at midnight and Batumi at 07.30; returning, it leaves Batumi at 15.25 and Tbilisi at 22.15, reaching Yerevan at 07.30. Women travelling alone have found it a frightening experience. One-way fares are between US$21 and US$45, depending on class; the best class, SV, can be a very civilised way to travel, if you're in no rush. There's even Wi-Fi nowadays!

Tbilisi should be connected by a direct line to Turkey late in 2015 (it was originally planned for 2010). This will link Akhalkalaki in southern Georgia with Kars in northeast Turkey and finally make a continuous route (although with a gauge change) between Baku and Istanbul (and Europe beyond) a reality. However, the new passenger carriages (to work on both standard- and broad-gauge tracks) will not be available until 2016 or 2017.

BY BUS Coming from Turkey, you're most likely to travel by bus (the rail link from Kars to Akhalkalaki will not open to passengers until 2016 at the earliest). There are two main routes, along the Black Sea Coast to Batumi, and by the Vale border crossing to Tbilisi; a less useful third crossing has opened at Çıldır in Javakheti.

For the first route, head for Trabzon (there are no-frills airlines plus several buses per hour from Istanbul, taking 15–18 hours for the 1,110km journey and costing US$28–35; flying is usually not much more expensive); from here buses run east to Hopa every half-hour, taking 3 hours to cover the 165km (US$10). From Trabzon Airport head south (with the sea behind you) to the main road; just to the right is the stop for minibuses to the bus terminal and town centre, while 200m to the left (at an overpass) is a stop for buses to Hopa. There are a couple of decent hotels, and various fleapits, in Hopa, which is also served by one or two buses a day from Erzurum, which is 5 hours to the south and can be reached by the *Dogu Ekspresi* sleeper train, which leaves Ankara at 18.00 daily (with a high-speed connection from Istanbul at 13.30) and arrives at 14.00. The border crossing at Sarpi, another 20km to the northeast, is effectively a huge bazaar, and there's plenty of transport on both sides of the border. It costs US$2 in a minibus, US$4 by shared taxi or US$15 by private taxi from Hopa to Sarpi, and GEL1 (US$0.50) by minibus or GEL10 by taxi onwards to Batumi; remember to put your watch forward 2 hours. There are direct buses from Trabzon's Otogar to Batumi (and on to Tbilisi), as well as minibuses leaving from just outside from mid-morning onwards.

To reach the Vale crossing, take a train or bus to Kars, then a minibus to Posof (*4hrs*), and a taxi or minibus via Türközü and Eminbey to the border (*30mins*) and finally a taxi to Akhaltsikhe (*30mins*). The Vale route is used by through buses from Istanbul and Ankara to Tbilisi (and on to Baku), costing US$25 from Ankara and US$40 from Istanbul (a 42-hour marathon). These are very comfortable air-conditioned, Turkish-built and Turkish-operated vehicles:

AST Turizm (Istanbul) Aydede Caddesi 24/2; \ +90 212 237 9463; e asttourism@tourkia.com. (Tbilisi) \ 32 233 4396; m 599 507032, 599 962564

Doghu Karadenizi Express (Istanbul) Dikmen Caddesi 29/37; \ +90 464 612 4253, 0850 840 3353; http://dogukaradenizekspres.com.tr

Luks Karadeniz (Istanbul) \ +90 212 658 3453, 658 3353, call centre 444 0053; (Tbilisi) \ 322 75 4179; m 599 552885, 555 442481, 599 278282; (Kutaisi) \ 04 312 63170; m 555 577980, 555 578010; (Batumi) m 593 931527, 577 780608, 593 951850; www.lukskaradeniz.com

Mahmut Tour Emniyet Otoparkı No. 5/C, Aksaray, Istanbul; \ +90 212 633 0220, 212 632 9979, 212 529 1193; www.mahmutturizm.com.tr

Mahmudoglu Turism (Istanbul) At the Otogar, office 3B; \ +90 212 658 3834–5; (Tbilisi) Shartava 7; \ 322 38 0475; (Ortachala) \ 32 275 4434; www.mahmudoglu.com

Metro Turizm toll free \ 444 3455; (Istanbul) \ +90 212 658 3232; e info@metroturizm.com.tr; (Trabzon) \ +90 462 325 7286, +90 462 325 7737; www.metroturizm.com.tr

Ulusöy (Istanbul) At the Otogar, office 128; \ +90 212 658 3000/1; & Inönü Caddesi 59, Taksim; toll free \ +90 212 444 1888; (Ankara) at the Otogar; \ +90 242 331 1310; (Trabzon) \ +90 462 325 2201, 321 1281, 212 692 1777; e musteri@ulusoy.com.tr; www.ulusoy.com.tr

Vardar Turizm (Istanbul) \ +90 212 529 5451/7/9, 212 658 3350; www.vardarturizm.com.tr

Buses from Greece to Tbilisi (US$80 from Thessaloniki/US$100 from Athens) are run by:

Elas Travel (Athens) \ 210 028 6268; (Thessaloniki) \ 231 522 5194

Kakheti Tur (Athens) \ 210 522 4410; (Thessaloniki) \ 231 055 1145

Manglisi Turi (Thessaloniki) \ 231 050 0702

In Tbilisi, contact Almazidi Tour, Athens Express, Borjomi Tour, Gomareti Tour, Irina Tour, Kakheti Tour, Nike Express, Nugzari Tour, Oktava Tour or Panaiotidi, all at the Ortachala bus station, from where each operates a weekly bus.

There are also minibuses and shared taxis between Yerevan (Armenia) and Tbilisi, as well as a train (page 60). Marshrutkas leave Yerevan's Central Bus Station on Admiral Isahakov Avenue every 50 minutes and take 5–7 hours, costing US$20. You can also wait until a shared taxi is full; this will take 5–6 hours and cost about US$35, as long as all four seats are taken. There are also buses from Yerevan's railway station that leave whenever they're full.

A few buses run from Vanadzor and Gyumri (in Armenia) to Tbilisi. There's also a daily marshrutka from Yerevan to Akhalkalaki (*8hrs; US$7*), continuing three times a week in summer to Batumi (*15hrs; US$25*). Take your own food and drink.

From Baku to Tbilisi there's less traffic so you're less likely to find a taxi; the train is slower and more erratic than the Yerevan service. There are a few buses (*US$15*), mostly overnight: these leave the Autovoksal (near the 20 Januari metro station)

between 20.00 and 22.00, taking 8 hours plus an hour or two at the border. See box, page 287 for the more scenic route via Lagodekhi and Shekhi.

Finally there are also buses, marshrutkas and shared taxis via Kazbegi between Tbilisi and Mineralni Vodi in the Russian Federation, some continuing all the way to Moscow (*US$60*).

BY SEA Another option is to arrive by ship; with the completion of new docks, train–ferry services were introduced in 1999 from Varna (Bulgaria) and Ilyichevsk (Ukraine) to Batumi and Poti, also carrying cars, trucks and passengers. The route from Ilyichevsk via Constanţa (Romania) to Poti and Batumi is served by the *Greifswald*, a large and comfortable ferry; built in Germany in 1988, it carries trucks and railway wagons and has a restaurant, non-smoking lounge, playroom and conference room as well as a swimming pool and sauna. There's a weekly circuit, leaving Ilyichevsk on Thursday morning and Constanţa on Thursday night and returning from Georgia on Sunday, so that it takes around 60 hours from Ilyichevsk to Batumi via Constanţa but only 40 hours for the direct return. Tickets can be booked through **Ukrferry-Tour** (*Sabanskyy Lane 4A, Odessa 65014;* \ *+380 482 347663, 348296;* e *ukf@ukrferry.com; www.ukrferry.com*). In Georgia book through UBG-Agency, which has offices in Tbilisi (*Kazbegi Av 12A, 0160;* \ *322 22 3987;* e *ubgagency@gol.ge*), Batumi (*Kutaisi St 34;* \ *42 227 4119;* e *ubgbatumi@gmail.com*) and Poti (*Gegidze 20/1;* \ *49 322 1060;* e *ubgcompany@ yandex.ru*). Fares start from US$95 per person in a four-berth cabin, including three meals; a car costs US$250.

Ferries (usually 'Kometa' hydrofoils, taking 6 hours) run from Sochi (in Russia, near the border with Abkhazia) to Batumi: contact **Batumi Express** (*Batumi* m *593 333966; Sochi* \ *+7 918 409 1296*); **Erekle 2008** (*Batumi* \ *42 227 9801*); or **Mikhail Svetlov** (*Batumi* \ *599 944504; Sochi* \ *+7 8622 959090;* m *+7 928 456 9090*). A new Russian company, **Paradise Cruise & Ferry** (\ *+8 800 333 2956;* e *sales@ cruiseisabella.com; http://paradisecruises.ru/en*) offers cruises from Sochi to Istanbul and Batumi (*5 days from US$720*) with passage from Sochi to Batumi available for US$25; it costs US$50 to take a car from Batumi to Sochi, but US$200 from Sochi to Batumi via Istanbul. Enquire directly for Istanbul–Batumi possibilities.

Finally, if you need to send goods or equipment to Georgia your best bet is either the Belgian company **Nomad Express** (*Belcrownlaan 23, 2100 Deurne;* \ *+32 3 360 5500;* e *info@gosselingroup.eu; www.gosselingroup.eu; Georgia:* e *info@ georgia.gosselinwwm.com; www.moving.gosselingroup.eu*), or **Georgian Express** (*Ketevan Tsamebuli 26/1, 0103 Tbilisi;* \ *322 74 5834;* e *tbilisi@georgia-express.com, georgiaexpress1@yahoo.com; www.georgia-express.com; Chavchavadze 40, Kutaisi;* \ *43 127 9015*).

HEALTH *with Dr Felicity Nicholson*

Reform and privatisation of Georgia's corrupt and run-down health service began in 1995; a state medical insurance company and 12 health funds were funded by a payroll tax of 3% on employers and 1% on employees. After the Rose Revolution any social safety net was abolished, so that those who could not afford insurance were sometimes forced to sell their homes; now there is state-backed insurance for all. In addition the abolition of the prescription system turned out to be a liberalisation too far, and it has been re-introduced. The health service is improving as the economy grows, and the share of GDP spent on health has risen from under 1% to just over 10%. Although British citizens are covered by a reciprocal agreement and need only proof of UK residence (ie: UK passport) for free treatment, they will still have to pay cash for drugs and many other services; as a rule US health insurance is not valid in Georgia without paying a substantial premium. Treatment is expensive (US$600 for a hernia operation). Embassies have lists of good English-speaking doctors in Tbilisi.

Pharmacies (*aptiaki* in Georgian) are plentiful and easy to find, and many are, in theory, open 24 hours. The Aversi, GPC and PSP chains have modern shops in many towns and all over Tbilisi – these show their names in Latin script, while others will at least have an *Apotheka* sign. You should expect generic drugs, but if you bring in an empty packet of whatever medicine you're looking for or name the main ingredient, the pharmacists will usually find a generic for you.

BEFORE YOU GO You are advised to be up to date with vaccinations against tetanus, diphtheria and polio, now available as an all-in-one ten-year vaccine (Revaxis). You should also be covered for hepatitis A and very occasionally typhoid for longer trips and more rural travel. Other vaccines that may be advised include a course of hepatitis B and rabies vaccine. Hepatitis B vaccination is essential if you will be working in a medical capacity or with children. Having the pre-exposure rabies jab is particularly important as there's a shortage of the rabies immunoglobulin used for treatment following bites, scratches or licks over open wounds from any warm-blooded mammal. The courses for rabies and hepatitis B comprise three injections over a minimum of 21 days (for hepatitis B you need to be 16 or over for this super-accelerated course), so you should go to see your GP or travel clinic specialist well in advance of your trip. Tuberculosis (TB) is spread through close respiratory contact and sometimes through infected milk or milk products. TB is very common in Georgia with 116 cases per 100,000 population (WHO, 2013). Experts differ over whether a BCG vaccination against tuberculosis is useful in adults and in most cases it will not be recommended if you are over 16: discuss with your travel clinic.

TRAVEL CLINICS AND HEALTH INFORMATION A full list of current travel clinic websites worldwide is available on www.istm.org. For other journey preparation information, consult www.nathnac.org/ds/map_world.aspx (UK) or http://wwwnc.cdc.gov/travel/ (US). Information about various medications may be found on www.netdoctor.co.uk/travel. All advice found online should be used in conjunction with expert advice received prior to or during travel.

HEALTH HAZARDS

Malaria Malaria in Georgia occurs solely in the benign form (*Plasmodium vivax*), and only occurs from July to October in some villages in the south-eastern part of the country beyond Sighnaghi and Davit-Gareja. Malaria had been eradicated in Georgia in 1970, but reappeared in 1996; since 2004 it has been largely dealt with and since these regions are seldom visited by travellers, taking antimalarial medication is not recommended. However, should you be going to these areas it is wise to seek advice from a travel expert. Malaria is transmitted by mosquitoes that emerge from dusk until dawn. Even if antimalarial medication is not recommended it is sensible to use insect repellents, wear trousers and long-sleeved tops and ensure that your accommodation is as mosquito-proof as possible when travelling in these remote areas.

HIV/AIDS HIV does not seem to be a big problem here so far (unlike in Russia); by the end of 2014 there had officially been 4,646 cases (of whom 966 had died), but the estimated total for the country was 6,000 or more. Transmission is through infected syringes in 50% of cases and heterosexual contact in 41%. Occasionally immigrants or long-term expats may be asked for proof that they are free from HIV infection. Check whether you need this when applying for visas or work permits.

Rabies Rabies risk exists in Georgia, especially in rural areas. Rabies is carried by any mammal and is passed on to humans through a bite, scratch or a lick of an open wound. You must always assume any animal is rabid, and seek medical help as soon as possible. Meanwhile scrub the wound with soap under a running tap or while pouring water from a jug for about ten minutes. Find a reasonably clear-looking source of water (but at this stage the quality of the water is not important), then pour on a strong iodine or alcohol solution of gin, whisky or rum. This helps stop the rabies virus entering the body and will guard against wound infections, including tetanus.

Pre-exposure vaccinations are advised for everyone, but are particularly important if you intend to have contact with animals and/or are likely to be more than 24 hours away from medical help. Ideally three doses should be taken over a minimum of 21 days. Contrary to popular belief these vaccinations are relatively painless.

If you are bitten, scratched or licked over an open wound by a sick animal, then post-exposure prophylaxis should be given as soon as possible, though it is never too late to seek help, as the incubation period for rabies can be very long. Those who have not been immunised will need a full course of injections and a blood product called rabies immunoglobulin (RIG). This product is expensive (around US$800) and may be hard to come by. However, if you have had the pre-exposure course then you only need two doses of vaccine which makes it very much easier to manage – another reason why pre-exposure vaccination should be encouraged.

Tell the doctor if you have had the pre-exposure vaccine, as this should change the treatment you receive. And remember that, if you do contract rabies, mortality is 100% and death from rabies is probably one of the worst ways to go.

Dentistry Some dental treatment should be provided free under the UK's reciprocal agreement, but Georgian dentistry is not recommended.

Drinking water Tap water is generally safe, but you may prefer to drink bottled water for the first few weeks while your system adapts to new strains of E. coli; meat and other foodstuffs are also safe, although care should be taken over milk and other milk products if there is doubt as to whether it has been pasteurised (see risk of TB above). About a third of the former Soviet Union's spas are in Georgia, and it's easy to find mineral waters such as Borjomi, Bakhmaro, Likani, Sno and Nakhalakhevi.

Smoking More likely health hazards include passive smoking and car crashes. Georgia has among the highest levels of tobacco use in the world, with most men (except monks) smoking most of the time, as well as 28% of pregnant women and 35% of breast-feeding women. Around nine billion cigarettes are consumed every year in Georgia, 2,200 per capita, against a world average of 1,600 per capita, and the 11,000 smoking-related deaths per year account for about 10% of mortality. Men now live a surprisingly long time but are generally in poor health. The excise on tobacco is relatively high at GEL0.90 per pack (three times Russia's) so 60–70% of the market is contraband; but tax is even higher in Turkey, so cigarettes are also smuggled there from Georgia. When the Ministry of Health tried a poster campaign in Tbilisi all the billboard sites were bought up at once by Philip Morris, manufacturers of Marlboro cigarettes.

In 2005 smoking was banned in public places, but this does not include restaurants or bars. Thankfully, the metro, theatres and parliament are smoke-free. Marshrutka drivers may smoke, but usually with the window open. It's acceptable for women to smoke in restaurants, but only a few smoke on the street.

Other dangers There's apparently been a rise in thyroid gland illnesses in western Georgia, which may be linked to strontium from Chernobyl.

Accidental death rates are surprisingly low in Georgia, under half the rates in Russia and the Baltic States. This is undoubtedly linked to the low rates of vodka consumption. The Russian response to economic collapse in 2014 was to cut vodka prices, as in previous crises. Even in 2011 there were half a million alcohol-related deaths in the Russian Federation, and too few to record in Georgia.

Given the undisciplined and excessively macho approach to **driving**, the constant use of mobile/cell phones, and the refusal to wear seat belts properly (many drivers sit on the lap strap), it's not surprising that the death toll is high on Georgia's roads (16.8 per 100,000 people per annum). Pedestrians are at risk too, as drivers assume they'll get out of the way – bad luck if your sight or hearing isn't too good. There are lots of three-legged dogs, as a warning to you.

SAFETY

Georgia is a very safe country, still with too few tourists for them to be targeted by thieves. **Abkhazia**, which has effectively seceded, is more problematic, and with no diplomatic representation you are very much on your own there if you get into trouble. The bordering area around Zugdidi is also considered to be risky. **South Ossetia** is closed to tourists, and crime levels are higher than elsewhere here too, partly due to the wide availability of guns; the same used to apply to Svaneti, where unwary tourists were almost routinely robbed until a few years ago, but this is now as safe as anywhere else in the country. Tusheti, Pankisi and Khevsureti are also safe – they were closed to tourists due to the Chechen war but there's no problem now. In **Tbilisi**, you should take the same commonsense precautions as in any other big city. There's little public drunkenness in Georgia, and there are usually plenty of people on the streets, even late at night; there is some pickpocketing, particularly in the metro, but few other problems. The days of Kalashnikov-toting Mkhedrioni (political gangsters) running the whole country as one big protection racket are long gone!

The **police force** used to be incompetent and corrupt, but after the Rose Revolution it was reformed and properly paid at last, and its popularity rose from 2% to 75% in polls. In particular, the new 'patrol police' (who deal with traffic and who should salute you when they pull your car over) have a good reputation – but the 'balaclava police' (part of the Security Ministry), who staged dramatic raids on tax dodgers and the like, often with television cameras in attendance, were seen as out of control under Saakashvili. In fact, there now seem to be too many patrol police, not doing much apart from driving around in new cars with loudspeakers telling stopped drivers to move on, but doing nothing about seat belts, mobile phones, red-light-jumping, speeding or dangerous driving in general.

Sexism in Georgia is as bad as anywhere in the world, but as a rule foreign women see only the positive, chivalrous side of the Georgian male's world view. In smaller towns and villages you may notice some stares and comments, but much less so than in neighbouring countries. Half of Georgia's judges are women, as are some leading politicians, notably foreign minister Tamar Beruchashvili and a couple of her predecessors, Salome Zourabichvili and Maia Panjikidze. Nevertheless, the proportion of women in parliament has fallen considerably from 30% in Soviet times, hitting a low of 5% in 2008 before recovering to 12%. In the 2006 local elections only 11% of those elected were women. According to UN research, one in 11 married women in Georgia has been subjected to domestic violence; but the real number could be much higher as victims rarely speak out. Three-quarters of Georgian women believe domestic violence is a private matter and should remain within the family, and police refuse to get involved.

Men may actually have a bit of a raw deal (it's not fair that when they dress in black they're said to look like gangsters while women in black are said to look like Medea) – but they've foolishly kept the bad jobs for themselves (manual labour, driving trucks and so on), as well as the mind-rotting ones like sitting around smoking in hotel lobbies, supposedly supervising or providing security, so it's no surprise the women are the ones getting ahead, especially in public service.

Despite the fact that discrimination against LGBT people is illegal, **homosexuality** is still viewed as a major deviation from Orthodox Christian values in Georgia – the Church itself is quite anti-gay and often protests against gay pride marches. Nevertheless, there are a couple of pro-gay bars in Tbilisi, such as Success (*Vashlovani 3;* \ *32 299 8230*), Café Gallery (*Griboedov 34;* \ *32 299 5747*), Salve (*Leselidze 25;* m *591 692727*) and Divan (*Tabidze 3/5;* m *599 018884; www.facebook. com/divantbilisi*). It is also normal for two men or women to share a room with each other.

The US embassy has useful, if over-cautious, advice online at http://travel.state. gov/content/passports/english/country/georgia.html.

Since 2012, there's now only one **emergency phone number** \ 112.

WHAT TO TAKE

Given the risk of power cuts, although they're not so common these days, it's sensible to bring a torch (flashlight) or candles. In addition, it's wise to have some toilet paper and your own soap or shower gel, and pens can be hard to find; a sheet sleeping bag may be a comfort in some hostels. You should also consider bringing presents for people you stay with (page 81).

MONEY AND BANKING

The unit of **currency** is the lari (GEL), which is divided into 100 tetri. The lari derives its name from the Latin *libra* or scales, while tetri simply means 'white'.

Banking hours are from 09.30 to 17.30 Monday to Friday. The main banks will change travellers' cheques, although they are choosy and erratic in the brands they accept; Thomas Cook and American Express are the most widely accepted. You should also bring some cash US dollars or euros (carried in a money belt or some other secure place). Sterling can only be changed in a few places in Tbilisi and Batumi (and only at poor rates). Russian, Armenian, Azeri and Turkish cash can be exchanged in a few places in Tbilisi and Batumi and near the border crossings, but other currencies are of little use. It's far easier to exchange cash than travellers' cheques, with exchange counters all over the place, especially around markets and bus stations.

ATMs can now be found in all cities and larger towns (not necessarily at the actual bank offices), and in many small rural towns; they are safe and reliable and the obvious way to fund your travels. You don't have to take your card back before receiving your cash, so don't forget it; in some machines you actually have to press 'Cancel' for it to be returned. Don't confuse ATMs with the Pay Boxes found in the streets everywhere for paying bills and topping up mobile phones and metro cards. Visa and MasterCard are accepted by the more expensive hotels, restaurants and supermarkets.

Western Union (*www.westernunion.com*) and MoneyGram (*www.moneygram.com*) have lots of agents in Georgia, all prominently signed, so it's easy but expensive to have money sent to you from abroad.

Costs are generally low. In restaurants, cafés and taxis, it's normal to tip by rounding up the total rather than by adding a percentage. It's usual to haggle in markets, where you can get up to 30% off (not for food).

GETTING AROUND

BY BUS The main mode of public transport is the marshrutka or minibus. These used to leave only when full (to bursting) but most routes now have a regular hourly service; there are more frequent departures between major towns, and at least one or two a day to most villages. These use fairly substantial bus stations in cities, while smaller places may just have a yard by the railway station or in the centre of town. Departure bays will show the destinations in Georgian, but if you look at the rear of this sign you may find the same information in Cyrillic or even Latin script. Comfortable modern buses (some overnight) run from Tbilisi to Kutaisi, Batumi and Zugdidi. Local services may be worked by ancient 20-seat yellow Paz vehicles, usually with a large area at the back cleared for luggage, as people take immense quantities of agricultural produce or building materials by public transport. The last bus from a town to a nearby village often leaves at about 17.00 or earlier, and the last service inbound to town may well be even earlier. Fares are generally about GEL1 per 20km, eg: GEL8 from Tbilisi to Lagodekhi, GEL18 from Tbilisi to Batumi or GEL10 from Kutaisi to Batumi.

Any bus or marshrutka with spare space (which doesn't necessarily mean a seat) will stop for anyone who flags it down; this can be tricky as it's hard to read the destination boards (only rarely in Cyrillic or Latin script as well as Georgian) until the last moment. Therefore (once you've learnt to read 'Tbilisi') heading towards the capital is an easier business than heading away from it! In most cases you'll pay as you get off at the front of the bus, so you should remember the name of the place where you boarded. If you have a ticket you may be expected to hand it in as you get off. Shared taxis are also available (faster and more expensive, but not vastly more dangerous than a marshrutka, as a rule), usually waiting outside bus stations, for instance at Telavi. Hitching is also possible, sometimes with a small payment expected, but rapes have been reported.

City transport City transport is also mainly by bus and marshrutka, although there's also a metro in Tbilisi. City buses take a long time at each stop; drivers won't open the rear doors (for boarding) until everyone has got off (and paid) at the front, but even so some people always wait to slip off at the rear, or to board at the front. Nevertheless, the buses will get you to your destination in the end, and they are very cheap. There are also plenty of semi-official taxis, without meters.

BY CAR Driving can take a bit of getting used to, given the poor state of minor roads and the excessive urgency of the other drivers. The cost of a car with driver is not high, so this may be the easiest solution; in Tbilisi it's easy to hire a taxi (including 4x4 vehicles) at the Didube bus station. You'll pay about US$40 a day for a car with driver in Tbilisi, and US$60 a day outside Tbilisi (plus fuel, and food and accommodation for the driver). The only major international car-hire chains represented in Tbilisi are Avis, Europcar, Hertz and Sixt (page 93), with cars costing from US$50 per day, plus insurance waivers, etc. A licence from almost any of the developed Western countries is valid in Georgia. Speed limits range from 50km/h in cities to 90km/h on highways, although these are universally ignored.

Contrary to general belief, Georgians are not totally lunatic drivers. They have some concern for life and limb, and perhaps more for their vehicles, skirting very carefully around speed-ramps and pot-holes and taking bends at fairly reasonable speed. Problems arise with laws and signals, which are widely ignored – I've hardly ever seen a Georgian wear a seat belt properly, as they prefer to sit on the lap-strap. Problems arise in relation to other cars; a Georgian's manhood (we can leave women drivers out of the discussion, as they are so few and they only drive locally as a rule) requires him to overtake at once; so drivers in both directions try to make a two-lane road into a three-lane one, with inevitable consequences. They also drive on the horn, not the brake, as it's always the other guy who is wrong or incompetent.

There are 20,000km of asphalt roads (93.5% of the total), although it can often be hard to tell the difference as most roads are in poor condition. Fuel prices have increased enormously over the past few years, costing around GEL2 a litre for normal, GEL2.20 for super and GEL2–2.20 for diesel; lead-free fuel is generally available now.

Distances are not great: by road it's about 85km from Tbilisi to Gori, 128km to Khashuri, 230km to Kutaisi and 384km to Batumi (349km by rail).

BY RAIL There has been a remarkable revival of Georgia's railways, making it the safest and most pleasant option for tourists travelling to the west of the country. The tracks were previously neglected and pounded by heavy trains transporting oil from Baku, but now the pipelines are open and new trains have been introduced, in

BICYCLE TOURING IN GEORGIA   *Alex Tilson*

Having toured throughout North America, Asia, Europe and Australia, I am convinced that there is no place on the planet as well suited for bicycle touring as Georgia. Georgians are the world's most hospitable people and there is no better way to be embraced by that hospitality than to arrive on a bicycle. Unlike any other method of travel, if you arrive as a 'velotourist' you will immediately command both curiosity and respect, and you will be welcomed with consistently open arms. We literally had multiple people grabbing us, pulling in different directions, begging us to stay with them – not for financial gain, but out of a genuine spirit of hospitality. It is awesome and will deeply influence the way you deal with guests for the rest of your life. In addition, Georgian food is amazing, a joyous celebration of life itself.

Georgia has a unique history that makes it a fascinating place to travel. This history is alive at every corner, discussed at every table, a veritable feast for the mind as much as food is for the belly, hospitality for the soul and scenery for the eyes. Now is an excellent time to travel before it is forever changed by the inevitable throngs of Western tourists.

Nevertheless, Georgia is not for the faint of heart. Though the human spirit is thriving, the infrastructure is not and the roads vary from bad to truly awful. Bring all of your own gear, tools and spare parts.

addition to the long-distance overnight trains – although there are still enough oil trains to cause delays. The main line from Tbilisi to Samtredia is double-track, and all Georgia's railways are electrified, though at one time power cuts were causing US$30,000 of damage a month to delicate traction equipment, and causing oil trains to take an average of 35 hours from Baku to Batumi instead of the scheduled 21 hours. Now, new day trains run from Tbilisi to Batumi (*5hrs 15mins*), Poti (*5hrs 10mins*), Ozurgeti (*8hrs 20mins*) and Zugdidi (*5hrs 30mins*).

However, it has to be said that there is a shortage of information about services. There's also a very poor service to Kutaisi, the country's second city, which is bypassed by the main line; you can use Rioni station, just south, as a sort of parkway station, especially to or from the west. The overnight train from Tbilisi to Zugdidi is one that is particularly worth considering: for the same price as being crammed in a minibus for a day (currently GEL18), you can enjoy a comfortable berth with clean sheets and good service.

The ticket offices are computerised, so you can go to any window; you'll have to give your name, so have a passport or credit card handy. The day trains are spacious, with overhead lockers and television in some; the seat numbers are hidden by curtains. There are three classes of accommodation on the night trains: *platzkart* is a hard seat, *coupé* is a four-bed compartment, and *spalny vagon* (SV or *esveh*) is a two-bed compartment. Fares from Tbilisi to Batumi range from GEL17.50/US$8.60 for *platzkart* to GEL25/US$12.50 for *esveh*. In Tbilisi it's possible to get rail information by phoning ✆35 1003, 56 6119, 56 4717 or 883 952527; only Georgian and Russian are spoken. The Georgian Railways website (*www.railway.ge*) has a journey planner (click 'English', then 'Online Services', then 'Train Schedule'), although it is not yet possible to book online. The entertainment tickets site Biletebi (*https://biletebi.ge*) now allows online train booking.

ADDRESSES Many street names have changed since independence, as communist figures such as Lenin have gone out of fashion; new signs have replaced worn and faded old ones, but these may only be in Georgian whereas the old ones were also in Cyrillic script. Some towns have signs with Latin script too, but elsewhere this may indicate there's a guesthouse or embassy on the street. In any case many people, especially taxi drivers, are more likely to recognise the old names than the current official ones. There are also grammatical differences between Georgian and Russian even where the names have survived unchanged. Likewise, streets named after people often have an 's' tacked on the end in Georgian. It's worth noting that street names are often shown not at the street corners but on house numbers, and many city buildings are very long, so that you may be told to go to, for example, No 20, third entrance; you may also be given a floor to go to (the ground floor counts as the first) as well as an apartment or office number. Six-digit Soviet postcodes beginning with 38 have been replaced with four-digit ones.

Out of town, places are located with reference to the kilometre signs along most roads; these count from both ends of the road (eg: km 2/154), so that the total on the two sides always adds up to the total distance (eg: 156km).Remember that 'street' is *kucha*, 'avenue' is *gamziri* and 'square' is *moedani*.

ACCOMMODATION

For a long time, finding somewhere to sleep was difficult outside Tbilisi; many of the older Soviet-period hotels were used to accommodate Georgian refugees from Abkhazia. Thankfully, there are now many new, better hotels, especially in Tbilisi. In any case this problem gave Georgia the chance to start again on a small-scale sustainable basis, with family homes opening as simple homestays. With a bit of improvement, many have become decent guesthouses. Many are well up to European standards, while those in remoter areas such as Svaneti and Tusheti are more basic, although this is compensated for by the ambience.

There are plenty of guesthouses in Tbilisi, but these evolved as upmarket abodes for businesspeople and official visitors. Some really are luxurious, and some might appear amazingly pricey for a country in which the standard of living is still low. Until recently there were few affordable alternatives, but in the last decade plenty of hostels and mid-range hotels have emerged to fill the gap. In hotels a single room often has a double bed, and you may just be able to pay a bit more for a second breakfast; but a double room often has twin single beds.

Details of local guesthouses can usually be obtained from tourist information centres. Otherwise two organisations are trying to coordinate and list rural homestays: **Elkana** has three offices (*Gazapkhuli 16, 0177 Tbilisi;* \ *32 253 6486/7;* e *biofarm@elkana.org.ge, www.new.ruraltourism.ge; Shalva Akhaltsikheli 9, Akhaltsikhe;* \ *79 050 6776;* e *farezi@elkana.org.ge, rop@elkana.org.ge; Guria* \ *79 053 6487;* e *guria@elkana.org.ge*); and the **Georgian Tourism Association** has an office in Tbilisi (*Melikishvili 18/II, 0179;* \ *32 220 195, 916793; www.tourism-association.ge/guesthouses*). See also www.davisvenot.ge. Houses in beach/spa villages often have signs offering *komnati* or *sdaetsya* ('rooms' in Russian). If in doubt, you can simply ask a taxi driver if he knows anyone who has a room free; in villages you'll never be allowed to go without a bed. Georgian hospitality is renowned, and you'll usually find liberal amounts of alcohol included in the cost of a homestay, as well as food. Although hotel beds can be absurdly soft, in homes they're usually firm enough, and washing facilities, which are quite clean in hotels, tend to be even more so in homes. Most hotels include value-added tax of 20% in their rates, but it's worth checking; smaller ones and guesthouses don't pay it.

EATING AND DRINKING

Georgian cuisine is far closer to that of Turkey and Iran than that of Russia, with plenty of garlic, walnuts, cumin and coriander; huge feasts are traditional, though not as huge as in the Brezhnev years, when food was absurdly cheap. Meat is central, but a Georgian meal is served with many dishes, including vegetable ones, on the table at once and everyone helping themselves to whatever they want. It's best to pace yourself, as it's likely to be a long evening with plenty of wine.

Menus are rarely displayed outside restaurants, especially in English. In Tbilisi there are fast-food joints selling shwarma (kebabs), burgers, hot dogs and a poor approximation to pizza. Cafés everywhere sell khachapuri and other traditional snacks. Street traders sell *marozhni* (ice cream) and *semichki*, the sunflower seeds which are chewed and spat out everywhere, and probably use more energy than they provide. Those who would like to try their hand at reproducing some of the dishes they enjoyed in Georgia will find a wealth of inspiring and knowledgeable food and wine bloggers discovering Georgia.

Traditional **meat** dishes include *kharcho* (a spicy soup of mutton or beef with garlic, rice and vegetables); *jigari* (a stew of liver, heart, kidney, onion and parsley); *ostri* (a stew of beef, tomato and onion); *chakapuli* (a stew of lamb, scallions and greens in their own juices with tarragon); *chakhokhbili* (a drier but equally tasty stew, originally of pheasant, but now usually chicken, with herbs, diced tomatoes, garlic and onion); *kupati* (kidney stuffed with minced meat and spices); *chanakhi* (lamb with tomatoes, greens, garlic and green peppers, baked in a clay pot); and *abkhazuri* (a meat purée with onion, garlic, pomegranate, herbs and spices). Chicken is also used, in the form of: *satsivi*, pieces of chicken (or turkey) in a sauce of walnut, cornflower, garlic and saffron (a traditional New Year dish); *tabaka*, pressed fried chicken; *chikhirtma*, chicken soup with egg; and *shkmeruli*, roast chicken in garlic sauce.

Mtsvadi, pork or mutton grilled on a vinewood fire (also known as *shashlik*), is very popular for outdoor feasts. *Basturma* (ie: pastrami, as used in New York delis) is air-dried pressed mutton. Finally, in the meat department, *khinkhali* are pasta envelopes of dough (shaped like little money bags) stuffed with minced meat (or cheese and caraway), historically associated with mountain villages such as Dusheti. Fish is also popular, notably sturgeon and trout, such as *kefalia*, small fried trout from the mountains of Adjara.

Vegetable dishes include several with aubergine (eggplant), for instance fried with walnuts, stuffed with hazelnut paste, or as *ajapsandali*, stewed with tomato and peppers. Bean dishes include *lobio* (kidney beans stewed with coriander), *karabakh loby* (green beans in sour cream and tomato sauce) and *mtsvane lobio niguzit* (a bean salad in a walnut dressing). *Pkhali* is a generic term for walnut and vegetable pâtés such as minced spinach with walnuts, spices, garlic and a topping of pomegranate seeds; similarly, shredded beetroot tops are served with red peppers and pomegranate seeds, and red beans with walnuts, garlic, celery and coriander. *Phklovani* is spinach and cheese; *soko ketze* is mushroom and cheese. Beetroot is also served with walnuts, or mashed with garlic. Salads include *tarkhun* (long green leaves with an aroma of aniseed, eaten with kebabs), raw cabbage salad, and the ubiquitous tomato and cucumber salad, often with walnut. Bunches of coriander (*kinza*) are used for sprinkling water over produce in markets, to keep it fresh, and it is eaten raw (for long life) as well as in cooking; dill is also popular. Food is spicier in western Georgia, and better for vegetarians, with more use of maize and nuts. Saying (*me*) *khortss ar v-ch'am* means *I don't eat meat*.

Practical Information EATING AND DRINKING

2

The programme known as Traceca (Transport Corridor Europe–Caucasus–Asia) was set up in 1993 by Georgia, Azerbaijan, Armenia and five Central Asian states, and has since been joined by Ukraine, Mongolia and Moldova. It's a sort of recreation of the Silk Route, with substantial funding from the European Union, which has mainly gone into refurbishing railways and ports and introducing new train-ferries across the Caspian and Black seas. Shevardnadze was a great enthusiast, rightly seeing Georgia as an essential link in any new Silk Route, which was both an economic opportunity and a way of reinforcing Georgia's international standing.

For cotton exports from Central Asia, a route via Georgia and a train-ferry across the Black Sea is around 2,000km shorter than the one through Russia to the Baltic ports. However, Russian Railways are still faster, and the Baltic States have uniformly low tariffs. Even so, traffic along the Traceca route rose from one million tonnes through Georgia in 1997 to 49 million tonnes in 2012 and was perhaps double that in 2004 and triple by 2009. You'll read quite a bit about Traceca in the papers, but its real significance is as a measure of Georgia's international status and its integration into the world.

Similarly, in 1995 the major companies involved in the extraction of oil from the Caspian and beyond announced that their 'early oil' would be moved through improved pipelines through both Georgia and Russia (which both opened in 2001), while continuing to debate the route to be taken by the larger modern pipeline needed for bulk flows. The best route is through Georgia to Ceyhan on Turkey's Mediterranean coast (as it removes tankers from the Bosphorus, which is 700m wide at its narrowest, with nine sharp bends, and faces a possible five-fold increase in tanker traffic); however, Russia did all it could to promote its route to Novorossiysk, even though this passes through Daghestan and close to Chechnya. This promotion may have included fomenting instability in neighbouring countries, perhaps even abetting an assassination attempt on Shevardnadze. Iran has also offered a route to the sea, but this was vetoed by the USA. The Ceyhan route is the longest, at 1,700km, and the most expensive. Its viability was thrown into doubt by the oil price plummeting from around US$20 a barrel to US$10 in a year. The Caspian oil reserves have also been reassessed, and may be 'only' 25–30 billion barrels (3.7–4.5 billion tonnes), not 200 billion barrels (30 billion tonnes). However, Turkey managed to halve its estimate of the construction cost, claiming that it had been using German labour costs and hadn't realised that Turkish wage rates could be used.

The oil price rose again and, in 2001, BP finally committed itself to the US$3 billion Ceyhan Project (in which it has a 30% share), after three years' hesitation; this was perhaps linked to BP's shift from being a British company to being an American one. The 'early oil' or Western Route Export Pipeline (also 34% owned

There's a range of **pastes and sauces** eaten with shashlik and other dishes; the best known is *tkemali*, a sour plum sauce with *ombalo* or pennyroyal. Others are *adjika* (a hot red pepper and coriander paste from the west of Georgia, which also comes in a green variety), and *bazha* (a sauce of crushed walnuts with a combination of spices with garlic and saffron known as *tkhmali-suneli*). *Masharaphi* is a pomegranate dressing. On the table you may find a small pot of *svanuri marili* (Svan salt), a blend of salt, garlic, fenugreek, coriander and red chili pepper, perhaps with black pepper, caraway, saffron or dill.

by BP), a refurbished Soviet pipeline from Baku to Supsa, now carries 150,000 barrels a day (three million tonnes a year); the BTC (Baku–Tbilisi–Ceyhan) pipeline can carry between one and 1.5 million barrels per day. A refinery is also to be built in Poti, opening in 2019.

The BTC pipeline, opened in 2005, was followed the next year by the parallel South Caucasus Pipeline to take Azeri gas from the Shah-Deniz field to Erzurum via Tbilisi, breaking the Russian monopoly of supplies to Georgia. In fact, Georgia is entitled to 5% of the seven billion m³ of gas passing annually through the pipeline, which will supply half its needs. BP's Shah-Deniz-2 project to expand the SCP (worth US$2 billion of investment to Georgia) will triple its capacity by 2018.

In parallel with Traceca, from 1996 Georgia, Ukraine, Azerbaijan and Moldova began to form a bloc of nations seeking to escape Russia's overpowering influence; Uzbekistan also joined, and the GUAM charter was adopted in 2001, followed by a free trade pact (without Uzbekistan) the next year. In 2006 Saakashvili again antagonised Russia by meeting the presidents of Ukraine, Azerbaijan and Moldova to revive GUAM and discuss the potential for new pipelines from the Caspian avoiding Russia. It received new impetus from the US-led anti-terrorism campaign after 11 September 2001; oil was already crucial to Bush's foreign policy (indeed the 'multiple pipelines' policy dates from the Clinton administration), but secure supplies have become even more important, and so Azerbaijan and the countries through which pipelines could run are seeing more American support. For a while the US embraced Russia as an ally in the war against terrorism, adopting a see-no-evil policy to human rights abuses in Chechnya and to the bullying of Georgia; but Putin's adventures in Georgia and Ukraine have ended that. The US$45 billion Southern Gas Corridor (or Euro-Caspian Mega Pipeline) project will allow gas from Azerbaijan to cover nearly 20% of western-European demand from 2019, using the upgraded South Caucasus Pipeline through Georgia, the new 2,000km Trans-Anatolian Pipeline (TANAP) through Turkey, and finally the new Trans-Adriatic Pipeline (TAP) from Albania to Italy. There's also talk of a Trans-Caspian Gas Pipeline to feed in gas from Turkmenistan and possibly Kazakhstan. In December 2014, Putin announced the abandonment of the South Stream pipeline, under the Black Sea from Russia to Bulgaria, due to EU opposition; instead Russia plans to send its gas via Turkey and Greece.

Georgia is also the route for most of Armenia's trade, as Armenia's borders with Turkey and Azerbaijan are closed. Most of this also takes the main railway line to Batumi; Armenia is particularly keen to see a resolution of the Abkhaz conflict and the reopening of its rail route to Russia. Armenia is also in favour of an Iran–Armenia pipeline project, to secure Armenia's fuel supply and possibly carry gas from Iran to Europe.

CHEESE AND BREAD There are various cheeses, divided into *brindza*, the bog-standard salty factory cheese found in shops everywhere, and far more interesting local and largely homemade cheeses. *Imeruli qveli* (Imeretian cheese) is a salted cow's-milk cheese that crumbles easily when cool and melts smoothly when hot. *Sulguni* is a mozzarella-like cheese associated with Mingrelia (where it should be made from buffalo milk) and Svaneti, and *sulguni shebolili* is a smoked version; *chechili* is also mozzarella-like, produced in dense strings that are usually braided and rolled into a figure of eight. *Gudiskweli* is a very salty cheese made of sheep's milk in Tusheti in a bag (*guda*) of sheepskin (with the wool inside). *Nodun* (or *naduri*) is whey curd (like cream cheese) with mint (or tarragon), *matsoni* is yoghurt, and *kefir* is the equivalent of the Central Asian buttermilk known as *kumiss*. Breads are also excellent; in addition to *zavatskoy* or regular 'Georgian bread', there are also various types produced in the *tone* or clay oven set in the floor, like an oversized tandoor (now often with electric elements rather than wood fuel). These include the spear-shaped *shoti*, and the flat, unleavened Armenian bread known as *lavash*. In Kakheti you'll find thin flattened

TAMADOBA

The set-piece Georgian feast is known as the *supra*, meaning literally 'tablecloth', from the Arabic *sufratun*; it's a marathon of food and drink in which men will drink up to four litres of wine over three to five hours. In theory they're not allowed to leave the room, but in practice an excuse can usually be found.

The key feature of the supra is the ceremony of toasting, led by a *tamada* or toastmaster (assisted by a *merikipe*, who fills the glasses and stokes the conversation but stays sober; both, of course, are always male). It's almost sacramental, with the first dozen or so toasts (of 20 or more) following a prescribed order. The first will be proposed by the master of the house to the tamada (unless he's playing this role himself), then the tamada will propose toasts to the person being celebrated, if any (for example, for a homecoming or a birthday), to his family or the host family, to the elderly (if any are present), to siblings, to the ancestors, to the dead, to children (ie: the future), to the parentland, to women and mothers, to the winemaker, and to 'our son' (any local hero, which could include Stalin or Tamar). For the toast to the dead, wine is poured on to bread, or on to the ground, and men may stand; for the toast to women those slaving in the kitchen will emerge to join in for a few minutes. After this, things become more flexible, with toasts to specific people, present or not, and guests may ask for permission to propose a toast themselves (a sure way for a foreigner to win approval). In regions such as Svaneti the pattern differs slightly, with, for instance, a toast to St George. Between the toasts there may well be singing.

Each *sadghegrdzelo* or toast is in fact a speech of ten to 15 minutes, during which it's not permitted to touch your wine (although water or soft drinks are always available); when it's done the tamada will drain his glass, or ideally a horn, and turn it upside-down, everyone says '*gaumarjos*' (victory), and you will have to drain your glass in one swallow too. Never have I drunk so much and tasted so little as at a Georgian supra; it's largely irrelevant whether Georgian wine fits contemporary Western tastes when so little of it makes contact with the taste buds. When it gets too much for you, ask permission to propose a toast, toast the host family, and leave.

Most meals are, of course, informal family affairs, but wine will be produced for a guest, and one-line toasts will be proclaimed: 'To Britain!', 'To Georgia!', 'To Thatcher!', 'To Stalin!' being a hardly atypical exchange. As at a supra, you should not drink wine outside toasts, and you must then, at least initially, drain your glass in one. Wine is never drunk without toasting, while beer is never drunk with toasting (except for a toast to 'the police and the president'), except in remote places like Khevsureti where they have to drink beer instead of wine.

loaves, a bit like unleavened baguettes. In the west of the country maize is used rather than wheat, both for *chadi*, a heavy but delicious crusty cornbread, and for *ghomi*, a form of polenta served with sulguni cheese; in Svaneti *elargi* is like ghomi, a mix of maize flour, cheese and milk. The national snack is *khachapuri*, literally cheese-bread, which takes many forms: in homes and restaurants it's usually a cheese-filled bread, while on stalls nationwide (though especially associated with Tbilisi) it's pelovani, a folded cheese-filled pastry. Cooks will tell you that there are four varieties: *imeruli* (ie: Imeretian), like a cheese calzone; *megruli* (ie: Mingrelian), similar but with cheese on top too; *achma*, made of thin layers of filo-like pastry (boiled then baked) interleaved with goat's cheese and folded into a square, much like pelovani; and *adjaruli* (ie: Adjaran), boat-like with a lightly fried egg on top swimming in molten butter. In Kazbegi and Ossetia they make *khabajini*, a potato khachapuri, and in Svaneti khachapuri is stuffed with greens; *kubdari* is the Svan national dish, bread stuffed with meat. *Chebureki* are pies (like the Ukrainian and Russian *pirozhi*) of unleavened dough and filled with spiced mutton; *lobiani* is bread stuffed with beans, and *kartushki* are greasy potato rolls found in bus stations.

DESSERTS AND FRUIT Desserts such as *halva* and *baklava* show influence from the south; walnuts are also used in many ways, such as in cakes, crushed and wrapped in a flour and honey paste, and best of all as *nigozis muraba*, picked green, marinated in slaked lime and water, and boiled in the shell with sugar, until you can easily bite through the shell and the nut is the texture of marron glacé. Also quintessentially Georgian is *churchkhela*, made by threading walnuts or hazelnuts, almonds and raisins on a string, covering them in flour, dipping them repeatedly in simmering grape juice and hanging out to dry; made at the grape harvest each year, they look like brown candles. The definitive version comes from Kakheti, where it's made with wheat flour and walnuts (*k'ak'ali*); in Imereti they use maize flour and hazelnuts (*tkhili*).

Fruit is also excellent, and all sorts of health benefits are now being discovered; in addition to the citrus fruits grown by the Black Sea, there are various relatives of the persimmon (*Diospyros lotus* and *D. kaki*), such as the *karalioke* (Russian for 'royal fruit'), similar to the Israeli sharon fruit, which can be eaten hard, with no need to peel; and the *khulma*, which looks similar but must be soft when eaten. November is the season for these, producing the striking effect of trees with no leaves but large numbers of golden fruit. The pomegranate (*Punica granatum*) grows wild between the Caucasus and the Middle East and bears many-seeded red fruit up to 13cm in diameter. In addition to being eaten fresh, its seeds and dark red juice are used in cooking. It's associated with the goddess of love, fertility, spring, youth and eternity, and does in fact contain lots of antioxidants while the seeds are high in potassium, vitamin C and polyphenols, which protect the heart. The medlar (*Mespilus germanica*) is a small tree up to 6m in height, with brown acidic fruit, like apples, up to 5cm in diameter. The fruit remains hard until frost, after which it is picked and kept in a cool dry room until soft, when it is eaten raw or in preserves. Figs and soft fruits are used for conserves, served with tea after dinner.

WINE There's been wine in Georgia almost as long as there have been Georgians: around 6,000–7,000 years. Stone wine presses and clay containers have been found dating from the 3rd millennium BC, and vine leaves and stems have been found in Bronze Age tombs. It seems that our word 'wine' derived from the Georgian *ghvino*. Wine is absolutely central to the Georgian lifestyle and to their self-image, and everyone (especially men) drinks large quantities and will want you to do the same. In theory Georgians drink red wines in winter, and whites in summer, but in practice it can be hard to tell the difference, as even 'red' (literally 'black' or *shavi*) wines may in fact be straw-coloured. Most families make their own, storing it in *qvevri*, large sealed clay vessels set into the floor of a room known as the *marani*. In every ancient site you visit, such as Vardzia or Uplistsikhe, there'll be a marani or three.

There are at least 500 varieties of grape in Georgia, with up to 38 in common use, and more or less every village produces its own wine, effectively semi-organic – draught wine accounts for 80–90% of the domestic market. Farmers will sell theirs in Tbilisi markets for GEL1.20 a litre (bring your own container), but a regular bottle will cost you about GEL6–10 (US$4–6).

In the Soviet period, Georgia produced large quantities of cheap wine for consumption in Russia above all, notably the dreaded semi-sweet red which has now largely vanished. After independence there was a move to modern techniques at the upper end of the market, with temperature-controlled stainless-steel tanks replacing concrete, leading to some very good wines suited to foreign tastes and the world market. What is happening now is more interesting, as many wine-makers are rediscovering the ancient qvevri method of natural wine-making – although the few remaining manufacturers can barely keep up with demand. In 2013, qvevri wine-making was added to UNESCO's list of world intangible heritage. The largest qvevri are three or four 'tonnes' (3,000 or 4,000 litres), treated with beeswax for hygiene while still allowing the clay to breathe, so that the wine is at the temperature

THE MONGOL RALLY   *Oliver Moss*

On 22 July 2006, I set off from the familiarity of London's Hyde Park along with 200 other drivers and cars, on the road trip of all road trips: the Mongol Rally. The purpose of the rally is to make your own way from London to Mongolia's capital Ulaanbaatar to raise money for various charities, in a car with an engine size below 1,000cc (eg: Nissan Micras, Fiat Pandas, Ladas, Minis, Ford Escorts) which would normally be deemed wholly unsuitable for such a journey. The route you take is largely up to you.

After reaching Prague on the second night, the teams started to head off in different directions according to their planned route. Some headed north through Scandinavia, St Petersburg, across the Urals and down into Mongolia; others headed across Poland to Moscow and through Kazakhstan; others through Ukraine and Central Asia; and others down through the Balkans, across Turkey, the Caspian and Central Asia. I, with my team of four Fiat Pandas, decided to take the last of the described routes. We spent a total of three days in Georgia, which under normal circumstances would barely seem sufficient. But the innate sense of hospitality and friendliness for which Georgians are well known, and the fact that we crossed the entire country from the western border with Turkey to the eastern border with Azerbaijan, meant we left this compact and stunning country with huge reluctance and a longing to return in the future.

On our first day, after a long wait at the border, we sat down to a late lunch in a beachside café overlooking the Black Sea. Having heard of the banquets that are the average Georgian meals, and the local wines of which they are so proud, we had to ask the staff to halve the dozen or so courses they were trying to lavish on us. The food was superb and very filling, with enormous amounts of cheese and meats and wine: it seemed rude to turn them down when they attached such devotion and pride to their meals.

of the earth that holds it and is imbued with the essence of its terroir. There are no additives; only the natural yeasts on the grape skins are used, with dead cells gathering in the narrow foot of the jar, for the duration of the winter or longer.

The classic Georgian (ie: Kakhetian) grapes are Saperavi (for red wine), which has deep colour, rich plummy flavours and crisp natural acidity, and Rkatsiteli (mainly for whites), acidic with spicy and floral notes and a very dry aftertaste. Other well-known varieties include Tsolikouri, Kisi and Mtsvane, but there are many more, with some villages having their own varieties.

Rkatsiteli goes with most foods, likewise Tsolikouri in western Georgia; and modern wines made with Mtsvane, Khikhivi, Kisi or Tsitska go well with salads and fish. Qvevri wines are high in tannins, so should not be drunk without food; in particular they go well with heavier fatty meals including most meats and mature cheeses. This also applies to Saperavi – some Saperavis are particularly good when young, going well with almost any food. In the centre of Georgia, Kartli is known for the Chinuri grape (for dry white wines), as well as other Georgian and indeed French varieties. The red wine from Kvanchkara, in Racha, goes well with cakes and desserts and is famed as Stalin's favourite (and costs twice as much, as it should); the dry Alexandrouli and Mujuretlui wines go well with typical Racha dishes such as smoked ham, rabbit, goose kharcho or lobio.

At the far end of the country, in Imereti, they make lighter, more flowery wines using the Aladasturi, Otskhanuri Sapere and Odzhaleshi grapes for red wines and

The first night we spent in the port city of Batumi, an interesting place rather than beautiful, with colourful markets set against crumbling grey Soviet apartment blocks, and dilapidated buses pushing their way through the thronging streets. The next day we embarked on a memorable journey to Tbilisi, crossing mountain passes where medieval castles overlooked long-abandoned Soviet factories, driving through stunning, green, wooded valleys with crystal-clear rivers winding and roaring their way down from the Caucasus Mountains, and passing through villages where pony and trap and horse and plough were still in widespread use.

When we got to Tbilisi, we were taken out on a city tour by a contact of mine, proud to show off his city and culture. Unlike the other major cities, Tbilisi is a beautiful old city, the jewel of the Caucasus, with grand buildings, windy cobbled streets, and ancient castles nestled in a deep valley. We went out for another traditional Georgian feast complete with toasts every few minutes, before heading to our hotel.

The main concern before entering Georgia was the reports of potential violence surrounding the disputed breakaway republics within the country. However, we never felt unsafe – in fact, we were made to feel so welcome that the image we had before we arrived was quickly forgotten, and we forged a new one of a beautiful, welcoming and fascinating country.

Unfortunately not all of our cars made it to Mongolia, as was perhaps expected. The first burst into flames on a particularly dodgy Azeri road, the second finally gave up the ghost in northern Kazakhstan, but the final two limped over the line some five weeks after setting off from London: battered, dusty and falling to pieces, but covered in hundreds of good luck messages from people along the way who had helped us to complete such an incredible journey.

For more information, visit www.mongolrally.co.uk.

Tsitska, Tsolikouri and Krakhuna for whites; here vines are allowed to grow high on trees and the grapes are collected in a pointed basket known as a *gideli* which is lowered down on a rope. This doesn't affect the taste, but does give rise to a specific genre of worksongs. Sparkling wine ('Georgian champagne' or *champanska*) is produced in factories nationwide rather than in homes; it's inexpensive and ranges from more or less dry to ultra-sweet in taste.

OTHER DRINKS The national **beer** was Kazbegi, a nice tangy German-style brew which has been produced in Tbilisi since 1881; Argo, a premium beer, is produced by the same company, as well as a porter, ice tea and a version of *kvass* (supposedly a weak malted rye beer), which tastes more like a bitter cola. Founded in 2005, the Natakhtari brewery produces *chekhuri* (Czech-style) beers such as Mtieli, better and these days more widely available than the Kazbegi brews; Russian beers such as Baltika are also available, as well as German Krombacher and Czech Staropramen at high prices.

Vodka is drunk in Georgia, but far less than in Russia and the other Slav countries; the national spirit is *chacha*, a firewater made at home, as a rule from grain, although in Svaneti, where grain doesn't grow, they use bread instead! It's intriguing to wonder whether there's any linguistic connection with *chicha*, the fermented maize drink of the Andes. Although the Georgians love to drink, there's very little public drunkenness and few of the alcohol-related problems that are found north of the Caucasus.

Soft drinks are easily available, both the ubiquitous Coca-Cola and Fanta, and local fruit juices, which are slightly cheaper as well as rather healthier. Borjomi mineral water is also sold almost everywhere, costing a bit more at GEL0.70 (US$0.40) for a half-litre bottle (for some reason a poster was produced entirely in Georgian except for the words 'Borjomi 0.5L not returnable'!); the milder Borjomi Light was introduced in 2001. Nabeghlavi and Sairme are other excellent mineral waters. Coffee (instant or Turkish) is available in cafés, and you'll usually be able to find tea – it's generally from Sri Lanka, as while Georgia produces tea, it's all green tea for the Russian samovar market.

PUBLIC HOLIDAYS AND FESTIVALS

1 January	New Year's Day
7 January	Christmas (Orthodox Church)
19 January	Epiphany (Orthodox Church)
3 March	Mother's Day
8 March	International Women's Day
9 April	Remembrance Day
April	Easter Sunday and Monday (Orthodox Church): 1 May in 2016, 16 April in 2017, 8 April in 2018 and 28 April in 2019
26 May	Independence Day
28 August	Assumption of the Virgin (Mariamoba) (Orthodox Church)
14 October	Sveti-tskhovloba (Mtskhetoba) – Mtskheta town festival
23 November	St George's Day (Giorgoba), now also celebrated as the anniversary of the Rose Revolution, and of Aslan Abashidze's departure from Adjara a year later

SHOPPING

Larger shops open from 09.00 to 20.00 Monday to Saturday. Kiosks and house-front 'markets' are usually open from 08.00 at the latest until in some cases midnight or later, and are usually open on Sundays too.

In Tbilisi there are quite a few 'antique salons', in which you can buy items such as ceramics, wood- and metalwork, and carpets. An export permit (and attached photo) is needed from the Ministry of Culture (*Rustaveli Av 37, 3rd floor, room 16, Tbilisi; ⟍32 299 0285*) to export carpets and some other items. You may find it simpler to take wine to your loved ones, or, if you really want to perplex them, sticks of churchkhela (strings of nuts coated in grape syrup that look like knobbly candles), but be aware that wine will have to be put in your checked-in luggage if you are flying – a risky business.

Among the more interesting items are the male national dress, the *chokha* and *akhalukhi*, a sort of frock coat with a row of pockets across the chest to hold cartridges, and a silk inner coat. More exotic perhaps is the *nabadi* or *burka*, the shaggy sheepskin cape worn by mountain shepherds. A dagger or *khandzali* is always worn by men with the national dress: it should have an elaborately decorated side, for weddings, and a plain one, for funerals. A winehorn or *khantsi* is another possible present. See pages 116–17 for suitable shops in Tbilisi.

MEDIA AND COMMUNICATIONS

MEDIA Several English-language **newspapers**, largely business-oriented, are published in Tbilisi, and subscriptions are available for most: *The Messenger* (GEL3) and the *Georgian Times* (GEL2) appear Monday to Friday; *Caucasian Business Week* (free) appears on Mondays; *Georgian Journal* (GEL2) appears on Thursdays; and *Georgia Today* (GEL2.50) appears on Fridays. All have websites that are updated most days, and agenda.ge is a web-only news source. The amount of world news you'll find in them is minimal, but they're a useful window onto Georgian life, politics and business. The papers can be picked up free in major hotels. Friday's *Messenger* is good for culture and what's on.

Nationwide, the dominant **television** broadcaster is Sakartvelos Sazogadoebrivi Mauts'q'ebeli or the Georgian Public Broadcaster; its Channel 1 reaches 85% of the population and Channel 2 reaches 55%. Having been a state system, and hardly neutral, it is now making the transition to being a genuinely public broadcaster (which seems to consist largely of pumping out Turkish serials). Other channels are Adjara, Imedi, Maestro, Mze and Rustavi-2, and satellite and cable TV is available in almost every hotel and elsewhere. The independent Rustavi-2 television station earned a good reputation towards the end of the Shevardnadze era, especially for its hard-hitting investigative programme *Sixty Minutes*, but then became tediously pro-government under Saakashvili; it still peddles his scare stories about crime waves and the Russian threat.

TELEPHONE The telephone system has traditionally been so decrepit that most people ignore it, using mobile phones instead. However, there has now been investment in modern equipment, with Siemens, Alcatel and Daewoo installing new exchanges and a fibre-optic line under the Black Sea from Varna (Bulgaria) to Poti, now extended across Georgia to Azerbaijan, *en route* to Shanghai. In Tbilisi in particular there are now good connections for broadband internet. The number of lines has risen to over 830,000 (around 20 lines per 100 people in urban areas, around four per 100 in rural areas), but some villages still don't have phone lines.

Mobile phones work on a GSM system using Siemens-Motorola kit that is compatible with Western systems. Probably the most reliable supplier is MagtiCom, a joint venture with the American company Telcell that was run by Shevardnadze's son-in-law, Georgi Jokhtaberidze. After the Rose Revolution he was arrested at the airport and only freed after paying US$15 million to the state treasury, allowing it to pay

2

salaries and pensions on time at last. The main alternatives are Geocell and Beeline; together they cover 98% of Georgia's populated area and have three million users.

Bring your own phone, and buy a SIM card for GEL10 at most, including GEL5 credit, from a corner shop. In truly remote areas such as Khevsureti there's no mobile (or fixed) phone coverage, but some satellite phones are available, at GEL9 per minute. Public coin or card phones have disappeared.

Georgia's **country code** is 995, and the code for Tbilisi is 32, so from most countries you'll dial 0099532, followed by the seven-digit number. All other places have six-digit numbers; other codes are 422 for Batumi, 431 for Kutaisi, 493 for Poti and 350 for Telavi. Within the same town, just dial the number; otherwise dial 0 then the code and number. Mobile numbers begin with 5 and two digits, then a six-digit number; you'll need to prefix this with +995 (rather than 00995).

Special numbers include:

Police, fire or ambulance ✆112	**Directory enquiries for Tbilisi** ✆09,
Long-distance operator ✆07	elsewhere ✆05
Taxi ✆008	

The emergency service should have an English-speaking operator, but otherwise you'll need to speak Georgian or Russian.

POST AND COURIERS The state postal service had virtually disappeared, but has now re-invented itself as **Georgian Post** (✆ *32 224 0909; www.gpost.ge*); post offices are few and far between, but at least there is now a vaguely reliable service. Whether sending to or from Georgia, you should stick to postcards if possible. Airmail to western Europe costs GEL5 (US$2.50) and takes about ten days; it's possible to buy pre-stamped envelopes for internal mail for GEL2 at cigarette kiosks. Blue-and-white letter boxes can be found on main streets, but you'll need to find stamps before leaving Tbilisi (page 112). Incidentally, the first Georgian stamp was the 'Tbilisi Unica' of 1857, which was the first in the Russian Empire; now it survives nowhere in the former Soviet Union, and only in two collections in the world. It's featured on a GEL0.80 stamp, against a photo of 19th-century Tbilisi. Letters to UK cost GEL5, domestic postage is GEL2.

The courier companies DHL, TNT, UPS and FedEx all have offices in Tbilisi (page 112) and they offer the most reliable international mail service.

OTHER PRACTICALITIES

TIME Georgia is four hours ahead of GMT. Georgians are not early risers, but can be lively well into the night.

PUBLIC TOILETS Public toilets are few and far between. Where you do find one, the doors are likely to be marked with Cyrillic symbols, M for men and Ж for women.

ELECTRICITY Electrical power is supplied in theory at 220v 50hz, using European-standard two-pin plugs; however, it's subject to surges, and in winter there may be power cuts.

BUSINESS

Georgians are known as wheeling-dealing businessmen, and Russians in particular also associate them with organised crime – unfairly, as most of the gangsters in

Moscow are in fact Chechens and indeed Russians. Laws and accountancy norms are being brought into line with EU standards; but to do business here you will have to come to terms with a culture of clannish loyalties.

Economic data can be obtained from the Economist Intelligence Unit (*www. eiu.com*). In Tbilisi, the International Chamber of Commerce is at Kakabadze 29 (✆ *32 298 8176; www.icc.ge*). AmCham, the American Chamber of Commerce in Georgia, is at Asatiani 36A, Tbilisi (✆ *32 222 6907; www.amcham.ge*); they have an online database of businesses in Georgia, and publish the useful and interesting *AmCham News* every two months (available free online).

For **casual work**, about your only option is teaching English – try International House Tbilisi, Centre for Language Studies (*26 May Sq 2, Tbilisi;* ✆ *32 294 0515; www.ihtbilisi.ge*); the Byron School (*Griboedov 2, Tbilisi;* ✆ *32 298 3478; www. byronschool.ge*); the English Language Centre (*Barnov 51A, Tbilisi;* ✆ *32 222 2326;* e *ELC@geo.net.ge; www.the-elc.com.ge*); and Teach and Learn with Georgia (*Gmir Kursantta 1, Tbilisi;* ✆ *32 220 0220; www.tlg.gov.ge*).

CULTURAL ETIQUETTE

CULTURAL DOS AND DON'TS   Perhaps the most important rule is to learn to accept a drink even when it's the last thing you want. Restaurant bills are never split; they're always paid by one person, almost always a man.

Adult Georgians don't wear shorts except for sport. In churches shorts and low-cut dresses are unacceptable, and this is true in general in the remoter mountain areas. Women cover their heads in church (though not always in Tbilisi) – perhaps pack a scarf to cover your shoulders, although often they are provided. Queues are surprisingly orderly.

INTERACTING WITH LOCAL PEOPLE   Georgians, though poor, are fantastically hospitable people; this is in some cases a form of subconscious domination or possession rather than pure generosity, but you still have to deal with the question of how to pay them back. Payment with money will never be accepted and may be seen as offensive, but presents for children are usually welcome (postcards or picture books about your home country, coloured pencils, toys, chocolate, etc). American cigarettes will usually be accepted by men, but the hardest problem is to find suitable gifts for the women who work so hard for so little in the way of thanks; in the remoter villages even make-up is inappropriate, but headscarves, napkins and tablecloths are much appreciated.

GIVING SOMETHING BACK

The best way to find out what's going on in the Georgian NGO scene is by reading the excellent newsletters published (on paper and online) by the Caucasus Environmental NGO Network (CENN). Details for this and other organisations are listed below.

Caucasus Environmental NGO Network (CENN) Betlemi 27, 0105 Tbilisi; ✆ 32 275 1903–4; www.cenn.org

The Noah's Ark Centre for the Recovery of Endangered Species (NACRES) Abashidze 12A, 0179 Tbilisi; ✆ 32 223 3706; www.nacres.org

Sabuko Society for Nature Conservation Akhmed Melashvili 5, Batumi 6010; ✆ 42 224 1777; m 558 217706; www.birdlife.ge

World Vision Georgia Imedashvili 18/17, 1060 Tbilisi; ✆ 32 215 7515; e ana_chkhaidze@wvi. org; www.wvi.org/georgia. Working mainly with children of poor families.

WWF-Georgia Aleksidze 11, 0193 Tbilisi; ✆ 32 223 7500; e atsintsadze@wwfcaucasus.org; www. panda.org/caucasus

Part Two

THE GUIDE

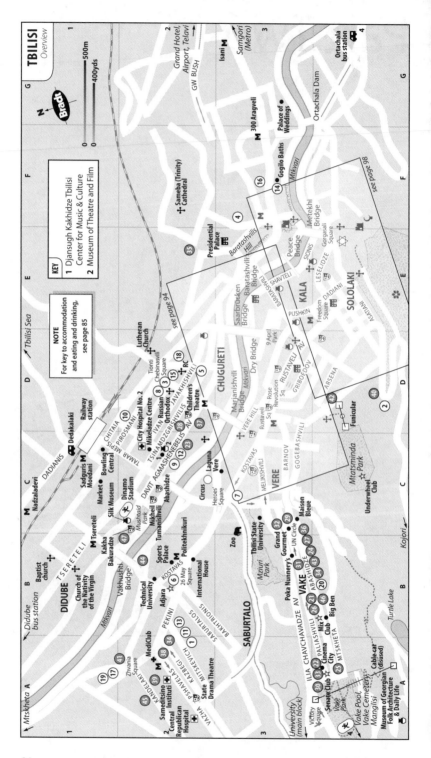

Tbilisi თბილისი

Telephone code: 32 (followed by a 2 and six digits)

Tbilisi lies at about 380m altitude, on the same latitude as Rome, Barcelona, Boston and Chicago. It stretches for 20km along the River Mtkvari (the Kura in Russian), with mountains on three sides: Mtatsminda to the southwest, Mount Tabori and the Solalaki Ridge to the southeast, and the low undulating Makhat Ridge to the northeast, beyond which is the so-called Tbilisi Sea, now a reservoir, and then the Samgori steppe.

The average temperature in Tbilisi is 13.2°C (24.4°C in July and 0.9°C in January), and average annual precipitation is 505mm (the wettest months are May with 75mm and April with 61mm). A damp spring is followed by a summer which can be oppressively hot and stuffy, then a fine autumn with lower humidity; the first snow appears on the mountains in mid-October, but winter in the city tends to be damp and misty with minimal snowfall, but higher pollution levels. This is a seismically active zone: seismologists reckon that the strongest earthquake likely to occur here will be 4.5 on the moment magnitude scale, and this was tested in April 2002 when a quake of magnitude 4.3 (Richter 4.8) struck. Six people died (two from heart attacks) and over 2,000 buildings were damaged in the old city, but none actually collapsed.

Perhaps the most evocative accounts of Tbilisi come from the 1930s, because of the contrast it offered to the rest of the USSR: the author Arthur Koestler said:

> I loved Tbilisi more than any other town in the Soviet Union, perhaps because it was still so untouched by the drabness and monotony of Soviet life. The town has an irresistible charm of its own, neither European nor Asiatic, but a happy blend of the two.

TBILISI *Overview*
For listings, see pages 95–108

🛏 Where to stay

1	Bu	A2	10	Khatuna's	D2
2	Diplomat	D4	11	Medea	B2
3	Dodo Kevlishvili	D2	12	Mirobelle	C2
4	Georgian House	F3	13	Nika	B2
5	Green Stairs	D2	14	Old Tbilisi	F3
6	Holiday Inn	B2	15	Prestige	D2
7	Iliani	C3	16	Sheraton Metechi Palace	F3
8	Irina Japaridze	D2	17	Sympatia	A1
9	Istanbul	C2			

18	Tamuna's Homestay	D2
19	Tbilotel	A1
20	VIP Victoria	B4

Off map

	Grand	G2

✖ Where to eat and drink

21	Acid Bar	B4	31	English Tea House	B3
22	Amira	A4	32	Fantastico Pizza	C3
23	Ankara	C2	33	Il Garage	A4
24	Art-Café Sfumato	B3	34	Literary Café	A2, B4
25	Assorti	A4	35	Luca Polare Finest Ice Cream and More	B4
26	Café Frâiche	B4	36	May Thai	C3
27	Cecilia	B3	37	Plekhanov	D2
28	Deniz	D2	38	Prego	A2
29	Dom*	C3	39	Ronny's Pizza	A2
30	Don Giuseppe	A4			

40	Shavi Lomi	D4
41	Sianggan	A2
42	Squirrels Gallery-Café	D4
43	Sushi Tokyo	B4
44	Taglaura	B2
45	Taste of India	A2
46	Vong	B4
47	World Sport Café	B2

Fitzroy Maclean, who came here a dozen times or more, called it 'one of my favourite towns anywhere'. Of his first visit he wrote:

> Immediately the town took my fancy. It had a graceful quality, a southern charm, an air of leisure, which I had so far found nowhere else in the Soviet Union. In the old city the houses, crazy structures with jutting verandas, hang like swallows' nests from the side of a hill. Beneath them a mountain stream tumbles its rushing waters and more houses cluster on the far side.

HISTORY

The city's name derives from *tbili*, meaning warm, referring to the 30 hot springs on the northeastern slopes of Mount Tabori – which produce three million litres of water a day, at between 24°C and 46.5°C – and in the 12th century supplied 65 bathhouses. Tiflis is the Persian name, also used by Russians and Armenians; the locals (or Tbilisebi) just say *kalaki* or 'the town'.

Legend has it that King Vakhtang Gorgasali ('Wolf-Lion'; AD446–502) went hunting from his capital in Mtskheta, and wounded a deer or pheasant, which was miraculously cured (or alternatively cooked) by a hot spring. Vakhtang decided to move his capital to this health-giving spot (the water is even said to restore eunuchs), though it was his son King Dachi who completed the walls of the new city and moved the capital here. In fact there's evidence of habitation since at least 3000BC, and it's not surprising given the combination of defensible hills with the hot springs. The city suffered 40 invasions between AD627 and 1795, by Persians, Byzantines, Arabs, Khazars and Seljuk Turks (many of them several times); in 1121 King Davit IV (the Builder) recaptured the city and rebuilt it (allowing the Muslims to stay), building his palace across the river in the Isani ('fortified place') district. The next year Tbilisi became capital of the most powerful state in the Near East, and then centre of Georgia's cultural flowering under monarchs such as Tamar. Then the invasions recommenced, with the Mongols in the 13th century, Temur Leng in the 14th and the Ottomans in the 15th. Georgia was divided into weak principalities, and from 1632 Tbilisi was governed by imposed Shahs (including Khusran-Mirza, an illegitimate member of the Bagratid family who had converted to Islam and who ruled for 26 years as King Rostom I). In 1744, they were driven out by King Teimuraz II and his son Erekle II, and in 1762, Tbilisi became capital of eastern Georgia. In 1795 the Shah of Persia, Aga Mohammed Khan, utterly destroyed Tbilisi (almost nothing survived; the churches you see now were rebuilt afterwards) and drove out the entire population.

After this disaster Erekle appealed for protection to the tsar and Georgia entered the Russian Empire. Tiflis (as the Russians know it) recovered but was soon largely inhabited by Armenians and Russians, with Georgians mainly in the Avlabari quarter, across the river beyond the Metekhi Church, which had been the Armenian quarter in Tamar's time, and is again now. The Russians developed the Garetubani area (the present centre, around Freedom Square and Rustaveli Avenue) only in the 1850s, when merchants' villas began to creep up the foothills of Sololaki and Mtatsminda. Across the river, towards the railway station, the Chugureti district was settled by Poles and Germans; the latter were invited to settle in the Russian Empire in 1817, and their influence can perhaps still be seen in the popularity of Doberman pinschers in Tbilisi. During this period it was the capital of the entire Transcaucasus, and many great figures came here. In 1829 Pushkin passed through on his way to Erzurum, in 1851–54 the young Tolstoy wrote his first significant stories here, and Gorki also wrote and published his first story here in 1892; he called Tbilisi his second home. The city was also visited by Tsar Nikolai I in 1837.

There are some fine Art Nouveau buildings (known as Moderne here), notably the National Library. Huge changes came in 1933–41, under Stalin's henchman Beria, when the Mtkvari embankments were built and Tbilisi became much longer, stretching along the river. The Circus, Dinamo Stadium and Rustaveli Cinema were built, and the first high-rise apartment blocks appeared; from 1951 the so-called 'attractive new housing developments' of Digomi, Varketili, Avchali and Gldani were built. Varketili is an extremely deprived area which has developed a particularly good community organisation to tackle its problems; if you should happen to go there, note block No 303, the Leaning Tower of Tbilisi, which has a cant of 1m. A few buildings in the Freedom Square/Rustaveli area were destroyed in the civil war of 1991–92, but most gaps have been filled by new developments, such as the Courtyard by Marriott Hotel. Nearby, the old town is decaying, with some pastiche restoration under Saakashvili, but less action and more stagnation under the Georgian Dream government. The city's population was 71,000 in 1865, 120,000 in 1900, 194,000 in 1913, and 519,000 in 1939; it reached a million in 1977, and now has about 1.4 million inhabitants, 40% of whom are not ethnically Georgian.

GETTING THERE AND AWAY

BY AIR Tbilisi's **Lochini Airport** (*formerly Novo-Alexeyevka; TBS; www.tbilisiairport. com*) is 18km east of the centre, reached by bus or taxi along the Kakheti Highway (a short stretch of which is now named George W Bush Avenue), or by train from Voksal, Tbilisi's central station. There are signs in English from the city centre and a tall monument of a woman holding a sun at the turn-off. From the air, see if you can spot the *kurgans* (Bronze Age burial mounds) near the airport. A new international terminal opened in 2007, able to handle aircraft as large as A330 and A340 Airbuses, and 1,500 passengers an hour. There's now an Avis car-rental counter (92 3594; m 595 587000) and ATMs, but the exchange desk is unlikely to be open when most planes from western Europe arrive; they are open by 05.30, however.

For **departures** check-in is 60–90 minutes before departure and flights within the former Soviet Union can suffer spectacular delays. Information (of sorts) is available by phoning 31 0421 or 31 0341. Up-to-date flight information is also available online at www.tbilisiairport.com. There's a coffee shop at departures (08.00–23.00) and a 24-hour restaurant at arrivals in addition to a Turkish-Georgian restaurant (08.00–22.30) and 'British' pub on the mezzanine floor. There are also two duty-free shops selling overpriced Georgian wines, various whiskies and a range of perfumes, cigarettes, sunglasses and electrical goods. Remember that duty-free goods bought in non-EU countries (ie: Georgia) can be taken into the EU, but there are limits.

It's also possible to take a low-cost airline to Kutaisi and then travel to Tbilisi with Georgian Bus (m 555 397287; www.georgianbus.com) or with any eastbound marshrutka on the highway outside.

Airline offices
✈ **Aegean Airlines** Paliashvili 66; 90 7090; http://en.aegeanair.com
✈ **Aeroflot** Gamsakhurdia 1; 37 2111; e tbstosu@aeroflot.ru; www.aeroflot.ru
✈ **Air Arabia** Chavchavadze 15; 40 0040;

e airarabia@gasa.ge; www.airarabia.com
✈ **Air Baltic** c/o Discovery Travel, Paliashvili 61; 90 0900; e airbalticgsa@discovery.ge; www. airbaltic.com
✈ **Alitalia** Kazbegi 14B; 93 7373, 93 73803; e customercare@alitalia.it; www.alitalia.com

✈ **Atlasjet** Abashidze 78; ☏ 25 0330; www. atlasjet.com

✈ **Azerbaijan Airlines (AZAL)** Chavchavadze 28; ☏ 25 1669; e tbilisi@swtravel.az; www.azal.az

✈ **Belavia** Davit Agmashenebelis 95a; ☏ 95 1685, 91 1791, 95 3815; e georgia@belavia.by; http://en.belavia.by

✈ **Czech Airlines** Use agent Berika International (page 90); ☏ 22 7941, 22 1341; e tbs@ czechairlines.com, berika@berika.ge; www.csa.cz

✈ **Fly Dubai** Kostavas 46/50; ☏ 40 0808, 40 0909; www.flydubai.com

✈ **Georgian Airways** (Still sometimes referred to as Air Zena) Rustaveli 12; ☏ 99 9130, 48 5577; e info@georgian-airways.com; www.georgian-airways.com

✈ **LOT** Chavchavadze 43 (Victory Sq); ☏ 55 4455; e lot@lottravel.ge; www.lot.com

✈ **Lufthansa** Abashidze 24; ☏ 24 3324; e lufthansa.tbilisi@dlh.de; www.lufthansa.com

✈ **Pegasus** Hotel Marriott Courtyard (Freedom Sq); ☏ 40 0040; www.flypgs.com

✈ **Qatar Airways** Pirimze Plaza Bldg, Vekua 3; ☏ 43 9608/09, 48 6000; www.qatarairways.com/ge

✈ **Turkish Airlines (THY)** Davit Agmashenebelis 147; ☏ 95 9022, 94 0703; e tbsmarketing@thy.com; www.turkishairlines.com

✈ **Ukraine International Airlines** Marie Brosse 2; ☏ 43 8614; e georgia@flyuia.com; www.flyuia.com

Airport transfer Bus route 37 (a yellow midi bus) runs from the airport every 20–30 minutes along the Kakheti Highway to Samgori (for metro and bus stations), Avlabari, the Baratashvili Bridge, Freedom Square, Rustaveli, Kostavas and Tamar avenues, giving a handy tour of the central area, and after half an hour reaching Station Square, where they leave from a relatively obvious stop in front of the railway station. The bus costs just GEL0.50 (US$0.30) – you'll need a MetroMoney card or coins. It operates from 07.00 to 21.30 (06.30–21.00 from the city); at other times you'll have to take a taxi or a train. **Taxis** cost around GEL20–25 (US$12–15) by day, or GEL30 (US$17) at night, usually after 20.00 (confirm the price before departure); cheaper transfers can be organised through hotels and hostels, also for GEL25–30. A **railway** branch to the airport's armadillo-like station opened in 2008. Trains currently leave only at 08.00 and 17.20 from the city's central station, taking around 35 minutes and returning 40 minutes later; pay the fare of GEL0.50 on board. Alternatively, it's under 2km to the highway, if you want to flag down a **marshrutka** east to Kakheti.

From Kutaisi Airport, used by low-cost flights, **Georgian Bus** (m *555 397287*; *www.georgianbus.com*) runs connecting minibuses direct to Pushkin Square, taking 5 hours; return tickets can be bought across the road at Bar Warszawa (⊕ *10.00–04.00*).

BUS AND RAIL International buses from Azerbaijan, Armenia, Turkey and Greece arrive at **Ortachala** [84 G4] (*www.avtovagzal.ge*), southeast of the centre, in theory the main bus station, with exchange desks but no ATM, and some cheap hotels. Ortachala also handles some services to Kakheti, and the Metro Class buses (☏ *42 224 2244; http://geometro.ge; GEL20*) go every couple of hours to Batumi, with Wi-Fi, air conditioning and reserved seats. The main terminal is in fact at **Didube** (☏ *34 4924*), to the northwest, but it is a disgraceful mess; emerging from the metro station through a crush of stalls and traders, you'll find in front of you a yard full of minibuses and shared taxis. Marshrutkas for Akhaltsikhe and Gardabani wait just to your left, and taxis to Davit-Gareja and marshrutkas for Mtskheta are about 50m ahead and to the right. Beyond them you can find marshrutkas to Kazbegi (sometimes with signs in Latin or Cyrillic scripts). The bus station proper is several hundred metres to the right; first you'll come to the new Autovoksal Okriba, which is just as chaotic as the rest of the site, with what should be ticket offices rented out as shops, and then the old terminal, where you'll find vile toilets and left-luggage and exchange facilities. Marshrutkas leave hourly to Batumi (☉ *09.00–17.00*) and every 30 minutes or so to Gori and Kaspi, and the really quite decent coaches to Kutaisi run hourly, as well as frequent marshrutkas. Marshrutkas to Borjomi leave on the hour from near the metro entrance, with others to Tqibuli (the 09.00 departure continuing to Oni) and elsewhere.

Buses for destinations in the **west** of the country, and **north** to Kazbegi, leave Didube in the mornings; in the early afternoon there'll still be some minibuses and shared taxis leaving from here, but later on you're best off going to the Dedakalaki (Capital) bus station on the rear (or north) of the main railway station [84 C1] (✆ *18 0567*). This is much more orderly and pleasant than Didube. A couple of ticket kiosks serve timetabled buses for Chiatura, Kutaisi, Senaki, Samtredia, Poti, Zugdidi and Ozurgeti, as well as marshrutkas that leave when full, with the last departures at about 19.00. Buses to Batumi leave at 10.00, 13.00, 16.00 and midnight, and marshrutkas leave roughly every 2½ hours from 09.00 to 19.00, and at midnight; there are also hourly marshrutkas to Batumi from the Sports Palace.

Marshrutkas **eastwards** to Kakheti leave from Ortachala (in front of the terminal), and from the Samgori metro station, east of the centre (local buses to Sagarejo, for instance, from right outside, and longer-distance buses from a small terminal to the right). Some also leave from the square just behind (north of) the Isani metro station (*Atskhuri 47*), where services from Samgori also pick up passengers, although they may already be full at this point. From Ortachala, marshrutkas leave from 08.00 to 18.00 every 40 minutes for Telavi (*GEL7*), every 20 minutes for Kvareli (*GEL8*), hourly to Dedoplis-Tskaro (*GEL7*), to Akhmeta (*GEL8*) at 10.00, 14.00, 17.00 and 19.00, to Gremi (*GEL8*) at noon, 15.00 and 16.00 and to Duisi (*GEL10*) at 07.30. From Samgori they leave from 09.30 to 16.45 every 45 minutes to Telavi (*GEL7*), every 20 minutes to Sagarejo (*GEL3*) and six times daily to Sighnaghi (*GEL6*). From Isani marshrutkas leave for Gurjaani every 20 minutes (*08.30–19.00; GEL6*), to Tsnori every 40 minutes (*GEL6*) and to Lagodekhi (*GEL7*) 15 times between 08.00 and 18.15.

The occasional bus to Tsiteli Khidi (the Krasni Most or Red Bridge, the main border crossing to **Azerbaijan**) also leaves from Samgori and from opposite the Isani metro station; they connect with minibuses on the far side of the border. Marshrutkas for Manglisi leave from Station Square at 11.00 and hourly from 13.00 to 18.00 and from Victory Square (Gamarjvebis Moedani). Marshrutkas to Marneuli and Bolnisi leave from the Ortachala roundabout. Buses to Rustavi leave from Didube and the Dinamo Stadium.

Heading towards **Armenia**, there are buses from Ortachala to Yerevan (*GEL30*) every 50 minutes from 07.30 to 15.00, to Stepanavan at 08.00, to Artiki at 08.45, to Vanadzor at 09.20, to Gyumri at 10.30 and to Spitak at 15.00, plus to Yerevan from the rear of the railway station at 11.00 and 17.00. However, the easiest way to get to Yerevan is with the comfortable cars waiting opposite Avlabari metro station (*09.00, 11.00, 13.00; GEL35*). For Baku (Azerbaijan), there's a departure from Ortachala at 14.00 daily plus at 16.00 on Mondays (*GEL30*).

Buses to **Turkey and Greece** (very long haul) leave from Ortachala; see page 61 for details of operators (it's best to buy tickets a day ahead). Buses leave Ortachala for Trabzon at 17.00 and 20.00 (*around 12hrs; US$30*), for Ankara at 10.30, 18.00, 18.30 and 19.00 (*around 26hrs; US$50*), for Istanbul at 08.00, 10.00, 10.30, 11.00 and noon (*34hrs; US$59*), and for Antalya (*31hrs; US$80*) and Izmir (*29hrs; US$70*) at 10.00. For Thessaloniki (*36hrs; US$80*) and Athens (*42hrs; US$100*) there are departures on Monday at 14.00, Tuesday at 13.00, Wednesday, Thursday and Friday at 10.00, and Sunday at 09.00.

Heading north to **Russia**, there are shared taxis from Didube to Mineralni Vodi, and daily buses from Ortachala at 11.00 to Mineralni Vodi and at 14.00 to Vladikavkaz (*GEL60*), Pyatigorsk (*GEL80*), continuing on Monday, Tuesday, Thursday, Friday and Sunday to Rostov-on-Don (*GEL140*). There's a through bus from Ortachala to Moscow (*GEL200*) on Thursdays at noon. Finally, there's a bus at noon daily from Ortachala to **Tehran** (*US$50*).

In 2010, the **railway station** [84 C1] was converted into a modern shopping complex with a supermarket and jewellery shops on the ground floor, and clothing retailers on the first and second floors. From the metro station go up the external ramp road to the second floor (at platform level), from where escalators give access to the station concourse, on a bridge over the tracks; upstairs is a food court with a variety of fast food stands, all reasonably priced, plus a play area. There are English-language timetables; a monitor next to the ticket counters shows the availability of tickets and berths on night trains, although only in Georgian. For rail information, call ✆ 313 on the phones provided, or see www.railway.ge which gives a brief outline of services. Left-luggage is on Platform 1, otherwise little used. Trains leave for Borjomi at 06.45 and 16.35, for Batumi at 08.45, 10.25 and 18.15, for Poti at 08.20 and 17.50, for Zugdidi at 08.55 and 21.10, and for Ozurgeti at 08.55 and 21.10, although precise times may change. For those arriving late at night there's a hotel up on the sixth floor.

TICKET AGENCIES The leading Georgian ticket agency is **Sky.Ge**, an amalgamation of four companies, also known as BusinessTravelCom, offering air and hotel reservations, car and bus rental and other travel services; they're at Mtskheta 17 (✆ 99 9662; e *info@sky.ge; www.sky.ge;* ⊕ *10.00–17.30 Mon–Fri, 10.00–14.00 Sat*). **Georgian Avia Service Agency** (*GASA; Chavchavadze Av 15; Courtyard Marriott Hotel, Freedom Sq 4; Radisson Blu Hotel, Rose Revolution Sq 1; Davit Agmashenebelis Av 172; all* ✆ *209 or 40 0040;* e *contact@gasa.ge; www.gasa.ge*), **Levon Travel** (*Chavchavadze Av 20;* ✆ *25 0010;* e *sales@levontravel.ge; www.levontravel.ge*) and the slightly less slick **Berika International** (*Chavchavadze Av 50;* ✆ *22 0941;* e *berika@berika.ge; www.berika.ge*) are travel agencies that deal more with residents than visitors, but can book flights with all major airlines.

Promethea Voyages (*formerly CGTT Voyages; Besiki St 4;* ✆ *22 1425/6;* e *contact@promethea-voyages.com, www.promethea-voyages.com*) is a French-owned company operating across the CIS.

See pages 55–7 for tour operators.

GETTING AROUND

Tbilisi has a two-line metro system, as well as buses and swarms of private marshrutka minibuses. Public transport runs from 06.00 to midnight.

METRO The metro (*www.metro.ge*) opened in 1966 and extends for 27km, with 22 stations. There are two lines, mostly deep underground, meeting at Station Square (Sadguris Moedani), and trains run roughly every 5 minutes.

Since 2010, all metro users must use a MetroMoney card. These can be bought at the booth just before the turnstiles; the minimum initial payment is GEL4 (GEL2 for the card deposit and GEL2 credit) and these can be topped up as necessary at stations or pay machines. Each journey (up to 90 minutes in length, with free transfers between lines or to buses) subtracts GEL0.50 from the total value of credit on the card.

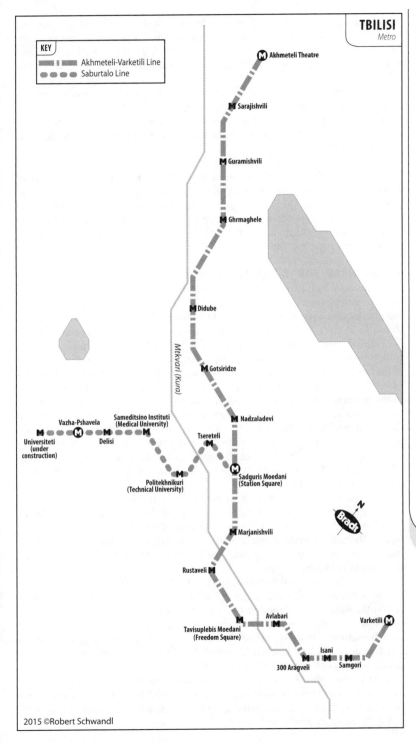

The principal line runs largely parallel to the Mtkvari from north to southeast, from Akhmeteli to Didube, Station Square, Marjanishvili, Rustaveli Square, Freedom (or Liberty) Square, Avlabari, Isani, Samgori and Varketili; the other line runs westwards from Station Square through the Saburtalo district mostly along Vazha-Pshavelas Avenue. There's currently a temporary terminal at Delisi while a 1.2km extension from Vazha-Pshavelas to Universiteti is completed. The system seems to have been built on the cheap, with stations unusually far apart and platforms only five carriage-lengths long (and three- and four-carriage trains); however, the trains and four central stations were refurbished in 2006, and announcements and signs are now in English as well as Georgian.

TAXIS There are thousands of taxis on the road in Tbilisi at any time, all unregulated, although a few do have meters. You shouldn't pay more than GEL6 (US$3) around town or GEL10–15 (US$3.50–5) to go to Turtle Lake or the Tbilisi Sea (fares double late at night). Two dependable taxi companies that may be pre-booked are **Gig Taxi** (↖ 78 7878; www.gig21.ge) and **NBO Taxi** (↖ 42 0111). **Taxi.Ge** (↖ 74 7474; www. taxi.ge) is also good but slightly pricier at GEL0.60/km.

MARSHRUTKAS AND BUSES Marshrutkas (yellow Ford Transits) are a phenomenon which barely existed under the Soviet Union: the franchise for each line is owned by someone (often a member of parliament, for some reason), whom minibus owners/drivers pay for the right to work. They run from dawn to 23.00 (later in summer). Fares are GEL0.80, compared with GEL0.50 for buses. A fleet of 500 relatively new, yellow Dutch **buses** were introduced in 2006 to replace tram and trolleybus services, and marshrutkas were summarily banned from the main axis of Rustaveli, Kostavas and Chavchavadze avenues. The marshrutkas (which should have been reorganised to be feeders to the metro and the new buses) simply moved to the inadequate parallel streets, with no information available about where they could be found or their destination other than the basic route information board (in Georgian) displayed in their front window. They're now back on the main avenues, but stop only at designated stops. Buses run every 10 minutes or so. They're slower and cheaper than marshrutkas, but have more space and in general provide a more relaxing experience; you can feed coins into the payment machine as you board, or use a MetroMoney card.

Bus stops have dot-matrix screens giving live updates on the next departures (in Georgian and English alternately), or you could try phoning ↖ 72 3433 for information. Bus route 87 is a handy loop, from Baratashvili Street via Freedom Square, Rustaveli Avenue, Kostavas, Pekini and Vazha-Pshavelas Avenue to Delisi metro, then around by the university to Chavchavadze Avenue and back along Rustaveli to Baratashvili Street.

Ortachala **bus terminal** is served by buses 44, 71 and 80 from Baratashvili Street and by a dozen marshrutka routes; some of these terminate at the roundabout just to the west. The Didube bus station is best reached by metro, but many bus routes pass it, notably 15 and 27 from Station Square, 20 from Orbeliani Square, 33 from Baratashvili, 46 from Avlabari (via Rustaveli) and 51 from Vake. The Samgori bus station is also best reached by metro, but buses 25 and 39 come here from Baratashvili, as well as the 101 from Ortachala.

Electric **trolleybuses** and **trams** were abolished in the city at the end of 2006 as one of the early reforms following the Rose Revolution. However, as the yellow buses that replaced them are polluting and barely able to cover their costs, there's talk of laying down new tram lines.

There's a modern **cable-car** from Rikhe Park to Narikala, and a funicular up to Mtatsminda. There are also two **sightseeing bus** companies, Bus Hopper (m 595 170502; http://hoponhopoff.ge/en; GEL25 for 24hrs) and City Sightseeing (Rkinis Rigi 11; 43 8088, 43 8808; m 514 217722; http://csstbilisi.com; GEL35 for 24hrs). City Sightseeing, which uses an open-top double-decker, is pricier but has more frequent services (five a day) and also offers a boat tour below the Metekhi Cliffs for an extra GEL15. Both buses go out to Mskheta too, costing an extra GEL10 with Bus Hopper or GEL25 with City Sightseeing; this is the cheapest and easiest way to get up to the Jvari Church.

CAR RENTAL As well as the international chains, there are local companies offering jeeps, saloon cars and minivans, with or without drivers, for US$95–110 (US$25 more to include a driver). A far cheaper option, however, is to look on the noticeboard at Prospero's Books (Rustaveli Av 34) where drivers offer themselves and their cars from US$20 per day. There are 24-hour petrol stations at the airport junction, Ortachala, and on the Mtskheta Highway, and there are plenty of others on the river embankments.

International companies

Avis Freedom Sq 4; 92 3594; m 599 580368; e reservations@avis.ge; www.avis.ge; at the airport: 92 3594; m 595 587000

Europcar Samghebro 6; 75 4471; m 551 348844; e geuropcar@yahoo.com; www.europcar.com

Hertz Inc Dollar & Thrifty; Leselidze 44/II; 99 9100; e hertz@georgia.com.ge; at the Radisson Blu Hotel: Rose Revolution Sq; 30 7890; m 557 455 1133

Sixt Samghebro 5; 43 9911; sixt.com.ge

Local companies

Cars4Rent Chavchavadze 34; 47 6399; m 577 441159; www.cars4rent.ge

Geo Rent Car Lermontov 9; 93 0099; www.georentcar.ge

GSS Car Rental Dadiani 10; m 571 446644; gsservices.ge

Info-Tbilisi Cars Nikoladze 6; 18 2244; m 599 333353; e cars@info-tbilisi.com; www.airport-transfer.ge

Jeep Rent Ltd Tatishvili 19; 10 6310; m 551 106310; www.jeeprent.ge

TOURIST INFORMATION

Tbilisi has an efficient **tourist information centre** [98 B2] (15 8697; m 595 997752; e tictbilisi@gmail.com; ☉ 10.00–18.00 daily, until 19.00 in summer) opposite City Hall on Pushkin Square. The helpful English-speaking staff has free maps and booklets to give away, and can advise on transport and help book accommodation in the city and beyond.

⌂ WHERE TO STAY

After the Abkhazian War, the Soviet-era block-hotels in Tbilisi and across Georgia were taken over by refugees and for a while there was almost nowhere to stay. Soon a crop of small, pricey guesthouses sprouted up for businessmen; these often have no sign on the street (both for security and for tax evasion), and should be booked in advance. In the last few years a new generation of backpacker-oriented homestays and hostels has appeared, mostly in Old Town and the Marjanishvili district of the city, and there are also plenty of new small hotels, as well as a couple of new Marriotts for the business market. Now that the refugees have been relocated from the Soviet-era hotels, these are being rebuilt as modern facilities: the Radisson and Holiday Inn towers are now open, but plans for Novotel, Intercontinental and Park

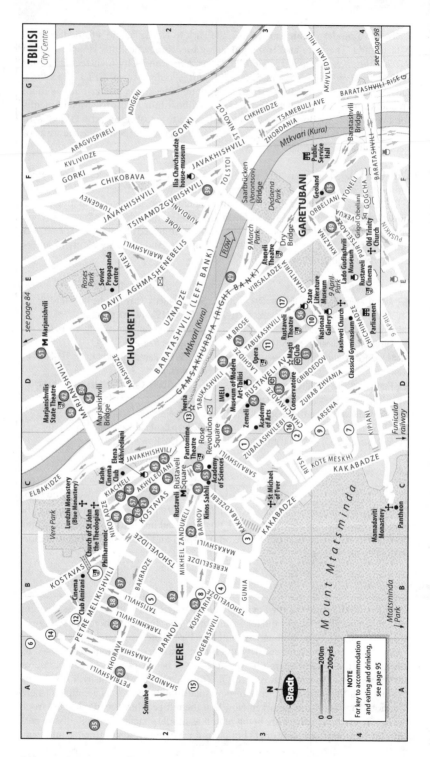

see page 98

G 1 2 3 4

ARAGVISPIRELI

KVLIVIDZE

GORKI

CHIKOBAVA

TURGENEV JAVAKHISHVILI

ADIGENI

GORKI

CHKHEIDZE

TSAMEBULI AVE

ZHORDANIA

ZO IOHN ST

BARATASHVILI RISE

Mtkvari (Kura)

AKHVLEDIANI HILL

BARATASHVILI
Bridge

BARATASHVILI

Public
Service
Hall

GARETUBANI

Geoland

ATONELI ORBELIANI

VEKUA KHAZINA

Rustaveli PUR Cinema Grigot Orbeliani

PUSHKIN

GOGCHA

Old Trinity
Church

ILIA

F

Marjanishvili

ARAGVISPIRELI

JAVAKHISHVILI

TSINAMDZGVRISHVILI

Ilia Chavchavadze
house-museum

TOLSTOI

Saarbrücken (Vorontsov)
Bridge

Dedaena
Park

Dry
Bridge

Ateneli
Theatre

9 March Park

State
Literature
Museum

9 April
Park

Lado Gudiashvili
Museum

National
Gallery

Kashveti Church

Classical Gymnasium

CHICHINADZE

Parliament

9 APRIL

E

see page 84

Roses
Park

Soviet
Propaganda
Centre

DAVIT AGHMASHENEBELIS

KURDIANI

ROME

MARIASHVILI

Mtkvari (Kura)

FLOW

VIRSALADZE

M BROSE

Rustaveli
Opera

TABUKASHVILI

Magti
Club

Rustaveli AV.

GRIBOEDOV

ZURAB ZHVANIA

CHAVCHAVADZE

Conservatoire

ARSENA

KIPIANI

Funicular
railway

D

Marjanishvili
State Theatre

MARJANISHVILI

CHUGURETI

ABASHIDZE

UZNADZE

BARATASHVILI (LEFT BANK)

GAMSAKHURDIA (RIGHT BANK)

Iveria

TABUKASHVILI

IMELI

Museum of Modern
Art-Tbilisi

Zemeli

Academy
of Arts

LAGHIDZE

ZUBALASHVILI

CHAVCHAVADZE

KOTE MESKHI

KAKABADZE

RTSA

Mamadaviti
Monastery

Pantheon

C

ELBAKIDZE

Vere
Park

Lurdzhi Monastery
(Blue Monastery)

Church of St John
the Theologian

Kashe
Cinema Club

Elena
Akhvlediani

JAVAKHISHVILI

KIACHELI

AKHVLEDIANI

KOSTAVAS

NIKOLADZE

Philharmonic

Pantomime
Theatre

Rustaveli
Square

Rose
Revolution
Square

Academy
of Sciences

Kinos Sakhli

BARNOV

MIKHEIL ZANDUKELI

MAKASHVILI

SARAJISHVILI

St Michael
of Tver

KAKABADZE

KAKABADZE

Mount Mtatsminda

B

KOSTAVAS

Cinema
Club Amirani

PETRE MELIKISHVILI

BAKRADZE

TATISHVILI

TARKHNISHVILI

KOSHTARIANT

TSHOVELIDZE

GUNIA

GOGEBASHVILI

VERE

Mtatsminda
Park

A

JANASHIA

KHORAVA

PETRISHVILI

SHAIDZE

BARNOV

Schwabe

N

NOTE
For key to accommodation
and eating and drinking,
see page 95

0   200m
0   200yds

Bradt

Hyatt hotels seem to be on hold. It might seem as though Tbilisi now has a huge over-provision of hotels, but very few have more than a dozen rooms.

Most **hotels** cater for Georgian tastes with huge (cold) rooms and echoing apartments; a few, such as the Kartli, have smaller, snugger European-style rooms. All but the very cheapest have their own generator; few have lifts. Remember that you'll have to pay an extra 18% tax in many cases.

Many of the **hostels** listed offer free internet access, tea, coffee and cooking facilities. Most can be booked online through sites like www.hostelworld.com, www.hostelplanet.com or www.hostels.com. There are many other hostels in Tbilisi, many of which are lucky to last one season.

For **budget** travellers looking for something slightly better than a hostel bed, the best bet is probably a private room in a city homestay. For longer stays you might want to rent an apartment – see www.besttbilisiapartments.com or www. rental.ge/apartments.htm; there's also the Citadines apart-hotel behind Freedom Square 4 (\ *54 7030;* e *tbilisi@citadines.com; www.citadines.com*). And of course, AirBnB (*www.airbnb.com*) is a great source of apartments, rooms and bed-and-breakfast options.

HOSTELS & HOMESTAYS

Map, page 84, unless otherwise stated

🏠 **SKAdaVELI** [map, page 98] (4 rooms, 1 en suite) Vertskhli 27; m 595 417333; e Skadaveli@gmail.com; www.ska.ge. Rooms (with Wi-Fi & AC) & a kitchen (with washing machine) along a traditional Tbilisi balcony in the lower Old Town. Erekle is very helpful & rooms are spacious with tables, desk lamps & lots of power sockets (& no TVs), so ideal for longer stays. **$$$**

🏠 **Formula 1 Guest House** [map, page 94] Kote Meskhi 13a; \ 93 8959; m 574 456789; e f1bed.com@gmail.com, info@f1bed.com; www. formula1georgia.com. A little hard to find, up a steep hill in the Mtatsminda district a 10min walk west of Rustaveli; you may want to take a taxi up at night. Steps also lead down from west of the Mtatsminda funicular station on Chonkadze. It's clean, modern & friendly, with en-suite sgls & dbls as well as 4- & 5-bed rooms, all with TV & Wi-Fi. Price inc b/fast. **$$**

🏠 **Green Stairs** Tsinamdzgvrishvili 53; \ 94 1552; m 593 331236; e vazha@lycos.com; http:// greenstairs.info. Another small hostel close to

---

TBILISI *City centre*
For listings, see pages 95–108

Marjanishvili metro, though in a very untouristy area, this one has private rooms rather than dormitories. It's simple but comfortable & owner Vazha is very helpful. **$$**

🏠 **Waltzing Matilda Hostel** [map, page 94] (8 rooms) Chavchavadze 11; ☎ 98 8343; ▥ 593 997957, 597 730642; www.cityhostel. ge. A popular & very lively hostel near the Opera, Russian- rather than Australian-owned, this has 2 large dorms & 6 smaller rooms, plus common room, kitchen & roof terrace. **$$**

🏠 **Dodo Kevlishvili** (7 rooms) Marjanishvili 38; ☎ 95 4213. This is half a block north of the Russian church. Dodo is a warm-hearted & extremely helpful woman who speaks excellent English & has shared rooms. The place underwent modest improvements in 2010 & now has Wi-Fi, but is still basically what Tbilisi guesthouses were like 2 decades ago – bring your own towel. **$**

🏠 **Irina Japaridze** (12 rooms) Ninoshvili 19; ☎ 95 4716; ▥ 599 111669; e irina5062@gmail. com; www.facebook.com/guesthause.irina. This is the 1st street on the left after the Russian church (taking Marjanishvili north from the metro). It's clean & spacious, with a dozen rooms (dorms & doubles), 4 bathrooms & 2 kitchens, TVs & great views over the city, plus free internet access & a washing machine (GEL5 for a full load). It's very popular with Israelis & even hosts celebrations of major Jewish holidays. **$**

🏠 **Khatuna's** Chitaya 12, on the main road from the Dry Bridge to the rear of the Voksal; turn left at the top of Marjanishvili, & it's on your left. From the Voksal, turn hard left (east) to take Pirosmanis, which leads into Chitaya. Long known to Japanese travellers, this is probably the cheapest place in the city. **$**

🏠 **Old Town Hostel** [map, page 98] Beridze (formerly Khodasheni) 7; ▥ 571 004002; e tbilisioldtownhostel@gmail.com. This friendly & relatively long-established non-smoking hostel charges GEL20 for dorm beds & from GEL65 for private rooms. In 2015 they also opened the 10-room **Urban Oasis** boutique hotel at Shavteli 8 (▥ *596 122255*; **$$$$**), with a café with a Steinway grand piano & a huge terrace with a view over the old town. **$**

🏠 **Tamuna's Homestay** (2 rooms) Chikobavas 32; ▥ 599 183555, 590 527818; e Tamuna.Georgia@gmail.com. Within walking distance of Marjanishvili metro, this small apt with

dbl rooms, shared kitchen & sitting room is best booked in advance. **$**

🏠 **Tina Muradashvili's Homestay** (2 rooms) Sulkhan-Saba 5; ▥ 593 139122; e t_gotsiridze@hotmail.com; http:// tbilisihomestay.com. Just off Freedom Sq, at the rear of the Marriott Courtyard Hotel. Tina works at the National Museum & Zviad is a taxi driver, so excellent & affordable tours can be arranged as well as airport pickups. Dbl rooms with shared bathroom, kitchen, washing machine & a filling b/fast. **$**

🏠 **Why Not? Hostel** [map, page 94] Tabukashvili 15/4; ▥ 599 007030; e whynot. tbilisi@gmail.com; www.whynothostels.com. With Polish, American & Georgian staff, this is one of the funkier & more cosmopolitan hostels in Tbilisi, although it needs more showers & toilets; sheets & towels inc. Close to Rustaveli Av, it's an old house with traditional balconied Tbilisi courtyard, terrace & common room – & an excellent b/fast. It incorporates the Tubo Party Bar. **$**

HOTELS

The hotels below are listed broadly from east to west, on the left/north bank & then the right bank. To book from abroad, prefix phone numbers with +99532.

East of the city
Map, page 84

🏠 **Grand Hotel** Kakheti Highway at Tvalcherelidze; ☎ 77 8864; e grandhotelgeorgia@ gmail.com; http://grandhotel.cityplaza.ge. A 10min drive from the airport towards the city (& not to be confused with the Grand Hotel in Avlabari), this is a large, modern hotel that makes an acceptable stopover before or after a flight. **$$$**

Avlabari (handy for the airport)
Map, page 84, unless otherwise stated

🏠 **Sheraton Metechi Palace Hotel** (140 rooms) Telavi 20; ☎ 77 2020, 0800 960501 (UK); e smpht@sheraton.com; www.sheraton.com/ tbilisi. The city's premier hotel for many years, this has packed a lot of living into its short life, & is now closed for refurbishment until early 2016. Opened in 1989, in 1994 it was taken over by Kalashnikov-toting Mkhedrioni, supposedly there to guard the place; instead there were lurid stories of shootings in the bar & drug dealing in the corridors. The US embassy banned its officials from going there (although the EC office was there); famously, a sign on the door read 'Handguns allowed, semi-automatics to be left at reception'. In 1997 the Marco Polo group sold the building to Sheraton, never having made any profit. Now it's like any other international business hotel, with its 7-storey atrium & glass lifts, & is home to various embassies & airline offices; nevertheless it's been overtaken by the Marriott downtown. $$$$$

🏠 **Kopala** [map, page 98] (47 rooms, 2 suites) Chekhov 8–10; 📞 77 5520, 77 5590; e hotel@kopala.ge; www.kopala.ge. In a fantastic setting above the Metekhi Church (not to be confused with the newer Kopala on Rikhe Park), views are best enjoyed from the roof-top terrace rather than the restaurant, which serves small portions of average food. The rooms are nice, with AC, satellite TV, minibar, internet access, safe & hairdryer; there's a gym, sauna & business centre. $$$–$$$$, *apts* $$$$$

🏠 **Dzveli (Old) Metekhi** [map, page 98] (15 rooms) Metekhi Rise 3; 📞 99 0536; 93 4571; e dzmetekhi@hotmail.com; http://oldmetekhi. tripod.com. A historic building set on the cliffs of the Mtkvari River, 10 of the rooms have balconies with a view of the city. All have AC, minibar, safe & satellite TV; there's also a good restaurant, which offers a 10% discount for hotel guests. Inc b/fast & tax. $$$–$$$$

🏠 **Lile** [map, page 98] (8 rooms) Ghvinis Aghmarti 19; 📞 77 3856; e lilehotel@posta.ge; www.lilehotel.ge. On the south side of Ketevan Tsamebulis Sq, Avlabari, this has 8 rooms (1 en suite), in a good, slick, modern style, with cable TV & AC. It's clean & friendly, with some English spoken, although cheaper rooms can be a little noisy. They also offer cheap tours with their own 4x4 & minibus & guides who charge US$5/hr, about half the tour agencies' rate. Rates inc tax, plus b/fast after 2 days. $$$–$$$$

🏠 **Georgian House** (12 rooms) Vakhtang VI 38; 📞 79 1919, 79 1920; e hotel@extour.ge; www. exotour.ge. Conveniently situated just uphill from Avlabari metro, close to Sameba Cathedral, this good-value small hotel has decent en-suite rooms with Wi-Fi, satellite TV, AC & minibar. Inc tax & b/fast. $$$

🏠 **GTM** [map, page 98] (32 rooms) Metekhi Rise 4; 📞 27 3348/9, 79 040 4221; e hotel-

gtmkapan@mail.ru; www.gtm.ge. A modern, business-style hotel in a prime location, with views over the river & Old Town; rooms are good & clean with cable TV & free laptop internet access. There's a restaurant, conference hall, swimming pool, sauna, gym & billiards. Rates inc b/fast. $$$

🏠 **Mirobelle** (14 rooms) Samreklo 14; 📞 77 4977; m 568 888918; e mirobelle@live.com; www.mirobelle.co. Just a couple of hundred metres from the Sameba Cathedral, this is new & squeaky clean but a bit over-priced, with friendly English-speaking staff & a good b/fast. $$$

🏠 **Old Tbilisi** (24 rooms) Ketevan Tsamebuli 27; 📞 77 3840–3; e hoteloldtbilisi@yahoo.com; www.hoteloldtbilisi.ge. On the cliffs above the Mtkvari River on the main road to the airport, this is a new & very nouveau hotel that is not particularly aimed at Westerners. Rates inc b/fast & internet access. $$$

Chugureti
Map, page 84

🏠 **Istanbul** (16 rooms) Davit Agmashenebelis 148; 📞 91 1182–3; e info@hotelistanbul.ge; http://hotelistanbul.ge. In a former military school on the Turkish section of Davit Agmashenebelis, this has a cramped staircase & lift, but decent rooms with TV, minibar, free laptop connection & good bathrooms. English is spoken & there is a restaurant & bar. B/fast inc. $$$$

🏠 **Prestige** (25 rooms, 5 suites) Marjanishvili 51; 📞 94 0505, 294 2974; e hotelprestige_ge@ yahoo.com; www.hotelprestige.ge. Fairly handy for the railway station, this small hotel has AC rooms with satellite TV & minibar, plus a restaurant-bar & parking. $$$, suites $$$$

The Old Town
Map, page 98

🏠 **Courtyard by Marriott** (118 rooms) Tavisuplebis Moedani (Freedom Sq) 4; 📞 77 9100; e courtyard.tbilisi@marriotthotels. com; www.courtyardtbilisi.com. Opened in 2002, this 4-star sidekick to the Marriott proper offers all necessary amenities at a slightly more affordable price. All rooms have 2 phone lines & dataport, voicemail, cable/satellite TV, AC, safe, hairdryer & iron. There's a health club, swimming pool & sauna, & a bar & brasserie, notable for its Sun brunch (🕐 *noon–16.00*). Price inc b/fast & tax. $$$$$

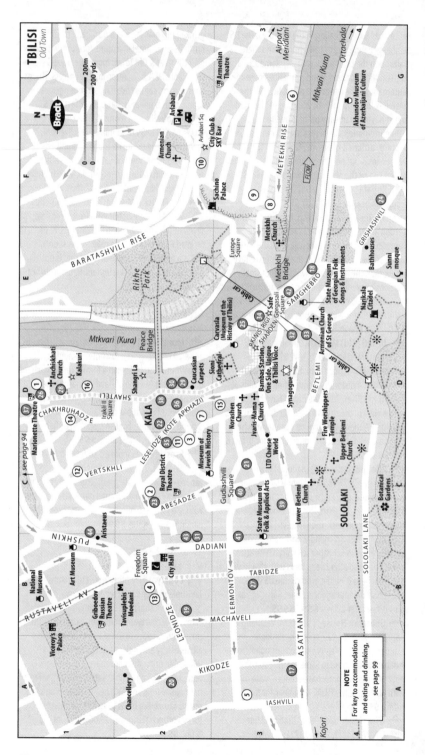

TBILISI
Old Town

Bradt

0 ——— 200m
0 ——— 200 yds

BARATASHVILI RISE

Rikhe Park

Mtkvari (Kura)

Peace Bridge

Europe Square

Cable car

Airport, Meridiani

Mtkvari (Kura)

Ortachala

Kojori

METEKHI RISE

FLOW

Sachino Palace

Armenian Church

Avlabari Sq

City Club & SKY Bar

Avlabari

Armenian Theatre

Metekhi Church

Metekhi Bridge

Carvasla (Museum of the History of Tbilisi)

Safe

Caucasian Carpets

Sioni Cathedral

Shangri La

Kalakuri

Anchiskhati Church

Marionette Theatre

Irakli II Square

Royal District Theatre

Museum of Jewish History

Norashen Church

Jvaris-Mama Church

Bambas Station, One Side, Unique & Tbilisi Voice

Synagogue

LTD Cheese World

Gudiashvili Square

State Museum of Folk & Applied Arts

Lower Betlemi Church

Upper Betlemi Church

Fire Worshippers' Temple

Armenian Church of St George

State Museum of Georgian Folk Songs & Instruments

Narikala Citadel

Akhundov Museum of Azerbaijani Culture

GRISHASHVILI

Bathhouses

Sunni mosque

SAMGHEBRO

BETLEMI

SOLOLAKI

SOLOLAKI LANE

Botanical Gardens

ASATIANI

IASHVILI

KIKODZE

MACHAVELI

LERMONTOV

TABIDZE

DADIANI

ABESADZE

Freedom Square

City Hall

National Museum

Art Museum

Griboedov Russian Theatre

Tavisuplebis Moedani

Viceroy's Palace

Chancellory

RUSTAVELI AV

PUSHKIN

Aristaeus

LEONIDZE

VERTSKHLI

CHAKHRUHADZE

SHAVTELI

KALA

LESELIDZE (KOTE APKHAZI)

Shangri La

ABKUMIS RIGI

SHARDEN

Gorgasali Square

NOTE
For key to accommodation and eating and drinking, see page 99

For listings, see pages 95–108

TBILISI *Old Town*

Where to stay

1	Ambasadori.....................D1	6	Dzveli (Old) Metekhi.......G3	12	SKAdaVELI......................C1
2	Ata................................C2	7	GT....................................D2	13	Tina Muradashvili's
3	Boutique Hotel No12......C2	8	GTM.................................F3		Homestay.................B2
4	Courtyard by	9	Kopala..............................F3	14	Villa Mtiebi.....................D1
	Marriott.....................B2	10	Lile...................................F2	15	VIP..................................D3
5	David Sultan....................A3	11	Old Town Hostel..............C2	16	Urban Oasis....................D1

Where to eat and drink

17	87 Café A3	26	Gabriadze's Café............D1	36	Moulin Electrique........D2
18	Alani Restaurant	27	Ghvino Underground.....B3	37	Mukhrantubani............D1
	& Brewery......................E4	28	The Hangar Bar................D1	38	Naxvamdis Café............D2
19	Arsad...............................B2	29	Kala.................................D2	39	Newsroom Caffé..........C3
20	Azarpesha.......................A2	30	KGB..................................D2	40	PurPur.............................C3
21	Bauhaus...........................C3	31	Khinklis Samkaro.............B2	41	Racha...............................B3
22	Café Le Toît.....................D2	32	Leffe................................E3	42	Samikitno......................... E3
23	Café Linville.....................C2	33	Machakhela.....................D3		Tartine.................(see 42)
24	Chaikhana........................F4	34	Maidan............................E3	43	Veliaminovi....................B2
25	Chardin 12.......................E3	35	Mirzaani Brewery............C2	44	Warszawa.......................C1

Ambasadori (39 rooms, 3 suites) Shavteli 13; 92 0403, 18 0110, reservations 43 9494; e info@ambasadori.ge; http://tbilisi.ambasadori. ge/en. Close to Baratashvili Bridge, this is the grandest of Tbilisi's locally owned hotels, with a roof-top swimming pool, lift & business centre. All rooms have AC, & the more expensive suites inc b/fast in the 4th-floor terrace café (*until 02.00*). **$$$$–$$$$$**

Boutique Hotel No12 (12 rooms) Beridze (formerly Khodasheni) 12; 55 2212; m 599 125520; www.no12hotel.com. A beautifully contrived patio, above the basement b/fast room, leads in to this charmingly decorated little place, with smallish rooms in Andalusian style with stained-glass lampshades & tiles; the upstairs rooms are quieter. The b/fast is excellent. **$$$$**

GT (21 rooms) Leselidze 28; 47 8166; m 599 478160, 593 269920; www.gthotel.ge. In a quiet courtyard just off the Old Town's main drag, this is a squeaky clean & remarkably good hotel, with efficient reception staff, rooms with huge balconies & a roof terrace with great views. **$$$$**

Villa Mtiebi (8 rooms, 1 suite) Chakhrukhadze 10; 92 0340–2; e tbilisi@ hotelmtiebi.ge; www.hotelmtiebi.ge. In a discreet & beautifully restored 19th-century building, with a lovely b/fast hall/winter garden, rooms all have AC, satellite TV, CD player, minibar, laptop access, free umbrella, hairdryer & orthopaedic mattress plus a large bathroom. There's also free internet access, gym, sauna & small swimming pool. Rates inc b/ fast but exc tax. **$$$$**

Ata (5 rooms) Leselidze 17; 98 7715; e hotelata@gmail.com; www.hotelata.com. A modern block on a side road off Leselidze, the adequate large rooms have small TVs, metal doors & electric water-boilers; Nana speaks fair English. Inc b/fast. **$$$**

VIP (7 rooms, 1 suite) Leselidze 31; 92 0040, 98 9809; m 599 574207; www.facebook. com/hotelvip. In another courtyard off the old town's main drag, this hotel is accustomed to international business visitors & some English is spoken. Rates inc b/fast & tax; dinner can be ordered, & there's free internet access. **$$$**

The New Town

Map, page 94, unless otherwise stated

Marriott Tbilisi (110 rooms, 17 suites) Rustaveli 13; 99 7200, 77 9200, toll free 0800 221222 (UK), 1 888 236 2427 (US); www.marriott.com/tbsmc. Built in 1915 as the Majestic & reopened in 2002, this is Tbilisi's finest hotel. Innovations inc Tbilisi's first wine bar, the Patio open-air summer restaurant & ice machines on each floor (one of which is smoke-free). **$$$$$**

Radisson Blu Iveria (249 rooms & suites) Rose Revolution Sq (Vardebis Revolutsis moedani) 1; 40 2200; e tbilisi.info@ radissonblu.com; www.radissonblu.com/ hotel-tbilisi. The run-down Hotel Iveria, which housed internal refugees for many years, has been transformed into a stylish, glass-fronted tower, Tbilisi's other 5-star hotel. The wide range of rooms & suites include 62 that connect with each other & 10 with facilities for guests with disabilities. There's free Wi-Fi throughout, a spa, health club & indoor pool, & also smart Italian & Asian-fusion restaurants, the Surface Bar (at ground level) & the Oxygen Bar (the highest bar in the city, on the 18th floor). **$$$$$**

🏠 **Diplomat** [map, page 84] (9 rooms, 1 suite) Bolo Agmarti 4; ☎92 2088; e hoteldiplomat@gol.ge; http://diplomat.ltd.ge. A very comfortable modern hotel up in Sololaki, the Diplomat's rooms are AC with satellite TV & minibar. There's a business centre with internet access & a sauna, gym & pool are available. It's on the Kojori Highway just above the terminal of marshrutkas 41 & 137. Prices inc parking & laundry. **$$$$–$$$$$**

🏠 **David Sultan** [map, page 98] (11 rooms, 2 suites) Iashvili 16A; ☎93 5006; m 574 646600; e hoteldavid5@gmail.com; www.davidhotel.ge. Opened in 2001, rooms are a little Soviet-style, but in other respects the style is oriental. Rooms have satellite TV, fridge & internet access for laptops, & the bathrooms have tubs. The corridors are spacious & airy, & there's a pleasant little tea house. **$$$$**

🏠 **Opera** (10 rooms) Vaso Abashidze 4; ☎99 6799, 99 0751; m 599 155554; www. hotelopera.ge. Just off Rustaveli, next to the opera house, this is in a prime location & not too noisy. 4 rooms are 'luxe' with balcony & bath. **$$$$**

Vere

Map, page 94, unless otherwise stated

🏠 **Betsy's Hotel** (45 rooms & 12 suites) Makashvili 32/34; ☎93 1404; www.betsyshotel. com. Founded in 1993, for many years Betsy's Guesthouse was a Tbilisi institution & Betsy herself Georgia's best-known expat; now she has retired but the name lives on. Having expanded into adjacent blocks, it's now too big even to be a boutique hotel & is used more by NGO workers than by business visitors or tourists; the Friday Happy Hour is still a key part of expat life here. Most rooms have balconies & views across the city; some are executive suites with free fibre-optic broadband. There's a lift, spa, sauna & outdoor pool, plus a restaurant & a branch of Caliban Coffee. **$$$$$**

🏠 **Vere Palace Hotel** (42 rooms, 9 suites, 2 apts) Kuchishvili 22/24; ☎25 3340–2; e hotelvp@verepalace.com.ge; www.verepalace.

com.ge. Recently expanded,this luxurious hotel has seen the Pope, the Patriarch of the USA & Canada, & the rock group Uriah Heep amongst its clientele. Beyond the lobby with its antique chairs, there's a business centre & Wi-Fi, restaurant & bar plus swimming pool, fitness centre & sauna. **$$$$–$$$$$**

🏠 **A and M** (Manana Skhirtladze's guesthouse) (6 rooms) Zubalashvili 51; ☎93 6397; m 599 656397; e anano@inbox.ru; www.anano.ge. Manana claims to have been the first to open a guesthouse in Tbilisi (6 months before Betsy) although she has now moved a block downhill to this building, with en-suite rooms, as well as meeting rooms, bar, gym & pool & a roof terrace with a good view. There's free Wi-Fi with a scanner & printer. Book ahead; rates inc meals & laundry. **$$$$–$$$$$**

🏠 **Beaumonde** (11 rooms) A Chavchavadze St 11; ☎98 6003; http://hotelbeaumonde.com. This is a comfortable, friendly place with an atrium sitting area (with fireplace), free beer & wine, both European & Russian billiards tables, & big fish in a tank in the dining area. **$$$$**

🏠 **British House** (8 rooms) Chovelidze (formely Belinski) 32; ☎98 8783, 92 3998; e hotelbritishhouse@gmail.com; www.british-house.ge. Just a short walk up from Rustaveli Av, this smart hotel (originally British-owned) is popular with both tourists & expat business visitors alike. **$$$$**

🏠 **Demi** (7 rooms) Ananauri 10; ☎22 0619; e demi@access.sanet.ge; www.demi-hotel.com. A nice, friendly guesthouse on a quiet lane with lots of greenery; all rooms are dbl, with a tiny balcony. There's AC, satellite TV, & English is spoken. Rates inc b/fast but not tax, with discounts for stays over 4 nights. **$$$$**

🏠 **Iliani** [map, page 84] (24 rooms) Anjaparidze 1 (at Nikoladze); ☎23 4086, 33 5710; e info@iliani.com; www.iliani.com. This modern block, just off Kostavas, has simple rooms with AC, balcony, cable TV & minibar. There's free Wi-Fi; the friendly staff speak English, but the lift & corridors are cramped. There's a pleasant garden & an extension inc conference facilities & a roof-top terrace. **$$$$**

🏠 **Lia's Guesthouse** (8 rooms) Arsena 35; ☎92 0858; m 577 499449; e arsena35@yahoo. com; www.welcome.ge/guesthouse_lia. A classy guesthouse where rooms have ornate antique-style furniture (& TV). Prices inc b/fast; dinner is also available if required. **$$$$**

🏠 **Primavera** (22 rooms, 4 suites) Kuchishvili 8; ☎ 25 1146; e primavera@primavera.ge, www. primavera.ge. An American–Georgian joint venture, this is a fine, modern building on a less fine street close to the Philharmonic. There's a free swimming pool, gym & jacuzzi on the 5th floor & a Georgian-Italian restaurant, & there's a lift with afterthought wheelchair ramp. **$$$$**

🏠 **Classic** (8 rooms) Gurgulia 18; ☎ 22 7415; e info@classic.ge. Down an alley formerly known as 2nd Barnov Lane at Barnov 43, the Classic has AC, free Wi-Fi & a friendly, family atmosphere; English is spoken. **$$$–$$$$**

🏠 **Victoria** (9 rooms) Petriashvili 42; ☎ 25 1235. 29 0304; http://victoria.com.ge. A new hotel with cable TV & balconies in all rooms. There's a small garden, conference & business centre. Good English spoken, but service & cleanliness are variable. B/fast inc, dinner available for US$15. **$$$–$$$$**

🏠 **Kartli** (5 rooms) Barnov 32; ☎ 99 5429; m 598 801999; www.hotel-kartli.com. German-owned, this is one of the more switched-on places in town with an excellent restaurant, a German-style pizzeria & beer garden. Tours are available (*www.erkareisen.com*) plus airport transfers. **$$$**

Vake

Map, page 84

🏠 **VIP Victoria** (12 rooms, 3 suites) Arakishvili 3; ☎ 29 1877, 25 1247; e http://vip-victoria.com. A modern, tastefully decorated hotel just off Abashidze, reasonably close to the centre, that caters mostly for a business clientele. En-suite rooms with balconies, cable TV, AC & free internet. Good b/fast inc. **$$$–$$$$**

Saburtalo

Map, page 84

🏠 **Holiday Inn** (270 rooms) 26 May Sq 1; ☎ 30 0099; www.hi-tbilisi.com. Far more upmarket than

you might expect, this glass-fronted tower was full of refugees just a few years ago; now it has a spa & swimming pool, & rooms featuring rain showers & work stations. Half the rooms are non-smoking; only 3 cater for visitors with disabilities. The metro station is across the (busy) road. Wi-Fi inc, b/fast extra. **$$$$$**

🏠 **Medea** (6 rooms) Mitskevich 40; ☎ 37 0125; e hotelmedea@posta.ge; www. hotelmedea.co.nr. A pleasant suburban house with a friendly, spacious feel, perhaps not the most slickly managed of places. Rooms have dbl beds (as well as the more usual twin sgls), balcony, satellite TV & bath; laundry & car service are available, & a minimum of English is understood. Price inc b/fast, tax & internet access. **$$$–$$$$**

🏠 **Sympatia** (14 rooms, 12 suites) Daraselia 4, nr Zhvania Sq; ☎ 37 0590, 99 5588; www. sympatia.ge. A big, modern business hotel, with a lift (but lots of steps to reach it), conference halls, billiards, gym, sauna, jacuzzi, & a roof terrace with indoor & outdoor pools. All rooms have AC, Wi-Fi, satellite TV & minibar, & the price inc b/fast & tax. **$$$–$$$$**

🏠 **Tbilotel** (20 rooms, 7 suites) Daraselia 8, nr Zhvania Sq; ☎ 38 7804–6; e tbilotel@ tbilotel.ge; www.tbilotel.ge. A well-run place with good English spoken at reception, AC, satellite TV, Wi-Fi & lift (without steps!). Rates inc b/fast. **$$$–$$$$**

🏠 **Bu** (9 rooms) Mitskevich 40A; ☎ 38 1739, 38 0230; e hotelbu40@yahoo.com, http://hotelbu. webs.com. This is a viable alternative if the others on Mitskevich are full; they're friendly but don't speak English. **$$$**

🏠 **Nika** (6 rooms) Mitskevich 38; ☎ 38 2931; m 899 914223; e nikaguesthouse@yahoo.com. Reached by bus 47 from Station Sq, this friendly guesthouse is popular with Peace Corps Volunteers visiting Tbilisi. Rooms are small but have TVs, some English & German are spoken, & there's a nice garden with safe car parking. Rates inc b/fast. **$$–$$$**

✕ WHERE TO EAT AND DRINK

RESTAURANTS   As with the hotels, these are listed from east to west, with the right bank first. Unless otherwise stated, restaurants are usually open from around noon until 23.00 or midnight. More basic cafés tend to close earlier while fancier, trendier places stay open until the early hours.

The **Old Town** is better served by cafés and bars than places for a proper sit-down meal; nevertheless, there are a few decent choices along pedestrianised Sharden and

Erekle II near Sioni Cathedral. There are plenty of restaurants, bars and cafés in the vicinity of **Rose Revolution Square** (formerly Republic Square). Akhvlediani Street (still best known as Perovskaya) leads west from the square towards the Philharmonic, in what was the academic and literary quarter; Kiacheli runs parallel to Akhvlediani to the east. Many of Tbilisi's most popular bars can be found along these two streets, most of which offer live bands plus food of some type, although it tends to be a featureless blend of Georgian and international styles. There is a whole row of cellar restaurants along Dadiani that dish up delicious Georgian staples like khinkhali at low prices.

Not surprisingly, there is a good range of places to eat and drink in the affluent residential quarter of **Vake**. Many of the smarter places serving Mediterranean and European food (often at western European prices) are lined up along Abashidze Street west of the UN Circle; there's not much Georgian food available here, however. In **Chugureti**, the area around Marjanishvili metro station on the left bank has a number of simple restaurants and fast-food places, particularly along Davit Agmashenebelis where there is a concentration of small, good-value Turkish cafeterias, although most do not serve alcohol.

The Right Bank
Old Town
Map, page 98, unless otherwise stated

✗ **Chardin 12** Sharden 12; ☎ 93 1556; ⊕ 11.00–01.00 daily. French-style café with live jazz; it's popular for drinks & a chat, but the food has recently got a lot better. $$$

✗ **Gabriadze's Café** (aka the Sans Souci) Shavteli 13; ☎ 98 6594; http://gabriadze.com; ⊕ 11.00–02.00 daily. A nice, stylish place with a few interesting dishes such as sturgeon shashlik, although it's best for a drink on the balcony overlooking the church. $$$

✗ **Leffe** Sharden 14; ☎ 30 3030; ⊕ noon–02.00 daily. One of the better places in this very commercial strip. As well as the eponymous Belgian beer, they also serve steak frites, pizza, pasta & salads, as well as a good range of cocktails & shots. $$$

✗ **Maidan** Rkinis Rigi 6 (on the embankment); ☎ 75 1188; ⊕ noon–01.00 daily. Deceptively rustic, Maidan serves expensive Georgian food, with live music from 20.00. $$–$$$

✗ **Mirzaani Brewery** Leselidze 25; ☎ 43 9646; ⊕ 09.00–23.00 daily. Good-value Georgian food (& a nice smoky dark beer) in a pleasant setting of brick walls & cast iron, with quiet background music. Also in Chugureti at Uznadze 41 (*at Chorokhi*; ☎ 95 0001; ⊕ 11.00–23.00). $$

✗ **Prego** [map, page 94] Vazha-Pshavelas 2A at Pekini; ☎ 37 3610; ⊕ 11.00–22.00 daily. An adequate & affordable Italian restaurant-pizzeria that also has branches at Erekle II 15 (☎ 99 9723,

93 1411), Marjanishvili 2 (☎ 99 9723), Paliashvili 10 (*near the UN Circle*; ☎ 25 2258), & Tarkhnishvili 25 (☎ 25 2516). The daily specials are the best bet. $$

✗ **Tartine** Maidan Sq; ☎ 43 8968; e omaintartine@gmail.com; ⊕ 08.30–00.00 daily. French-owned, with a classic bistro menu (excellent onion soup!), this is also very popular for brunch, with an accordionist from 11.00 on Sun. Also at Abashidze 22 in Vake (☎ 22 6669). $$

✗ **Machakhela** Leselidze 26; ☎ 10 2119; www.vdcapital.ge/en-machakhela; ⊕ 10.00–23.00 daily. A chain of what look like fast-food joints but they actually take their time producing excellent khacahapuri & acharuli 'boats' with aubergine stew, spinach & cream or meat sauces; there's also Wi-Fi. Also nearby on Maidan Sq & at Marjanishvili 16, Lagidze 1 (at Rustaveli), Kostavas 77, Davit Agmashenebelis 106, Arakishvili 5, Tsereteli 77, Gulia 1 (Ortachala), Kazbegi (at Tamarashvili) & Vakhushti Bridge (right bank). $

✗ **Samikitno** Maidan Sq; m 577 710788; http://vdcapital.ge/en-Samikitno; ⊕ 24rhr. A chain of budget restaurants serving the classic Georgian menu; there's a great upstairs terrace here. Also at Rustaveli 24/1, Davit Agmashenebelis 106, Pushkin 5/7, Kostavas 77, Kazbegi 26. $

Sololaki
Map, page 98, unless otherwise stated

✗ **Azarpesha** Ingorovka 2; ☎ 98 2346; m 579 704080; www.azarpesha.com; ⊕ 11.00–23.00 daily. Two blocks uphill from Freedom Sq, Tbilisi's first wine restaurant is a place for you to experience the range of Georgia's wines in conjunction with fine food, offered as soups & small plates such as bruschetta, *moutabal* (aubergine spread) & leek mimosa (GEL7–12), large plates such as lamb saddle ragu, pork loin, pkhlovani & other vegetarian dishes (GEL12–20) & divine desserts such as lavender crème brûlée (GEL8–10). $$–$$$

✕ PurPur Abo Tibilebi 1; ☎ 47 7776; ⏰ 11.00–02.00 daily. There's a great atmosphere here, upstairs in one of the few buildings on Gudiashvili Sq that isn't crumbling; the food doesn't always match the friendly service & retro/shabby-chic setting. There's often live jazz. $$

✕ Shavi Lomi [map, page 84] Amagleba 23; ☎ 93 1007; e shavilomi@gmail.com; ⏰ noon–02.00 daily. Right at the top of Sololaki, this cellar (with no sign other than the eponymous Black Lion painted on the wall) is renowned for its modern Georgian cooking, especially its stews. $$

Dadiani Street
Map, page 98

✕ Racha Lermontov 12 (at Dadiani); m 577 460532; ⏰ 11.00–22.00 daily. Food & wine from Racha, of course, in this popular cellar dive; no English spoken. $$

✕ Khinklis Samkaro Dadiani 12; m 993 274412. Serves traditional Georgian fare. $–$$

✕ Veliaminovi Dadiani 8; m 551 906920. Very popular, often filled with locals. $–$$

Towards the Dry & Baratashvilis Bridges
Map, page 94, unless otherwise stated

✕ Mukhrantubani [map, page 98] Baratashvili 23; ☎ 99 7474. One of Tbilisi's best & most expensive restaurants; it has an English-language menu & private rooms, making it ideal for business meals. There's also a German biergarten, & a converted tramcar in front selling shashlik kebabs. $$$$

✕ Dzveli Sakhli (Old House) Sanapiro 3; ☎ 92 3497; ⏰ noon–midnight daily. Down by the river just west of the Dry Bridge, this is one of the best Georgian restaurants in town. It might be a bit too touristy for some tastes, with music & a dance display on w/end evenings, but the food is delicious. $$$

✕ Baan Thai Tabukashvili 35; ☎ 29 9780; ⏰ 11.30–23.30 daily. One of Tbilisi's best Thai

restaurants; staff speak English & it's non-smoking! Also does deliveries & take-aways. $$

✕ Ben Chelero Mtkvari 6; ☎ 99 9003; www.facebook.com/BenChelero; ⏰ 10.00–20.00 daily. Opposite the Public Service Hall, this is one of Tbilisi's more interesting vegetarian/vegan options, serving modern Latin American food (inc fish) in a pleasant wooden-panelled setting (non-smoking upstairs). $$

✕ Shemoikhede Genatsvale (Step In, Darling) Pushkin 10; ☎ 99 7887; www.facebook.com/shemoikhedeams; ⏰ 09.00–23.00 daily. A branch of this popular & affordable Georgian chain, known for excellent khinkali; service can be patchy but the price is right. The central branches (also at Maidan Sq, Kakabadze 2 & Marjanishvili 5) seem all to be in cosy cellars, but those out at Kazbegi 16A, Oniashvili 2 & on Zhvania Sq are modern buildings. $–$$

Rustaveli Avenue
Map, page 94

✕ Marco Polo Rustaveli Av 44; ☎ 93 5383; ⏰ 09.00–01.00 daily. Georgian & European food in a tastefully furnished city bar. $$$

✕ Sake Sushi Bar Besiki 4; ☎ 51 9966. Tbilisi's first genuine sushi bar, just off Rustaveli, has Japanese dishes adapted to Georgian tastes. Also offers business lunch packages. $$$

✕ Khinkhlis Sakhli (The Khinkhali House) Rustaveli 37, at the south entrance to the Rose Revolution Sq underpass; m 790 561532; ⏰ 24hrs. This Tbilisi institution is the place for a huge meal of dumplings (inc vegetarian options) at low cost. $

Close to Rose Revolution Square
Map, page 94

✕ Csaba's Jazz-Rock Café Vashlovani 3; ☎ 92 3122; ⏰ noon–04.00 daily. On a side street off Akhvlediani, this café offers Hungarian food as well as music (⏰ 20.30–23.30). $$$

✕ Maharajah Akhvlediani 24; ☎ 99 9799; ⏰ noon–late daily. A curry house serving fairly authentic dishes. Live music & belly dancing at w/ends. $$$

✕ Dublin Akhvlediani 8; ☎ 98 4467; ⏰ 11.00–03.00 daily. A fairly generic Irish pub serving sandwiches & salads along with various Russian, Georgian & even Mexican dishes. $$–$$$

✕ Picasso Miminoshvili 4; ☎ 98 9086; ⏰ 11.00–00.00 daily. Chinese restaurant with

Wi-Fi, between Kostavas & Akhvlediani by the Super Babylon department store. $$

Vere

Map, page 94

✖ **Le Cabernet** Tatishvili (formerly Kazbegi) 8; ☎ 90 4094; ⏰ noon–23.30 daily. A fine French restaurant that specialises in steaks; the fixed lunch is good value. $$$$

✖ **Green Terrace** Kekeldize 11; ☎ 24 0203; ⏰ noon–midnight daily. Below the Barnov viaduct, this stylish, new, wood-faced building covered in greenery, houses a café (with great cakes) downstairs & a spacious restaurant upstairs serving international cuisine such as goulash, pizza & pasta. $$–$$$

✖ **Café Goethe** Zandukeli 16; ⏰ 11.00–20.00 Mon–Fri. Also run by Rainer Kaufmann. Serves good, cheap food in a great garden. $$

✖ **Rainer's Pizzeria & Biergarten** Barnov 39; ☎ 98 5439; www.hotel-kartli.com; ⏰ noon–23.00. Just up the hill from the Philharmonic facing the Hotel Kartli, Rainer's serves a mix of German, Italian & New Georgian cuisine & also delivers pizza. $$

Vake

Map, page 84

✖ **Vong** Abashidze 29; ☎ 30 3030; ⏰ 13.00–02.00 daily. A smart place offering French–Asian fusion food & seafood. Also **Buffet** (☎ *22 4961; ⏰ noon–midnight; $$$*), a classy Italian restaurant, is next door at Abashidze 31. $$$–$$$$

✖ **Amira** Mosashvili 24; ☎ 90 7701; m 599 179699; ⏰ 11.00–midnight. An excellent & fairly upmarket Lebanese restaurant; plenty of veggie options inc the meze. $$$

✖ **Cecilia** Abashidze 10; ☎ 30 9559; ⏰ 11.00–23.00 daily. Excellent Italian food, thanks to importing authentic ingredients (though at a cost) – they serve pizza, pasta, soup, cakes & ice cream, plus fine coffee. $$$

✖ **Don Giuseppe** Mosashvili 13; ☎ 24 4727; www.giuseppe.ge; ⏰ noon–02.00 daily. A popular modern Italian restaurant, with a Neapolitan owner, by the side entry to Vake Park. $$$

✖ **Sushi Tokyo** Abashidze 14; ☎ 25 0343; m 597 010733; ⏰ 10.00–01.00 daily. Pricey but reliable sushi. $$$

✖ **Il Garage** Mosashvili 26; ☎ 22 7588; ⏰ noon–22.00 Mon–Sat. The most authentic

Italian restaurant in Tbilisi; it's moved from the original garage but is still intimate & relaxed. A free portion of bruschetta is followed by huge portions of pasta or pizza – & don't miss the homemade limoncello! $$

✖ **May Thai** Mtskheta 1; ☎ 23 2372; www. facebook.com/RestaurantMayThai; ⏰ 11.00–22.30 daily. This Thai place is probably more use as a take-away than as a restaurant. $$

✖ **Fantastico Pizza** Napareuli 3A; ☎ 29 4675; www.fantastico.ge; ⏰ 11.30–23.00 daily. A great, cheap Italian place (for pizza, pasta & desserts) on a side street near the university & UN Circle. It's smoky, but they do take-away. Also at Kazbegi 14 (☎ *72 8908; ⏰ 10.00–02.00 daily*). $–$$

Saburtalo

Map, page 84

✖ **Taste of India** Kandelaki 23; m 577 587333; www.tasteofindia.ge; ⏰ 10.00–midnight. Formerly Little India, this is perhaps the most authentic & most expensive North Indian restaurant in Tbilisi; non-smoking area, deliveries available. $$$

✖ **Sianggan** Pekini 41 (Zhvania Sq); ☎ 37 9688; ⏰ 11.30–01.00 daily. A flashy Chinese place in the Las Vegas casino; serves Hong Kong specialities & Beijing smoked duck. $$–$$$

✖ **Ronny's Pizza** Vazha-Pshavelas 3 (at Pekini) ☎ 47 2472; www.ronnyspizza.com; ⏰ 11.00–23.00 Mon–Sat, 14.00–23.00 Sun. Tiny pizza place with just 3 tables that serves authentic American-style pizza with thick crusts & real mozzarella. $$

✖ **Taglaura** Mtkvari right bank near Vakushti Bridge; m 555 207700; http://vdcapital.ge/en-taglaura; ⏰ 10.00–late daily. With 3 more branches in Ortachala, Okrokana & Digomi, this offers Georgian food & ambience in a spacious rustic setting. The wide-ranging menu features home-baked bread, BBQ, a choice of 4 types of khinkhali among many other Georgian favourites, plus home-brewed pale & dark beer. $$

The Left Bank

Chugureti

Map, page 84, unless otherwise stated

✖ **Ankara** Davit Agmashenebelis 130; ☎ 95 7281. One of several dependable Turkish lokantas along this stretch. $–$$

✖ **Deniz** Davit Agmashenebelis 63107; m 593 982783; ⏰ 08.00–midnight daily. Another good Turkish cafeteria with no menu but helpful waitresses & excellent food. Beer is available in the upstairs section. $–$$

✘ **Shemoikhede Genatsvale** (Step In, Darling) [map, page 94] Marjanishvili 5 (on the ramp left down to the embankment); ✆91 0005; ⏰ 09.00–23.00 daily. This chain specialising in khinkhali has other branches (page 103) but this bierkeller-style place is probably the best of the bunch. $–$$

✘ **Luca Polare Finest Ice Cream and More** Davit Agmashenebelis 125; ✆38 0802; www.lucapolare.com; ⏰ 08.00–02.00 daily. Probably Tbilisi's best, certainly its priciest, ice creams. The 'more' includes salads, cakes, juices & coffees, including iced soya-milk frappés & the like, plus Wi-Fi. Also at Leselidze 34, the UN Circle & Pekini 7A. $

FAST FOOD AND TAKE-AWAYS If you need food on the run, Georgia's first branch of McDonald's [94 C2] opened in 1999 next to the Rustaveli metro station, and there are now others on Marjanishvili Square and at Tsereteli 34 and Kostavas 71; they're smoke-free, have Wi-Fi and good toilets so make a popular meeting point for expats. The area around Marjanishvili Square [94 D1] must also have the greatest concentration of take-away khachapuri places in the entire city – a cheap way to fill up at breakfast or lunch.

BARS AND CAFÉS Most bars simply serve their locals and don't bother with any sign beyond that supplied by Heineken, Guinness or Grolsch; others make more of an effort and can really be quite stylish and even pricey (these are more likely to have signs promoting their Czech beers). Many bars serve food and may be listed in the previous section.

On the **left bank** there are various bars and cafés, none of any great distinction. There's more excitement in the **lower Old Town**, where Sharden (with Rkinis Rigi and Bambis Rigi) is now the city's trendiest street, with cafés and bars all offering very un-Georgian hookahs. Nearby, as mentioned previously, the pedestrianised Erekle II is lined with pleasant cafés. The **upper Old Town** starts with the pretentious nouveau lounge-bars and restaurants on the pedestrianised lower block of Galaction Tabidze, above which more interesting venues are slightly more scattered. You won't find any pubs in **Vake**, but there are some classy café-patisseries and also roadside coffee stands.

Left Bank

Map, page 94, unless otherwise stated

▯ **Folk Garden** Davit Agmashenebelis 68; ✆74 3274; ⏰ noon–midnight daily. In the attractive garden of the Folklore State Centre of Georgia, with an interesting gallery, it serves decent Georgian & European food, & hosts a folk group playing 'Tbilisi city music' on Fri from 21.00. $$

▯ **Marjanoff Express** Marjanishvili 8; ✆36 9516; ⏰ noon–late daily. An elegant café with Art Nouveau features attached to the Marjanishvili Theatre; Orient Express-style interior & a terrace. $

▯ **Public Coffee** Davit Agmashenebelis 96 (Marjanishvili Sq), also Pekini 4; ⏰ 08.00–midnight Mon–Sat, 10.00–midnight Sun. An American-style coffee bar that actually seems to specialise in chai latte, as well as pizza & omelettes. $

▯ **Madliani Brewery** Tsinanamdsghvrishvili 14; ✆95 7574; www.madliani.ge; ⏰ 11.00–23.00 daily. This historic tavern a block above Saarbrücken Square now houses a microbrewery using imported German malt & hops. The beer is good, the food & service not. $$

▯ **World Sport Café** [map, page 84] Kipiani 5; ✆95 0236, 95 8062; e wsportcafé@hotmail.com. In the Mushtaid Garden near the Dinamo Stadium, this café-bar has big-screen TVs, a Formula 1 car stuck to the high ceiling & the best ribs in Georgia. $$

▯ **Plekhanov** [map, page 84] Davit Agmashenebelis 98. At the western exit from Marjanishvili Sq, this is a good local bar with food. $

Old Town

Map, page 98, unless otherwise stated

▯ **Café Le Toît** Leselidze 22; m 559 497497; ⏰ 11.00–01.00 daily. This lovely new café looks like your granny's front room with its retro chintzy wallpaper & furniture; there's a small bar, an enterprising kitchen, Wi-Fi & nice roof-top views. There's quiet-ish music in the day & often live piano or guitar from 19.00. $$

Café Linville Abesadze 2; ✆ 93 3651; m 593 32 2221; ⏰ noon–02.00 daily. Arty café-restaurant with a vintage-apartment style ambiance & comfy sofas (plus a fish tank in an old TV); there's good jazz & a varied menu including excellent crêpes. $$

Naxvamdis Café Erekle II 7; m 591 902576; www.facebook.com/naxvamdis; ⏰ 13.00–05.00 (winter from 15.00) daily. An arty café with photographic displays & rooftop bar; snacks such as sandwiches, burritos & Mexican potatoes are available, plus alcoholic drinks & unlimited free tea & coffee. Big-screen football, too. $$

Chaikhana Grishashvili 14; ✆ 72 2172. A Persian teahouse near the baths, run by an Armenian couple, but very authentic for all that. $

Kala Erekle II 8; m 599 799737; http://kala.ge; ⏰ 10.00–02.00 daily. A trendy bar with Western prices & beers; jazzy music live nightly 21.00–23.30. $$$

The Hangar Bar Shavteli 20; ✆ 93 1080, 91 1080; ⏰ noon–late Mon–Sat, from 10.00 Sun. One of the main expat drinking holes, with free Wi-Fi & major sporting events screened live. It incorporates the Old Love café, once renowned for its oriental sweetmeats & startling décor, with plaster lion heads in the jaws of which a cigarette can conveniently be perched. $$$

Alani Restaurant & Brewery Gorgasali 1; ⏰ 09.00–midnight daily. On the embankment between the baths & Maidan Sq, this is the place for great Ossetian khinkali & khachapuri (with cheese & potatoes) & for their own excellent beer. There's also a smoky, noisy cellar. Service is poor & there's a risk of overcharging. $$

Gabriadze's Café (aka the Sans Souci) Shavteli 13; ✆ 98 6594; http://gabriadze.com; ⏰ 11.00–02.00 daily. A great place for a drink, although it only has foreign beers as well as lots of teas; there's Wi-Fi, & one of Georgia's best pianists plays here from 22.00 nightly. $$

KGB Erekle II 10; m 599 674488; www.kala.ge; ⏰ noon–02.00 daily. With the slogan 'We're still watching you' above the door, the emphasis here is on ironic Soviet kitsch, with dishes such as Lenin's Favourite & Proletarian Pizza. $$

Moulin Electrique Leselidze 28; m 551 722323; ⏰ 10.30–01.00 Mon–Fri, 11.30–01.00 Sat–Sun. A very hip place in a courtyard, with outdoor seating or a smoky interior; it's most popular for snacks & drinks, especially Illy coffee & iced tea, but the food is also good, with several vegetarian options. $$

Pirimze [map, page 94] Atoneli 18, 3rd fl; m 557 631310; ⏰ 17.00–02.00 daily. A laidback hipster bar in a retro apartment near the flower market, with interesting art & a balcony; food & drinks are not bad & quite reasonably priced. $$

Warszawa Pushkin 19; m 574 805564; www.facebook.com/barwarszawatbilisi; ⏰ 10.00–04.00 daily. Tbilisi's first shots bar (basically vodka, of course) – drinks at GEL2–5, knock 'em back & be on your way. But, in fact, there's a cellar bar too with long shared tables where you can order wine, or bring beer & food down some tricky steps. $$

Sololaki
Map, page 98

87 Café Asatiani 33; ✆ 30 5785; ⏰ 11.00–23.00 Mon–Sat. This non-smoking Iranian café serves excellent coffee, a great choice of herbal teas & alcoholic drinks, with a range of 'Persian tapas' (mainly vegetarian but including meatballs); there's also a monthly gourmet dinner plus live music on occasion. Excellent English is spoken & the vibe is relaxed & welcoming. $$

Newsroom Caffé Asatiani 13; ✆ 98 8819; www.facebook.com/newsroomcoffee; ⏰ 08.00–22.00. The owner of this café/photo gallery is a very suave former foreign correspondent who has created a relaxed but stimulating atmosphere here, with copies of The New Yorker & The Economist, plus books on Georgian culture; you can sit for hours working on a laptop with the occasional shot of their excellent coffee. $$

Ghvino Underground Tabidze 15; ✆ 30 9610; m 551 944841; www.vinounderground.ge; noon–23.00 daily. Just above the pedestrianised section of Tabidze (next to Tea Underground) 'Wine Underground' is an attractive cellar owned by a group of Georgian natural winemakers & stocks a good range of their wines (to drink in or take away, with plenty of tasting advice) plus some hardcore artisanal cheeses. $$$

Arsad Machabeli 2; m 595 507001; www.facebook.com/nowhere.arsad; ⏰ 18.00–02.00

daily. Meaning 'Nowhere' in Georgian, Arsad has no sign outside, but you'll find your way easily enough down to this rather dingy cellar full of wild youngsters. $

♀ **Bauhaus** Abo Tibilebi 5; m 551 908318; ⊕ 16.00–01.00 Mon–Thu & Sun (until 02.00 Fri/Sat). A wild arty café, with snacks available as well as drinks; there are live & DJ gigs. $

On & near Rustaveli
Map, page 94, unless otherwise stated

🍴**Caliban's Coffeehouse** Rustaveli 34; ☎ 92 3592; ⊕ 09.30–21.00 daily. Coffee shop attached to Prospero's Books that is very popular as a meeting place for expats. The coffee is pricey but good; also at Betsy's Hotel (page 100). $$

🍴**Entree** Rustaveli 20; m 591 709022, 599 215383; www.entree.ge; ⊕ 08.00–22.00 daily. This Franco-Georgian bakery-café offers delicious baked goods like croissants & quiches, pizza, pasta, saltimbocca sandwiches, Italian ice cream, a variety of b/fasts & excellent coffee. No smoking. Also at Leselidze 47, Chavchavadze Av 78, Davit Agmashenebelis 68 (Marjanishvili Sq), Taktakishvili 13 (at Abashidze, in Vake), Petriashvili 19 (at Barnov) & Pekini 7 (Saburtalo). $

🍴**Family & Friends Art Café** Griboedov 17; ☎ 92 3772; e familyandfriends.ge@yahoo.com; ⊕ 10.00–23.45 Mon–Sat. Popular with the Conservatoire kids, there's interesting, quiet-ish music here & a good menu of affordable snacks & drinks, plus Wi-Fi. $

🍴**Squirrels Gallery-Café** [map, page 84] Chonkadze 29; ☎ 98 9721; m 599 757791; ⊕ 11.00–23.00 Tue–Sun. Supporting & employing people with mental disablilites, this is Tbilisi's first 'social café', well placed opposite the funicular's lower terminal (& wheelchair-accessible, of course). A plain, quiet space of white-painted concrete (smoke-free & with Wi-Fi), it serves b/fast (inc matsoni & honey from Samtskhe-Javakheti), lunch (combos for GEL12–14, ⊕ 13.00–15.00), quiches, khachapuri & salads. $

🍴**Sophia Melnikova's Fabulous Douqan** Stamba Dead End 22; ⊕ noon–02.00 daily. Just down the hill from Rustaveli, left on Tabukidze & all the way to the rear of the Literary Museum (the sign on the gate is only visible when it is closed), this bohemian outdoor café offers good home cooking & chilled vibes to an arty, alternative crowd. $

♀ **Dive Bar** Lagidze 12 (at Mari Brosse); m 597 067473; www.facebook.com/DiveTbilisi; ⊕ 18.00–01.00 Mon–Thu & Sun (until 03.00 Fri–Sat). An American bar with a slightly older crowd of friendly expats & Georgians who've travelled. A bit of an underground feel, with its concrete floor & seating on wooden crates; no food but cheap beer & cocktails & occasional live music. $

Along Akhvlediani & Kiacheli
Map, page 94

🍴**Mukha Café** Akhvlediani 15; ☎ 92 0053; m 577 737440; www.facebook.com/Mukhatsakatukha; ⊕ 11.00–01.00 daily. Essentially a café-deli in the daytime, selling baked goods & juices from bare pine shelves, this offers more leisurely dining in the evenings, with French-oriented dishes based on local products, & jazz; there's no smoking. $

♀ **Buffalo Bill** Akhvlediani 16; ☎ 93 6052; ⊕ noon–late daily. A Wild West-themed bar with rock & country music (live from 20.30 nightly) plus Wi-Fi. $$

♀ **Dublin** Akhvlediani 8 (on the corner of Ekaladze); ☎ 98 4467; ⊕ 11.00–03.00 daily. Another Irish pub with live music nightly; odd, then, that its menu is more Georgian than you'd expect. $$

♀ **Nali** At the angle of Kiacheli 4/1; ☎ 43 0420; www.nali.ge; ⊕ noon–03.00 daily. Near Rose Revolution Sq, this pub has a 'happy hour' from 16.00 to 19.00 & live music at 21.00 daily. There's a good range of affordable food. In the same building is the Althaus tea house, serving 80 types of tea, with non-smoking area & a terrace (⊕ noon–midnight). $$

♀ **Oil Drop** Akhvlediani 18; m 595 232393; ⊕ 13.00–03.00 daily. For some reason this pub seems to have an oil-painting theme, with information panels on Brueghel, Vermeer, Bosch et al, but the beer & steak on offer is plain & satisfying. $$

♀ **Old London** Akhvlediani 6; m 571 882225; ⊕ noon–late daily. Wood-panelled 'English' pub theme with live music. $$

♀ **Wheels** Akhvlediani 16; ☎ 98 8733; ⊕ 13.00–01.00 daily. Tbilisi's first Irish pub, this has a wood-panelled bar & a homely dining area. $$

♀ **Canudos Ethnic Bar** Samaia Sq (at the top of Javakishvili); m 598 262670; ⊕ 15.00–02.00 daily (until midnight Sun). Linked to a backpackers' hostel, this is a party place for alternative young travellers & their local equivalents, with a bright, wood-floored interior plastered with travel-related items & a garden with fountain. There's cheap beer & snacks including a huge Italian sandwich. $

Vere
Map, page 94

🖵 **Café Petozi** Petriashvili 20; 📞 25 1120; ⏲ 09.00–23.00 daily. A nice but slightly smoky little café with Lavazza coffee, 3 types of khachapuri & salads. $

🖵 **Factory 27** Zandukeli 27; m 595 255552; ⏲ noon–01.00 daily. A pleasantly post-industrial café, serving excellent light meals; there's a small courtyard below street level, enlivened by graffiti art, where you can sit wrapped in a blanket on summer evenings. $

♀ **Rainer's Pizzeria & Biergarten** Barnov 39; ⏲ noon–midnight daily. Beer & pizza – what more do you need?

Vake
Map, page 84

🖵 **Assorti** Abashidze 81; m 579 16 5151; ⏲ 09.00–23.00 daily. A pricey but classy bakery, producing its own bread, khachapuri, pastries & cakes, as well as salads & tarts. Also at Mosashvili 1 (*near Chavchavadze 64*; m 579 165252), Mtskheta 8 (m 579 162244), Nikoladze 5 (m 579 165353), Nutsubidze 86A (m 579 161188), Chavchavadze 50 (📞 22 2913) & Pekini 22 (m 579 168282). $$

🖵 **Dom*** Eristavi 16; 📞 22 6836; m 557 770542; ⏲ 11.00–23.00 daily. On the UN Circle (or Round Garden), this friendly & stylish café-bar is good for lunch (lovely soup) & snacks at other times. $$

🖵 **Art-Café Sfumato** Abashidze 10–12; 📞 90 7711; ⏲ 10.00–23.30 daily. A genteel café with art exhibitions & piano (live music from 20.00 Fri–Sun). $

🖵 **Café Frâiche** Abashidze 39; m 577 443362; www.facebook.com/fraiche.ge; ⏲ 09.00–22.00 daily. Attractive European-style café-patisserie that also sells frozen yoghurt. $

♀ **Acid Bar** Abashidze 37; m 599 41 19 80; ⏲ noon–02.00 daily; also at Kazbegi 3A, Chavchavadze 16 & Leonidze 9. These are among the coolest bars in town, with creative décor including bench sofas & booths; Georgian & international food & drink available. $$

Other coffee houses
Map, page 94

🖵 **Book Corner Café** Tarkhnishvili 13B; 📞 23 2430; www.bookcorner.ge; ⏲ 11.00–03.00 daily. Similar to the Literary Cafés but with better food (soup, flatbreads, vareniki cheese dumplings & cake). $

🖵 **Literary Cafés** www.literaturuli.com. Branches at Tarkhnishvili 2 (📞 44 4546; ⏲ 10.00–01.00); Kostavas 36 (*near the Philharmonic;* 📞 99 0746); Pekini 31 (*at Kazbegi;* 📞 31 3057); & Abashidze 22 (📞 22 0276). All of these cafés incorporate interesting bookshops & hold book launches & talks. $

🖵 **Whittards of Chelsea** There are several outlets, variously known as English Tea House, or Elite Tea House, at Marjanishvili 5 (📞 94 1620), Paliashvili 32 (📞 22 1109) & Vekua 3 (*in the Georgian Trading Centre;* 📞 93 6138). $

ENTERTAINMENT

NIGHTCLUBS Cafés and bars often stay open until 02.00, but after that Tbilisi doesn't have a wild nightlife, with just a couple of clubs open to 06.00. As well as the places listed, some of the bars and cafés on Akhvlediani and in the Old Town also have live music. From July to September some close to move their operations to the Black Sea coast. There's also a concentration of commercial DJ and karaoke clubs in the Rkinis Rigi area (near the Maidan and Metekhi Bridge).

☆ **Bamba Station** [98 D3] Bambis Rigi 12; m 555 713888; www.facebook.com/ bambastation1; ⏲ 22.00–04.00 Thu–Sat. A cool groove bar.

☆ **City Club & SKY Bar** [98 F2] Metekhi 22; m 592 323232; ⏲ 19.00–late Thu–Sun. In

Avlabari, this has theme nights, live bands & DJs playing '80s & '90s hits. No under-21s admitted.

☆ **Kalakuri** [98 D1] Shavteli 13; 📞 99 6683; m 571 223333; http://kalakuri.info-tbilisi.com; ⏲ 22.00–late Thu–Sat, 20.00–late Sun. DJs, karaoke & live music, & European & Japanese food.

☆ **Magti Club** [94 D3] Rustaveli 22; m 599 500022; ⏰ 21.00–06.00 Tue–Sun; GEL25 inc cocktail. Cellar club with live jazz, blues, soul & even 'ethno-folklore' & experimental music.

☆ **Mix Club** [84 D2] Javakishvili 2; m 597 211211; ⏰ restaurant & lounge bar 19.00–22.00 daily, nightclub 22.00–07.00 Thur–Sat; GEL20. DJs, live music & Ukrainian erotic dancers.

☆ **One Side** [98 D3] Bambis Rigi 7; m 579 493 434. Originally Two Side (with all-male staff on one side, all female on the other), this is now a straightforward DJ club.

☆ **Safe** [98 E3] Rkinis Rigi 11; m 595 5620050, 557 700044; ⏰ lounge 15.00–late, club 22.30–07.00 daily. Behind the big bank vault door there are DJs & dancing girls.

☆ **Senate Club** [84 A4] Mishveladze 5; ☎ 22 3344; ⏰ lounge noon–05.00 daily, club 23.00–06.00 Thu–Sat. On the edge of Vake Park, this mock-Roman farrago is popular with the residents of this affluent area.

☆ **Tbilisi Voice** [98 D3] Bambis Rigi 8; m 597 211211; ⏰ 16.00–06.00 daily. Karaoke.

☆ **Underwheel Club** [84 C4] Mtatsminda; www.facebook.com/Club.Underwheel. A wonderful setting, under the Ferris wheel high above the city.

☆ **Unique** [98 D3] Bambis Rigi 8; m 577 662028; ⏰ 15.00–02.00 daily. Two DJ sets per night.

CASINOS

☆ **Adjara** [84 B2] 26 May Sq 1; ☎ 33 5519; www. casinoadjara.com. Attached to the new Holiday Inn, for blackjack, poker & roulette.

☆ **Iveria** [94 D2] Rose Revolution Sq 1; ☎ 40 2245; www.casinoiveria.com. A glass box attached to the Radisson, this is the classiest of Tbilisi's casinos.

☆ **Shangri La** [98 D2] Mtkvari right embankment, by the Peace Bridge; ☎ 20 0701; http://shangrila.ge. A garish blaze of neon by the river, this is the city's most modern casino.

THEATRES These close at the end of June for the summer.

🎭 **Abashidze Music and Drama State Theatre** [84 C2] Davit Agmashenebelis 182; ☎ 34 8090; www.musictheatre.ge

🎭 **Atoneli Theatre** [94 E3] Atoneli 31; ☎ 93 3238

🎭 **Dumbadze State Children's Theatre** Davit Agmashenebelis 99/1; ☎ 95 3927, 95 7874; e childrentheatre@gmail.com; www.mozardi.ge

🎭 **Griboedov Russian Theatre** [98 B1] Rustaveli 2; ☎ 93 5811, 93 1106; www. griboedovtheatre.ge; also the **Liberty Theatre** (*Sulkan-Saba 11;* ☎ *98 5821; www.theatre.ge*) at the rear, with a ship's bow & portholes.

🎭 **K. Gamsakhurdia Sukhumi State Drama Theatre** [84 A2] Vazha-Pshavelas 16; ☎ 37 1650; www.teatrisokhumi.ge

🎭 **Kakha Bakuradze Movement Theatre** [84 C2] Davit Agmashenebelis 182 (Mushtaid Park); m 599 015567

🎭 **Marjanishvilis State Theatre** [94 D1] Marjanishvili 8; ☎ 95 5966; www.marjanishvili. ge; ⏰ box office 11.00–19.00 Tue–Sun. This is also home to performances & rehearsals of Fingers Theatre (*www.fingers-theatre.net*) – dancing

fingers that perform Georgian dance, the cancan & a version of *Hamlet*, all in great costumes.

🎭 **Mikheil Tumanishvili Movie Actors' Theatre** [84 C2] Davit Agmashenebelis 164; ☎ 35 0203; m 599 501816; e info@ tumanishvilitheatre.ge; www.tumanishvilitheatre. ge. Home to GIFT, the Georgian International Festival of Theatre in honour of Mikheil Tumanishvili (*www.giftfestival.ge*).

🎭 **Pantomime Theatre** [94 C2] Rustaveli 37; ☎ 99 6314

🎭 **Rezo Gabriadze's Marionette Theatre** [98 D1] Shavteli 13; ☎ 98 6590; http://gabriadze. com. Puppet theatre for adults with 3 shows in repertory: *The Battle of Stalingrad, The Autumn of my Spring* & *Ramona*.

🎭 **The Royal District Theatre (Samepor Ubenese Teatri)** [98 C2] Abesadze 10; ☎ 99 6171; e rd_theatre@caucasus.net. This theatre was built as a caravanserai in 1898, became a cultural centre under Beria, & was abandoned in 1987. In 1992 Isa Grigoshvili, leading lady of the Rustaveli Theatre for 30 years, was sacked for going on a tour of Germany without permission, although she claimed it was because of her Zviadist politics; she, her husband, actor/director Mairab Tavadze, & their son Nico Tavadze, decided to set up an independent company in the Royal District Theatre & were ready to reopen in 1995, when a Jewish group claimed it as a former synagogue. A furious legal battle erupted & all the city's unemployed actors joined an 'act-in', 24hrs a day for 10 days, until they won the right to open as a theatre. It is now a venue for some of the city's liveliest drama.

🎭 **Shota Rustaveli State Theatre** [94 D3] Rustaveli 17; ☎ 32 6868; www.rustavelitheatre.

ge; tickets GEL10–40. Newly refurbished, with 2 modern theatres seating 300 & 800 people, plus a studio theatre.

🎭 **Tbilisi State Armenian Dramatic Theatre** [94 G3] Avlabari Sq, Ketevan Tsamebuli 8; ☎ 74 7764, 74 7696; www.tbilarmtheatre.ge

🎭 **Theatre Veriko** Anjaparidze 16; ☎ 99 9896

🎭 **Zakaria Paliashvili State Opera House** [94 D3] Rustaveli 25; ☎ 93 1654, 93 3743; www.opera. ge, www.ballet.ge. The opera should reopen very soon after refurbishment.

CINEMAS
The Georgian film industry is having a bit of a revival at the moment, and the numbers going to the cinema are rising, with the odd new cinema opening, too.

Akhmeteli Near the metro station of the same name; ☎ 58 6669

Astra Park entertainment centre Chachava 8; ☎ 37 3737; www.facebook.com/AstraPark. Well north of the centre, this promises 7D cinema.

Cinema City [84 A4] Mosashvili 24; ☎ 43 0250; http://cinemacity.mymovies.ge

Cinema Club Amirani [94 B1] Kostavas 36; ☎ 99 9955; e amirani@amirani.ge; www.amirani. ge. Under the Philharmonic, this is the main venue for art films (mostly dubbed into Russian) & home of the Tbilisi International Film Festival in

December (www.tbilisifilmfestival.ge).

Kashe (or Cache) Cinema Club [94 C1] Kiacheli 9; ☎ 99 0551.

Kinos Sakhli (Kolga Cinema House) [94 C2] Kakabadze 2; 99 9460, 99 6013. In the west end of the Academy of Sciences on Rustaveli Sq across from McDonald's (the top door, above the restaurant).

Rustaveli (Century 21) [94 D3] Rustaveli 5; ☎ 55 5000, 92 0357; http://rustaveli.com.ge. The best commercial cinema.

Sakartvelo Guramishvili 2/9; ☎ 69 6647/51, 30 8080

MUSIC
Classical music is performed at the **Philharmonic**, now officially known as **Tbilisi State Concert Hall** [94 B1] (*Melikishvili 1;* ☎ *99 0099; www.tbilisiconcerthall. com; box office at rear,* ⊕ *11.00–14.00, 15.00–19.00 daily*), and at the **Djansugh Kakhidze Tbilisi Center for Music & Culture** [84 C2] (*Davit Agmashenebelis 123;* ☎ *95 0119;* e *tmc@caucasus.net; www.kakhidzemusiccenter.com*). The Tbilisi Symphony Orchestra was founded in 1993 by Djansugh Kakhikdze (1935–2002), splitting away from the Georgian State Symphony Orchestra, and is now conducted by his son Vakhtang. The Georgian Philharmonic Orchestra, directed by Nikoloz Rachveli, plays at the **Mikeladze Centre** [84 C2] (*Davit Agmashenebelis 127;* ☎ *91 5505; www.mikeladzecenter.ge*). Other venues are the **opera house** (led by the Italian conductor Gianluca Marciano) and the **Rustaveli Theatre** [94 D3], the **summer theatre** [84 C2] at Davit Agmashenebelis 123, and the **Conservatoire's concert halls** [94 D3] at Griboedov 8 (☎ *93 4624;* e *grandhall@conservatoire.edu.ge; www.conservatoire.edu.ge; box office* ⊕ *11.00–14.00, 15.00–17.00*.

FESTIVALS
The city's festival, **Tbilisoba**, is held on a weekend in late October, with food, music, dancing and other events in the Rikhe Park and elsewhere. The **Autumn Tbilisi Music Festival** (*www.kakhidzemusiccenter.com*) runs from mid-September to mid-October each year, followed in November by the **Tbilisi Wind Festival** (*www.tbilisiwindfestival.com*). The **Art Gene Folk Festival** (*www.artgeni. ge*) is held in July at the Museum of Ethnography and the **Tbilisi Jazz Festival** (*www.tbilisijazz.com*) in October. The film festival in December, and a month-long theatre festival in October and November (pages 48 and 109).

BATHS Most of Tbilisi's hot baths date from the 19th century and have always been central to community life; they've long been used for checking that prospective sons/daughters-in-law have no physical defects, and for gay cruising. Bathing in the single-sex public section (traditionally for women only on Tuesdays and Wednesdays) costs just a few lari, but to enjoy the full experience you and a few friends should take a private room, for GEL50–80 per hour – in fact two rooms, one for (un)dressing and resting, the other with a large tub with hot sulphur water flowing through it. Most baths also offer larger 'luxe' rooms, for GEL90–120/hour. There's not much point in paying for a massage (more of a brutal scrub really), especially as they communicate only with signs, but ordering tea is definitely part of the experience.

The best-looking ones are the **Chreli ('Motley') Baths** at the top of Abanos kucha, but sadly these were restored then closed. The older baths in the brick domes just below, including the **Sulphur Baths** and the **Royal Baths** (signed in English; private rooms only) are welcoming, and just beyond them are the cheaper **Public Baths no.5** in Aliyev Park, beneath the Tiflis Palace Hotel. It's worth going a block east up Grishashvili and turning right towards the Bohema restaurant to find the **Orbeliani Baths** (⊕ 07.00–00.30 daily); built in Moorish style, these have attractive stained glass but smaller rooms than most.

On the left bank are the **Gogilo Baths** [84 F3], across the road from the Sheraton Metechi Palace Hotel, which has a health club with pool and sauna, available to non-residents for a daily charge. There's another sauna on Ghvinis Aghmarti, between Avlabari Square and the Metekhi Church.

SPORTS The main spectator sport (other than watching other people work) is **soccer**: Lokomotiv (http://fcloco.ge) play at the Mikheil Meskhi Stadium, Vake Park [84 A4], while Dinamo Tbilisi (www.fcdinamo.ge) and the national team play at the Boris Paichadze Stadium [84 C2] (page 130); this was refurbished in 2006, just before the World Cup finalists France and Italy visited.

The Paichadze and Meskhi stadiums are also used by the Lelos, the national **rugby** team (*lelo* also means a try), who are doing remarkably well in the second tier of European competition, qualifying for the 2003, 2007 and 2015 world cups (not totally surprising, as almost the whole team plays professionally in France, and Bidzina Ivanishvili's Cartu Charity Foundation has invested over GEL100 million in the sport). A new 30,000-capacity stadium is planned in Didi Digomi. The Georgian team are currently ranked 13th in the world. The country's leading clubs are Tbilisi Caucasians and Lelo Saracens (formerly Lelo Tbilisi), who both play at the Avchala Stadium, in Gldani on the way to Mtskheta.

The most quintessentially Georgian sports are **wrestling**, **weight-lifting** and **power-lifting**, with major tournaments held in the Sports Palace on 26 May Square [84 B2] (www.sportspalace.ge).

The city's main **tennis** clubs are the newly renovated Jan Homer Tennis Complex (*Ljubljana 18;* ☏ *54 0077*) and the Leila Meskhi Tennis Academy (*Marjanishvili 29;* ☏ *95 3800*); courts (from GEL2/hour) are also available at the Mtkvari embankment (☏ *99 5905*), and in the Vere and Vake parks.

The city's main **swimming** pool is the Laguna Vere [84 C3] (*Kostavas Lane 34, between Heroes' Square and Vere Park;* ⊕ *07.00–21.00 daily*). The outdoor Vake Pool [84 A4] at Chavchavadze Avenue 49B has natural warm water and is popular with expats before work, all year round; there's also a covered pool and fitness club here (☏ *25 2575;* ⊕ *07.00–23.00 Mon–Fri, 09.00–22.00 Sat & 09.00–21.00 Sun*). You can also take the kids to Europark, out towards Didube at Ninua 3 (☏ *92 3388; www.*

europark.ge; ☺ *10.00–20.00 daily),* which has pools with slides, wave machines and artificial rivers.

Bowling and **billiards** are available at Bowling Central [84 C1] on Station Square (☏ *20 0383),* the Kopala Entertainment Centre (*Rustaveli St 3, Lower Tskneti;* ☏ *22 8062; www.kopala.ge*) and Astra Park well north of the centre at Chachava 8 (☏ *37 3737; http://astrapark.ge/en/;* ☺ *noon–midnight daily*), which also offers karting and air-rifle shooting.

OTHER PRACTICALITIES

MONEY AND BANKING There are now plenty of **ATMs** around town; some machines dispense US dollars as well as Georgian lari. There are **exchange offices** all over the city, especially on Rustaveli and Chavchavadze avenues, as well as on Tamar Mepis below the Voksal, opposite the Samgori and Isani metro stations and at the airport, where you can exchange cash – euros, dollars, roubles and sometimes British pounds – for Georgian lari.

$ **Bank of Georgia** Pushkin 3; ☏ 44 4444; e customerservice@bog.ge; http://bankofgeorgia. ge. On the north side of Freedom Sq, with a beautiful hall (dating from 1902).
$ **Bank Republic** Abashidze 2; ☏ 90 9090; e info@republic.ge; www.republic.ge. Now part of the French Société Générale Group.
$ **Cartu Bank** Chavchavadze 39A; ☏ 92 5592; e info@cartubank.ge; www.cartubank.ge. Formerly AbsoluteBank.

$ **Liberty Bank** Chavchavadze 74; ☏ 55 5500; e info@libertybank.cge; www.libertybank.ge. Formerly the People's Bank of Georgia.
$ **Progress Bank** Baratashvili 8; ☏ 38 8888; e info@progressbank.ge; www.progressbank.ge
$ **TBC Bank** Marjanishvili 2; ☏ 27 2727; e info@ tbcbank.com.ge; www.tbcbank.com.ge/en; also Leselidze 22; ☏ 27 2727. Founded in 1992, now the largest bank in Georgia, & the second largest in the Caucasus.

COMMUNICATIONS

Post office Technically the main post office is the one at Davit Agmashenebelis 44 [94 E2] (☺ *09.00–17.00 Mon–Fri, 10.00–14.00 Sat*), which is where you should check for poste restante. Others (same hours) are at Chavchavadze 21 and Pekini 39.

Couriers

DHL Tsereteli 105; ☏ 69 6060, 69 9966; e info@ dhl.ge; www.dhl.com; ☺ 09.30–18.00 Mon–Fri
Federal Express Ketevan Tsamebuli 39; ☏ 74 8240, 274 8940; e fedexge@post.ge; www.fedex. com/ge; ☺ 10.00–18.00 Mon–Fri, 10.00–19.00 Sat
Georgian International EMS Davit Agmashenebelis 44; ☏ 94 3797; e ems@caucasus. net; www.ems.ge; ☺ 09.00–19.00 daily. Also at Rustaveli 31 (☏ *30 8723*) & Chavchavadze Av 21 (☏ *22 7403*).

TNT Express Worldwide Davit Agmashenebelis 25; ☏ 91 0220; e tamuna.khelaia@tnt.com; www. tnt.ge; ☺ 10.00–18.00 Mon–Fri
United Parcel Service (Meridian Express) Ketevan Tsamebuli 15–17; ☏ 18 0144; e info@ mexge.com, www.ups.com; ☺ 10.00–18.00 Mon–Fri

Internet All hotels and hostels have Wi-Fi, as do many cafés. There's also the city's Tbilisi Loves You free public Wi-Fi service, which seems to work in metro stations but rarely connects elsewhere. Alternatively, Tbilisi has some cybercafés: there are a couple of good places close to Marjanishvili metro station, in the courtyard between Marjanishvili 28 and 30, and at Davit Agmashenebelis 81, 108, 109 and 120. Across the river, there are places down an alley at Rustaveli

ⓔ Armenia Tetelashvili 4, 1 block west of Marjanishvili Sq; ℡ 95 1723, 95 9443; e armemb@caucasus.net; http://georgia.mfa.am/en; ⊕ 09.00–18.00 Mon–Fri

ⓔ Azerbaijan Gorgasali 4; ℡ 24 2220; e tbilisi@mission.mfa.gov.az; www.azembassy.ge

ⓔ Canadian consulate Rustaveli 34; ℡ 98 2072; e ccogeorgia@gmail.com

ⓔ China Barnov 52; ℡ 25 2670; e zhangling@access.sanet.ge; http://ge.china-embassy.org/eng

ⓔ European Union Chkheidze 38; ℡ 94 3763, 94 3769; e delegation-georgia@eeas.europa.eu; http://ec.europa.eu

ⓔ France Krtsanisi 49; ℡ 72 1490; e ambafrance@access.sanet.ge; www.ambafrance-ge.org

ⓔ Germany Due to earthquake damage the embassy is semi-permanently on the 4th floor of the Sheraton Metechi Palace Hotel, Telavi 20; ℡ 44 7300; ⊕ 08.30–17.30 Mon–Thu, 08.30–14.30 Fri. Consular/visa section is temporarily at Davit Aghmashenebelis 166; ℡ 43 5399; ⊕ 09.00–13.00 Mon–Fri

ⓔ Iran Chavchavadze 80; ℡ 91 3656–8; e iranemb@geo.net.ge

ⓔ Israel Davit Agmashenebelis 154; ℡ 55 6500; e press@tbilisi.mfa.gov.il; http://tbilisi.mfa.gov.il

ⓔ Russian Federation c/o embassy of Switzerland, Chavchavadze Av 51; ℡ 91 2406, 91 2645; e russianembassy@caucasus.net; www.georgia.mid.ru

ⓔ Turkey Chavchavadze Av 35; ℡ 25 2072; e turkemb.tbilisi@mfa.gov.tr; http://tbilisi.emb.mfa.gov.tr

ⓔ Ukraine Chavchavadze Av 76; ℡ 31 1161; consul ℡ 31 1454; e emb_ge@mfa.gov.ua; http://georgia.mfa.gov.ua

ⓔ UK Krtsanisi 51; ℡ 27 4747; e british.embassy.tbilisi@fco.gov.uk; http://ukingeorgia.fco.gov.uk; ⊕ 09.00–17.00 Mon–Fri except Georgian & British holidays

ⓔ United Nations Eristavi 9 (on the UN Circle); ℡ 25 1126; e uno.tbilisi@unic.org, www.ungeorgia.ge

ⓔ USA Balanchini 11, Didi Dighomi; ℡ 27 7000 (embassy), 27 7724 (consular section); e support-georgia@ustraveldocs.com, askconsultbilisi@state.gov; http://georgia.usembassy.gov; ⊕ consulate 08.30–17.30 Mon–Fri

18, Leselidze 6 and Chavchavadze Av 22. The main providers for home use are Caucasus Online (*Vazha-Pshavelas 37;* ℡ *220 0000;* e *info@co.ge; www.co.ge/en*) and Geonet (*Vazha-Pshavelas 41;* ℡ *47 0000;* e *info@geonet.ge; www.geonet.ge*).

MEDIA
Newspapers There are several free English-language newspapers, largely business-oriented, that you can pick up in the better hotels – the best established is *Georgia Today* (*www.georgiatoday.ge; issued every Fri*), along with *Georgian Journal* (*www.georgianjournal.ge; issued every Thu*) and *Caucasian Business Week* (*www.cbw.ge; issued every Mon*). An online-only equivalent is Agenda.ge, which is updated daily. There's also Investor.ge, a glossy mag from the American Chamber of Commerce in Georgia that can also be picked up in major hotels every two months.

MEDICAL SERVICES There are plenty of *aptekas* (**pharmacies**), most now part of the Aversi, GPC and PSP chains, and many open 24 hours (with a night window). Medicinal herbs are sold at Leselidze 53. The Stomatological (Dental) Clinic is at Davit Agmashenebelis 126 (℡ 95 3282); there are lots of private dental clinics in Vake and Saburtalo (especially on Mitskevich, it seems).

✚ **Central Republican Hospital** [84 A2] Vazha-Pshavelas 29; ☎ 39 5714
✚ **Cito Medical Centre** [84 A3] Paliashvili 40; ☎ 29 0671, 25 1948; www.cito.ge. A Swiss–Georgian joint venture.
✚ **City Hospital No. 2** [84 C2] Constitution St 2; ☎ 95 4423

✚ **David Tatishvili Medical Center** [84 B3] Tabuladze 20; ☎ 91 3119, 91 3242
✚ **MediClub** [84 A2] Tashkent 22; ☎ 25 1991; m 599 581991; http://mcg.ge
✚ **Tbilisi State University Medical Diagnostic Centre** [84 B3] Chavchavadze 5; ☎ 822 25199; http://tsmu.edu/tsmu2; emergency doctor m 599 581991

SHOPPING

MARKETS Tbilisi's **central market** (Bazroba) [84 C1] is by the station, a bustling place, where you'll find better quality (at higher prices) upstairs; beware pickpockets in this area. There's an open-air flower market, between Baratashvili and 9 April Park, but the old food market here has closed and there is now a branch of Carrefour on the ground floor and fashion outlets upstairs. The **Lilos bazroba** is a huge flea market 20km east beyond the airport on the Kakheti Highway, where you can find anything you need; don't forget to bargain. This is really the wholesale market for the whole country, with direct buses from cities such as Kutaisi, and several marshrutka lines terminate here, as well as bus 41 from Samgori metro.

Artists sell their work at weekends at the **Vernissaj**, the open-air market in the park by the Dry Bridge; above, by the road between the bridges, there is a thriving street market where Soviet-era memorabilia, military uniforms, second-hand books, magazines, coins, banknotes, records and cameras are all sold alongside household items and all manner of bric-a-brac. The lingua franca here is predominantly Russian and this is the place to come if you are in search of a Stalin bust or communist lapel badge. There are also people carrying labels advertising houses and flats for sale. Around the corner is a car bonnet market that mostly deals in tools and spare parts.

FOOD SHOPS Most Tbilisebi buy food at markets and corner shops, but there are some joint-venture supermarkets, many open 24 hours, the best of which are listed below. The excellent Populi and Ioli neighbourhood supermarkets will all be converted to 24-hour Spar outlets by 2016. There are also a couple of shops selling artisan Georgian cheeses.

Hypermarkets
Carrefour ⏲ 09.30–22.00 daily. This French giant has a huge store in the Tbilisi Mall (on the edge of town at km13 of the Mtskheta Highway), & smaller branches at the rear of the railway station (*Tsotne Dadiani 7*) & on the lower level of the Georgian Trade Center (GTC), home to the former central market, now with fashion & jewellery boutiques on the upper level.
Goodwill Branches at Parnavaz Mepe 1, Didi Dighomi, by the highway northwest to Mtskheta, & in the Pixel Business Centre, Chavchavadze 34; ⏲ 10.00–22.00 daily. Georgia's first hypermarket (with some interesting German foods), it's now been taken over by Carrefour.

Supermarkets
Big Ben [84 B4] Abashidze 46
Nugeshi 90 branches across the city.
Schwabe [84 A2] Petriashvili 28
Smart www.smart.ge. Mainly found at petrol stations, but also has 24hr branches in the old post office at Rustaveli 31, at Chavchavadze 37 & on the Kakheti & Mtskheta highways.
Zemeli [94 D3] Rustaveli 37, opposite McDonald's

Artisan shops
Aristaeus [98 B1] Pushkin 19; ⏲ 10.00–21.30 daily
Grand Gourmet [84 C3] Eristavi 9; ⏲ 10.00–22.00 Mon–Thu, 11.00–23.00 Fri–Sun. This deli on

Armenian Church of St George [98 E4] Samghebro 5, Gorgasali Sq; ⊕ 09.00 daily
Baptist [84 B1] Kedia 4; ⊕ 10.00 (Russian), noon (Georgian), 14.00 (Armenian) Sun
Cathedral of the Assumption of the Virgin [94 F2] Abesadze 4, in the Old Town;
⊕ 10.00 daily, noon & 18.00 Sun, 17.30 winter/18.00 summer Mon–Fri
Georgian Orthodox Sioni Cathedral [98 D3] ⊕ 09.00 Sun (magnificent singing)
Lutheran [84 D2] Terenti Graneli 15; ⊕ 11.00 Sun
Mosque [98 E4] Botanikuri 32; ⊕ 13.00 Fri
Roman Catholic Church of SS Peter and Paul [84 D2] Ivan Javakhishvili 55; ⊕ 09.00
Mon–Sat (in Georgian); 10.00 (English), 11.00 (Georgian), 17.00 (Latin) & 18.00 (Polish –
summer only) Sun
Russian Orthodox Church of St Alexander Nevsky [84 D2] Ivan Javakhishvili 69;
⊕ 09.00 daily
Synagogue [98 D3] Leselidze 47; ⊕ 09.00 daily
Tbilisi International Christian Fellowship Eristavi 1, Didube; ⊕ 17.00 Sun
(interdenominational, in English)

the UN Circle sells imported goodies such as caviar, sushi & salmon.

LTD Cheese World Puris Sq
Poka Nunnery's [84 B3] Paliashvili 30

WINE Shops selling Georgian wine and carpets tend to have a sign in English; there are lots of **wine shops** along Leselidze, mostly open 10.00–22.00, and there a number of other good options elsewhere, as listed below. Various **wineries** also have their own outlets – these close earlier at about 19.00. There are some good wine bars that also sell some interesting bottles.

Along Leselidze
Georgian Wine Legend Leselidze 27
Mukuzani at Gocha's Winery Cnr of Anton Katalikosi & Leselidze
Vinomania Wine Gallery Leselidze 45
Vinotheca Leselidze 31
Vintage Leselidze 11. New shop with bottles up to GEL250.
Wine House Leselidze 55

Elsewhere in Tbilisi
Alco Room Abanos 13
Diwine Metekhi Rise 2
Georgian Wine Culture Centre Bakhtrioni 11A
Vino Vera Chovelidze 3
Wine World at Lagidze 2

Winery outlets
Château Mukhrani Samghebro 6, Maidan Sq
Château Telavi Amagleba 21

Eniseli Gudiashvili 11
Gurjaani Paliashvili 66
Khareba Rustaveli 50
Khvanchkara Vazha-Pshavelas 41
Kindzmarauli Marani Chavchavadze Av 56
Marani Pushkin 19
Sachashniko Kostavas 60
Shumi Saburtalo 36A
Tibaani Janashia 18/11
Tolibashi Kazbegi 35A
Vazi + Tsinamdzgvrishvili 4; ☎65 8756; www.binekhi.ge. Stocks the Binekhi collection of wines, chahchas & liqueurs in addition to traditional wines like Saperavi, Tsinandali & Muzukani.

Wine bars
Georgian Accent Pushkin 25
Ghvino Underground Tabidze 15. See also page 106.
Schuchmann Sioni 8

BOOKS As well as those listed, other good bookshops are at Sharden 17 and Rustaveli 16.

Tbilisi SHOPPING

3

Biblus Books www.biblusi.ge. Branches at Rustaveli 40, Kostavas 47, Chavchavadze Av 10, Davit Agmashenebelis 121, the railway station foyer, major shopping centres & half a dozen sites across the city.

Caliban's Coffeehouse See page 107. The noticeboard is a good place to look for rooms, drivers & so on. Also found at Betsy's Hotel (page 100).

International House [84 B2] 26 May Sq 2; \ 94 0515. Well stocked with classics, modern literature & language-learning books.

Parnassus www.parnasi.ge. Branches at Leselidze 33 & Chavchavadze 22.

Prospero's Books [94 C3] In the courtyard at Rustaveli 34; \ 92 3592; e info@ properosbookshop.com; www.prosperosbookshop. com; ⊕ 09.30–21.00 daily. This is the best place for English-language guides & novels, as well as news magazines & maps; they also buy & sell secondhand books. There's also a branch at Betsy's Hotel (page 100).

MAPS For detailed Georgian maps, the best place to look is **Geoland** [94 F4] (*Telegrapis chichi 3, just off the right bank facing the Public Service Hall;* \ 92 1493, 92 2553; e info@geoland.ge; www.geoland.ge; ⊕ 10.00–19.00 Mon–Fri). It produces excellent 1:200,000 travel maps (GEL10, or GEL50 for all 6 covering the whole country), 12 1;50,000 hiking maps, a road map of the country and a Tbilisi map (all GEL10 each). They will also print off (in about 20 minutes) old Soviet military maps (with place names in Latin script, and a modern UTM grid) and other maps from the 1970s and 1980s. They also stock Garmin GPS gear and Camping Gaz canisters.

SOUVENIRS

Handicrafts For souvenirs such as daggers, drinking horns and national costume (page 79), look in the shop in the Opera underpass and the pavement in front of the Academy of Science, or the souvenir shops on Leselidze. For cloisonné enamel, try the galleries at Sharden 12 (⊕ *noon–19.00 daily*) and Erekle II 6 & 7 (⊕ *11.00–20.00 Mon–Sat*), or The Enamel Gallery in the courtyard next to Prospero's Books at Rustaveli 34. Artworks and handicrafts can also be bought at the following places.

Art Salons Shops at Baratashvili 12, Griboedov 11 & Davit Agmashenebelis 68

Caucasus Nature Jewels In the Tbilisi History Museum, Sioni 8; ⊕ closed Mon. Supports local artists & craftspeople & also national parks. Another branch in the Radisson Blu Hotel (page 99).

Maison Bleue [84 C3] Barnov 94, at the UN Circle; \ 35 9941; e tbmaisonbleue@yahoo.co.uk; ⊕ 11.00–18.00 daily. This produces high-class textiles, but there's also a small shop at Vertskhli 26, just off Leselidze, selling Georgian costumes.

Carpets Carpets are, of course, a speciality throughout the Middle East; although they're common in the Islamic countries, they are made in Georgia too. The best places to buy carpets (including Georgian ones) are across the Caspian in the bazaars of Bokhara, Ashgabat and other cities. As well as the places listed below, you can buy carpets at Leselidze 10, 27 and 42 (at Sioni), and under the Dry Bridge.

Caucasian Carpets [98 D2] Erekle II 8; m 577 753069; e carpetsgallery@posta.ge; ⊕ 10.00–20.00 daily.

Firma Narikala [98 E4] Abanos 1. Sells carpets, but is not as good as Maidan.

Maidan 91 [98 E3] On the south side of Gorgasali Sq, Samghebro 5; \ 72 3546. This is the best place in Tbilisi to buy a carpet. It has good pieces at very high prices which can be reduced with several days of bargaining.

SPORTS GEAR There are sports shops around the Dinamo Stadium, and there's also an Adidas outlet at Chavchavadze 58 and the Competitive World of Sport at Vazha-Pshavelas 12. The Magellan Sport Shop (*Mitskevich 68;* ✆ *37 1919; www. magelani.ge*) stocks a range of specialist gear for skiing, snowboarding, fishing and other outdoor pursuits.

A DAY'S TOUR OF TBILISI

This provides an outline of a tour of Tbilisi which should take about a day, although if you visit all the museums as you go around it'll take far longer; it can also be speeded up by taking minibuses along the main streets, and by omitting its western extremities.

THE OLD TOWN The Old Town of Tbilisi (the Kala) lies higgledy-piggledy on the crowded slopes between the river and the citadel of Narikala. Here, in an area inhabited, at various times, by Persians, Tatars, Jews and Armenians, you can visit a mosque, a synagogue, and Armenian and Georgian churches, all still in use, and a Roman Catholic church, built in 1804 and reconsecrated by the Pope in 1999.

Freedom Square to the Metekhi Bridge
The best starting point for a day walk is **Freedom Square** [98 B2] (Tavisuplebis Moedani), one of the busiest stations on the metro (which calls it Liberty Square). Laid out by the Russians between the 1820s and 1870s, it was originally known as Yerevan Square, then Theatre Square and was then Lenin Square until 1990; the statue of Lenin in its centre was replaced by a grassy roundabout, on the site of the city's first opera house, built in 1846 (the south wall was unearthed 30 years ago when the Rustaveli Avenue/Pushkin Street pedestrian underpass was built). A very tall column, the **Monument of Freedom and Victory**, with a kitschy gilded statue of St George and the Dragon by the sculptor Akaki Tsereteli atop it, now has pride of place in the centre of the square. The square is dominated by the **City Hall** [98 B2], built as a police station in the 1820s and remodelled in 1882–86 by the German architect Peter Stern, with a third storey and clock tower added in 1910–12; this is an attractive building with stripes of sandy green and white and mauresque stucco. The west side of the square was gutted in the civil war, but new buildings such as the Courtyard by Marriott Hotel have now filled the gap. To the northwest is Pushkin Square, really an extension of Freedom Square where the chaotic oriental bazaars were cleared away by Beria; now, old men play backgammon here beneath the trees and a bust of Pushkin. There's also a **tourist information office** here with plenty of free booklets, maps and helpful English-speaking staff, as well as the grave of Kamo, a Bolshevik activist who was killed by a car in 1922, in what was almost certainly a murder organised by Stalin. The **Art Museum** [94 B1] (pages 132–3) faces Pushkin Square, in a Neoclassical building which was built in 1827–34 as a hotel, then served as a seminary until 1908, and became an art gallery in 1933. Noe Zhordania, the prime minister of independent Georgia from 1918 to 1921, studied here, as did Stalin.

To the left of City Hall (across Dadiani Street), Leselidze Street leads down into the Old Town – it's recently been renamed Kote Apkhazi Street (as Konstantin Leselidze was a Soviet general), but even those who've noticed are ignoring the change. A 19th-century Russian construction, this was roughly the dividing line between the Upper and Lower parts of the Old Town and is now lined with souvenir shops and snack bars.

However, the Old Town's historic main street is Shavteli, parallel to the river; US$1.3 million has been spent to pedestrianise and beautify the pleasantly shabby area through which it runs. To reach it, continue down Pushkin (on the east side, opposite the Art Museum), on a walkway over the 12th–13th-century ruins of the

Dighomi Gate, unearthed only in 2012. The blocks on the west side of Pushkin date from the 1950s and 1960s, while on the east side many houses were built into the **city wall** in the 19th century and now host touristy restaurants, as well as a wedding registry. The west end of Shavteli is marked by the Misrule statue (seemingly children playing) that used to indicate the Children's Art Gallery and Dolls Museum; turning right you'll pass the rather contrived, surrealist tower of the **marionette theatre** [98 D1]; turning right again at the junction just beyond and then left, you'll come to the house-museum (rarely open) where the poet Nikoloz Baratashvili lived from 1841 to 1845.

Continuing on Shavteli, immediately on the left at No 7 is the **Anchiskhati Church** [98 D1], the oldest and one of the most loved in Tbilisi, with the best choir, singing on Saturdays (⊕ *16.00–19.00*) and Sundays (⊕ *09.00–noon*). Dating from the early 6th century, it's a three-nave basilica with two pairs of bare brick columns and stone walls flanking its narrow three-bay aisles. It has been rebuilt several times, most notably in 1675; the present frescoes (with wording in Old Church Slavonic script) probably date from the 18th century. Its name means 'the icon from Ancha', after a wonderful 6th-century icon in a golden frame (now in the National Museum), which was moved here in 1664 from Ancha, in Turkish-occupied territory. The gate-tower, with a residence above the gate, was built in 1675 and is most unusual with its Islamic-influenced brickwork.

Shavteli continues past an attractive park and an old people's home and chapel, before leading into **Erekle II Square** [98 D1], the historic centre of old Tbilisi, with a cast-iron fountain from France, once the site of open-air courts and punishment. On the north side of the square is the balconied palace of Giorgi XII (well restored but now semi-permanently closed); semi-underground towards the embankment are the remains of the 17th-century baths of King Rustum and Vakhtang VI's press (1709). To the east is the former governor's palace (built in 1802 and now a police building).

Passing through an ugly unfinished area at the rear of the Shangri-La casino, a path leads left to the **Peace Bridge** [98 D2], an arresting if somewhat over-sized footbridge, opened in 2010, which stretches across the Mtkvari River to Rikhe Park. The bridge is supposed to symbolise Georgia's transition from the past to a better future, but due to its unfortunate resemblance to a giant sanitary towel is referred to by some WAGs as 'Always Ultra'. Across the river, **Rikhe Park** [98 E3] was a resting place for camel caravans from Persia, and has recently been beautified with dancing fountains and quirky sculptures, as well as the giant 'tubes' of Saakashvili's performing arts centre, still standing closed. Remaining on the right bank, you'll enter **Erekle II Street**, now pedestrianised, with trendy art galleries and bars and lots of tables and chairs on the street; it's very nice at weekends, especially Sundays, the only time you see expats strolling in jeans instead of driving in 4x4s.

Forking left at the end of Erekle II on to Sionis Street (instead of joining Leselidze), you'll come to the **Sioni Cathedral** [98 D3], seat of the Catholicos of Georgia, who lives in the villa immediately to the west. The original Church of the Assumption was built between AD575 and 639, but little of that is left; the present church is a typical domed Georgian church built of tuff stone from Bolnisi in the 12th century, but it's nothing special architecturally. However, it is the centre of religious life in the city, partly due to the presence of St Nino's Cross, which she made by binding two vine branches together with her own hair (hence the drooping arms of the Georgian cross); a replica is displayed to the left of the iconostasis, but it's hard to see much as even this is in an ornate early 14th-century reliquary. The frescoes and iconostasis (1850–60) are by the Russian Grigori Gagarin. Across the road is the handsome bell-tower or *kolokolnaya*, the first example of Russian neoclassicism in Georgia but now in very poor repair; it was built in 1812 at the wish of the Russian viceroy prince Paul Tsitsiani, who had died in 1806 and been buried in the cathedral. This is also where the playwright Griboedov married Alexander Chavchavadze's daughter Nina. To the north of the cathedral (towards the river) is the original bell tower, built in the 13th century and 1425, and restored in 1939.

On the west/right side of Sioni (on either side of the kolokolnaya) are two caravanserais or trading centres for visiting merchants (at numbers 36 and 40), supposedly being restored, and then on the left at No 8 is the Tbileli caravanserai or **Carvasla** [98 D3], built in 1650, rebuilt in the 1820s and again in 1912 with an Art Nouveau façade, which now houses the Museum of the History of Tbilisi (page 134). The interior has a high atrium and three galleries overlooking a fountain, which was once a drinking pool for pack animals. Immediately beyond, on the left, Bambis Rigi curves right to continue as Rkinis Rigi to the Metekhi Bridge; parallel to the right is Sharden Street (named after the French traveller Jean-Baptiste Chardin, who visited Tbilisi in 1671). This area is packed with rather commercial bars, restaurants and art galleries; in particular on Bambis Rigi, a wonderful unified piece of Art Nouveau architecture (1905), has been ruined by tasteless clutter.

Maidan and Abanotubani At the end of Sharden, steps lead up to **Gorgasali Square** [98 E3], popularly known as the Maidan, at the west end of the Metekhi Bridge. In medieval times this was the site of the city's bazaar, and it is still surrounded by Silversmiths' Street, Blacksmiths' Street and so on, marking where various trades were once concentrated. There were two bridges across the Mtkvari here, and a mosque, until 1951 when Beria replaced them with the present Metekhi Bridge; but when the river is low the foundations are still visible to the west. Just to the left of the south side of the square is the **Armenian Church of St George** [98 E4], founded by the Armenian merchant Umek in 1251, although what you see now is largely 18th century and fairly standard in form, apart from the choir gallery. Continuing eastwards on Samghebro, the first turning to the right leads up to the **Narikala Citadel** [98 E4] (page 127); you'll emerge on Botanikuri, which leads steeply up the hill to the right through the old Azeri quarter to (as you might expect) the **Botanic Gardens** [98 C4] (pages 135–6), passing the **Sunni mosque** [98 E4], the only one left in the city (with Sunni and Shia now worshipping together), at No 32. Built in 1895, it's red brick with a relatively discreet minaret, opposite a memorial to the Turkish artist Ibrahim Isfahanli (1897–1967).

Immediately across Botanikuri, beyond the carpet shop, is Abanos kucha, named after the **bathhouses** [98 E4] found here. At the end of the road just to the right you'll see the most striking bathhouse, the late 17th-century Chreli ('Motley') Baths (famously visited by Pushkin in 1829), with a façade of bright-blue tiles and two short minarets, recalling the design of a mosque. The other old bathhouses are underground, their presence betrayed only by rows of brick domes which you can walk over. The oldest surviving is the Erekle, on the corner of Abanos and Akhundov; opposite this is the early 17th-century Simbatov baths, while the 18th-century Bebutov baths are on Akhundov. In 1817 Sir Robert Ker Porter, court painter to Alexander I, was able to bribe his way into the women's baths and was shocked to find that 'they seemed to have as little modest covering on their minds as on their bodies'. The area immediately around the bathhouses and mosque has long been at the centre of the city's **Azeri quarter**: the small park in front of the bathhouses bears the name and bronze bust of Heydar Aliyev, the former president of Azerbaijan. In 2011–12 this area was nicely repaved and pedestrianised, with the

Tsavkisistksali riverbed opened up, creating a pleasant promenade up the gorge to a waterfall below the Botanic Gardens.

South of Gorgasali Square and Narikala Returning to the Maidan, there are two churches at this end of Leselidze, the first of which is the Georgian **Jvaris-Mama Church** [98 D3], built in the 16th century and modified in 1825; it's small and tall, with a gravel floor and interior walls now repainted, and a brick iconostasis. The other, larger, church is the Armenian **Norashen Church** [98 D3], built in 1793 and now closed for repairs. The **synagogue** [98 D3] (1913) at Leselidze 47 has a blue and gold lower hall for daily services (at 09.00) and a brighter upper hall with large chandeliers for Sabbath and festivals. In the courtyard of Leselidze 28, there's also the Bet Rachel or Ashkenazi synagogue, reopened in 2009.

For the best sense of how Tbilisi's Old Town used to be, you should explore the back alleys of **Kala**, on either side of Leselidze. Many of the buildings here fell into poor repair in the latter part of the 20th century, due to neglect and earthquakes, and the area was placed on the list of the world's most endangered monuments and sites. There's been extensive restoration work in the last few years, but under Saakashvili this too often involved demolition and rebuilding with a pastiche version of the original façade and balconies. It's still possible to get a feel for how life used to be in this densely populated area, with its narrow winding streets and multi-storey houses with *musharabi* balconies and stained-glass windows overlooking courtyards. Historically, Kala fell into two parts – Zemo Ubani (the Upper District) centred on Batonis Moedani (King's Square, now Erekle II Square) and the largely Armenian Kvemo Ubani (the Lower District) around Tsikhis Moedani (Fortress Square, now Vakhtang Gorgasali Square) up to Narikala.

The Betlemi area, on the slope below the Narikala Fortress, has been inhabited since the 5th century but the oldest houses now extant date from the 17th century, and most are 19th century, with far older churches hidden in between. From Leselidze, take Asatianis kucha (formerly Bebutov) up to the left of the Jvaris-Mama and Norashen churches; there are good Moderne (Art Nouveau) buildings at Asatiani 38, 44, 50 and 66. You'll pass the tiny Tumanian Square on the left and soon emerge into Puris (Bread) Square, which is not much bigger. From the corner of Asatiani and Betlemi you can climb steps to the **Ateshga or Fire Worshippers' Temple** [98 C4], a rock-cut altar built by the Persians between the 5th and 7th centuries, and converted to a mosque in the 17th century. From here, an alley leads on to the **Upper and Lower Betlemi (Bethlehem) churches** [98 C4] (founded in the 7th century but both now largely 18th century, and both painted inside in the last few years). There's a bell tower to the east of the upper church, and there is a fine view from its charming garden over the roofs and wooden balconies of the Kala and across the river to the Presidential Palace and Sameba Cathedral. Just behind the church you'll find steps leading up to the *Mother Georgia* statue. More steps lead down to the lower church and back to Asatiani; at No 28 is the striking former Girls' College (opposite the end of Dadiani, which leads to Freedom Square), now the Tbilisi Institute of Law and Economics. Immediately north of Asatiani on Machabeli are two of the earliest and most exuberant examples of Art Nouveau in Tbilisi: No 13 was built in 1905 for the cognac magnate Davit Sarajashvili who left it to the Writers' Union; and No 11, Beria's residence in the 1930s, now houses the **Georgian Olympic Committee and museum** (⊕ *10.00–17.00 Mon–Fri; free*), which has lots of interesting electronic displays (and wrestling videos) but only in Georgian, alas.

It's three blocks further downhill to Gudiashvili Square, currently the Ground Zero of dereliction and neglect – bizarrely, the city has created a tranquil haven in the centre of the square, while the buildings around it are collapsing. The most notorious is No 2, the **Lermontov House** (one of the city's finest balconied houses, built in the 1830s), where the writer stayed in 1837. Continuing from the square downhill and at once turning left, you can go back down Anton Katolikos to Leselidze, through a nicely restored area with the new Georgian Museum of Jewish History (not yet open at the time of writing).

Garetubani and the Dry Bridge If you go down Pushkin from Freedom Square to Baratashvili Street (leading to the **Baratashvili Bridge** [94 F4], rebuilt in 1966 as the Stalin Bridge, with a lower urine-stinking pedestrian level) and turn left, you'll pass the city's former central market, the former US embassy (in the splendid 1860s Orbeliani Palace) at the foot of 9 April Park, and the **Dry Bridge** or Mshrale Khidi (1851); this crosses a former channel of the Mtkvari (now a busy highway) to **Dedaena Park** [94 F3] (formerly Madatov Island), where artists display and sell their works en plein air and there is a street market devoted to Soviet-era bric-a-brac on the road above. Returning by the river towards Baratashvili Bridge, the new **Public Service Hall** [94 F3] (also known as the House of Justice) appears to have been air-dropped in, with its parachutes (more often compared to mushrooms) still on the roof. It's actually bustling and very useful, with fast, corruption-free service (*www.my.gov.ge*).

THE NEW TOWN
Rustaveli Avenue Rustaveli Avenue (Rustavelis Gamziri in Georgian) leads off to the northwest from Freedom Square. Laid out in 1810, almost 1.5km long and lined with plane trees, it's a fine, stately avenue that's spoilt by the amount of traffic roaring up and down it these days. There are pedestrian underpasses, but not many and not at the metro stations. On the north/right side at No 3 is the **National Museum** [98 B1] (pages 131–2), built in 1923–29, that houses the national collections of archaeology, history, natural history and ethnography, based on the collections of the Caucasian Museum, founded in 1852. A treasury houses a superb collection of pre-Christian gold; jewellery and icons from the Christian era are in the treasury of the Art Museum. Just beyond the museum is the **Rustaveli Cinema** [94 E4], built in 1939 by Nikolai Severov (who also designed the National Museum), with idealised statues of Soviet youth on the façade. Behind them is the **National Library**, housed in three imposing former banks (all built 1907–15) along Gudiashvili Street; the easternmost block is a fascinating neo-Romanesque creation with lovely murals on its ceiling (including an external arcade). Below the library is the **Old Trinity Church** [94 E4] (built in 1790, with more recent frescoes and a Baroque iconostasis), busy with weddings at weekends.

Immediately on the left at the start of Rustaveli is a modern trade centre, with the **Griboedov Russian Theatre** [98 B1] behind it; originally a caravanserai, there's been a theatre here since 1845. At its far end is the Freedom Square metro station at Rustaveli 6, and steps up to the Chancellery, then Rustaveli rises to the Young People's Palace, built in 1807 as the Russian **Viceroy's Palace** [98 B1], with an arcade in front added in 1865–68. Stalin installed his mother here at one time and it then served as the Pioneers' Palace, housing the Soviet youth organisation and a Museum of Children's Toys. It's still used for youth activities, and is the best place to find classes and displays of Georgian folk dance and the like.

Beyond this is easily the most dominating building on Rustaveli, the **Parliament Building** [94 E4]. This was built as a U-shaped block in 1938 (on the site of the Alexander Nevsky Church, built in the 19th century for the Russian army); a very solid portico of tuff was built by German prisoners of war and the building opened in 1953. It was on the steps before the Parliament that the massacre of 9 April 1989 took place, and you'll still see memorials to the dead here. This was also the focus of the civil war, with Gamsakhurdia and his supporters holed up inside; the side wings were gutted, but the portico resisted the National Guard's shellfire, giving rise to comments on the superiority of German building to Soviet efforts. It stands opposite the site of the Artists' House and the lovely Hotel Intourist (built in the 1870s), both sadly destroyed in the civil war; a new national art gallery is being built here, as part of a future Museums District.

Immediately beyond the Parliament is the **Classical Gymnasium** [94 E4] or High School No 1, founded in 1802 as the first European-style high school in Transcaucasia; it educated many of the leading figures of recent Georgian history, including Kostavas, Gamsakhurdia, Sigua and Kitovani. It's a good example of Russian neoclassicism, with statues of Ilia Chavchavadze and Akaki Tsereteli (1958) in front; you might want to look inside and enquire about the Museum of Education housed there, although it's unlikely to be open. A plaque commemorates those killed by Soviet security forces on 9 March 1956.

At No 9 on the north side is the **Kashveti Church of St George** [94 E4], built in 1904–10 by the German Leopold Bielfeld, on the site of a 6th-century church demolished as unsafe at the end of the 19th century. It was based on the 11th-century church of Samtavisi, and the altar apse was decorated in 1946 by Lado Gudiashvili (who lived just behind the church and for his pains was expelled from the Communist Party and lost his job at the Academy of Art). There's a separate church in the crypt, used for Russian-language services. Henry Mowatt, a Scottish engineer who worked on the Surami rail tunnel and married a Georgian, is buried here.

The attractive 9 April (formerly Alexandrov) Park is behind the church (with decent public toilets), and next to it, at Rustaveli 11, is the **National Gallery** [94 E4] (page 134) in a fine building known as the Khram Slavi (Temple of Glory), built in 1885, with a modern rear extension added in 2011. Beyond this, at No 15 (opposite the 1950s Ministry of Transport and Communications) is the Hotel Tbilisi, built in 1915 as the Hotel Majestic and gutted in the civil war. It reopened in 2002 as the luxurious Marriott Hotel (page 99). Behind it at Chanturia (formerly Georgiashvili) 8 is the **State Literature Museum** [94 E3] (✆ 99 8667; ⊙ 10.00–18.00 Tue–Sat), a nice 19th-century building facing the park, which houses temporary art shows, although the literature displays are closed.

Beyond the hotel, at No 17, is the splendid French neoclassical façade of the famous **Rustaveli Theatre** [94 E3], built in 1899–1901 and refurbished in 1920–21 for the new Rustaveli Theatre Company and again in 2002–05. It boasts marble staircases, classical statues, and frescoes by Lado Gudiashvili, Moise Toidze and David Kakabadze in the Kimerioni (Chimera) café. Rustaveli 19 was built as the Palace Hotel in 1910; No 27 (built in 1909 as a military school, then the national archives) houses the new **Museum of Modern Art-Tbilisi** [94 D3] (*www.momatbilisi.ge*; ⊙ 11.00–18.00 Tue–Sun, noon–19.00 in summer; GEL3) created by the ubiquitous Zurab Tsereteli (page 48). There are temporary displays by other artists on the ground floor, with Tsereteli's powerful paintings and sculptures in the large upstairs space; a mezzanine displays lots of photos of him schmoozing with the famous and powerful.

On the south side of the avenue, behind Rustaveli 24 at Griboedov 8, stands the **Conservatoire** [94 D3] (music college), built in 1904; there's a museum (*in room*

301, up one flight and at the end of the corridor to the right; ⊕ *noon–17.00 Mon–Fri; free*) with Rachmaninov's piano and lots of vintage photos and drawings of opera sets. On the ground floor at the east end of the building are the newly refurbished Grand Hall and a lovely chamber recital hall where Horowitz played. The poet Titsian Tabidze lived at Griboedov 18 from 1921 to 1937, where his friend Boris Pasternak allegedly did many of his translations of Georgian poetry. The imposing Supreme Court stands on the next street uphill, Brothers Zubelashvili. You can continue along Griboedov to Rose Revolution Square, passing the **Academy of Arts** [94 D3] at No 22 – a very fine building erected in 1858, with a display of students' work upstairs; there are rather splendid murals in the hall and mosaics above the staircase.

If you continue from the theatre along the north side of Rustaveli, you'll pass the permanent crowd of smoking students outside the Georgian State Institute of Theatrical Arts and come to the **Zakaria Paliashvili State Opera House** [94 D3] at No 25. Founded in 1851 and burnt down in 1874, it was replaced with the present Moorish building in 1880–96; it saw the start of Shalyapin's career before it too burnt down again in 1973. It was rebuilt in 1977, and is currently closed for another refurbishment (but will reopen very soon). On the first floor are a few cases of memorabilia of Zacharia Paliashvili's operas. Outside is a statue of Paliashvili (by Merab Berdzenishvili, 1973); this is next to his grave and that of Vano Saradzishvili, the first great Georgian singer. On the same side of Rustaveli, at No 29, is an imposing colonnaded building built in 1938 as the **Institute of Marxism–Leninism (IMELI)** [94 D3], which housed the obligatory Lenin Museum, with a copy of his Kremlin study; there are four blank cartouches high on the façade where the heads of Marx, Engels, Lenin and Stalin were removed in 1991. It was the seat of the State Council when Shevardnadze returned to take power, then the constitutional court, before it was sold to developers who removed the roof, expecting the building to collapse and allow them to raze it and replace it. It failed to oblige, and public outcry finally forced them to restore it, while building an ugly tower (to be a Millennium hotel) at the rear that will blight the whole city. Beyond this is a brutalist block built in the late 1970s, housing the main post and telephone offices and the PostBank. Opposite at Rustaveli 42 was the first major Soviet public building in Tbilisi, constructed in 1926–28; it's also brutalist plain concrete but with a few Neoclassical details, and very modern for the period, perhaps influenced by Czech functionalism.

Here, the modern plaza of Rose Revolution Square opens up to the right while Rustaveli kinks to the left past the **Academy of Sciences** [94 C2], a large, pompous building (built in 1953–58) in which 7,000 research staff once laboured. In its courtyard is a flattened, circular building (1960) housing the terminal of the cable-car to Mtatsminda, built in 1958 with British cables and closed in the early 1990s after collapsing. The avenue ends at the small **Rustaveli Square** [94 C2], on the site of the former Moscow Gates, where a statue of the poet (by Koté Merabishvili, 1937) now stands by the Rustaveli metro station, next to Tbilisi's first McDonald's. Above this is **Vere**, an attractive district that is popular with younger expats and professionals.

Rose Revolution Square to the Philharmonic Rose Revolution Square [94 C2] (then Republic Square) was laid out in 1981, above a road underpass and a shopping complex (now closed and very dark); in 1991 it was the rallying point for the opposition to Gamsakhurdia. It's now been pleasantly landscaped, with metal planters and wooden benches, and offers fine views across the city to the High Caucasus (to the northwest). To the north is the high-rise glass tower of the

Radisson Blu Iveria, the product of a total renovation of a very run-down Soviet-period hotel built in 1967 that was inhabited, for many years, by the internally displaced and refugees from Abkhazia. At the west end of the square, most traffic swings left to Rustaveli Square; ahead are two minor streets, Kiacheli (to the right) and Akhvlediani (still better known as Perovskaya), lined with some of the city's liveliest pubs. Confusingly, the Elena Akhvlediani house-museum, one of the most enjoyable in the city, is at Kiacheli 12. Traffic from Rustaveli Square passes under the Rose Revolution Square plaza and drops down Vere Hill to the Marjanishvili Bridge, leading to the left/north bank of the Mtkvari.

The city's main traffic axis continues west as Kostavas kucha (the former Lenin Street), and soon splits in front of the striking circular building of the **Philharmonic** [94 B1], otherwise known as the Tbilisi Concert Hall, built in 1969–71, largely of glass; a bronze sculpture, *The Muse* (1971, by Merab Berdzenishvili), stands in front of it. To the right/north of the square in front of the Philharmonic is the **Vere (formerly Kirov) Park** [94 C1]; to the right in the park (ie: at the end of Kiacheli) you'll find a flight of steps that descend to the petrol station on the embankment road, passing the **Lurdzhi Monastery** [94 C1], and the very Russian **Church of St John the Theologian** [94 C1] (1901) next to it. The Lurdzhi Church is smaller, and can be identified by the faded blue roof that gives it its name. Built in 1155 and rebuilt in the 16th and 17th centuries, it's high with virtually no nave, and an unusual round cupola added in 1873; it's richly decorated and a modern belfry has been added. In communist times it housed a museum of medicine, while the Russian church was quite clearly left untouched; now the tables are turned and it's the Russian church that externally looks abandoned. This is entered from the far side and is painted in eggshell blue and white, with a gold iconostasis that just manages not to be too over the top. From here you can go up to the Vere district (page 123), or continue to the newer parts of the city.

Around 26 May Square Forking right in front of the Philharmonic (behind which is Phikris Gora or Dream Hill, an enclave of nice hotels), Kostavas soon drops down to the ugly roundabout, underpass and flyovers of **Heroes' Square** [84 C3] (Gmirta Moedani), in a ravine filled in in the 1930s; there's a modern white obelisk in the centre and an Eternal Flame with guards at the heroes' memorial. To its left is the **zoo** [84 C3] (page 136) and the Mziuri (Sunshine) children's park, and to the right is the **circus** [84 C2] (built in 1940) and (by some massive new tower blocks) the bridge across the Mtkvari to Tamar Mepis Gamziri (Queen Tamar Avenue) and the railway station [84 C1]. Carrying on straight ahead, Kostavas climbs again past some very decent Stalinist/Neoclassical buildings to **26 May Square** [84 B2], laid out from 1940, with the Sports Palace (1961; with a statue of a buff naked athlete in front) and the Technical University metro station to its right and the high-rise Holiday Inn ahead (this was the Hotel Adjara, cleared of refugees in 2005, totally rebuilt and re-opened in 2010). The main road continues to the left of the hotel as Pekini Avenue, passing through the affluent but unlovely Saburtalo district and becoming the main road towards Mtskheta. To the right of the hotel, Kostavas leads to the main building of **Georgia Technical University** [84 B2], a fine white-and-ochre Neoclassical pile, behind which the Saakashvili Presidential Library overlooks the Vakhushti Bridge, crossing to Didube on the left bank.

Vake The Vake (Plain) district is the city's most affluent area, with many of its best restaurants and patisseries on streets such as Abashidze, parallel to the left of Chavchavadze. The district was built by Beria on top of the mass graves of the victims of his purges; the Bolsheviks executed many of the Georgian aristocracy here in 1923, and a public toilet was built on the site, now replaced by a memorial. Vake was once home to the communist bourgeoisie, and now, because it still has the city's best phone/internet and power supplies, is home to most of the city's expatriates and NGOs.

Forking left in front of the Philharmonic, Melikishvili kucha (widened in 1948) leads past the massive Soviet-era ex-Hotel Sakartvelo and the Tbilisi No.1 wine cellars to the **Tbilisi State University** [84 C3], the country's leading academic institution, housed in a fine domed building built in 1900–16, as well as some rather less attractive blocks behind this and a large modern complex on the western edge of the city, beyond Saburtalo. There's always a crowd of students blocking the pavement here, a great social coming and going which is the nearest thing to a *passeggiata* that Tbilisi offers. The main road continues west as Ilia Chavchavadze Avenue, lined with upmarket shops and coffee bars. To the right at No 21, marked with a jokey statue, there's an entrance to the **Mziuri Park** [84 B3] (pleasant but with an unfinished feel, and surrounded by tatty high-rises), and nearby the statues of the poets Galaction Tabidze and David Guramishvili (1966, by the omnipresent Merab Berdzenishvili).

After 3.8km (with frequent buses) Chavchavadze finally reaches Victory Square (Gamarjvebis Moedani), overlooking **Vake Park** [84 A4] to the left/south. This is a spacious and well-tended area of 226ha, where the grave of the Unknown Soldier lies at the foot of a flight of steps up to the statue of Victory, erected in 1976. A derelict cable-car rises over the park to Kus Tba (Turtle Lake), where there are cafés. There's a small charge for swimming, which is good if you can avoid being run down by a pedalo (*GEL20/hr*) or row boat (*GEL8/hr*). The lake can also be reached by a 3km road, from just beyond the park, halfway along which is the open-air **Museum of Georgian Folk Architecture and Daily Life** [84 A4] (page 134), which has a restaurant with a great view. There's also the Squirrels' Park, opened in 2006, with free children's games and wooden picnic huts. Just beyond the park, at the western end of Chavchavadze Avenue, is the **Vake Cemetery** [84 A4], with its tall cypresses, grand tombstones and ivy-clad mausoleums, which featured as a setting for the 2013 film *Repentance*. The main road climbs through pine forest to the so-called 'mountain resort quarter' of Tskhneti (now swamped by tasteless dachas built with illegal money after 'accidentally' burning down an area of forest) and to Manglisi and Akhalkalaki.

OTHER AREAS It is of course possible to extend this brief tour of Tbilisi in various directions if you have the time and stamina.

Mtatsminda If you turn right/south from Kostavas up Tamriko Tshovelidze (still better known as Belinskis), you can turn left on to Gogebashvili and at its end right onto Makashvili, which runs along the slopes of Mtatsminda. With wide views over the city, Makashvili then Chonkadze pass the Russian church of St Michael of Tver (1910) and a few houses before reaching the crossroads just below the **Mamadaviti (Father David) Monastery** [94 C4], up a few tight cobbled hairpin bends. It's named after St David, one of the Syrian Fathers, who lived here in a cave in the 6th century before moving on to Davit-Gareja (pages 285–8). The present church was built in 1859–79, in plain brick on an artificial terrace. However, what's of interest here is the **Pantheon** [94 C4] or graveyard, a repository of the remains of the leading figures of Georgian culture. These include the poets Nikoloz Baratishvili, Galaction Tabidze, Akaki Tsereteli and Georgi Leonidze, painter Lado Gudiashvili, dissident Merab Kostava and educationalists, critics and philosophers such as Iacob Gogebashvili,

Niko Nikoladze and Vazha-Pshavelas, as well as Stalin's mother. Grottoes in the cliff face house the Russian playwright Griboedov and his widow Nina, daughter of Alexander Chavchavadze, and the secular saint Ilia Chavchavadze (no relation).

A little further along Chonkadze is the mosque-like lower terminal of the Mtatsminda **funicular** [84 D4] (⊕ *09.00–04.00 daily; GEL2 each way, midnight–04.00 GEL3; you need to buy a stored-credit card per group for this & the amusement park rides*) which was built in 1903–05 by Belgian engineers, an odd contribution from so flat a country, and recently rebuilt; it climbs at 55° for 5 minutes (with a path winding up and criss-crossing it) to reach its upper terminal, at an altitude of 727m on the edge of Mtatsminda, the Holy Mountain, so called because of St David's Cave. Above the terminal is the vast restaurant complex (⚲ 98 0000; www.funicular.ge) built by Beria (an 80m-high statue of Stalin was planned on top). The Funicular Restaurant (⊕ *18.00–midnight*) is the best here, with the cafeteria-style Puri Guliani (⊕ *13.00–midnight*), serving a great range of snacks such as khachapuris on the other side, and a lounge bar and terrace above (⊕ *18.00–02.00*).

There are other restaurants in the spacious but rather lame **amusement park** (*www.park.ge;* ⊕ *summer 11.00–04.00 daily, 11.30–21.00 Sat–Sun, from 11.00 winter*) behind the terminal, with attractions such as a rollercoaster, water ride, climbing wall, trampolines and ice rink that all have to be paid for (GEL1–2) with the stored-credit card. The main attractions are, in fact, the stunning views (as far as Kazbek, weather permitting, best seen from the Ferris wheel) and the fact that in summer the temperature is up to 5°C cooler than the city, so that it's lively until 04.00. Behind it is the massive TV Tower, like a 210m oil rig visible from all over the city; this had lurid flashing lights put up for Christmas in 2005, and they have not been turned off since. The Pantheon and Funicular Restaurant (and the Kartlis-Deda statue, Parliament, Presidential Palace, Chancery, Peace Bridge and Sameba, Sioni and Mtskheta churches) are also lit at night.

Buses 90 and 124 come up here from the city; there's an ATM and ticket office at the bus terminal. Otherwise, it's a pleasant 20-minute walk through pine woods to reach the Kojori road. If you happen to be coming up by car, it's a very sharp right turn into the park at a no-entry sign, virtually opposite a yard with a wire sculpture of an elephant with a mahout on its back.

East to Ortachala From Gorgasali Square, the main road to the east along the Mtkvari embankment is Gorgasalis kucha, built in 1851 as Vorontsov ulitsa. About 100m beyond the bathhouses it passes the kneeling statue of the painter Pirosmani (1975, by Elgudja Amashukeli), the Tbilisi Balneologic Health Resort (founded in 1938 by Shevardnadze's father, and apparently run now by Saakashvili's father!) and at No 17 the **Akhundov Museum of Azerbaijan Culture** [84 F4] (⚲ 72 1571; www.azmuseum.ge; ⊕ *10.00–18.00 Tue–Sun; free*). This is part of a newly renovated complex with wine-bar, café and art gallery, in the house where the writer Mirza Fatali Akhundzade (1812–78) lived from 1834. Not far beyond is the huge Azerbaijan embassy and then the '300 Aragveli' monument, a 23m-high stela raised in 1961 on the spot where, in 1795, King Erekle II was rescued from Aga Mohammed Khan by 300 men from the Aragvi Valley (on the Georgian Military Highway), who were all killed in the process. This was also the scene of one of the closer assassination attempts on Shevardnadze. Note that the 300 Aragveli metro station is actually on the far side of the river.

Continuing eastwards, you'll pass the equestrian statue (1982) of Pyotr Bagration, who distinguished himself in the campaign against Napoleon in 1812. To the left is the Ortachala Dam, and on the cliff top beyond this is the former **Palace of Weddings** [84 G3]. Built by the communists in 1984 to attract couples away from church weddings, it's very modernist, but with a classical statue (of a naked male) in front of the blatantly phallic carillion tower. The palace was bought in 2002 and used as a private mansion by the reclusive oligarch Badri Patarkatsishvili until his death in 2008, and its future is now uncertain. It can be reached by going straight across the road from the 300 Aragveli metro station, but you can no longer get inside.

To the east, the road now follows the course of the channel that used to make a small island, past the Finance and Justice ministries, the Public Prosecutor's Office and the city's main prison. The **Krtsanisi Palace**, built by Beria and home to the president until Shevardnadze neglected to move out, is hidden away just to the south. In fact, Saakashvili refused to move in, preferring to build the new Avlabari Residence. This area is becoming the new embassy quarter, with the British, Germans and Swiss moving here. The highway continues past the Ortachala bus station, built in 1973 to replace the cramped former terminal by the Marjanishvili Bridge; however, most bus services use the chaotic yard at Didube, and Ortachala's echoing hall is used mainly by international services, to Azerbaijan, Armenia and Turkey. On the façade you can see *The Wheel*, a mosaic by Zurab Tsereteli; to the rear there's another fine mosaic (1979) on a fire station.

Beyond Ortachala the main road continues along the river and then splits, to Rustavi and Baku to the left, and Marneuli and Yerevan to the right.

Narikala Perhaps the best way to reach *Mother Georgia* and the Sololaki Ridge is by the cable-car (☉ *11.00–23.00; GEL1 with MetroMoney card only*) from Rikhe Park to Narikala, opened in 2012; this gives great views, especially from the one car with a glass floor, although the journey takes under 2 minutes. Otherwise your options are the steps and pathway up from the Upper Betlemi Church; Orbiri Street, climbing steeply from near the Armenian church to the Narikala Citadel; or Sololaki Lane, a road, lined with lime and cypress trees, that turns off the Kojori Highway and passes beneath the eyesore of Ivanishvili's business centre with its flying saucer helipad. It takes 5 minutes to reach the ruins of some medieval fortifications and a view to the right over the Botanic Gardens (there's a turnstile and a rough path down); and the 20m-high aluminium statue of *Kartlis-Deda* or *Mother Georgia*, visible from all over the city. There's a great view down to the Old Town, marred by huge amounts of litter; there are lots of charms tied on a tree behind the statue. This was made in 1958–63 by Elgudja Amashukeli; sword in one hand and bowl in the other, it shows Georgia as hospitable but ready to defend herself. Also nearby are the ruins of the ancient Shakhtakhi Fort (from 'Sahis Tahti' or Throne of the Shah), which was used as an observatory in the 7th–9th centuries.

Heading east along the ridge, you'll pass the cable-car terminal then fork left onto a rough path around to the gate of the **Narikala Citadel** [98 E4]. This was built in about AD360 by the Persians (who called it Shuris-tsihke), expanded by King David the Builder and restored by Mustafa Pasha's Turks in the second half of the 16th century, before being ruined by an earthquake in 1827. It's always open and entry is free, although there's a minimal charge for parking. Locals often come up here for picnics and to enjoy the evening views of the city. Near the car park is the 12th-century **Church of St Nicholas**, rebuilt in 1997, with a painted interior and a simple, modern, stone iconostasis. The fort walls are either over-restored or untouched; you can walk along the battlements, although there are some very steep steps. At the citadel's south end, you'll see the square Istanbul tower which was a prison under Turkish rule.

The left bank of the Mtkvari The left or north bank of the Mtkvari is, with the exception of the Metekhi Church and the area immediately behind it, relatively recently developed; although it contains little of touristic interest, there is much of practical use here. Its heart is the area to the south of the railway station, along Davit Agmashenebelis Gamziri (David the Builder Avenue), laid out by German colonists in the 19th century.

Avlabari To the east, the highway from the airport and Kakheti runs in alongside the railway and then turns and dives under it to turn right on to Ketevan Tsamebulis Gamziri, just east of the Sheraton Metechi Palace Hotel, and then Avlabari Square and metro station, the heart of Tbilisi's Armenian quarter. At its west end is the Echmiadzin Church, named after the Armenian equivalent of Canterbury; built in 1804, it was cracking apart due to vibration from the metro trains passing underneath, but has recently been repaired.

To the left, Meskhishvili leads towards the massive new **Sameba (Trinity) Cathedral** [84 F2] on Mount Elia, begun in 1995 and finished in 2004. Regarded as an eyesore by many people, it is equally venerated by many others, who cross themselves whenever they glimpse it on the far side of the city. It was built on the Armenian Khojavank cemetery, which was treated with a scandalous lack of respect. It's the largest religious building in the Southern Caucasus, with an interior area of 2,380m². It's certainly way out of scale for a Georgian church, even though it's in an exaggerated traditional Georgian style; a long esplanade with fountains leads past a belfry to the cathedral with a sort of triple-decked west end. The apses are very high but the windows only reach two-fifths of the way up; the dome is supported by eight freestanding pillars. The interior is now full of icons, priests and people; there are five additional chapels in the crypt.

Opposite the Armenian church, a flight of steps and an alleyway lead to the Chapel of the Transfiguration, set on the battlements of the **Sachino Palace** [98 F3]; although the Avlabari cliffs have long been fortified, all that remains is this chapel and a round pavilion both built in 1776 for Queen Darejdan, wife of Erekle II. They're set in an attractive garden, from which there are views stretching from the bathhouses to Tbilisi State University. The chapel has a simple, vaulted nave and sanctuary with a very low dome at the west end under a belfry with external bell ropes. There are some early 20th-century frescoes, and plenty of whitewashed areas.

The Metekhi Church There are two routes from here to the Metekhi Church [98 E3]. Firstly, you can go back down the steps and turn left and left again down Ghvinis Aghmarti (Wine Hill), a steepish street that drops down below the walls of the Sachino Palace, mostly made of rows of riverbed stones alternating with double rows of brick. Alternatively, you can head east along an alley to turn right onto Metekhi Street, and then right down Metekhi Rise, lined on the left with the fine merchants' homes (now hotels and restaurants) whose triple-decker balconies you may already have admired from across the river. In either case you'll end up at the north end of the Metekhi church precincts, set on a crag over the Mtkvari; the view of this church, with the equestrian statue of Vakhtang Gorgasali (1967) overlooking the city he founded, is one of the most widespread images of Tbilisi.

The earliest churches on this site were built in the 5th and 8th centuries, but the present Church of the Virgin was built in 1278–89 by King Demetre II the Self-Sacrificer (so called because he answered a summons by the Mongols to near-certain death rather than cause an invasion). The ground plan is actually quite complex, with a cross filled out to a square, and lateral apses projecting at the eastern end. Four free-standing pillars support a central dome (rebuilt in 1748). The external stonework is very worn, and the interior is bare.

The present churchyard was long occupied by a castle which was ruined by Shah Aga Mohammed Khan in 1795 and rebuilt in 1819 as a prison, which housed Beria's offices and less willing guests such as Kalinin, Gorki and Kamo, the last of whom escaped down the cliff on half a dozen sheets tied together. This was demolished in 1937 when the present bridge and the Mtkvari embankment road were built. The church was used as a youth theatre until it was finally restored for worship in 1988. Below, by the bridge, is the tiny chapel of St Abo Tbileli (a 7th-century Arab convert, killed here by Muslims), recently built by hand.

Upstream, beyond the Europe Square roundabout at the north end of the Metekhi Bridge and the mouth of the tunnel under the Avlabari Cliffs, is Rikhe Park, site of the **Tbilisoba Festival** on the last weekend of October (page 110), when stages are set up for performers and the whole area is hidden by the smoke from shashlik stalls (also up on Rose Revolution Square); this was a scruffy area but is now very attractive. You'll see the Narikala cable-car terminal and the Peace Bridge (page 118), and beyond them, the giant 'tubes' of Saakashvili's performing arts centre, still standing closed. To the right, Baratashvili Hill descends to the bridge of the same name from Avlabari Square; to the north, looking down on the bridge, is Saakashvili's new presidential palace with its striking egg-shaped glass cupola, like a mini-Bundestag. There has been much speculation as to how much this building cost, although Saakashvili himself claims it was a mere GEL13 million; it may be used to house a new Technological University. This part of Avlabari is prone to earthquakes and was rather run-down, but is now seeing some regeneration on the back of the palace and the Sameba Cathedral, with quite a few small new hotels opening. You can get here from the north side of the Echmiadzin Church along Meskhishvili and to the left.

Just west, Akhvlediani Hill (formerly Uritskis Hill) leads down to the river beyond the Baratashvili Bridge and a nice little park with a statue of the poet Nikoloz Baratashvili, by Boris Tsibadze (1975).

Chugureti To the west is the Chugureti district, largely settled by Germans and Poles from around 1820; one block inland at Chkheidze 38, the EU embassy is a surprisingly beautiful three-storey building (built in 1888) quite out of keeping with this tatty brick district. The main road swings away from the river, soon passing the **Ilia Chavchavadze house-museum** [84 F2] (*Javakhishvili 7; supposedly* ☉ *10.00–18.00 except Mon; free*) and continues to the railway station and out towards the northwestern suburbs.

However, soon after a relatively uninteresting early 19th-century church on the embankment, Tolstoy kucha leads off to the left to Saarbrücken Moedani, at the north end of the **Saarbrücken Bridge** [94 F3] (formerly Vorontsov, then Marx), and on as Davit Agmashenebelis Avenue. This was built as Mikhailovskaya in the 1830s, and was then known as Plekhanov under communism. Despite appearances, it's not a one-way street – a few marshrutkas do go the 'wrong' way, so be careful. At this eastern end there are a few local bars and a couple of shops selling antiques and wedding dresses, but it's hardly Knightsbridge. However, the avenue's western end has seen major modernisation in a bid to make it the city's major shopping street. The first buildings of real interest are No 60, the **University Hospital**, a neo-Gothic pile built in the 1860s, and opposite it at No 61 the former **Soviet Propaganda Centre** [84 E1], a brutalist block built in 1977 with, on its façade, a lurid high-relief mosaic (42m by 12m) by Zurab Tsereteli, celebrating the 60th anniversary of the Bolshevik Revolution.

A little further along Agmashenebelis you'll come to Marjanishvili Square, laid out in 1948–56, with a metro station in its northern corner facing the city's second McDonald's; Yevgenii Primakov, Russian prime minister in 1998–99, grew up nearby on what was then Leningrad Street. A block towards the river at Marjanishvili 7, the striking **TBC Bank HQ** was built in 1912 as the Economic Society of Caucasian Officers, and shows temporary exhibits in a gallery upstairs (⊕ *13.00–17.00 Mon–Fri; free*); opposite is the Marjanishvili Theatre, built in 1907 with fine Moderne ironwork and newly refurbished.

Marjanishvili kucha (formerly Kirochnaya) leads north from Marjanishvili Bridge and Square and, after two blocks, crosses Ivan Javakhishvili (formerly Kalinin); on the corner to the left (at No 69) is the city's main **Russian Orthodox church** [84 D2] (1864), and just to the right at No 55 is the **Roman Catholic church** [84 D2], a low-key Neoclassical building (1870–77), both now in great condition, thanks to foreign funds. A block to the east on Chitaia is Chikobava (formerly Sovietskaya) Square; on its far side, beyond the statue of Gorki on Terenti Graneli, is the modern **Lutheran Church of the Reconciliation** [84 D2], built in 1997. The Germans' first church was where Marjanishvili Square now is, but this was replaced in 1897 with a larger church (by Leopold Bielfeld, who also designed the Kashveti Church on Rustaveli Avenue), and then demolished in the 1940s when the square was laid out.

Continuing westwards from Marjanishvili Square on Davit Agmashenebelis, there are some grander Art Nouveau buildings, such as No 108 (with stucco pilasters) and No 101 (with caryatids supporting a balcony; built by Bielefeld in 1897 as a hotel), and a nice park behind. Beyond some Turkish fast food cafés, No 123 houses the Composers' Union and the **Djansugh Kakhidze Tbilisi Center for Music & Culture** [84 C2], with a garden in which the State Symphony Orchestra gives summer concerts. Just beyond it at No 127 is the **Mikeladze Centre** (home to the Georgian Philharmonic Orchestra) [84 C2], a fine Neoclassical pile built as the Cultural Centre of the Railwaymen of Georgia in 1950 and set back from the road in front of a park. Here, too, is the Tumanishvili Movie Actors' Theatre and documentary film studios, in a pseudo-medieval castle and tower built in 1930. Just behind the splendid former Apollo Theatre (1909) at No 135 is the **Museum of Theatre and Film** (⊕ *11.00–17.00 Tue–Sun; GEL2*) at Kargareteli 6, a mansion built in 1895 by Peter Stern; temporary exhibits are inside the main entrance, then you'll come back outside, turn right and go upstairs to six period rooms furnished with film costumes, lots of portraits of actors and singers, and paintings by Gudiashvili, Pirosmani and Kakabadze. At Davit Agmashenebelis 150 (right at the back) is the Observatory in which Stalin worked in 1899–1901, just before the junction with Tamar Mepis, leading from the railway station to the river.

Didube Beyond Tamar Mepis, Davit Agmashenebelis soon reaches the well-kept **Mushtaid Park** [84 C2] on the left (with dodgems, a Ferris wheel and a miniature railway) and the **Silk Museum** (page 135) on the right, overshadowed by the Paichadze National Stadium, better known simply as the **Dinamo Stadium** [84 C2]. This was built in 1937 and then rebuilt in 1976 to accommodate 70,000 fans. It is here that you enter the Didube district, also settled by Germans in the 19th century. The main road is Tseretelis Gamziri, a block to the right/northeast, which passes first the Orthodox **Church of the Nativity of the Virgin** [84 B1] (1883) where there's another pantheon of lower-league celebrities such as football players (and poet Terenti Graneli), and then the **Baptist church** [84 B1], before reaching the huge modernist **Exhibition Centre**, which now houses furniture showrooms and the like. It's quite a bit further to the Didube bus station, which is best reached by metro.

Rather than heading into the wilds of Didube, it's probably preferable to turn either left to the Tamar Mepis Bridge and Heroes' Square, or right to Station Square, where you can catch the metro. The **railway station** [84 C1] is a huge brutalist concrete block, renovated and essentially turned into a shopping centre in 2010. It is also a terminal for many of the city's marshrutkas and buses, and the **main market** [84 C1] is immediately to the southwest, so the whole area is always heaving with people. Behind the station roads lead up past the Gypsy palaces of Lotkin to the **Tbilisi Sea** (Tbilis Tskalsatsavi), the natural Lake Djairan enlarged in 1951 to form a reservoir (fed by the Iori River); there are restaurants and beach resorts here, but the water is not really clean enough for swimming. However, it is good for windsurfing, though you have to bring your own board. The massive Tbilisi Sea Plaza is being developed by China's Hualing group to be the most important trading centre in the Caucasus. In the Tbilisi Sea New City (also known as Olympic Village), the Hotels & Preference Hualing Tbilisi luxury hotel opened in 2015, with a massive recreation centre and gym, gardens with an artificial lake, and of course a Chinese restaurant. Nearby is the **Gino Paradise Aquapark** (\ *15 8585;* m *599 880989; www.ginoparadise.ge;* ⊕ *noon–23.00 daily; from GEL39 for 3hrs*), opened in 2013, with a 25m pool, wave pool, waterfall, 'wild river' and six slides up to 30m high, as well as a spa.

WHAT TO SEE AND DO

MUSEUMS
National Museum [98 B1] (*Rustaveli 3;* \ *99 8022; www.museum.ge;* ⊕ *10.00–18.00 except Mon & holidays; GEL5*) Reopened after refurbishment in 2011, the National Museum now has a nice modern foyer with a tiny coffee stand and two shops (selling books, postcards and Geoland maps), and a display of the earliest hominid relics found outside Africa, including the skull of an old man who survived for years after losing his teeth, suggesting care for the elderly and hence compassion and social structure. The first stone tools at Dmanisi, over two million years old, were found in 1984, followed by bones from at least five 1.77 million-year-old hominids and from sabre-toothed cats, short-necked giraffe, giant ostrich, giant cheetah, elephant, rhinos, horses and deer.

The museum's star attraction, however, is the amazing treasury of largely **pre-Christian gold and silver**. Whereas the Greeks preferred filigree decorations and the Persians encrustation, the Georgians chose granulation (*tsvara*), with tiny lumps creating texture; they also set their jewellery with semi-precious stones, such as cornelian (found all over Georgia). Going around to the left, the display falls into three parts, the Culture of Great Barrows (3rd–2nd millennium BC), 'Colchis rich in gold' (8th–3rd centuries BC) and Kartli-Iveria (3rd century BC to 4th century AD). Gold-mining in fact began in the 4th millennium BC; in the 3rd millennium the Barrow Culture of the Trialeti Plateau produced tiny pins (plain or with semi-precious stones and granulation), then diadems, pendants and vessels. A tiny golden lion with an intricately worked mane, dating from 2600–2300BC, is one of the most remarkable pieces in the whole collection; slightly later pieces include a king's sceptre, a silver cup with a frieze of religious ritual and hunting, and a gold bowl from about 1800BC encrusted with precious stones. A millennium then passed without gold- or silverwork until the Colchian culture developed in the west – finds from Vani, produced in the 5th century BC, include a superb diadem and very finely granulated necklaces, including one with 31 tiny turtles (symbolising longevity) hanging from it, others with swastikas, and an enamelled pendant, the oldest in Georgia. There are also hooped earrings, gold bracelets with cornelian beads, signet rings, and coins imitating Greek and Roman originals. Also from the 5th century BC, there's jewellery from Iveria, including silver bowls, earrings, gold buckles and sheep's-head rings, a lovely pair of gold pendants showing horses with a type of harness only used in Georgia, and a necklace of frogs (symbolising fertility). You'll also see an imported pectoral with cloisonnée inlay from Achaemenid Egypt.

From the mid 4th century BC Colchian goldsmithery changed, with new styles of bracelets and signet rings, and wreath-like headdresses replacing diadems. Rich burials from the 4th and 3rd centuries BC have been found in eastern Georgia, yielding discoid plaques from horse harnesses, torques and silver *phialai* (dishes) from Iran.

The display then leaps forward to the 2nd century AD, and a tiny part of the Hellenistic-style treasure buried with the royal family and ruling elite of Kartli in the Armaziskhevi cemetery in Mtskheta, such as the sheath of Aspavruk the Pitiakh's dagger, his gold and cornelian signet, and an intaglio buckle. There's also fine Roman silverware and a cameo, Roman and Sassanian silver *phialai*, glass pitchers, agate vessels and cloisonné inlays. Finally, by the early 3rd century, granulation was giving way to encrustation, and gold served mainly as a support for precious stones: from the late 3rd to early 4th century AD there's a writing set found in the Svetiskhoveli churchyard in Mtskheta, consisting of a silver box, gold plaque and a gold inkpot case.

On your way out, you can see a silent video on the technique of cloisonné enamel, developed in Vani from the 2nd century BC.

Upstairs there are temporary shows plus the **Oriental Collections**, with a small first room showing Egyptian pieces then a larger galleried room with 18th–20th-century Iranian paintings and steel ewers with gold overlay, and finally a room devoted to East Asia, with 19th-century bronzes and gouache on silk from Tibet, a 14th-century celadon bowl, 18th to 19th-century porcelain, jade, ivory and gouaches on rice paper from China, and 18th-century Satsuma porcelain, netsuke, and Samurai armour and swords from Japan, as well as an Utamaro print. Finally, the new **Museum of Soviet Occupation** covers the period from 1921 to 1991, with images, documents and items depicting the brutal Soviet rule that led to 80,000 Georgians being shot, 800,000 deported and another 400,000 killed in the Great Patriotic War, with examples of prominent musicians, artists and poets lost in Stalin's terror, along with Nagan revolvers used to kill them. Finally there's coverage of the rather ineffectual dissident movement led by Zviad Gamsakhurdia and Merab Kostava. In the centre, a long carpet leads to a Stalin-era desk from where you might learn your fate; around the upper gallery original documents are displayed, including the Certificate of Merit awarded to Stalin's henchman Kamo in 1928. The atmosphere is powerful but the displays should be much better – English labels are patchy and videos are without sound.

Art Museum [98 B1] (*Gudiashvili 1;* ✆ *99 9909;* ⏰ *10.00–18.00 except Mon; GEL3, plus GEL10 (up to 10 people) for the required guide; catalogues are available in English, French & German for GEL20*) The Art Museum houses the Treasury of gold- and silverware and cloisonné enamel from the Christian era, which is if anything even more amazing than the collection in the National Museum. There's little else here now other than temporary shows, as the building is being prepared for major restoration. Naturally most of the exhibits are icons, in fine golden frames – three-dimensional sculptures of the saints were forbidden by the Orthodox Church, but relief was permitted. Many are of St George, who is often shown lancing the Roman emperor Diocletian rather than a dragon or devil, as a symbol of the triumph of Christianity over paganism; St George is also shown being tortured. Encaustic enamels, in which the colours were mixed with wax, were (from the 6th century) another speciality, reaching a peak in the 10th to 12th centuries; the technique of firing them so that the colours were melted, but not the gold frame, was lost in the 15th century.

After passing full-size copies of frescoes from Betania, Svaneti and Davit-Gareja, you'll start in a small room with a selection of jewellery (and decorations from horse bridles) from 5th-century BC Colchis, similar to the treasures from Vani in the National Museum's treasury and with an equally superb range of techniques such as granulation, filigree and inlaying.

The long second room starts with some Byzantine- and Assyrian-influenced crosses and Hellenistic heads, then highlights include the Zarzma icon of the Transfiguration (AD886) and a 9th-century encaustic enamel of the Virgin Agitria (Showing the Way) with Child. There's also a 10th-century cloisonné Virgin and icons from Racha and Svaneti, then the superb chalice from Bedia (in Abkhazia), made in AD999 from a single piece of gold with a relief of Christ, the Virgin and Apostles. Then there's the famous 11th-century tondo from Gelati, a circular silver plaque with a high relief of St Mammes on a lion (it wouldn't eat him so he was martyred by soldiers). There are more incredibly fine cloisonné enamels (with a lapis colour that's typical of Georgia), notably 13th-century ones of St George from western Georgia.

Queen Tamar's pectoral cross has almost mystic significance for many Georgians, as a tangible link with one of their greatest rulers; it was made at the end of the 12th century, of gold set with emeralds, rubies and pearls, and has a 13th-century starotech or case. The triptych Icon of the Saviour from Ancha was enamelled in the 6th century and brought to the Anchiskhati Church in Tbilisi in the 17th century; its frame was made for Tamar in the second half of the 12th century, with a grape motif that never repeats itself. The wings of the frame were added in the 14th century, well after the Georgian Renaissance but still proof of good craftsmanship, while the cherubim on top are from the 19th century.

The Khakhuli triptych has a similarly tangled history: the head of Christ is a 6th-century encaustic wax painting, to which the Virgin (the largest piece of cloisonné enamel in the world) was added in the 10th century. These, with 115 cloisonné enamel medallions mostly dating from 1125–55, were set in a gold frame (with gilded silver wings) in the first half of the 12th century, after it was brought to Gelati from Khakhuli, now in Turkey. The Russian governor of Imeretia, Levashev, tore out much of the gold and jewels in 1859; only the Virgin's face and hands have been recovered. The Martvili Icon of the Virgin, dating from the first half of the 12th century, is of gold with small enamels of the Evangelists in the corners and in the middle of the right side a medallion of St Peter from the 9th century, the oldest known Byzantine enamel.

The third room shows how Georgian metalwork lost its way somewhat after the Mongol invasions of the 13th century, when the secrets of enamelling were lost; good pieces were produced again from the 15th century and, from the 16th century, icons from eastern Georgia show Persian influence, with floral motifs rather than vines. The 15th-century cross of Gori-Jvari is 2m tall and bears 16 silver plaques, with reliefs of St George. The Atskuri triptych is unusual in depicting the birth of the Virgin; the faces are sadder than in the Golden Age, hinting at hard times in 16th-century Georgia.

By the 18th century, emphasis was on secular jewellery; in the fourth room there's a display of the jewels of Katarina Dadiani, daughter of Alexander Chavchavadze, and possessions of other notable families. Finally, there's a small room of embroidered clerical robes.

National Gallery [94 E4] (*Rustaveli 11;* ✆ *15 7300;* ⊕ *10.00–18.00 except Mon & holidays; GEL5*) With a modern extension added in 2011, this now houses the Georgian art collection that was held in the former seminary on Pushkin Square. Entering at the rear, there are temporary exhibitions on the ground floor (as well as a simple café and a shop), then you'll go upstairs to the original Temple of Glory (page xxx), with one room devoted to Pirosmani, another to Kakabadze (including three 'Imeretian Landcsapes', a very avant-garde still life and some Constructivist work) and another to Gudiashvili. The central room houses sculptures, including half a dozen by Iacob Nikoladze, with photos of other works by him across Tbilisi. On the far side, there's another roomful of Pirosmanis.

The Museum of the History of Tbilisi (or Carvasla) [98 D3] (*Located in the caravansarai at Sionis 8;* ✆ *99 80228;* ⊕ *10.00–17.00 except Mon; GEL3*) Rooms are situated around the atrium (a wonderful space with cast-iron pillars) and display a range of interesting models, costumes, musical instruments, paintings, interesting historic photographs and replica shops and restaurants. The upper floor (presumably once displaying the history of communist Tbilisi) now houses temporary exhibits, offices and empty rooms, while on the lower level there are craft shops and a wine bar.

The Museum of Georgian Folk Architecture and Daily Life (also known as the Ethnographic Museum) [84 A4] (*Turtle Lake Rd;* ✆ *70 9045;* ⊕ *10.00–18.00 except Mon; GEL1.50*) This open-air museum displays about 70 buildings from all over Georgia, in vernacular local style and traditionally furnished. The lower houses, nearer the entrance, are furnished and open, while those further up can usually be safely viewed from a distance. At weekends and in summer costumed staff will be cooking or baking bread. You'll see *darbazi*-type and flat-roofed houses from the east of Georgia, gable-roofed wooden houses from the west, and three roof types: thatch in western Georgia, red channel tiles, and shingles.

Going around to the left (clockwise), you'll come first to a big, open-plan house from Abacha in Mingrelia, with a sleeping platform; then a farmstead, also from Mingrelia, with attractive, wooden panelling around a bukhari or chimney. An 18th-century house from Imereti is built of logs on a stone base, also open-plan with a central chimney; above is a house from Lanchkhuti (in Guria), which has an ingenious babywalker on the veranda, and a smithy which is still in use.

The shorter route back passes another Imeretian house, with the traditional Georgian marani or wine store; the alternative is to climb up the hill to a restaurant by the road, near large and impressive houses from Adjara and a Svan defensive tower (a copy of the 28m tower of Etseri) on the ridge. Returning down the hill you'll pass a house from Teliani (near Kaspi) just before the ruined 6th-century Sionis Church from Tianeti and a row of tombs (one, with an inscription in Old Georgian, under glass); beyond this a stone building half-set into the hillside is from Kakheti. Finally, hidden away right at the bottom is a 2m phallic stone from Abkhazia.

You may find Ivan Togonidze at work in the smithy, where he makes striking metal sculptures, or Gia Akhvlediani (great-nephew of the famous Elena Akhvlediani) selling his woodcuts and sketches in the house below. As you go around you'll also see odds and ends such as old muskets, wooden claws to protect the fingers while scything, and cots with a pipe leading to a gourd for urine below.

There's a good restaurant, Rachis Ubani, open seasonally in a restored house from Racha.

Lado Gudiashvili Museum [94 E4] (*Gudiashvili 11, just below the Kashveti Church;* ✎ *93 2305; www.ladogudiashvili.ge;* ⊕ *11.00–18.30 Tue–Sun; GEL5*). The fantastical painter's home has been rebuilt as a modern gallery, with a display of his work, mainly from private collections and changing every year, plus temporary shows. See also the dandyish statue of Gudiashvili in the adjacent (southeastern) corner of 9 April Park.

Elena Akhvlediani Museum [84 C2] (*Kiacheli 12, one flight up and on the right, with posters on the door;* ✎ *99 7412;* ⊕ *10.00–18.00, closed Mon; free*). The best of Tbilisi's house-museums is the home of Elena Akhvlediani (1901–75), where you'll find a room with a huge wooden column in the middle, modelled on peasant architecture, as well as small wooden galleries and hanging rugs. Akhvlediani's paintings are hung up to five high on the walls, and you'll also see examples of her theatre and film designs and book illustrations, as well as photos and mementoes. Although not the most challenging of artists she did have a very wide range of styles, and is loved for her warm depictions of daily life.

State Museum of Folk and Applied Arts [98 B3] (*Dadiani 28;* ✎ *99 9722; 10.00–18.00 Tue & Thu–Sun, 10.00–21.00 Wed; GEL2*). Founded in 1913 as the Museum of the Caucasian Kustar (craftsmen) Committee to encourage crafts in the Russian Empire, this displays carpets and *kilims* (most made in the 1930s), costumes, silver and ceramics upstairs (ask for English-language information); downstairs are historic photos and temporary shows.

State Museum of Georgian Folk Songs and Instruments [98 B3] (*Samghebro 6;* ✎ *45 7721;* ⊕ *10.00–18.00 Tue–Sun; GEL3*) Just off Maidan Square, this small museum is good for children, who can touch and even play instruments such as a *calliope*. The first room has displays of traditional Georgian wind, string and percussion instruments, the second has Asian instruments, used by Armenian, Azeri, Jewish, Assyrian and Yezidi musicians, and the third has 19th-century European classical and mechanical instruments, such as an orchestrion, accordion, mandolin and banjo, and musical boxes.

Silk Museum [84 C2] (*Tsabadze 6;* ✎ *40 963/7; www.silkmuseum.ge; 11.00–17.00 Tue–Sun; GEL3*) In the shadow of the Dinamo Stadium, this is one of the oldest museums in Georgia, built in 1892 to help develop the silk industry and still using the original display cabinets. A helpful guide will explain the silkworm's life cycle and show machines for chopping leaves to feed them, plus a butterfly-sexing carousel, 4,000-odd cocoons from across China and elsewhere, natural dyes and finally the textiles and embroideries that are the final product.

OTHER PLACES OF INTEREST
Botanic Gardens [98 E4] (✎ *72 3406/9; www.nbgg.ge;* ⊕ *09.00–19.00 except Mon; GEL3*) These gardens are one of Tbilisi's least-known treasures, a beautiful place to wander for an afternoon, with both cultivated beds and greenhouses and wilder, quieter areas higher up the slopes. The main entry is at the top of Botanikuri, above Gorgasali Square, and it can also be reached by paths from the second hairpin of the Kojori Highway, at the junction to the Sololaki Ridge, or near the Kartlis-Deda statue; if you enter this way guards will send you down to the main gate to pay.

The gardens were established as a royal pleasure ground in 1636 on the right bank of the Tsavkistiskhevi (Fig Ravine), with a natural waterfall, and became a municipal

3

garden in 1801, growing vines, vegetables and fruit. In 1845 it was taken over and expanded by the Russian Viceroy Mikhail Vorontsov (who also founded the lovely gardens in Yalta), using the steep valley, and a Muslim cemetery. In the 1890s it became an academic body, publishing its proceedings and a seed exchange list from 1895, and the *Bulletin of the Tbilisi Botanic Garden* from 1905; from 1897 it was organised into bio-regional sections (such as pine grove, saline soils and Turkestan). In the Soviet period it expanded on to the right bank of the stream and became more practical in outlook, as well as opening sections in Kutaisi and Zugdidi. Taken over by the city in 2000, it was desperately short of money and in a terrible state until being rescued by oligarch Bidzina Ivanishvili. There are still virtually no labels on plants and no signs or maps.

In its 128 hilly hectares (of which 85ha are cultivated) there are 4,500 species, including 2,300 species and forms of trees and shrubs, and over 900 species of tropical and subtropical plants in greenhouses (⊕ *Tue–Thu afternoons*). Local people see the gardens mainly as a venue for picnics and wedding photos; an EcoCentre, funded by the Worldwide Fund for Nature, is being set up here, as a key part of an environmental education programme.

There's a fine specimen of Pitsunda pine (*Pinus pithyusa*) inside the entrance, from where a gravel path leads up the valley to bridges below the waterfall; the main building and greenhouses are across the valley to the left, with a winding asphalt road continuing up the valley, not very interesting at first with fields and scrubby shrubs, as well as some succulents and thorny shrubs, and some hidden gardens stumbled across at random. Things improve near the head of the valley where you'll enter conifers (with bamboo) and then untended scrub of birch or alder, ending at a locked gate. It's possible to loop back to the left, below the cliffs, or to the right down a cypress alley (on a gravel path).

Zoo [84 C3] (*Kostovas 64, at the Heroes' Sq roundabout;* ↘ *33 2901; www.zoo.ge; ⊕ May–Sep 09.00–21.00 daily, Oct–Apr 10.00–18.00 daily; GEL2*) Tbilisi's zoo was criticised in the past for its small, concrete-floored cages, but since 2006 it has moved the animals to more suitable housing and opened a veterinary centre. It had a few camels, lions, tigers, hippos, zebras, gibbons, baboons, bears, hyenas and peacocks, and also a kids' funfair, which needs to be moved away from the animals. The elephants were moved to more natural surroundings in 2008. Proposals for a New York-style 'central park' to link the Saburtalo and Vake districts mean that the zoo may be moved to a new location at the Tbilisi Sea; this became more urgent after a flash flood virtually destroyed the zoo in June 2015, drowning three keepers, and a dozen others outside the zoo. Some animals escaped and a lion and a tiger were shot by police, after the tiger had killed a man.

4

Shida (Inner) Kartli
შიდა ქართლი

Heading west from Tbilisi, you pass through the heartland of Georgia, beginning with Mtskheta, the country's spiritual capital. Most tourist agencies in Tbilisi run day trips to Mtskheta and Gori, with your car or theirs.

MTSKHETA მცხეთა *Telephone code 32 (followed by a 2 and six digits; same as Tbilisi)*

Named after Mtskhetos, son of Kartlos, and overlooked by Mount Kartli, supposedly still home to the soul of Kartlos, Mtskheta (pronounced 'Skayta') is at the heart of Georgia's spiritual identity. Inhabited for 5,000 years, the site at the confluence of the Mtkvari and Aragvi rivers was the centre of the pagan cult of Armazi (the local version of the Zoroastrian fire god Ormazd of Persia), adopted in the 4th century BC by King Parnavaz I of Kartli, who established his capital 2km southwest of present-day Mtskheta. It was known to the ancient Greeks as Armosica and to Pliny as Armasicum, and is now Armazistsikhe (Armazi Castle). There are traces of older Hittite and even Sumerian cults; the surrounding hilltops all housed pagan shrines which have now been replaced by churches. From the 4th century BC until the 5th century AD this was the capital of Iveria (present-day Kartli), the scene of the royal family's conversion to Christianity, and continued as seat of the Georgian Church until the 12th century. The town's churches are included on UNESCO's World Heritage List. The main cathedral, though no longer seat of the Catholicos, is far more impressive than Tbilisi's Sioni Cathedral, and effortlessly dominates the town (now little more than a village), especially as seen from the main highway across the river. There's another fine ancient church in Mtskheta, and the Jvari Church, high on a crag across the Aragvi, is one of the most architecturally important in Georgia, setting the pattern for virtually all those built in the following centuries.

GETTING THERE AND AWAY At the Didube **bus** terminal in Tbilisi there's always a marshrutka loading for the 25–30-minute trip to Mtskheta; buy tickets (*GEL1*) at the cash desk before boarding. Marshrutkas also leave roughly every 30 minutes for Gori and more frequently for Kutaisi, passing below the Jvari Church.

Buses cross the Didube Bridge heading for the statue of King David the Builder (and a spectacular statue of St Nino above) where they join the main highway. If you come directly from the city centre along Pekini you'll first pass the most striking piece of modern architecture in Tbilisi, the Highways Ministry (now the headquarters of the Bank of Georgia), composed of towers and horizontal blocks of offices built into and out of the hillside in 1977, the modernist effect now spoilt by the new (traditional-style) church in front.

After the usual outskirts clutter of restaurants, petrol stations and big-box shops, as well as the new US embassy (an ugly, big, white building away to the right), the dual-carriageway leaves the city limits at km16 and swings left along the right/south bank

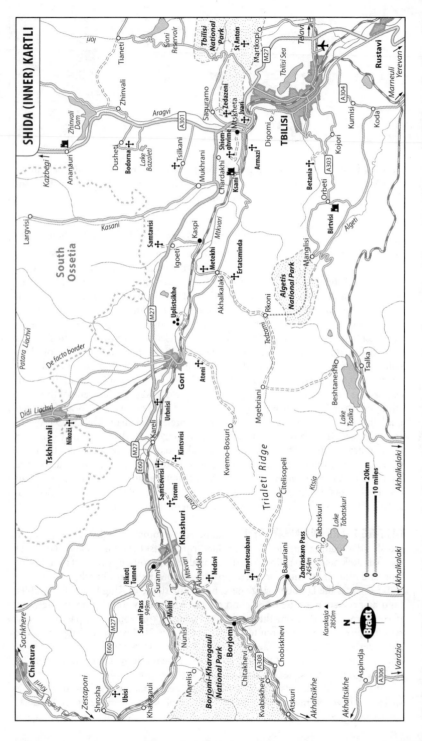

SHIDA (INNER) KARTLI

of the Mtkvari (passing the Zahesi hydro-electric station, built in 1927 and now very small and old-fashioned). After just 2km, the Jvari Church is signed (in Latin script) to the right, but it's still 7km away and you shouldn't get off the bus here. It's just 1km more to the turning to Mtskheta, which takes off to the right and goes under the main highway just before it crosses the Mtkvari. Coming by road from the west you should get off here, immediately after the bridge, and go 200m west to a bus stop; marshrutkas from Tbilisi are often full, but there will eventually be a bus, or a taxi may be waiting.

It's a deceptively long way into town from here, following the river past the town, then after 4km crossing a bridge (with what seems to be a statue of a skateboarding eagle at its south end; the foundations of Pompey's Bridge, dating from 65BC, are visible when the water is low) and doubling back. The main highway passes below the Jvari Church, high on its rock, crosses the Aragvi at km25.5, and meets the local road from Mtskheta after a pedestrian underpass leading to bus stops on the highway. It's another couple of kilometres to the flyover at the start of the Georgian Military Highway, just after the km27 marker.

Entering into Mtskheta, you'll cross the bridge and swing right to continue for 1km to the post office at the start of the one-way system. You'll glimpse the cathedral on your right and then the Armazi cinema (with a colourful fresco depicting Georgian history) on your left; it's built over the remains of the Old Town gates, visible beneath. Immediately afterwards, you'll arrive at a plaza with the Samtavro Church to the left, where you should stop.

Returning to Tbilisi, marshrutkas pass Samtavro and the cinema and pick up along Davit Agmashenebelis, the next road up the hill.

The railway station lies just southwest of the bridge, and a couple of **trains** a day still call here, leaving Tbilisi at 08.55 and 21.10, arriving 25 minutes later, and continuing on to Gori and stops along the route to Ozurgeti.

WHERE TO STAY
The tourist information centre can organise accommodation in one of the guesthouses (all **$$–$$$**), and there may be signs for rooms in houses close to the cathedral; otherwise there are just a few hotels.

Hotels

Hotel Mtskheta Palace (8 rooms, 3 suites) Davit Agmashenebelis 7,500m west from the north end of the bridge; 91 0202, 51 3131, 51 2777; m 593 078585, 599 111246; e mtskhetapalace@gmail.com; http://mtskhetapalace.ge. Still the best hotel in Mtskheta, though it now seems dated. It has a covered pool & sauna, & 3 dbl rooms with AC, TV & a good bathroom with toiletries & hairdryer, 5 larger ones & 3 suites with massage shower, like a vertical jacuzzi. All inc b/fast. **$$$–$$$$**

Bagineti Kostava 39; m 592 007500, 593 631786; www.hotelbagineti.ge. At the northwestern corner of the cathedral wall, this small, new place is pretty amateur but has decent rooms with TV, AC & Wi-Fi. **$$$**

Old Capital Erekle II 7; m 593 631786. Just to the right from the cathedral gate, this comfortable, new hotel has TV & AC in all rooms; it also offers a luggage storage service. **$$$**

Homestays

Ekaladze Gia Arsukidze 85; 51 2582; m 598 449255

Guesthouse David Arsukidze 67; m 551 707172

Guesthouse Mtskheta-Kapanadze Arsukidze 63; m 595 380898

Kapanadze Nazi Kostava 22, opposite the cathedral gate; 51 2865; m 551 512865

Khamkhadze Amirami Arsukidze 37; 51 2623; m 555 969070

Khizanishvili Zaqro Arsukidze 93; 51 2402; m 593 360609

Mtskheta Sanapiro Sanapiro 6; m 597 182244. New & squeaky clean in 2014.

Tamarindi (7 rooms) Arsukidze 23; 51 2764; m 579 037772. Also offers jeep tours.

✕ WHERE TO EAT AND DRINK Once upon a time a restaurant opposite the cathedral gates supposedly served the best shashlik in Georgia, but now there are few services in Mtskheta. As well as those listed, there's also a decent **café-bar** (m *599 250125*; $) at Gamsakhurdias 17, west of the cathedral.

✕ Old Tavern (Dzveli Taverna) At the top of Arsukidze. A perfectly decent but not particularly fast place to try the usual Georgian dishes (note that the beet soup is actually beef). $$

✕ Opizari Mamulashvili 2. Modern & fairly upmarket restaurant on the way to Samtavro. $$

✕ Salobio Restaurant About 4km towards Tbilisi by the riverside. This has always been a favourite outing for the people of Tbilisi, offering a wide range of traditional dishes such as lobio (for which Mtskheta is famed), chadi, pirozhki, khinkali, shashlik & khachapuri. The nearby Metropol & Serafin restaurants are similar. $$

✕ Café Guga Mamulashvili 6. The best food in town, with indoor seating & private wicker summer huts. $

OTHER PRACTICALITIES The United Georgia Bank is at Davit Agmashenebelis 37, where there's an **ATM**; you'll find another at People's Bank, opposite Samtavro, and more on Arsukidze. There is a **tourist information centre** (*Arsukidze 3;* ✆ *51 2128;* e *ticmtskheta@gmail.com*) with English-speaking staff, plus toilets and a couple of souvenir shops in the pompous wedding hall opposite the cathedral.

The **Mtskhetoba Festival**, usually attended by the president and Catholicos as well as over 100,000 others, is held in October; there's also a **Festival of Performing Arts** in early June.

WHAT TO SEE AND DO
Sveti Tskhoveli (⊕ *08.00–20.00 daily*) The Sveti Tskhoveli Cathedral of the Twelve Apostles rises on the site of the palace of the kings of Iveria, to which part of Christ's crucifixion robe was brought soon after his death by Elias, whose sister Sidonia died of joy clutching it so tightly that it had to be buried here with her. The cedar which grew out of her grave was felled to build St Nino's first church here, and one column supposedly hovered in the air until Nino brought it down by prayer; in addition, miraculous sap is said to have flowed from it at her behest.

The church derives its name of Sveti Tskhoveli or 'Life-giving Column' from this; it could also be said that the name is clearly pagan in origin. The first church here was built of wood in the 4th century AD; this was replaced by a three-nave basilica by AD575, and the present church was built for Patriarch Melchisidek in 1010–29, incorporating the tiny 6th-century building. It was damaged by an earthquake in 1283 and again by Tamerlane at the end of the 14th century before being restored in 1412–31 and 1656; in 1837 the narthexes to the south and north were removed. Built just a few decades before the great Norman cathedrals of England, you may find some similarities in style.

Perfectly proportioned, with its great pepper-pot dome of greenish stone rising high above the village and the river, it sits in a large square of walls added by Erekle II in the second half of the 18th century The main entrance (to the west) was added in the 11th century and above it you'll see two carved bulls' heads, which are pagan fertility symbols. The exterior of the church is well decorated, with carvings of red stone set in limestone, but not excessively so; note particularly the beautifully carved trees on the western façade, and a hand holding a bevel-square over the central arch of the northern façade. This illustrates the story of the builder Arsukidze's hand being chopped off by his jealous teacher (though there are various versions of this story).

The church has a three-bay nave that seems huge by Georgian standards; incorporated into the second bay to the right is a 14th-century copy of the chapel of the Holy Sepulchre in Jerusalem. In the next bay is a high-sided 17th-century pavilion built over the tomb of Sidonia, and to the east of this is the patriarch's stone throne, also 17th century. Immediately ahead you'll find the royal tombs, of which three (all of grey marble) can be identified: the last two kings, Erekle II (1720–98) and Georgi XII (1746–1800) lie on either side of the altar steps, and Vakhtang Gorgasali, founder of Tbilisi, is the second back from Erekle.

The most notable frescoes are in the centre of the south wall of the south transept, although much is missing; what's left of this 17th-century Apocalypse is a wheel of the zodiac radiating out of a central Christ figure, with the Apostles to the right and a sea with monsters to the left. Intriguingly, the writer Daniel Farson states that there were undeniably two flying-saucers painted at eye level on the altar fresco of the crucifixion, and another over the arch; others felt they were just floating faces shining down. In any case they had been whitewashed over by 1991.

There is excellent singing here on Saturday and Sunday mornings; knees, shoulders and women's hair should be covered at all times, and shawls are available in the porch.

Samtavro Just 5 minutes north, beyond the plaza with the Armazi cinema, the Samtavro nunnery (also a royal residence and administrative centre) stands on the site of Georgia's first church, which is now a royal residence and administrative centre, with a tiny 4th-century chapel (with poor frescoes) in the grounds marking the spot where Nino lived in a log hut. The main Church of the Redeemer dates from the first half of the 11th century (the dome was restored after damage by a 13th-century earthquake); the most notable feature is the richly carved tombs of King Mirian and Queen Nana, the 4th-century founders of the Chosroid dynasty, incongruously set under a 19th-century Italianate marble and mosaic canopy in the church's southwest corner, just left of the entrance. Otherwise the church is big and spacious, with bare walls and some very battered frescoes in the dome and above the altar. Externally, there are good decorative carvings on the north and east walls and the dome; the bell-tower (obviously shaken by earthquakes) dates from the 13th century.

Mtskheta Archaeological Museum (*Davit Agmashenebelis 54;* ❧ *22 2360;* ⊕ *10.00–19.00 Tue–Sun*) The museum is currently closed for refurbishment but has a good collection of exhibits from excavations in the area: agricultural tools, prehistoric children's toys and bronze jewellery.

Jvari The Jvari (Cross) Church stands on a spur of the Saguramo Hills, 150m above Mtskheta, and now seems to grow out of the rock. It's one of the finest examples of old Georgian architecture, a marvellously simple but sophisticated edifice, in advance of most European ecclesiastical architecture of the period. Built between AD586 and 604 by Patriarch Stephanoz I, it was the first 'apse-buttressed' cruciform church, in which the gaps between the arms of the cross are filled by small chapels, producing a virtually perfect square ground plan; this allows a wonderfully lofty and spacious interior in which four pillars support an octagonal drum and a round dome covering the entire central space. It stands on the spot where Nino first set up her cross overlooking the pagan shrines of Mtskheta; the ruins of a late 6th-century church survive just north of the present church, with the remains of a defensive tower to the northeast. It was also the first Georgian church where reliefs played a significant role on the façades – there's an exceptionally fine bas-relief of a pair of winged angels bearing a cross above the south door, and other carvings on the east end. Closed in 1911, it was reconsecrated in 1988, and still appears partly ruined, the main columns seemingly hewn out of raw rock. Inside there's the huge plinth of St Nino's Cross in the centre, and a low wooden iconostasis.

Getting there and away Mtskheta and the Jvari Church are quite close as the crow flies, but they're separated by the Aragvi River. If you don't have a car the easiest option is certainly to take a **taxi** from Mtskheta to Jvari (*GEL20, inc waiting time*), but you could also take a **marshrutka** along the main highway (for instance, to or from Gori or Kutaisi) and ask to be set down at the roadside immediately below the church, at about km21, from where you can hike up in about 15–20 minutes. By car, you'll turn right/east on the Tbilisi bypass (the E60, signposted to Telavi) then take a very sharp turn left; the road takes a long, looping route, ending at a large car park, with a tiny drinks stall and a toilet below it.

Walking back to Mtskheta Once you've seen the church, it's possible to descend, either by the road, or directly down the northern hillside, by a clear 4x4 track that turns left off the tarmac road just off the top. Once on the flat, follow the track across the meadow to an underpass a little way south of the Aragvi restaurant on the far side of the highway; it'll take 30–45 minutes. A path leads down beyond the restaurant to a footbridge (where locals swim); once across the river, turn right along the road and then cut through to the left to the road past the derelict campsite, or continue for 5 minutes along the road to the open-air theatre below the 14th-century castle of Bebristsikhe. This rises beside the road between the historic village and the modern town of typical communist blocks, set tactfully (for once) 1–2km to the north; from the castle it takes 10 minutes to walk to the left/south to the Samtavro Church.

For those who wish to do the walk to the church in reverse, from the centre to Jvari, head north past the Samtavro Church and turn right around the north side of the derelict Univermag shop. Then, go right following the tarmac road past the former campsite, and right again at the junction to find the footbridge on your left.

AROUND MTSKHETA To the northeast of Mtskheta, beyond the main highway and the Jvari Church, is the Saguramo Nature Reserve, which became the **Tbilisi National Park** in 2007; it's mainly of recreational importance and not very species-rich, although there are wolves and bears, and a wildlife rescue centre.

At km24 on the main highway a road turns to the right/north to Saguramo, where there are some luxurious holiday homes and a modern winery; you can visit the **house-museum of Ilia Chavchavadze**, the reformer who became a secular saint after his murder nearby at Tsitsamouri in 1907 by agents either of the Tsarist regime or of the Bolsheviks (pages 17 and 278).

From here, a track leads about 7km south to the **monastery of Zedazeni** (also known as Aktimo), set on a hilltop at 1,390m in the heart of the reserve. It was founded by Ioane of Zedazeni, one of the Syrian fathers, who lived here in a cave from AD501 to 531; the monastery was built over his tomb in the 7th–8th centuries and has a 7th-century fresco of St George and the Dragon. Ioane's disciple founded Kvemo (Lower) Zedazeni at the foot of the mountain, and a three-nave basilica was built in the AD860s and 870s; now reopened, it's sending out monks to repopulate other disused monasteries.

In the hills 12km west of Mtskheta, the **monastery of Shiom-ghvime** is built into the hillside in a spectacularly picturesque manner, though the buildings look more like a farm than a monastery; it was founded in the 6th century by the Assyrian monk Shio Mgvimeli, another of the Thirteen Syrian Fathers, who voluntarily spent 20 years in a cave. A church was built over his grave in the 11th century, as well as the Monastery of The Virgin, built by Davit Agmashenebelis in 1103–23, a 12th-century refectory, and a 7km aqueduct at the end of the same century.

The road to Shiom-ghvime is signed (12km) between the Armazi cinema and the Samtavro nunnery; there are no buses, but taxis wait near the nunnery. This passes the Gvtismshobeli and Mgalobliant-Kari churches (both just to the north of the road and both 17th century), then the Tsminda Demetre and Kaloubiani churches (both to the south and both 12th century). The first three are within 2km of Mtskheta and make a pleasant walk.

THE ROAD WEST FROM MTSKHETA

From its junction with the Georgian Military Highway, the main highway west to Kutaisi and western Georgia runs to the north of the hills along the north side of the Mtkvari; it's a fast road through fairly empty, featureless countryside, except for the spectacular 16th-century **castle of Ksani** visible to the south as the road crosses the river of the same name at km40.5. A few kilometres before Ksani is the village of **Chardakhi**, where you can visit Iago's Winery (m 593 352426; e chardakhi@gmail. com), one of the best places outside Kakheti to discovery traditional *qvevri* wines (made with organic Chinuri grapes). An alternative, if you want to meander along rough back roads, is to follow the south bank of the Mtkvari, visiting ruined castles and ancient churches in villages that see almost no visitors despite being just a few hours from Tbilisi.

ARMAZI The road from Mtskheta to Tbilisi crosses the Mtkvari and turns to the left; to the right/west a minor road passes the closed railway station and continues towards Armazi, Akhalkalaki and, after 57km, Gori. About 1km west of the station a road turns left across the railway towards the **Armazi Monastery**, 3km south; for a pleasant hike up to it, continue another 1km west to the 'Archaeologists' House', where the site of Parnavaz's capital (page 137) is being excavated. On the hillside across the river is the Kaloubiani Chapel, off the road to Shiom-ghvime, but sadly there's no way across the river here. Virtually opposite the archaeologists' gate you can take a tiny path diagonally up over the railway embankment to the km0.3 marker. A path, and for a while a water pipe, run along the true right side of a dry ravine into low forest of oaks and hornbeams, with lots of birds in residence and the odd squirrel. The path continues on either side of the stream bed; after about 15 minutes it turns right at some shacks and climbs steeply uphill for a couple of minutes before dropping back to the stream bed. You'll see **Armazi Church** on the far bank; fork left at a junction to reach it after about 30 minutes in all. It's a simple brick structure dating from the 12th century, now reclaimed and being refurbished by monks. If you cross the stream and fork left, following the stream and then climbing up to your right, you'll come in about 20 minutes to a saddle below the ruined tower of **Armazistsikhe** (Armazi Castle), spectacularly set amid cliffs of dramatic strata, with views to the chapels on the hilltops around Shiom-ghvime. It's possible to climb down on the far side of the saddle and loop back to the stream, but I wouldn't recommend doing it alone.

AKHALKALAKI AND AROUND At the west end of Armazi village (all modern concrete blocks) a comical eagle sculpture points the way left under the railway; the road, fairly well served by marshrutkas, soon heads south away from the wooded

4

river valley into dry sandy hills, and at km36 reaches **Akhalkalaki** (New Town – one of many), where there's an EU-funded home for children with disabilities at the road junction.

From here, a road follows the Tedzami Valley southwest for 24km to **Rkoni**, where there's a 7th–8th-century church (altered in the 11th century), a medieval bridge and an 18th-century fort. From Rkoni it's possible to hike or mountain bike through the Algetis National Park, across the Trialeti Ridge, to Manglisi. A three-day hiking route follows the Tedzami Valley to Mgebriani and then takes an ancient trail south across the Trialeti Ridge by the Kldecari (Rocky) Pass to Lake Tsalka, by the main road from Akhalkalaki (the other, more important one) to Tbilisi.

By the graveyard at the south end of Akhalkalaki is a simple 10th-century basilica church, with traces of frescoes on its west wall; another 2km to the south (20km from Kaspi) the **church of Ertatsminda** was built in the 13th and 14th centuries. It's a cruciform church, with carved crosses on all four façades, and a blind Romanesque-style arcade above the aisle roof line. This is a settlement of stone houses which has something of the feel of a real mountain village. It's known for a priest who was martyred after leading invaders the wrong way to save the village.

Akhalkalaki is a long thin village with a topless defensive tower near its northern end; just beyond this a road that turns left to Gori (22km, passing the Uplistsikhe cave-city), while straight on to the north it's 15km to Kaspi; marshrutkas run between Kaspi and Gori. It's just a couple of kilometres along this road to the village of **Metekhi**, where the 13th-century Metekhis Sioni Church has a unique tapering pepper-pot dome design. Otherwise it's a simple cruciform shape within a square plan, with carved crosses on all four façades. The other feature of interest in the village is a golden statue of Stalin to the west of the road just north of the church.

KASPI AND SAMTAVISI
Kaspi is a small town with a chemical plant on the railway 48km west of Tbilisi; however, there's nothing to see and no services for travellers. The only trains are to Tbilisi at 06.30 and back at 21.00. It's 9km south of Igoeti at km54.5/494.5 on the Tbilisi–Kutaisi highway. About 200m east of the junction there's a small 9th-century basilica of brick on stone foundations; about 600m west (still within Igoeti) is the junction to the superbly decorated **church of Samtavisi**, definitely a worthwhile stop for anyone taking the road between Tbilisi and Kutaisi. Without a car this is more easily done eastbound, as any marshrutka will stop and take you on to Mtskheta and Tbilisi, while westbound you'll have to struggle with reading destination boards.

The Samtavisi road continues straight ahead where the highway swings left (formerly known as the Curve of Death) to the River Lekhura Bridge, and curves to the right/northwest. The church is soon visible, but is bigger than it seems; in fact, it's about 1.5km away (and 11km from Kaspi). Stick to the main road through the village, then turn right where a bridge comes into view ahead, to reach a gate on the north side of the church complex. To the left as you enter are the remains of the bishop's palace; the bell-tower under which you enter dates from the 17th century, but the church itself is a unified structure dating from 1030–68. Outside, the north, west and south sides are relatively simply decorated, although the north side has what seems to be a fake clock; the east end is richer (perhaps the best stone-carving in Georgia), with the two deep recesses that are typical of Georgian architecture marking the shape of the altar apse within and the lateral apses on either side. They draw the eye upwards to the incised cross and the dome above, stressing the verticality of the building. Inside, the church is high and bare, with the central dome set on four free-standing pillars that are not quite parallel. There are some battered fragments of 17th-century frescoes in the altar apse, and in the cupola (you'll notice that the figure of Christ is always the right way up for the priest, not the congregation), and tombstones dating from the 11th century. If you want to spend more time in the area, there's a fine-looking **fort** which is easily reached by a track northeast from the next village to the north, Pantiani.

GORI გორი *Telephone code 370*

The dual-carriageway from Tbilisi to Kutaisi runs several kilometres to the north of Gori, a fairly unattractive city known above all as the birthplace of Georgia's most infamous son, Stalin. Even if you choose to boycott the Stalin Museum, Gori is nevertheless the base for visiting the cave-city of Uplistsikhe and several fine historic churches, notably Ateni Sioni.

There have been fortifications on the hill dominating Gori since the first half of the 1st millennium BC; the Roman general Pompey besieged it in 65BC, but there was no real civilian settlement here until 1123 when King David the Builder established a city, partly settled by Armenian refugees. In 1892, when Stalin was 13, Gorky described Gori as: 'quite small, no bigger than a fair-sized village … The whole place has a picturesque wildness all its own. The sultry sky over the town, the noisy, turbulent waters of the Kura, mountains in the near distance with their 'City of Caves' and further away the Caucasus range, with its sprinkling of snow that never melts.' The population at this time was 9,000 at most, but is now 54,000, with a relatively high proportion of Roman Catholics.

Gori is not a particularly attractive town and these days seems to have a somewhat schizophrenic attitude towards its historical connection with Stalin. Until 2010, a 17m-tall statue of Stalin stood in the central square, the only survivor of thousands of similar edifices that once graced every city square throughout the Soviet Empire. Although the others were removed elsewhere in the Soviet Union in the years following Khrushchev's denunciation, the Gori statue remained, defended by the town's citizens on the premise that however dreadful the despot's crimes against the Soviet people may have been, he was still, in Georgia at least, a hero of sorts in the 'local boy makes good' mould. Attempts to remove the statue were thwarted by proud locals and it was not until 24 June 2010 that cranes were brought in to remove it. The operation took place at night without debate or warning – clearly the act of a young government in a hurry to demonstrate its pro-West credentials. President Saakashvili had plans to erect a monument to the victims of the 2008 Russia–Georgia war in its place, although for the time being Stalin Square is devoid of any statuary (although it still bears the dictator's name). The statue may have gone but Stalin's shadow will remain for long years to come, it would seem.

Gori was quite badly damaged during the conflict with Russia in August 2008; although several military targets were attacked by Russian planes, bombs also fell in the town centre, causing considerable damage to residential buildings and an estimated 60 civilian deaths. Many residents fled the city as Russian forces and South Ossetian militia moved in following the aerial attack – troops that are accused of carrying out widespread looting and arson before their eventual withdrawal on 22 August. Scars from this episode can still be seen in the town, as can the human fallout of the conflict in the shape of large estates of prefab refugee housing across the Gori district.

GETTING THERE AND AWAY There are eight **trains** a day from Tbilisi (*GEL1*), four of them leaving the capital between 08.00 and 09.00; they take 52 to 72 minutes. The town centre lies on the left/east bank of the River Liakvi at its confluence with the Mtkvari, and its railway station is on the far, south side of the Mtkvari. From here take a minibus or yellow bus route 2, or climb the steps at the west end of the platform to reach the bridges over the tracks and the river, and carry on northwards along Stalin Prospekt for 15 minutes to reach Stalin Square.

From the north side of the square, Chavchavadze Street leads past the theatre and a circular Public Service Hall to the **bus** station about 500m west, south of the market; some buses leave from a second terminal across the bridge to the west. There are also **marshrutkas** every 30 minutes from Didube, taking around an hour (*GEL4*). Marshrutkas for Tbilisi wait by a ticket kiosk outside the main terminal.

Heading west – to Kutaisi, say – from Gori is a trickier prospect as most transport passes the town on the main highway without diverting into the town itself. Apart from taking a train – they pass through on their way west at around 09.00, 10.00, 17.00, 19.00, 22.00 and 02.00 – the best bet is to take a local marshrutka to the junction of Khashuri.

The junction to Gori is at km472/80 (about 60km west of Mtskheta), and it's 4km more to the centre; from the west turn off at km468.5/83.5 if you have your own wheels, or continue to the Tskhinvali junction, where taxis (*GEL6*) wait.

WHERE TO STAY
Guesthouses are generally better than hotels here – ask at the tourist office. All charge GEL25pp plus GEL5 for breakfast (**$$**). See map, page 147.

Hotels

Hotel Gori (10 rooms) 3km from town on the highway to Tbilisi; m 590 776669, 599 131205; www.hotelgori.ge. You'll see this hotel, the best place to stay in Gori, on the left as the bus from Tbilisi begins to turn off into Gori; you can loop under the dual-carriageway to reach it. It's a very nice 4-star place, about the standard of a European Best Western & much more affordable. The staff speak enough English, & there's a good restaurant, with Georgian dishes from about GEL6 (or GEL30 for caviar). **$$$$**

Hotel Georgia Stalin Av 26; 70 7576; m 599 396163; e sastumrosaqartvelo@mail. ru; www.hotelgeorgia.blogspot.com. Centrally located on the north side of the old Hotel Intourist (now closed), this has friendly staff & good soundproofing. **$$$**

Hotel Victoria (16 rooms) Tamar Mepis 76; 827 07 5586; m 877 402372. To reach the Victoria, continue south from Stalin Sq towards the rail station for 300m, then at the lights go 200m or so to the left. Rooms are huge & have TV, shower & fridge. It's rather run-down but adequate for a stopover. Rates inc b/fast & tax. **$$$**

Guesthouses

Kalifornia Rustaveli 79; m 593 300802, 551 300802; e okalifornia@mail.ru

Levani Agmashenebelis 29; 27 3147; m 598 268 045; e kapanadze.tamar@gmail.com; http://guesthouselevani.blogspot.co.uk

Nitsa Kutaisi 58; 27 7567; m 599 142488; e liazauta@gmail.com

WHERE TO EAT AND DRINK
As well as those listed, there are also a couple of places being built on Chavchavadze near the theatre and the new cathedral, and a few bars on Stalin Avenue near the war memorial (such as **Bar Shardin** at No 17). Outside town, the **Hotel Gori** (above) has an excellent restaurant, and the **Venezia** (*m 595 507870, 599 726902*) and **Nacharmagevi** (*m 577 257711*), 5km north on the Tskhinvali road (1km beyond the highway junction) are spacious, rural places that specialise in family parties. See map, page 147.

Hunter Restaurant Stalin Av 6 (south of Stalin Sq). Decorated with dead animals rather than serving game; it actually offers the usual khachapuri, khinkali & kebabs, but with slow service. **$$**

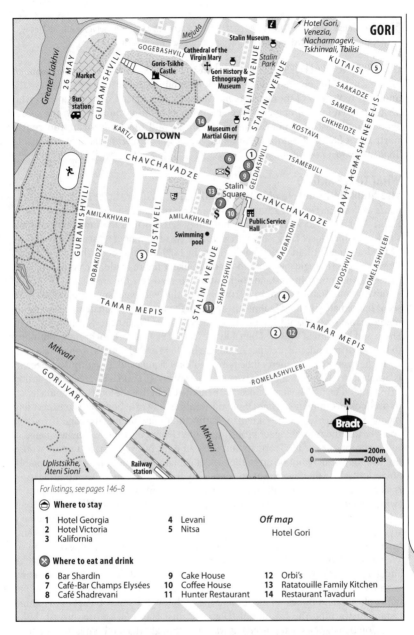

For listings, see pages 146–8

Where to stay

1 Hotel Georgia
2 Hotel Victoria
3 Kalifornia
4 Levani
5 Nitsa

Off map

Hotel Gori

Where to eat and drink

6 Bar Shardin
7 Café-Bar Champs Elysées
8 Café Shadrevani
9 Cake House
10 Coffee House
11 Hunter Restaurant
12 Orbi's
13 Ratatouille Family Kitchen
14 Restaurant Tavaduri

✕ **Orbi's** Tamar Mepis 78 (next to the Hotel Victoria). Popular with locals, has good food, locally brewed beer & a terrace. To reach it, head south along Stalin Av from Stalin Sq & turn left. **$$**

✕ **Restaurant Tavaduri** Tsereteli 9; m 599 425157. The nicest place to eat in the 'old town'. **$$**

✕ **Café-Bar Champs Elysées** Stalin Sq, opposite the City Hall. A fancy café that serves good pancakes & salads & has Wi-Fi. **$**

✕ **Café Shadrevani** Stalin Av 24. Serves good drinks & snacks. **$**

✕ **Cake House** Stalin Av 22. Despite its name, this also serves beer & Turkish coffee. Free Wi-Fi. **$**

✗ Coffee House Stalin Av 13. Also serves pizza. $ corner of Chavchavadze. Serves warm food ready
✗ Ratatouille Family Kitchen Stalin Sq, at the   to take away or eat in. $

OTHER PRACTICALITIES There are plenty of **ATMs**, including at the Bank of
Georgia and TBC on Stalin Square, Bank Republic at the post office (*Stalin Av 15*)
and ProCredit west of the centre (*Chavchavadze 10*). Peace Corps Volunteers who
visit the town for training also rave about the **swimming pool** behind the sports
school southwest of Stalin Square. There's a helpful **tourist information centre**
north of the Stalin Museum (*Kutaisi 23A;* ✆ *27 0776;* e *ticgori@gmail.com;* ⊕ *10.00–
18.00 daily, to 19.00 in summer*).

WHAT TO SEE AND DO
The Stalin Museum (*Stalin Av 32;* ✆ *07 5215;* ⊕ *10.00–18.00 daily; GEL10 inc
guide, railway carriage GEL5 extra*) To the north of Stalin Square, the large plaza of
Stalin Avenue, lined with imposing buildings, has replaced the jumble of slummy
shacks in which Josef Djugashvili grew up; the two-room house, then Sobornaya (or
Cathedral Street) 10, in which he was born in 1879, remains beneath a glass-roofed
Doric temple (thought by some to be more like a metro station) erected by Beria
in 1939. An empty plinth stands in front of this ready for the erection of the statue
removed from Stalin Square in 2010; whether this will ever happen remains to be
seen. Immediately behind Stalin's birthplace is the massive Italianate museum to his
memory that was defiantly built in 1957, the year after Khrushchev's denunciation of
Stalin and his crimes. This was officially closed in 1989, but school groups continued
to be shown around; the pretence of closure has long ended and it's open to all again.

To the people of Gori there's little purely political significance to the museum: Stalin
is simply the only important thing ever to come out of Gori, and is revered as the 'strong
man' rather than for his views or deeds. There's no doubt that the locals are far too quick
to overlook his immense crimes, but you would in any case be foolish to expect any
mention of the gulag or the Ukrainian famine in a museum like this, and if you ask
you'll be told they're waiting for proof, much like George W Bush on climate change.

Most captions are in Georgian and Russian only, but you'll have a guide whose
English may or may not be up to the task of explaining things; most take a suitably
Soviet attitude to their work, but one or two are friendly and open. The building itself
is as cold as most of the staff, and clearly not maintained. The displays are upstairs
(without a lift); the first floor deals with Stalin's youth and pre-revolutionary career
– it's remarkable what a good-looking youth he was (in a romantic revolutionary
style), and how literary, writing quite passable poetry, working in secret presses and
then being the first editor of *Pravda*. In the second room, bringing events up to
World War II, he gradually becomes more Stalin-like, with the bristling moustache
and bushy eyebrows and hair (which prevented his hats from fitting for many
years). Kalinin and Gorky remain prominent, but Trotsky can only be seen in one
of the photos, and there's no mention of the Molotov–Ribbentrop Pact or of Lenin's
testament warning the Communist Party against Stalin ('a coarse, brutish bully
acting on behalf of a great power'). It was once thought that Stalin might have been
a double agent for the tsarist secret police in the pre-revolutionary period, but it's
less clear which foreign power Lenin might have been thinking of – quite possibly
Britain, which was vilified for its occupation of Transcaucasia.

The third room deals with the Great Patriotic War – even if we can't forgive Stalin's
crimes, we should give him credit for saving us in the war. The next room is dominated
by tributes from a motley collection of world figures such as Kirov, Ordjonikidze,
Ibarruri, Barbusse, Roosevelt, Churchill and de Gaulle, and the museum culminates

with a sort of symbolic lying in state by a bust of Stalin. After this there are more miscellaneous photos, and off the grand staircase a room of cabinets displaying gifts to Stalin. Finally, the museum has responded grudgingly to pressure to cover Stalin's crimes by converting a basement room into a mock NKVD office with limited coverage of the Terror and gulags. Naturally you can buy Stalin postcards and badges here, and those with a strong sense of irony might even want a bottle of Stalin-brand Saperavi wine for a souvenir. Beside the museum it's also worth glancing at Stalin's massive private rail carriage, on six axles to carry the weight of its armour-plating. There is an additional charge if you want to go inside.

Gori History and Ethnography Museum (*Kirion II 12;* ⊕ *09.30–17.30 Tue–Sun; GEL3*) This is hidden behind Stalin Avenue 29 and has a remarkable collection of relics from the early Bronze Age Kura-Araxes culture, much of it from a burial mound about 7km away, and then the early Kurgan period, from the mid 3rd millennium BC. More recent artefacts include bronze bulls from the 8th or 7th centuries BC, Greek and Parthian coins and Roman luxury goods. From the top of the stairs, where there's a copy of a drawing of Gori Castle made for the Pope in the 17th century, you should go around to the left and then right to the ethnographic display of mainly 20th-century clothes, weapons, musical instruments and jewellery.

Elsewhere in Gori Just southwest of the History and Ethnography Museum is the Neoclassical **Cathedral of the Virgin Mary**, and rising beyond it is the **Goris-Tsikhe Castle**, colourfully lit up at night. This is best reached from the east side: just south of the cathedral, turn right at a stone cross to follow a paved pathway that curves up to the castle gate. Just to the right of here, beneath the fortified walls, is an interesting sculpture of giant warrior figures. Another path leads up from the road by the market to the entrance on the south side of the castle. The best view of the castle from below is from the west, where the walls form a series of defensive enclosures tumbling down the hillside. Although the fortifications (mostly from the 7th and 13th centuries) have been rather over-restored, the castle offers good views of the Mtkvari Valley, the solid snowy wall of the Caucasus beyond South Ossetia to the north, and, on a high spur across the river to the southwest, the 6th-century **Church of Gori-Jvari** (⊕ *May–Nov on Tue, with a festival on 6 May*). This was rebuilt in the 12th century and the 1980s; taxis charge GEL20, although it's a delightful walk of around 3 hours there and back. To reach it, head south along Stalin Avenue, cross the river and railway then follow the Ateni road that winds up the hillside and eventually becomes a dirt trail leading to the church. There's also a **Museum of Martial Glory** (*Stalin Av 19;* ⊕ *10.00–17.00 Tue–Sun; GEL3*) by a ceramic relief memorial to the dead of 1941–44 and an eternal flame. The museum contains a lot of dull photos with Georgian and Russian captions, the odd mortar and a statue of Stalin. There's minimal coverage of the 2008 war (a few bombs in the foyer, uniforms and photocopied medal citations), but the intention is to create a Museum of Russian Aggression. Behind the museum, east of the castle, is the so-called '**old town**', essentially comprised of the heavily renovated 19th-century brick buildings lining Tsereteli.

AROUND GORI

UPLISTSIKHE (⊕ *10.00–18.00 Tue–Sun*) About 10km east of Gori along the Mtkvari Valley, visible from trains along the main line, is the unmissable cave-city of Uplistsikhe (meaning the castle of the mythical Uplos, son of Mtskhetos). The Silk Road ran along the hills to the north (hence the positions of Gori, Kaspi and

Mtskheta, all on the north side of the Mtkvari), and Uplistsikhe was a religious centre by 1000BC and a trading centre by at least the 5th century BC. It was also a major centre, with a population of perhaps 20,000, in the Hellenistic and Roman periods. Later it became more isolated and was inhabited by monks until it was destroyed in the 13th century by Chinghiz's son Khulagu. Over the centuries the site has suffered greatly from the elements, although channels were built to carry off storm water and prevent flash floods (drinking water was brought 5–6km from a spring just 44m above, through a beautifully engineered system of ceramic pipes and a tunnel). Most of the caves have been at least partly eroded away, so that it takes a considerable feat of the imagination to really understand what the city was like.

The tour of the ruins is only for the able (and requires gripping footwear), starting with steps, then scrambling up rocks and following an ancient pathway past grain pits to the remains of a theatre built in the 2nd or 3rd century AD, complete with orchestra pit; the auditorium side has now all collapsed into the river and been washed away, and the stage roof is held up by concrete pillars. There's even a bread oven in the middle of the stage. The 'Blackberry Hall', so called because of the bramble roots dangling from cracks in the ceiling, may have been a pagan temple. The largest hall in the city is known as Tamar's Hall, although Queen Tamar never lived here; its front wall has gone, but it's otherwise intact. The marani (wine-storage room) next to it, one of three in the city, dates from after her time. There's an underground prison, 8.5m deep, just below Tamar's Hall, and to the south is what must have been a pharmacy, with eight layers of storage spaces (about 15cm cubes), where traces of herbs and wrapping parchments have been found. To the north of Tamar's Hall is another hall, now roofless, which was once a church – there's very little left except for the stumps of four columns, and a basin for the blood of sacrificed animals. Further up there's a very obvious conventional church, a three-nave basilica built of red brick in the 9th–10th centuries, which survived the Mongol onslaught, although all 5,000 resident monks were killed. The church's frescoes were all whitewashed in the 19th century. At the highest points of the site you'll see scraps of medieval defensive walls.

On the way back down you'll pass the market, with its stone stalls, and finish by going down through a 41m tunnel (designed to be used by water carriers, as well as for emergency exits) to emerge on the track beside the river. This leads to a village immediately to the west, whose inhabitants were removed in 1968 (though at least one house is clearly in use again). You might be tempted to set out to walk back to Gori along the north bank of the river, but you should be aware of the deep gullies blocking the way.

A World Bank cultural heritage project paid for an interpretation centre (often locked; ask to see the video with English subtitles, a useful preparation for visiting), walking itinerary and better guides. The cave complex has been on the tentative list of potential UNESCO World Heritage Sites since 2007. At present there are reasonably well-informed guides, whose services cost GEL20 on top of the ticket price of GEL3; some speak English although most have only Georgian and Russian. There are plenty of people flogging postcards, but no real interpretative materials. In addition, cracks are developing in many of the caves, which may soon crumble away; some are supported by concrete pillars, and metal roofs protect some excavated sites, but there's no fencing or limitation on where you can explore.

Getting there and away A return **taxi** from Gori to Uplistsikhe costs around GEL30 including a reasonable amount of waiting time, or GEL10–15 one-way. Alternatively, a local **bus** (*GEL1; with a sign in Latin script*) leaves the bus station in Gori at 30 minutes past the hour, passing the railway station (by an odd one-way system), forking left in the first village, Khidistavi, and then turning left at an English sign to Uplistsikhe. After a bridge across the railway the bus heads to the right through the village of Velebi and follows the river for 1.5km to Kvakhvreli; get off after 25 minutes where the bus turns right (away from the river) and head left over the bridge, from where it's a 15-minute walk to the site. To take the bus back to Gori, you should walk back another block to a junction by a bend in the river. A café and restaurant are being built by the road; there's a souvenir shop and toilets by the ticket office. The road runs below cliffs of weathered yellow sandstone which act as a heat trap, with bushes in bloom and bees and butterflies even in winter, as well as rare lizards and two species of hamster; there are eagles in the hills to the north. The best time to visit is late afternoon or early evening, when the setting sun brings a special warmth to the rocks; in summer it can be very hot in the middle of the day.

ATENI SIONI From the road junction at the west end of Khidistavi, an asphalt road, also served by regular local buses from Gori (*GEL 0.70*), leads south to Ateni following the left/west bank of the Tana stream. The village of Patara (or Little) Ateni stretches from km2.5, with metal frames training Atenuri vines out over the road from almost every house. At km6.5 the tiny Ateni Church hides to the left of the road; built of green tuff in the 7th century, with a dome added in the 9th or 10th century, it's just 5m by 6m in area and very sparsely decorated.

It's another 1.5km to the Church of Ateni (or Atenis) Sioni: this is one of the loveliest churches in Georgia, due, above all, to its setting at a bend of the narrow Tana Gorge, which is especially stunning in winter. Terraced fields by the river give a Central Asian feel, while just to the south there's a great view down the valley to Mount Kazbeg. The writer Fitzroy Maclean said of it that it made:

> [...] as great an impression on me as any [church] in Georgia; [...] architecturally Ateni Sioni impresses by its simplicity, but what struck me most of all was its magnificent position and the feeling it gave me of age, serenity and strength.

It was built by a certain Todos in the first half of the 7th century in the new style initiated at Jvari (Mtskheta) at the end of the 6th century; its decoration is finer than at Jvari, and it's in a better state of preservation. The lower parts are in red sandstone, with yellow-green tuff above. The ground plan is a tetraconch cross, its arms ending internally in four half-circles, with corner rooms rather than aisles and transepts. The spacious interior effectively has eight columns, supporting four squinches and a relatively low dome. There's just a low minimalist iconostasis. The interior was entirely painted in the late 11th century; the image of the Archangel Gabriel in the apse, painted in 1080, is a highpoint in Georgian art, as is the *Dream of Joseph* in the south transept. Externally, the façade is a copy of Jvari in local stone, restored in the 16th century; note also the two carved stags (pagan symbols) in the tympanum of the north door, and a hunter in a Sassanid headdress and a herd of stags on the west façade.

Taxis charge about GEL30 return from Gori, including waiting time (or GEL 50 combined with Uplistsikhe); but it's well worth taking a marshrutka (hourly from Gori) all the way to the end of the road, in the heart of the rugged Trialeti range, and then back to Ateni Sioni; then you can walk down to the village to catch a bus back down the valley.

A booklet and map entitled *Walking Tracks in Ateni Valley* (free from tourist offices) was published by the National Tourism Administration in 2013 and is key to a project to develop green tourism in the area. The Tana (or Ateni) Valley, rising from 600m to 2,200m in the Trialeti range, offers opportunities for rock-climbing (and even ice-climbing, on a waterfall near Biisi), birdwatching, horseriding and mountain biking. The booklet describes ten hikes, of which three are easy; one of these (5km total) starts from a bridge near the south end of Ateni village and climbs gently southeast to the lower Danachvisi Church, just below the 9th-century Vere Fortress. Two harder routes continue from here: one (12km) swinging right/south to the upper church of St George on a 1,643m hilltop (a wonderful viewpoint), the other (11km) looping left to the Ghvtimshobeli Church and returning down the next valley to the north to Chechelantubani. There are longer routes starting further along the valley, and multi-day hikes (not in the booklet) to Borjomi, Manglisi or Tsalka.

SOUTH OSSETIA Gori would also be the base for visits to **Tskhinvali**, capital of Samachablo or South Ossetia, if the political situation were normal. However, travel to the breakaway region is ill-advised to say the least for the time being and also next to impossible from Georgia (although apparently just about do-able from North Ossetia in the Russian Federation). From a tourism perspective, there's little to see in Tskhinvali anyway, which was a drab place of typically communist concrete blocks even before the 2008 conflict reduced much of it to ruins. However, there are a few things worth seeing around Tskhinvali. In the Georgian village of **Nikozi** (south of the de facto border, but too close for comfort) there's a 5th-century cruciform cathedral, rebuilt in the 14th century, and the ruins of an episcopal palace built in the 9th and 10th centuries. There's also fine walking in the hills to the north of the South Ossetian capital, which have largely escaped the erosion of the Kazbegi area, although at the present time this is unreachable. Roads continue northwards to Oni in Racha, and towards the Roka Tunnel into North Ossetia, although both are closed to foreigners. Java, the first major village on the Roka road, was the epicentre of an earthquake in 1991.

WEST OF GORI

Continuing westwards from Gori, within a few kilometres of rejoining the main road, you'll pass another village church that is well worth a brief halt. From the **Urbnisi** intersection, at km94, follow the asphalt road south through the village until you see the church to your left. Passing through a stone gateway topped by an octagonal brick bell-tower, you'll enter a churchyard in which a surprising number of large qvevri wine jars are lying around. The church is a relatively long three-nave basilica, built in the 6th century; the lower part is of stone, with the upper part of thin Roman-style bricks, supported by two brick arch-buttresses on either side, an unusual sight in Georgia. There are also a few inscribed stones on the exterior and a high relief cross on the east end. Just to the west, at km96, a sign marks the turning to **Ruisi Church**, just north of the highway, a typically Georgian cross-and-cupola church built in the 7th to 9th centuries.

SOUTH OF KARELI There's a group of interesting and attractive churches south of the Mtkvari between Gori and Khashuri, at Samtsevrisi, Tsromi and Kintsvisi. From km101.5 (km450.5 from the west) a road leads a couple of kilometres south to Kareli, a small town on the railway on the south side of the Mtkvari. Minibuses and taxis shuttle the 2km to the bridge and level crossing just beyond, and then left to the rail and bus stations. Marshrutkas run hourly to Gori until 16.00 (some continuing to Tbilisi), six times a day to Khashuri (the last at 14.40), and at noon, 15.00 and 18.00 to Zguderi, to the south beyond Kintsvisi.

From the T-junction 100m south of the level crossing, this road heads right/southwest to the modern town centre and left at a roundabout. At km2 a minor road leads right for 2km to **Samtsevrisi**, at the far end of which two old churches (visible from the Tbilisi–Kutaisi highway and railway to the north) stand on hillocks on either side of the road. The first, in a cemetery to the left/south, is a tiny dome church built in the first half of the 7th century, with a small bit of 16th-century stonework to the southwest; it's a 'free-cross' church, with a horseshoe apse in a cross plan, and is simply a perfect example of its type. The other, about 1.5km from the junction, is a small, simple basilica beside the well-preserved ruins of a 16th-century castle, with a circular underground chamber which could have been a dungeon or water cistern. The road continues parallel to the Mtkvari for another 8km to Akalsopeli (reached by a couple of buses a day), and perhaps 5km more to **Tsromi**. The Church of the Redeemer here, built in AD626–634, is the oldest of its kind in Georgia, with four free-standing columns to support the cupola; its roof has mostly been ruined by earthquakes, but it's important as the model for many churches in Georgia and far beyond. It can also be reached across a footbridge from Gomi, at about km118 on the main road from Tbilisi to Khashuri and Kutaisi.

Continuing south from the junction at km2, you'll see a couple of very odd towers on the hillside to the east, and after 6km more you enter the village of **Kintsvisi**, where a sign by a bridge marks a road to the left leading to the Kintsvisi Monastery in 3.5km. With the help of a few short cuts, it takes about 40 minutes to walk up, climbing from fields to oak and beech forest to the lower edge of the conifer belt. The monastery has reopened, with lots of restoration work under way, and you'll first pass the priest's modern house before curving right up to the church at the end of the road.

Built in 1207–13, of brick despite standing on limestone hills, the church has a single-bay nave and aisles, with a large porch to the west and others to the north and south. The three apses at the east end are the same length, the central one being distinguished only by being slightly wider and by its solid stone iconostasis. The church's frescoes are absolutely magnificent, if damaged by mould (now being treated), in particular the 13th-century Resurrection (a copy of which you can see in Tbilisi's Art Museum), and a Virgin and Child in the apse, as well as portraits of royalty and the 14th-century encyclopaedist Zasa Panaskerteli-Tsitsishvili; the painting of the cross inside the dome is typically Georgian. There's also a small stone chapel to the west of the main church, and the eastern half of a former church poised on the edge of the hill to the west, with a fantastic Virgin and Child, in Sutherland-esque swirling robes, rather exposed to the elements but still in good condition.

It's a long way on a very rough road, but theoretically it would be possible to continue south through the village to Zguderi and on to the churches of Tkemlovani and Timotesubani (page 181); perhaps a route best suited to the hardier type of mountain bikers.

KHASHURI AND SURAMI Continuing westwards, the main road passes through an unattractive district of light industry (although there is the modern Silk Road Hotel in Agara at km108/444), and then, from km118, a stretch of road with several Turkish truck stops. **Khashuri** (km126; pronounced 'Hashuri') boasts glass and textile factories, but its chief significance is as the junction of both road and rail routes west to Kutaisi and southwest to Akhaltsikhe and the Turkish border. The road passes to the south of the centre, and at km129/423 (45km from Gori, 113km from Tbilisi, 32km from Borjomi) reaches the road junction (at a roundabout with a big cross on a fountain), as well as a 24-hour fuel station and ATM. Trains take just under 2 hours from Tbilisi (*GEL2*); the station has been nicely renovated, and there's an ATM opposite. Marshrutka 1 runs from the railway station to the roundabout, about 10 minutes' walk west. Marshrutkas to Kutaisi and Batumi halt just west of the roundabout, and those to Borjomi wait about 100m down the road to Borjomi and Akhaltsikhe. The town has no other services or features of interest.

The main road to Kutaisi and the west soon climbs to the Rikoti Pass and into Imereti, bypassing the climatic resort of **Surami**, which is a far better bet than Khashuri for food, drink and accommodation; they're linked by frequent local marshrutkas. The poet Terenti Graneli was detained in the TB/mental hospital here in 1930–34. First, as the main road climbs up on to the hillside to the north of the town, it passes a dramatic small castle, which served as residence of the dukes of Kartli in early medieval times, to the south of the road at km133. This can be easily reached by a lane past a small brick church, built in the 18th and 19th centuries, with barrel domes – not the more recent church just west of the road on a rock in the pine forest. The film *The Surami Fortress*, by the Tbilisi-born Armenian director Sergei Paradjanov, tells the legend of a young man built into the castle's walls to preserve them. There are scores of wicker stalls baking and selling excellent sweet bread by the roadside (and after the tunnel there are lots of beehives and stalls selling honey to go with the bread); you can also ask here for a room. The **Hotel Surami** (*Mshvidobis 12;* \ *36 823 2269;* **$$$**) claims to have non-stop lighting and hot water.

After being reunited with the road through the town to the left, the road soon reaches the **Rikoti Pass** where, at km141 there's a choice of a tunnel, 1.75km long, or the more scenic old road over the 997m pass, 4km of tight, hairpin bends signposted as the Rikoti Tunnel Bypass. Trains use a far longer tunnel to the south, leading to Kutaisi via Manglisi and Kharagauli, and there's also a back road from the town of Surami over the Surami Pass (949m) and on beside the railway.

The Gergeti Trinity Church sits high on a mountaintop overshadowed by Mount Kazbek, and is the destination of one of Georgia's finest hikes
(P/S) pages 165–7

left   Borjomi-Kharagauli National Park is now a protected wilderness area and home to a vast variety of habitats (KG) pages 176–81

below left   The High Caucasus offers a range of beautiful and exciting hikes for all levels of ability (MGI/S)

bottom   The yellow Turk's cap lily (*Lilium monadelphum*) (JAD/DT) and fragrant orchid (*Gymnadenia conopsea*) (AF/S) are both endemic to the High Caucasus page 9

right At 2,000m, Gudauri is Georgia's main ski resort (A/DT) pages 158–60

below right Carved crosses have dotted the landscape since Georgia's conversion to Christianity in the 4th century (WC/S) pages 43–5

bottom Davit-Gareja Monastery, near the border with Azerbaijan, is surrounded by an almost lunar landscape of dry steppe (IT/DT) pages 285–8

above   The Bagrat Cathedral, controversially refurbished and re-roofed, overshadows the city of Kutaisi (WB/S) page 205

left   Tbilisi's Orbeliani Baths are covered in intricately patterned tiles (S/DT) page 111

below   Surami Fortress, the former residence of the Dukes of Kartli, has given rise to a legend that a young man was built into its walls to preserve them (AB/DT) page 154

above   Kintsvisi Monastery's frescoes are magnificent (IV/AWL) page 153

right   The majestic interior of Tbilisi's synagogue (RB/S) page 120

below   Shiom-ghvime was one of the first monasteries founded in Georgia (SI/S) pages 142–3

above left Traditional clay *qvevri* vessels are key to the huge revival in natural wines in Georgia (MaP/S) pages 75–8

above right *Churchkhela*, made of nuts on a string dipped several times into grape juice, are the symbol of the autumn grape harvest (M/S) page 75

left At Tbilisi's Dry Bridge flea market you can buy carpets, Stalin busts, houses and flats, bad art and anything else you want (MaP/S) page 114

below Chess players in Sukhumi, Abkhazia (AC/A) page 225

above Musicians playing the *duduki*, a clarinet-like pipe from Armenia, at Davit-Gareja Monastery (AC/A) page 51

below Adjaran dancing, from the southwest of Georgia, is even more athletic and exhibitionist than elsewhere in the country (tk/S)

above left — White-winged redstart (*Pheonicurus erythrogaster*) (L/DT) page 12

above right — Bearded vulture or lammergeyer (*Gypaetus barbatus*) (E/S) page 12

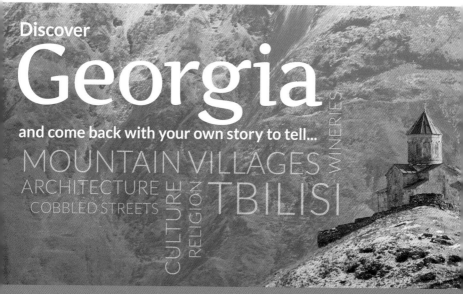

5

The Georgian
Military Highway

საქართველოს სამხედრო ხა

The Georgian Military Highway has existed as a route since before the 1st century BC, but had only evolved into a bridle track by the time the Russians finally converted it, by the Herculean efforts of 800 soldiers, into a carriage road in 1783. In 1829 Pushkin followed this route, as did many other great Russian writers, such as Lermontov, Gorky, Tolstoy and Mayakovsky, all inspired in various ways by the experience. In 1846, Shamyl attempted to close the highway in his rebellion against Russia, and it was his failure which persuaded the other tribes of the northern Caucasus not to join him, though his rebellion continued until 1864. The route finally lost much of its importance with the opening of the railway via the Caspian coast in 1883. Just over 100 years later the Roki Tunnel opened between South and North Ossetia, although given the instability of these regions it never became a major through route and now only links the two Ossetias.

The Georgian Military Highway still serves as a link to the province of Khevi (The Valley), around Kazbegi, which lies on the northern slope of the Caucasus, and offers the easiest access from Tbilisi to the high mountains. Unfortunately the hillsides are heavily eroded in this area, due largely to overgrazing but also to tourism, and the road is in an appalling state for much of its length, especially north of Gudauri. It suffers greatly from snow and ice and the pass is frequently closed in winter.

NORTH OF MTSKHETA

The highway starts with a flyover junction just after km27 on the highway from Tbilisi to Kutaisi, immediately to the northwest of Mtskheta. From here it's 58km to Pasanauri, 124km to Kazbegi, and 168km (just over 100 miles) to Vladikavkaz in Russia.

The road runs along the right/west bank of the Aragvi, in a wide valley between sandy foothills; it's lined at first with large wedding-style restaurants and conference-type hotels, of which the best is the Kapiloni at km5/134 (*Misaktsieli; 15 rooms;* m *595 771177, 596 755777; www.kapiloni.ge;* **$$$**), with conference facilities and a swimming pool. Just before km3 a side road leads 5km west to **Tsilkani**, where there's a church built as a basilica in the 5th and 6th centuries and remodelled as a dome church in medieval times. Founded by one of the Syrian Fathers in the 4th century, this was one of the first churches in Georgia, and was famous for its icon of the Virgin painted by St Luke on a board from Christ's cradle. This road continues to the Mukhrani Valley, where champanska is produced on what was the Bagration family estate (more usually visited from the Tbilisi–Kutaisi highway).

At km15.5/123.5 another road leads 8km west to **Lake Bazaleti**, formed according to legend by the tears of the Georgians at the death of Tamar's child; it's too full of weeds for swimming, but fishing is popular. The Bazaleti Lake Hotel

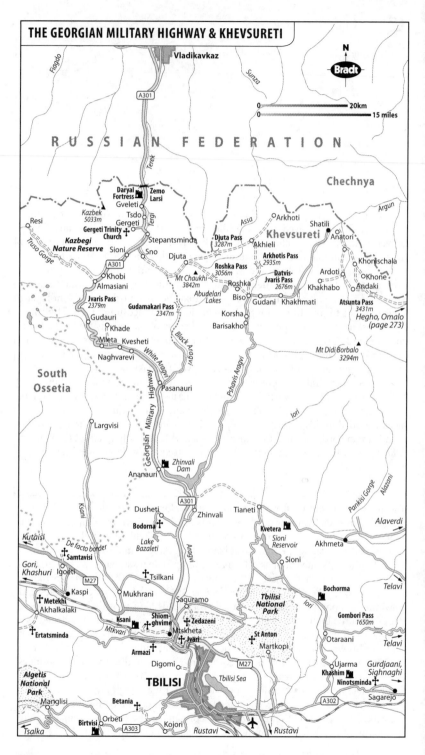

THE GEORGIAN MILITARY HIGHWAY & KHEVSURETI

N

Vladikavkaz

A301

R U S S I A N   F E D E R A T I O N

0 — 20km
0 — 15 miles

Chechnya

Friago

Sunza

Terek

Argun

Daryal Fortress
Zemo Larsi
Gveleti
Kazbek 5033m
Tsdo
Gergeti
Gergeti Trinity Church
Resi
Stepantsminda
Kazbegi Nature Reserve
Sioni
Sno
Djuta
Assa
Arkhoti
Shatili
Anatori
Khevsureti
Djuta Pass 3287m
Akhieli
Arkhotis Pass 2935m
Khonischala
Truso Gorge
A301
Khobi
Almasiani
Roshka Pass 3056m
Mt Chaukhi 3842m
Roshka
Datvis-Jvaris Pass 2676m
Ardoti
Khakhabo
Khone
Andaki
Jvaris Pass 2379m
Gudamakari Pass 2347m
Abudelari Lakes
Biso
Gudani
Khakhmati
Atsunta Pass 3431m
Hegho, Omalo (page 273)
Gudauri
Khade
Korsha
Mleta
Kvesheti
Barisakho
Naghvarevi
Mt Didi Borbalo 3294m
White Aragvi
Black Aragvi
South Ossetia
Pasanauri
Pshavis Aragvi
Largvisi
Iori
Ksani
Georgian Military Highway
Zhinvali Dam
Ananauri
Dusheti
Zhinvali
Tianeti
Alaverdi
Pankisi Gorge
Alazani
A301
Bodorna
Kvetera
Sioni Reservoir
Akhmeta
Kutaisi
De facto border
Lake Bazaleti
Sioni
Gori, Khashuri
Samtavisi
Igoeti
Tsilkani
Bochorma
Telavi
M27
Kaspi
Mukhrani
Saguramo
Tbilisi National Park
Iori
Gombori Pass 1650m
Metekhi
Akhalkalaki
Ksani
Shiom-ghvime
Zedazeni
Gurdjaani, Sighnaghi
Ertatsminda
Mtkvari
Mtskheta
Jvari
St Anton
Martkopi
Otaraani
Telavi
Armazi
Digomi
M27
Ujarma
Khashim
Ninotsminda
Algetis National Park
TBILISI
Tbilisi Sea
Sagarejo
Manglisi
Betania
A302
Tsalka
Birtvisi
Orbeti
A303
Kojori
Rustavi
Rustavi

156

complex (\ *32 275 5366;* e *info@bazaletilake.ge; www.bazaletilake.ge;* **$$$$$**) has boats and bikes as well as a swimming pool and three-room apartments for four to five persons in four-star 'cottages', plus one- and two-room hotel suites; all prices include three meals a day. To the north of the lake is **Bodorna Monastery**, where the medieval dome Church of St Mary (rebuilt in the 18th century) has a row of hooks outside for hanging sacrificed sheep, and caves in oddly shaped yellow cliffs were used as refuges from the Tatars. Further north (10km from the lake) is **Dusheti**, which was the capital of the Aragvi princes in the 17th century and received a municipal charter late in the 18th century; now it's just a small village with some Art Nouveau buildings. From here it's 5km back to the Georgian Military Highway, at km19.

At km26 a minor road turns right to follow the Pshavis Aragvi Valley to Khevsureti (pages 168–70); the Georgian Military Highway rises above the right bank to pass the **Zhinvali Dam** at km28; this has flooded the area of the confluence of the Aragvi and the Pshavis Aragvi, where the forested mountainsides begin to press in on either side. Companies from Tbilisi are now organising rafting trips on the Pshavis Aragvi.

ANANAURI The highway climbs along the hillside to km34 (where there's a restaurant with good views), then descends past the crenellated Restaurant Ananauri (m *577 968896, 577 455022;* e *ananuri.rest@hotmail.com*) at about km35, before dropping to cross a modern viaduct and reach the amazing churches of Ananauri just before km37 (ie: after km102 from the north; 45 minutes from Tbilisi). These stand within a crenellated wall at the head of the reservoir; the village, which stood below, has largely been destroyed and relocated to the north. Amazingly, it was seriously proposed to build the dam higher and flood the churches too, but a popular protest movement of a kind that was almost unheard of in Soviet times managed to defeat this plan.

The entrance on the south side of the wall leads you to the **lower church**, the larger and more recent of the two crammed together here. Dedicated to the Dormition of the Mother of God, it was built in 1689 and is big and bare inside, with two pillars supporting the barrel dome, and frescoes of saints and the Last Judgement on the south wall. The interior was damaged by fire in the 18th century, and many fine frescoes were lost. However, its carved external decorations are superb, above all on the south wall where a huge cross stands on the backs of two dragons, flanked by two vines (being eaten by deer) above two odd moustachioed angels and two lions; there's another angel up at the top left corner. The pagan elements in the design clearly show Persian influence. There are also stones with carved rams' heads, an older pagan motif, now piled up inside the gateway.

Immediately above this church is a 12th-century **watchtower**; the west wall of the church pressed up against this carries wonderful carvings, presumably for the eye of God alone. Above that is the smaller **Hvtaeba** or **Saviour's Church**, built in the 1650s. Although externally of stone, the interior is of brick and it too is bare, with the remaining frescoes largely ruined by graffiti, mainly Russian. It has a two-bay nave and aisles, with a barrel dome above the crossing, lit by deep-set lancet windows. At the top of the slope, set into the ring wall, is the solid Sheupovari (Intrepid) **tower**, which has five chambers, one above the other, all made safe with concrete and connected by wooden ladders. It's well worth climbing to the top for views of the church domes and the surrounding hills, and you can also walk most of the way around the battlements. At the lower end of the complex is a small 17th-century **bell-turret**, nowadays looking out over the lake as well as a ruined

Armenian church. Down some steps by the bell-turret is a hiding place where soldiers could lurk before rushing out to attack intruders.

Ananauri was in the wars many times, most famously in 1717 when Prince Bardsig, the Eristav of Aragvi, seized the wife of Prince Chanche, Eristav of Ksani. Chanche allied himself with the Lesghians of the northern Caucasus, and captured Ananauri; he reclaimed his wife successfully, but the Muslim Lesghians burnt the churches and destroyed many of the frescoes.

PASANAURI The road continues between thickly wooded hillsides that Fitzroy Maclean found rather reminiscent of Perthshire. Small villages offer the occasional café, while footbridges give access to walks on the eastern side of the valley. At km53 you'll see the first of the remaining watchtowers, which once stood at every curve in the valley, providing a relay chain of signal stations for times of danger. The only town between Mtskheta and Kazbegi is Pasanauri, which consists of just two streets, Rustaveli (northbound) and Kostava (southbound) between km59 and km60.

This is a climatic resort at 1,014m, where the White (Tetri) Aragvi, the main river, is joined by the Black (Shavi) Aragvi from the northeast; the water of the Black Aragvi is often noticeably darker, with the two flowing side by side before merging. There's little to do here other than rest and walk to the **Chabarukh Gorge** (where there's a waterfall) and the **Gudamakari Gorge**, and to the **Church of St George of Lomisi**, at 3,000m on a ridge to the west; this is the centre of a pagan cult, where boys are taken at the age of 11 or 12 for initiation, a ceremony apparently described by the anthropologist Margaret Mead.

Where to stay and eat The **Hotel Aragvi** (*Rustaveli 77*; 📞 *92 0529*; 📱 *899 233220*; **$$**) is very run-down, but there are various unpretentious family-run hotel-restaurants along the road just north, which provide decent and friendly accommodation. The Pasanauri area is famed for its khinkhali, so don't miss them.

🏠 **Hotel Kvesheti** (14 rooms) km75; 📱 599 543288, 599 114377; www.kvesheti.ge. Can arrange trekking, horseriding & rafting. Rates are HB. **$$$**

🏠 **Guesthouse Korugi** (7 rooms) km62; 📱 599 540139, 579 540139; e korugi@pasanauri. ge; www.pasanauri.ge. Also offers rafting & mountain biking. **$$**

GUDAURI Continuing northwards in the Mtiuleti district, the valley is still relatively wide. Near km66 you'll see a watchtower high to the left; at km73 you'll see one to the right and another pair ahead, and near km74 there's a tower to the left and a chapel and then a tower to the right. The road passes through the villages of **Naghvarevi** at km75–76 (followed by stalls selling comical sheepskin hats) and **Kvesheti**; then there's another tower to the west, and after Zemo (Upper) Mleta (1,556m; km79), above which there's a spring and roadside stalls selling drinks, woolly socks and sheepskin hats. The road then climbs 640m up the Mleti cliff, with the help of six hairpin bends from km82. As you climb, the High Caucasus finally comes into sight; first the Red Mountains, and then the Seven Brothers, both massive ranges of red volcanic rock. Near the top (just after a roadside shrine at a hairpin) is a viewing platform with metal rails giving great views as you lean out over the abyss.

At the top are the scattered Ossetian villages of Qumlistsikhe and then Gudauri which, at 2,000m, is the highest settlement on the Georgian Military Highway, and one of Georgia's two main ski resorts. Two hours from Tbilisi at km89/50, it's an unplanned mess: the centre is marked by a petrol station, supermarket and police post, with a road west to a new church and scattered chalets and hotels. Hairpin bends lead up to some modern hotels by the turning to the mid-station of the main chairlift, before leaving Gudauri at km 92/47.

Where to stay Prices for hotels are high, but most do include meals (normally breakfast and dinner in ski season). Alternatively, there are a few cheaper hostels.

Hotels

Hotel Carpe Diem (53 rooms) 32 251 0770; www.carpediem.ge. 130m from the main road near the mid-station, this is a comfortable place with brightly-coloured rooms & a decent restaurant. **$$$$$**

Hotel Club 2100 (38 rooms) m 571 210000; www.club-2100.com. New in 2013, this big, modern hotel above the centre of the resort (at 2,100m, of course) is non-smoking throughout & has a sauna/jacuzzi (⏰ 24hrs). You can also book through AlpinTravel (+41 81 720 2121; www.alpintravel. ch) who operate heli-skiing packages. **$$$$$**

Hotel Truso (14 rooms) 32 214 6900; m 599 276644; e info@hoteltruso@com; www. hoteltruso.com. A simple, older place right in the centre, 100m from the lifts. FB, Wi-Fi, satellite TV & sauna. **$$$$$**

Marco Polo (123 rooms) 32 220 2900; m 599 111900; http://marcopolo.ge/en. Turning right/east at the Wissol petrol station/Smart supermarket, there's a short, unsigned road to this 4-star establishment, built by an Austrian entrepreneur in 1988. It struggled to survive in the absence of direct flights from western Europe to Tbilisi, but it may now have a brighter future. Renovated in 2011, it offers all the comforts required of a hotel of this class, inc an indoor swimming pool & tennis courts, gym, sauna & jacuzzi. Although primarily established for skiing (with the lifts starting immediately behind the hotel), it's also an ideal base for walking in summer. **$$$$$**

ApartHotel New Gudauri m 577 245 245; e booking@newgudauri.ge. The centrepiece of the New Gudauri development, at the base of a new gondola, with luxury apartments. Kitchen, Wi-Fi & upmarket Georgian/European restaurant. **$$$$**

Gudauri Hut (33 rooms) m 595 939911; e gudaurihut@gmail.com; www.gudaurihut.com. Rooms are en suite with TV & there's a sauna in the basement. **$$$$**

Hotel Good Aura (16 rooms) m 571 503011; www.hotelgoodaura.com. A modern

place towards the church, there's a restaurant, sauna, climbing wall & transfers to the lifts. **$$$$**

Hotel Ozone (20 rooms) Qumlistsikhe km88; m 599 550983; e gakozon@yandex.ru. Down at 1,850m, they provide a free shuttle to the chairlift, 500m away. There's a sauna & a bar in a separate building. **$$$$**

Hotel Shino (19 rooms) m 599 534420, 599 267733; www.gudauri.info/accommodation/hotels/shino. At km92, just before the police post (with an English sign), an asphalt road turns right, leading in a couple of hundred metres to this biggish chalet-style building with a cosy lounge & en-suite twin rooms. Meals are about GEL10 each. **$$$$**

Skihouse-Panorama (10 rooms) Qumlistsikhe km88; m 599 330003; e info@skihouse-panorama.com; www.skihouse-panorama.com. Run by a paraglider pilot, this hotel is 500m from the chairlift; all rooms have satellite TV. It also has a minibus, a small pool & sauna. Rooms are FB, & are a little cheaper in Apr. **$$$$**

Hotel Shamo (16 rooms) m 599 500142; e info@allgudari.ge; www.allgudauri.ge. Further from the lifts in Qumlistsikhe, this family-run place has a lounge & bar, & offers good meals. Rates are HB. **$$$–$$$$**

Hostels

Gudauri Dacha (5 rooms) m 597 032396, 599 709203; www.facebook.com/GudauriDacha. This snowboarders' place has a couple of rooms with en-suite bathrooms while others have shared facilities; filling Georgian b/fasts & dinners. **$$$**

Snow House (10 rooms) m 599 170104, 599 153577; e carva@caucasus.net; www. snowhouse.ge. Above the centre near the mid-station of the lifts, this hostel also houses a ski-school & equipment rental, & for just US$5/day extra you can avail yourself of an instructor's services. **$$$**

Gagieti Hostel (10 rooms) m 599 579099, 590 232335; e ninobuchukuri@gmail.com; www.

gagieti.ge. Immediately below the police station on the main road, this very welcoming place has a good restaurant serving healthy food, organic where possible. $$–$$$

🏠 **Happy Yeti Hostel** (6 rooms) Qumlistsikhe; m 571 268800; e booking.gudauri@gmail.com;

http://happyyetihostel.com. Run by a Polish/Ukrainian crew, this comfortable, modern place has shared dorms each with their own bathroom, a bar & washing machine; 2 hearty meals included. $$–$$$

✖ Where to eat and drink
There are good restaurants at the **Hotel Truso**, **Gagieti Hostel** and the **Gudauri Hut**, all in the centre, just above the 24-hour Smart supermarket, which also has a café. On the mountain, there are various places to eat near the lift stations, such as the renowned **Khade (or Khizhina) Hut** at 2,650m, which serves Georgian and Uzbek cuisine, as well as cocktails.

What to see and do
In winter the place is heaving with skiers and snowboarders, of course, many of them from Poland and Ukraine. The Sukhia ski race, effectively the Georgian championship, is held here in odd years (in even years it's in Bakuriani). Good Doppelmayr chairlifts run northeast from the Marco Polo Hotel to a mid-station and then the Khade Hut (2,650m) and on to a col at 2,860m and to Mount Sadzele (3,307m), from where skiers have a vertical drop of almost 1km. The New Gudauri development of chalets and apartments is at the base of a new ten-seat gondola to a new snow park just above the Khade Hut. There are 50km of pistes, the longest at 5km, with plenty of snow at least until the end of April. It's not much further north to Mount Sadzele, and **heli-skiing** is available from 4,200m with Heliksir (*Pekini 28, Tbilisi;* ✆ *32 224 3503;* m *595 350900; www.heliksi. travel*). Gear can be rented through hotels and hostels and at the bases of the lifts. Instruction is available through hotels and hostels or from Kankavebi (m *599 153577*), Mtis Skola (m *599 929113*) or Skiniki (m *599 364647*).

A ski pass for the 2014/15 season was GEL30 per day or GEL174 per week; the chairlifts run from 10.00 to 17.00 and on Saturdays from 19.30 to 22.00, and on summer weekends from 11.00 to 17.00 (*GEL5, day GEL10*).

In summer you could stop for the odd day's **hiking**, but not more. It's possible, on foot or horseback, to cover the distance between the Khade Hut and the Khade Gorge (1,600m) in about 3 hours. Khade Gorge still has more than 50 defensive towers in seven villages. A 12km dirt road leads down to Kvesheti on the highway below the Mleti cliff. Paragliding is possible all year with experienced pilots, from GEL140 – contact Fly Gudauri (m *568 114453; www.flygudauri.com*) or Georgia Sky Atlantida Paragliding Co (m *597 035421, 597 067948;* e *skyatlantida@gmail. com; skyatlantida.com*).

INTO THE TERGI VALLEY From Gudauri, the road climbs slightly to an avalanche gallery then dips briefly into the Devil's Valley, which as the poet Lermontov explains is really a mistranslation of Frontier Valley; above to the right is the original Russian road, which makes a pleasant short hike. From km96 a short road leads to the left to a large viewing platform (and a small one without rails, to be avoided) looking over the 'Stone Chaos' of the Gudaur Abyss and the 'zebra-striped' summit of Gud-Gura. If the view is too much for you, there's a 70m-long Soviet mural on the inside of the platform, created in 1983 to celebrate the 200th anniversary of the Treaty of Gurgievsk; some of the colour has gone but the outlines are clear.

From here it's not far up to the **Jvaris Ughelt** or Cross Pass, better known in Russian as the Krestovy Pereval (2,379m, 127km from Tbilisi); open only from May to November, it's the highest point of the route and there are many fine descriptions, notably by Lermontov and Dumas, of the struggle to cross the pass in foul weather. There's a small marker at the pass on the present road, but visible to the east at km99 is the cross erected by Yermolov in 1824, replacing the so-called Tamar's Cross, in fact erected by King David the Builder. This stands on the old road, rather higher than the present one, and is visible from the Devil's Valley at the top of a steep rise.

Descending the Bidara Valley into the watershed of the Tergi (Terek in Russian) River, you'll pass five avalanche galleries, which traffic uses only in winter; you could hike the old road, across the valley to the left. The alpine meadows are interrupted by rocks stained red by the sweet mineral waters that are common here; the bearded vultures seem to dye their 'beards' red by drinking the iron-rich water.

Almasiani (1,960m), the first part of the village of **Khobi**, lies to the left of the road at a police post, by some caravan-cafés. This is the start of a superb hike (signed in English by the WWF at the junction) to the west up the **Truso Gorge** (nicely described by Tony Anderson as 'a geological fantasy on the duel between water and rock'), which follows a dirt track alongside the Tergi to the village of Nogkau. Beyond here there was until recently only a 4x4 track through the very tight gorge to the hamlets of Ketrisi, Abano and Resi in the lovely wide upper valley. Now, a new road goes over the ridge to the south, but it is also possible to hike through the gorge. This is wonderfully spectacular scenery, with the steep slopes of this glacial valley on the southwestern flank of Mount Kazbek rising high above the defensive towers of the villages; there are many more mineral springs at the foot of the cliffs to the south side, especially before Ketrisi and at Abano (ie: Bath, about 25km up the valley), where there's a mineral lake. The valley is an excellent spot to see bearded vultures and other alpine specialities like wallcreepers. There's good camping here too, unlike the Sno Valley where you allegedly need to keep a fire alight all night to keep wolves away. The upper valley is inhabited in summer by Ossetians, and the borders of South and North Ossetia meet at the top of the valley; do not go beyond a Georgian flag.

At about km106 the Military Highway passes the centre of Khobi (1,932m); you'll have your first view of the immense Mount Kazbek ahead (just as on the beer labels), before the road passes through the Baidari Gorge (named after Toti Baidarashvili, an Ossetian mountaineer posted here in the 18th century by King Erekle to rescue travellers from snow). The only villages are away to the west, perched on the cliff on the left bank of the Tergi, crossed by a cableway.

The next village by the road (148km from Tbilisi) is **Sioni**, where you'll see the church and watchtower on a crag overlooking the road (at km116) more or less opposite the turning to a bridge to the villages across the river; to reach them you need to continue to a junction by a green caravan. From here, head right/east for 500m to a T-junction, then follow the road back southwards for 1km, all on asphalt except for the final zigzags up to the church. This is a three-naved basilica built in the late 9th and early 10th centuries; externally it is quite rectangular, although internally there is an apse behind the altar, as well as a five-arched stone iconostasis. The watchtower, beyond an abandoned modern building, is a late medieval construction; at ground level there's no door (a ladder having been used for access), but tasteless Russian graffiti instead.

SNO, DJUTA AND HIKING EAST TO KHEVSURETI

The northern end of Sioni is **Arsha**, where there's a 9th–10th-century fortress and the Hotel Tergi (*km119*; m *599 987675, 595 326527*; e *levan_pitskhelauri@yahoo.com*; **$$**), which is simple, friendly and very cheap (you can book through AirBnB). Just to the north, another dirt track leads east through Achkhoti, just off the highway, and to the villages of

Sno and Djuta, another highly recommended hiking route (you can start from the north side of the bridge at km122). **Sno**, where the asphalt ends, is about 4km along the wide glaciated valley, beyond a bizarre sculpture park that has the heads of local writers strewn around the hillside like glacial boulders; it's the birthplace of Ilia, the Catholicos of the Georgian Church. There's a ruined fortress (built in the 16th or 17th century) within a circular wall here and not a lot else.

It's about 18km further to the end of the side road at **Djuta**, the highest village in the area at 2,200m and one of the highest in Europe (page 240). It is home to 20 Khevsur extended families, mostly named Arabuli due to having traded with 'Arab' caravans, living in solid houses with verandas. Immediately southeast of Djuta is the seven-peaked Mount Chaukhi (3,842m), the north face of which offers 800m-high cliffs for climbers (best in September/October); the base camp is at 2,600m, 2 hours' hike from Djuta. There are a few basic **homestays ($$)** in the village; ask for Soso Arabuli (m 595 515149), Iago Arabuli (m 599 533239, 593 422951) or Maia Chincharauli (m 593 203716) if you want to stay here. In summer, you can also stay in a hut or big solid tents at Zeta Camp (m 577 501057; e zetacamp@yahoo.com; http://zeta.ge; **$$**), which offers organic meals and hot showers, in a stunning setting a 10-minute hike up the valley from Djuta at 2,300m. A well-marked track leads on to a climbers' campsite at 2,250m on a plateau below the Chaukhi Massif, where there's lots of good, accessible climbing.

From July onwards, it's also possible for trekking groups to cross into **Khevsureti**; the paths have largely vanished, so a guide is needed, but it's safe otherwise. In fact it's just a 10-hour hike to Roshka (2,050m) by the direct route over the Chaukhi or Roshka Pass (3,056m), but it's more interesting to cross the Djuta Pass (3,287m) north to the headwaters of the River Assa and Akhieli (just four houses and an abandoned tall tower); it's part of the three-hamlet community of Arkhoti, a beautiful valley that's very isolated, with fairly easy access to Ingushetia to the north but only two hard passes into Georgia to the south. It's a 10-hour hike across the Arkhotis Pass (2,935m) south to Roshka, where there are two huge erratic boulders, the smaller of which measures 19m by 5m by 7m. It's also possible to hike south along a pony track from between Sno and Djuta over the 2,347m Gudamakari Pass to the Black Aragvi Valley and Pasanauri.

STEPANTSMINDA (KAZBEGI)
სტეფანწმინდა (ყაზბეგი)   *Telephone code 245*

Another 4.5km brings you to Stepantsminda (Kazbegi), at 1,797m and km124/15 (153km from Tbilisi); this is the only town in Khevi province (or Mokhavia) and the only place with anything resembling shops and accommodation. However, with a population of just 4,000 and relatively little through traffic to Russia, commercial opportunities are inevitably limited, although it's worth looking for the local woollens, such as socks and hats.

It's a small, sleepy place, dominated by free-range highland cattle and pigs. Known in the 19th century as Stepan-Tsminda (St Stephen), the town was then named after Alexander Kazbegi (or Qazbegi; 1848–93), a local noble who became a much-loved pastoral poet, living as a shepherd for seven years; it has now reverted to Stepantsminda, but Kazbegi remains the more widely used name. The square, dominated by a monument to Kazbegi, is lined with 4x4 taxis and marshrutkas, as well as a couple of cafés and hotels.

GETTING THERE AND AWAY Marshrutkas leave from the Didube terminal in Tbilisi every hour until 17.00, as well as shared taxis from the same place; services back from Stepantsminda leave hourly from the square. Others run from Tbilisi as far as Pasanauri, and one goes as far as Gudauri, returning at about 16.00. If you want to go from Kazbegi to Gudauri you may be forced to pay the full fare to Tbilisi. Marshrutkas take around 3 hours and charge GEL10; **shared taxis** (which might even stop for you to take a photo) charge GEL15. There are local marshrutkas south from Stepantsminda as far as Khobi, but none go northwards. Local **taxi** drivers at the central square offer excursions to Djuta and the Russian border; be sure to bargain.

TOUR OPERATORS Various operators in Tbilisi (pages 56–7) offer multi-day trips to climb Mount Kazbek. On the main square in Stepantsminda you'll find the **Mountain Travel Agency** (m *555 649291, 599 269291;* e *dkhetaguri@gmail.com; www.mtainfo.ge*) who have guides available, as well as climbing gear, bikes, tents and horses.

WHERE TO STAY As well as the hotels, there are various homestays in Stepantsminda village and better ones across the river in Gergeti. Naturally, it is always worth looking at the rooms and checking out facilities like hot water before making a commitment. Prices are fairly standard: around GEL20 for a bed or GEL30–40 for half-board.

Hotels

Rooms Hotel (156 rooms) Gorgasali 1; 322 71 0099, 322 40 0099; http://roomshotels. com/kazbegi. Now one of Georgia's finest hotels, it's hard to believe that this was once a run-of-the-mill Intourist block. Up a cobbled street just north of the square (before Liberty Bank), a right & a left & a surprisingly bad road leads up to the hotel on the left, a 10–15-min hike (or a taxi) above the town. Inside, the ground floor is a lovely flexible library-style space with views across the valley to Kazbek & the Gergeti Church. There's a bar with sofas & shared tables, & more of a real restaurant beyond the bar, though still informal. There's a casino too, but it's unobtrusive. Below, there's a swimming pool (& sauna) that also has a view to Kazbek. Bedrooms, also with views of Kazbek, are spacious & comfortable, although missing details such as bedside lights. **$$$$$**

Hotel Stepantsminda (20 rooms) m 599 646880, 182296; e kazbegihotels@yahoo.com. This comfortable, new hotel on the square has large Western-quality en-suite rooms, with TV & stunning views. Mainly used by groups but it may have short-notice availability. English is spoken (ask for Nata). **$$$**

Shorena's Hotel 34 525 2607; m 598 398274, 599 074074; e shorenashoka@gmail.com. At the south end of the square, a friendly little place with a bar-restaurant. **$$$**

Hotel Lomi (Lion) (5 rooms) Behind the green gate at the northern end of the square; m 599 403264. Basic (with shared bathrooms) but a friendly, family-run place, although no English is spoken. GEL15 extra for HB. **$$**

Homestays

Anano's Guesthouse Vazha-Pshavelas 7; m 595 099449, 593 344274, 598 589662; e ananoqushasvili@yahoo.com. Also offers tours & has rooms with private bathrooms; b/fast is an extra GEL10.

Gogi Alibegashvili Tabidze 44; m 551 901085. An attractive big house with Wi-Fi but no English spoken.

Guesthouse Gergeti Khevisberi 7; 345 25 2480; m 598 382700, 599 265813; e ssujashvili@yahoo.co.uk; www.hotelgergeti. com. Clearly signposted on the same street that runs left to the HQ, this is a welcoming guesthouse, also known as Nazi Chkareuli's or Shorena Sujashvili's homestay. It's very popular with backpackers & somewhat crowded.

HQ of Nove Sujashvili 25 2418; m 591 400211, 593 199200. One of the best homestays (although oddly named), this is across the river in Gergeti, about a 15min walk from the square – head north across the bridge on the road to Russia, turn left & after crossing a stream either go diagonally left up a path between 2 walls &

turn left, or keep going & take the road to the left. In either case, it's a decent 2-storey house just up to the right, opposite a cross & above No 25. They have 4- & 8-bed dorms & a private dbl, or you can camp in the garden, below a cliff with fine vertical strata. English is spoken, & Nana knows a lot about traditional cures & recipes.

🏠 **Luisa's House** Vazha-Pshavelas 38; 🔌 25 2353. Also has a minivan for tours.

🏠 **N & M Guesthouse** Tabidze 5; m 598 761016

🏠 **Nunu Maisuradze** 🔌 25 2593; m 558 358535. This homestay is on Kazbegi, the road leading up from the main square, & offers rooms for GEL15 & HB for GEL30.

✕ **WHERE TO EAT AND DRINK** For food, meals at your hotel or guesthouse are the best bet, although there are one or two places on the main square.

✕ **Restaurant Khevi** Kazbegi 29; m 551 171736, 598 259330; www.facebook.com/restaurantkhevi. Slightly more modern & upmarket than Shorena's. $$

✕ **Tsanareti** In the nearby village of Arsha; 🔌 790 70 7162. The best restaurant in the area, which serves large portions of fantastic Georgian food. $$

✕ **Shorena's** On the main square; ⏰ 08.00–23.00 daily. This friendly restaurant-bar serves huge portions of the classic Georgian dishes. $

✕ **Taverna** Kazbegi 15. Just north of the war memorial, this is a friendly bar-restaurant with free Wi-Fi. $

OTHER PRACTICALITIES A few minimarket-type shops close to the central square sell the usual range of goods; there's no obligation to patronise the one that calls itself 'Tourist Shop'. There are **exchange kiosks** on the square giving poor rates, but there is now also an **ATM** at Liberty Bank, just north. There's a **post office** (⏰ 09.00–17.00 Mon–Fri, 09.00–15.00 Sat) further north just beyond the museum, and a hospital to the west at the south end of town, opposite the police station.

WHAT TO SEE AND DO At the far end of the square the Georgian Military Highway forks left, while the road to the right leads past the church and the **Stepantsminda Museum** (⏰ 10.00–17.00 except Mon; GEL3) to the town hall. The church is a very simple basilica, built in 1814, with a few nice external carvings and a separate gate-tower. The museum is in a large stone building with a veranda and attractive garden with Kazbegi's grave. Downstairs are manuscripts, photos of Kazbegi and his three brothers whose home this was, and stills from films of his stories, and upstairs is his furniture. The ethnographic section has material on the Mokheve people, the gates of the Betlemi Monastery and information on the 'Kazbegi Treasure', a hoard of gold and bronze. Behind the museum is the post office and behind this stands what remains of the lower terminal of the former cable-car.

Immediately to the south of the church is Rustaveli kucha, just south of which, one block above the square (at Vazha-Pshavelas 24) is the **Kazalikashvili Museum of Alpinism** (ie: mountaineering), which is small and unpretentious and may be left open and untended (or, equally, locked and untended), but gives a good insight into the allure of rock and ice.

For a short **local walk**, a good option is to head up to the graveyard that stands above Stepantsminda to the north-east. Simply make for the massive Rooms Hotel and just beyond it you will come to a gate into the cemetery. There are superb morning views over the village, Gergeti and Mount Kazbek from here; the graves, some quite elaborate with etched faces copied from photographs of the deceased, are also interesting. A track continues up to the hilltop shrine of Elia, with views towards Mount Kazbek.

The Kazbegi Nature Reserve The Kazbegi Nature Reserve was established in 1976, covering an area of 8,707ha. It lies at the divide between the Central and Eastern Caucasian ranges, with average precipitation in Kazbegi town of 640mm per year and temperatures of –5.2°C in January and 14.4°C in August (an annual average of 4.9°C). At 3,652m (the Gergeti glacier weather station) it's far colder, with temperatures of –15°C in January, 3.4°C in August, and an annual average of –6.1°C.

There are 1,347 plant species in the reserve, of which 105 are trees. Around half the trees are birch, with pine, beech, and large areas of Rhododendron caucasicum, and smaller areas of barberry, buckthorn, aspen, willow, maple and juniper. There are many alpine flowers in the hay meadows, with campanulas and gentians above the treeline, and cushion alpines on the scree slopes. Mammals include the brown bear (*Ursus arctos*), Caucasian goat or tur (*Capra caucasica*), chamois (*Rupicapra rupicapra*), hare (*Lepus europaeus*), fox (*Vulpes vulpes*), marten (*Martes martes*), weasel (*Mustela nivalis*), wildcat (*Felis silvestris*), squirrel (*Sciurus* sp) and birch mouse (*Sicista kazbegica*).

Bird species include lots of raptors, such as the bearded vulture or lammergeyer (*Gypaetus barbatus*), Egyptian vulture (*Neophron percnopterus*), Eurasian black vulture (*Aegypius monachus*), Eurasian griffon vulture (*Gyps fulvus fulvus*), golden eagle (*Aquila chrysaetus fulva*), imperial eagle (*A. heliaca*), lesser spotted eagle (*A. pomarina*), white-tailed eagle (*Haliaetus albicilla*), pallid harrier (*Circus macrourus*), long-legged buzzard (*Buteo rufinus*), lesser kestrel (*Falco naumanni*), peregrine (*Falco peregrinus*); also the jay (*Garrulus glandarius krynicki*), black francolin (*Francolinus francolinus*), chukar (*Alectoris chukar*), Caucasian snowcock (*Tetraogallus caucasicus*), Caucasian black grouse (*Tetrao mlokosiewicz*), great rosefinch (*Carpodacus rubicilla*), white-winged redstart (*Phoenicurus erythrogaster*) and red-fronted serin (*Serinus pusillus*).

The meadows are presently overgrazed and increasingly suffering from erosion; from Kazbegi southwards sheep flocks migrate along the verges of the Georgian Military Highway in spring and autumn as they move between their home villages and the high meadows, and the damage done can easily be seen. On the other hand, the provision of natural gas has reduced the damage done to forests by the cutting of fuel wood. The WWF (Worldwide Fund for Nature) is involved with projects here, including an ecotourism scheme. GCCW (the Georgian Centre for the Conservation of Wildlife) is also active, bringing groups of birders almost daily in May and June, and the economic impact has largely ended the poaching of Caucasian snowcock. June and July are also a good time to visit, with the rhododendron in bloom.

The Gergeti hike The WWF started conservation work in Kazbegi, but has now been replaced by the US Agency for International Development (USAID); they did produce a map of hiking routes up the Truso Valley and to the Gergeti and Devdoraki glaciers but this is no longer available. The Gergeti route is an extension of the near-compulsory hike up to the Gergeti Trinity Church, which sits high on a ridge west of the town of Kazbegi, silhouetted against the massive bulk of Mount Kazbek. This was reached by a cable-car built in 1988 and very soon abandoned; no-one here ever wanted it, seeing it as an imposition from outside and an assault on the religious identity of the Gergeti Church. The lower terminal behind the Kazbegi Church is now derelict, while the upper one beside the Gergeti Church has already virtually vanished.

North towards the church (*1hr 15mins; moderate*) The route starts by taking the Georgian Military Highway from the square in Kazbegi and across the Tergi and turning left up the road to the attractive mountain village of Gergeti. Following the road up the left/south side of the village, heading straight for the Trinity Church, you'll come to a point where a ruined defensive tower can be seen in a small side valley to the left; although it is possible to go up here on a steep path to the rear/west of the Trinity Church, it's far easier to turn right to cross on the level through the village and then swing up to the left, following green arrows with the Kazbegi logo. From here a track leads up to the village cemetery, about 30 minutes from Kazbegi; *en route* you should ask for Genri Chiklauri's house, to ask for the key to the church; he or his wife may well come with you, in which case you should give them GEL3–5. Just above the village you'll pass the **Kazbegi Mountain Hut** (m 599 497764; *www.kazbegi-hut.ge*; ⊕ *May–Oct*), funded by USAID, where you can ask for information and arrange a guide (hiking GEL150/day, climbing GEL250/day) and rent gear; there's also accommodation (GEL25pp).

At the cemetery the track crosses a jeep track and climbs past crooked birch (*Betula litwinowii*) trees then pines, with Caucasian chiffchaffs and green warblers, reaching the jeep track again in 20 minutes. From here the most direct route is to head left for 5 minutes and then take a steep path up through the forest for five more minutes (a minimum of 1hr from Kazbegi); this emerges from scrubby birch and on to the ridge, where you'll see the church to the left, less than ten minutes away across the alpine grassland.

An easier route is to head to the right on the gravel track, which loops up to the left to reach the ridge in 15–20 minutes (with short cuts possible).

The churchyard is entered through a gate-tower (with a chimney shaft) which opens directly on to a blind porch on the south side of the church; the main door is to the west. The Church of Tsminda Sameba or Holy Trinity was built in the 14th century, with the tower added a century later, and a big separate belfry; it's a remarkably large construction for such an isolated location, at 2,170m. In fact the ruins of another church were found in 1913 at 3,962m on the slopes of Mount Kazbek. Paganism is alive and well in these remote areas, with crosses made of rams' horns; when I was first here a freshly decapitated sheep's head sat on the parapet of the churchyard. Monks are living here now, and there are even reports of solar panels. The church's festival is held on 28 August, when sheep are sacrificed (attracting vultures for the next day or two).

This is a popular hike throughout the summer, and although there was a report of a tourist being raped several years ago, it's usually busy enough to be safe. Jeeps and horses are also available.

Above the church (*2hrs 45mins; moderate–hard*) Coming out of the church and turning left at a pile of stones, follow the gravel track which climbs to the ridge, turns sharply to the right, and continues westwards just above the treeline (with a steep drop to the north but pastures and alpine flowers to the south), to reach the Gergeti Glacier at about 2,950m, 3 hours (10.5km) from the village of Gergeti. Near the snout of the glacier it's easy to see Caucasian snowcock, wallcreepers, snowfinch, twite, Guldenstadt's redstart and great rosefinch, as well as lammergeyer soaring overhead. It's a straightforward hike as far as the Sabertse Plateau (3,050m), but only those experienced on ice, or with competent guides, should continue up the right/south side of the glacier (about 7.3km long but retreating fast) and then across it to reach the huge former meteorological station, which was the highest in the Soviet Union at 3,675m. Now it's a climbers' hut, run since 1998 by Caucasus Travel, who have replaced the roof, and it is known as Mtis Qokhi Betlemi or the **Betlemi Hut** (m 599 497764); rooms cost up to GEL40, although it's possible to sleep on a mattress on the floor for GEL10; camping is also possible but it can be very windy. There's heat and light but no food available.

Nearby, at 4,100m, is the **Betlemi (Bethlehem) Cave**, the setting of Ilia Chavchavadze's poem *The Hermit*, where a new metal chapel has been deposited by helicopter. It's possible to climb from the hut to the summit and back in an 8–12-hour day, starting at 04.00.

Mount Kazbek, more properly known in Georgian as Mkinvartsveri ('Ice-Top'), is a long-extinct volcano 5,047m in altitude, and is by far the highest peak in this section of the Caucasus. It's laden with mythology, firstly of Amirani, the Georgian Prometheus, who was chained to the mountain as a punishment for his pride and whose shape can be made out in the rock from far away, and secondly of the tent of Abraham which was said to stand on the summit, protecting the Holy Manger, or the Tree of Life – or treasure. There are also legends of lost treasure connected with the Betlemi Cave.

Kazbek was first climbed in 1868 by Douglas Freshfield with colleagues from the Alpine Club of London and guides from Kazbegi; it's a UIAA (International Climbing and Mountaineering Federation) grade II climb (PD, with just 100m of ice climbing in the final couloir) and is best tackled in September or October; the classic route on the icy south face is UIAA grade III+. Kazbek is far easier than peaks such as Uzhba in Svaneti; climbing it takes four days as a rule – one day to the hut, one day training and acclimatising, one day to the summit and back to the hut, and a day to return to town. It's a 1,855m climb from the town of Kazbegi to the Betlemi Hut – a good day's work if carrying food and climbing gear – and 1,381m more to the summit. It's also possible to turn left at the top of the glacier to climb Ortsveri (4,258m), another UIAA grade II peak, which makes a useful warm-up. A guide will cost about US$250, or about US$800 for four clients.

The Arsha hike *(Full day; no experience needed)* This is actually a very pleasant and easy stroll (now signed as a mountain-bike trail) up the west side of the Tergi Valley to the south of Kazbegi. An obvious path starts from the road bridge at the north end of Kazbegi; it's also possible to start from the Gergeti homestays, simply turning right and following the track southwards, to reach the floodplain after 5 minutes. From here a gravel track leads south but you'll soon take a path to the right to reach an obvious wellhead, surrounded by boggy patches and pools full of frogs and tadpoles, after 10 minutes; it's another 5 minutes to a new pool (about 15m by 30m) beneath a scree slope, full of fresh-tasting mineral water, by an unfinished concrete building. It's a good place to relax and watch the vultures soaring above.

Continuing, you'll join a gravel track below a tiny, newly restored chapel and a defensive tower, passing the few houses of Pansheti village, and reaching a junction after 20 minutes; turning left you'll cross a new road bridge to reach the highway at km121/18, 3km south of Kazbegi and a few hundred metres north of the junction to Sno. Carrying on along the west side of the valley, you'll pass 1½ towers (and the starts of some good paths up into the mountains), go through a hamlet, and then briefly go up to the right above a marsh and past a cross, before following a gravel road straight to a bridge, 25 minutes from the junction. To the west there's a view directly up a valley with good waterfalls, which would be easy and fun to explore. Crossing the bridge, you'll reach the highway in a couple of minutes, opposite a pharmacy north of the centre of Arsha, a few kilometres north of Sioni.

Alternatively, it may be easier to start by taking a taxi south from Stepantsminda and then walk back: from the bridge at km121 you can either turn right on to a gravel road after a couple of minutes or go on to some houses and turn right below a chapel, then after almost 1km take a path to the left to pass below scree and reach the mineral pool in 20 minutes. Go to the right around the boggy patch to the gravel track, then after a couple of minutes fork left to reach the first houses of Gergeti in 5 minutes more.

NORTH OF STEPANTSMINDA

The Georgian Military Highway continues north from Kazbegi on the left/west bank of the Tergi, passing through Tsdo (1,767m) and then Gveleti (1,850m), where griffon vultures nest on the cliff; just southwest of Gveleti you'll see a fine waterfall. The road crosses to the right bank here (12km from Stepantsminda), but immediately before the bridge a track turns left to continue along the left bank, then follows the Amali Valley as a good hiking trail through subalpine birch forest to reach the **Devdoraki Glacier**. This is the lowest of all those in the Caucasus, its tongue reaching an altitude of just 2,300m; the trail is 9km each way, taking a minimum of 4 hours return. Beyond the Zemo Larsi border checkpoint the highway enters the **Daryal Gorge**, its wildest section, where the road runs for 12km on a narrow shelf below granite cliffs up to 1,500m high where lammergeyers nest. The gorge takes its name from Dar-i-Alan or 'Gates of the Alans', named after the forefathers of the Ossetians, who arrived here in the 5th century AD. Before that it was known as the Sarmatian gates or the Iverian gates, the point at which Pompey's advance into Asia was halted in 65BC. At the southern entrance to the gorge, to the west of the road, are the ruins of the **Daryal Fortress**, popularly known as Queen Tamar's Castle, although it's far older than the 12th century. It was restored by the Russians and successfully held by General Gurko against Shamyl's forces in 1846.

The frontier between Georgia and Russia at Zemo Larsi was closed by Russia in July 2006 and remained so until March 2010 when it was reopened for Armenian traffic. The border facilities were modernised with USAID funding in 2009. For those wishing to take a look, two or three people could take a taxi from Kazbegi most of the way to the border and back for about US$10. The old border crossing is at **Chertov Most** (Devil's Bridge), about 20km beyond Kazbegi, and the highway ends after 168km at Vladikavkaz ('Rule the Caucasus'), founded in 1783 to be the base for the subjugation of the Caucasus. It was renamed Ordjonikidze after the Georgian revolutionary Sergo Ordjonikidze, Stalin's hatchetman, whose brutality horrified Lenin and who was in the end killed off by Stalin himself. Although there are still traces of the fashionable 19th-century climatic resort and garrison town, it has been surrounded by soulless communist tower blocks and was then knocked about during the first Chechen war.

KHEVSURETI ხევსურეთი

Khevsureti is one of the most remote and least changed areas of Georgia, a country where adherence to ancient traditions is very highly prized. The Khevsurebi are known for their unique textiles, with beautifully embroidered stars and crosses, probably a simplification of the pagan sun motif. The men are popularly supposed to have worn Crusader-style chain mail until the 1930s, and at the time of the protests after the 9 April 1989 massacre they certainly appeared in Tbilisi wearing 'knee-length, richly patterned tunics with half-metre silver daggers strapped to their waists'.

In the 1920s the population of Khevsureti was about 4,000, but nowadays many actually live in Tbilisi and only about 400 still live full-time in the mountains. You may still be able to buy socks made from the wool of their aboriginal strain of sheep, and dyed only with natural products. The Khevsurebi are known for their brevity and straightforwardness, and for their unique poetry; they may actually speak in verse on day-to-day matters.

Their religion is still very pagan; icons are forbidden, and there are no real churches, only tiny sanctuaries for strange sacrificial rituals which may involve the *dekanozi* or priest drinking blood and 'sacred beer'. Beer is brewed to an ancient recipe (utterly unlike the Germanic lager found elsewhere in the region); the Khevsur firewater is *zhipitauri*, like vodka but more lethal. On the altar you're likely to find deer antlers and ram's horns instead of a cross. They are surrounded by spirits or *vohi* such as Sakhlis Angelosi, guardian of the household; Mparveli Angelosi, guardian of wanderers; Goris Angelosi, guardian of the mountains; and Did Gori, the Father of the Great Mountain, responsible for storms and avalanches. Others are Otchopintre, a version of Pan, and Dali, the Georgian Artemis, while St George is identified as the god of war.

Despite the Chechen war Khevsureti is safe enough as there are plenty of Georgian frontier troops (who will check your papers) and OSCE observers (unarmed foreign military officers) based here. The OSCE's daily helicopter flights will occasionally remove people who manage to hike in from places like Djuta.

GETTING THERE AND AWAY Khevsureti is reached by the road up the Pshavis Aragvi Valley from an underpass at km26 on the Georgian Military Highway, south of the Zhinvali Dam; take the road at right angles which soon heads south down to a bridge, and then turns north through the village of Zhinvali. It turns right up a side valley, crosses the stream and soon swings left to a junction about 3km from the highway. The Khevsureti road heads left here, while another turns right to Tianeti, in Kakheti.

A daily **bus** from Didube in Tbilisi (at 10.30 or 13.00) runs as far as Barisakho, the administrative centre of both Pshava and Khevsureti; it stops at the bottom of the hill, from where you climb up to the village, busy with free-range pigs, dogs with clipped ears and a few bored soldiers.

WHERE TO STAY AND EAT There are guesthouses in Korsha, 2km further up the valley. Only about 40 families live here, but it's a good base, giving access to three valleys.

Batria Arabuli m 599 686510. He speaks Russian but not English. **$**

Shota Arabuli m 595 503134. Just before the museum in Korsha, which he runs. Shota is also an artist & rents rooms for up to 5 or 6 people with shower & washing machine. **$**

Shota Tsiklauri m 599 399380. At the top of the village; speaks Russian but not English. **$**

WHAT TO SEE AND DO In **Korsha**, there's a museum in the former church (there's an English sign; GEL1). The museum houses rare Khevsur chain mail, remarkable traditional costumes with patterns unique to each clan (like tartans), fearsome spiky knuckledusters and agricultural implements.

Beyond here there's not even a kiosk and you have to find your own transport. You may wait days for a lift, but it's great country for **walking**, and there's no shortage of water. You can walk north up the Pshavis Aragvis to the hamlet of Biso and then west on a terrible track to Roshka, 30–40 minutes from Barisakho; hikers can continue to Djuta (page 162). There's also a lovely **day hike** to the Abudelauri lakes, one green, one blue and one white. In Roshka you can stay with Shota Tsiklauri's brother Badri.

From Biso, you can go northeast up the Gudantistsqali Valley to Gudani and Khakhmati, the last village in Pshavi; there are defensive towers in both Gudani and Khakhmati, and a guesthouse in Gudani.

From here a 4x4 track continues eastwards, climbing 1,000m or so with hairpin bends up to the Datvis-Jvaris (Bear Cross) Pass (*2,676m, ⊕ from May/Jun–Oct/Nov only*), and then swings north into Khevsureti to follow the Argun down the northern slope of the Caucasus through Kistani to a bridge where trucks stop below **Shatili** (1,395m), the main village of Khevsureti. It's less than 100km from the Georgian Military Highway (under 50km from Barisakho), but it takes 4–5 hours to drive this distance. It's an almost unspoilt complex of over 50 defensive towers and ancient houses with wickerwork balconies (some dating from the 6th century, though most are from the 10th–12th centuries) huddled together on a low cliff, facing another of Tamar's castles. They were largely abandoned in the 1950s then partially restored in the 1970s, when Shevardnadze also built a new village around the corner beyond a soccer pitch-cum-helipad; bizarrely, there's a row of villas with big balconies overlooking the Argun River. Now 15 towers have had urgent repairs, and one is to become a museum. The World Bank and UNESCO have a cultural heritage project here, with a new ecotourism hotel in two renovated towers, with a kitchen and real bathroom on the ground floor and a ten-bed room above (GEL20pp plus food); you should book in advance, by calling Mindia Tsiklauri in Tbilisi (m *593 144644*). Vazha Chincharauli (m *577 729362*; e *vabula@posta.ge*) also provides accommodation, but speaks only Georgian and Russian. The lovely Nana Gogochuri also has a guesthouse, with spectacular views towards the defensive towers. The road continues north down the Argun Valley from Shatili through a border checkpoint and soon, below the necropolis of Anatori, swings southeast up the Andaki Valley. It's about 8km (with shrines marking excellent mineral springs) up the Andaki to **Mutso** (1,590m), the only other real settlement in Khevsureti, perhaps the finest (though most ruinous) of Khevsur villages. Almost completely abandoned over a century ago, it had around thirty medieval tower dwellings on near-vertical terraces, but many have collapsed. You'll climb up past massively built tombs (about 2m by 2m and 4m long), to a few towers on a narrow ridge, now being renovated.

The valley splits immediately south of Mutso, with Khone in a bowl to the southeast beyond Khonischala and two plague huts still containing human bones; it's just 2km further to Chechnya, but the border is (officially) open only to incoming refugees – there's a road just 3km beyond the border, north of Mount Tebulos. Two hours south of Mutso is **Ardoti**, a few defensive towers with a church above, after which the valley splits again: to the southwest in the Chanchistsqali Valley is **Khakhabo**. The lower village is still inhabited, while Upper Khakhabo (2,150m) is a tiny cluster of ruined 11th-century towers. From the tiny hamlet of Andaki, to the southeast, hiking groups can make the tough crossing over the 3,431m Atsunta Pass into Tusheti, reaching Parsma in about 12 hours.

The track north from Shatili across the border into Chechnya is of course closed, and even in quieter times you should not attempt to cross the border here. You'll see abandoned helicopters and armoured cars in the area, and maybe some traces of a quixotic 1980s railway project, and a half-built tunnel, used by Chechen fighters to store arms in the 1990s.

6

Samtskhe-Javakheti
სამცხე-ჯავახეთი

This chapter covers three historic provinces: firstly the tiny and virtually forgotten **Tori**, around the spa of Borjomi; secondly **Samtskhe** or Meskheti, the high volcanic tableland around Akhaltsikhe; and then **Javakheti**, on the border with Armenia. Although part of Georgia's historical heartland, with the cave-city of Vardzia at its centre, the present region of Samtskhe-Javakheti has a population that is 90% Armenian and is in many ways autonomous. In 1624, the Georgian ruler of Samtskhe converted to Islam for political reasons; many Georgians left the area, but many of those who remained also converted. These so-called Meskhetian Turks lived here until their deportation to Central Asia in 1944 and have not yet been allowed to return; their villages are now largely populated by people from Racha and Lechkhumi. When the Russians took control of the area in 1829, some Muslims emigrated to Turkey and Armenians came here from Turkey to take their land. Thanks to its bleak climate and poor transport links, it remains a poor and isolated region, although the roads have been improved recently.

NEDSVI

From the junction with the Tbilisi–Kutaisi highway at the west end of Khashuri, it's 32km southwest to Borjomi, following the Mtkvari into the Borjomi Gorge. Marshrutkas for Borjomi (*GEL2*) wait by a ticket kiosk a couple of hundred metres down the Borjomi road from the roundabout.

The road passes through the long thin village of Akhaldaba, from where you can hike up to the **Nedsvi Sanctuary**. At km12, by the Akhaldaba Restaurant and (on the far side) a ruined tower, there's a junction where a bridge crosses to the right bank; this road crosses the railway, continues to the right as Rustavelis kucha, and then swings right again to cross a stream and carry on up the valley as Kazbegis kucha. Just before km3 you should be able to find a path up to the ridge on your right/southwest side, to **Tamar's Castle**, a small group of dramatically located ruins. It's another kilometre to the end of the road at km4 (measured from the start of Kazbegis); a very muddy forestry track continues up the valley, reaching some fields and houses after an hour's hiking.

Just beyond these the track crosses to the right bank, and after about another 15 minutes you'll reach some summer-only houses at the meeting of two valleys; after crossing a stream you'll find some graves and a ruined church in a grove of trees on your left, as well as a table and shelter. This is all that remains of the Monastery of Nedsvi and its three-naved basilica, built in the 9th century by Grigol Kandzdeli; forestry tracks continue up steep-sided conifer-lined valleys which offer very attractive hiking and camping. The monastery is in the Nedsvi Sanctuary, a new 9,000ha enclave of the Borjomi-Kharagauli National Park (pages 176–81); it's unmanaged but wildlife should be recovering.

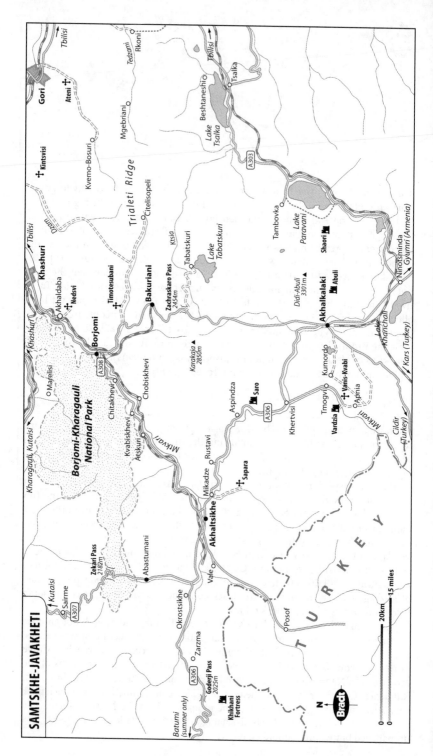

SAMTSKHE-JAVAKHETI

Just before km29 the main road up the left/west bank of the Mtkvari reaches the centre of the spa town of Borjomi, with shops, a market, and a bus station, just south of the centre. This has departures more or less hourly to Tbilisi and Akhaltsikhe, eight a day to Bakuriani, and to Gori (*07.45 & 10.45*), Batumi (*09.00*) and Vardzia (*Jun–Sep 08.45*). The railway station has closed but you can buy tickets on board the amazingly cheap trains to Gori (*GEL1*) and Tbilisi (*GEL2*), which leave at 07.00 and 16.45.

At an altitude of 800m the spa offers both health-giving waters and a bracing mountain atmosphere; in August the average temperature is 20°C, but it freezes from late October until March or later, and in January the average temperature is –2°C.

It's a town of 16,000, with a large plant bottling the water which used to be shipped all over the Soviet Union. Baths were built here in the 1st century AD but the springs were forgotten from the 15th century until a Russian army, returning from fighting the Turks, rediscovered them in 1810; a bottling plant was built in 1896 and, from 1900, carbon dioxide was added to extend the water's life and allow exports. In 1995 a French–Dutch joint venture, the Georgian Glass & Mineral Water Company, bought it with the Borjomi brand name, only to find that others had also been given licences to use the name; this was sorted out, but the company then lost US$7 million when the Russian economy collapsed in 1998. It merged with two Ukrainian companies in 2004 and had 8% of the Russian market until it was banned from Russia for political reasons in 2006; determined marketing elsewhere has brought sales to 15% above their level before the ban.

WHERE TO STAY The homestays are mostly unmarked but the tourist information centre (page 174) can advise on their whereabouts (the staff here claim there are over 100 – probably an exaggeration).

Hotels

Crowne Plaza Borjomi (84 rooms) Baratashvili 9; 22 0260; www.crowneplaza.com. Another 5-star place opening in mid-2015 just outside the spa park. **$$$$$**

Hotel Natali (19 rooms) Vepkhadze 20, Likani; m 597 706613, 551 581 1353; e hotelnatali1@gmail.com; http://hotelnatali. ge. On a track leading in to the national park, 3km south, this new place is very peaceful & has large, comfortable rooms, all with balcony, fridge, kettle, hairdryer, toiletries & lots of power sockets. There's a meeting room for 60 on the 2nd floor & a more utilitarian restaurant below. **$$$$$**

Hotel Rixos (149 rooms) Meskheti 16; 29 229; m 555 555505, 599 489888; e Natalia. Khatiashvili@rixos.com; http://borjomi.rixos. com. A brand-new 5-star place in the former Likani sanatorium that boasts of being the most expensive hotel in Georgia. It has a particularly fine spa, with supposedly the best of Borjomi's mineral springs. **$$$$$**

Borjomis Khoeba (28 rooms) Rustaveli 107A; 22 3072; m 599 323247, 568 777020; e info@ borjomiskhoeba.com; www. borjomiskhoeba.com. The best place in town until the new 5-star hotels opened, this modern place just to the north of the town is also a medical centre & guests have access to the health centre. It has en-suite rooms with satellite TV & a restaurant, bar & swimming pool. **$$$–$$$$**

Hotel EcoRest Likani Palace (5 rooms) Meskheti 27A, 1km south, immediately beyond the national park headquarters; 22 4249; m 577 990075, 599 994459; www.ecorest.ge. This hotel occupies the top 2 floors of a modern chalet, with its entry at the rear; there are 2 luxe rooms (with fireplace, kitchenette & a children's bedroom) & 3 others. Rates are FB, although there's a kitchen available too, & there are discounts in winter. **$$$–$$$$**

Hotel Borjomi (11 rooms) Tsminda Nino 3; 22 212, 21 487; m 899 456463; e gentleman@ caucasus.net. This elegant wood-sided house next to the museum has a private mineral spring in the courtyard; it's a very welcoming old-style place. The en-suite dbl rooms have good TVs (with a huge choice of satellite channels), hairdryer & a fold-up child's bed. Rates inc b/fast & tax. **$$$**

🏠 **Hotel Meidan** (6 rooms) Kostava 2; 📞 22 3908; m 593 152939. In the centre near some decent bars & restaurants, this small place is the best of the budget hotels. **$$–$$$**

🏠 **Firuza Sanatorium** Baratashvili 3; 📞 22 3935; m 599 151898. Parallel to 9 April, rooms are available here from May–Oct, but it's rather dated. **$$**

Homestays

🏠 **Ate's Homestay** (1 room) Rustaveli 89; 📞 22 0027; m 599 302513; e borjomigoldentours@gmail.com. A recommended option; has 1 cosy room for 4 people & runs excursions to Vardzia. **$$**

🏠 **Marina Zulmatashvili's Homestay** (3 rooms) Shromis/Ketevan Tsamebulis 2; 📞 22 2323; m 598 184550; e marinasguesthouse@gmail.com; www.facebook.com/MarinasGuesthouse. A good option; rooms have shared bathroom & English is spoken. Marina's can be reached by taking the rough stony track uphill to the right that leads off Kostova before it plunges downhill; turn left at the top of this to reach the house at the end. **$$**

🏠 **Nino Chkhartishvili** Gogias Tsikhis 9; m 595 915073, 596 790681. Climb the steps across the road from the suspension bridge near the tourist information centre, follow the path above the road under the grapevine & it is the gate at the very end. Nino's daughter speaks some English; the big family dog is actually gentler than he might at first appear. **$$**

🏠 **Levan Jangiroshvili** (Leo's Homestay) (2 rooms) Pirosmani 18; m 574 861516, 593 981595, 551 414422; e jango.geo@gmail.com. Just behind the museum, the owner speaks excellent English & is full of information; unfortunately he's also a bit of a sharp operator & very pushy with travellers he finds on the street. Rooms for up to 8 people. **$**

✖ **WHERE TO EAT AND DRINK** There are several cafés along Robakidze, parallel to the south bank of the river west of the suspension bridge. All of these serve decent khachapuri, khinkhali and other Georgian staples. Also on Robakidze is the Wine House.

Along Robakidze

🍴 **Aguna** Robakidze 2; 📞 22 2340 $
🍴 **Orkidea** Robakidze 1; m 855 596905 $
🍴 **Taverna Nia** Robakidze 1A; 📞 22 2114. Probably the nicest of the cafés on this street. $

Elsewhere

✖ **Café Turisto Beer-Bar** At the rear of the Hotel Meidan on Dumbadze, on the next street south. Georgian menu. $

✖ **Inka Café** 9 April 2. In a nicely restored period building. Serves excellent cakes, pizza & khachapuri, & has good coffee. $

✖ **Merabiko** 📞 20 723. In the park opposite the railway station, this café-bar (with a roof terrace) is a good place for shwarma. $

✖ **Old Borjomi** Kostava 19. This café, facing the park, has decent Georgian food, is slightly more expensive than those on Robakidze but has a wider choice & better décor, plus Wi-Fi. $

OTHER PRACTICALITIES There's a **tourist information centre** (📞 22 1397; m 599 302513; e ticborjomi@gmail.com, https://travelinborjomi.ge; ⊕ 09.00–18.00, until 19.00 in summer) on Rustaveli just north of the suspension bridge that crosses the river to Borjomi Park station. The helpful English-speaking manager provides maps and information on accommodation and travel, runs tours to Vardzia, and can also supply permits for the Borjomi-Kharagauli National Park when the national park headquarters (page 176) is closed.

There are several **banks** with ATMs along Rustaveli, including TBC Bank at No 121 (📞 21 902; e borjomi@tbcbank.com.ge), ProCredit Bank at No 125, Bank Constant at No 145 and Liberty Bank at No 147 (📞 23 042). There's an **internet café** (⊕ until 23.00) at Rustaveli 26 next door to the tourist information centre; it's full of local kids playing shoot-'em-up games but it has a good connection.

WHAT TO SEE AND DO The **Museum of Local Lore** (*Tsminda Nino 5;* ⊕ *10.00–17.00 except Mon, Jun-Sep to 19.00; GEL3, GEL1/photo*) is signed to the west from the square north of the market; although dark, largely without captions, and with no English spoken, its exhibits do give interesting insights into the life of the Borjomi region. Starting at the top with tatty stuffed animals, there's then the Romanov porcelain collection on the floor below, and Bronze Age jewellery and agricultural implements, photographs of ancient churches and 19th-century spa life, and by the entrance, furniture made for the Romanovs from the antlers of deer they'd shot. You can also see a video made in 2002.

In the small park on Rustaveli below the museum stands a statue of Pyotr Ilyich Tchaikovsky, who used to holiday here, looking rather dandy.

Borjomi Spa At about km28.5, a bridge crosses the river and the railway to the spa; this road, Kostava, passes an attractive park on the left, with the beautifully refurbished Borjomi Park station and a new church.

Kostava soon reaches the Borjomka stream and 9 April, lined by trees and late 19th-century villas, which leads up to the right with little seated pavilions jutting over the river, ending (after about 5mins) at the gates of the **Ekaterina Park** (⊕ *Jun-Sep 06.00–midnight, Oct-May 09.00–22.00; Jun-Sep GEL0.50, Oct-May free*). The last villa on the left (No 48) is in the same style as the others but with glittery arabesque decoration in the ceiling of the balcony. It belonged to Grand Duke Mikhail Nikolayevich Romanov, brother of the Tsar and viceroy of the Transcaucasus; he renovated the spa in 1862, built a summer residence in 1871 and then the Likani Palace in 1892–96. The railway opened in 1894 and Chekhov, Tchaikovsky, Mme Blavatsky, other members of the tsar's family and Stalin were among those who came to take the waters here.

Inside the park a stately pile on the left now houses a library, and a covered pavilion on the right has taps spewing out the famous Borjomi water. Together with Narzan (from the northern Caucasus) this was the former Soviet Union's favourite mineral water, with 300 million bottles a year being filled when times were good. It's flavoured with sodium carbonate, tasting something like Vichy water – slightly warm and salty.

A bridge crosses the stream to new toilets and a hall with a 3D panoramic model of Georgia (*GEL2*), while the main promenade leads on up the right side of the valley past cafés, bars and restaurants, a cinema and a play area, added when the park was refurbished in 2006. This also gives access to the **Sadgeri Arboretum**, on the plateau immediately above the park, which covers 136ha and is laid out for invigorating walks for the spa patients in pine forests with splendid views. You'll also see the remains of a fortress, and the simple barn-like Church of St George, built in the 15th and 16th centuries. Outside the park gate a stylish little terminal houses a **cable-car** (*GEL1.50*) to lift visitors the 100m to the arboretum and a Ferris wheel. Sadgeri can also be reached by a winding road which starts from 9 April and passes the 'Composers' House' where the next Tchaikovsky could seek inspiration on his summer holidays; it continues to Tsemi on the road to Bakuriani (page 181).

Walking to Likani Ignoring the modern viaduct above the bus station and continuing up Meskhetis, the main road southwards, take the steps to the right at km29.2, and just after the first bend (to the right) you'll find yourself in a cemetery with a brightly painted chapel and good views of Borjomi. Higher up, where the gravestones mingle with pines, there's a Soviet-period archway that leads left to a war cemetery and statue of a smug-looking Stalin on a plinth. Next to this stands a more recent Georgian statue of a grieving woman; whether or not she is weeping for victims of the Great Patriotic

War or victims of Stalin himself is open to debate. The ruined **Gogiatsikhe** (Castle of St George) on the ridge immediately behind the market is also visible from the cemetery; it's quite easy to scramble up to this. In medieval times this was the stronghold of the feudal lords of the Avalishvili family, looking across the valley to the 11th–12th-century **Petristsikhe** (Castle of St Peter). From the museum in Borjomi, you can follow green-striped hiking markings to the fortress and a viewpoint (1,140m) over Borjomi; blue-striped markings lead through the town to the Ekaterina Park and Sadgeri.

The headquarters of the Borjomi-Kharagauli National Park is just north of km67/30, under 1km from the viaduct. You're already in Likani, and it's just another 500m to the gate of the former **sanatorium**, now the Rixos Hostel. Once reserved for the elite of the Soviet Communist Party, this was used for conferences and for Shevardnadze's meetings with Lyudvig Chibirov, then leader of South Ossetia. It was bought by Kazakh investors in 2006 and closed for renovation, although this was delayed because of the Georgia–Russian 2008 conflict, finally opening in January 2015. With luck you should still be able to walk through the lovely park and to the quasi-Tuscan Romanov **mansion**, built in 1895 of grey-painted stone and pink-painted brick, at the south end of the park; still owned by the state, this is where Saakashvili stayed when skiing at Bakuriani. At some point it should be restored and opened to tourists; Stalin's bed is still there, and even the nail he hung his hat on, and there's a table made by Peter the Great himself, without nails. There's a sharp bend where the road south leaves Likani at km31/66, where you can glimpse a Romanov folly/viewpoint to the left.

BORJOMI-KHARAGAULI NATIONAL PARK

For a distance of 60km the Mtkvari River runs northeast from the Meskheti Plateau down to the central valley of Inner Kartli; this is the Borjomi Gorge, marking the division between the humid Colchic habitats of western Georgia and the drier landscapes of the east. There's also influence from the arid Anatolian Plateaux to the south, so there's an intriguing mix of species here, as well as Tertiary relics and some endemic species (such as *Gladiolus dzavacheticus* and *Corydallis erdelii*). In 1880 Prince Mikhail Romanov established a royal hunting reserve, building rangers' huts and appointing a German chief forester; it became a nature reserve in 1935 and a national park in 1995, opening to the public only in 2001. What's more, this was the only protected area in Georgia to have a management plan, thanks to the help of the WWF and the German government. It now covers 85,000ha with a buffer zone of 450,000ha, now including Abastumani and Sametskhavario, the highest peak in the region at 2,642m.

Trips can be booked through tour agencies in Tbilisi or through the national park – its headquarters are 1km south of Borjomi at Meskheti 23, Likani (m 577 640480, 577 101857, 577 640444, 577 101857; e borjomkharagauli@gmail.com; http://apa.gov.ge; ⊕ 09.00–18.00 Mon–Fri, 09.00–14.00 Sat–Sun). Staff speak very good English and can arrange guides, bikes, horses, tents, snowshoes and accommodation. Rhododendrons bloom in April and May, and autumn colours are spectacular too.

GEOLOGY AND NATURAL HISTORY The area is composed mostly of Tertiary sediments (clay, marl, sandstone) and Quaternary volcanic bedrock (andesite, basalt, dolerite), with plateaux of petrified lava flows. There are 30 mineral springs, of which Zvare, Mitarbi and Nunisi are supposed to have medicinal properties, in addition to Borjomi water. The climate is moderately humid, with cold snowy winters and long cool summers, lasting 3½ months below 1,100m and just two months above 1,500m, where snow lies for at least 150 days a year. Average precipitation is 687mm a year, although it's higher to the north with 1,842mm at the Rikoti Pass and 1,366mm at Kharagauli, and lower to the south with 576mm at Atskuri. Temperatures are also higher to the north, with an average in August of 23°C at Kharagauli, 19° at Borjomi and 16° at Bakuriani.

Forest covers 75% of the national park, mostly climax conifer forest. However, more than 60 species of Colchic trees and shrubs have been recorded here, including cherry-laurel, holly, chestnut, *Rhododendron ponticum*, yew and buckthorn. Forests dominated by oak (*Quercus iberica*), beech (*Fagus orientalis*) and hornbeam (*Carpinus caucasica*) can be found at up to altitudes of 1,800m, though mostly at lower levels, while spruce (*Picea orientalis*) and pine (*Pinus kochiana*) can be found from 1,000m to 1,800m, and Caucasian fir (*Abies nordmannia*) from 1,400m to 1,800m. From this altitude to 2,400m there's subalpine forest of crook-stem birch (*Betula litwinowii*), mountain ash (*Sorbus caucasigena*) and *Rhododendron caucasicum*, with alpine grasslands above 2,400m. To the south, the slopes of the Trialeti are dominated by the pine *Pinus sosnowskyi* with smaller species such as juniper, *Astragalus caucasicus*, meadow sweet, hawthorn, cornelian cherry and dog-rose. In addition the Nariani marshes, at 2,050m, are home to many wetland species. The Nedsvi and Ktsia-Tabatskuri reserves (9,000ha and 22,000ha respectively), described on pages 171 and 184, are detached from the main body of the national park, which lies to the west of the gorge.

The 55 species of mammal in the national park include red and roe deer, chamois, brown bear (*Ursus arctos*), wild cat, lynx, wolf, boar, badger, otter, pine marten, squirrel and some endemic species of bat (*Myotis emarginatus*, *Nyctalus lasiopterus*, *Barbastella barbastellus*). Nine bezoar goats (like small ibex) were reintroduced to the Atskuri section of the park in 2006.

Among the 95 species of bird are the golden and white-tailed eagle, black vulture, blackcock, crossbill and six types of woodpecker.

There are also snakes, three endemic lizards, newts and Caucasian salamander.

HIKING IN THE NATIONAL PARK

Meadows are found as high as 2,500m on the flanks of Mount Sametskhavario, and are still used for seasonal grazing. Problems of overgrazing, leading to erosion, have been reduced by the national park, and hunting and logging are also less of a problem than they were. There are nine four-man ranger stations around the edges of the park, notably (in a clockwise direction from Borjomi) at Kvabiskhevi, Atskuri, Abastumani, Marelisi, Nunisi, Kvishkheti and Zanavi. There should always be a ranger on duty, guarding against illegal logging more than poaching or anything else.

Atskuri lies at 950m on the road from Borjomi to Akhaltsikhe (page 184); Kvishkheti (600m), at the northeastern corner of the national park, is 1km west of the Khashuri–Borjomi road at km7/96; and Zanavi (850m) is 1km west of the same road at km19.5/83.5, south of Akhaldaba.

Specifically for tourists, there are guesthouses in Atskuri and Marelisi (pages 184 and 180) and a visitor centre at the park headquarters in Likani (page 176). There's a pleasant 3km **Interpretive Trail** from the rear of the headquarters, with wooden sculptures by students of the Academy of Fine Art and labelled trees; it starts to the left of the building with poor switchbacks for a couple of minutes before taking a better path. This trail can be done self-guided or with a national park guide if preferred. There's a map at the start and nine educational boards.

There are also twelve **hiking trails**, each marked with a different colour on maps and trail markings, and mostly open to horses too, with rangers' stations and tourist

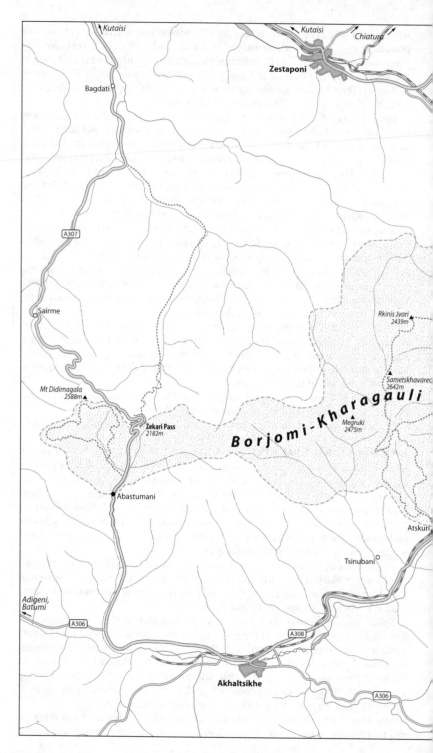

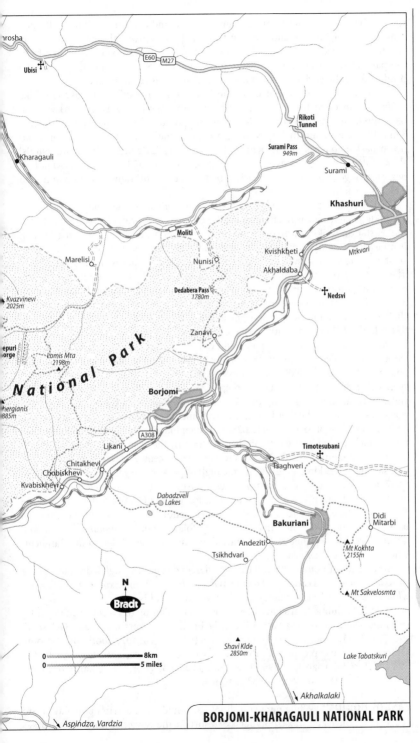

BORJOMI-KHARAGAULI NATIONAL PARK

179

shelters (where you have to bring your own food and bedding). Hiking without a ranger was not initially allowed, but this has been relaxed; the park still prefers you to hire a freelance local guide. Detailed trail maps can be downloaded from the park website (*www.apa.ge*), and an excellent GPS-compatible map has been produced for the park by Geoland, with gradient profiles on the back.

At the eastern end of the park, the isolated **Trail 4** offers an easy day hike (*12km; about 6hrs*) from Zanavi north to the village of Nunisi (400m) with an old church and thermal springs which are supposed to heal eczema; it follows the Samotkhisgele stream then goes along a ridge to the Dedabera Pass (1,780m) and down past shepherds' summer huts (1,380m) to reach Nunisi. The Samta Nunisi Park Hotel is here (m *599 225580, or Tbilisi* \ *32 47 5202;* e *nunisi90@mail.ru; www.nunisi.ge*), which can be reached by trains to Moliti railway station and then a 6km transfer.

Trail 1 (*Nikoloz Romanov Trail; 43km; about 14hrs; blue-&-white stripes*) from Likani to Marelisi leads north through the Likani Gorge (you can take a taxi to the ranger station, 1.5km north of the highway) to a campsite, where you can get water. It then climbs and swings west to reach (after 5–6 hours) the Lomis Mta tourist shelter where you can stay the night (or you can camp; water is about 500m away). The next day you can either go over Lomis Mta (2,198m) or loop around to the east, with a short detour to St George's Chapel. It is mainly downhill, reaching the Shavtwala Valley in 5–6 hours; to the left it's half an hour to the Sakhvlari tourist shelter, or you could go to the right and reach the Marelisi guesthouse (m *599 951421, 577 101994*) in another couple of hours.

From Marelesi or Sakhvlari you could return south on the longer, harder **Trail 2** (*St Andrews Trail; 40km; about 15hrs; red-&-white stripes*) to Atskuri: this follows the Shavtwala through the Bjoliskhevi Gorge to Sakhvlari (950m) and the Megruki tourist shelter (1,018m) at the mouth of the Stepuri Gorge, an exciting side trip (especially if water levels are high after rain) of 5.5km each way. From here the trail climbs to the northwest, past the shepherds' summer settlements of Shertuli and Chishkara to a 1,920m pass west of Kvazvinevi (2,025m). It then follows a ridge past the Kvazvinevi ranger shelter (1,800m) to Rkinis Jvari (2,439m), the Iron Cross Peak on which St Andrew the First-Called placed a cross in the 1st century AD. It continues to the east side of Samteskhvario (2,642m), the highest peak in the park, and over Megruki (2,475m). After a steep descent it reaches the Amarati tourist shelter (1,910m, with views to the Turkish mountains), and then follows the Ochora Ridge and and the Barghebis Ghele Valley to the Atskuri ranger station (*6hrs*). Alternatively, you can backtrack slightly from the Amarati shelter to follow **Trail 3** (*Panorama Trail; 16km; about 6 hrs; blue-&-white stripes*) south along the Ochivari Ridge to the Barghebis Ghele Valley and the Atskuri ranger station.

From south of Lomis Mta you can also descend south through a dramatic gorge to Kvabiskhevi on **Trail 6** (*Following Wildlife Traces Trail; 13km; 6hrs; yellow-&-white stripes*), which also makes a good day hike from Likani.

Since 2013, **horse tours** have been provided by a group of Polish-trained guides (*www.horsetoursge.kaukaz.net*) – the only English-speakers are Vazha Gelashvili (m *595 116343*) and Jemal Ghonghadze (m *595 188461*), both in Borjomi. Otherwise if you can cope with Russian or Georgian you can call m 551 865019 or 593 120289 (Bakuriani); m 595 111005 or 558 231936 (Borjomi–Likani); or m 557 231722, 577 101828 or 592 946533 (Atskuri).

EAST OF BORJOMI While here you should also make a side trip up to **Bakuriani** (page 181), once the most popular ski resort in the Soviet Union. Marshrutkas leave from Borjomi's bus station, with taxis waiting by the square just north. The road starts at about km26.3, 2km north of the centre of Borjomi; a bridge crosses the river to the Borjomi-Works station, where the Tbilisi–Khashuri–Akhaltsikhe railway connects with a rather amazing **narrow-gauge railway** on which tiny carriages are hauled by a large and ungainly electric locomotive at a very leisurely pace. Opened in 1902, the 920mm-gauge line was electrified (at 1.5kV dc) in 1972. The first 18km to Tsemi (where it crosses a 34m-high steel bridge designed by the Eiffel company) were upgraded in 2002 to allow the dizzy speed of 25km/h, but the next 19km are limited to 15km/h. There's also a narrow-gauge steam loco set on a plinth near the Borjomi station.

The road and railway pass the sprawling water-bottling plant and then follow a valley to the southeast. At km9 they pass the minuscule hamlet of **Daba**, with the very simple basilica of St George, built in 1333, with some nice carvings, which can be seen from the railway, on the left/west side of the valley, or reached by road from km8.5. At km11 the road enters the village of **Tsaghveri**, where it swings right and climbs in hairpin bends out of the valley; the railway takes a far longer route, heading west to cross the Gujareti Gorge and winding slowly through dense pine forests. A new 10km circular walk takes you along the railway from Tsaghveri to the Eiffel viaduct, down to Daba church and back beside the railway.

A minor road (Toreli kucha) continues due east up the valley from Tsaghveri, through an impressive short gorge (with a ruined fort high above the left bank) and then past fields, reaching the village of **Timotesubani** (17km from Borjomi) in just over 3km; turning left at the junction in the centre, it's another 1km to the **Monastery of St Timothy**, just beyond the edge of the village at the end of the asphalt. Here the Church of the Virgin, built at the end of the 12th century, is famous for its frescoes, painted in 1205–15. The gate-tower, older than the church and now rather ruinous, is of red brick; the church is also red brick but with a band and crosses of turquoise mosaic on the barrel dome. Entering through the south porch, built later in limestone, you'll see plenty of bare brickwork, but also plenty of fine surviving frescoes, including a Virgin and Child above the altar, a Crucifixion to the south of the iconostasis, and Paradise at the west end; there are also plenty of saints and a flute-player in the north transept. The frescoes have recently had emergency work to treat mould. The monks have recently returned, living in an unattractive new house, and some speak a little English. Three buses (*GEL1.50*) a day leave from Borjomi at 10.30, 13.30 and 17.00 but only two return, at 12.30 and 15.20.

A rough road follows the main valley eastwards all the way to Citelisopeli, which was inhabited by Ossetians until the secession of South Ossetia. Hardy mountain bikers could turn left/north at Sinubani to cross the ridge to Tkemlovani and ultimately Kintsvisi (page 153), a church which is similar to that of Timotesubani. There's a signed mountain-bike route north over a ridge from Bakuriani to Timotesubani, allowing you to make a loop. Keti Gelashvili-Verulava has a guesthouse in Timotesubani (m 599 799476; **$$**) with five bedrooms and two shared bathrooms.

BAKURIANI ბაკურიანი *Telephone code 367*

The road climbs steadily from Tsaghveri, passing the spa of Tsemi, and eventually reaches Bakuriani, Georgia's second most important ski resort, 27km from the main road. Established in 1932 at 1,700m, Bakuriani is still largely a traditional village, subsisting on grazing and logging, with large hotels built in the last two or three decades set at a respectful distance across the subalpine meadows. There's snow from November to March, or even May, with the heaviest falls in December;

in January the average temperature is –7.2°C, but in August it's a pleasant 15°C, making it ideal for walking.

GETTING THERE AND AROUND **Marshrutkas** from Borjomi (*GEL3*) take 40–50 minutes while the trains take around 2½ hours to cover 37km. Marshrutkas leave at one- to two-hour intervals through the day, the last in either direction leaving at 17.00. The train journey is a fascinating and cheap (*GEL2*) alternative but *very* slow, perhaps stopping to load someone's firewood in the forest. Departures are at 07.15 and 10.15 from Borjomi, returning at 10.00 and 14.15, although there may be seasonal variations. Fares are collected on board and you are more or less guaranteed a seat; one coach even has panoramic windows. Direct marshrutkas from Tbilisi's Didube station (*GEL9*) take between 2½ and 3 hours.

Buses usually turn right at the wood-faced police station and terminate 50m along Tamar Mepe opposite the Hotel Santa Claus, but some continue straight along the main road, Tavisuplebis and Davit Agmashenebelis, to pass near the slopes *en route* to the village of Andesiti. Arriving at the railway station, you should turn left and go uphill past the waiting taxis to the bus station at the junction of Tamar Mepe, Rustaveli and Mta; from here head left/east to the main road and turn right towards the slopes. It's not far to the junction with Tsakadze, which leads east past the Villa Palace Hotel (not recommended), gear-hire shacks and the nursery slope, known as Otsdachutmetriani or the Twentyfive-metre-Field, where there's a 40m drag and lifts up to 420m long. It passes the turning to Kokhta I, the original lift and runs, and continues to make a 3km loop around a large meadow, lined with disused communist hotels, to finish just above km26 on the Borjomi road.

Alternatively, Davit Agmashenebelis continues southwards and then splits; the right fork continues (past the Hotel Melisi) towards Akhalkalaki, while the other, lined with new hotels, leads to the Kokhta II lifts (to the left – also known as Tatra-Poma) and the new Didveli lift to the right.

In winter, in addition to taxis, there are **horse-drawn sleighs** which cost about GEL1 per minute, if you negotiate well (*min GEL5*). You can also rent a Buran snowmobile, which will do 80km/h (US$100/hr), or slower ones for kids, plus quad bikes, toboggans and horses.

WHERE TO STAY AND EAT There are a few simple places to stay right in the centre, but the big modern hotels are all a kilometre or two to the south near the slopes. The main road southwards, Tavisuplebis, is lined with traditional wooden cottages, in which rooms are available in the ski season; however, there are only the simplest restaurants and cafés here, so you'll have to arrange meals too. On the road parallel to Davit Agmashenebelis to the left are plenty of private houses, all of which rent rooms in winter; you'd be sure to find one in summer too, for about GEL15.

The best restaurants are in the hotels, with few alternatives. Two good ones are the **Mgzavruli Bistro** (*Tsakadze 1;* m *592 220520*) and **Sopro's Restaurant** (*Tsakadze 11;* m *595 975398, 595 975399*), and there's Italian cuisine at the **Hotel Tovlis Babua** in the centre (*Mta 1;* m *597 700055, 597 727755 for deliveries*). The nice **Iceberg Bakery and Café** is at Davit Agmashenebelis 3 (m *599 105429*).

Hotel Crystal (23 rooms) Near the Didveli funicular; ⊠ 24 0376/7; m 595 461461, 596 500500; www.hotelcrystal.ge. Bakuriani's first 4-star hotel, this has a fine modern spa & an excellent restaurant. **$$$$**

Vere Palace (36 rooms, 7 suites) Tsakadze 12; ⊠ 24 0050; m 599 116045; e vpbhotel@ mail.ru; www.davisvenot.ge/verepalace. Opened in 2002, this was an offshoot of the hotel of the same name in Tbilisi but has since been taken over by new investors. It has a swimming pool, sauna, gym, cinema, disco, business centre, nursery, laundry & ski rental & all rooms have satellite TV, hairdryer & minibar. **$$$–$$$$**

🏠 **Hotel Melisi** (17 rooms, 5 suites) Davit Agmashenebelis 55; ☎ 322 45 1848; m 599 228499; www.welcome.ge/hotel_melisi. A new spa hotel, with sauna, gym & tennis courts (in summer). **$$$**

🏠 **Hotel Tbilisi** (70 rooms) Davit Agmashenebelis 23; m 599 909305; e hoteltbilisi73@mail.ru. A modern package-style hotel with small rooms with balconies, TV & fridge-freezer. They're very friendly, although there's no English spoken. GEL5 extra for a buffet b/fast. **$$$**

🏠 **Villa Fagus** (12 rooms) Tamar Mepis 3; m 593 715855, 595 244300; www.welcome.ge/fagus. A chalet block, close to the bus & train stations; rates include 3 meals a day. **$$$**

🏠 **Villa Park** (20 rooms) Rustaveli 25; ☎ 24 0405; m 579 826862; e hotelvillapark@yahoo.

com. Central, but with facilities such as swimming pool, sauna & gym, & a buffet b/fast. **$$$**

🏠 **Hotel Apollon** (17 rooms, 2 suites) Davit Agmashenebelis 21; m 599 571108, 577 730772; e info@apollon.ge; www.apollon.ge. South of the village centre, this hotel is open all year & is rightly popular with expats in Tbilisi; it comprises 2 buildings (& 2 dining rooms), with a nice simple style & pine furniture, & en-suite rooms for 2–4 people plus families. There's Wi-Fi, TV in all rooms, plus video & an open fire in the common area, sauna, billiards & table tennis as well as parking, a warm boot room & a garden. They're very friendly & efficient & will do vegetarian food given notice, & Inga speaks good English. Price includes 3 meals a day. **$$–$$$**

🏠 **Hotel Tovlis Babua** (Santa Claus; 32 rooms) Mtis 1; m 599 142783, 568 142783; e dima.mikaberidze@mail.ru. Right in the centre; no English is spoken. Rooms are en suite, with TVs. **$$**

OTHER PRACTICALITIES There's a helpful **tourist information** office at Davit Agmashenebelis 2 (m *593 335058;* e *ticbakuriani@gmail.com*) that can provide information on hotels, skiing and tourist trails around the town. There are **ATMs** at Tavisuplebis 19, Davit Agmashenebelis 26A and at the Hotel Villa Palace, Tsereteli 1.

WHAT TO SEE AND DO Bakuriani has 8km of runs (2.4km easy, 3.8km intermediate, 1.8km difficult) in three main areas. A ski pass costs GEL30/day, GEL174/week, or GEL5 for a single gondola ride. Many of the hotels rent downhill skis for GEL5–10 per hour, but you'll have to bring your own cross-country skis, snowboard or snowshoes.

There's a 1.3km run (very difficult at the top) on Kokhta Gora (Pretty Hill; 2,255m) and also ski jumps; an old lift takes you to a restaurant and the radio masts on top. Behind, on the peaks' southern side, is the Kokhta II or 'Tatra-Poma' lift (owned and renovated by the Kazbegi brewery) by the Trialeti Palace Hotel, which has a good restaurant (but not recommended as a hotel). You can also take a 3.5km run from the top of Mount Tskhra-Tskharo (2,711m) and from Mount Imerlebi (2,500m). The new Didveli slope is 3km to the southwest (GEL8 by taxi) at the end of Davit Agmashenebelis. It's owned by oligarch Bidzina Ivanishvili, who provided free skiing for the first season (when the lift was not yet open to the top). An eight-person Leitner gondola takes you up to a quad Doppelmayr chairlift and then a funicular to the summit, and four interconnecting pistes, between 1,200 and 2,200m long. There's snow-making, and it's also possible to skate on a natural pond in January and February.

Otherwise, the big winter sports event here is the **Sukhia ski race** held in early March of even years (in odd years it's in Gudauri).

In summer there's good **walking**, of course, although chairlifts don't start until 11.00. The best access to the peaks is by a jeep track to the left from Davit Aghmashenebelis by the Tatra-Poma lift; there's a pleasant hike to the right/south to the next two peaks. Unusually for a ski resort, Bakuriani also has a fine alpine

Botanical Garden (*Borjomi St 57;* m *899 573830;* ◷ *10.00–17.00 in theory*), founded in 1910 and reached through the green gates at km25.9 on the road to Borjomi; in an area of 17ha they have over 800 subalpine species of flowering plants, including around 100 trees and shrubs. Incidentally, Bakuriani is known for a sort of 'chewing gum' made from pine resin.

There's a **cinema** at Davit Agmashenebelis 5, near the Entertainment Center (with billiards and DJs) at no 25 by the Hotel Tbilisi. Joyland (*www.joyland.ge*) is a new **tubing park** in the centre of the village (between Davit Agmashenebelis and Rustaveli) which is open daily 11.00-20.00 for children and then in the evening for their parents with a bar, restaurant and disco.

Around Bakuriani
The village of **Tsikhdvari**, 9km west (signposted as a mountain-bike route), is lovely, with a mineral bath built by Mikhail Romanov. Turning right off Davit Agmashenebelis, an unsurfaced road continues southwards through the Trialeti range and eventually down, through a Greek-populated area, to Akhalkalaki; immediately beyond the 2,454m Zachraskaro Pass an even rougher road leads east to **Lake Tabatskuri**, at 1,990m. The lake (14.2km^2 in area) and the headwaters of the Ktsia River, to its north, are an important stopover for waterbirds such as grey heron, velvet scoter, Eurasian crane, black and white stork, great white egret, red-beaked swan, and also griffon-vulture; they're protected in a detached part of the Borjomi-Kharagauli National Park. It takes about 2 hours by 4x4 (not in winter) to get from Bakuriani to the east side of the lake, where the birds are most numerous.

SOUTHWEST FROM BORJOMI

Beyond Likani, the main road to Akhaltsikhe passes Chitakhevi, just north of which in the Khitakhevi Gorge is the lovely **Mtsvane (Green) Monastery**, a simple 9th-century basilica partly in a cave, with a deacon's nave to the south and porches to the south and west. It's a short drive from just north of km37.

From km39/52 (10km south of Borjomi), a road is signed to **Chobiskhevi**, across the river 3km south; here, by the Gogichant stream, are the most important secular buildings in the national park, lantern-vaulted houses (a style associated primarily with the historic Tori province) built in the 8th–10th centuries. With horses, it's a lovely excursion to the southeast up the Chitakhevi Gorge to Lake Tabatsveli, which was reached by a cable-car in Soviet times but has been largely abandoned since then.

The A308 continues to the small village of **Kvabiskhevi** from where, as mentioned above, a trail leads to Lomis Mta, starting near the rangers' shelter and campsite, behind which you can climb up to the Mariamtsminda (Holy Virgin) Church, a three-naved basilica built in the 9th and 14th centuries. It takes 90 minutes to the Kvabiskhevi fortress (1,150m), from where you can continue to Lomis Mta. In Kvabiskhevi, Rusudan Khutsishvili has a guesthouse (m *555 726386;* **$$**) with two double rooms.

As the road emerges from the Borjomi Gorge, and gets rougher, there's a clear change to the dry, bare landscape of the Anatolian highlands. At about km51 the railway (now on the left bank) passes through a tunnel under a castle, and at km56 the road and railway reach **Atskuri** (950m), a small, dusty village under the remains of a 10th–13th-century fortress high on a crag. Atskuri was an important trade centre from the 6th century BC, with Greek pottery coming via Vani; St Andrew is said to have brought an icon of the Virgin Mary here, and a bishop's church was built later. The fortress was a Turkish stronghold until 1829, but then fell into ruin. Hiking routes lead north into the Borjomi-Kharagauli National Park from 2.5km east of the village, as described on page 177. Guesthouse Nick & George, at Atskuri 45 (*3 rooms;* m *555 259355, 551 916237;* e *maiaaitsuradze@gmx.com; www. nickandgeorge.com;* **$$**) works closely with the national park.

AKHALTSIKHE The Mtkvari passes through the short Tsnisi Gorge and swings away to the southeast (along with a short cut to Vardzia), while the road and railway briefly head west to the small city of Akhaltsikhe, 77km from Khashuri and 200km from Tbilisi. Its name means 'New Castle', but the fortifications on the easily defensible hilltops actually date from the 12th century, long before Paskevich stormed the Turkish defences in 1828 and built a new fort. The town was an important centre for the Circassian slave trade in the 18th century. It's now a city of 20,000, about a third of whom are Armenian – the Meskhetian Turks who were numerous in the region in the period following the Ottoman occupation have long gone, exiled to Central Asia by Stalin in the early 1940s. These days, Akhaltsikhe is somewhat down-at-heel, but it's hoped that the massive refurbishment (or Disneyfication) of the fortress will bring many more tourists; there are certainly some decent new hotels. In any case there is enough interest here for an overnight stay and it makes a good base for visits to Sapara Monastery and Vardzia cave-city.

Getting there and away There's a fairly new road crossing to Turkey at Posof, and Mahmut Turizm **buses** from Tbilisi to Turkey can be caught at the Akhaltsikhe bus station at 13.00, costing US$15 to Trabzon or US$50 to Ankara. Alternatively, **marshrutkas** run hourly to Vale, 7km before the border (*GEL1; 15min*), from where you should be able to get a ride to the border (or a taxi from Akhaltsikhe costs about GEL20); however, there are unlikely to be taxis waiting on the Turkish side.

There are also daily marshrutkas to Batumi (*via Borjomi; GEL18; 08.30, 11.30*), Vardzia (*GEL5; 10.20, 12.30, 16.00, 17.30*), Kutaisi (*via Borjomi; GEL10; 2/3 a day*) and Akhalkalaki (*GEL6; 09.30, 11.00, 13.30, 16.30, 17.45*); almost all Tbilisi traffic (*GEL10; at least 2 dozen marshrutkas, between 06.20 & 18.00*) takes the faster route via Borjomi. To Vardzia you can also take a taxi for GEL50–60 round trip including waiting time; the drive takes about 90 minutes each way.

There are also buses to Yerevan (*GEL25; 07.00*) and Gyumri (*GEL15; 07.00*) in Armenia. Armenian buses to Gyumri have the old name Leninakan written in Cyrillic on their destination board.

Where to stay There's a hotel upstairs in the bus station (m *599 108144*), charging GEL15 each for a very basic room and cold showers; the only television is the one always blaring by the entrance, but they're friendly and speak some German. You may also be offered a homestay at the bus station, otherwise there are quite a few cheap hotels opposite the bus station and on and near Rustaveli, the road to Vardzia and Akhalkalaki.

Lomsia (63 rooms) Kostava 10; ☏ 365 22 2001; m 577 327825; e lomsia.reservation@ gmail.com; www.lomsiahotel.ge. Easily the classiest place in this area, with a good bar & restaurant, although the b/fast is not as good as you might expect. **$$$$**

Gino Wellness Hotel (38 rooms) Kharischirashvili 1; m 599 880960, 599 880924; www.gino.ge. This new fake-oriental palace, complete with purdah balconies, is just inside the Rabati fortress & you have to park outside & carry luggage in. It's grandiose, with a luxury spa, but service can be poor. **$$$–$$$$**

🏠 **Hotel Rio** (13 rooms) Akhalkalaki Highway 1; 📞 32 31 9101. A modern hotel 2km east of the centre, this has bright, largish rooms with Wi-Fi; fitness club & swimming pool. Price inc b/fast. **$$$**

🏠 **Meskheti Palace** (24 rooms) Natenadze 2; 📞 365 22 2210; m 577 244046; e meskhetipalase@mail.ru. On the left as you go up Kostava, this is a comfortable but somewhat impersonal new hotel, with a PC available at reception & English-speaking staff. **$$$**

🏠 **Hotel Prestige** (18 rooms) Rustaveli 76; 📞 22 0570 m 593 937125; e otelprestige@gmail.com. A solid old building of pink stone, all rooms have AC, cable TV & private bathroom & some have balconies. Rates inc b/fast. **$$–$$$**

🏠 **Hotel Shin** (9 rooms) Sts Davit & Konstantine 2A at Aspindza; m 579 174174; e qkurtanidze@gmail.com. Down by the river north of Rustaveli (not far from the Borjomi road, but about a 15min walk from the centre), this solid building of pink tufa has good plain rooms, Wi-Fi & a beer garden. **$$–$$$**

🏠 **Diana Kurtanidze's Village House** (4 rooms) m 555 775434. In Kide, a couple of kilometres north of the Borjomi road & 6km from Akhaltsikhe, the dbl rooms have 2 shared bathrooms. It's a charming place to sample village life & enjoy organic food. **$$**

🏠 **Guesthouse Edelvais** (3 rooms) Aspindza 7; m 574 228820. A self-contained flat with 8 sgl beds in all & a basic kitchenette & poor Wi-Fi. No b/fast. **$$**

🏠 **Hotel Meskheti** Kostava 8; 📞 365 20 420; m 570 100671. Formerly the Intourist, this Soviet-era hotel in the centre has gloomy corridors but fairly clean rooms with TV, shower & Wi-Fi. **$$**

🏠 **Hotel Old Rabati** Tsikhisdziri 6. More like a hostel, though you'll probably get a nice room with AC & a huge bathroom to yourself; some English spoken. **$$**

🏠 **Guesthouse Edemi** (7 rooms) Rustaveli 105A; 📞 365 22 0035; m 599 185159, 599 937338. A long way east on the Vardzia/Akhalkalaki road; some rooms have shared facilities, others en suite, inc 1 small chalet in the yard. **$–$$**

✖ **Where to eat and drink** Other than in the better hotels, there are few places to eat in Akhaltsikhe: just a handful of simple places on Kostava that serve Georgian snacks and, if you're lucky, burgers and shwarma. On the north side of town there's a **German beer-bar** (🕐 *11.00–22.00 daily*) where you go under the railway and turn left towards to Rabati fortress, and there are a couple of touristy restaurants between the tourist office and the entry to the upper part of the citadel.

✖ **Dzveli Sardaph** On the right near the top of Kostava. Similar to the Old Pub, serving a good range of Georgian classics such as kharcho, ostri, mtsvadi, chikhirtma & of course khinkali & khachapuri. $

✖ **Paemani** Just a little further up Kostava, this has more of a more cafeteria ambience but serves

decent enough food. $

✖ **Restaurant Old Pub** Orbeliani 2 (on the corner of Kostava). Good cellar restaurant with Wi-Fi. Traditional Georgian menu. $

✖ **S + L Pizzeria-Bar** Rustaveli 120. Basic but adequate. $

Other practicalities The **tourist information** office (m *555 777241*; e *ticakhaltsikhe@gmail.com*; 🕐 *10.00–18.00 daily*) is just inside the entry to the Rabati Castle but is fairly useless and has no maps; there are good toilets behind, although the entry to the disabled WC is ridiculously narrow. There are a couple of **ATMs** on Kostava.

What to see and do Turning right out of the bus station and then right under the railway, you can make your way up to the left through a historic district characterised by narrow, roughly cobbled streets and darbazi houses that have the enclosed loggia-style balconies typical of the region. Kazbegi leads to the hilltop **Rabati Castle**, controversially refurbished in 2011–12 in what was more like a total rebuilding and re-imagining – everything is very new and slick, in authentic

Saakashvili style. The upper part of the 7ha site contains a gold-domed mosque, madrasah, church and a superb new museum which makes a visit worthwhile whatever you think of the rest of the fortress.

Inside the main gate is the tourist information office (*where you should buy entry tickets for the upper citadel;* ⊕ *10.00–18.00 Tue–Sun; GEL5*) and a clinically neat garden feature at the east end of the fortress beyond an open-air performance area; stairs lead up inside a rebuilt tower (with concrete floors) and onto the walls, with views across the city (the rebuilding did not extend to making the steps health and safety-compliant, so watch your children).

To the right, a bit of a maze leads past new hotels and restaurants to the upper citadel, where the keep and the mint (with a double gallery) just beyond the bare Ahmadiyya Mosque (built in 1752) are relatively authentic; the gardens and pavilions are not. Below the keep is the excellent **Museum of Samtskhe-Javakheti** (*same ticket/hrs as upper citadel*) with spot-lit displays that work very well as long as the bulbs are replaced as required. They start with clay idols with rather spooky obsidian eyes from the first half of the 3rd millennium BC and obsidian arrowheads, metal and pottery from the same period, followed by a priestess's ornaments and some clay vessels from the mid 2nd millennium BC. The end of the 2nd millennium BC saw the rise of the Daiaeni kingdom (part of the Hittite cultural sphere), with ritual axes of copper and antimony, and then the use of iron. From the 5th century BC the area came under Greek influence, with the kingdom of Arian Kartli developing as a rival to Mskheta, which came out ahead and created the proto-Georgian kingdom of Kartli. There are stone carvings from churches, founded in Javakh from the 10th century and in Samtskhe from the 13th century, and ended by the Turkish conquest in the late 16th century. Finally, there's Georgian weaponry from the 17th to 19th centuries and tiles, copper vessels and musical instruments.

There's a minaret outside the upper gate of the citadel (between the mosque and an equally bare 9th–10th-century church) – if you come out of the gate and take the dirt road to the left of the paved road you'll come directly to an **Ottoman hammam** that's now used as a wood store. It is interesting to note that this structure has been dutifully patched up with recycled chunks of church-style stonework – a true palimpsest of the first order. If you carry on, turn right and cross the asphalted road (Kazbegi Street) and fork right again you'll come to a very ruined little church with a separate belfry, from where you can go on down to Kazbegi by a basketball court. If you explore the backstreets on the far side of Kazbegi below the fortress you should also come across an austere 18th-century **synagogue**.

Turning right from the bus station and then left at the same roundabout, you'll cross the river to the centre; keep to the right up Kostava from the statue of Tamar (outside the House of Culture), and at the top of the hill you'll pass the market to your right. If you go on and turn left and left again to return on the other side of the pseudo-one-way system, you'll have seen all there is to see here – not a lot, although the neatly built houses of volcanic tuff are very Armenian in style. Heading down Naidze (opposite the Hotel Meskheti) you'll reach the large **Armenian church**, silhouetted on a small hilltop that's even more dramatic than the one occupied by the fort; built in 1868, its interior is bare and cold and not worth seeing, but the view is good. You can reach it by the rough steps up from the end of Naidze, or take a big loop left to reach it from the rear.

WEST FROM AKHALTSIKHE Heading west from Akhaltsikhe, a road soon forks left to **Vale** (where there's a 10th-century cruciform church, remodelled in the 14th century) and the Turkish border. The main road continues westwards and then divides, with the A307 heading north to Kutaisi; this passes Amara, west of which you'll see the Amaravepe castle ruins on a hill, and enters **Abastumani**, a tiny spa which is the site of Georgia's main astronomical observatory (previously a Romanov villa and a TB sanatorium). At km9 (to the east from a statue on a rock) is the *banya* or spa, and at about km10 the Observatory Hotel (m *577 230475*) is on the east side of the road opposite No 56. About another 1km to the north, opposite No 7, a track leads 100m west to a footbridge and a tiny cable-car which runs up to the observatory every few hours (the last, at 18.30, connecting with a marshrutka from Akhaltsikhe). Alternatively you can take a path parallel to the cable-car, 20 minutes downhill and probably double that uphill, or a taxi, costing GEL5 – a 3km road turns left to the north of the village. There are four or five telescopes and typically Soviet apartment blocks in usual post-Soviet disrepair, plus a nunnery and a few nice new guesthouses, all strewn along a thin ridge which offers great views of the forested hills just to the north, now part of the Borjomi-Kharagauli National Park. The Kapa guesthouse at Rustaveli 31 (m *599 518760*) has ten en-suite rooms, plus a summer cottage with three more rooms.

From a ranger shelter about 7km north of Abastumani a marked trail leads northwest and upwards, making a 10km loop on the south slopes of Mount Didimagala (2,588m) via the Didimagala tourist shelter, about 3km west of the road just south of the Zekari Pass. Mountain bikes are allowed here, but not in the main part of the park.

There's an unmarked **three-day hike** from Abastumani to Tsinubani, near Atskuri, starting with a 22km road up the Baratkhevi Gorge to shepherds' summer huts where you can camp at 2,100m on the north side of Mount Tsikhisdziri. The next day takes you over the summit (2,252m), where you'll find the ruins of a fortress, to the south plateau, then eastwards to Mount Amagleba (2,277m), with a good site for camping on its north slope at about 2,050m; the next day you'll come down through the Kombekhi Gorge to the Tsinubanis Valley.

Organised groups also make a **five-day hike** west to Bakhmaro (page 222), with great views to the High Caucasus and Ararat, via mounts Mamlismta (2,489m), Mepistskaro (2,850m) and Gomistsikhe (2,380m), then down along a ridge to the village of Grdzelgori (2,200m) and Bakhmaro resort (2,000m).

Two or three minibuses a day run from Akhaltsikhe as far as Abastumani, but none continue northwards to the 2,182m **Zekari (Sun Gate) Pass** over the Lesser Caucasus; this is often closed by snow between October and June, but if you can get here a short hike to the east soon gives superb views. There's accommodation in the national park's Zekari tourist shelters (2,080m), about 50m above some shepherds' huts south of the pass; from here it takes 5 hours (return) to climb Mount Didimagala (2,588m), the highest in the region, to the west of the road. The road descends through Sairme, known for its mineral waters, and Bagdati (page 210), to Kutaisi.

The Batumi road, the A306, continues westwards up the Kvabliani Valley below Okrostsikhe (Golden Fortress), the stronghold in early medieval times of the lords of Samtskhe-Javakheti province and an important obstacle to the Turkish invasions of the 15th and 16th centuries. Its huge towers and powerful walls are still visible. Crossing the river, you'll come to **Zarzma**, 29km from Akhaltsikhe, and see to the left the early 14th-century Church of the Transfiguration, with 16th-century frescoes, a fine large bell-tower and four smaller churches. Beyond here the road is very bad, and unsigned – in summer a marshrutka goes this way to Batumi, leaving Akhaltsikhe at 08.30. It climbs southwest out of the valley, entering Adjara just before the 2,025m Goderji Pass (92km from Borjomi, 115km from Batumi), which is often blocked by snow between October and May.

EAST FROM AKHALTSIKHE TO VARDZIA To the east of Akhaltsikhe, the Akhalkalaki road (the A306) soon rejoins the Mtkvari Valley, crossing it at the first village, Mikadze, and entering a dramatic gorge; on the north side of this you can see caves which prefigure those you're heading for at Vardzia. Before this you can turn off to **Sapara**, where there's an ancient monastery similar to that at Zarzma; turn right/ south on the edge of Akhaltsikhe along a rough road up a side valley, fork left after 3km and continue up the valley for another 8km. There's been a monastery here since the 10th century, but the present Church of St Saba (the largest of ten) dates from the late 13th century, with fine early 14th-century frescoes in the Byzantine Paleologue style. Dramatically set on the edge of a gorge, with a fort above, it is a good example of the cruciform ground plan. It's possible to hike here from Akhaltsikhe in about 3 hours, or you can take a taxi (*GEL20 return*).

Soon after emerging from the gorge, at about km143, you'll see a statue of the national poet Shota Rustaveli, marking the entrance to the village of Rustavi, just to the left/north of the road. Here, not the post-war industrial city of Rustavi southeast of Tbilisi, is where he was born. Although the river is still fairly sizeable, the country becomes increasingly arid and unpopulated, although you'll see several ruined castles. The landscape is extraordinarily beautiful here in autumn when the hornbeam forest that cloaks the hills turns a fiery red. Entering **Aspindza** at km30/80, the castle ruins on a hilltop to the north are easily reached from just west of the centre; there's also a rough, fairly old basilica at the eastern exit from the village. There's accommodation here at the Chiko (m *593 906405*) and Bermukha (m *599 181763*) guesthouses, plus a couple of cafés on the main road at Vardzia 33 and 35. About 1 hour from Akhaltsikhe, just before km44/66, traffic to Vardzia forks right off the A306 at **Khertvisi**, with the famous fortress directly ahead; it's immediately to the left after the bridge at the confluence of the Mtkvari and the Paravani, and can easily be reached by a road on its far side. There were fortifications here by the 2nd century BC, long before a church was built in AD985, when it was the administrative capital of the Meskheti region. The two main towers (one recently restored) were built by Tamar, and the present walls were added in 1354–56, according to the plaque over the entrance. Beyond it you'll see cave cells in the cliff above the houses to the left and field terracing to the right. Now running south along the right/east bank of the Mtkvari, after about 10km the road reaches a junction to the village of Nakalakevi then climbs steadily to Tmogvi village.

Just after the village is a dramatic defile known as Tamar's Gates, on the far side of which is the medieval castle of **Tmogvi**, wonderfully well placed to defend the approaches to Vardzia. It's best seen from a distance to the north, but from the road immediately opposite you'll see the curtain walls and the caves in the cliffs below, near the river. It's also possible to reach the castle in an hour or so following a track along the left/west bank of the Mtkvari from Vardzia; you could continue up to a track on the plateau above and eventually descend to the Jolda Bridge just north of Nakalakevi – quite a hike, and you should be sure to carry plenty of water. The castle was built in the 10th and 11th centuries and destroyed by the Persians in the 16th century; subsequent earthquakes have more or less completed the job of reducing it to rubble. The Tirebi guesthouse (m *599 338871*; **$$**), is across the river from Nakalakevi, a pleasant 30–40 minute hike from Tmogvi fortress; it's a peaceful spot, with friendly owners who serve delicious meals of their own organic produce. They have two en-suite rooms and two sharing a bathroom. In Tmogvi itself, guesthouses (all **$$**) include the Village House (m *595 285750*), Tsiskari (m *598 968687, 790 606047*) and Imedi (m *595 285750*).

From here the road descends for 3km to the turning to the cave-nunnery of **Vanis-Kvabi** (or Kvabebi) to the left, a smaller equivalent of Vardzia itself, built, or excavated, between the 8th and 13th centuries.

VARDZIA ვარძია

It's another kilometre along the valley to Vardzia, one of Georgia's most impressive sights. It is the most famous cave-city in Georgia, which, largely because of its connections with Queen Tamar, is a place of almost mystic importance for most Georgians. Having been in a closed border zone throughout the Soviet period, it's now receiving plenty of visitors, at least in summer. It's said that its name derives from 'Ak var, dzia' or 'Here I am, uncle' – Tamar's call when lost in the caves. First established by King George III in 1156 and consecrated in 1185, his daughter Tamar made it into a monastery, which became the chief seminary of southwestern Georgia (housing 2,000 monks) until an earthquake ruined it in 1283, slicing away a large portion of the rock face, weakened by tunnelling. Another quake in 1456 was followed by a Persian army in 1551, and it was abandoned after an attack by the Turks in 1578, so that now around 600 chambers survive of a total 3,000, which included stables, barracks, bakeries, wine presses and stores. Likewise, only half a dozen levels remain of the 13 which once penetrated 50m into the cliffs. It's been protected since 1938; there was some heavy-handed restoration with concrete in the 1970s, but work now under way should be more sensitive. Heavy rain in 1998 caused a large section of cliff to collapse from 40–50m up; the Dutch government rapidly provided US$50,000 for emergency repairs, including to the stairs to the monastery bell-tower. Egyptian vultures are nesting in the caves, making their management yet more complex.

GETTING THERE AND AWAY Getting here is certainly much easier these days, with daily marshrutkas from Akhaltsikhe (*4 in summer, 2 in winter; GEL5*), taking about 1½ hours; they return at 08.30, 10.00, 13.00 and 15.00. You can also take a taxi for GEL50-60 round trip including waiting time (or GEL130 from Borjomi) – this means you do not have to rush around the site in order to catch the last bus back at 15.00.

 WHERE TO STAY

 Hotel Taoskari (7 rooms) m 599 543540, 598 242403. Near the Vardzia bridge, with en-suite rooms. **$$**
 Valodia's Cottage (10 rooms) m 599 114506, 599 116207, 595 642346; e welcome@

psity.ge. This is the best place to stay, about 2km beyond Vardzia on the left bank. It's a big, new place with en-suite rooms & a lovely garden, where you can feast on their own trout & vegetables; rafting is also available. **$$**

WHAT TO SEE AND DO Crossing the road bridge and turning right, it's a few hundred metres to the car park for the cave-city of Vardzia, at about 1,400m altitude. There's a simple but relatively decent toilet block, as well as souvenir stalls. The site is officially open from 10.00 to 17.00 except on Mondays, but they can be pretty tardy opening up out of season and can stay open till 19.00 in summer; nor are they likely to have change except in summer. Having paid your GEL3 (and GEL10 if you want an audio guide, or GEL15 for a guide), you have to walk up a road past two hairpin bends. This ends at the Ananauri sector of Vardzia, which, dating from the 10th century, is older than Vardzia proper, but was swallowed up by it; immediately above the end of the road is a cave used as stabling for horses (note the holes in the rock used to attach head ropes), while a small path (from the top bend in the path leading north) leads to a church. This is usually locked but you can peer in and see its smoke-blackened 16th-century frescoes.

The main path leads northwards below the cliffs to a bell-tower (built after the 1283 earthquake) and the refectory, and then (after a stretch where you're encouraged not to hang around, due to occasional rock falls) to the **Church of the Assumption** (1184–86), the pivotal point of the complex; in front of you is a famous fresco of Tamar (one of just four painted in her lifetime) and her father, together with what seems to be an Annunciation but for the fact that the Virgin already has the child Jesus on her knee. You can head down a tunnel (with electric lights) outside, forking left to the pool known as 'Tamar's Tears', with beautifully cool and sweet water, or right to go much further to a refuge and ultimately to the upper level of the city (see below).

Returning outside, you can continue to the right to the top of a ropeway at the entry to some caves, now inhabited by monks, and then either head down the steep steps to the paved path below that leads back to the ticket office, or climb up to a much higher level with cliff face walkways. Either way you're pretty free to explore, although safety railings are beginning to appear; some of the chambers are interconnected, but thanks to the earthquakes most of them are now open to the outside world. Compared with the honeycombed hillsides of Cappadocia, in Turkey, this isn't really very exciting. There are a few frescoes, although most of the chambers are smoke-blackened; what are more interesting than the walls and ceilings are the floors, which are pitted with a surprising array of channels and receptacles for water and, of course, wine.

BEYOND VARDZIA The road crosses to the left bank of the river and about 1km further south it reaches a hot spring, now feeding a swimming pool in a barn-like shed, where you can luxuriate in the warm sulphurous waters for next to nothing. Turning right, you'll eventually reach **Zeda Vardzia** (Upper Vardzia), where the writer Peter Nasmyth reported finding an old church surrounded by fields of marijuana; now nuns here make cheese and farm fish.

A road winds its way up from half a kilometre back to the northeast from the Vardzia bridge to the top of the cliff on the east side of the Mtkvari Valley, and on to the village of Apnia. From here a very rough road leads to **Kumordo**, 12km southwest of Akhalkalaki, where there's a fairly large and complex cathedral built in AD964, with a large apse above the altar, two side apses at the east end and two more to the west; in the centre six pillars support the dome, which collapsed in the 16th century and was restored. At the west end an ambulatory was added in the second quarter of the 11th century.

The road on to Akhalkalaki is slightly better, but without a 4x4 you're best advised to travel from Vardzia to Akhalkalaki via Khertvisi. This is a delightful journey up the Paravani Valley (there's a new hydro-electric station on the edge of Khertvisi, but it hasn't ruined the valley above). At km64.5, 3km short of Akhalkalaki, there's a footbridge created by placing an entire railway carriage across the river.

AKHALKALAKI ('New Town'; 1,716m) This is a small town of no importance now that Javakheti is governed from Akhaltsikhe, except as the site of a Russian military base, which was once vital to the local economy. This closed in 2007, despite the protests of locals who were bitterly opposed to this because of the loss of jobs and the perceived loss of security from Turkey, in an area that is 90% Armenian (street signs are in three scripts, Georgian, Armenian and Cyrillic). It was also the terminus of a painfully slow railway from Tbilisi, a 160km-long branch completed in 1986, but as part of the project to build a railway to Kars in Turkey a new Akhalkalaki International Station has been built midway between Akhalkalaki and Ninotsminda, and the spur into town has lost its services. A new road crossing to Turkey has also opened at Çıldır, 34km to the southwest (and the road from Tbilisi improved), so the town may benefit a little.

Where to stay and eat

Artsegi Hotel (Art-Seg) (9 rooms) Mashtots 31; 362 22 3707; m 579 743411, 593 713033; e art-seg@mail.ru. This is a surprisingly good hotel, with a decent restaurant; turning off the main street by the church, it's across a small park next to the town hall. **$$$**

Guesthouse Anank (10 rooms) Darbinian 5; m 599 101835 **$$**

Hotel Ararat (18 rooms) Kamo 13; m 592 618575, 593 618575 **$$**

Hotel Gold Javakishvili 11; m 579 150985. Just to the left as you leave town towards Ninotsminda, this also has a friendly café-bar. **$$**

Café Lux Charents 9; m 599 777212. By the school at the top of Tamar Mepe. **$**

Restaurant Kavkaz Where the road to Turkey leaves town, opposite the ruins of an Ottoman fort. **$**

What to see and do Akhalkalaki is a drab town with lots of slots and betting shops, but there's a remarkably vibrant street market on Nalbandian. There are a couple of ATMs at Privat Bank (*Svoboda 4*) and the Bank of Georgia (*Nalbandian 35*). There's no tourist office, but there's a useful information board (in English) at the start of the Ninotsminda road.

Other than the remains of a **fort** there's nothing much for tourists in the town itself; however, there's growing interest in the megalithic 'Cyclopean ruins' dotted across the Javakheti Plateau. These massive structures of basalt blocks 3m across remain enigmatic, their purpose and building techniques still largely unexplained. They date mostly from the 2nd millennium BC, although some are much more recent.

The easiest to visit is at **Abuli**, a dozen kilometres east of Akhalkalaki and easily reached by taxi on a rough road. There seem to be defensive and residential structures here, overlooking the Javakheti Plateau and Lake Paravani; it's not far as the crow flies from another important site at **Shaori**, at 2,760m on the slopes of Mount Patara Abuli, but this is reached from Poka on the shores of Lake Paravani (page 193). The third major site is at **Saro**, just north of Khertvisi (and 3km to the right/east on the Khizabavra road), where there are also cave dwellings and food stores; nearby is a twin-nave church dating from the 7th–8th centuries. Here, as well as in Khizabavra and elsewhere, you'll also see *darnebi* or cave shelters, connected by tunnels, for protection from invaders. The villages of the Javakheti Plateau are also notable for their darbazi houses, with three sides buried in a hillside and a flat earth- and grass-covered roof; in the centre is a pyramidal chimney of stepped logs, and of course there are pits for storing wine and grain as well as cheese. There are also *menhirs* dotted across the bleak Javakheti Plateau, notably at Chikiani and Tezi (now Avranlo).

NINOTSMINDA AND BEYOND ნინოწმინდა

To the east, the railway and the A303 cross a high arid plateau dotted with a surprising number of lakes; the road was known for its terrible state but has been rebuilt thanks to the US$100 million Millennium Challenge fund, also providing bilingual education in this poor and largely Armenian area. It's 18km to **Ninotsminda** (or Bogdanovka) a town of 7,000 and, at 1,940m, one of the highest and remotest in Georgia. There are few direct marshrutkas from Tbilisi (*13.00 from Didube, 08.00 & 17.30 from Samgori; GEL3*) and it's usually easier to travel via Akhaltsikhe to Akhalkalaki, a GEL4–5 taxi ride away; the railway from Tbilisi to Turkey (opening in 2016) passes the edge of town but the only stop will be the Akhalkalaki International Station, midway between the two towns. The only hotel is the basic Ararat (*5 rooms; Teryan 2A; m 555 777905, 599 539956; $$*), one block south of the main drag. Just southeast of the central crossroads is the Boutique-Café-Ground Coffee ($), which may also have rooms.

Just 1km southwest of Ninotsminda is **Lake Khanchali**, which also has a sad and complicated history. Until 1961 it covered 1,310ha and was home to lake trout, Caucasian herring, barbel and migrating ducks, but in that year it was drained to be adapted for fish farming. It remained dry until 1964, by which time the wildfowl had moved to Lake Çıldır, in Turkey, on their migrations. As the lake was shallow and warm, the fish farming was successful, but even so it was abandoned in 1968, and the lake gradually reverted to its natural state. In 1985 a dam was built across the lake and two-thirds was drained again to grow hay, while the southeastern third was used for fish farming until 1990; in 1997 the dam began to collapse and the whole lake was drained for a year while it was patched together.

Amazingly, 40 bird species still stop here on their migrations, while another 24 (of which four are threatened with extinction) nest at the lake, including cranes and white storks. The Georgian Centre for the Conservation of Wildlife is campaigning for the restoration of the lake and buying 900ha of the lake bed, which will be the first private reserve in the Caucasus; although the mainly Armenian population at first wanted the land for farming, 77% now want the lake restored.

This is part of the **Javakheti Protected Areas**, a loose collection of lakes on the bleak plateau that are vital habitat for migrating birds; this is now being transformed into the Javakheti National Park (m *577 640482*; e *tkarapetiani@apa.gov.ge*), linked to the new Lake Arpi National Park in Armenia, with an expensive new visitor centre opening on the edge of Akhalkalaki (3km to the southwest) in 2015.

Just west of the lake in **Sulda**, on the road from Akhalkalaki to the Turkish border, birdwatchers and international drivers can stop at a couple of guesthouses, Flora (m *595 211136*) and Misha (m *599 492967*) which both charge GEL40 for a double room including breakfast. Similarly, just short of the Armenian border on the A306, the Guesthouse Madatapa (m *551 550941; GEL40/room B&B*) by Lake Mada, is also ideal for birders.

From Ninotsminda the A306 leads southeast to the Armenian border, passing through **Gorelovka**, the goal of Philip Marsden's quest in *The Spirit Wrestlers*. Here in 1895, on what they called the Sacred Heights, the Dukhobors, a Tolstoyan Quaker-like sect of Russians, burnt their guns and refused to serve in the tsar's army, starting a long saga of persecution and eventual emigration to Canada (via Siberia, as a rule). Now some of their turf-roofed cabins remain, but few of the people. In 1990 nearly 7,000 Dukhobors lived in eight villages in this region, but today their community has shrunk to only a few hundred (still half of the population of Gorelovka). When collective farms were broken up in 1997 the Dukhobors chose to stick with the principle of co-operative work and established the Dukhoborets collective farm. Unfortunately they left no land for the local Armenians, and in 2006 the local council removed almost 5,000ha, leaving the Dukhobors with only 600ha, between 6ha and 15ha per family. They're now talking of moving back to Russia.

The A303 and railway head northeast from Ninotsminda past Georgia's largest lake, **Lake Paravani** (2,047m), which is also threatened by a plan to farm non-native fish; at its southern end is Poka, known for the **convent of St Nino** (*www.phokanunnery.ge*) whose nuns make excellent cheese of all kinds that can be bought in Tbilisi or at their shop here, just to the west. This is also the access to the Shaori megalithic ruins (page 192). At the lake's northern end is the Dukhobor village of Tambovka. The villages on this cold and treeless plateau are notable for their savage speed-bumps, and for their grass-roofed houses. From km 46/100, after Lake Paravani, the road drops fast to Tsalka (page 293; 81km from Ninotsminda) and on to the outskirts of Manglisi, where the old road

6

takes a rather hilly route passing near to Birtvisi and Betania (page 293), before descending to Tbilisi, while the railway takes a loop to the south. A minor road from Manglisi to Koda, south of Tbilisi on the main road to Armenia, was rebuilt (and launched by Saakashvili with great fanfare as the new Silk Road) and is now the fastest route, used by the few marshrutkas that head up on to the plateau.

Imereti, Racha, Mingrelia and Guria

IMERETI იმერეთი

Imereti lies cradled between the High and Lesser Caucasus and the Surami range, inland from the coastal plains; it's a fertile, well-watered region that was one of the cradles of Georgian civilisation. The Imeretians are known as the most voluble and temperamental people in Georgia, and they also consider themselves the most hospitable. Its capital is Kutaisi, Georgia's second city, an attractive, friendly place which has a few creature comforts to offer the traveller.

The main road from Tbilisi crosses the Rikoti Pass from Khashuri and Surami (page 154) and descends steadily to Zestaponi, while the railway (and a back road) follows the next valley to the south. The main road has been improved, with lots of new bridges cutting off sections of road that take a much longer route along the curves of the river. Many of these still form village streets, and they can be used to make a far more enjoyable route for cycling; as most of these loops are to the north of the main road, cyclists should head westwards (ie: downhill). With a good, solid bike it would be possible to return by the Kharagauli road to the south, making a very pleasant loop. This was a bad road, but it is better now that repairs have been made.

HIKING TO THE NORTH OF BORJOMI-KHARAGAULI NATIONAL PARK On this route, the tiny village of **Marelisi** (450m) is becoming a centre for hiking into the Borjomi-Kharagauli National Park (page 176); there's a park guesthouse (m 599 951421; e welcome@borjomi-kharagauli-np.ge; ☾ spring–autumn; $$) 4km south of the station and 3km north of the park gate (a taxi is available and can also shuttle your baggage). It has four double rooms with food and hot water available, plus camping in the yard, and is becoming popular with Tbilisi expats at the weekends. Horses can be rented for easier forays into the park. The trails leads south up the Shavtwala Valley and then to either Lomis Mta and Likani, or Rkinis Jvari and Atskuri – see page 180 for details.

Kharagauli is the northern centre for the Borjomi-Kharagauli National Park, with special responsibility for the buffer zone. Rather more substantial than Marelisi, it consists of two main streets (across the river from the station and to the right) with some fine buildings of dressed stone built in 1933, one of which is now a park office and visitor centre. Further west there's the large *Muza* sculpture by someone who'd obviously never seen a naked woman; the road heads into a gorge, passing a very odd sculpture, half-covered in ivy but seeming to represent grotesquified pagan myths. Thankfully the 10km road from Dzirula on the main highway to Kharagauli was rebuilt in 2005.

Marelisi, Kharagauli and Moliti (the station for Nunisi – see page 180) are served by marshrutkas from Didube (the last at 15.30) and trains, with the 08.55 and 21.10 departures from Tbilisi taking about 2 hours to Moliti, 2 hours and 50 minutes to

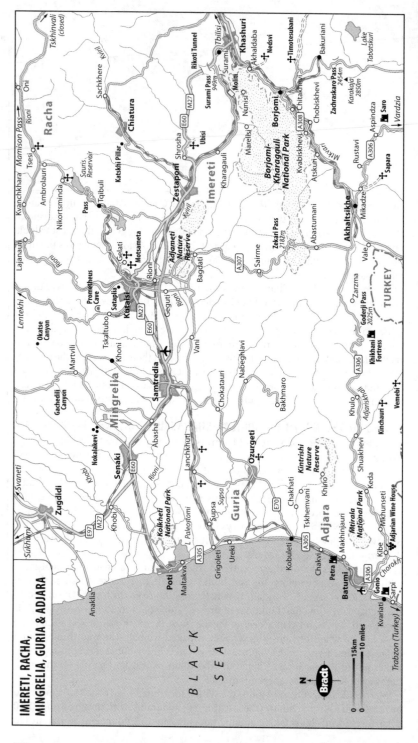

IMERETI, RACHA,
MINGRELIA, GURIA & ADJARA

Marelisi and 3 hours to Kharagauli. From the west, trains leave Zestaponi at 02.00 and 13.50, taking 45 minutes to Kharagauli, 70 minutes to Marelisi and 80 minutes to Moliti.

UBISI Emerging from the toll tunnel at km143.5 (or the old road over the pass), the main highway passes beehives and their keepers camping beside the road in summer and criss-crosses the Rikotula and the Dzirula streams many times, passing a new restaurant at about km149 and then attractive villages such as Khonevi (km155) and Boriti (km167).

Immediately after passing the piers for an unfinished concrete viaduct, to the left at km170/382, a road to Goresha turns left on a bend and drops to a bridge; it's well worth halting here to visit the charming little **church of Ubisi**, just before the bridge. Heading east, there's a good view of the church and the remains of fortifications above the unfinished viaduct. Built in AD826 by one Grigor Kansteli, it's a single-nave basilica, but with a double porch that more or less constitutes a southern aisle. The gate-tower, built of rounded river stones, has been doubled as well, and there are various other extensions tacked on to the main building. However, the bell-tower, a three-storey dwelling built by Demetre I in 1141 (when the church was also restored), with a ladder to reach the entrance, is separate. The 14th-century frescoes by Damiane, reaching almost to the floor, are lovely and rival the finest Byzantine paintings with a supple grace that seems very Western, especially the Last Supper above the altar and the Annunciation (with the Virgin turning in surprise) to the north.

TO ZESTAPONI In the long village of **Shrosha**, huge quantities of red ceramics are for sale, especially in a lay-by at km174 (km378 from the west), although the village itself is at km177; this is virtually the only place in western Georgia where qvevris are made for wine-making. The good Imereti Restaurant is just west of km180. The railway soon appears from the valley to the southeast (before the junction with the Kharagauli road at km183) and cuts across a bend in the river through a new tunnel; to the north the traces of the old single-track railway can still be seen and could also be used for a hiking or mountain-biking route from km184. At km189, a road bridge leads right into the village of **Shorapani**, while the highway (lined with stalls selling engine oil) loops to the left; to the right at km190 you'll see a ruined castle, then a rusty steam locomotive (a 0-6-0 tank engine) on a plinth above the rail junction to Chiatura.

Another kilometre to the west, at km192, the road enters **Zestaponi**, a sprawling, grimy industrial town at the junction to Chiatura and Sachkhere, with a decent soccer team but not much else to recommend it. The transit route (lined with Western-style coffee shops) turns right over the first bridge crossing the Kviril River, while buses pick up and set down here, continue on the south bank, then take the second bridge and turn left to pass the railway station and a park (through a colonnade to the south). At the western end of town they head under the railway to the bus station at km195.5 (the end of the transit route), then pass the metallurgical works (now American-owned and supplying 6% of the world's demand for ferroalloy) and finally leave the town at km199 (km353 from the west). At km204 the road passes the turning north to Tqibuli and Racha (pages 211–14); the new Khareba winery is just another kilometre west. For accommodation in this area, the Hotel Savane is in the centre at Davit Agmashenebelis 11, and there's another hotel by a supermarket in the western outskirts.

CHIATURA This small town, 40km north of Zestaponi (an hour by marshrutka), sits amid one of the world's richest manganese deposits, perhaps 222 million tonnes;

Bidzina Ivanishvili, who's worth about US$4 billion, also comes from Chorvila, just east of Chiatura, so the town is not in the state of total post-communist decline you might expect. Many of the mines are on the cliffs around the town, reached by a network of cable-cars which are becoming an offbeat tourist attraction. The first manganese ropeways were built in the 1930s and the oldest cable-car (No 25) dates from 1954, just after the mines were turned into a modern Stalinist industry; this was in part a reward for their having been the only Bolshevik stronghold in overwhelmingly Menshevik Georgia. Stalin himself hid here in his revolutionary days, holding up trains to steal the mines' pay chests.

Getting there and away Marshrutkas run roughly hourly (*GEL6; until 18.00*) from the Okriba terminal at Didube in Tbilisi to the bus station at the first hairpin on the Zestaponi road, taking about 3½ hours. They also run from Kutaisi until about 15.00, taking an hour and a half but also charging GEL6, although some continue through town to Sacchere. There's a daily train from Kutaisi I at 09.00, returning at about 15.00, amazingly slow but cheap (*GEL1*).

Where to stay and eat Tourist services are minimal: about a kilometre north of town, continuing on the main road (Maiakovski), there's a nameless hotel (m *598 432190, 599 759528;* $$) opposite the bridge to Perevisa, which has basic but adequate en-suite rooms and weak Wi-Fi, and a similar place about 75m up the side-road to the left (☎ *599 475608, 555 393052;* $$). The only place to eat is the tiny Café Sophie Comme Il Faut on the main street ($), Ninoshvili, which doesn't offer much beyond beer, cakes and khachapuri.

What to see and do At least a dozen **cable-cars** are still in operation; those owned by the town charge a small fee (*GEL0.20*) while those owned by the mine are free. By the bridge just north of the main square, one cable-car rises southeast across the river while a tiny blue one climbs north to a clifftop mine from where you can hike down in a very long zigzag to the south. From the main square, you can cross a bridge and go under the railway to another small terminal, and there's a triple terminal, linking the cliffs to the east with a terminal just above the Zestaponi road, near a footbridge just to the south.

Another unusual attraction is perhaps 7km along the road to Zestaponi and Kutaisi at the point where it crosses the Kashura River: about 500m to the north you'll see the 40m-high **Katskhi Pillar**, a limestone monolith with a small church and hermit cells on top. A monk called Maxime has lived here alone for almost 20 years, hauling up food that's supplied by local followers. He's not a total recluse and does climb down a metal ladder twice a week. It seems that the hermitage was abandoned from the Ottoman invasions of the 15th century until 1944, when a way up was found again.

A couple of kilometres north of town and up to the left in the village of **Mghvimebi**, there's a cathedral founded in the 10th or 11th century where Queen Tamar once hid, apparently; it's richly decorated inside and out.

KUTAISI ქუთაისი *Telephone code 431*

Kutaisi dates from perhaps the 17th century BC and was established as a Greek colony by the 7th century BC; by the 3rd century BC it was capital of Colchida, and from AD978 to 1122 it was the capital of the united Georgia, Tbilisi being occupied by the Turks. It was again capital of Imereti from the late 15th century to 1810.

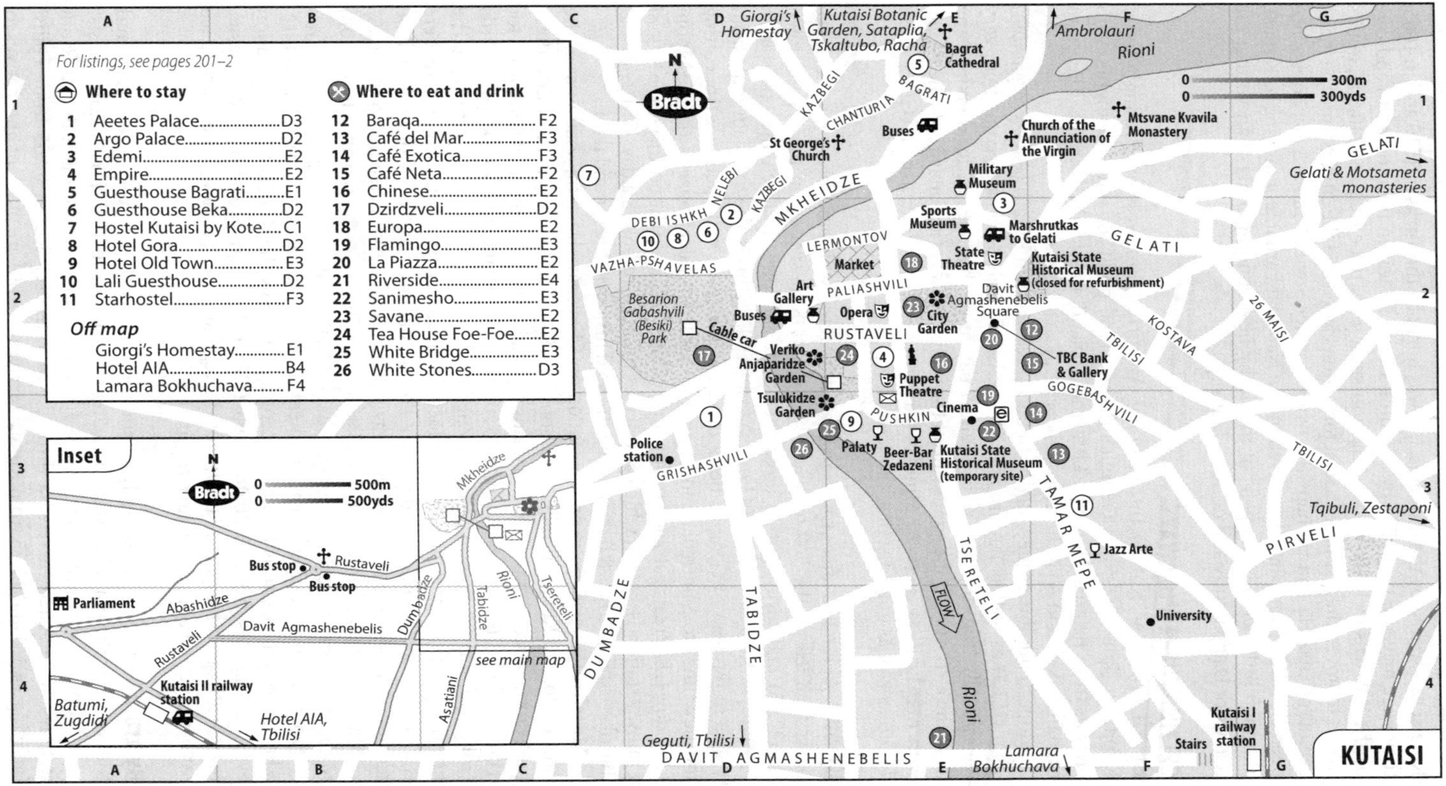

KUTAISI
For listings, see pages 201–2
Where to stay
1 Aeetes Palace D3
2 Argo Palace D2
3 Edemi E2
4 Empire E2
5 Guesthouse Bagrati E1
6 Guesthouse Beka D2
7 Hostel Kutaisi by Kote C1
8 Hotel Gora D2
9 Hotel Old Town E3
10 Lali Guesthouse D2
11 Starhostel F3
Off map
Giorgi's Homestay E1
Hotel AIA B4
Lamara Bokhuchava F4
Where to eat and drink
12 Baraqa F2
13 Café del Mar F3
14 Café Exotica F3
15 Café Neta F2
16 Chinese E2
17 Dzirdzveli D2
18 Europa E2
19 Flamingo E3
20 La Piazza E2
21 Riverside E4
22 Sanimesho E3
23 Savane E2
24 Tea House Foe-Foe E2
25 White Bridge E3
26 White Stones D3
Inset
Bus stop
Rustaveli
Parliament
Abashidze
Davit Agmashenebelis
Dumbadze
Tabidze
Rioni
Tsereteli
Mkheidze
Asatiani
see main map
Kutaisi II railway station
Batumi, Zugdidi
Hotel AIA, Tbilisi
0 500m
0 500yds
Giorgi's Homestay
Kutaisi Botanic Garden, Sataplia, Tskaltubo, Racha
Bagrat Cathedral
Ambrolauri
Rioni
0 300m
0 300yds
Mtsvane Kvavila Monastery
Church of the Annunciation of the Virgin
St George's Church
Buses
KAZBEGI
CHANTURIA
BAGRATI
GELATI
Gelati & Motsameta monasteries
Military Museum
Sports Museum
Marshrutkas to Gelati
State Theatre
Kutaisi State Historical Museum (closed for refurbishment)
MKHEIDZE
NELEBI
DEBI ISHKH
LERMONTOV
Market
VAZHA-PSHAVELAS
Art Gallery
PALIASHVILI
Davit Agmashenebelis Square
Besarion Gabashvili (Besiki) Park
Opera
City Garden
Cable car
RUSTAVELI
KOSTAVA
26 MAISI
TBILISI
Veriko Anjaparidze Garden
Puppet Theatre
TBC Bank & Gallery
Tsulukidze Garden
GOGEBASHVILI
PUSHKIN
Cinema
Police station
Palaty
Beer-Bar Zedazeni
Kutaisi State Historical Museum (temporary site)
GRISHASHVILI
TAMAR MEPE
Tqibuli, Zestaponi
Jazz Arte
PIRVELI
DUMBADZE
TABIDZE
TSERETELI
FLOW
University
Geguti, Tbilisi
DAVIT AGMASHENEBELIS
Lamara Bokhuchava
Stairs
Kutaisi I railway station

Kutaisi was spared by the Mongols, but was burnt by the Turks in 1510 and in 1666; they were driven out in 1770 by Solomon II, but he was in turn forced to abdicate by the Russians in 1810. Under communism it grew to be a city of 240,000, but its main employer, the Kamaz truck factory, soon closed and the city became the mafia capital of Georgia and perhaps the whole former Soviet Union. It has long since been cleaned up and may be revived by the National Parliament moving to Kutaisi, although little actually happens in the flashy new building other than voting; the real work is apparently still done in Tbilisi.

GETTING THERE AND AWAY

By air The new Kutaisi International Airport, 14km west on the highway at Kopitnari (km255/297), is Georgia's main arrival point for low-cost flights, with arrivals from Belarus, Hungary, Lithuania, Poland, Russia and Ukraine. There's an exchange desk and ATM here, as well as a café.

Modern minibuses meet flights to take passengers to Kutaisi (*www.georgianbus. com; GEL5*) as well as Batumi and Tbilisi; bus 777 also seems to come here very occasionally from the city. You shouldn't pay more than GEL20 for a taxi. In any case, the airport is on the south side of the main highway (ie: Kutaisi is to the right), with marshrutkas every 20 minutes between Kutaisi and Samtredia (*GEL2; until 18.30*) as well as long-distance services.

By bus At km223, after crossing a plateau covered with pine forest, long-distance buses turn left on the E60 to reach the Bagdati–Kutaisi road on the edge of town (km227.5) and turn right to cross the Rioni and directly reach the bus station [199 A3] of Kutaisi, 232km (142 miles) from Tbilisi. This is also the main route from Tbilisi to the west of Georgia, but a bypass to the south will open in 2016, cutting journey times to Samtredia and beyond by an hour. **Local buses** from Zestaponi (*15 a day; GEL2*) carry straight on for 5km to enter the city to the north, via the Kutaisi I railway station [199 G4], which also serves buses to Tqibuli (8 a day; GEL2.50) and Terjola (*6 a day; GEL1.80*). Bus tickets are sold inside on the ground floor.

Marshrutkas use the main bus station on Chavchavadze, 3km southwest of the centre, close to Kutaisi II railway station. This is perhaps Georgia's most disorderly bus station, a scene of third-world chaos especially when it rains. Frequent buses for Tbilisi (*GEL8–10*) leave from several locations, long-distance marshrutkas westwards (roughly hourly to Batumi, Poti and Zugdidi) leave from a concrete platform at the northwestern end, and those to more local destinations to the southeast, where there is a rusty ticket booth. Coming from Tbilisi, marshrutkas leave from the Didube terminal and also the rear of the railway station and the Akhmeteli metro station.

Marshrutkas for more local destinations like Oni in Racha province leave from Mkheidze, north of the river beneath Bagrat Cathedral.

From the bus station, turn left then right up Rustaveli to reach the centre. Alternatively, bus 1 runs to the city centre and below the Kutaisi I railway station every 5 minutes from 07.30 to 21.00 (*GEL0.30*); there are also slightly faster marshrutka minibuses (*GEL0.40*), but the regular buses are new, have more space for baggage and are particularly cheap here.

By train Kutaisi has two railway stations: Kutaisi I [199 G4] facing east, and Kutaisi II, by the main bus station, facing west. Trains to Tbilisi (*GEL7.50*) consist of a couple of carriages from Kutaisi I trundled down to the main line at Rioni station and attached there to a through train; the services at 08.55 from Tbilisi (arriving 14.15) and 12.25 from Kutaisi (arriving 18.00) are pleasant alternatives to a scary marshrutka ride, and the easiest way to get to Gori or Mtskheta. Going to or from western Georgia, you could use Rioni as a sort of parkway station; it's about 500m west of the road from Kutaisi to Bagdati, served by several marshrutkas every hour. Kutaisi I also has two trains a day to Sachkhere. The Kutaisi II railway station [199 A4] is barely functional (buy tickets on the train) and only handles local trains to Tskaltubo (*4 a day; GEL1*) and a daily train to Batumi (*GEL6*).

From Kutaisi I railway station, turn right to walk 1km into the centre.

WHERE TO STAY *Map, page 199*

As well as the hotels listed, there are nice homestays on Ukimerioni Hill west of the Bagrat Cathedral, where large houses have secure parking and balconies with great views of the city.

Hotels

Empire Hotel (25 rooms) Pushkin 1; 24 2328; www.empirehotel.ge. Also facing the Tsulukidze Garden, this excellent new hotel has AC rooms (14 luxe), conference room & a classy bar-restaurant with terrace. **$$$$**

Aeetes Palace (28 rooms) Tabidze 34; 25 3533, 24 4407; www.aeetes-hotel.com. A modern, centrally located hotel close to the cable-car station, with restaurant, bar & conference hall. **$$$**

Argo Palace (18 rooms) Debi Ishkhnelebi 16; m 599 779797, 599 376525; https:// argopalace.wordpress.com. A friendly, modern place with excellent homemade food, AC, parking & fast Wi-Fi. Rooms (& bathrooms) are smallish but each floor has a shared balcony overlooking the city. **$$$**

Hotel AIA (7 rooms) Chavchavadze 8, just over 1km east of the bus station; 22 3676; m 599 293676, 570 104149; e teonchi@mail.ru; http://hotelaia.com. A comfortable, new place that's handy for drivers in transit, but is linked to the city centre by bus 1 & various marshrutkas which run up Asatiani to the centre & back on Ninoshvili. There's good Georgian food a 5-min walk west at the Delikatessen Restaurant, Chavchavadze 20. B/fast is GEL10 extra. **$$$**

Hotel Gora (43 rooms) Debi Ishkhnelebi 22; 25 2170; m 599 574625; e hotelgora@gmail. com; www.bigsale.ge/hotelgora. A grandiose new building, totally out of place in this area of low-rise family homes & guesthouses, but it gives good views towards the Bagrat Cathedral. Rooms are simple but come with en-suite facilities. Price inc meals. **$$$**

Hotel Old Town (9 rooms) Grishavili 3/4; 25 1451; m 595 300024, 599 516056;

e dzvelikalaki@gmail.com; www.oldtown.ge. New hotel primarily aimed at a business clientele, facing the Tsulukidze Garden. Rooms with AC, minibar & cable TV. Rates inc b/fast & Wi-Fi. **$$$**

Edemi Brosse 9; 25 2823; m 599 563825; e merabi661@gmail.com; www.edemihotel. ge. A fairly simple place with small rooms & tiny balconies, but good value for this central location, opposite the Gelati marshrutka stop. **$$**

Hostels

Hostel Kutaisi by Kote (14 rooms) Gorki 18; m 593 548507; e hostel.kutaisi@mail. com; https://hostelkutaisien.wordpress.com. On Ukimerioni Hill, not far from the Bagrat Cathedral, a small shop serves as reception for dorms in 3 separate houses; shared bathrooms, kitchen, washing machine & Wi-Fi. **$**

Starhostel (9 rooms) Tamar Mepe 37; m 555 238893. In a pleasant old quarter between the river & Kutaisi I railway station; 6 dbl rooms & 2 small dorms sharing 5 bathrooms, a kitchen & laundry room; car-parking available. B/fast & towels inc plus unlimited tea & coffee. **$**

Homestays

Guesthouse Bagrati (4 rooms) Bagrati 25; 24 9278; m 551 164162, 555 767698; e ghbagrationi@mail.com. This friendly & comfortable new place (in a historic house) could hardly be closer to the Bagrat Cathedral, with views from the terrace; some rooms also have balconies. **$$**

Guesthouse Beka (5 rooms) Debi Ishkhnelebi 26; 24 6923; m 568 105262; www. bigsale.ge/beka. They're very friendly & some English is spoken. 4 rooms are en suite. Price inc dinner & b/fast. **$$**

Lali Guesthouse (12 rooms) Debi Ishkhnelebi 18; 24 8395; m 599 376525. Lali Jalaghiana has built a new wing here with nice big twin rooms with showers opposite (with solar water heating), but only Georgian & Russian are spoken. Price inc 2 excellent meals. **$$**

Lamara Bokhuchava (3 rooms) Tsereteli 152 (on the left at the end of a short alley); 22 5550. Near the Kutaisi I railway station. 2 twin rooms & a trpl, with shared toilet & shower. The paint is peeling a bit, but the plasterwork is great. Price inc food. **$$**

Giorgi's Homestay (8 rooms) Chanchibadze 14; m 595 591511; e giorgihomestay14@yahoo. com. A hospitable & comfortable family home 5mins' (uphill) walk from the Bagrat Cathedral. Giorgi Giorgadze speaks good English & can show you how to play Georgian dominoes as well as arranging tours & transfers. Price inc 2 good, filling meals. **$–$$**

✗ WHERE TO EAT AND DRINK *Map, page 199*

There are attractive cafés at either end of the pedestrianised Tetri Khidi (White Bridge), by the Veriko Anjaparidze Garden; the **White Bridge** bar has a terrace close to water-level, while the **White Stones**, at the west end, was the meeting place between 1915 and 1930 of the Symbolist writers known as the Tsisperkantselebi (notably Grigol Robakidze, Paolo Iashvili, Titian Tabidze, Gogla Leonidze, Galaktion Tabidze, and the painter Lado Gudiashvili).

Riverside Davit Agmashenebelis 16/18; m 597 02020. This is the best restaurant in Kutaisi, & is indeed right by the Rioni just south of the centre. It serves classic Georgian dishes such as khinkali, khachapuri, shashlik & aubergine salads, with live music at w/ends. **$$$**

Baraqa Tamar Mepe 5; m 597 225522. Another popular place that specialises in khachapuri from around the country – imeruli, adjurali, etc – & in particular Svan kubdari. Service is excellent, & there's a choice of foreign beers & free Wi-Fi; it's even non-smoking. **$$**

Chinese Restaurant Tsereteli 10. This has Chinese owners & does what you'd expect; opened in 2014, it's not cheap but there's free tea & it's all authentic & tasty. **$$**

Dzirdzveli Vazha-Pshavelas 1; 24 1735; m 590 498940. In Besarion Gabashvili Park, by the Ferris wheel, this is a local favourite with its rustic style & semi-rustic location. **$$**

La Piazza Davit Agmashenebelis 2; m 557 667047. A place to pose & be seen, with its 1920s décor & bartenders' tricks. It does serve good desserts, & puts on jazz nights. **$$**

Europa Paliashvili, opposite the City Garden. Offers live music plus a cocktail & beer bar. **$–$$**

Café del Mar Tamar Mepe 21. Serves khachapuri & Turkish coffee, made in hot sand. **$**

Café Exotica Tamar Mepe 15. Has a good choice of cheap Georgian fast food, notably acharuli (Adjaran) khachapuri. **$**

Café Neta Tamar Mepe. Serves coffee & cakes. **$**

Flamingo Pushkin/Tamar Mepe. A glass building with self-service cakes, drinks & snacks. **$**

Sanimesho Tamar Mepe 16. Self-service bakery/café. **$**

Savane In the City Garden. This café is a pleasant place to take a break, especially at its outdoor tables. **$**

Tea House Foe-Foe Rustaveli 5; m 555 689989. In the foyer of the former Hotel Kutaisi, this has an arty junkshop vibe, with mismatching chairs & tables, lots of books, & large paintings including on the ceiling. They serve a long list of teas (from GEL4) & snacks, & have Wi-Fi. **$**

NIGHTLIFE AND ENTERTAINMENT The best nightlife in town is to be found on Pushkin, a newly refurbished and cobbled 'old town' street, where **Palaty** [199 E3] at No 2 (24 3380; m 595 909806) is a hip little bar-restaurant that serves khachapuri and pizza and often has live bands; the **Beer-Bar Zedazeni** [199 E3] at No 16 (24 3899) is linked to the brewery of the same name and also serves good khinkali. There's also the **Che** bar, the **Kozell Pub** and the **Bon Appetit** bar-café on the same street, and the flashy **Café Medea** by the opera on Tsminda

Nino. The **Jazz Arte** café-bar [199 F3], in a fine period house at Tamar Mepe 57 (\ *25 1910;* ⊕ *noon–02.00 daily*) plays to a slightly older crowd.

As for entertainment, the huge **State Theatre** [199 E2] (*www.meskhishvilitheatre. ge*) dominates Davit Agmashenebelis Square, and the **opera house** [199 E2] (*Tsminda Nino 17;* \ *24 2432*) has a horrid new exterior but puts on decent shows. The **Puppet Theatre** [199 E2] (*Tsminda Nino 11;* \ *45 205*) is always popular with children, and there's a new **cinema** [199 E3] on Pushkin between Tsereteli and Tamar Mepe. **Kutaisoba**, the annual city festival, is on or around 2 May.

OTHER PRACTICALITIES **Tourist information** is available from an office in the entrance to City Hall [199 E2] (*Rustaveli 3;* \ *331 241103;* e *tickutaisi@gmail.com;* ⊕ *10.00–18.00 daily, summer to 19.00*), and also at the airport (m *595 088219;* e *tickutaisiair@gmail.com*).

The best places to **exchange money** are between Rustaveli and the bus station, on Tsereteli, or north of the market on Tsminda Nino. There are plenty of **ATMs** along Rustaveli, Paliashvili and Tsereteli and elsewhere in the centre.

The **post office** is near the south end of Tsminda Nino [199 E3] (⊕ *09.00–17.00 Mon–Fri, 09.00–13.00 Sat*); **DHL** have an office at Rustaveli 165 (⊕ *09.30–18.00 Mon–Fri*). For **internet** access, Ciber House is on Pushkin at Tamar Mepe [199 E3]; there's open Wi-Fi at McDonald's at the bus station.

Flights and tours can be booked at the Wonderland Travel Agency at Tsereteli 8 (\ *25 5656;* m *597 355656;* e *kutaisi@wonderland.ge; http://wonderland.ge/ka*) or at Kolkha Tour, upstairs in the cable-car terminal at Veriko Anjaparidze Park (\ *25 1199;* m *593 902683; www.kolkhatour.ge*).

WHAT TO SEE AND DO

A tour of central Kutaisi Rustaveli forms the main axis of the city, leading from the Zugdidi road to the city centre; there are plenty of buses, but if you walk from the junction by the bus station it'll take about 30 minutes to a square where a brief one-way loop begins; almost at once you rejoin Rustaveli to cross the river by a stone bridge built in the 1860s, flanked by two steel bridges dating from 1866 and 1872. Beneath the bridges, the limestone slabs from which the city derives its name are visible – '*kwata*' means stony.

To the left, immediately before the river, is a monument to Galaction Tabidze (the young poet being sent on his way by his muse); to the right on the far bank of the river is the **Veriko Anjaparidze Garden** [199 D2], laid out as a royal garden in the mid 17th century and now named after a famous actress; from its southern side a cable-car (⊕ *noon–20.00 daily; GEL0.50*) ascends to the hilltop **Besarion Gabashvili (or Besiki) Park** [199 D2], where there's a small funfair and zoo. Next to it is the **Tsulukidze Garden** [199 D3], a small sculpture park.

To the left is the city's main marshrutka terminal at Tsitelikhidi or the Red Bridge, and beyond it you'll see an intriguing gable at the western end of the covered market passage that uses terracotta figures to detail the city's history and culture.

Continuing into the centre, the first building on the left is the **David Kakabadze Fine Art Gallery** [199 D2] (*Rustaveli 8;* ⊕ *10.00–18.00 except Sun; GEL5*). Temporary shows are held downstairs, while the main collection is in one large room one flight up; this gives perhaps the best overview of Georgian art of any gallery outside Tbilisi. Opposite the door are two Pirosmanis, then paintings by local hero David Kakabadze including two called *Imereti* (1912 and 1934). There's a portrait by Ketevan Maralashvili of the poet Titsian Tabidze, looking like Oscar Wilde with his red carnation and cigarette. Then there's Lado Gudiashvili's *Autumn Festival*, with people in national dress celebrating the grape harvest, and a painting by Robert Sturua, father of the famous theatre director. The works on the facing wall are less famous but possibly more attractive, such as Valeri Margiani's *Kutaisi*, with the white rocks built up in impasto, and a portrait of Pirosmani by Samson Nadareishvili.

Just beyond the Art Museum on the right is the Classical Gymnasium (1902), the school attended by the poets Akaki Tsereteli (1840–1915) and Vladimir Mayakovsky (1893–1930), whose father, an impoverished Russian noble, worked as a forester in Bagdati, south of Kutaisi.

Away from the gallery, the former **Radium cinema** (1911) on the right at the top of Tsisperkantselebi, is worth a look. Beyond this, at Rustaveli 5, is the Hotel Kutaisi, an old Soviet-era hotel that has now closed, and then a group of rather odd statues supposedly in praise of labour, although in fact one is also named *My Imereti*.

The centre of the city is the **City Garden** [199 E2] or Bulvari, a park full of trees where old men gather on benches and cafés serve the young. At its east end is **Davit Agmashenebelis Square** [199 E2], in the centre of which is a huge fountain based on gold jewellery found in the Vani archaeological site (pages 210–11). This replaced a statue of King David the Builder (who was crowned and started his campaign of unification here) by Elgudja Amashukeli, Georgia's best-known monumental sculptor, unveiled by Shevardnadze during the 1995 election campaign and moved by Saakashvili to a more dominant position in front of the Kutaisi I railway station [199 G4].

On the north side of the square is the huge, circular **Meskhishvili State Theatre** [199 E2] (⊕ *for performances only*), on the south side is the **TBC Bank and Gallery** [199 E2] (⊕ *11.00–20.00 Mon–Fri, 11.00–14.00 Sat; free*), hosting some impressive temporary shows, and to the east the **Kutaisi State Historical Museum** [199 F2] one of the best outside Tbilisi. This is currently closed for long-term refurbishment and there's a temporary display at the corner of Tsereteli and Pushkin [199 E3] (⊕ *10.00–18.00 except Mon, winter 11.00–16.00; GEL5*). On the ground floor is a cannon seized by Solomon I at the battle of Rukhi in 1799, a landau and music box and a huge wine press made from a hollowed linden tree trunk. In a beautiful hall upstairs you'll see stone implements from the Palaeolithic and Neolithic periods, qvevri burial pitchers used in Colchis for burying women (men were wrapped in leather and hung on trees) and then jewellery and ceremonial axe heads from the 2nd and 1st millennia BC, and a fertility figure from Bagdati, with both breasts and phallus, produced sometime between the 8th and 6th centuries BC, which is the museum's most famous exhibit. From the Antique epoch (6th–3rd centuries BC) there are ceramics, beads and a *rhiton* or silver cup of fighting soldiers from Gomi. However, the museum's pride and joy is its early medieval collection, above all icons from the 10th century onwards, many from Svaneti and Racha. Note the fine icon of St George from the 12th century, the big 13th-century icon of an archangel from Gebi, and a large 16th-century cross from Barakoni. Also from the 16th century is the great triptych of the Virgin from Gelati, its Nativity scene showing Joseph clearly wondering what's going on. There are too many photos of ancient documents, plus 17th-century ecclesiastical vestments, 18th-century costumes, 18th- and 19th-century weaponry (including the sword of King Solomon II) and 19th-century musical instruments. In a side room, beyond some medieval ceramics and 12th-century frescoes on plaster from Vani, there are agricultural implements, a chacha still and drinking vessels, an 18th-century door from Martvili Church, snowshoes, traps and guns, some 16th to 19th-century deeds and 18th to 19th-century coins. There's also a replica of an Imeretian peasants' house, with carpets on the wall and wooden vessels on the shelves. Finally, you'll see a priests' punishment belt and items of goldsmithery including decorations for horse harnesses.

It's also worth mentioning the **Kutaisi Sports Museum** [199 E2] (🕐 *office hours; free*), across the road to the west of the theatre, which has surprisingly eclectic coverage, with insight into social context as well as the usual cases of medals. A prize exhibit is George Best's shirt from a Northern Ireland–Soviet Union game, and there's also the bike of world champion cyclist Omar Kakadze. A couple of doors down there's also a **Military Museum** [199 E2] (🕐 *10.00–17.00 Tue–Sat; free*), honouring the dead of World War II.

A kilometre north of the bus station along 9 April, or west on Abashidze from Rustaveli, the appallingly expensive new **Parliament Building** [199 A4] (by Spanish architect Alberto Domingo Cabo) is an astonishing sight, like a giant frog's eye rising out of the ground. This was the site of a 1980s war memorial by Merab Berdzenishvili which Putin suggested should be moved to Moscow if Georgia was spurning it. Saakashvili had it blown up in 2009 out of personal pique, but unfortunately flying concrete boulders killed two people in the courtyard of their home a considerable distance away. Guided tours are available on Wednesdays, Thursdays and Fridays in weeks when parliament is sitting, at noon, 15.00 and 17.00; booking is required – contact ✆ 32 228 1690/3 or e toursparliament@gmail.com.

The Bagrat Cathedral

[199 E1] The city's great sight is the Bagrat Cathedral, which you'll see high on the Ukimerioni Hill across the river from the city centre; to reach it, head north on Tsminda Nino (Saint Nino Street) from the west end of the City Garden. This leads past the market and across the river on a mock-suspension bridge to Mkheidze kucha; the terminal for buses to Racha is just to the right here, and steps from behind here (or a road further to the right) lead up to Kazbegi kucha and the cathedral. There has been a fortress here since at least the 1st century AD; now there are remains from the 5th and 6th centuries, and late medieval fortifications. Occupied by the Turks, in 1769 it was bombarded by Solomon I and the Russian General Todleben from Mtsvane Kvavila. However, these are dwarfed by the Cathedral of the Assumption, commissioned by Bagrat III in 1003 (as recorded by the oldest Arabic numerals in Georgia), as a huge triconch cruciform church with a central dome. Later (although still in the first half of the 11th century), a portico was added to the west, with others to the north and south added in the 12th century. The cathedral was destroyed in 1691–92 by the Turks, leaving it roofless; it was disused, but immensely impressive, until 2008, when President Saakashvili launched a controversial plan to restore it as a working church. UNESCO, which had placed it on its World Heritage List in 1994, was very opposed to this (along with many other people and bodies) and in 2010 placed it on its list of World Heritage Sites in Danger. The restoration is now complete, with a horrid green roof and a modern tower discreetly added on the north side, but UNESCO has not yet actually removed the cathedral from the World Heritage List. To the west on the same hill is **St George's Church**, built in the 19th century, with a plain white interior.

Northern Kutaisi

There are other interesting churches on the left bank of the Rioni, to the east of the centre. Behind the State Theatre, Varlamishvilis (named after a local painter) leads to the **Church of the Annunciation of the Virgin** [199 E1], rebuilt by French Roman Catholics around the start of the 20th century. It's a Georgian Orthodox church, with an interior that seems at odds with its Baroque exterior and Latin inscription. Further north (from the far side of the State Theatre) at the end of Newport kucha (Mayakovsky kucha until it was named after Kutaisi's Welsh twin in 2000) is another attractive church, only a couple of centuries old;

it's very compact, with single-bay aisles, lateral chapels and a high barrel dome. Finally, just off Newport kucha, Jerusalem Street is the heart of what was the Jewish quarter, which had three synagogues in the 19th century; in 1926 a tenth of the city's population was Jewish, and 5% of Georgia's Jews still live here. There are still two synagogues on Gaponovis (one, built in the 1880s and recently restored, a block east of Newport). On the hill above is the **Mtsvane Kvavila (Green Flower) Monastery** [199 F1], with three churches including the 6th-century Church of the Archangels and a 17th-century church and bell-tower, as well as a pantheon that includes the grave of the composer Meliton Antonovich Balanchivadze (1862–1937), father of the choreographer George Balanchine. There's a good view back to the Bagrat Cathedral and northeast to a dam across the Rioni River.

Also on the west bank of the river, the **Kutaisi Botanic Garden** [199 E1] (↖ 245 079; www.bgk.ge; ⊕ 10.00–18.00 Tue–Sun; GEL3) is about 500m north from the chain bridge and the steps up to the Bagrat Cathedral. Founded in the mid-19th century, it became very run-down after the end of communism but has recently been refurbished. Even so, it's mainly about trees and shrubs, of which there are around 700 species; there are few non-woody plants here, apart from a small rose garden just to the left of the entrance. There are lots of fine Mediterranean cypress (*Cupressus sempervirens*) near the entrance, and further in various specimens of cedars (*Cedrus atlantica* and *C libani*), Eastern red cedar (*Juniperus virginiana*), box elder (*Acer negundo*), Nepal camphor trees (*Cinnamomum glandiferum*), Caucasian zelkova (*Zelkova carpinifolia*) and Chusan palms (*Trachycarpus fortunei*), as well as a big Osage orange (*Maclura aurantica*) with huge green fruit, and a box hedge (*Buxus colchica*). At first it's tidy and well organised, with labels in Georgian and English, and lots of solid bamboo benches; towards the river it gets wilder.

Returning towards the city on Leselidze, after a few minutes you can turn right for a steep climb up Petre Iberi to reach Bagrati Street, at the rear of the Bagrat Cathedral.

EXCURSIONS FROM KUTAISI

Gelati Wonderfully set in the hills just to the north of Kutaisi, the monastery of Gelati is one of the most beautiful spots in Georgia. Marshrutkas (*20mins; GEL1*) leave from the rear of the State Theatre in Kutaisi daily at 10.00, noon, 14.00, 16.00 and 18.00, returning 25 minutes later. The Gelati-bound marshrutka has a little church symbol on its windscreen; it is best to arrive 20 minutes before if you want a seat. Buses from Kutaisi I to Tqibuli also pass the Motsameta and Gelati turn-offs, although you're unlikely to get a seat if you board here heading north. The turn-off is 3km from the edge of Kutaisi, from where it's a 2km uphill walk to the monastery. A taxi will charge GEL15–25 for a combined trip to Gelati and Motsameta, including waiting time. You can stay in the very friendly Korena guesthouse halfway up the hill to Gelati (*signed to the left just before a small meat shop, between 2 sets of hairpins;* m 790 913194, 599 926026; e korena.office@gmail.com), for GEL50 per head with all meals. The rooms are simple with a modern bathroom outside under the stairs; there's a lovely garden and great views from the terrace to the monastery. Korena is a small local agro-tourism association and they offer tours to local sites.

Up a grassy slope from the road as you arrive at Gelati is a small church that's currently being restored. You may have to pay a nun a couple of coins to pass through the gateway. On the left as you enter is the Church of St George, built in the mid 13th century, burnt in 1510, and restored and painted in the 16th and 17th centuries. It tends to be shut except at weekends, when weddings are often held here.

The centrepiece is the great **Cathedral of the Virgin**, built by King David the Builder in 1106–25 (though in a style typical of the 11th century). The apses project

Western Georgia is the site of ancient Colchis, where Jason and the Argonauts went to obtain the Golden Fleece in the classical legend.

During the spring in northern Georgia, the upper reaches of many rivers flow fast and high with meltwater from mountain snows. At least until well into the 20th century, 'miners' from the area fixed sheepskins in stream beds to form a series of traps for particles of gold washed down by these torrents. The particles got caught up in the fleeces, and could be brushed out later to obtain useable quantities of gold. It is said that the fleece placed highest up such a stream course could become so laden with gold particles that it would come out looking as if it were indeed a real Golden Fleece.

As early as Roman times, commentators such as Strabo speculated that this was the source of the legend of the Golden Fleece. More recently, the adventurer and explorer Tim Severin describes seeing this method demonstrated to him at the end of his voyage to Georgia in a reconstruction of a 20-oared Greek galley, *Argo*. In his book *The Jason Voyage* he claims that most, if not all, of the basic features of the *Argo*'s voyage, as related by Appolonius of Rhodes and others, have been confirmed by modern archaeological discoveries along the probable route.

to the east in a manner reminiscent of Abkhazian churches such as Bichvinta (Georgian churches usually have a flat east end). The narthex was added to the western end later in the 12th century, followed by chapels to the south in the 13th century and to the north in the late 13th or early 14th century. Burnt by the Turks in 1510, and again by the Lesghians (from the north Caucasus) in 1579, it was restored, then closed under communism, and reopened in 1988.

The interior is full of light, and painted, mostly in the second half of the 16th century, in fantastic colours (although a blue background is unusual in Georgian churches). The cupola, supported by the walls of the apse to the east and two columns to the west, bears a fresco of Christ Pantocrater, and on the spandrels the four evangelists were painted by Tevdore in the 17th century; the narthex was decorated with paintings of the first seven ecumenical councils (now in poor condition) in the first half of the 12th century. The north transept was painted in 1291–93 and in the 16th and 17th centuries, with portraits of King David the Builder (haloed and holding the church), Bagrat III and Giorgi II (both kings of western Georgia) and, across the corner from David, the Emperor Constantine and his wife Helena; above these is a fresco of Palm Sunday and above this, between the windows, the two saints Theodore. The south transept was painted in the 17th century – note in particular the Death of the Virgin, below saints George and Dmitri. Above the west door you'll see Pontius Pilate washing his hands, and Judas hanging himself.

However, the pride of the church (and one of Georgia's greatest works of art) is a remarkable mosaic (containing 2.5 million stones) in the apse of the Virgin and Child with the archangels Michael and Gabriel. Created c.1130 in a Byzantine style with specifically Georgian features, it was damaged by earthquakes later in the same century and subsequently. The lower half was restored by painting – although this is often denounced as communist vandalism, it seems that it was genuinely impossible to restore it as mosaic.

Outside, the belfry stands to the southwest, built over a spring in the second half of the 13th century. Next to this, facing the west end of the cathedral, is the **Church**

Imereti, Racha, Mingrelia and Guria   KUTAISI

7

of St Nicholas, one of the oddest in design in Georgia. Also built in the 13th century, it's a two-storeyed construction that looks rather like an English market cross, with the church above an arcade in which you can see a section of tree trunk once intended for use as a coffin. Beyond this, to the west looking out over the valley (in good weather it's possible to see to the Black Sea), are the recently restored buildings erected in 1106 by King David to house the academy of Neo-Platonist metaphysical philosophy under Ioanne Petrisi; the portico, with four different types of column, was added in the 13th century. To the left is the south gate, built early in the 12th century; when King David died in 1125 he was buried as requested in the centre of the gateway, where churchgoers would walk over him and remember him for ever: an interesting way of combining self-abasement with a bit of egotism. The battered iron gate was made in 1063 in the Persian city of Ganja (now in Azerbaijan, on the main Tbilisi–Baku highway) and brought back by David's son Demetre I in 1129 from a campaign against the Persians.

From the gateway a track continues steeply into the trees; turning right near the top you can walk to a viewpoint overlooking Gelati and the valley beyond. In the hills to the south are two further small churches, St Saba and St Elijah, a pleasant 20-minute walk. The monastery car park has all manner of stalls selling souvenirs, religious knick-knacks, churchkhela and even hot dogs.

Motsameta Slightly closer to Kutaisi (a 2km walk to the right/east from the junction) is Motsameta Monastery. It's smaller and quieter than Gelati, although its cliff-edge setting is more spectacular by far. It commemorates the brothers David and Constantine Mkheidze, killed by Arabs in the AD720s for refusing to convert to Islam and then thrown into the gorge here. They are now saints, with their skulls in a casket behind the red velvet curtain, and your wish will be granted if you crawl three times under their tomb, set on two lions on the south side of the church, without touching it. The monastery was founded in the 8th century, but the present church and bell-tower were built by Bagrat III in the 11th century; the frescoes were destroyed by the Bolsheviks. To the left of the gatehouse is a steep path down to the river, which makes this a very popular excursion in summer, when Kutaisi swelters.

Walking between Gelati and Motsameta This is a pleasant hike that takes an hour or two and affords great views of both monasteries – it is best to start at Gelati. From the monastery gate, take the signed path to the right past a cemetery. The rough stone path descends and soon divides; take the right fork, which winds down through a village to reach the main road near the Gelati turn-off. Turn left to cross the river and walk along the road for about 600m before turning left into Motsameta village. You can then follow the railway track to the left (south) for about 500m until you reach the road to the car park and the path to Motsameta Monastery.

SATAPLIA, TSKALTUBO AND THE PROMETHEUS CAVE The most popular excursion from Kutaisi is to one or both of these spectacular karst caves just northwest of the city, both with spectacular stalactites, stone curtains and other formations. It's worth combining the two (GEL35–40 by taxi, waiting for 1½ hours at each) but remember that Prometheus is closed on Mondays and Sataplia on Tuesdays. The Prometheus Cave is bigger and has fancier lighting but there's not much else to it (other than a boat ride through part of the cave), whereas at Sataplia there are added attractions; it's best to go to Prometheus first as the electric boats' batteries run flat in the afternoons at busy times.

Sataplia (⏲ *10.00–18.00 Wed–Mon; GEL6*) Just 7km from Kutaisi in the 2,000-year-old Kolkhuri Forest is Mount Sataplia (Honey Mountain), a forested area in which a cave 300m in length (up to 10m high and 12m wide) and full of stalagmites was discovered in 1925 by Peter Chabukiani, a Kutaisi teacher. There are five karst caves here in all, although only the largest is open to visitors; in addition, about 200 footprints of dinosaurs have been preserved in Cretaceous limestone (120 million years old). This is said to be the only place where prints of both carnivorous and herbivorous dinosaurs are preserved together, although they are separated in time by several thousand years. Although Sataplia has been protected as a reserve since 1935, until recently it was mainly seen as an excursion for the people of Kutaisi, especially schoolchildren, and was not well preserved. New tourism infrastructure was completed in 2010 and visits are now properly controlled.

The reserve covers 354ha, on the slopes of Mount Sataplia (494m) and Mount Tsinara (520m), with a humid subtropical climate (with an annual average of 1,380mm precipitation). Nevertheless, the average temperature in January is as low as –5°C, and 24°C in August, with an annual average of 14.5°C (and 14° C in the cave). Colchic forest covers 95% of its area and 544 species of flora have been recorded (67 of them trees and bushes). These include hornbeam, alder, box (growing up to 15m high here), chestnut, beech, ilex, medlar, ivy, rhododendron, bilberry and blackberry. There are small mammals such as moles, squirrels, hedgehogs, hares, foxes, jackals and badgers, and birds such as larks, goldfinches, tits, jays, woodpeckers, hawks, sparrowhawks, cuckoos and hoopoes. The mountain bees that produced the plentiful honey that gave the mountain its name are now few in number.

To get there by public transport you'll have to take marshrutka 22 (*every 10mins; GEL0.30*) along Rustaveli and Javakishvili to the first major intersection on the edge of town from where marshrutka 45 (*Mon–Sat; GEL1.50*) may take you to the cave – or marshrutka 4 (*hourly; GEL1*) may leave you with a 2.5km uphill walk from the turning at the north end of Banoja village. At the entry there's a toilet and tiny shop; then the guided tour covers a total of 2km, starting with the hall over the dinosaur footprints (with sound effects) and then a cliffside walk, with views to Kutaisi, before heading to the cave where you'll see three halls carved out over 2,000 years, with an active stream still flowing in the second half. Outside again, there's a stylish café with a double terrace and an exhibition hall with good displays about the reserve; to the right the Colchic Forest Trail is a 300m loop, while to the left a trail leads 500m to a stunning new viewing platform looking out over Kutaisi and Gelati.

Tskaltubo A dozen kilometres northwest of Kutaisi (or 5km from the Banoja junction near Sataplia), Tskaltubo is a spa where mildly radioactive water at an average 15°C is used to treat arthritis, rheumatism, polio and fertility problems. In Soviet times none of the hotels in Kutaisi were open to Westerners, and they had to stay out here; when the hotels and sanatoria were taken over by refugees from Abkhazia, tourists staying in Kutaisi could come here for a day trip. Now one or two places to stay have been refurbished, such as the **Hotel Spa Kurorti** (*Rustaveli 23;* m *599 563115;* **$$$**), the **Argo Spa Resort** (*Rustaveli 8A;* m *595 509019;* e *hotargo@ gmail.com; www.hotelargo.ge;* **$$$**) and the **Hotel Imereti** (*Tsereteli 8;* ☏ *436 22 1122;* m *597 918422;* e *imeretihotel@gmail.com; www.hotelimereti.ge;* **$$$**).

Marshrutkas run from the junction of Chavchavadze and Rustaveli, near the bus station (route 22), and from the market (route 30; both GEL1) and after 15 minutes enter the spa, passing the station (served by a few trains a day from Kutaisi II) and a large park dotted with pines. The town is spacious and fairly modern with little to see; you can ask to try the waters at the big Stalinesque sanatorium. The main attraction is the **Prometheus (or Kumistavi) Cave** (*7km from Tskaltubo;* ⊕ *11.00–16.00 Tue–Sun*), found only in 1983. It's 145m deep, with 17 chambers, and a river (with waterfalls) runs through it; there are also ten to 12 species of bats living here. Marshrutka 42 (to Kumistavi) comes here from the market in Tskaltubo (*20min; GEL1*), and a guide will lead you on a 1,420m route through six chambers, with the option of taking an electric boat for the last 380m.

GEGUTI AND VARTSIKHE From Kutaisi's main bus station, marshrutkas (*GEL1*) leave regularly for **Geguti**, about 7km south in the plains of the Rioni, known in classical times as the Phasis. This gave its scientific name, *Phasianus colchicus*, to the pheasant, which was discovered here, perhaps by Jason. Geguti is the site of the great ruined palace of the Georgian kings, one of the few secular buildings left in Georgia from medieval times. Now, it's a jumble of ruins covering 2,000m², set on a plinth 2.5m high housing heating conduits; you may be able to identify the large fireplace of the 8th-century hunting lodge, as well as one shattered arch of the 14m-wide dome of the 10th-century hall, and other ruins from the 12th and 13th centuries, including a church. The royal chambers are to the southwest, the treasury to the southeast, and the church and bathhouse to the northwest. In 1179 George III proclaimed his daughter Tamar his co-ruler here, and in 1360 David VII died here; later it fell into disuse and was destroyed in the 17th century. Arriving by bus, get off at the Restaurant Venezia (on the left) 1.5km from the village of Geguti, and walk up the paved road to the left for 5 minutes to the end where a series of unlocked gates on the right lead to the 'castle', which does look a bit like a tumble-down Tudor manor house.

Marshrutka 211 continues south to a dam across the Rioni, on the south side of which is **Vartsikhe**, once the Greek fortress of Rodopolis; from the lane leading to the Geguti 'castle', you can follow a farm track for 1.5km then turn left on the road about 3km short of the dam. It's a dull walk, although buses are barely faster due to the lunar road surface. From the dam it's another kilometre on to Vartsikhe, but the ruins are on the left immediately after the dam. There's not a lot to see, just 100m of ancient wall, some partially rebuilt, and another chunk of wall in a cemetery behind, by a small church. The fortress dates from the 4th–6th centuries, with a royal residence built here in the 9th–11th centuries. Vartsikhe is also known for its brandy. From the village it's 100m to the main road, where you can pick up buses between Kutaisi (to the left/east) and Vani.

VANI On the far side of the Rioni, Vani is reached by hourly marshrutkas (*GEL2*), the last leaving at 19.00 from Kutaisi and 17.00 from Vani. It's also possible to go via Bagdati (10 marshrutkas a day), on the main road to Akhaltsikhe (via Sairme, known for its mineral waters), although there's now little trace of one of the 20th century's greatest poets, Vladimir Mayakovsky (1893–1930), who grew up here.

Beyond the Technical University the road follows the left bank of the Rioni, through beautiful oak forest, which forms part of the Adjameti Nature Reserve, and passes 500m east of the Rioni railway station. After 15km Vani buses turn right off the Bagdati road at a police post on to a rougher road, and after 2km (30mins from Kutaisi) pass Vartsikhe. It's 7km to the road from Bagdati, after which the surface is better, but you'll be glad to reach Vani, where there's a big market opposite the bus station. There's a much better road on from Vani, with marshrutkas taking under an hour to reach Samtredia, 25km west (page 214).

Cross the bridge over the River Sulori and the square beyond, and follow the sign (in English) to the 'Archeological Excavations'. You'll see the very obvious large **museum** (☉ *10.00–17.00 except Mon; GEL2*) on the hillside ahead, although it takes about 10 minutes to reach it, winding up Gorgasali; go under the footbridge and up the steps to the right to the entrance. Vani, known to the Greeks as Surium, was a major centre from the 8th to 1st century BC (at its peak from 600–400BC), and many of the finest artefacts from ancient Colchis were found here. The best are all in the Treasury of the National Museum in Tbilisi (page 131), but there are replicas here, as well as fine original pieces; what's more, captions are in English. By 1876 it was known that rain revealed gold objects on the hillsides here, and excavations began in the 1890s, with further work in the 1930s and from 1947 to 1963. Nowadays research is continuing, and the museum may also be closed for improvements, with a temporary display nearby.

The ground-floor displays are mostly of weapons and tools, and the oldest and finest pieces are up in the gallery. In the 7th and 6th centuries BC, gold jewellery by superb craftsmen was buried with nobles, together with fine ceramics from the 6th to 4th century BC. From the 4th century BC on burials were in *qvevri* (clay vessels or *pithoi*), making it easier to conserve the contents, which now included Greek imports from Sinope. By 100BC foundries were casting bronze statues; on the gallery there's a fine torso of a youth, in front of a small treasury of beautiful gold ornaments and lots of tiny silver coins from the 3rd century BC. Across the footbridge is a small area of ruins, including city walls and sanctuaries; a few are covered, but visitors can clamber over the rest. There's a fine view north to Kutaisi and the High Caucasus, with attractive wooded hills to the south.

It's also possible to visit the **house-museum of Galaction Tabidze** (1892–1959), one of Georgia's finest and best-loved poets, near the Rioni in Ckhovishe, about 4km north of Shuamta, on the main road about 3km west of Vani. It's a simple cottage with little on view; what's more, the replica of Jason's ship, the *Argo*, which Tim Severin sailed here from Greece in 1984 and was on display, has been burnt! However, it's worth coming here on Galaction's birthday, 17 November, when there's always a celebration (followed on 23 November by Giorgoba – a good time to visit Georgia!).

RACHA რაჭა

Immediately to the north of Kutaisi is the small province of Racha (or Racha-Lekhumi), along the upper reaches of the Rioni River. Hemmed in by mountains up to 3,600m, it's a beautiful area which is mild enough in summer to produce both wine and tea, but so harsh in winter that most of the population move temporarily to the lowlands. It's also apparently the best source of seeds for Christmas trees (*Abies nordmanniana*), which unfortunately requires local men to climb 30–50m up without safety equipment. The people here are known for their strong traditional culture, with superb icons, honey and a unique genre of bagpipe music. Racha is also becoming known as a great venue for adventure tourism.

NORTH FROM KUTAISI The main road runs from Kutaisi along the Rioni past Ambrolauri, the chief town of Racha, to Oni, and then over a pass (open all year) to Tskhinvali, capital of South Ossetia, although this road is now closed. From Oni the Ossetian Military Highway climbs to the summer-only Mamison Pass (2,820m), which you should not use to enter the Russian Federation.

Marshrutkas from Kutaisi to Ambrolauri leave from the minor bus terminal on Mkheidze, below the Bagrat Cathedral, at 09.00, 10.00 and 14.00 daily, returning at

13.00 and 17.00. The 09.00 continues to Oni (*GEL7.50*). Tickets can be bought from an office that also sells bread at the back of the grey concrete building.

Heading north along the right/west bank of the Rioni, you'll soon pass the Kutaisi Botanical Garden and the **Gumat Dam**, a typical Soviet hydro-electric scheme of the 1930s. About 25km from Kutaisi the road enters a fine limestone gorge, emerging before the village of **Mekvena** (km36) where a side road crosses to the left bank. The next village, **Tvisi**, known for its white wine, is the first in Racha; it lies below high cliffs on which you can see vertical lines caused by logged trees being slid down the slopes.

At km54.5 (2hrs from Kutaisi, on a pretty rough road), a road turns left to **Lajanauri**, known for its hydro-electric dam; this continues over a pass to Tsageri on the Tskaltubo–Lentekhi road. **Lentekhi**, at 800m, is nothing but a village, with the late medieval ruins of a Dadiani palace, but it is the capital of Kvemo (Lower) Svaneti; this is far lower than Svaneti proper and has far less of interest to visitors. The only old churches are a couple dating from the 10th century just north of Zachunderi, from where a very rough track continues over the 2,623m Zagar Pass (☉ *Jun–Oct; 4x4 only*) into Upper Svaneti. Buses to Lentekhi leave three times a day from Kutaisi's main bus station, and take 4 hours.

Remaining in the Rioni Valley, the first village, across a bridge to the right, is **Zeda-Ghvardia**, known for its large caves. In fact the whole of Racha is a caver's paradise, and two 5km-long caves were discovered in 2001. This is the site of the Shareula tourist complex (page 213), a great base for rafting, riding, and hiking, as well as the Hotel Vila Racha (page 213). At km74 the road enters the district of **Kvanchkara**, known for its wine, which everyone will proudly tell you was Stalin's favourite. Now the valley opens up and the road improves, passing the 14th–15th-century hall church of Bugeuli on the far (south) bank; and after another 12km you'll see the modern sprawl of **Ambrolauri** on the far side of the river, 14km from Kvanchkara (and at least 3 hours from Kutaisi). You can also get here by taking a bus to Tqibuli and then marshrutkas via Nikortsminda (pages 213–14), or directly from the Didube terminal in Tbilisi. It's still little more than a village, with a small daily market opposite the bus station and few other services. If you head south up Kostava, the main road, from the roundabout, Kvanchkara is the second street on the left and Rustaveli the third; then you'll pass an ATM on the right before the main square where you'll find a small and fairly simple new hotel plus various guesthouses (page 213).

Continuing eastwards up the Rioni, the next village is **Tsesi**, where you'll see the Barakoni Church of the Virgin (km91), a cruciform dome church built in 1753, on the right, and then the Mindatsikhe Castle, an easy scramble up to the left. Beyond this lies **Oni**, at the junction of the routes to North and South Ossetia. There are daily marshrutkas to and from Kutaisi (*GEL7.50*) and Tbilisi, and taxis charge just GEL4 from Ambrolauri. Oni is famed as a stronghold of the mountain Jews, living in isolation here for 2,000 years or more. The community has largely vanished to Israel, but around 20 families are said to remain, and there is still a synagogue to the north of the centre on Baazovi that dates from 1895 and was restored in 1991. This can be visited by asking for the key in the house facing the entrance. Further out on Baazovi is a cemetery with a mixture of Georgian and Jewish (and Soviet-era) grave markers. Northwest of the central square, there's a church with a wooden bell platform and a curiously large statue of Daniel and lion outside. High on the hill across the river is a small, new chapel that is worth walking up to for the view. The museum here is closed due to earthquake damage, and its treasures are in the Kutaisi Museum (page 204).

A very lovely road, lined with mineral springs, leads northeast into the Caucasus for 25km past **Utsera** (where there are beds at the Fazisi sanatorium) to **Glola**, site of another of Tamar's castles. **Shovi**, a few kilometres east of Glola, was a popular spa in Soviet times, but now there are only a few fine villas and some moribund blocks set about a lovely meadow. The hotels listed below offer basic rooms, but better accommodation should soon be available.

Just beyond is the Mamison Pass into North Ossetia, which is closed to foreigners. A rough track leads northwest up the Rioni Valley from west of Glola to Chiora and **Ghebi**, a large lively village surrounded by wildflower meadows and glaciers, from where you can hike to the turquoise Sasvano tarns. Ghebi is also known for its traditional singing, especially of harvest songs and funeral laments.

There's also a very bad road east from Oni to Tskhinvali in South Ossetia, which is presently closed and unlikely to reopen in the foreseeable future.

Where to stay and eat

Zeda-Ghvardia

🏠 **Hotel Vila Racha** m 598 604919, 593 238442; e qristineyurashvili@gmail.com **$$**

🏠 **Shareula tourist complex** m 790 890830, 599 703939; www.shareula.ge **$$**

Ambrolauri
Hotels

🏠 **Hotel Silovani** Kostava 37; m 790 224243. A communist-era building with service standards still stuck in that era. **$$$**

🏠 **Hotel Metekhara** Gamsakhurdia 2; m 599 181464. A boxy but comfortable modern place, with swimming pool & restaurant. **$$**

Guesthouses

🏠 **Ambrolauri** Chavchavadze 6; m 593 218212 **$$**

🏠 **Elo** Kobakhidze 15; m 599 408567 **$$**

🏠 **Sopo** m 514 700055 **$$**

🏠 **Tanini** Kvanchkara; m 595 486121 **$$**

🏠 **Tsibena** Rustaveli 46; m 555 526515 **$$**

Oni

🏠 **Hotel-Restaurant Orioni** (15 rooms) Davit Agmashenebelis Sq (at the junction of Kafianidze & Baazovi; m 591 255999, 599 343161. A big, modern place. **$$$**

🏠 **Hotel Sunset Shovi** (35 rooms) On the Ambrolauri road at km111 m 571 768855; www.sunsetshovi.ge. A comfortable new hotel set in its own nature reserve, with a good restaurant. **$$$**

🏠 **Famili Hotel Gallery** (8 rooms) Kafianidze (formerly Stalin) 18; m 599 231722, 593 660884; e nikagugeshashvili@gmail.com. Run by delightful artists Elene & Temur Gugeshvili. One of the best places to stay. **$$**

🏠 **Guesthouse M & B** (4 rooms) Baratashvili 7; m 599 157638, 558 385588. A nice place to stay, this has comfortable rooms, good meals & some English & German spoken. **$$**

Shovi

🏠 **Hotel Mamisoni** (28 rooms) m 599 514086 **$$**

🏠 **Hotel Racha** m 577 720808; www.shovi-racha.com **$$**

🏠 **Turbasa Shovi** m 599 921591. Basic. **$**

NIKORTSMINDA By far the greatest attraction of Racha is 15km to the south of Ambrolauri, at Nikortsminda, where there's a beautifully decorated church set on a ridge on the edge of the village. Marshrutkas run several times a day from Ambrolauri, crossing the bridge south from the bus station and labouring up a modernised road to reach the village on a high limestone plateau. It's also possible to come directly from Kutaisi, taking a bus past Gelati to the logging town of Tqibuli and continuing by marshrutka on the Ambrolauri road up a winding road to a pass (a great spot for advanced paragliders) and past the Sauris Reservoir to Nikortsminda, 40km and 50 minutes from Tqibuli. From Ambrolauri, marshrutkas leave at 09.00 for Tbilisi and 09.30 to Kutaisi via Nikortsminda.

Just down a lane to the east of the bus stop, the **Church of St Nicholas** is built of mellow golden stone reminiscent of Somerset or the Cotswolds. It was built by Bagrat

III in 1010–14 on a tight and tidy hexagonal internal ground plan; this was slightly spoiled in the mid-11th century by the addition of porches to the west and south, and a chapel to the south, which has a curved west end and Romanesque-style round arches. There was a porch to the north, but this has gone. None of this has interfered with the external carvings on all four façades. The finest is a figure of Christ on the north wall, above three perfectly proportioned blind arches. Inside, the hexagonal plan produces six apses radiating from the centre (instead of the usual four in the shape of a cross) which are all identical except that the eastern one (above the very simple blue-painted iconostasis) is marginally longer, and the western one leads into the porch. The dome is set on a splendid drum without squinches, pierced by 12 slim windows with finely carved architraves. The interior was fully painted in the 16th and 17th centuries, with the life of Christ (starting with the Nativity to the right of the entrance, together with a modern icon of the church's patron, St Nicholas) and portraits of local notables. The Annunciation is over the arch of the eastern apse, with Christ in Majesty beyond that; see also the wooden model church incorporated into the altar. The detached bell-tower, with its fireplace and spiral staircase, was added in the second half of the 19th century. Ask for the church key at the house with the two-storey glass front through the blue gate to the north of the church. It's half an hour downhill to Ambrolauri past the Khotevi Castle and Church of the Archangels at km9/63. There are also great mountain views to the west and northeast.

MINGRELIA სამეგრელო

The main highway westward leaves Kutaisi by the bridge over the railway next to the bus station and Kutaisi II railway station (with the new parliament and the High Caucasus visible to the right); there are some cheap Turkish truckstop-hotels along the road before it reaches the new Kutaisi airport (km255/297) after 20 minutes. At km256.5 it passes the end of the new Kutaisi bypass (opening in 2016), and at km258 the Hotel Tsiskhkhavi in a pleasantly rural setting by the Gubistskali River, at the start of the road north to Khoni.

TOWARDS SENAKI The highway rejoins the Rioni at **Samtredia**, an industrial town where the bus station is a few hundred metres west of the railway station. The Hotel Brend is a block north from the railway station at Javakishvili 7 (\ 411 220052; m 568 674044, 593 444445; e nikoleishvili53mail.ru; **$$**). There is a simple restaurant to the left/west at the end of the pedestrianised street, and an ATM at Rustaveli 28, at the railway offices.

Virtually all traffic into town uses the bridge at km264/288, about 500m east of the station, with vehicles heading west performing hazardous U-turns at the bottom; not an ideal spot to flag down marshrutkas but still feasible, and taxis do wait here. This is a major road and rail junction; traffic to Batumi turns left/south after km267 to cross the Rioni, while traffic to Poti and Zugdidi continues west and then northwest. This road is lined with long thin villages, each merging into the next, and each house has a garden full of citrus trees and a water tank on a tower (spot the polyhedral one painted like a football).

From Abasha (km280) a road leads 34km north to **Martvili**, where there's an interesting late 10th-century cruciform church (the centre of Mingrelia's religious life in medieval times) and another from the first half of the 7th century; Abasha's railway and bus stations are 200m west of the junction, opposite a huge, ugly monument.

In the foothills of the Caucasus, to the north of Khoni and Martvili, new tourist opportunities have opened up in 2014, with roads and visitor facilities at some stunning canyons where you can swim, hike, camp and take boats through virtually untouched nature. The **Okatse (or Gordi) Canyon** is in Imereti, north of Khoni on the Satsiskvilo River near the village of Zeda Gordi; it's 2km long and no more than 5m wide at its narrowest points – too tight for boating, but you can swim, although the water is chilly all year. It's known for its dramatic waterfalls, up to 35m high (and 70m high in a side valley). There's also a quite stunning new metal walkway high above the water that, at times, is up to 15m away from the cliff.

About 6km north of Martvili, in Samegrelo (Mingrelia), the **Gachedili Canyon** is also superb, with the added attraction of dinosaur footprints and Colchic forest. You can take a boat on the Abasha River, or float in wetsuits and helmets, through the canyon, 2.4km long and 20–30m deep; there's no shuttle service though, so after floating down you do have to paddle back up to your starting point. Slightly further into the foothills, you can hike to the Toba waterfall, plunging vertically into a circle of cliffs, and on to the Oniore and Abasha falls.

It's possible to get to Gordi and Martvili by marshrutka from Kutaisi, but it's generally easier to take a tour or to hire a taxi for the day (*GEL60–70*).

SENAKI This is another industrial town and the rail junction for Poti. Entering from the east, the highway crosses the Tekhura River (at km292/260) and the railway, then bypasses the town to the south; local marshrutkas turn off to cross back over the railway, then head down the old main road past the barracks where the 1998 mutiny began. In the centre they turn left to the rail and bus stations, then loop back over the railway by a level crossing, and stop again immediately across the tracks from the bus station; so if your bus appears to have left early, dash across the tracks and enquire at the ticket kiosk; through buses and minibuses also stop here. The road junction to Poti is at a level crossing at km301/251, 6km west of Senaki; from here it's 30km to Poti or 35km to Zugdidi.

Where to stay and eat Senaki's hotels are aimed more at the wedding market than at travellers, so big glitzy buildings have cavernous restaurants and only a few rooms.

Hotel EA Senaki m 595 002002; e georgian.hotel.ea@gmail.com. On the main road just southeast of the centre, this has cottages around a court. **$$$**

Hotel Oscar m 598 565683; e restaurantoscar@mail.com. This probably has the best restaurant, & is on the main road just southwest of the centre at km296/256. **$$$**

Hotel Versailles Tsminda Nino 2/4; \413 275260; m 597 255111, 597 089592; e versailes. senaki@yahoo.com. In the centre, just west of the station. **$$**

Around Senaki About 18km northeast of Senaki (30mins by bus towards Martvili) are the ruins of **Nokalakevi**, capital of Egrisi (Lazica) from the 4th to 8th century. In AD542–555 Shah Khusro I (and his famous general Mermeroes and his elephants) failed to capture the city; but in AD737 it was destroyed by the Arabs and remained in ruins until the first excavations in the 1930s by the German Alfons Maria Schneider, continued since 1973 by the National Museum, with the help of Cambridge University since 2001. Known to the Greeks as Archaeopolis (Old City), it's also been known as Tsikhegoji and Dzicha (Tsikhe and Dzicha meaning 'castle' in Georgian and Mingrelian respectively).

On a hill to the left a few kilometres north of Senaki, you'll see the ruins of **Shkhepi** (part of a chain of signal posts from the Black Sea, and a pleasant jaunt). Continue on a reasonable road through two villages, before reaching a museum and the gates of the ancient city to the left immediately after the bridge over the Tekhuri River. The archaeological site has now been fenced and there will probably be a fee of a couple of lari in the future. In the museum (⊕ *10.00–16.00 except Mon*), the first room on the left upstairs displays relics from the 8th to 1st century BC, including ritual clay animals, silver and bronze bracelets (there were gold ones too, now in Tbilisi) and Greek ceramics, attesting to trade links across the Black Sea. To the right are *pithoi* (funerary urns) from the 4th to 1st century BC, and replica coins, agricultural implements, weapons (sling and catapult stones, and arrow- and spearheads), and pipes from a 'calorifer' (underfloor steam heating), as well as a few ceramic pieces from the 6th to 18th century AD.

The ruins are entered by a right-angled trap area and a gateway through a massive triple wall; the outer wall, of big blocks, was built in the 6th century AD, and the next two, of smaller stones, date from the 5th and 4th centuries. The walls enclose an area of 20ha, including a 4th–5th-century citadel and two churches on the mountain behind. There are a couple of modern houses, with beehives, inside the walls; you'll also see a gatehouse with external stairs and the Church of the 40 Martyrs of Cappadocia (with tatty remains of frescoes, mostly hidden by a new iconostasis), both from the 6th century. Next to the church are the ruins of a tiny palace and the foundations of an older basilica, with those of a third church just to the west.

Beyond a house just outside the ruins, a tiny path leads up to a **fort** on a hill (as opposed to the citadel, higher up and reached by a jeep track to the north, a pleasant walk of an hour or so each way). At the far end of a very solid 19th-century girder bridge (for pedestrians and bikes only) across the river are the remains of a 5th-century bathhouse (with three rooms for three different temperatures, and red ceramic heating elements). As in most Georgian forts, there's a tunnel down to the river, to get water during a siege. On the far side of the river is a popular, if stony, beach, and a road leading up into a dramatic gorge with popular hot springs a kilometre or two along. It's possible to stay at the archaeological base if it's not full, or Aleko Janjgava has a homestay.

ZUGDIDI (*Telephone code 415*) Heading northwest from Senaki, the Zugdidi road crosses the River Khobi at km311/211 and soon reaches the bus station of **Khobi**, opposite a massive sculpture of the sun, moon and stars, just east of a theatre with a matching sculpted frieze along its front and fly-tower. Marshrutkas from Batumi and Poti to Zugdidi join the main road here; a couple of kilometres north across the railway are the ruins of Khobi Monastery, founded in AD554, and a church which dates from the 12th and 13th centuries, as well as medieval walls and a bell-tower.

It's just over 100km from Kutaisi to Zugdidi (322km from Tbilisi), a city of 51,000 plus, at present, about 72,000 refugees from the neighbouring Gali district of Abkhazia. It's full of men standing around with nothing to do, as well as plenty of soldiers, police and aid workers. Nevertheless, it's pleasant enough and there are a couple of things worth seeing if you decide to stay overnight. It's the capital of Mingrelia or Samegrelo, a province which has always gone its own way; it was ruled by the Dadiani family from 1046 at the latest until 1857 (paying tribute to the Turks from the 1460s until 1774, and nominally under Georgian rule at other times), and was the stronghold of the Zviadists (supporters of the ousted president Gamsakhurdia) and of the nationalists who wanted a military assault on Abkhazia.

Getting there and away The main bus terminal is 400m west of the main square at the railway station (reached by bus 1); tickets are sold in the hall opposite the railway ticket office. There are regular buses and minibuses to Kutaisi, Poti and Batumi, and some every few hours to Tbilisi (*6–7hrs*). There may be a bus or minibus for Mestia here but there's more likely to be something in the area by the Svan tower, where jeeps and minibuses heading up to Svaneti wait for passengers.

Where to stay

Hotel Samegrelo (20 rooms) Kostava 54 (almost opposite Hotel Zugdidi); 50 7445; e xxlsakune@gmail.com. Slightly more expensive than the nearby Hotel Zugdidi but better value & with its own restaurant. $$–$$$

Hotel Zugdidi (14 rooms, 1 suite) Kostava 5A (the 1st left off Rustaveli, just a block from the square); 54 2442. All rooms have clean, en-suite facilities with TV (not cable), hot water & towels, &

there's a good little café-bar. Still, it's pretty over-priced. Rates inc b/fast. $$–$$$

Zugdidi Hostel (4 rooms) Rustaveli 2; m 558 102688, 591 654036; e zugdidihostel@gmail.com; www.zugdidihostel.com. The last house on Rustaveli before the climb to the viewpoint & cemetery, this friendly place has some chilly dorms, a small kitchen & a bathroom outside & down the stairs. $

Where to eat and drink

As well as those listed, there are several decent cafés along Zviad Gamsakhurdias facing the park such as Kamea (25 1185) at No 13, and Atriumi (25 0141) at No 26.

Diaroni Meunargia 9; 25 1122; http://diaroni.ge. One block east of the central park at its northern end, this cellar restaurant is the best place for a full meal. $$

Mendzel Kostava 34; m 571 541515. This has been recommended for authentic Megrelian food. $$

Taverna Pirate Rustaveli 85 (not far from the Zugdidi Hostel). This is an oddly named but cheery place serving a familiar range of Georgian & more local dishes. $$

MG Bistro Across Rustaveli on the same street as Diaroni. Pizza to eat in or take away. $

Other practicalities There's a **tourist information centre** (10.00–18.00 daily) on Rustaveli a block east of Zviad Gamsakhurdias Square. The Bank of Georgia has an **ATM** opposite the Hotel Zugdidi at Kostava 6, PrivatBank has one by the bridge at the junction of Rustaveli and Gulua, and there are others on the square at Tabukashishvilis 1 and Zviad Gamsakhurdias 34, and opposite the tourist information centre. There are also money-changers outside the market. The **post office** is on the south side of Rustaveli immediately west of Zviad Gamsakhurdias Square. There's an **internet** café at Rustaveli 88 (*GEL1/hr*) and another on Zviad Gamsakhurdias at the northern end of the square.

What to see and do The main square, Zviad Gamsakhurdias Gamziri, is quite attractive; long and thin, it has trees in the centre and a few cafés and bars. Buses go three-quarters of the way around the square to continue on Rustaveli, the bad main road westwards, past a market and so-called trade centre, bustling with people heading for the de facto border with Abkhazia, just a few kilometres further west. A couple of hundred metres northwest of the bridge on Gulua you'll see a Svan defensive tower, built in the communist period to mark a Svan restaurant.

Heading northwards along the length of the main square, past the new esplanade behind the Public Service Hall to the right, you'll come in a couple of minutes to a park (with steps down towards the Svan Tower to the left) on the far side of which is the neo-Gothic palace of the Dadiani family, rulers of Mingrelia, until the Russians finally took over in 1857; it's now a **museum** (10.00–18.00 Tue–Sun; GEL2).

Alexander Chavchavadze's daughter Katarina (sister-in-law of the playwright Griboedov) married David Dadiani, the last prince of Mingrelia (although the poet Nikoloz Baratashvili was in love with her); their daughter Salome was the goddaughter of Catherine the Great and married Achille Murat, grandson of Marshal Murat and Napoleon's sister Caroline. Thus, one of Napoleon's three death masks has ended up here, together with other bits and pieces of Bonapartiana. The palace was built in the 17th century and extended in 1873–78; it became a museum in 1921. Together with the relics of Napoleon and the Dadianis, it also houses a notable collection of Colchian gold and silver coins. To the side is the small Church of the Icon of the Mother of God (built in 1838), with a bare interior and unusual semicircular sides to the porch so that its ground plan is a circle in a cross plan. The chasuble of the Mother of God, brought from Jerusalem to Khobi's Monastery of the Dormition, and now in the museum, is taken in procession to the church on 7 July.

On the right-hand side of the park is Nico Dadiani's **palace**, built in the 1880s, and the **Botanical Gardens** established in 1840 by Katarina Dadiani, complete with picturesque ruin, which are free and make a nice spot for a stroll, especially in spring.

It's not wise at present to continue along the main road towards Abkhazia, but when the situation is normalised again, it may be worth stopping in the village of **Rukhi**, where a fortress dominating the Enguri crossing dates from 1636 (and a new shopping mall is being planned).

POTI ფოთი *Telephone code 493*

From the road junction 6km west of Senaki, it's 30km (rough in parts) to Poti, founded by the Greeks (as Phasis) and re-established as a Turkish fort, which was the hub of the trade in Circassian slave-girls, the most highly prized in the Ottoman Empire. In a little-known episode, a group of Vikings once landed here; they had taken part in a Russian campaign against Constantinople in 1043 but were captured and ultimately released. In 1047 they were invited by Bagrat IV to join his army, fighting in the battle of Sasireti, after which they returned home, with Georgian coins which have since been found in Scandinavia. Development of the modern port began in 1858 and was boosted by the arrival of the Transcaucasian Railway in 1872. Nowadays it is Georgia's largest port, with a capacity of five to six million tonnes a year, largely containerised; a train-ferry terminal opened in 1999, to link Poti with Ilyichevsk (near Odessa, Ukraine), Constanța (Romania) and Varna (Bulgaria). The Korean Hyundai Group took a 99% share of the shipbuilding yard, and the port itself, occupied by the Russian army in 2008, which has also been sold to the sovereign wealth fund of Ras al-Khaimah (in the United Arab Emirates), with, surprisingly, the Russian oil company Rosneft buying 49% of the oil terminal.

It's a city of 50,000 people; unattractive and without much to see, but it does offer a couple of comfortable places to stay. It's also the base for the Kolkheti National Park (pages 220–1) whose headquarters and visitor centre are at Guria 222, south of town.

GETTING THERE AND AWAY There are comfortable day trains from Tbilisi (*GEL12.50; 5hrs*) via Gori and Rioni. Marshrutkas leave more or less hourly for Tbilisi (*GEL15*), Batumi (*GEL5*), Kutaisi (*GEL5*) and Zugdidi (*GEL5*) from the closed bus station, west of the train station. Marshrutkas for Batumi also wait by the Tsotne Dadiani statue.

The Ukrainian shipping company UkrFerry (e *poti@ukrferry.com; www.ukrferry. com*) has ferries that ply weekly across the Black Sea to and from Constanța (Romania) and Ilyichevsk (Ukraine); fares start from US$95 (page 62).

WHERE TO STAY

Hotel Ankori (24 rooms) Gegidze 22; 22 6000; e ankor.99@mail.ri. A good, modern hotel just to the right from the roundabout at the north end of Davit Agmashenebelis, with a nice restaurant & rooms with AC & cable TV with good Grundig sets. English is spoken at reception, & they'll exchange US dollars. **$$$**

Hotel Poti (10 rooms) Kostava 36; m 599 540815, 551 684455. A modernist glass box facing the Tsotne Dadiani statue, opened at the end of 2014. **$$$**

Golden Lake Hotel In the centre of Maltakva (by the bridge); 21 422. South of Poti by the lake, this is run-down but cheap, & in a peaceful rural setting. **$$**

Hotel Paleostomi 52 0929; e bartianatia@rambler.ru. A further 1km to the south from Maltakva, a road leads 50m east to the hotel from the Restaurant Iasoni (Jason; km81/40), where marshrutka 20 terminates. This is an ideal location for birdwatchers, as the national park boat launch on Lake Paleostomi lies immediately beyond the hotel. **$$**

Hotel Prime (9 rooms) Akaki 53; m 790 9022, 592 929202; e primepoti@hotelsprime.ge; http://hotelsprime.ge/en/poti. In an older building just southeast of the centre, this has adequate rooms with fast Wi-Fi & a bar & restaurant (reserve in advance for dinner). **$$**

WHERE TO EAT AND DRINK

Aragvi Gegidze 18; 24 2727. Just 100m east of the Hotel Ankori, heading towards the station, this red-brick beer-restaurant has a double terrace with a view of the docks. **$$**

Restaurant Old Ship Mshvidoba; m 790 936129. In a galleon just west of the cathedral by the rowing club, this is not gourmet, serving tapas & the usual Georgian dishes, but it's a pleasant setting & there's Wi-Fi. **$$**

Coffee House 1 block north of the canal bridge on Davit Agmashenebelis. Serves coffee & snacks. **$**

OTHER PRACTICALITIES There are banks with **ATMs** on Davit Agmashenebelis, including at the south end BTA Bank at No 10 and Liberty Bank at No 12, with PrivatBank and KSB across the road, and at the north end Bank Republic and VTB, with large TBC and ProCredit branches across the roundabout by the dock gates. South of the cathedral, Bank of Georgia, Bank Republic and KSB all have ATMs at the Aversi pharmacy.

The city is clearly increasingly used to foreign visitors, with groceries for instance now signed in English and street names translated.

WHAT TO SEE AND DO Turning right from the bus station on Samegrelo you'll come to the beautifully restored railway station; turn right to cross the bridge to the big equestrian **statue of Tsotne Dadiani** (who led an uprising against the Mongols and was killed by being coated with honey and left to be eaten by insects), with the market (and exchange stalls) immediately on your right. Head west on Chanturia past the market, and you'll reach a huge roundabout and the circular **cathedral**. Built in 1906–07 and loosely based on Hagia Sophia in Istanbul, it was a theatre under communism and has now been restored for religious use.

Heading north from the cathedral, you'll cross the Rioni Canal again on Davit Agmashenebelis, passing fine buildings built around the start of the 20th century, of which a surprising number are now being refurbished and repainted. A stadium is visible to the left, as well as the **lighthouse**, a cast-iron structure fabricated in London and erected here in 1864; refurbished in 2012, this is now open to visitors, with an exhibition at the base if you can't face the 153 steps. There is a theory that soccer was introduced to Georgia here, either from sailors or the English workers installing the light.

Eventually the road crosses a smelly channel to a roundabout where it swings left to reach the port in around 200m; here, there's a big, modern grey ferry terminal, and a small chapel. Immediately north of the terminal is the yacht club, with electricity, water and fuel available for yachts, plus a shower, sauna and café terrace for their crews; it also organises races and other events.

AROUND POTI

Maltakva To the south of the cathedral, Mshvidoba leads past a park with various statues, fountains, dodgems and an unserviceable Ferris wheel, to the sea. It's possible to walk south along the dirty grey beach for 3km to the Maltakva resort area, an impressively Modernist complex, built to hold water-skiing championships on the so-called Golden Lake. It's easier to follow the Batumi road, taking Akaki southeast from the cathedral and after about 1km turning right past a cemetery. Behind it is Lake Paleostomi, which is black with waterfowl in the migration seasons and in winter, although there's little to see at other times. From here, it's 2.5km south to the national park headquarters and another 1km to the Maltakva turning.

Marshrutka 20 from the market runs this way, mostly terminating 500m north of the Maltakva turning. You can walk through a turnstile to the right just south of this terminal, or take a road from km82/39 (opposite a large ugly monument of Jason holding the Golden Fleece, and an English sign to Maltakva). This leads through a wood and then after 200m right to the complex; from the beach you should turn inland at a half-built hotel isolated by the sea and cross a long, modern rusty-coloured footbridge to the derelict spectator facilities. The campsite at the north end of the complex has closed, as has the Pioneer Railway in the park behind it, but you could camp wild.

Kolkheti National Park Immediately east of Poti is the Kolkheti (Colchis) National Park, now recognised as globally important wetlands and listed as a Ramsar Site; the reserve is in four parts totalling 44,849ha (including 15,742ha of water). The coast both north and south of Poti and the wetlands inland, along rivers such as the Rioni, are very young, having formed only in the last 6,200 years. In other words, when Jason and the *Argo* came here from Greece in the 13th century BC, there was only open sea here. Then around 5000BC the connection from the Mediterranean to the Black Sea burst open, causing the biblical Great Flood, which in fact lasted for about 40 years and raised the sea level by about 100m. Now there is a coastal sandbank with peat bogs, up to 12m deep (ie: well below sea level) behind, with a system of lagoons. The largest is **Lake Paleostomi**, 18.2km^2 in area and up to 3.2m deep; it's a stopover for 21 threatened bird species, and there are 173 other bird species resident here. The best birdwatching is to the east of the lake, reachable only by boat. It was linked to the sea in 1934 by an artificial channel, the Kaparcha River, and the changes in salinity have wiped out many of the rare fish species; expansion of Poti port and the new Khulevi port to the north may cause further damage. Despite heavy human impact, there are still important communities of endemic and relict plant species in the wetlands. Among the most interesting is the wingnut tree, whose only relations are in China and Japan, as well as an endemic oak; it's also one of the only two remaining spawning grounds of the Atlantic sturgeon. You may also see three species of dolphin offshore. Many international and Georgian NGOs are now involved in the conservation of the Colchic wetlands, notably the WWF, the Poseidon Marine Association and the Georgian Centre for the Conservation of Wildlife. The park headquarters, with a modern visitor centre, is at Guria 222, 4km south of the centre of Poti, and a long way from Guria 212 (✆ *577 10 1837;*

e *zjibladze@apa.gov.ge; www.apa.gov.ge;* ⏰ *10.00–19.00 daily*). The friendly staff can arrange boat trips and kayak rental (*GEL10/1hr or GEL15/2hrs*), with maps of paddling routes.

GURIA გურია

Immediately south of the checkpoint at km40 you'll cross a bridge over the Kaparcha River from Lake Paleostomi to the sea, and another 3km further south you'll finally leave Poti municipality and the province of Mingrelia, and enter Guria. This is a small province, known both for its immensely complex polyphonic singing, and for its people who are both very political and very forthright, which many of us would see as a contradiction in terms; nevertheless, it was the home of Shevardnadze.

ALONG THE COAST ROAD The first village in Guria on the coast road is **Grigoleti**, populated by the descendants of Protestants exiled from Russia; here (at km48) it meets the direct road (and, just south, the railway) from Tbilisi to Batumi, via Samtredia and Lanchkhuti (31km from Senaki, with a fine Stakhanovite statue) and Supsa. Some very comfortable new resort hotels have opened here (see below).

Just inland of the coast road, and southwest across the river from **Supsa** village, four big storage tanks mark the terminal of the refurbished oil pipeline from Baku, opened in 1999. This carries just 80,000 barrels a day or four million tonnes a year, which could be increased to ten or 12 million tonnes a year.

When the land was privatised, the elite took the best farming land, and the rest got the marshy land across the Supsa River to the south, which was then required for the terminal; however, the compensation offered was derisory, leading to a lawsuit and the detention of their lawyer on thoroughly dubious grounds. Meanwhile, the Khulevi port and refinery are to be built on some 96ha of wetland north of Poti, home to migratory waterbirds and supposedly protected by the Ramsar Convention.

There are fish restaurants by the coast road south to Kobuleti, notably opposite the station of **Ureki**; this attractive little resort (also known as Magnetiti), on the coast, is famous for the healing properties of its iron-rich black sand. Soviet doctors sent patients for rest, relaxation and treatment at the resort's three sanatoria; then businessman Badri Patarkatshishvili started redevelopment aimed at creating a Western-standard resort. Crossing the tracks or following the road from south of the station where there's a seasonal tourist office (e *ticureki@gmail.com*), it's about 20 minutes' walk to the small park (refurbished by Patarkatshishvili) with modern toilets and lots of benches, beyond which alleys lead down to the beach.

The main road (Takaishvili) turns to follow the coast southwards only where there are hotels (page 222), but there are cheaper options available inland such as the Teodora (*Takaishvili Alley III;* m 557 248585; **$$**), and even cheaper rooms above a shop inland from the square at Takaishvili 118 (**$$**). The small restaurants near the park are adequate, pleasantly rustic but a bit samey, all serving fish kefalia and kambula.

🏠 Where to stay and eat
Grigoleti

🏠 **Hotel Andamati** (24 dbls, 6 half suites, 3 suites) 📞 293 30035; m 599 446097; www. andamati.ge. Suites have DVD & jacuzzi. Also has tennis court & seawater pool. **$$$–$$$$$**

🏠 **Hotel Spa Villa Reta** 📞 493 25 0555; m 571 250 555; www.villareta.com. This has all the creature comforts you might expect of such a place – AC rooms, Wi-Fi, swimming pool & health spa. **$$$–$$$$**

Hotel Central m 555 178201;
e grigoleticentral@gmail.com; www.centralhotel.
ge. Down a track towards the sea at the highway
junction, this is a cheaper option. **$$**

Ureki

Tbilisi (46 rooms) Takaishvili 200; m 590
222277, 557 134000; e marta-55@mail.ru, tsitso@
locks.ge; www.urekitbilisi.ge. Ureki's only 4-star
hotel. **$$$$**

Elegant Ureki Takaishvili 67; m 557
087788, 577 727377; e elegant.ureki@gmail.
com. A plain block not far from the beach &
with decent sized pool; there's a cafe but no
restaurant. **$$$**

George Takaishvili 107; m 597 806061, 592
806061. Overlooking the beach, this has a small
pool. **$$$**

Kolkhida (76 dbls, 12 suites, 3 apts) Takaishvili
117; m 790 302203, 599 205445;
e kolkhida.hotel@gmail.com; www.kolkhida.ge. Just
beyond the Edemi on the right, this was once the main
sanatorium but is now a large & rather faded hotel
complex, open all year, with 3 soccer pitches. **$$$**

Edemi (16 rooms) Takaishvili 138;
m 599 101393; e amiko1947@rambler.ru. This is
a 4-storey block with friendly staff. **$$–$$$**

BeachCamp m 571 300125; www.
blackseacamping.com; ☼ summer only. In
Kaprovani, 3km south of Ureki (the 1st right after
crossing a bridge over the railway). *€10pp/night*

OZURGETI The capital of Guria is Ozurgeti, south of Lanchkhuti; it's a drab,
uninteresting town, but the starting point for visits to some attractive old
churches in the hills just to the southeast. The closest is the medieval monastery
of Shemokmedi, 7km south. The others are to the north near Lanchkhuti (on the
main road from Samtredia to Batumi); from Chkonagora, 9km east of Lanchkhuti,
a road is signposted south to the nunnery of Sameba-Jikhetis – the road is steep and
passable only in good weather, but the views over the Kolkheti National Park are
great. It's best to take a guide with a 4x4 vehicle, and you may still have to walk the
last bit; the Festival of the Virgin on 21 September is a good time to visit. The Maral
monastery of Jumatis is to the south from km38, 7km west of Lanchkhuti.

Ozurgeti is now reached by a railway from the coast, with day and night
trains from Tbilisi (*from GEL8.50*) and a local from Batumi (*GEL3*), but it's a
very roundabout route and you're best off taking a bus (*GEL3*) from Samtredia
or Batumi. Lanchkhuti is on the main road and railway between Samtredia and
Batumi, and thus an easier stopping-off point.

BAKHMARO There's a better road southeast from Chokatauri, on the Samtredia–
Ozurgeti road, via the Nabeglavi mineral spring (famous for its sodium bicarbonate
water, available in bottles all over Georgia) to Bakhmaro, in the mountains a mile
above sea level just north of the Adjaran border. Once a Soviet children's health
resort, it's only accessible from mid-June to mid-October; in July and August it's full
of Georgians who come to hike, watch the sunset, drink wine and chat by a bonfire.
Rooms are cheap and you can buy some food, but you may want to bring extra food
and camping gear because there are no amenities.

ANAKLIA This stands on the sandbanks at the mouth of the Enguri River where
President Saakashvili decreed that a sparkling new pleasure resort should be built,
as part of a barely thought-out scheme for a tourist zone stretching from a new ski
resort above Mestia to the Black Sea, as well as a new port and international airport.
Alas, he ignored the man-eating mosquitoes and other problems, but a couple of
over-sized and over-priced hotels with casinos opened in 2012, and are mainly used
for weddings. It may be worth a jaunt from Zugdidi to enjoy the sense of space,
and to cross the dramatic modernist cycle-bridge (540m long) across the mouth
of the river to the **Aquapark** (☼ *11.00–19.00 daily; GEL15*), the largest waterpark

anywhere on the Black Sea coast, with wave pools, slides and a bar. The beach in front of the Aquapark was the site of the Kazantip Republic Festival, something like Nevada's Burning Man, in 2014, and it might return in the future despite the Orthodox Church's opposition. Just inland, the marshland that Saakashvili hoped to build his airport on is a haven for migrating birds.

About 15km south, the city of Lazika has a similar background, but consists of just one building, a very imaginative City and Public Service Hall on stilts above the marshland designed by the Anglo-Georgian firm, Architects of Invention. It's hard to believe that anything else will be built here.

Getting there and away Marshrutkas run a few times daily from opposite the Svan tower on Gulua in Zugdidi, 31km away; if you get off where the road turns 90° left at the seafront, you'll see the walls of a fortress built in 1703 that effectively blocked the trade in slaves from the Caucasus to Constantinople.

Where to stay and eat As well as those listed, a few houses offer rooms, and there's a café and a couple of food shops just inland from the fortress.

Golden Fleece Hotel (105 rooms) m 790 341401; http://goldenfleecehotel.ge. Just south on the seafront boulevard, this is a rather grandiose 5-star establishment, with spa, pools & sauna. **$$$$$**

Hotel Anaklia (42 rooms) \32 260 9990/1; http://hotelanaklia.com. Slightly Moorish-style luxury hotel with a large outdoor pool. **$$$$**

Hotel Palm Beach (52 rooms) m 596 007700; e palmbeach@myhotels.ge; www. pbanaklia.ge. This 4-star hotel (with organic restaurant) is on the seafront, & overshadows the fortress. **$$$$**

ABKHAZIA აფხაზეთი

Abkhazia, the beautiful westernmost district of Georgia, has effectively seceded and, having once been the Soviet Union's most popular area for beach holidays, is starting to lure back Russian holidaymakers attracted by its relatively low prices, good beaches and sunshine. Western, non-Russian, visitors are rare, although bodies such as the United Nations and the Red Cross are working here. Part of the reason for this is – quite reasonably – the region's perceived instability, but there are also serious problems with visas, as Russia and Georgia disagree about Abkhazia's claimed independence. From the Russian perspective, Abkhazia has every right to be independent and is recognised as such; Georgia (and most of the world) sees Abkhazia as merely an autonomous republic within Georgian territory. Naturally, such a divergence of views has led to enormous problems since Abkhazia's de facto independence in 1994. The situation remains volatile and subject to change but at the time of writing it was just about possible (albeit difficult) for foreigners to enter Abkhazia from either Georgia or Russia and then return to that same country.

GETTING THERE AND AWAY Entry to Abkhazia from Russia and continuing on to Georgia is not possible (and ill-advised as individuals would be subject to arrest as

A NOTE ON TRAVEL TO ABKHAZIA

It should be noted that both the British FCO and US Department of State **advise against** travel to Abkhazia and the area close to the border. At the time of writing, however, it was possible and safe.

illegal aliens) as Georgia does not consider the Russian–Abkhazian frontier an official entry point, nor the Georgian–Abkhazian border as a bona fide exit point. Boats no longer run from Trabzon in Turkey and so this is no longer a viable alternative.

However, short trips from Zugdidi are increasingly popular; you'll have to go to the Abkhaz Foreign Ministry's website at http://mfaapsny.org/en/council/visa.php, and download the visa form, fill it in and email it to their Consular Service. A free permit is usually emailed back within five days, which you should print out and present at the Enguri checkpoint 10km northwest of Zugdidi; within three days you must go to SberBank of Abkhazia in Sukhumi to pay the US$20 fee, and take the receipt to the Consular Service to receive your visa/exit permit.

Returning to Georgia proper, the guards are obliged, in theory at least, to let you back in as, in official terms, you have not left Georgian territory. Coming from Russia, it is only possible to return to that country (you will need a double-entry visa), although as there should be no evidence of ever having visited Abkhazia from Russia in your passport, you will still be free to visit Georgia at a later date. The border situation might well change in the future – for better or worse – but for the time being a visit to Abkhazia is just about do-able for adventurous types. Sukhumi is more dangerous than Georgia proper, especially after dark, when women should definitely not go out alone. The lingua franca in Abkhazia is Russian and the currency used, Russian roubles - be sure to take some with you as Georgian lari are of no use whatsoever. US dollars and euro can be changed in Sukhumi but not necessarily elsewhere; Abkhazian ATMs do not work with foreign credit cards, and your SIM card probably won't work either. A useful website for more information is http://abkhazia.travel/en.

On the food front, local specialities are *abhazura*, deep-fried spicy meatballs of pork and beef with pomegranate, and *ojakhuri*, grilled meat with fried potatoes, onion and garlic.

WHAT TO SEE AND DO It should be noted that both the British FCO and US Department of State advise against travel to Abkhazia and the area close to the border. Should you decide to go, here is a brief summary of the highlights.

South from Russia
Entering in the far west from Sochi in Russia, you'll immediately reach **Leselidze**, site of a huge children's holiday camp and a training centre for the Soviet team before the Moscow Olympics, and then **Gantiadi**, where the Tsandripsh basilica, built in the 8th century, has perfect acoustics due to resonating hollows built into its walls. From here the road runs below cliffs to the town of **Gagra**, which claims to be the warmest place on the Black Sea, with bathing from February to November; you can see the ruins of a 5th-century castle, a 6th–7th-century basilica and a park stocked with subtropical plants. It is then 14km to the road south to **Bichvinta** (better known by its Russian name of Pitsunda), where a modern resort abuts the only forest of the relict long-needled Pitsunda pine *Pinus pithyusa*, stretching east for 7km along the beach. By the 14-storey hotels is the late 10th-century Church of the Mother of God, large and externally very rounded. Large numbers of Russian tourists are once again visiting this area and there are now plenty of beach hotels; the season runs from May to October and hotel rooms can be had for just 200 Russian roubles (about US$7), with better rooms in guesthouses costing from about US$20 in April, May or October to double that in August.

Once back on the main road, this swings inland to run parallel with the railway, and in 7km reaches Bzyb (or Bzipi), where there's an attractive 10th-century church and the junction to **Lake Ritsa**. This road follows a valley into the hills inland for

41km to the lake, in a stunning location at 950m, below the 3,256m peak of Mount Agapsta on the border to the northwest. Stalin used to come here to relax, and you can still see his dacha beside the lake. In normal circumstances there's a motel open here, as well as boat hire; in the Ritsa Nature Reserve you may see boar, roe and red deer, plus mountain goats and trout. Some of the world's deepest caves are in the Bzipi Ridge, including the Kruger Abyss, only found in 2005, and the Krubera or Voronya Cave, now explored to a depth of 2,140m, currently the world record.

The main road returns to the coast at Musera (site of Gorbachev's dacha) and continues to Gudauta, a resort which is also the site of the 10th–11th-century Abaata basilica and a Russian army base. About 5km north is Lykhny, site of the 14th-century palace of the Abkhazian kings and a 10th-century Byzantine church. It's another 20km along the coast to **Novy Afon** (known in Greek as Anakopia and in Georgian as Akhali Atoni), where the 9th–10th-century Church of St Simon the Canaanite (who came to this area with St Andrew in AD55 and is buried in Komani near Sukhumi) was the seat of the Bishop of Abkhazia. There's also a tower built in the 13th century by the Genoese. In 1875–86 the monastery of New Athos was built by monks from Athos in Greece; it's been described as 'a delirious fantasy of a building with silver domes bubbling up out of the mountainside, its walls painted in rich yellows and red, crowned by spires'. Under the Soviet regime it was converted into a holiday camp, and suffered badly from 'official' vandalism. Just inland is the Psyrtskha holiday camp, and beyond it the Anacopia Cave in the holy Mount Iveri, which was discovered in 1961 and opened to visitors (except on Sun and Mon) in 1975, with an electric-train tour of its beautiful rock formations. There are nine chambers over 100m in length and 40–60m in height, and the longest is 140m long.

Sukhumi

The coast road soon crosses the Gumista River and enters Sukhumi, the capital of Abkhazia, which was founded in the 5th century BC as the Greek port of Dioscurias. The ruins of Dioscurias have been underwater for over 2,000 years, and are still sinking slowly; the remains of the Roman fort of **Sebastopolis**, built in the 2nd century AD, survive by the quayside, and the 10th-century castle of King Bagrat stands on a 600m hill by the remains of an 11th–12th-century church. Also here is the 15th-century **Turkish fort of Sukhum-Kale** (Turkish for 'Water Sand'), rebuilt by the Russians in 1810. The **Botanical Gardens** were created in 1840, and the 32ha Forest Park, on a low hill to the northeast, was laid out in 1941–51. The Botanical Gardens were very fine before the war of secession but are now fairly run-down; in an area of 25ha they had 5,000 species and varieties of plants, including 1,300 trees and shrubs and 2,800 herbaceous plants, as well as 500 species in greenhouses and 20,000 specimens in the herbarium. Abkhazia is known for the great ages its inhabitants can live to, and Sukhumi's Centenarians' Choir (Nartaa) had members up to 130 years in age. Also here is the Abkhazian State Museum, with Greek statues and local history.

From Sukhumi to Zugdidi

Continuing east along the coast, 6km from Sukhumi a rough road leads another 6km up the west/right bank of the Kelasuri River to **Kelasuri**, where you can see the Great Wall of Abkhazia, built by the 6th century AD as a defensive line along the river. You'll also pass the 11th–12th-century arched bridge of Besleti, 13km from Sukhumi. It's another 13km along the main road (passing Gulripshi, where there are dolmens dating from the 3rd and 2nd centuries BC) to **Dranda**, near Sukhumi's airport, where there's a 9th-century church by the River Kodori. About 30km further east a road leads inland to **Mokvi**, site of a cave-church built in the AD960s, with five aisles, and a cupola on four pillars.

Beyond the town of Ochamchire (54km from Sukhumi) the road heads inland through rich subtropical farmland and hazel trees, soon passing the turning north to **Bedia**, where a 10th-century church was home of the Bedia Chalice, now in the Art Museum in Tbilisi (page 133). The church's frescoes include the only portrait of Bagrat III (AD975–1014), the first king of a unified Georgia, to be made during his lifetime; unfortunately it was damaged after the fall of Sukhumi. Beyond Gali the road reaches the border at the bridge over the Enguri, not far short of Zugdidi; Unomig, the United Nations mission in Georgia, operates a free shuttle bus across the bridge several times a day. Coming from Georgia, it is advisable to cross the border as early as possible in order to catch one of the few marshrutkas (150 roubles) that ply between Gali and Sukhumi; otherwise, you may be at the mercy of ruthlessly overcharging taxi drivers. Taxis to the border from Zugdidi cost around GEL10, and marshrutkas, GEL4; minibuses from the other side of the border to Gali cost 50 roubles.

8

Svaneti სვანეთი

Svaneti, the land of the Svans or *Svanebi*, hidden in obscure recesses of the High Caucasus, is an area to which much mystery attaches itself. It's seen as more Georgian than Georgia proper, the repository of the country's soul, due to having been the last refuge from the Mongols – the holiest icons and richest treasures were carried up beyond the Enguri gorges for safe keeping in times of crisis, and artistic and religious traditions are felt to have been better preserved here than elsewhere. At the same time the Svans are seen as strong but unsophisticated, often disregarding the norms of law and order and speaking a language which split from Georgian by the 6th century and is largely incomprehensible to the people of Kartli and Kakheti.

The Svans' fearsome reputation for brigandage is not wholly without foundation; indeed crime flared up during the Shevardnadze period, and during the civil war in Abkhazia, when refugees were fleeing from the Svan-populated upper reaches of the Kodori and Sakeni rivers, some were greeted by soup kitchens at the passes, but others were robbed by their fellow Svans. Until 2003 tourists were sometimes held up and robbed here but the situation changed dramatically thanks to investment and a clean-up campaign by President Saakashvili.

The typical Svan name 'Kurdiani' means 'thief', although the family has actually produced many well-known Tbilisi architects and artists. In fact, the Svans are very hospitable and friendly, and given the amazing beauty of the surrounding peaks, the clusters of defensive towers that dominate the villages, and the frescoes and icons of the churches, it is hardly surprising that these valleys are now enticing many visitors, just as they did in Soviet times.

More and more independent backpackers are arriving and people can see the economic benefits of tourism: the total was still only 1,200 in 2005 but an estimated 50,000 came in 2014. The Saakashvili administration sought to develop tourism in Svaneti even further, turning the region into a 'Switzerland in the Caucasus', complete with reliable air access, ski slopes and modern hotels. One aspect of this was the enlargement of Mestia's airport to handle commercial flights. Another is the US$25 million spent in 2011 on rebuilding the rough, and occasionally frightening, 136km highway between Zugdidi and Mestia; journey time was cut from 5–8 hours to just 2½. Under the current government development has slowed, but the new facilities are at least being maintained well. Such changes will undoubtedly boost the region's economy, although the harm they will do to an age-old and formerly isolated culture such as this remains to be seen. The Svan culture is probably strong enough to survive, but it's still sound advice to get there as soon as possible.

CULTURE AND HISTORY

The Svan culture shows clear ties with ancient Sumeria and Mesopotamia, though many Svans are blonde with green eyes. They've lived here at least since the 2nd

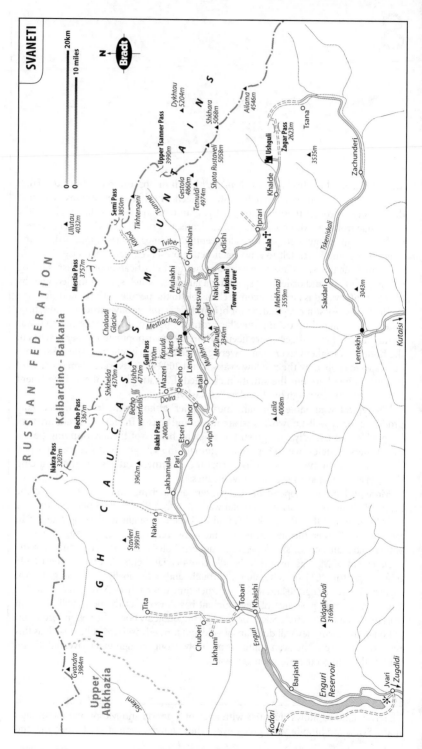

Death has always been nasty and premature for many Svans, even before the arrival of the motor car, so it's not surprising that many traditions have evolved to cope with it. Men don't shave for 14 days after a death, while widows wear black with a lapel badge bearing a photo of the deceased. In the home there is a shrine with more photos, and visitors will be given a drink, to pour a few drops on the floor, and toast the deceased with the rest. Forty days and three months after the death, family and friends go to the cemetery; a table is set up on the grave with food and drink (and perhaps other household items such as a radio). The women wail and cry, then the men line up, hats off, to say prayers and, of course, toast the deceased with chacha; then the table is removed from the grave, and the food is eaten.

As in every Orthodox church, tapers are lit by everyone who enters a church; those at the front left are for prayers for women, those at the front right are for prayers for men, and those at the back are for the dead.

The dead are commemorated on Mariamoba (St Mariam's Day, 28 August), and also in Khaishi on Jvedi Ham, the second Sunday in January, when the souls of dead relatives stay overnight with their families, and in Ushguli on Lipanali, the Monday after 19 January. Singing at funerals combines pre-Christian wailing traditions with Christian singing, by both men and women but not together.

millennium BC, supplying high-grade copper, gold and other metals to Bronze-Age Colchis, and the foundations of the oldest defensive towers can be dated to the 1st century BC. These towers are Svaneti's most distinctive feature, more elaborate than those in Khevsureti and elsewhere to the east, with fortified tops and roofs. There are now about 175 towers, dating from the 6th to 16th centuries (most being from the 9th to 13th centuries), and a couple of dozen have been restored. In Roman times the Greek geographer Strabo called the Svans 'a mighty people ... foremost in strength and courage'; they were formally Christian by AD523 but even today their religion retains strong elements of paganism, such as sacrificing rams on religious festivals and placing their horns on the altar. The Svan sun god Lile may well be the same as the Sumerian Enlil, and the village of Lakhamu may be named after the Sumerian water god. Now, St Barbara (Barbol) is seen as an equivalent of the sun god, while St George (Dzgraeg) is revered as an equivalent to the moon god. Nominally under the control of Colchis, then Lazika (Egrisi), Svaneti became part of Abkhazia then of a unified Georgia from the early 11th century; it shared in Georgia's golden age under Queen Tamar (who ruled from 1184 to 1213), who visited Svaneti several times and is still revered there. The Svans were largely undisturbed by the Mongols (although Tamerlane's horde passed through in 1397), and came under a Russian 'protectorate' in 1833, local autonomy surviving until 1847 when Prince Constantin Dadeshkeliani stabbed to death a Russian administrator and three of his staff, and was summarily tried and executed. The principality was abolished the following year and replaced by direct Russian rule; the last Tsarist governor was driven out in 1905, leaving Svaneti effectively independent again until 1924. The wheel and the aeroplane both appeared in Svaneti in 1935; given their eight-month winter and the poor state of the roads, many Svans are still happy to use heavy ox-sledges as a means of transporting goods. However, increasing numbers now live for most or all of the year in Tbilisi or other cities, as the disadvantages of the harsh mountain lifestyle become ever clearer. In Rustavi, built after World War II as a new industrial city, there are now Svan villages. In the winter of 1987 a terrible avalanche killed around 70 people at once, mostly children in a school in Ushguli, and the following year around 4,000 residents of Zemo (Upper) Svaneti left. In all there are 45,000 Svans in Georgia, of whom 12,000 remain in Zemo Svaneti, about 2,500 of them in Mestia. Logging (probably about double the official level of 60,000m³ per annum) is leading to more avalanches and landslides, and 75–80 families are still leaving each year.

However, it has to be said that the bulk of the death toll is entirely self-inflicted, as young men keep on killing themselves in road accidents; when I was first in Mestia three families were mourning three young men killed in entirely separate incidents. The Mestia cemetery has a number of grave markers that have etchings of young men proudly standing in front of cars, the same vehicles that took them to their death. The 136km road from Zugdidi to Mestia was notorious as the most dangerous in Georgia, and was lined with shrines at accident sites. Under the shrine was a shelf laden with bottles and glasses, and friends would stop and drink a toast of chacha in memory of the deceased; the absurdity of drinking firewater in memory of someone who was probably drunk when he went off the road is lost on the Svans. There's a sense that this was linked to lack of hope during the brigand period, and more recent economic stability has reduced the collective death wish somewhat. It's also reckoned that between 1917 and 1925, 5% of the population (600 people) were killed in feuds, so now politeness is ingrained, and 'fool' is the strongest insult the Svans allow themselves.

A typical Svan village is actually composed of perhaps half a dozen separate clusters of around 30 households huddled around their defensive towers. These are up to 28m tall (perhaps following a formula by which the height of the tower should equal the sum of the four sides), and unlike those of Ossetia and elsewhere they are crenellated and roofed. The standard tower also has three 'eye' windows in each of its four sides, for a total of 12. They were probably built by spiral scaffolding, with rocks hoisted up by oxen. In some villages the oldest and largest will be the 'war tower', standing separately on a hilltop. The traditional home or *machubi* consists of one spacious room with living space in the centre separated by carved wooden partitions from the livestock stalls around the walls. Churches are generally tiny, just 5–6m², and they're single-nave basilicas, mostly built between the 8th and 14th centuries, with frescoes painted between the 10th and 12th centuries, both on the inside and the outside of the churches. They tend to be opened perhaps twice a year for festivals, but the key holder may let you in. Svan icons are remarkable for the standard of their chased metalwork, and the finest examples, made at the end of the 10th century and start of the 11th century, are kept safe in the homes of the leading families.

The national dish of Svaneti is kubdari, bread stuffed with meat. They also make particularly fine khachapuri, known as *teeshdvar*. The local firewater is an especially horrible form of chacha, made from bread due to the lack of grain, although a better apple spirit is also produced.

Svaneti is known for its primeval and ethereal style of three-part singing, with pentatonic harmonies (unlike the rest of Georgia), often accompanied by the changi, the Svan harp, which looks as if it's come straight off a Greek vase, or the lute-like chianuri.

SVANETI FESTIVALS Until the 1950s there were 160 feast days a year in Svaneti; around 50 festivals are still celebrated, not to mention the various inescapable ceremonies remembering the dead (see above).

yes	*ah-du*	hello, good day	*khocha-ladegh*
no	*desa, maama*	thank you	*ivasukhari*
good	*khocha*		

- Jvedi Ham – in Khaishi on the second Sunday of January, a 'Long Night' when the souls of the dead stay overnight with their families
- Lipanali – in Ushguli on the Monday after 19 January, commemorating dead family members
- Lagami – in Latali and Lenjeri at the end of February, with a 'battle' of snow towers
- Lamproba – in all the Svan villages ten weeks before Easter, commemorating St George and the spiritual unity of the village with candles (*lampari*) for each male in the family plus one for St George
- Kashvetoba – in Lenjeri and Kala the third week after Easter, when women married in other villages return to their roots
- Kaishoba – in Nakra, Pari and Becho eight weeks after Easter, the festival of the Archangels
- Hulishoba – in Nakra, Becho and Ushguli ten weeks after Easter, the adoration of God the Father, with animal sacrifices and sports such as horse racing, arm wrestling and rock lifting
- Giorgoba – in all the Svan villages on 6 May, the birthday of St George
- Petre-Pavloba – in all the Svan villages on 12 July, the festival of Saints Peter and Paul
- Kvirikoba – in Kala on 28 July, the main religious festival of Svaneti, commemorating Saints Kvirike (in fact the pre-Christian deity Kviria – see below) and Ivlitta
- Eliaoba – in Lenjeri and Tzvirmi on 2 August, the feast of the Prophet Elia
- Livskhvari – in Ushguli on the first Sunday of August, marking the start of the grass-cutting season
- Mariamoba – in all the Svan villages on 28 August, the festival of the Assumption of the Virgin Mary
- Lalkhori – in Etseri on the first Sunday of October, a celebration of village solidarity
- Giorgoba – in all the Svan villages on 23 November, commemorating St George's martyrdom

For **Kvirikoba**, on 28 July, almost everyone in Svaneti descends on the mountaintop site of Kala for a real 'gathering of the clans'. As you'd expect, there's a lot of alcohol-fuelled singing and some religious observance involving the sacrifice of bulls or goats. Dating from Roman times or before, it's linked to the pagan deity Kviria, protector of the fertility of soil, man and animals. In addition you can buy hand-carved wooden drinking vessels, traditional Svan felt hats and other craftwork direct from the artisan, as well as traditional Svan food. Outsiders are welcome. Some of the Tbilisi travel agents should be able to offer tours to Svaneti that coincide with this event.

GETTING THERE AND AWAY

Now that Mestia Airport has been expanded there are regular **flights** to Mestia from Tbilisi, though only in good weather (at 09.00 Mon, Wed, Fri from the Natakhtari

Svaneti GETTING THERE AND AWAY

8

aerodrome near Tbilisi, with a free transfer from Rustaveli metro (*07.30, returning from Mestia at 11.00; GEL75*); this is operated by Vanilla Sky, at Rkinis Rigi 11 (↘ *322 42 7427;* m *599 659099; www.vanillasky.ge;* ⊕ *10.00–18.00 Mon–Fri, 10.00–14.00 Sat*). Otherwise, the only other way in is by road via Zugdidi. There's a **marshrutka** from Tbilisi's main railway station at 06.30 daily (*GEL30; 8hrs*), but it's far more comfortable to take the overnight **train** to Zugdidi, and make your way to the Svan tower near the river from where marshrutkas leave for the drive up the Enguri Valley to Mestia (*3–4hrs; GEL20*). Although there are no official departure times – it could be any time between 07.00 and 11.30 – it is best to arrive as early as possible; buy your ticket from the kiosk with the 'Mestia' sign. If you miss the marshrutkas you'll probably be able to get a ride in a jeep until early afternoon (page 217). On the return journey, you'll be stuck in Zugdidi for about 8 hours if you plan to take the night train to Tbilisi; far better to get a marshrutka to Kutaisi and break your journey there. Most marshrutkas returning to Zugdidi leave early in the morning, from around 06.00; if you ask nicely they may drop you off at the railway station where the Kutaisi marshrutkas leave from, otherwise it is a 10-minute walk. There are a couple of marshrutkas from Seti Square in Mestia to Tbilisi at 07.00 and 08.00.

FROM ZUGDIDI TO MESTIA

By road, Svaneti is best reached from Zugdidi, although there is also a very poor road (4x4 only) from the less interesting region of Kvemo (Lower) Svaneti. From Zugdidi the road heads north across the plains straight towards Elbruz (across the border in Russia, and the highest peak in Europe at 5,642m), between two near-continuous rows of houses, then climbs up a side valley before cutting across to the west to reach the Enguri Valley at Georgia's largest hydro-electric station. Many vehicles will go the hundred-odd metres to the left to a viewpoint over the dam at km30 (half an hour from Zugdidi); they also tend to make a café-stop at km53 (Barjashi), km63 or km99 (the Restaurant Mariami). The road, often strewn with rock falls, follows the side of the valley high above the reservoir, passing through half a dozen new tunnels. Above the head of the reservoir (km61; where you can see how quickly it's filling with silt) the road relatively soon reaches **Khaishi**, the first of the Svan villages (comprising 20 separate little settlements), 71km and about 80 minutes from Zugdidi. Khaishi is known for its honey, but may be submerged by a proposed dam. The road crosses to the right/north bank after 5 minutes at Tobari, where a road leads north to Chuberi and the Lakhami and Nenskra valleys, as the valley closes in; **Dizi** (km90) is the site of the quarry which produced much of the marble for the Moscow metro's fabulous stations. At about km94 a road turns north up the Nakra Valley towards the Nenskra Pass. The valley opens out and becomes more heavily populated as it turns east into the upper Enguri Valley, with fantastic views of Elbruz, Ushba, Tetnuldi and Shkhara. At km101 it passes **Lakhamula** (centre of a group of 11 hamlets), then below the village of **Pari**, once inhabited by notorious robbers who were eventually driven out by Cossacks.

At the **Etseri** crossroads (km112) there's the remains of a Soviet bus stop and signs in English and Georgian north to Mazeri via the Bakhi Pass; an unpaved side-road climbs fairly steeply for 10 minutes to the Etseri school where more bilingual signs point to the Archangels' Church of Pkhutreri (600m left) and St George's Church of Kurashi (1.3km ahead). Continuing northwards up the road to Iskari hamlet, the second house on the right, at about 1,550m altitude, is Hanmer House (↘ *790 33 7065;* m *599 629789;* e *a.hanmer@gmail.com; www.facebook.com/hanmer.house.svaneti*), a welcoming guesthouse that's an ideal jumping-off point for the lovely hike over the Bakhi Pass to Becho (see below) and also for visiting the two churches and the highest Svan tower. The Anglo-Canadian-Zimbabwean and Georgian owners offer accommodation in sizeable rooms (one en suite) for GEL20 per person (GEL60 full board) as well as camping; there's a small shop, shared kitchen and kettles with tea and coffee in the rooms.

The lovely Archangels' Church is at the end of a ridge at the far end of the hamlet of Pkheutreri, with an open porch around three sides. Continuing up the hill from Hanmer House into the hamlet of **Barshi**, you'll see the Dadeshkeliani tower, the highest in Svaneti at 28m and newly restored; not far behind it are a small private family church and a fortified house. Turning right at the top of Barshi, near the northern end of Etseri village, a track leads across to **Kurashi**, basically an extended family farm, where St George's Church is an odd double structure with an open porch all around. There's also homestay accommodation in Barshi with Beka Gurchiani (m 599 917623) and in Kurashi with Vakhtang Khorguani (m 599 744663).

Horses are available for the trek over the Bakhi Pass (2,400m) to **Becho**, which can be reached by road from km119 of the Zugdidi–Mestia highway (until 2011, a bulldozer was always waiting to repair the Etseri–Becho stretch of the road). On the east side of the bridge over the Dolra in Mazeri (the northernmost of the eleven hamlets of Becho), at about 1,620m, the Grand Hotel Ushba (m 598 599930, 598 633864; www.grandhotelushba.com/EN) is grand only in the ambition of its name and in its warmth and hospitality; run by an energetic Norwegian in co-operation with a local family, it's a great base for hiking west to Etseri, east to Mestia over the Guli Pass, or up to the Ushba Glacier (page 242). Double rooms cost from €69 with shared bathroom or €104 with private bathroom, including breakfast. Hiking with local guides and other activities are available from GEL25 per person. There are also various homestays, including with Jena and Lela Kvitziani (m 599 139072) in Ushkhvanar, halfway between Mazeri and the main highway.

It's not much further up the main road to **Ienashi**, a biggish settlement with defensive towers; this is the central part of the village of **Latali** (km127–130) which means 'guard' and is the first of the truly Svan villages, having always been free from the feudal system. Latali, spread across the tongue between the Mulkhura and Enguri rivers, is perhaps the loveliest part of Upper Svaneti. The Matskhvari Church of the Saviour, a small one-nave basilica built in 1140 on the hilltop above the settlement of Matskhvarishi (at the west end of Latali), has fine 12th-century frescoes, including one of the coronation of Demetre I by the Svan painter Mikhail Maglakeli (1142), the only medieval painting on a secular theme in Svaneti. There's also the church of Jonah in Ienashi itself. Just 2km further on, the road passes above **Lenjeri**, the first of the 'villages of Mestia' (and itself the centre of six hamlets) with half a dozen towers; just south of the road the Lashtkhveri Church of Taringzel (the Archangels) has a famous fresco of Amirani (the Georgian Prometheus) killing the devil Devi, painted on the northern façade in the 14th and 15th centuries, and a contemporary fresco of St George killing the pagan Roman emperor Diocletian (in place of the dragon) inside. At the eastern end of Lenjeri, the Matskhvari Church of Nesgun has 9th–10th-century frescoes by a master called Giorgi.

MESTIA მესტია

It's another 2km to the town of Mestia itself, at 1,470m, where the old town sits above the modern Seti Square on the right bank; at its west end, by the road from Zugdidi (once Stalin Street, now Pharjiani Street), are the striking police station and Public Service Hall, both built in 2012 by the German architect Jürgen Mayer H.

At the town's east end, beyond a hideous statue of Queen Tamar, is a commercial block that has stood unoccupied since around 2012. The new museum and airport (also by Jürgen Mayer H) are on the far left bank, along with some apartment blocks. The old town's backstreets are pure Svan, with steep stony alleys, hairy, free-range pigs, rough stone houses and defensive towers – in 1887 the climber Douglas Freshfield counted 80 towers in Mestia alone, but now there are 66 at most, with just 175 in all Svaneti.

WHERE TO STAY
Marshrutkas will drop you in the square, where in summer you're likely to be met with offers of accommodation. There are now plenty of adequate homestays and guesthouses here and in the surrounding villages, and a few hotels.

Hotels

Hotel Tetnuldi (36 rooms) Margiani 9; ☎790 12 3344; www.tetnuldi.ge. Reached by the unpaved Avtandil Khergiani St & opened in 2010, this is Svaneti's premier hotel: a ski-lodge-type chalet that is squeaky clean but not perfectly maintained. All rooms have satellite TVs, Wi-Fi access & balconies with great views. Local tours can be arranged & there's also a restaurant & bar. **$$$$**

Hotel Mestia (14 rooms) Seti 27; m 577 721252, 599 949419. Immediately east of the square, this is newly renovated & has bike rental & internet facilities. The hotel may function in winter only, but the restaurant is usually open. **$$$**

Hotel Svaneti (12 rooms) Tamar Mepe 5; m 599 648822, 599 549142. An odd-looking but perfectly comfortable structure just east of Seti Square; there's a decent bar-restaurant. **$$$**

Homestays

Davit Zhorzholiani (5 rooms) Seti III 1, right next to St George's Church; ☎790 858505; m 599 344948. Rooms for up to 4 are available inc all food & hot showers; they have a car available & can organise treks & trips, & make their own chacha! **$$**

Guesthouse Koka (6 rooms) Betlemi Alley 4; m 599 910831; e kokachartolani@yahoo.com; www.mestiahotel.com. Now being extended, with a big entry hall & rooms with 1 power socket & a rather cramped bathroom; there's good food & drink with free tea & coffee. Tours & transfers as far as Batumi can be arranged; you'll need a torch to walk outside after dark. **$$**

Irma Jatchvliani (6 rooms) Gabliani 9; m 551 143516, 599 708872. Another comfortable homestay in the centre. **$$**

Nino Ratiani (10 rooms) Jondo Khaftani 19; ☎41 042 1182; m 599 183555, 590 527818; e ninoratiani@gmail.com. Nino is very well connected, & speaks some English, while her daughter Tamuna is fluent; they're located at a mini-market only 2mins from the square back along the Zugdidi road, with clean, white, light, airy rooms, modern bathroom & large quantities of delicious Svan food. Nino's is understandably popular & sometimes completely full & so it is best to book in advance. Price inc 2 or 3 meals. **$$**

Roza Shuqvani (6 rooms) V Sella 17, Lekhtagi; m 599 641455, 598 309919; e rozashukvani@gmail.com; www.roza-mestia.com. Mestia's best & friendliest guesthouse, with clean, simple rooms for up to 6 (with big old beds & 1 power socket) plus shared modern bathrooms. Access is by a steep lane that's a bit muddy but vaguely lit. **$$**

Tsiuri Gabliani (4 rooms) Gabliani 20; m 599 569358. Tsiuri is an English teacher who also speaks German, with a good library. The street, formerly Rustaveli, was renamed after her father, a fine mountaineer; it's next to the 'hospital', 2mins from the square, down the lane by the Public Service Hall. **$$**

Camping

SvanLand Davit Agmashenebelis 17; m 599 912573, 591 699629; e merabson@yahoo.com, campinglegabi@yahoo.com. About 1km upriver from central Mestia (but before Lakhrami), this is Svaneti's only dedicated campsite (although various guesthouses allow camping on their lawns). There's a good washblock (with hot showers) & Wi-Fi, & the helpful owners are fluent in English, French & Russian & can organise horses, 4x4 vehicles & hiking guides. *GEL10/tent*

⚑ Manoni's Guesthouse Camping Hostel Boris Kakhiani 25; m 599 568417, 551 664821, 590 602040; e manonisvaneti@yahoo. com. To the right just beyond the bridge on the airport road, this very hospitable guesthouse allows camping in the garden. *GEL5pp*

✗ WHERE TO EAT AND DRINK All guesthouses and homestays provide large quantities of food, and independent restaurants are beginning to open up in the town as tourist numbers grow. The local honey and *matsoni* (yoghurt) are excellent, and it might be worth trying *khevi*, a sort of chewing gum made of fir-tree resin, which sells for GEL1 and takes a lot of work to get chewy.

✗ Cafe Laila Seti Sq; m 577 577677; e swanuka@yahoo.de; www.facebook.com/ CafeBar.Laila; ⊕ 09.00–03.00 daily. The most modern & tourist-friendly place in town, with Wi-Fi plus live music most evenings in summer, but there's a limited menu & service can be sulky, while the local drinkers can also be annoying. $$

✗ Café Ushba Tamar Mepe. Just beyond the Hotel Svaneti, this is a fair restaurant with a terrace above the street. $$

✗ Sunseti Tamar Mepe. Just east of Seti Square, with a quiet terrace at the rear on the lane leading to St George's Church, this bar-restaurant is one of the nicest places to eat in town, with friendly, competent service. $$

✗ Café-bar Riho Tamar Mepe. This Polish-owned café has free Wi-Fi for customers. $

✗ Café Old House Beqnu Khergiani St. One of the few options for a break away from Seti Sq. Wi-Fi. $

OTHER PRACTICALITIES The **tourist information centre** at 7 Seti Square (m 790 357375) is pretty useless and usually has no local maps, but you will find good maps of the town at the east end of Seti Square (although they don't show the new road to the museum and Ushguli). Maps can be bought at the souvenir shop behind the Café-bar Riho. There are two 24-hour **filling stations** in Mestia (on the Zugdidi road) and two **ATMs** (at the Seti pharmacy just west of the police station, and at Liberty Bank to the east just before the bridge) and an **exchange office** (⊕ 09.30–17.00 *daily*) immediately east of Seti Square. The **hospital** is a few hundred metres west along Gabliani from the Public Service Hall; it's behind the rather grander Pharmadepot – there's a small 'Emergency' sign (in English) on the left at the end of the road.

WHAT TO SEE AND DO One of the greatest pleasures here is to roam the town's backstreets, which, away from the sterile central square, show all the characteristics of any typical Svan settlement – defensive towers, wandering pigs and dung-rich farmyards. There is a handful of specific sights too, however.

Church of St George East of the main square down Seti III Alley is the Church of St George, built in the 19th century to replace an 11th-century ruin; this is where the museum's icons were housed until the church reclaimed its building. Now it has a plain interior and a minimalist iconostasis; there's a good metal icon of St George killing Diocletian and painted icons of Christ and the Virgin and Child from the 12th century. Outside, the grandest memorial is a boulder commemorating the climber Mikhail Khergiani (1932–69), who died in the Italian Dolomites when he got bored with climbing on a rope; there's now a museum in his home (pages 236–7).

Museum of History and Ethnography (*Ioseliani 7;* ⊕ *10.00–18.00 except Mon; GEL5; GEL10 for an optional English-speaking guide*) Now part of the Georgian National Museum, this has a smallish but exquisite collection that's beautifully displayed (and you're free to take photographs, without flash). Its impressive new home, opened in 2013, is totally unsigned under 1km up the new road to Ushguli; it can also be reached by following Ioseliani south from between Seti Square and St George's Church and crossing two bridges.

The six exhibition halls begin with archaeological displays, including 'stones of sin', rocks with holes in them to be hung around the neck to atone for crimes and found only in Svaneti. There are also medieval signal-arrow heads with a hole to make sound, and two-pronged ones for hunting game. Coins, found mostly in church treasures, include a 5th-century BC Colchian silver hemi-drachma and a gold stater of Alexander the Great from the 4th century BC, as well as English and French coins and, bizarrely, Malaysian coins from 1948. The highlight is the collection of icons from the 10th century onwards, all showing a remarkable quality of metalworking – most are from the 11th to early 13th centuries, the so-called Georgian Renaissance or Golden Age. One of the finest, though not made in Svaneti, is of the Forty Sebastian Martyrs, from the 11th or early 12th century. Note also the 13th-century icon of the Archangel Gabriel from Latali, an 11th-century Christ from Mestia, and 11th- and 13th-century icons of St George from Ipari.

There are also some astounding Gospels from the 9th–13th centuries – perhaps only the Labskaldi one quite matches the *Book of Kells* for artistic richness, but to have half a dozen ancient books of such grace and finesse in one place is amazing. Among them are the famous Adishi Gospels, the oldest surviving illuminated manuscript of the Gospels in Georgian, produced in Tao-Klarjeti (now in Turkey) in AD897 and later removed for safety to Adishi in Svaneti. Also here are 14th–15th-century documents on wood from Kala, and psalms printed on Solomon II's press in Tbilisi in the early 18th century. Finally, the cultural exhibits, from the 17th to 20th centuries, include armour, daggers, saddles, hunting arrows, snowshoes, musical instruments, costumes, jewellery and powder horns. There are also fascinating photos of Mestia in 1890, showing very little sign of change since. You'll exit to a lounge and café, with sofas, good toilets and great views of Mestia's towers to the northeast.

Margiani Museum of Architecture (⊕ *When the main museum is open (in theory); GEL1; you'll have to pay at the Museum of History & Ethnography*). This museum, where you can visit both a defensive tower and a machubi house, is at the top northeastern corner of central Mestia, above the road to Lakhrami; it's the house with a silver gate, just beyond a cemetery chapel and the defensive tower, which is left open, with fixed external steps then five flights leading up to the roof. The machubi house, which dates from the 12th century, has a central fireplace (with a chimney of fireproof *mukhra* wood, and a metal plate for cooking bread, by a wooden basin for mixing dough). The fire would have been virtually the only source of light, although there is now a sole electric bulb. Around the room, clockwise from the chest between the windows in which dishes are kept, there's a store for food and chacha, then stalls for sheep along one wall, and larger stalls for cows along two walls. Between 12 and 20 people would have lived in this room, sleeping above the animal stalls for warmth; yet there's only one chair, reserved for the oldest man of the family. Carved on the wooden stalls is a repeated sun or eternity motif, like an orange or apple flan seen from above, which also appears on Georgian coins.

Khergiani Museum (⊕ *10.00–17.00 Tue–Sun; free*) Not far below the Margiani Museum, Khergiani Street leads from the main part of Mestia eastwards to a cluster of nine towers, the hamlet of Lakhrami. Here you can visit the Khergiani Museum, beyond the 13th-century Matshovris Church, which has a fresco of Adam and Eve

visible on the façade. The museum is both a memorial to Mikhail Khergiani, one of the world's leading climbers when he died, and a traditional Svan house; however, opening hours are erratic. You can return by the main road, Davit Agmashenebelis, on the valley floor, passing the high school, where you can pop over a stile to a *narzan* (mineral water) spring in the yard.

Skiing The old Zuruldi ski resort, immediately south of Mestia, fell into disuse around 1993, but was re-invented as Hatsvali, as the centrepiece of President Saakashvili's plans for transforming Svaneti. An Italian high-speed quad-lift (⊕ *all year*) runs from the base at 1,800m to a mountaintop restaurant at 2,345m. Open from January to the end of April, there are 2,600m of red runs and 2,565m of blue runs. The new Tetnuldi resort is being built above Mulakhi, with a first phase due to open in December 2015.

Hikes around Mestia
The Chalaadi Glacier (*10km; 3hrs each way*) The easiest and most popular hike from Mestia follows the Mestiachala Valley beyond the airport before crossing the rushing river by a shaky Soviet-era pedestrian suspension bridge and continuing for 2km up to the Chalaadi Glacier. Walk or get a ride along Davit Agmashenebelis, past Lakhrami to the road bridge just beyond the airport, then follow the jeep track along the left/east bank (past Lavladashi village) to the footbridge (at 1,627m). Soon after crossing this, you'll pass a border guards' post and then climb up the side valley to the glacier, now somewhere above 1,800m altitude; return the same way (or via the airport). You can climb on to the ice, covered with rocks and gravel, with the fully-fledged river flowing from beneath the glacier.

From the bridge it's also possible to make a multi-day trip following the Mestiachala and Tyuibri valleys to the northeast towards the Lekzyr Glacier and ultimately the Mestia Pass (3,757m), which would be open from June to October if one could freely cross the border, but this is not currently possible.

Koruldi Lakes (*16km; 8hrs return*) A wooden cross was erected on a hill high above Mestia in around 1994, and it's an excellent, if exhausting, walk up, taking about two hours to climb 800m over 4km. Having got this far, it makes sense to continue along the ridge to the lovely Koruldi Lakes, giving a total of 16km (which can also be done by horse or mountain bike).

There are two possible routes out of town, the better probably being to take Lanchvali Street past the Margiani Museum of Architecture, then bearing away to the right before crossing a stream and returning to the left to the cross and viewpoint at Tskhakvazagari, popularly known as **Mount Mestia** (2,200m). At the top you have a bird's-eye view of Mestia, an astounding panorama of the High Caucasus and the Enguri Gorge, and lush alpine meadows full of cows and brightly coloured plants, as well as a surprising number of cowherds' huts. The path (now marked with red-and-white stripes) continues via the Lamaaja signpost (2,400m) to the small lakes in a grassy basin. Returning to the Tskhakvazagari cross, you can descend more directly to Vittorio Sella Street (in Lekhtagi) and Seti Square.

Mount Zuruldi (*9km; 8hrs return*) From Seti Square signs lead south along Ioseliani and across the main road beyond the museum, up the hill south of Mestia. Crossing the Ushguli road again, this swings sharply left/east, passing the Hatsvali resort at the foot of Mestia's ski runs and continuing to climb steadily to Mount Zuruldi (2,340m), on the ridge between the Mulakhi and Enguri valleys. You can also return by following the ridge via the top station of the Hatsvali chairlift to the abandoned village of Heshkili, from where a track soon joins the Hatsvali road.

The Soviet alpine lodge (*8km; half-day*) This is an enjoyable excursion from Mestia. Cross the bridge from the central square and instead of heading uphill right to the museum, fork left on Revaz Margiani St past a new church with a graveyard containing an unusual pyramidal grave marker. Pass the Hotel Tetnuldi, named after the 4,974m-high pyramid-shaped peak at the head of the valley, and after passing a souvenir shop sign, fork right to climb gently, keeping Tetnuldi peak in the gun-sight of the road. When you meet a path to the right next to some chain-link fencing, continue straight on, following a jeep track and telephone lines. As this track climbs higher, you'll notice the twin peaks of Ushba surfacing above the Mestia ridge like a terrier's perky ears. Soon you arrive at an abandoned Soviet-era alpine lodge complete with rotting three-tier accommodation, the remains of a swimming pool and a curious semi-circular restaurant. Everything is close to collapse and unlikely to survive many more years – there are even trees growing out of the decaying restaurant roof. Nevertheless, the view is wonderful here (the site is sometimes used as a picnic spot by locals). Just before reaching the lodge, you will pass a steep track rising to the right that climbs up to alpine meadows and over a ridge to Mulakhi village – this is the start of the four-day hiking route from Mestia to Ushguli.

From Mestia to Ushguli (*40km; 4 days*) This increasingly popular trek, now marked with red-and-white painted stripes, can be done with overnight stops in homestays in remote villages, or by camping. The full trip starts by hiking from Mestia to Mulakhi, as above, but many people choose to take a jeep or marshrutka to Zhabeshi, the top hamlet of Mulakhi, and start a three-day trek there.

From Seti Square it takes around 7½ hours to Zhabeshi, going past the Hotel Tetnuldi and the Soviet alpine lodge then climbing to the right over the Chkhuti ridge to the Mulakhi Valley. The trail passes above the hamlet of Zardlashi then through Murshkeli, Zhamushi (the centre of Mulakhi), Cholashi, Majdeveri and **Chvabiani**, where there is a Makhtsovari Church, the oldest in Svaneti, dating back to the 4th century. It's a simple basilica with a three-sided apse, although it once had aisles to the south and north, and a porch to the south. Now it has a modern metal roof, to protect the frescoes and icons inside; ask for the key at the last house in the village. There's also a tower, built in the 10th century, and you may notice the tiny St George's Church, isolated in the fields to the left as you enter Chvabiani.

Continuing, you'll then arrive at **Zhabeshi**, at about 1,600m at the head of the valley. Here, there's accommodation with Mariana Ioseliani (m *595 323508*), Temur Gujejiani (m *599 255997, 591 228572*), Sopho Chartolani (m *598 919236*), Mamuka Naverani (m *595 563155*), Avghan Naveriani (m *598 465846*), Lola Kakhiani (m *591 352477;* e *irmanaveriani@gmail.com*), Mevlud Kakhiani (m *591 952487*) and Zurab Kakhiani (m *591 816772*). There are other homestays in Cholashi and Chvabiani, and in Lakhiri, just above Zhamushi.

From here the trail leads southeast, climbing steadily through birch forest for 8km to a plateau at about 2,700m (with great views of Tetnuldi, only about 5km to the southeast, and many other Caucasian peaks), before dropping to the south for 4km to the very remote village of **Adishi** (1,900m), 9km from the nearest road and cut off by snow for six months of the year. Now only eight families live here, and the village's maze of alleys, towers and wooden balconies is in desperate need of restoration. Although tiny, it has four churches (notably the Saviour and St George churches) and eight towers, in which treasures from all over western Georgia used to be brought to be kept safe from invasion. There's accommodation in summer with Gia Avaliani (m 598 126469), Mukhran Avaliani (m 599 186793), Mamuka Kaldani (m 595 305953), Omar Kaldani (m 599 309055), Elisabed Kaldani (m 599 931418), Tarzan Kaldani (m 790 870794) and Zhora Kaldani (m 599 187359).

Next the trail leads southeast, climbing up the Adishchala Valley for 5km before crossing the river and climbing steeply south for 2km to the Chkhutnieri Pass (2,720m). From here it drops steeply to the Khaldeshala Valley and follows it downstream (southwest) through **Khalde**, a rebel stronghold finally burnt down by the Russians in 1876, where the Lalhor Church is worth a visit, to **Iprari** (1,890m), 15km from Adishi. There's accommodation here with Ucha Margveliani (m 595 557470, 599 250578; e uchaiprali@yahoo.com), Jokola Pirveli (m 599 197207) and Erekle Pirveli (m 599 328505).

The final stage, of only 10km, climbs gently up the Enguri Valley, parallel to the road, reaching Ushguli (at almost 2,200m) after a couple of hours.

TOWARDS USHGULI Seti Square in Mestia is the place to look for a jeep (in fact a Mitsubishi Delica, as a rule) to Ushguli. A return trip should cost around GEL150 (GEL200 if you stay overnight) – not bad if this is shared between four. Your guesthouse will probably be able to hook you up with a group, or ask at the Café Laila (page 235), which arranges day trips in summer for GEL30, leaving at 09.00 and returning at 18.00. The 46km road has been improved so that even a day trip gives time for a bit of a hike, but it's better to stay overnight. A public marshrutka also runs at least once a week from Mestia to Ushguli – call one of the Ushguli guesthouses for information.

A new road starts to the west of Seti Square and crosses the narrow gorge of the Mulkhura River before joining the old road from the left by the modern museum. The road is newly paved with concrete past the junctions to the Hatsvali ski resort (6km to the right) and the top of Mulakhi (also being developed for skiing), and up to the Ughveri Pass (1,923m). There's a *narzan* (mineral spring) to the right 500m along the Ushguli road (marked by red stains on the rocks), by a washed-out bridge. Following the south/left bank of the Mulkhura River, you'll pass the various hamlets of **Mulakhi** village, all with small groups of defensive towers, on the right bank – first Ghvebra, then Zardiashi, Artskheli and Zhamushi (also hit by a lethal avalanche in 1987). The road crosses briefly to the right bank then back before Cholashi, as the towers of Chvabiani come into sight ahead, in front of the giant peaks of Tetnuldi (4,974m) and, to the right, Shkhara (5,068m, the highest peak in Georgia). At the junction to Chvabiani (with two ancient churches – page 238) and Zhabeshi, the Ushguli road hairpins sharply right and climbs to the pass (⊕ *Apr–Dec only*), with good views of Ushba. The concrete ends here and a rough, narrow road switchbacks down into the Enguri Valley at Bogreshi (27km from Mestia, at the start of the track to Adishi – page 238), opposite **Nakipari**, where there are seven towers and the Jgrag (St George) Church, decorated with frescoes in 1130 by Tevdor, supposedly the court painter of King David the Builder (although there's no real evidence); these have survived untouched since then, and there are also some fine icons including a silver one of St George.

The road follows a power line by the Enguri River, passing the isolated **Kukdiani 'Tower of Love'** after 5 minutes; legend has it that a girl shut herself up here after her lover (who was married to another) drowned in the river while hunting. It's worth a visit (*GEL1*) if you haven't climbed up one of the towers in Mestia. It's another 30 minutes up the wooded valley to Khe (39km from Mestia), the first part of the village of **Ipari**, where the 9th-century St Barbara's Church houses a 6th-century icon and 12th-century frescoes; there's also a café here.

After a wet, muddy stretch of road, a bridge crosses to the right bank and the Taringzeli (Archangels) Church of Iprari, 1km up the road to Khalde (page 239); this also has frescoes painted by Tevdor in 1096, as well as ancient icons. The next hamlet, as the road follows the increasingly precipitous Enguri Valley, is **Kala**, where the hilltop Lagurka Church of Sts Kvirike and Ivlita is up a steep track to the south. Built in 1112, with splendid frescoes painted then by Tevdor, it hosts Svaneti's most important pilgrimage and festival, Kvirikoba, on 28 July (page 231). Inside, there's the fabulous gold Shalkiani icon of the Crucifixion; outside, there are great views of Ushba. It's possible to hike on southwards all the way to Mami, on the Ushguli–Lentekhi road in Lower Svaneti.

From here it's just 4km to Ushguli, the road switchbacking up a cliff face to reach a high pasture, something over 2 hours' drive from Mestia. The road passes above Murkmeli, the first part of Ushguli (almost uninhabited, with ten towers, one close to collapse), before crossing the Enguri by a bridge between Chazhashi (to the right) and Chvibiani and Zhibiani, the main parts of Ushguli (to the left).

USHGULI უშგული

Finally, almost 50km and at least 2 hours from Mestia, the road reaches Ushguli, claimed to be Europe's highest permanently inhabited settlement at an altitude of almost 2,200m, although there is a contender for the title on the other side of the Caucasus in Daghestan. It's also a stunningly beautiful spot, with small clusters of towers huddled together amidst alpine pastures and beneath the highest peak in the country; fittingly, it's a UNESCO World Heritage Site. It is divided into three main settlements, with a total of seven churches built and painted between the 9th and 12th centuries. Ushguli has more towers per capita than elsewhere in Svaneti (about 33 for around 50 families or 220 inhabitants), and they show far more variation than elsewhere; one in Chazhashi, possibly the oldest in Svaneti, has 18 'eyes', as do the joined 'Twin Towers' of the Ratiani family in Zhibiani.

To the right of the bridge, Chazhashi was terribly damaged by the avalanche of 1987 but still has many medieval buildings, including the 'war tower' dominating from a hillock. The much-needed restoration of Ushguli's historic buildings began in 2014 with the tower of the ethnographic museum (*GEL10*), which houses some beautiful gold and silver icons and crosses, many from the 11th and 12th centuries, some from the 6th century and some even older. On the ridge above are some isolated towers that are supposed to have been Queen Tamar's summer home; her burial place is unknown, but the Svans naturally hope that it's here. When television arrived in Svaneti in 1975, the communists took great pleasure in installing the relay (now long gone) on Tamar's Towers. Across the bridge to the left is Chvibiani, and beyond it Zhibiani, the last and most spectacular part of Ushguli, where domestic artefacts, icons and a magnificent 11th-century carved door are displayed in another barn-like ethnographic museum (*GEL10*). On the far side of the village is the Jgrag Church of St George, and isolated on the ridge to the east is the Lamaria Church of the Assumption of the Virgin, set against the backdrop of Shkhara in the finest setting of any Svan church. It's a small basilica built in the 9th century, with a defensive tower and 10th–12th-century frescoes, somewhat deteriorated, including a portrait of Queen Tamar, plus scenes from the Amirani legend on the exterior. Pridon or Vladimir Nizharadze and Nanuli Chelidze are the people to ask for to open the museum and church.

If you visit Ushguli in wet or snowy weather be sure to have good footwear as the village streets, such as they are, tend to be permanently covered with a thick layer of cow manure; some have a stream flowing along them; some have both. Locals recommend wellington boots but slurry-proof hiking boots are probably the best option.

The road (4x4 only) passes to the south of Zhibiani and continues to the Zagar Pass (2,623m; 9km from Ushguli) and Lower Svaneti. After passing through various abandoned villages, this reaches the asphalt a few kilometres before Lentekhi (the main town of Lower Svaneti) and takes a recently modernised road down to Tskaltubo and Kutaisi.

WHERE TO STAY AND EAT As well as those below, others that have been recommended are Giorgi Ratiani (m *599 971194*) and Malkhaz Khachvani (m *598 153538, 599 111425;* e *shorenadevdariani@gmail.com*) in Zhibiani; and Gogi Charkviani (m *598 939359*) and Otar Nizharadze (*Guesthouse Caucasus-Ushguli;* m *599 317086, 596 119132;* e *solomonmdivnishvili@gmail.com*) in Chvibiani (*all* **$$**).

Guesthouse Lileo (4 rooms) m 599 912256; e ratiani.dn@gmail.com, likuna-788@ mail.ru. A welcoming homestay, close to the museum in Zhibiani, with excellent food & a cosy atmosphere. Dato Ratiani is quite a character but it is his hard-working mother who is the real dynamo driving this place. **$$**

Guesthouse Ushguli (6 rooms) m 599 974873, 599 773094, 595 710164; e teagigani47@ gmail.com. Laert Charkviani runs the best

guesthouse in Chvibiani, with easy road access & a café. **$$**

Guest & Art House Gamarjoba (4 rooms) m 599 209719 (Russian), 595 229814 (English); http://gamarjoba-ushguli.com. A relative of Nana in Mestia, Temraz Nizharadze offers rooms in his house just below the small church of St George of Zhibiani, with hot water & lots of excellent food, as well as an art display. **$–$$**

HIKES AROUND USHGULI The most popular hike is to the **Shkhara Glacier** (*16km; 6hrs return*), source of the Enguri River. From the Lamaria Church a track drops to a bridge to the right/north bank of the Enguri and then follows it northeast through grassy meadows to where the freezing-cold river gushes from beneath the ice. You can climb on to the glacier and explore an ice-cave, with the bulk of Shkhara (5,068m), just a few kilometres away, looming overhead (you're at about 2,600m here). Climbers can camp here at 2,280m to enjoy the many challenging routes on the Shkhara wall.

It's possible to hike to **Iprari** either directly down the valley (*14km; 5hrs one-way*) or by a full day's hike along the ridge to the southwest via the peak of Latpari (2,830m) and the Lagurka Church.

Finally, you can hike northwest from Ushguli over the **Khalde Pass** (*over 3,000m; 35km; 2 days*), from where there are great views to Elbruz, past the huge Adishi Icefall to the village of Adishi, below the peak of Tetnuldi, and over another ridge to Chvabiani.

BACKPACKING AND CLIMBING IN SVANETI

This is the prime area for backpacking and climbing in Georgia, and the possibilities are described in a couple of guidebooks. Those published before independence assumed that hikers can freely cross the watershed into the Russian Federation – these hikes have to be adapted as there-and-back trips. Peter Nasmyth's *Walking in the Caucasus* and the booklet *Mountaineering Routes of Georgia*, produced by Geoland for the Georgian National Tourism Administration in 2014, both have more current coverage of Svaneti. The Svaneti Trekking website (*www.svanetitrekking.ge/eng/index.htm*) is a useful online resource. Nevertheless, routes are still hard to follow and the terrain is extremely rough in places.

From west to east, the easiest crossing of the Caucasus is by the **Nakra Pass** (3,203m, practicable from July to October), starting from Lakhani on the Zugdidi road – but of course you can't cross into Russia. Finishing at Terskol, in the valley immediately south of Elbruz, this gives fantastic views of Europe's highest peak (5,642m). This route was taken by British climber Douglas Freshfield in 1868, and was the scene of fierce fighting in 1942, when the Germans tried to break through from the north to seize the oil fields of Baku. It's also possible to hike from the Nakra Valley east to the Dolra Valley Pass via the Ledesht Valley, glacier and pass. The Nakra *turbasa* (a sort of climbers' basecamp hostel) is in fair condition and may be privatised.

It was Freshfield who explored this area and made the first ascents of most of the peaks, in wool and tweed and with alpine guides from Chamonix, as was the norm. In 1868 he climbed Kazbek and the east peak of Elbruz, then in 1887 Tetnuldi, Gulba, Shoda, and a reconnaissance of Shkhara, and in 1889 Laila, while searching for fellow climbers Donkin and Fox, lost on Koshtantau. In 1888 John Cockin made the first ascent of Shkhara, while Albert Mummery climbed Dykhtau, then the highest unclimbed peak in the Caucasus at 5,180m.

The **Dolra Valley**, above Becho and Mazeri, gives superb views under the distinctive twin peaks of Ushba (4,710m), a beautiful mountain with the reputation of being a 'killer queen', which was only climbed in 1903 by a Swiss–German expedition (the lower north peak (4,694m) was climbed in 1888 by Cockin). Now, the south summit (the higher and easier one) is rated as French TD, UIAA grade IV–V, and can be climbed in a trip of four days (six days from Tbilisi), such as those run by Caucasus Travel in Tbilisi (page 57). Starting from Mazeri, the first camp is at 2,367m, above the 200m-high Becho waterfalls, and the second is on the Ushba Glacier at 4,000m (the main difficulty is the crossing of a suspended glacier between 3,000 and 3,800m); then the route follows the northwest ridge for 600m before some hard ice-climbing for 400m to the final ridge and snow dome. Shkhelda (4,370m), just to the north of Ushba, is rather easier (UIAA II–IV); between these two peaks is the Ushba Pass (4,100m), a very hard and high route. The glaciers in this area are retreating and the upper part of the Ushba Glacier is now dangerous.

Easier routes from Mazeri involve hiking to the foot of the Ushba Glacier (2,500m) and the waterfalls, or to the Guli Glacier (2,900m); it's possible to swing east to the Guli Pass (3,100m), south of Ushba, and then down to Mestia. From Mazeri the route follows the left/east bank of the Dolra and passes through a gorge to the confluence of the Dolra with the Becho, from the north, a couple of hours from Mazeri. From here routes lead west to the Nakra Valley, north to the Becho Pass (*3,367m; ☻ Jun–Sep*) and the Baksan Valley, northeast to the Akhsu Pass (3,830m; crossed by Freshfield in 1889), and east to Ushba and Mestia. It's another 2 or 3 hours to the Guli Glacier and bivouac, start of the climbing routes on the south side of Ushba; it's not much further to the Guli Pass, from where it's about 4 hours down to Lenjeri or Mestia.

There are **two possibilities from Chvabiani** to the Semi Pass and the Upper Tsanner Pass, at the top of Mulakhi, both starting by following the right/north bank of the Tviber through a gorge known as the Gates of Georgia, where the trail follows a metre-wide shelf for about 50m, to the confluence of the Tviber with the Kitlod at 2,400m, 5 or 6 hours from Chvabiani. You should cross the Tviber using the ruins of a bridge, unless there's a snow bridge upstream, then continue up the left/east bank of the Tviber, reaching the Tviber Glacier in about 6 hours. Again, it would be possible to continue to the pass (3,580m) and down to Chegem if politics permitted. It's an easy pass, with safe glaciers and no need for anything more than a rope.

Having made the crossing of the Tviber, a path follows the right/north bank of the Kitlod to the Kitlod Glacier; with a short climb on snow, it takes about 6 hours to reach the Semi Pass (3,850m). From here there's a stunning view of the sheer white Bezengi Wall, 12km long, and the lovely pyramids of Tetnuldi (4,974m) and Gestola (4,860m), as well as Elbruz and Ushba to the west. It's possible to continue northeast and then east along the watershed for 4 or 5 hours to the Upper Tsanner Pass (3,990m), from where there's a view of the other side of the Bezengi Wall and the 5,204m peak of Dykhtau to the north. This is the most spectacular of the hikes currently possible in this region.

Tetnuldi (4,974m) is approached from Adishi, starting up grassy slopes to the north, then bypassing moraines to the left after 3–4 hours and reaching the first camp at 3,013m after another hour or two. Alternatively, it's possible to drive a jeep from the Ughveri Pass to a hut at 2,786m (or to hike from the pass in 5–6 hours) then take a horse track to the camp.

9

Adjara აჭარა

In the far southwest of the country, Adjara (or Achara) is the warmest and wettest of Georgia's provinces, with 2.4m to 2.8m of rain per year. Average temperatures on the coast range between 4°C and 6°C in January and 20°C and 23°C in July, and it's horribly humid in summer. It's cloudier than Abkhazia, which claims 100 more sunny days per year.

Christianity arrived here in the 1st century AD; the region has been under Turkish domination for much of its history and now many of the population, especially in the mountains, are Sunni Muslim in faith although ethnically and linguistically Georgian. People are fairly religious in the mountains, but less so in Batumi, where there's only one mosque. The Adjaran men's traditional costume (as seen in dance troupes) is particularly camp with its tight trousers. Russia took over in 1878, and after the convulsions of the war and revolution (including a brief British Protectorate), created an autonomous republic within Georgia in 1921 as a condition of peace with Turkey. Nevertheless 340,000km² of historically Georgian territory still lie within Turkey, including many of the finest Georgian churches (see the ITM/ERKA map of Georgia), and the Georgian population of Turkey has not always been well treated.

After the break-up of the Soviet Union Adjara was ruled as the personal fiefdom of Aslan Abashidze, whose family had been in charge here since the 15th century, and never tolerated much opposition (Tbilisi streets are named not after Aslan but other Abashidzes who were fine poets). Abashidze was appointed chair of the Adjaran Soviet by Gamsakhurdia in 1991, and always had strong support from the generals commanding the Russian (nominally CIS) base outside Batumi. He ruled firmly, keeping the Mkhedrioni out of Adjara, and handed over very little tax to Tbilisi; nor did he go to Tbilisi himself – although elected as a deputy, he never attended parliament and should technically have been dismissed. Meanwhile the Adjaran opposition lived in Tbilisi, due to threats against them in Batumi. It was unclear why Shevardnadze didn't stand up to him, given all Abashidze's insults and his talk of challenging for the presidency; as he had plenty of funds due to his take of the trade passing through Batumi from Turkey, he easily persuaded opposition parties outside Adjara to throw in their lot with him. Abashidze claimed to have been the target of frequent assassination attempts, which he blamed on the Shevardnadze government. No-one outside Adjara took this very seriously, but the streets of Batumi were full of young toughs in plain black clothes wielding Kalashnikovs.

All this changed after the Rose Revolution – in May 2004 Abashidze staged a confrontation with Saakashvili and had three bridges linking Adjara to the rest of Georgia destroyed. Saakashvili gave him ten days to disarm and return to constitutional rule, sending the army to conduct a major exercise just across the border, while activists were smuggled in to lead protests and seduce Abashidze's guard away from him. Fortunately he was also persuaded to go peacefully and was flown to Russia, and Adjara returned to being a normal part of Georgia.

On the coastal road from Poti or Samtredia, the new Kobuleti bypass takes off to the left at km62/59, just before you enter Adjara (map, page 196) at the bridge over the Choloki River at km65. This is also the terminal of the minibuses that run the length of Kobuleti from the station. The dunes just south cover the Pichvnari archaeological site (page 256), while a thin strip of bog inland from the road forms the 770ha Kobuleti Nature Reserve. This protects the Ispani Marshes, ecologically valuable wetlands similar to those near Poti (page 220); rangers are happy to take you for a guided walk (you're not allowed in alone) from Davit Agmashenebelis 642 (m 577 101897). The road enters the long, thin coastal sprawl of Kobuleti 2km from the bridge. A settlement has existed here since the 5th century BC; now it's chiefly a beach resort, although there is also a small port. With the closure of Abkhazia, this is currently Georgia's prime resort on the Black Sea, although the beach is black sand and everyone is aware of the polluted state of the Black Sea. The residents insist on cladding their buildings, even blocks of flats, with corrugated galvanised iron, which is perhaps not to all tastes.

GETTING THERE AND AWAY There are plenty of marshrutkas up and down the coast road; services to Tbilisi (*Didube; GEL20*) leave every hour from the railway station (served by trains to Makhindjauri, ie: Batumi).

WHERE TO STAY The main road along the coast, Davit Agmashenebelis (formerly Lenina), is lined with hotels and guesthouses – there are plenty to choose from. There are also quite a few signs advertising 'komnaty' (Russian for rooms) on the stretch of road north of km73/142.

Georgia Palace Hotel (156 rooms) Davit Agmashenebelis 275; 24 2400; e info@gph. ge; www.gph.ge. Just south of km71, this former sanatorium has been refurbished & reopened as a 5-star luxury hotel. It still functions as a health spa with all manner of treatments available. Guests have included Katie Melua as well as the Polish & Ukrainian presidents. All rooms with AC, Wi-Fi & cable internet, minibar & satellite TV. **$$$$$**

Kobuleti Beach Club (9 suites) Davit Agmashenebelis 373A; m 599 569677; e kbchotel@gol.ge. Near km66.5 & the last of a number of other isolated hotels to the north, this British-owned place is the best in town, with a Moroccan restaurant & a swimming pool. **$$$$$**

Hotel Condori (32 rooms) Davit Agmashenebelis 280; 26 6444; m 577 448882; e hotel-condori@mail.ru; www.condori.ge. A decent, mid-range hotel built in 2006 that has rooms & suites with cable TV, minibar & internet connection. **$$$–$$$$**

Hotel Chveni Ezo (9 rooms) Davit Agmashenebelis 492; m 599 791907; e chveniezo@mail.ru. Simple, clean en-suite rooms with generous balconies; there's beach access directly opposite. **$$$**

Hotel Palermo (35 rooms) Davit Agmashenebelis 448; 750 722 2224. A big comfortable place, in garden well set-back from the road; Georgian & Lebanese food. **$$$**

Hotel-Restaurant Chero Davit Agmashenebelis 454; m 599 616168. A mini-hotel that's of note mainly for its excellent restaurant (page 246). **$$$**

Solidarity (51 rooms) Davit Agmashenebelis 269; 26 9407; m 558 503207; e rusiko_m@mail.ru, hotel.solidarity@profkurort. ge. A modern façade hides fairly standard rooms with garden views as well as a conference hall; it's very close to the beach. **$$$**

Hotel Edemi Davit Agmashenebelis 288; 26 6763. A modern hotel with large balconies down an alley across the road. **$$–$$$**

Astoria Hotel (6 rooms) Tamar Mepe 100 (rear of Davit Agmashenebelis 213); 26 7560. At about km72.7, a slightly tatty small hotel in a large house on the beachfront promenade. **$$**

🏠 **Caffe Princessa** (20 rooms) Davit Agmashenebelis 390; 📞 26 6656; m 593 315273. Simple, clean & comfortable rooms, some with 3 or 4 beds making it ideal for families or groups. **$$**

🏠 **Kolkheti** (300 rooms) Davit Agmashenebelis 285; 📞 26 7620; ⏱ May–Sep. A huge block with rooms for between 2 & 6 people, with a shower in each room but TV only in luxe rooms. **$$**

🏠 **Savane** (25 rooms) Davit Agmashenebelis 362; 📞 26 6538; m 599 568665; www.savane. ge. Comfortable but noisy rooms; restaurant & café-bar, & a luxuriant garden with small outdoor pool. **$$**

🏠 **Nani's Guesthouse** (12 rooms) Davit Agmashenebelis 338; m 599 228906. Basic rooms above the Kafe Bar Martvili. **$**

✖ WHERE TO EAT AND DRINK

✖ **Hotel-Restaurant Chero** (See also page 245) Davit Agmashenebelis 454. This hotel has an excellent restaurant, serving fantastic khinkali, shashlik (with sulguni), khachapuri, BBQ chicken & grilled fish. **$$**

✖ **Bora-Bora** Davit Agmashenebelis 466. A bit fast-foody in style, but with live music in summer; it's next door to the lively Lounge Bar Monroe. **$**

✖ **Green Café** Davit Agmashenebelis 134 (km73); m 595 018757; ⏱ 10.00–midnight. Affordable snacks such as khachapuri. **$**

OTHER PRACTICALITIES There are several **ATMs** north and south of the museum, and to the north at Davit Agmashenebelis 478 and 492. The town centre lies just north of km74/45, 500m north of the modern railway station, but this is a fairly dull area. There is a helpful **tourist information** kiosk here, facing the main square (with cinema and supermarket) at Davit Agmashenebelis 121–139 (📞 422 29 4414; m 593 937991; e tic@welcomebatumi.com; ⏱ 09.00–19.00 daily). Just south is the **Kobuleti Museum** (⏱ 10.00–14.00 & 15.00–18.00 Tue–Sun; GEL2), a surprisingly grand building housing good archaeological and ethnographic displays.

TOWARDS BATUMI The road south from Kobuleti begins after 4km to climb away from the coast into the fringes of the Lesser Caucasus in a steep series of hairpins, while the railway follows an equally lovely route along the coast. Due to the influence of the mountains, it's cooler in summer and warmer in winter than in Batumi; there's thick subtropical vegetation, with groves of bamboo as well as plantations of tea and citrus fruits. Thanks to this mild climate the road is in far better condition than similar roads elsewhere in Georgia. The road climbs past the ruins of the 6th-century Byzantine fort of **Petra** (or Tsikhisjiri; ⏱ always; free) at km80, then drops from km82/37 to **Chakvi**, a small coastal resort with a station at km86/33 and the Hotel Oasis (155 rooms; Batumi 16; 📞 322 47 2233; m 592 296060, 592 847272; www. hoteloasis.ge; **$$$–$$$$**) to the west from the main bus stop at km87.5/31.5, 1.5km south of the railway station. In 2005, a 657m-long road tunnel was opened through the ridge south of Chakvi; a second bore was added in 2010. If you stay on the old road, it climbs again, then begins to drop towards the gate of the Agricultural Institute of the Academy of Science, which houses one of the best Botanic Gardens in Georgia (page 257). The road is reunited with the railway at **Makhinjauri**, a pleasant small resort of 15,000 residents; south of the station (km94/25; the terminus for passenger trains from Tbilisi and elsewhere), the most striking building is a restaurant built in 1917 by a Japanese architect, with a wrap-around veranda and nicely carved wooden lattices. Behind this is the Hulus Castle Hotel (Tamar Mepe 20; 📞 422 25 5560; e huluscastle@ mail.ru; **$$$$**), a retro-styled place with swimming pool. Finally, after passing the Chess Palace and very kitschy Batumi Art Center, the road and railway swing west along the shore of a bay to Batumi (km102/19), one of the most attractive and relaxed cities in Georgia. Most people will arrive by the route described above, but it's also possible to arrive from the Turkish border crossing at Sarpi, 19km south, and served by plentiful taxis and minibuses, or by the rough highway from Akhaltsikhe, to the southwest of Borjomi, untouched by public transport except in summer (page 188).

BATUMI ბათუმი Telephone code 422

Batumi, with its sheltered natural harbour, existed as a Greek trading colony by the start of the 2nd century BC at the latest; its name is probably derived from the Greek words *bathys limen* (deep harbour). Under Turkish rule from the 16th century it was just a tiny fishing village, but once the Russians arrived in 1878 it began a very rapid development. It was a free port from 1878 to 1886 and became the terminal of the railway from Baku in 1883 and of the oil pipeline in 1906. In 1902, Stalin organised a strike after the sacking of 400 workers from the Rothschild refinery; 15 lives were lost, and Stalin was sent to Siberia for three years. A week after the Armistice of November 1918, 15,000 British troops landed in Batumi to protect Georgia and the Caspian oilfields from Germany and Bolshevik Russia; the last troops left on 9 July 1920, leaving the way open for the Bolshevik invasion and the takeover of Georgia. The democratic prime minister Noe Zhordania and his government fled from Batumi early in 1921. Now, it's a city of around 130,000 people, perhaps the liveliest in Georgia, and handles a great deal of trade with Turkey, both by land and sea.

From 2009, the Saakashvili government used an array of incentives to trigger a building boom aimed at turning Batumi into the Atlantic City of the Black Sea, or the new Beirut. The new architecture is glitzy, verging on kitsch, particularly around Evropus Moedani (Europe Square) and especially all along the seafront, from the towers in Miracle Park to the New Boulevard well south of the city. The Sheraton and Radisson hotels now dominate the city skyline and there are even plans for the American mogul Donald Trump to co-finance, with the Silk Road Group, the building of a Georgian 'Trump Tower' development here (or in Tbilisi, or in both cities) in the near future.

GETTING THERE AND AROUND Until July 2015 passenger trains to and from Batumi actually only ran as far as **Makhinjauri**, 5km north of the city centre, which has a tourist information office, a baggage store and computerised ticketing, and there's an ATM across the road. In addition to the day trains to Tbilisi (*at 08.05 and 16.40; GEL24.50 1st class, GEL17.50 2nd*) there are stopping trains to Kutaisi (*17.00*) and Ozurgeti (*07.55*), and a sleeper train runs daily from July to October directly between Batumi and Yerevan via Tbilisi. You'll need to book several days ahead for this. Bus 8, 10, 13 and 15 (*GEL0.80*) and marshrutkas 20, 21 and 31 (*GEL1*) run between the station and the city centre; taxis cost about GEL15. Just as this book went to press, a new rail and bus terminal opened; it's called **Batumi Central**, after the attached shopping mall, but is in fact about 2km north of the city, immediately south of the Batumi Art Center (page 246). As well as the trains that previously terminated at Makhinjauri, this will also serve international and domestic buses. In addition to the ticket office at the station, there is also a booking office at Mazniashvili 5 in central Batumi (⊕ *09.00–13.00 &14.00–18.00 daily*).

The **bus station** [248 G3] (✆ *30162/3*) lies just off Tsereteli, not far east of the centre next to the railway lines; the ticket hall is closed so you have to buy tickets from kiosks at the relevant bay. Look out for the Soviet-era hammer and sickle on a plinth in the yard. Marshrutkas leave for Tbilisi, Kutaisi, Poti and Zugdidi almost hourly until 18.30, with some later overnight departures to Tbilisi (*GEL18*); marshrutkas to Akhaltsikhe run via Kutaisi, leaving at 08.30 and 10.30 (*6hrs; GEL18 to Borjomi or Akhaltsikhe*). Other marshrutkas for Kutaisi and Tbilisi leave when they're full from the junction of Gogebashvili and Chavchavadze (by the cable-car),

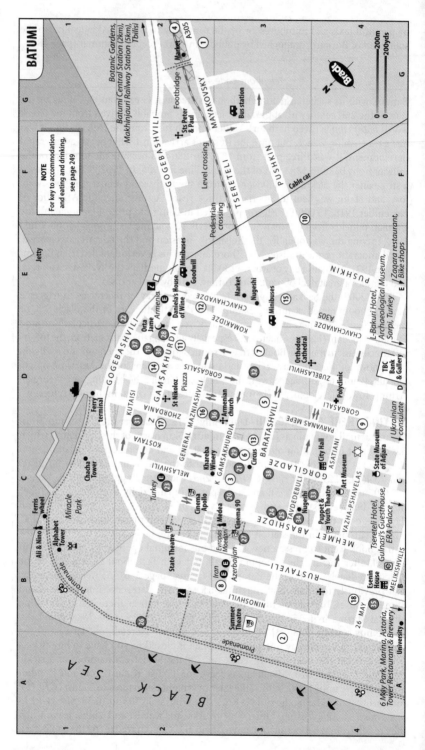

BATUMI

NOTE
For key to accommodation
and eating and drinking,
see page 249

and marshrutkas and shared taxis leave from the rear of the old railway station (Zubelashvili/Vazha-Pshavelas); the Georgian Bus service to Kutaisi airport leaves from the Radisson Blu hotel (book in advance). Buses run up the Adjariskhali Valley as far as Khulo. There are also comfortable Turkish buses to Trabzon (*3hrs; GEL25*) that leave fairly regularly throughout the day.

Metro Georgia (\ *24 2244; http://geometro.ge*) operate buses to Tbilisi, with Wi-Fi, air conditioning and reserved seats, from a new terminal a little further east on Mayakovsky at Gogoli 1 (\ *24 2612*), at 01.00, 09.00, noon, 15.00, 20.00 and midnight. They take longer than the marshrutkas, but are far more comfortable and restful; fares are currently GEL20 by bus or GEL18 by marshrutka. Metro and other companies also have buses to Turkey from the Gogoli terminal. Tickets can be reserved through Adjara Tour at Chavchavadze 48 (*Melikishvili;* \ *22 8778;* m *577 788888;* ⊕ *09.30–19.00 Mon–Fri, 09.30–18.00 Sat–Sun*).

The newly refurbished **airport**, 3km south at Khelachauri (*bus 10;* \ *23 5100; www. batumiairport.com*) at present has flights from Ukraine with Ukraine International Airlines and Georgian Airways, Minsk with Belavia, Tbilisi with Air Batumi and Georgian Airways, and Istanbul with Pegasus and Turkish Airways, which has a sales office at Baratashvili 27 (\ *22 3222;* e *batummd@thy.com; Mon–Fri 09.30–17.30*).

It's also possible to arrive by sea, at the stylish **ferry terminal** [248 D1] at the north end of Zhordania – see page 62 for details of services (or ask at the 'Inquiring Office' in the terminal). Some cruises call here, too.

There's no shortage of **taxis**, but for more comfortable and reliable vehicles try Taxi 2 (\ *27 0594*), Taxi 777 (\ *23 1070;* m *577 511070*), or Taxi 929 (m *599 929929*).

The Batumi Velo **bike-sharing** system has automated stations around town and all along the Boulevard. You have to register at the tourist information centre (with your passport), and pay GEL10 for ten days, which gives you three free hours plus top-ups at GEL2 per hour, or GEL20 per year with five free hours. It may be easier to just rent bikes the old-fashioned way, with various types of bikes and tandems for rent opposite the tourist information centre and at various places along the boulevard.

City transport is provided by both buses and marshrutkas; the latter race around more or less everywhere while buses stop only at designated stops meaning they are slower (but cheaper). Marshrutkas cost GEL0.50 (pay the driver as you leave) while

---

BATUMI
For listings, see pages 250–3

Where to stay

1	Batumi 2000	G2
2	Batumi Tennis Club	A3
3	Batumi Surf Hostel	C3
4	Boni	G2
5	David	D3
6	G Bakuri	C3
7	Iliko	D3
8	Intourist Palace	B3
9	Irise	D4
10	Lavro	F3
11	Luna	D2
12	Mercury	E2
13	Metropoli	C3
14	Oskar	D2
15	Peria	E3
16	Rcheuli Villa	D2
17	Ritsa	D2
18	Sheraton	B4

Off map

Astoria	B4
ERA Palace	C4
Gulnasi's Guesthouse	C4
L-Bakuri	D4
Marina	B4
Tsereteli	C4

Where to eat and drink

19	Arhavi	D2
20	Bar 32	C3
21	Batumi Pizza	C3
22	Bereg Café	E2
23	Boulangerie	C2
24	Café Batumi	C3
25	Café Saamo	C3
26	Dzveli Gemi	B2
27	Espresso Bar Sinatra	B3
	Kafé Bar Maspindzelo	(see 21)
28	Istanbul Fish Restaurant	D2
29	Literaturuli	C3
	Mamapapuri	(see 21)
30	Mevlana	D2
31	Munich	D2
32	Porto Franco	D3
33	Prague Pub	C4
34	Princess Café	C3
35	San Remo	B4
36	Seven	D3
37	Sofra Lokantası	D2
38	Temelas Dukani	C3

Off map

Tower Restaurant & Brewery	B4
Zaqara	E4

Adjara BATUMI

9

bus tickets cost GEL0.80 for two rides – in the central area (including the airport) you validate just one whereas to go out to Makhinjauri or Sarpi you validate both.

TOURIST INFORMATION The tourist information office is at Ninoshvili 2 [248 B2] (↳ *29 4412;* m *577 909091;* e *infocenterbatumi@gmail.com, ticbatumi@gmail.com; www.welcomebatumi.com;* ⏲ *09.00–20.00 daily*), at the entrance to the seaside park; the helpful staff speak English and can provide excellent maps and leaflets. There's also a kiosk at the airport (↳ *29 4414;* m *593 937991;* ⏲ *09.00–18.00 daily*) and others (*both* ⏲ *24hrs*) by the cable-car on Gogebashvili (↳ *29 4410;* m *577 909093;* e *ticbatumi@gmail.com*) and at the Sarpi border post (m *577 909093;* e *ticbatumi@ gmail.com*).

⌂ WHERE TO STAY Map, page 248

Batumi has a good choice of hotels, due to the flow of businessmen across the border from Turkey and to serious promotion of its casinos in Turkey, Iran and Russia, where gambling is banned. Some of the flashier ones not only offer prostitutes, but are said to take serious offence if guests fail to avail themselves of their services. Currently, there is serious multi-million dollar investment from Armenian, Kazakh and Tbilisi business concerns in southern Batumi and all along the coast south to the border, and even US billionaire Donald Trump has expressed an interest in building here (page 247). Refugees from Abkhazia were paid US$7,000 per family to move out of communist blocks such as the Hotel Medea, which have been gutted or demolished and rebuilt. Hilton and Radisson hotels have recently opened, and a Kempinski is planned. Just 75,000 tourists visited Batumi in 2004, a figure which climbed to 1.6 million in 2012, and continues to rise rapidly.

Hotels are listed from north to south.

Hotels

⌂ **Boni** (34 rooms) Mayakovsky 4; ↳ 27 1939, 27 4820; m 577 125206. Surprisingly good for its location just beyond the market, this is a modern block with a sauna (with cold pool), café-bar-restaurant & billiards, & English is spoken. **$$–$$$**

⌂ **Batumi 2000** (28 rooms) Mayakovsky 15; ↳ 27 2568, 25 4132; e batumi2000@yahoo.com. Signed as the Hotel-Disco Batumi, this is not as good as the Boni but pricier. **$$–$$$**

⌂ **Oskar** (9 rooms) Gorgasali 6; m 557 537842, 593 959476. A small place; rooms with shower & TV, & some with AC. Everything's basic but clean. **$$**

⌂ **Ritsa** (14 rooms) Z Gamsakhurdia 16; ↳ 27 3292; m 594 14293; e hotelritsa@hotmail. com; www.hotelritsa.com. Opened in 2007, a stylish, city-centre hotel with luxe rooms (with nice wrought-iron balconies) as well as standard. **$$$–$$$$**

⌂ **Mercury** (32 rooms) Chavchavadze 10/12; ↳ 27 7501–3; www.hotelmercurybm.ge. A good new city-centre hotel that satisfies both business

folk & Peace Corps Volunteers, this has a bar, bistro, sauna (GEL12/hr), roof-top swimming pool & PCs with internet access. In addition to standard rooms & suites it has sgl & twin 'student' rooms. **$$–$$$$**

⌂ **Rcheuli Villa** (10 rooms) Zhordania 31; ↳ 27 0707; m 599 637662; e info@rcheuli.ge; www.rcheuli.ge. One of a chain of smart, new boutique hotels, this is attractive & conveniently located, with stylish rooms with marble floors & antique furniture, but suffers from poor maintenance. **$$$–$$$$**

⌂ **G Bakuri** (28 rooms) Baratashvili 23; ↳ 27 4788; m 577 125209; e bakuriltd@yahoo.com.

NOTE ON STREET NAMES

Note that in its wisdom the city has named two streets Gamsakhurdia (Konstantin and Zviad), two for Abashidze (Mehmet and Haidar) and two for Khimshiashvili (Selim and Sherif).

A decent modern block, with a bar but no other facilities; rooms are with shower, TV, & phone. **$$–$$$**

🏠 **Metropoli** (15 rooms) Nodar Imnadze 5 at Baratashvili; ☎ 27 3794; m 599 161815; e metropol_hotel_batumi@hotmail.com. A good, modern building with twin rooms; also a huge AC apt with a remarkably small TV & 3 balconies. Snacks are available in the top-floor bar; limited English is spoken. **$$–$$$$**

🏠 **Iliko** (7 rooms) K Gamsakhurdia 42; ☎ 27 3892; m 593 574260; e hoteliliko@mail. ru. A small, slightly grubby place shoehorned into a courtyard, with cramped twin rooms with bathroom, Wi-Fi & TV. **$$**

🏠 **David** (12 rooms) Baratashvili 33; ☎ 27 1718; m 592 091010; e hoteldavid_11@mail. ru. The best in town until the Intourist Palace and Sheraton opened, with big stylish rooms & a good restaurant, sauna, & tennis facilities; a café is being built next door. Good English is spoken, & there's internet & cable in all rooms. With standard twin rooms (good Sony TVs, full bath, minibar, hairdryer), & deluxe rooms (with jacuzzi), inc b/ fast (no credit cards). **$$$–$$$$$**

🏠 **Peria** Zurab Beridze Seshakhveri (formerly Pereulok Kalieva) 13; ☎ 25 1576; m 599 262870. A new building with restaurant-bar & Wi-Fi, pretty decent but no English spoken. Rather post-Soviet sgl rooms. **$$–$$$**

🏠 **Luna** (4 rooms) Zubelashvili 4; ☎ 27 7277. A small, new pension, in an orange-painted house on a square near the mosque. There are 2 bathrooms, a living room & kitchen, with fans but no AC. **$$**

🏠 **Intourist Palace** (146 rooms) Ninoshvili 11; ☎ 27 5525, 21 7878, 27 6608; m 577 947720; www.intouristpalace.com. A Stalinist block of 1939 (on the site of the Alexander Nevsky Cathedral) totally remodelled & reopened in 2006 as a Turkish-run 5-star hotel, with gym, hammam & 4 swimming pools (2 indoor, 1 outdoor & 1 for children). It's come a long way from the days when staff refused even to tell me the phone number for reservations. Rooms all inc b/fast, tax, plasma-screen TV & power showers. **$$$$–$$$$$**

🏠 **Batumi Tennis Club** (14 apts) ☎ 22 1661; m 593 241085; www.btc.ge. Set in the park off Ninoshvili, these are lovely motel-style apts (but without car access), each with a terrace, small garden & pavilion. There are 8 artificial grass courts, costing US$10/hr, & a bar above reception in the centre of the courts. Prices inc b/fast & an hour of tennis daily. **$$$–$$$$$**

🏠 **Irise** (formerly Piramida; 15 rooms) Vazha-Pshavelas 39 at Gorgasali; ☎ 23 2204; m 893 732923. A small, newish hotel over a café-bar, with only Georgian & Russian spoken. Basic twin rooms with shower & TV, inc b/fast, or larger rooms are available. **$$–$$$**

🏠 **Sheraton** (202 rooms) Rustaveli 28; ☎ 22 9000; www.sheratonbatumi.com. An unmistakable & tasteless building that can be seen from all over town, especially at night when it is illuminated. This state-of-the-art 5-star hotel has everything you might expect: conference facilities, 2 restaurants, 3 bars, health centre, business centre, spa & outdoor & indoor swimming pools. Rooms have hypoallergenic pillows, minibar, satellite TV & complimentary high-speed internet. Prices inc taxes & b/fast. **$$$$$**

🏠 **L-Bakuri** (40 rooms) Chavchavadze 121; ☎ 27 6930, 27 6921; m 593 402844. A block south of Lermontov, a friendly, well-run 6-storey place with rooms ranging from sgls & dbls to 4 suites, all with bathroom, AC, fridge & TV. There's an adequate bar-restaurant, too. Room rates inc b/fast. **$$$–$$$$**

🏠 **Tsereteli** (12 rooms) Gorgiladze 33; ☎ 27 6684; m 557 247575. A small place in a period building with dbl rooms (each with 2 beds), & 3 suites. All have AC, with satellite TV, minibar & balcony. There's a restaurant & bar, & parking & laundry are available. Prices inc b/fast. **$$$–$$$$**

🏠 **ERA Palace** (39 rooms) Gorgiladze 77; ☎ 22 0000, 27 8221; e erapalace@gmail.com; www. erapalace.ge. A stylish, new, 8-storey, 4-star hotel of modernist design with a good range of rooms – suites, semi-suites & standards, all with AC, satellite TV, minibar & bath. Rates inc b/fast. **$$$$–$$$$$**

🏠 **Marina** (33 rooms) Selim Khimshiashvili 10; ☎ 24 4400; m 599 136565; e hotelmarina@ marigroup.ge; www.marigroup.ge. South of the city centre on the New Boulevard (hidden behind a Bank of Georgia branch) but close to the beach, this is part of a complex (built in 2006) that also includes a Mexican restaurant, cafés, tennis courts, fitness club & swimming pool. All rooms come with cable TV, internet, AC & balcony. **$$$**

Astoria (10 rooms) Selim Khimshiashvili 41; 📞23 2066; m 579 273739; e hotel_astoria@mail. ru. Also south of the centre, has 8 dbls, a 4-bed room, & a luxe room, all with AC, cable TV & fridge; internet access is available. **$$–$$$**

Guesthouses

Gulnasi's Guesthouse (20 rooms) Lermontov 24A; m 557 065859, 599 797224; e homestay@mail.ru. Through the gate under a 2-storey house, it's the house on the right of the yard at the back. The best budget option, with en-suite rooms for up to 6 plus camping space & use of a kitchen, with free tea, coffee & wine/chacha to taste. Tours, transfers & meals can be arranged. **$**

Lavro (8 rooms) Pushkin 29; m 558 551453. Primitive but cheap, this guesthouse has rooms for 2 or 3 people. **$–$$**

Hostel

Batumi Surf Hostel (2 dorms & 3 dbls) Melashvili 33/35; m 599 104094; e batumisurf@gmail.com; www.facebook.com/batumisurf. This welcoming ground-floor hostel opening onto a courtyard (rather than the adapted apts that often pass themselves off as hostels) has rooms for 5, 7 or 8, plus two 4-bed rooms that can serve as private dbls; excellent English. **$$**

✕ WHERE TO EAT AND DRINK   *Map, page 248*

There are relatively few good restaurants in Batumi, although you'll see signs with pictures of khachapuri outside cafés serving the cholesterol-laden Adjaran version of this snack. Other local snacks include *borano* (a fried cheese), *sinori* (a dough coil filled with curd and garlic), and honey-soaked *baklava* as a dessert. For a special occasion or a splurge, the **Veronica Restaurant** at the Sheraton Hotel is worth considering, as is the **Winter Garden Café** at the Intourist Palace. More humbly, there are several cheap and characterful **Turkish lokantas** along Khulo and Kutaisi, near the mosque – most of these serve the standard Turkish cheese-and-olives breakfast and Turkish *çay* (no alcohol, as a rule). There are plenty of cheap **cafés** around the market and in the bus station, some serving the Turkish version of pizza and strong coffee made the Turkish way in a bed of hot sand.

Restaurants

✕ **Munich** Kutaisi 8; 📞22 7284; ⏱ 09.00–01.00 daily. Occupying a whole red-brick block (between Zhordania & Kostava), this is a lively place serving German-style sausages, pork, schnitzel & beer, & also fish. Service varies, & it's not particularly cheap. **$$$**

✕ **San Remo** Rustaveli 34; m 790 505270; ⏱ 11.00–02.00 daily. On a glass-floored pier south of the centre, this is a great place for evening drinks; it's also a slightly pricey fish restaurant. **$$$**

✕ **Porto Franco** K Gamsakhurdia 40; 📞27 6222; ⏱ 09.00–22.00 daily. Excellent restaurant serving Georgian food such as (Adjaran) khachapuri & khinkali in a very slick setting with an open kitchen. **$$–$$$**

✕ **Bereg Café** Gogebashvili 9; 📞27 1549, 23 1271; ⏱ 08.00–02.00 daily. Pavilion-style fish restaurant with terraces overlooking the entrance to the harbour; very popular for drinks but the food & service are less enticing (no toilet). **$$**

✕ **Dzveli Gemi** (Old Ship) Seaside Park; m 599 417758, 558 323787; e img333@mail.ru; ⏱ noon–midnight daily. In a (new) wooden galleon on the Boulevard, serving Georgian food. **$$**

✕ **Espresso Bar Sinatra** Dumbadze 12; m 557 566050; ⏱ 08.00–01.00 daily. A great place for b/fast (with omelettes or pancakes) & above all good coffee in many forms (from GEL2.50 for a takeaway espresso), as well as sandwiches, pasta & other light meals. **$$**

✕ **Kafé Bar Maspindzelo** Melashvili 33; m 593 789235; ⏱ 09.00–02.00 daily. Named after a dish of ground fried meat with sour cream, they also serve good fish; like **Mamapapuri** (m 598 092906; **$$**) immediately north & **Batumi Pizza** (m 599 50 23 86; www.batumi-pizza.tk; **$$**) immediately south it's next to the Batumi Surf Hostel & accustomed to foreigners. **$$**

✕ **Tower Restaurant & Brewery** Khimshiashvili 9/11; m 558 177676; ⏱ 10.00–01.00 daily. To the south on the New Boulevard, a surprisingly small tower (it's still worth climbing the spiral stairs) rises from the terrace over the glass-sided little brewery; unexpectedly, it produces a good dark beer as well as pale ones, & German-style food. $$

✗ **Princess Café** M Abashidze 45; ☎ 27 3733. A fairly basic place selling standard Georgian fare. $

✗ **Sevan** Zhordania 20; ☎ 21 3005; m 568 763667, 551 810310; ⏰ 10.00–23.00 daily. A simple Armenian restaurant in a plain room (with Wi-Fi). Armenians constitute 7.5% of the population of Batumi but are far less gastronomically visible than the Muslim/Turkish community. $

✗ **Zaqara** Vazha-Pshavelas/Pushkin; ⏰ 10.00–midnight daily. A busy & smoky local restaurant with good khinkhali & draught beer. $

Turkish lokantas

✗ **Arhavi** Khulo 2; m 577 585385; ⏰ 10.00–01.00 daily. A very clean & efficient cafeteria-style place, with menu & prices displayed above the counter. Wi-Fi. $

✗ **Istanbul Fish Restaurant** Kutaisi 36; ☎ 27 0688; ⏰ until late daily. On a row of good restaurants, this one obviously more fish-oriented. $

✗ **Mevlana** Khulo 3; m 577 535369; http:// mevlanabatumi.com; ⏰ until late daily. Spick & span cafeteria-style place, immediately north of Antalya Fast Food. $

✗ **Sofra Lokantası** Kutaisi 27; ⏰ until late daily. One of the better lokantas on this street. $

Cafés

✗ **Literaturuli** K Gamsakhurdia 18; ☎ 27 2013; ⏰ 10.00–23.00 daily. For American- or Italian-style coffee, cakes & savouries in a bookish setting (some English titles for sale), this is expensive but good. $$

✗ **Boulangerie** M Abashidze 11. Wonderful cakes, pastries & real coffee; nice terrace but awful service. $

☕ **Café Batumi** M Abashidze 39; ☎ 27 7766; ⏰ 10.00–00.30 daily. Also known as Privet iz Batuma, a good, relatively pricey café with nice historic photos of the city. $

☕ **Café Saamo** M Abashidze 37. Opposite the Batumi, brightly lit & less interesting, but with decent coffee, beer & snacks. $

Bars

🍷 **Bar 32** Melashvili 32; m 557 945160, 598 901758; ⏰ 15.00–03.00 daily. A nice cellar bar opposite the Batumi Surf Hostel. $

🍷 **Prague Pub** Marjanishvili 8; ☎ 27 4415; m 558 286060; ⏰ 11.00–late daily. Near the Art Museum, a cheery place with outside seating, Wi-Fi, & karaoke on Fri & Sat nights. $

🍷 **Temelas Dukani** Baratashvili 43; m 599 640027; ⏰ 10.00–02.00 daily. Wine is produced in Adjara, but in this pleasant wine cellar you'll mainly be drinking Kakheti's finest. $

ENTERTAINMENT Occasionally there's something worthwhile on at the **State Theatre** [248 B2] (*Rustaveli 1*; ☎ *27 4280; www.batumitheatre.ge*) or the **Summer Theatre** [248 B3] on the boulevard west from Tavdedebuli, and the **Puppet and Youth Theatre** [248 C4] at Mehmet Abashidze 49 (☎ *27 0593*) is still active. There are two cinemas, the new **Cinema 9D** [248 C3] (*Gorgasali 2 at Tavdedebuli*; m *555 560179*), and the **Cinema Apollo** [248 C2] (*M Abashidze 17*; ☎ *22 7227*).

OTHER PRACTICALITIES
Currency exchange   It's easy to exchange money in Batumi; there are exchange counters everywhere, even folding tables on the pavement around the market and Tbilisis Moedani, at the top of Chavchavadze and also at the bus station and the Hopa Bazaar. In addition to the standard dollars, euros and roubles, some of them will also exchange pounds sterling, though at an awful rate. There are **ATMs** across the town, with many on Konstantin Gamsakhurdia and Chavchavadze.

Consulates

🅔 **Armenia** [248 E2] Gogebashvili 32; ☎ 21 6302; http://batumi.mfa.am/en
🅔 **Azerbaijan** [248 B3] Dumbadze 14; ☎ 27 6700; e huseyn_n_najafov@yahoo.com
🅔 **Iran** [248 B3] Dumbadze 16; ☎ 27 7200/2

🅔 **Turkey** [248 C2] Mehmet Abashidze 8; ☎ 27 4789/90; e consulate.batumi@mfa.gov.tr; ⏰ Mon–Fri 09.30–13.00 & 14.00–18.00
🅔 **Ukraine** [248 C4] Melikishvili 71; ☎ 23 1600

Communications The **post office** is at Chavchavadze 90 at Lermontov. There are a few **internet** places on Zviad and Konstantin Gamsakhurdia and Chavchavadze. UPS is at Tavdedebuli 36 (☏ 27 7358; ⊕ 10.00–18.00 Mon–Fri, 10.00–14.00 Sat), TNT at Gorgiladze 40 (☏ 22 3275; ⊕ 10.00–19.00 Mon–Fri, 10.00–13.00 Sat) and DHL at 26 Maisi 44 (☏ 27 4608; ⊕ 09.30–18.30 Mon–Fri, 10.00–14.00 Sat).

Shopping There's a good **food market** to the east along Tsereteli and beyond the bus station. Goodwill (www.goodwill.ge) is a large 24-hour **supermarket** at Chavchavadze 3 [248 E2]; Nugeshi is a smaller supermarket on the north side of Tbilisi Moedani [248 E3] and the north end of Marjanishvili [248 C3]. There are also some decent **wine shops**: Daniela's House of Wine at Zviad Gamsakhurdia 43 [248 E2], and Khareba Winery on Konstantin Gamsakhurdia at Melashvili [248 C2]. There are bike sales/repair shops at Pushkin 59 and Pushkin 61.

A TOUR OF BATUMI If you leave the bus station and cross Tsereteli and the railway, you'll reach Gogebashvili, the main road along the harbour front. To the right is the modernist **church of Sts Peter and Paul** [248 F2], opened in 2000 and easily the most active Roman Catholic church in Georgia, with Sunday Mass at 10.00 in English, 11.30 in Georgian, 14.00 in Armenian and 17.00 in Latin, and also services at 09.00 in Georgian (except Sun). Confusingly, you head due north from the bus station to the sea, and the town lies to the west on a headland projecting into the Black Sea. Turning to the left/west, opposite the north end of Chavchavadze you'll find the terminal of the new Doppelmayr **gondola** [248 E2] (⊕ 11.00–midnight; GEL5 return), which takes 10 minutes to climb to a 257m hilltop southeast of the city, where there's a café-bar (serving good pastries, cakes and real coffee in the morning, then shashlik, pizza and other meals); there's nothing else to do but enjoy the view from the terrace (with telescopes).

Continuing along the coast, you'll pass the port headquarters on your left and the ferry terminal on the right, always crowded with anglers. This is the start of the seafront promenade to the west and then south. The new **Miracle Park** [248 B1] occupies the headland at the entry to the harbour, dotted with various exotic mismatched towers, all elaborately illuminated at night; you'll pass first the **Chacha Tower** [248 C1] on your left, a 25m-high clocktower that marks 19.00 each evening by spouting chacha from its fountains for 10 minutes. Next is the **Ferris wheel** [248 C1], 55m high and taking 10 minutes for each revolution; going for a spin (⊕ 10.00–20.00 daily; GEL3) is an enjoyable and convenient way to get an overview of the city. To the right by the water is the **Ali and Nino statue** [248 C1], named after the romantic novel by Kurban Said (page 298), comprising two human forms that move together and become one. Beyond the 21m-high lighthouse, built in 1882, is the **Alphabet Tower** [248 B1], a 130m-high double helix bearing the Georgian alphabet with a globe and viewing platform at the top. To the south of the park are the Radisson Blu hotel (and the future Kempinski) and another tower with, bizarrely, another Ferris wheel set into its side; this was built to house a Technical University but is to be sold and converted to a hotel.

Running south from here for 7km is one of the city's finest features, the **Seaside Park** that stretches along the shore; laid out from 1881 by German and French gardeners (plus a Georgian who'd worked at Kew), it's now dotted with funfairs, cafés and restaurants, as well as toilets and bike rental stations; the beach, unfortunately, is stony, but still popular. Looking south along the boulevard the skyline is dominated by the rocket-like, rather Stalinist-looking tower of the Sheraton Hotel, with the twin towers of the Hilton beyond and then the apartment blocks of the New Boulevard.

Running east to the tourist information kiosk on Ninoshvili is a series of dancing fountains; continuing inland just north of the Intourist, on Konstantin Gamsakhurdia (formerly Lenina), you'll cross Rustaveli to the square behind the theatre, with a large statue of Ilia Chavchavadze to the left (where there was previously a statue of Lenin) and then the plaza of Evropas Moedani (Europe Square) on the right, lined with pastiche buildings and a new astronomic clock. It's named after the Association of European Regions, the only international body to treat Abashidze's Adjara as a real entity, earning his eternal gratitude. At the centre of Evropas Moedani stands an enormously tall plinth with a **statue of Medea** [248 C3] holding a glistening Golden Fleece, a controversially expensive monument by Davit Khmaladze that was unveiled by Mikheil Saakashvili in 2007. Continuing inland, the tree-lined Konstantin Gamsakhurdia also hosts some of the city's more expensive shops, and the **Armenian church** [248 D3] at No 25, built in the 1880s; it continues through the Old Town to Tbilisis Moedani, the square which serves as the terminal for most of the city's marshrutkas. Beyond this is the central **market** [248 E3], heaving with people and more like a Turkish bazaar than anything Soviet.

If you head north on Parnavaz Mepe from Konstantin Gamsakhurdia you'll enter the (relatively) Old Town, a tightly packed area of Neoclassical houses, with balconies, columns and pediments, built about a century ago, and pass the newly restored **Church of St Nikoloz** [248 D2], built in 1865. Opposite this is the **Piazza** [248 D2], the only really outrageously kitsch development to be shoehorned into the Old Town (the others are safely out of the way on the New Boulevard); modelled on Venice's Piazza San Marco, it's ringed by expensive shops and restaurants and an Irish pub, and the campanile houses a luxury hotel. Then you'll see the **Orta Jame mosque** [248 D2] to the right at Chkalov 6, just before reaching the harbour front again. Built in 1866, it's not particularly ancient and much like any small-town Turkish Mosque, but it's more unusual in Georgia.

To the south of Tbilisis Moedani is the former **Roman Catholic church** [248 D4]. Built at the start of the 20th century in a sort of Baltic-Gothic style, with Arts and Crafts-like murals and stained glass, it's now the busy Orthodox cathedral, although it remains largely unchanged. The church is brightly lit at night. Just beyond it is the former railway station, now the **TBC Bank and Gallery** [248 D4], with occasional exhibitions. Turning right/west here you'll come in three short blocks to the **synagogue** [248 C4] at Vazha-Pshavelas 33, opened in 1904 and reopened in 1998 after a thorough refurbishment; on the right-hand side of the street opposite, Chincharadze, at No 4, is the **State Museum of Adjara** [248 C4] (✆27 1175; ⊕ 10.00–17.00 daily). This is a very old-fashioned (and easily missable) collection of stuffed wildlife (without scientific names), archaeological relics, tools, Arab metalwork and other odds and ends. Upstairs are some weapons, a display on the tea industry (including relics of the Chinese merchant Lan Chun-Chao who established the first plantations in Adjara), and photographs of Batumi's development in the 19th and 20th centuries; there are also some Byron-esque paintings of battling Turks. In the yard, there's a whale's skeleton and a few medical monstrosities, as well as the toilet. Staff here used to hold the key to the two-room Stalin Museum, in the little white wooden house at Pushkin 19 where he stayed for a couple of months in 1901–02, but this is currently closed; it took a reverential viewpoint now out of fashion in the rest of the world, with paintings and photos depicting him as the idealistic, youthful union organiser, rather than the paranoid dictator he later became.

Immediately to the west, Vazha-Pshavelas crosses Gorgiladze (formerly Gorki, then ERA kucha or Association of European Regions Street); across it to the right is the **Art Museum** [248 C4] at Gorgiladze 8 (✆ *27 3894;* ☉ *11.00–18.00 except Mon; GEL2*), which opened only in 1998, in a lovely building built in the 1930s to house a Museum of Communism. The upstairs gallery displays the older paintings, including pieces by Akhvlediani, Gudiashvili, Kakabadze and Pirosmani (a cow being milked, instantly recognisable), as well as local prodigy Rusudan Petviashvili; downstairs are pieces by more contemporary painters. Diagonally opposite it, facing Roses Square, is the **City Hall** [248 C4], built around the start of the 20th century.

Gorgiladze continues south to Khimshiashvili and the new promenade, but a block to the right, by a statue of a female aviator flying a one-winged toy plane with a child, is the main entrance to **6 May Park** [248 B4] (*www. parkbatumi.ge*), surrounding a large lake; the oligarch Bidzina Ivanishvili paid for its refurbishment, with very funky low-level lighting, and also for a high-tech rebuild of the dolphinarium at its far end. There's a small Zoo Corner (☉ *closed Sun & Mon; free*) on the inland side, with primates, birds, marsupials and hoofed animals. The Russian poet Sergei Esenin lived at Melikishvili 11 (formerly Engelska), on the northern side of the park, in 1924–25 between his fourth and fifth marriages (not to speak of his homosexual affairs); born in 1895, he was one of the most radical of the young poets at the time of the Revolution and an ardent supporter of the Bolsheviks, although he was refused party membership as he considered himself too much of an individualist. In 1922 he married the American dancer Isadora Duncan and set off to travel in Europe and America, but he suffered a nervous breakdown and declined into alcoholism, with hallucinations. He then married Galina Benislavskaya, travelled to Batumi and Baku, then in 1925 married Sofia Tolstoya, Leo Tolstoy's granddaughter, and on 28 December 1925, hanged himself in Leningrad, leaving a suicide poem written in his own blood. In Nice, in September 1927, Isadora was strangled instantly when her scarf caught in the wheel of her sports car.

In the southwestern corner of the park, the modern **dolphinarium** puts on a show (☉ *17.00 Tue–Fri, 14.00 & 17.00 Sat–Sun, more in season; GEL15*), and you can also swim with dolphins for 15 minutes (*ages 3–12 GEL80, 12–18 GEL100, 19+ GEL150; box office* ☉ *10.00–14.00 & 15.00–18.00 Tue–Sun*). Immediately south at Rustaveli 51, the **aquarium** (☉ *11.00–18.00 except Mon; GEL2*) stands on the campus of the State Maritime Academy and the Marine Ecology and Fisheries Research Institute; it's worth a visit, although many of the fish are in fact from the tropics. Bus 1/1A and marshrutkas 116, 120 and 155 come this way. South of the Maritime Academy the road turns 90° left and right, at the start of a new seaside boulevard, Sherif Khimshiashvili (not to be confused with Selim Khimshiashvili, running east from 26 May Park), where the city has built the fabulous 'Splashdance' animated fountain and lightshow, installed at great expense by a French company to be the centrepiece of the new tourist zone, with cafés, discos, bowling, tennis courts, a casino and so on. There's a Dutch-themed restaurant, marked with a windmill, and the Tower Brewery (page 252). There's also a new Public Service Hall by Ardagari Lake and regional government offices have been moved here to open up space in the city centre for development.

Returning to the centre, a new **Archaeological Museum**, behind Soviet arches at Chavchavadze 77 [248 D4] (✆ *27 6564;* ☉ *10.00–18.00 daily; GEL2*) displays finds from Pichvnari, on the coast between Kobuleti and the Choloki River, where a joint Oxford University/Georgian team has been working since 1988. Meaning 'Place of the Pine Trees' in Georgian, Pichvnari is the site of a Greek trading settlement from the mid-5th century BC, on the site of an earlier Colchian settlement; there are late Bronze Age, early Iron Age, Classical and

Hellenistic levels over an area of 100ha. Visitors would be made welcome at the site but there's not a lot to see, as the digs are in sandy soil and quickly filled in. The museum has photos of the dig, Stone Age pottery, Greek- and Roman-era articles including drinking bowls and medieval Arabic coins, and finds from graves at Gonio (see below); upstairs a large gallery is used for temporary shows.

One of Batumi's most interesting attractions is in fact 9km to the north: the **Botanic Gardens** at Green Cape (Mtsvane Kontskhi), reached by bus 15 (*GEL0.80*) or minibus 31 (*GEL2*) from Parnavaz Mepe, which turn off along the old road before the tunnel. Get off at the hairpin at km28/93, go through the main gate and then right (the green gate to the left leads to the Agricultural Institute, which has beautifully labelled plants but they're mainly standard herbs and palms, bamboos and so on. Fork left to the gate and *kassa* (ticket office) (☏ *27 0033; www.bbg.ge*; ⏰ *10.00–21.00; GEL8*), and go on to the administration building halfway down the hill. From here the main part of the garden is ahead to the north, with a rose garden, Australian, New Zealand, Himalayan, Mediterranean, East Asian, Mexican and North American sections, and at the far end a park. If you return and gradually go down to the south, through some big mature eucalyptus trees as well as citrus plantations, you'll cross above the railway tunnel to the Green Cape, with attractive viewpoints. You can leave by the Mtsvane Kontskhi gate from where marshrutka 101 (*GEL0.70*) leaves frequently, reaching the old road in 500m, just before its junction with the new highway from the tunnel. Guides are available, and there's an electric shuttle which will carry you from end to end of the garden for GEL6.

Founded in 1912, the gardens cover 113ha with over 5,000 species of plants (and 1,200 varieties of rose) from around the world, as well as 40,000 specimens in a herbarium. As well as Caucasian flora, there are species from moist subtropical climes around the world, including Japan and the Himalayas. It's a great spot for a picnic in wonderfully lush surroundings, and the presence of the sea just below the trees always adds an extra frisson.

TO GONIO AND THE TURKISH BORDER

Gonio Turkish trucks and businessmen in black Mercedes race up and down the main road south from Batumi to the Turkish border; this starts by turning right off the road east to Akhaltsikhe at km107/14, at the entry to the village of Angisa. At km109 there's a turning to Batumi's airport, 200m to the west, before the road crosses the Chorokh River at about km110. At exactly km115/6 you'll find the gate to the fortress of Gonio on the left, with a mini-fort aptly placed in a playground across the road. Founded in the 3rd century BC as Apsaros (after the son of King Aeetes killed by Jason), a Roman fort built in the 1st century AD was home to five cohorts, or 1,200–1,500 men, until it was abandoned in the 4th century. What is seen now is the outer wall of the Byzantine (from the AD540s) and Ottoman (after 1548) fort of Asparunt; it's a square of about 200m, with oranges, plums, strawberries and palms being grown inside, and mature eucalyptus trees outside, against a backdrop that's reminiscent of the gentler parts of the Nepalese foothills, with luxuriant vegetation.

There's a ticket kiosk (⏰ *10.00–18.00 Tue–Sun; GEL3, audio guide GEL5*) and toilets inside the gate, from where a paved path leads to the centre, where there's a museum (with poor English captions) and souvenir shop. The earliest finds are from the 8th century BC, and you'll also see sling/catapult stones, amphorae and coins, and photos of the wonderful 2nd-century AD Colchian goldsmithery of the Gonio Treasury, found in 1974. Nearby are the remains of Roman baths and barracks (with underfloor heating) and perhaps a temple; in the southwest corner are the remains of Roman handmills and a kiln. Excavations by the south gate have revealed lots of Roman, Byzantine and Ottoman pipework. Outside the south wall a 5th-century burial site has been found, as well as a theatre and hippodrome from the 1st–3rd centuries. The grave of St Matthew the Apostle (Matthew Levi) is said to be by the cross to the left of the museum; he was one of 70 Minor Apostles who replaced Judas, and came to Georgia with St Andrew the First-Called and Simon the Zealot. It's possible to climb up onto the 5m-high walls behind the ticket office and walk around the square, with 18 of the original 22 towers surviving.

There's a beach at Gonio but it's not that attractive – a bit of pebbly wasteland with wrecked Soviet-period bunkers, grazing cows and frogs splashing about in ponds – and it's known for its Uzbek prostitutes. You're better off continuing south to Kvariati if you're after sun and sand.

Getting there and away **Marshrutkas** charge GEL1 to Gonio or to the Turkish border at Sarpi, 19km south of Batumi, and bus 16 costs GEL0.80. A **taxi** to the border shouldn't charge more than GEL10, and coming from the border you may be able to share. It's a very busy route, and you'll be accosted by drivers yelling '*Sarpi Sarpi Sarpi*' as you arrive at Batumi's bus or train station. Minibus 142 (often with *Sarpi* on a sign in Latin script) runs from Tbilisis Moedani, in the centre of town, and along Chavchavadze; you should be across the border in Hopa within a couple of hours, and in Trabzon in another 3 hours.

⌂ *Where to stay and eat*

⌂ **Guesthouse Gonio** (7 rooms) m 899 577360. 1.5km south of the fortress & 5mins from the beach, with a swimming pool & summer café. **$$$**
⌂ **Hotel Eva** (16 rooms) ☎ 52 4040; m 877 456666, 593 353727. A new hotel with a restaurant & bar, 1km from the sea at the south end of Gonio. All rooms come with TV, minibar & AC. **$$$**

⌂ **Hotel Magnolia** (19 rooms & suites); m 574 482181; e info@hotelmagnoliagonio. com. More peach-coloured than magnolia, this new place on the main road, not far south of the fortress, has simple rooms with satellite TV, minibar & bath; AC in the suites. **$$$**

Kvariati

To the south of Gonio (14km from Batumi) is Kvariati, also being developed for tourism, with a some spacious new beachfront hotels. At the moment it's still a very pleasant resort for those looking for rest and contact with nature, and better for swimming than Batumi; in addition to the buses to Sarpi, marshrutka 33 comes here.

⌂ *Where to stay*

⌂ **Egrisi** (21 rooms) m 790 335000, 598 657545; www.hotelegrisi.com. A large, new, 4-storey place with excellent service, & a couple of independent restaurants nearby. **$$$$**

⌂ **Hotel Martini** (12 rooms) m 577 556464; www.martini.ge. With 4 sgls & 6 dbls, & a cottage with 2 trpl bedrooms. All rooms are en suite with satellite TV, fridge & balcony. Large swimming pool, billiards, restaurant & bar. **$$$**

Sarpi

The road finally runs below a cliff to reach the Turkish border at Sarpi (km0/119), crammed into a tiny space below hills before the Customs Terminal, a funky jigsaw tower built in 2011 by Jürgen Mayer H, the German architect responsible for the new look of Mestia in Svaneti. There is a **beach**, where the water is cleaner than in Batumi. Right behind the gate of the customs area is a **tourist information** kiosk (m *577 909093*), with helpful English-speaking staff who can book beds in Sarpi, Kvariati or Gonio, as well as Batumi. A bed in a private house in Sarpi will cost US$10–15 in August or US$5–10 at other times; most of the houses on the road up to the right from the border crossing rent rooms. A kiosk sells tickets for bus 16 to Batumi, or you can just jump on a marshrutka. Sarpi holds the **Kolkhoba Festival** on 20 August (in theory – check the date), a Laz festival based on the legend of the Golden Fleece that was revived in 1978.

INLAND FROM BATUMI The humid mountains immediately east of Batumi protect tertiary relict forests with some of the highest levels of endemicity in Georgia. Rare species include lynx, golden eagle, black vulture, falcon, Caspian snowcock, great rosefinch and Caucasian salamander. In addition the mountain villages inland from Batumi are home to the bulk of Adjara's Muslims.

Mount Mtirala ('Weeping'; 1,336m) is the rainiest place in Europe, with 4.1m of precipitation per year. The mountains of the Lesser Caucasus, with its ravines and thick forests, block the passage of clouds from the sea and make this the greenest corner of Georgia. It would be worth protecting as a national park anyway, but there's the added interest of the autumn migration of up to 280,000 raptors a day at a bottleneck on the coastal flyway. This is dominated by European honey-buzzards and steppe buzzards (over half a million each), but you may also see black kite, Montagu's harrier and various eagles. In September and October the **Batumi Raptor Count** (*www.batumiraptorcount.org*) is becoming a well-known attraction, countering the local tendency to shoot birds. Organised by Bird Conservation Georgia (*Sabuko, Melashvili 5, 6010 Batumi;* ✆ *24 1777;* m *558 217706; www.birdlife.ge*), their main counting posts are in the villages of Sakhalvasho and Shuamta, where they have set up guesthouses (m *599 216 580;* e *visit@batumiraptorcount.org; €140 for 5 nights all-inclusive*).

To reach Sakhalvasho, take the main road north from Batumi and turn right on the first road after the tunnel, then take the gravel road to the right below the school to a house marked with the BRC logo (or ask for Ruslan's house, 'Ruslanis sachli'). The nearest hotel is the Oasis in Chakvi (page 246); you can buy snacks and drinks in the village. In Shaumta (7km inland), the Adjaran Department of Tourism has constructed a viewing platform with stunning 360° views; it's a steep walk from the car park, but there's a shelter and toilet.

Access to the 15,806ha **Mtirala National Park** (*http://apa.gov.ge*) is to the east from Chakvi; there's a visitor centre at the park headquarters just east from km 87/32, at Chavchavadze 13 (m *577 101889;* e *mtiralapa@yahoo.com, nino_khakhubia@yahoo.com*). Inland from Chakvi the park has another visitor centre in Chakvistavi; there's also a small hostel, campsite and a family-run restaurant (m *593 967495*). Marshrutkas from Batumi (every 30mins) run only as far as Khala. Guesthouses in Chakvistavi are run by Gela Kontselidze (m *557 651764*) and Guram Kontselidze (m *558 466828*). Enthusiastic local rangers can lead you on a 3-hour loop trail (also a 2-hour hike to a 12m-high waterfall), and there's a longer circuit (15km) to the Tsivtskaro shelter, that can be tackled with mountain bikes.

To the north is the **Kintrishi Reserve** (18,893ha), reached by a long drive inland from Kobuleti. The visitor centre is at Tskhemvani, 24km east (marshrutkas run only as far as Chakhati), and the road continues through the Kintrishi River Gorge, with a dozen wonderful old bridges attributed (as always) to Queen Tamar, to Khino, where there's a ruined cathedral. It also lies on a new east–west horseback itinerary through the mountains.

To the south of Mtirala the road from Batumi to Akhaltsikhe follows the Adjariskhali River inland to the Goderji Pass (2,025m), which can be closed by snow any time between October and May, forcing a lengthy detour via Kutaisi. This is a luxuriantly fertile region, with a profusion of vines, tangerines and watermelons, as well as magnolia, oleander, eucalyptus and cypress trees. Along the Adjariskhali there are also ten well-preserved Turkish bridges, built in the 10th to 12th centuries, spanning side-streams with surprisingly slender stone spans.

South of Batumi airport, the road heads inland up the valley of the Chorokh River (flowing out of Turkey) then forks left/east at Adjariskhali (km15); to the south on the border is the new **Machakhela National Park**, with little infrastructure as yet. At km16, the **Adjarian Wine House** (*www.awh.ge*) is an attractive new winery with a small vineyard of local grape varieties such as Chkhaveri; they also make chacha and serve food. Continuing up the lovely wooded valley, at km24/135 the little Restaurant Chadrebi serves traditional Adjaran dishes. In **Mkhunseti** (km28) a sign in English leads left up a bad track to a museum in a modern barn to the right and then left to a dramatic waterfall (behind a café-restaurant with a tank to keep the trout fresh). Across the main road and down some steps is **Tamar's Bridge**, a simple 19.5m span of volcanic stone without parapets.

At **Keda**, about 42km from Batumi, there's a seasonal tourist office and various ruined fortresses in the hills around; the area is known for its pink tomatoes and wines from Tsolikauri and Chkhaveri grapes. About 5km on up the valley is **Vaio**, known for its knitting and wicker baskets, as well as wine and chacha; there is a guesthouse here and nearby at Gobroneti (see below). There are also **mineral springs** (good for intestinal conditions) in this area at Kokotauri and Gundauri.

At Dandalo, there's another famous bridge and just above to the north is the 11–12th-century **Takidzeebi (or Otolta) Fortress**, with ruined walls (18m by 52m) and a tower; from here a dead-end road leads north up the Chvanistskali Valley. It's not far up the main valley to **Shuakhevi**, a small spa where there's another seasonal tourist information centre; there are guesthouses nearby in Nigazeuli, 6km north of the road and 78km from Batumi (see below). Just beyond, at Zamleti, a minor road leads southeast up the Skhalta Valley to the **ancient churches** of Kinchauri, Skhakta, Vemebi and Kalota. It's not much further to **Khulo**, centre of an area known for its 19th-century wooden mosques, *chiponi* bagpipes and plaited cheese; there's a small museum and a seasonal tourist information centre. This is as far as marshrutkas come, apart from a summer-only service over the Goderji Pass to Akhaltsikhe.

Near the pass at 2,635m is **Khikhani Fortress**, with the ruins of 11th-century walls, towers and a church. Traces of fossilised trees can be found near the pass; Goderji is also the newest of Georgia's ski resorts (still under construction), with the country's longest ski trail.

🏠 Where to stay and eat

Gobroneti
🏠 **Guesthouse Tskarostvali** m 599 944662. Owned by Amiran Bolkvadze. **$**
🏠 **Guesthouse Zebo** m 593 933403. Owned by Zebur Bolkvadze. **$**

Nigazeuli
Rooms start at GEL15–25 without meals or GEL35–50 with 3 meals (**$**).

🏠 **Avto** m 577 203468
🏠 **Imedi** m 555 12819
🏠 **Kvemourebi** m 577 290848
🏠 **Mtsvane Sakhli Guest** m 558 793307

Vaio
🏠 **Lado Shavishvili** m 599 783659 **$**

10

Kakheti კახეთი

The easy-going, wine-growing province of Kakheti, to the east of Tbilisi, is justifiably popular for easy excursions of a couple of days (or even day trips from the capital), but it also gives access to Davit-Gareja and Tusheti, much harder trips along very rugged roads, but well worthwhile if you have the time. The *rtveli* or grape harvest in September and October is a fine excuse for a visit.

EASTWARDS FROM TBILISI

The main road from Tbilisi runs to the south side of the Gombori Mountains, around their eastern end and then back to the northwest to reach Telavi, the capital of Kakheti; almost all marshrutkas and tour buses take this route, but it is also possible to cut directly across the 1,650m Gombori Pass by a quiet, winding road that has seen considerable improvement in recent years. This is a glorious route with expansive views towards Tbilisi that you are only likely to experience if you drive yourself or charter a taxi. However, some shared taxis between Telavi and Tbilisi also go this way in preference to the longer route via Gurdjaani.

In either case, you'll head out of Tbilisi on the airport road, past the Isani and Samgori metro stations (terminals for marshrutkas to Kakheti – see page 89) with the white tower blocks of Varketili along the ridge to the left. There's some striking Saakashvili-era modern architecture along this road: first the green-glass Interior Ministry (security police) headquarters (by the Italian architect Michele de Lucchi, 2009) to the left/north, then the offices of his party, the UNM, to the right, and the treasury of the National Bank of Georgia to the left. After the flyover junction to the airport, with its needle-like monument, the six-lane dual-carriageway becomes a four-lane highway, passing the huge Lilos Bazroba or open-air flea market to the left (page 114), and the Castel brewery to the right, before leaving the city at about km21/139, by the intersection with the city's eastern bypass; from here it's single carriageway, with overtaking lanes up some hills. From km23, it's 22km north to Martkopi, 5km northwest of which, on Mount Ialno, is the **Monastery of St Anton**, who spent his last 15 years as a hermit in a tower that still stands to the east; the church, founded in the 6th century, was rebuilt at the end of the 17th century (the belfry was built in 1629). At the top of a hill at km27 on the main A302, the direct route to Telavi via the Gombori Pass turns left/north, passing through **Ujarma**, on the Iori River 45km from Tbilisi, where you can see an old stone church, the remains of a two-storey palace and fortifications with nine square towers (at km47.5). This was the residence of King Vakhtang Gorgasali, who died here in AD502; destroyed in the 10th century by the Arabs, the fortifications were restored in the 12th century. The road to Shuamta and Telavi turns right in Otaraani, but if you continue up the left/east bank of the Iori to km56 it's possible to hike up to the 10th-century castle of **Bochorma**, with its six-apse domed church built in the 7th century.

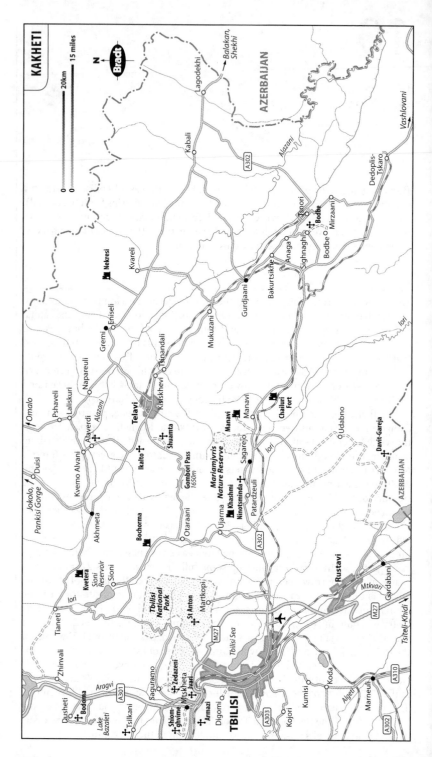

KAKHETI

The main road soon descends from the Samgori steppe to cross the Iori and enter Kakheti at km35/125; you'll see the ruins of the 6th–7th-century fort of **Khashmi** to the north from a viaduct, and a few oil wells, and pass south of the village of **Patardzeuli**, with the new KTW winery's tasting rooms at km39, before, at km45.3, the old road turns left to run through Ninotsminda and Sagarejo. Buses to Telavi use the bypass to the south, stopping for passengers only at the roundabout at its far end; if you want to visit Ninotsminda you should take one of the local marshrutkas to Sagarejo, leaving from immediately outside the Samgori station.

There are no house numbers or street signs, so look out for small signs with a monastery symbol leading up to the solid tower of Ninotsminda, to the left of the old road around 2km from the junction, and 3km west of the centre of Sagarejo. The site of **Ninotsminda Church** has been used for Christian worship since the 5th century, and the present cathedral was built in AD575. It was largely ruined by earthquakes in 1824 and 1848, but is nevertheless profoundly impressive, the earliest large cruciform church to survive (anticipating the Jvari Church of Mtskheta). It has a tetraconch ground plan with corner niches, and because the church is half ruined this is a good place to study the detailed arrangements. In the eastern apse are the remains of a 16th-century fresco of the Virgin and Child, and the western end of the church has recently been converted into a chapel. The bell-tower was built in the mid 16th century by Levan I; it shows strong Safavid-Persian influence, although it seems oddly primitive and almost African in feel. Around these are well-preserved defensive walls built in the 16th and 17th centuries.

Continuing across the Tvaltkhevi Bridge into Sagarejo, a roundabout marks the town centre, with a market just north; following the main road east, you'll fork right after 5 minutes and go downhill for almost 20 minutes to reach the roundabout at the end of the bypass (km50/110), where you can catch a bus onwards towards Telavi (marshrutkas for Tbilisi via Ninotsminda wait here too). Halfway down the hill you'll pass a small and very attractive old basilica.

EASTWARDS FROM SAGAREJO
Continuing eastwards, a left-turn at km51.5 gives access to the **Mariamjvris Nature Reserve**, one of the country's older reserves, protecting endemic pines in 1,040ha of the Gombori Mountains, and to the 10th–11th-century **Manavi Fortress**, once the summer residence of the kings of Kakheti (known as 'Come and See Castle', as enemies always failed to take it). This is visible from km58 on the main road, high on a hill to the left/north, with the Church of Giorgi-tsminda (Saint George) below it. At km64.5 you can go up to the restored 16th-century **Chailuri Fort** just to the right; the walls are in good shape but there's nothing to see inside. The Hotel Ambasadori Kachreti is a luxury hotel and golf resort in the middle of nowhere at about km84 (m *591 225004; http://kachreti. ambasadori.ge*).

Eventually the main road climbs out of the Iori Valley, and then from km94/66 drops steeply through woods into the Alazani Valley, past the junction to Sighnaghi (page 280) at km 94.5, the Nakeduli Restaurant (km99.5), and Vardiskheli (Cool Water) at km101.5, where there's a fountain and stalls, before reaching a roundabout at Bakurtsikhe (km103/57, 1½ hours from Tbilisi). The name implies that there is a castle here, but it is in fact known for its *kurgan* or burial mound from the 3rd millienniun BC. In theory, the main road is the one to the right, towards Azerbaijan, but most traffic turns left towards Telavi, 45km northwest.

GURDJAANI This road passes through Bakurtsikhe and at km6/66 a road leads up to the west; turning right after 1.5km you'll come to the **Kvelatsminda Church**, the only ancient double-domed church in Georgia and perhaps Gurdjaani's main claim to fame. Built in the 8th century, it's a three-aisled stone basilica rather than a cruciform church, with two octagonal brick domes over the nave which are too small to dominate it. The church also has external galleries and lateral chapels, one of which projects to the northeast. Just west at km6.5, the main road passes a turning (signed in English) up to the west to the house-museum of the great actress Nato Vachnadze, opened in 1989 due to the efforts of her sons, the film directors Eldar and Giorgi Shengelaia.

At about km8/64, you'll reach the centre of Gurdjaani, a large town known as a spa and a centre of winemaking; there is not a lot to see, but it's a pleasant place with lots of trees lining the streets. The second roundabout (with bus stand) marks the centre of town, and immediately to the right is the Aktala *kurort* or **health resort** (*Tamar Mepe 9;* \ *353 22 3948;* m *599 231774;* **$$$$**), with mini-volcanoes belching forth healing mud. You can have treatment here for an hour, or have daily treatments for up to two weeks, except on Sundays; the mud is at its best in the mornings. Past this, the pedestrianised Rustaveli leads downhill to the former railway station.

Heading back towards Tbilisi, the **market** is to the left of the main road, more or less opposite the terminal of a disused cable-car that once led up to a cool hilltop park; the road signposted to Arashenda also leads into the foothills to the west, where there's plenty of space for wild camping. At km12 on the road to Telavi, in Chumlaki, a tiny old **chapel** stands on the right; there's no lock on the door, and inside it's very dark, totally blackened by smoke. There are no specific features of interest, but the place has an intriguingly pagan feel to it. At km18, just beyond the turning into the village of Velistsikhe, a road turns right to Kvareli (page 277), 17km to the northeast. The Telavi road crosses the railway and enters Mukuzani, where there's a simple basilica to the left of the road.

🏠 Where to stay and eat

🏠 **Wine House** (5 rooms) Rustaveli 28; m 790 512244, 599 512244; www.winehousegurjaani.ge **$$$**

🏠 **Guesthouse Gurjaani** (4 rooms) Tabidze 19; m 599 567840 **$$**

🏠 **Juisher Mikeladze's Guesthouse** (5 rooms) Gonashvili 32; m 595 154780 **$$**

TSINANDALI There's a near-continuous string of villages, with vineyards behind them (and elaborate war memorials with images of Stalin), until km36.5, at the far end of Tsinandali, where you reach the entrance to the **Alexander Chavchavadze house-museum** (*www.tsinandali.com;* ⊕ *10.00–17.00 daily, to 19.00 in summer; park GEL2, park & museum GEL5*). You'll cross a typically communist irrigation channel, huge and out of place, before following a cypress-lined avenue to a handsome pair of wrought-iron gates and the ticket office. The house is set in an ornamental garden of 12ha with many fine, mature examples of rare trees, including umbrella pines, cedars, magnolia and lime trees, as well as bamboos and palms. To the right as you enter, the garden is relatively formal, leading to a big villa which was a government guesthouse, and is now a hotel (*21 rooms;* \ *322 25 3581–3;* m *570 701212;* e *nikamumlauri@yahoo.com;* **$$$$**). A Radisson Blu hotel is to open here by the end of 2016. There's more affordable accommodation in Tsinandali village (*Tsinandalis Edemi;* \ *350 23 5200;* m *599 260215;* **$$**), where they make good wine.

To the left the garden is slightly less formal, with a box maze; however, it's too densely planted with trees to be an 'English park', as claimed. Behind the house to the northeast are industrial buildings which house the famous **Tsinandali winery**, founded in 1884 by Alexander Chavchavadze's father. It can be visited by tour groups, who can taste the dry white wine, although not the 1814 vintage, which is the oldest in the collection.

The house itself is a relatively small and unpretentious two-storey manor house of local sandstone, built in the early 19th century by the poet Alexander Chavchavadze, leading spirit of the Romantic Movement in Georgia. Born in St Petersburg (where his father was Georgian ambassador) in 1786, he joined the Russian army and served against Napoleon and the Turks before settling in Georgia, marrying Salome Orbeliani, a member of one of Georgia's grandest families. This was a summer house, and his main residence was in Tbilisi; although he wrote poetry, Chavchavadze's main importance was as translator of the poetry of the French Romantics and as chief animator of the circle of writers and critics who created Georgian Romanticism. Many of the leading Russian Romantic writers also came to Tbilisi, usually with the army or government; these included Alexander Griboedov (1795–1829), who married Chavchavadze's daughter Nina when she was just 16. He was a notorious philanderer and is generally supposed to have seduced her (although the museum staff might disagree) and then been forced to marry her; almost at once he was sent on a diplomatic mission to Tehran which went tragically wrong when a mob stormed the Russian legation and killed all the Russians, brutally hacking Griboedov's head off. The teenage widow became a symbol of grief, and is portrayed as such on their shared tomb in Tbilisi's pantheon.

Chavchavadze himself died in 1846 in a bizarre accident in Tbilisi, when his cloak caught in the wheel of his carriage and he was thrown out, hitting his head on the ground. In 1854 the house was burnt by Chechen rebels, who kidnapped the Chavchavadze princesses and their children and servants and rode off into the Caucasus with them lashed across their saddles. Their leader Shamyl demanded the return of his son Djemmal-Eddin (or Jamal Al-Din), who had been handed over to the Russians as a hostage 15 years before, at the age of eight, and given a Russian education and then a commission in the army. Negotiations took nine months, but eventually the hostages were exchanged (together with 14,000 silver roubles for the rebels); alas, the last thing Djemmal-Eddin wanted or was suited to was a life in a rebel village in the Caucasus, and deprived of the glittering social life of the court he faded away and died within six months. Just one of the Chavchavadze children avoided capture by hiding in a hollow tree, which can still be seen beyond the maze. You'll be given a guided tour of the house, still with original furniture and lots of grand pianos, including the French one (with a folding keyboard) given as a wedding gift by Griboedov to Nina, supposedly the first piano in Georgia. There's also a reproduction of the Winterhalter portrait of Chavchavadze's wife Salome, and embroidery by their daughters. The former drawing room is now an exhibition hall (also used for concerts), after which you'll emerge into a new summer gallery over the wine cellar and toilets. There's a café (⏲ *until 18.00*) with a terrace on the side of the house near the ice-house.

KISISKHEVI Crossing the bridge (at km35) from Tsinandali, you'll have the Shumi winery on your left and the Marani winery to the right. Beyond them is Kisiskhevi, home to a church with a circular tower built of river stones.

🏠 Where to stay

🏠 **Schuchmann Château** (8 rooms)
m 790 557045, 577 508005; e i.datunashvili@schuchmann-wines.com; www.schuchmann-wines.com. Attractive to the upmarket wine enthusiast, this has 50 stainless-steel fermentation tanks, some 3,000-litre qvevri & a huge cellar

(inc a riddling rack for sparkling wines). You can take a 15–20min tour of the winery followed by a tasting (with bread, cheese & olives); or there's a good restaurant (⏲ *10.00–22.00 daily; $$$*). They also offer classes in baking and making churchkhela & chacha, & in Sep you can try barefoot grape-pressing. You can stay the night in attractive wood & stone rooms (with no need for AC). **$$$$**

🏠 **Villa Alazani** m 577 414842; www. villaalazani.com. A simpler option, this is owned by a group of former foreign correspondents (& therefore well stocked with interesting English books, as well as old rugs draped over the gallery); they also make wine, but only about 500 litres a year, & don't bottle any. **$$$**

TELAVI ოჯელავი *Telephone code 350*

From Tsinandali it's 5.5km to the city limits of Telavi, and 3km more to the centre. The city sits at 568m on a hilltop above the Alazani Valley. In the 2nd century, it was mentioned by the Greek geographer Ptolemy as 'Telada', and was the capital of Kakheti in the 11th century and again from 1615 (when Gremi was destroyed by the Persians) to 1762 (when Tbilisi took over); with a population of just 28,000 it's still the largest town in Kakheti.

GETTING THERE AND AWAY There are two **bus** stations on either side of Alazani immediately below the market; to the left is a small yard packed with buses to most destinations, including the frequent marshrutkas to Tbilisi (there's a *kassa* and toilets at the bottom end), while a little further down and to the right is a large yard used only by buses and minibuses to Akhmeta, Alaverdi, Gremi and Kvareli, and buses to Tbilisi (every hour or so until at least 17.00). **Shared taxis** to Tbilisi wait at the crossroads by the market on Chavchavadze. Heading up the hill from the market (which has stalls selling good hot snacks) is a broad boulevard (Ketevan Tsamebuli) with a stream and trees in the middle; at the first crossroads you can turn right/west into a residential quarter recently refurbished with cobbles and single and double balconies. Turning left takes you along Erekle II past government buildings to reach Erekle II Square and the walled enclosure of Batonistsikhe citadel (the best of the city's four fortresses – page 268).

🏠 **WHERE TO STAY** As well as the hotels, there are also some good homestays (although not all of them speak English), especially along Nadikvari, the road above the Public Service Hall (turn right off Erekle II Square past the theatre).

Hotels

🏠 **Château Mere** (15 rooms) Vardisubani 15; m 595 990399, 595 990390; http://mere. ge. The best place to stay in the area is this fake castle on the road to the Gombori Pass; it has large rooms with a rather bohemian style, a fairly grand restaurant & its own winery & cellar. **$$$$**

🏠 **Rcheuli Marani** (24 rooms) Chavchavadze 154; ☎ 27 3030; m 592 758899; www.rcheuli. ge. The oldest of this small chain (with sister hotels in Batumi, Tbilisi & Sighnaghi) is just west of the centre in an attractive red-brick building with traditional balconies. It has spacious, nicely furnished rooms decorated with Pirosmani prints & with Wi-Fi, TV, minibar & bath, & there is a good restaurant. Prices inc b/fast. **$$$–$$$$**

🏠 **Teliani Valley** (5 rooms & 2 suites) Tbilisi Highway km3; m 599 363600; e nana-teliani@ mgroup.com; www.telianivalley.com. One of the more modern & dynamic Georgian wine companies, Teliani Valley has a modern guesthouse at its winery on the eastern edge of town. Prices inc b/fast & winery tour with a tasting. **$$$–$$$$**

🏠 **Alaznis Veli** (Alazani Valley; 30 rooms) Alazani 74; ☎ 27 4144; m 599 007704; www.elgitour.ge. This plain, white building, just north of the bus station, has rooms with satellite TV, minibar, AC & bath; conference hall & sauna. The same company owns the homelier Kakhuri Ezo (Kakhetian Yard) just off the Tbilisi highway at Davitashvili 15

(27 4144; m 599 007704; **$$$**), with 4 dbls & a wine cellar. **$$$**

🏠 **Old Telavi** (34 rooms) Cholokashvili 1; 27 0707, 27 9009; m 596 440707, 596 450707; www. oldtelavi.ge. In 2 blocks (one 19th-century, one modern) on either side of the road; rooms have all comforts for business & leisure travellers. **$$$**

🏠 **Kakheti** (20 rooms) Vardoshvili 1; 27 0151; m 599 135511; e hotel.kakheti@gmail.com; www.hotelkakheti.ge. Across the road to the west of the market, this is a fairly functional 3-star, with decent rooms with Wi-Fi, & a restaurant (⊕ from 09.00). **$$**

Homestays

🏠 **Eto Jajanidze** (4 rooms) Akhvlediani 27; 27 7070; m 598 782050; e familyhoteleto@ yahoo.com. Just uphill from Nadikvari, the very hospitable Eto speaks English & has a comfortable traditional house. Good meals, internet access & a nice shady garden. **$$**

🏠 **Marleta's B&B** (4 rooms) Bagrationi 13; m 577 722771. To the east of the market off Chavchavadze, the excellent café-restaurant has closed, but is still a fine guesthouse, & the food is good, thanks to their nearby farm. **$$**

🏠 **Merab Milorava** Akhvlediani 67; 27 1257; m 599 737371. Just uphill from Nadikvari.

Merab works in the regional government building at the start of Kostava (up 2 flights & to the right) & offers rooms in a cottage in a lovely garden for 4 or 5 people, with safe parking, or a car is available. **$$**

🏠 **Nana Shaverdashvili** Nadikvari 9; 27 2185. Pleasant, clean rooms. English also spoken. **$$**

🏠 **Asmat Sekhniadze** 9 April 83; 27 3137; m 599 565074. **$–$$**

🏠 **Lali Khosroshvili's Guesthouse** (5 rooms) No 4 on the 2nd lane off 26 May, which runs uphill from Kostava east of the theatre; 27 1824; m 593 981862; e ingabel2020@yahoo.com. Has a wine marani. **$–$$**

🏠 **Nana Kviriashvili** 26 May 39; 27 3552. **$–$$**

🏠 **Svetlana Tushishvili** Nadikvari 15; 27 1909; m 577 756625; e sspiridon@rambler.ru; www.globalsalsa.com/telavi. They have beds in a lovely AC apt, cable TV (inc BBC World!) & swimming pool. English spoken. 1–2-day trips to wineries, Davit-Gareja & Kakheti can be arranged with a neighbour from GEL30. B/fast is GEL5 extra, or you can pay more for HB (inc wine). **$–$$**

🏠 **Guesthouse Marinella** (6 rooms) Chavchavadze 131; 27 3946; m 577 516001; e maria.marinella@mail.ru; www.marinella.ge. A solid grey house on the main road west, with good food & views over the Alazani River. **$**

✗ WHERE TO EAT AND DRINK

✗ **Old Marani** In the wine cellar at the Rcheuli Marani hotel. Probably the best restaurant in town. **$$$**

✗ **Dzveli Galavani** Cholokashvili 6; m 790 230363. A friendly place serving excellent Georgian food. **$$**

✗ **The Best Café** North side of Cholokasvhili; 27 6363; ⊕ 09.00–21.00 daily. Serves pizza, burgers, & coffee to go. Has Wi-Fi. **$**

✗ **Blitz** North side of Cholokashvili. Serving the usual fast-foody options. **$**

✗ **Café Madison** North side of Cholokashvili. Slightly better than the other café options, this serves khachapuri, pizza, ice cream & cakes. **$**

✗ **Media Café** Erekle II 4; 27 2803. It shares its cellar space with local newspaper Kakhetis

Khma (Voice of Kekheti), so you can watch the journalists at work & enjoy newspapers & magazines with your coffee & cakes; there are interesting talks & workshops as well. **$**

✗ **Pirosmani** Chavchavadze 52; m 574 878777; www.telavipirosmani.com; ⊕ 10.00–late daily. A cheery & reliable place serving standard Georgian dishes. **$**

✗ **Restaurant Paradise** Opposite the post office on Erekle II. This brick & wood-panelled cellar has the usual range of Georgian dishes (& an English menu). **$**

✗ **Starz Café and Restaurant** North side of Cholokashvili. Good pizza & shawarma, a salad bar, plus good coffee & cakes. **$**

OTHER PRACTICALITIES There's a helpful **tourist information centre** (27 5317; e tictelavi1@gmail.com; ⊕ 10.00–18.00 daily, summer to 19.00) at Erekle II 9, clearly signed, upstairs in a traditional house on the main square; they're accommodating and have free Wi-Fi, but no city maps. **ATMs** are along Erekle II and at Kostava 7 and

Ketevan Tsamebulis 11. The **post office** (⊕ *09.00–17.00 Mon–Fri, 09.00–14.00 Sat*) and DHL (↖ *27 0991*) are by the town hall at Erekle II 12.

Internet access is available at Telavi Internet Club at Kostava 1 and Internet Café and Games (*both ⊕ until late*) at the corner of Saakadzis and Erekle II. There are a couple of other places on both sides of Erekle II (like 1001 Computers at No 3) and at Tsamebuli 5. You can buy wine at **Shumi Wine Co** (*Sulkhan Tsintsadze 18;* ↖ *27 5333; www.shumi.ge*).

The city's **festivals** are Telavkalakoba at the end of October and Erekleoba on 7 November; there's also the Telavi International Music Festival in October.

WHAT TO SEE AND DO It's now hard to find the quaint old streets lined with elms (*tela*) and wooden-balconied houses which used to characterise Telavi, but there are traces here, as well as the zigzag patterns of river stones that are still typical of the region.

Turning left at the crossroads south (uphill) of the bus station, you're on the city's main street, Erekle II, lined with relatively tasteful post-war blocks, housing the post office and so on, which leads to the large **Freedom Square**, with the **Batonistsikhe citadel** to the left. Closed for refurbishment until sometime in 2015, this contains various churches and palaces, now housing a school and museum. If you turn left (past a statue symbolising the wine harvest and towards a striking Neoclassical hall) to enter on the near side, you'll pass the school on your left and

WINE TOURISM IN KAKHETI

Interest is growing fast in the wines of Kakheti, increasingly famed as the home of natural qvevri wines; new hotels are opening, in both the towns and the vineyards themselves. The wines are widely available, so it's strange that tours of the wineries are so awkward and expensive; the only winery to offer free visits is Kindzmarauli in Kvareli (see below). The Kakheti Wine Guild runs a Wine Tourism Center at Rustaveli 1 in Telavi (↖ *27 9090; www.kwg.ge;* ⊕ *10.00–19.00 daily*) which organises winery visits with a driver. Alternatively, Dato (David) Luashvili (m *551 300620, 593 761216;* e *davi.luashvili@gmail.com*) is an excellent guide in Telavi who speaks good English, drives carefully and doesn't smoke when with clients; he charges GEL80 per day for four people and can also take you to Davit-Gareja (*GEL120*) and elsewhere. In Sighnaghi, Goga Shabalaidze (m *598 722872;* e *goga_shabalaidze@mail.ru*) is also a good guide.

On the edge of Telavi are big industrial wineries that produce export-quality wine, but aren't very interested in independent tourists; to the east, there are some smaller, more welcoming places. Alternatively, some family winemakers also welcome visitors (but probably won't speak English).

OUTSKIRTS OF TELAVI

GWS Achinebuli village; ↖ *27 6051; www.gws.ge.* Charges GEL30.

Telavi Wine Cellar Kurdghelauri village; ↖ *23 6111; www.marani.co.* Charges €11 & really only want big groups.

Teliani Valley ↖ *23 4848; www.telianivalley.com.* This is the only winery you need to book for (1 day in advance); charges GEL30.

EAST OF TELAVI

Schuchmann Château m *790 557045.* Charges GEL15–35 for a very professional tasting of 3–7 wines. Also offers accommodation (page 265).

Shumi m *599 289982; www.shumi.ge.* Across the river from Tsinandali, they charge GEL10, which includes a visit to their museum. This houses a good collection of items, starting with a sculpture park on the right, and find the **Ketevana Iashvili Art Gallery** (*GEL3*) in front of you; opening hours are erratic, but it's worth a visit. In addition to the works of local painters (there are lots of views of Gremi and Alaverdi) and five paintings by Elena Akhvlediani (born in Telavi in 1901), it houses lots of 17th- to 19th-century German and French paintings, a few Dutch ones, and Russian landscapes. Continuing to its left side and past various other buildings, you'll find the **palace** of King Erekle II, a relatively small and low two-storey building built in the 1750s in the Persian style, one of the least expected buildings in Georgia. The correct procedure is to go on around the outside of the citadel to enter at the east end and buy a ticket (*GEL6 foreigners, GEL1 Georgians*) for a tour of the palace and the small museum of history and ethnography it houses. Beyond the palace are two **churches**: a tiny and very simple basilica, built of stone in the 17th and 18th centuries, which is always open although there's little to see, and a larger brick church, built by Erekle in 1758, which is abandoned and shut up. There's also a pantheon, bringing together the graves of sundry Kakhetian notables, and the ruins of the 11th-century royal baths.

Leaving the citadel by the east gate beyond the palace, you emerge by the large **equestrian statue** of King Erekle II, by Merab Merabishvili. There's an excellent view to the east from here, and about 100m below is a small park with a famous 900-year-old plane tree, below the ruined shell of the Hotel Telavi. On the far side of the hotel, Nadikvari runs through a pleasant residential area that has a number

ceramics dating from the 4th to 2nd millennia BC & silver sleeves from the 3rd millennium BC for grafting, & qvevri from the 12th century; in front is a collection of 294 varieties of vine, 200 Georgian & 94 'European'. They're only just beginning to make qvevri wines, & don't always have an English-speaking guide available.
Tsinandali winery At the museum; www.tsinandali.com. Charges GEL20, with a museum tour & tasting of 5 wines.

WEST OF TELAVI
Alaverdi Monastery m 599 155002; e keti.khizanishvili@gmail.com. Charges GEL80pp with a minimum of 4.
Château Mere hotel-winery m 595 990399; e winiveria.mere@gmail.com; http://mere.ge. This upmarket winery charges GEL60 for tour & tasting.
Danieli Winery m 599 624411; www.danieliwinery.com. It's well worth visiting this boutique winery in Argoichki, just north of Kvemo Alvani especially for their dry white Kisi. No set prices – be sure to call ahead.
Graneli Near Kvareli m 577 419585; e meghvineobagraneli@mail.ru. Charges GEL10, with a tasting of 6 wines & sometimes their brandy.

Khareba m 790 120001, 593 303636; www.gvirabi.ge. In Kvareli, they charge GEL3 to visit their tunnel, & from GEL10 for tastings.
Kindzmareuli Corporation ✆ 252 50555; m 595 330433; http://kindzmaraulicorporation.ge. In Kvareli, these offers free visits (although they have to charge for larger groups).
Kindzmarauli Marani ✆ 322 36 1850; www.kmwine.ge. This has a tasting room with ethnographic display & a demonstration plot of rare Georgian grape varieties. Charge GEL20 for a minimum of 5 .
Twins Winery m 599 170929; www.cellar.ge. In Napareuli, this excellent winery charges GEL15–20, including a visit to the nice museum of *qvevri*-making.

FAMILY WINEMAKERS
Avtandil Abuladze Eniseli; m 599 398733
Niko and Vadja Nikolaishvili Tsinandali; m 599 260215
Nunu Kardenakashvili Gurdjaani; m 599 767071
Paata Lachashvili Ikalto; m 599 108467
Petriaant Marani Zemo Khodasheni; m 593 197355

of homestays and past another citadel wall to **Nadikvari Park**, nicely done up with a funfair, open-air theatre and viewpoints over the Alazani Valley, and the terrace of a modernist white café-bar (which has step-free access all the way from the road).

WEST OF TELAVI

Shuamta Heading west from Telavi, it's about 2km to the city limits, and another 1km to the junction (at about km7) of the road south to Tbilisi via Gombori. Taking this road for about 8km to km57 and turning left on to the old road (not served by buses), after 2km you'll come to the **monastery of Akhali (New) Shuamta**, where you can see a cruciform brick church built in the second quarter of the 16th century and decorated with frescoes of the founders King Levan of Kakheti, Queen Tinatin and their son Alexander. Tinatin became a nun and was buried here; her tomb was found in 1899, and she is remembered on 3 September. Alexander Chavchavadze is also buried here, by the north wall. However, the nuns who have returned here are somewhat fierce and unwelcoming.

The real attraction is another 3km up the road, the **nunnery of Dzveli (Old) Shuamta**, beautifully set on an isolated hilltop amid hornbeam forest. There are three churches here; the southernmost is a triple-church basilica dating from the 5th–6th century, with a barrel vault and its original alabaster iconostasis. Immediately to its north is a tetraconch cruciform church with an octagonal dome, dating from the early 7th century (and modelled on the Jvari Church), and to the east is a smaller version of the same, also 7th century. There is supposedly a tunnel from here to Ikalto.

Families from Telavi often come to the lovely **Tetris Khlebi Waterfall** above Shuamta on the side of Mount Tsivgombori; it's a good spot for a picnic and a stroll, or even taking a ride on one of the horses for hire.

Ikalto Marshrutkas head west from Telavi every 15 minutes or so to Akhmeta and Alaverdi, all passing through the village of Ikalto, famed as the site of the academy at which the national poet Shota Rustaveli studied in the 12th century; students kept a jug of wine under their desks, to renew their inspiration as required. At km53/19 (8km west of Telavi) there's a signpost to the academy, 1.7km south up a good road along a valley. Halfway up you'll see the tiny chapel of St Stefane on the far left bank which, although open, is of no real interest. At the end of the asphalt you'll find the three churches and the ruins of the academy crammed together in a relatively small compound, beautifully set among cypress trees.

Ikalto was founded in the third quarter of the 6th century by St Zenon, one of the Syrian Fathers who established Christianity in Georgia, but the main church is the 8th–9th-century **Church of the Transfiguration** (Gvtaeba), which is the oldest in Kakheti to have a central dome supported by four free-standing pillars. The belfry over the porch at the west end was added in the 19th century; its interior was whitewashed by the Russians, also in the 19th century, so there's little to see, although Zenon is buried to the right of the altar. To the east is the original 6th-century **Church of the Trinity** (Sameba), a small basilica with an odd interior plan, with apses off the side of the sanctuary, and steps to a chamber over the porch. In the northeastern corner of the complex is the 8th-century wine-press, with qvevris on the ground. Just to the south of the main church is the 7th-century **Kvelatsminda Church**, another bare, undecorated basilica, and behind it the ruins of the academy's **refectory**, built at the start of the 12th century and destroyed by Shah Abbas in 1616. It lost its roof a long time ago, but the stone walls and window arches remain; Georgians find the ruins very moving because of the association with Rustaveli, but although they are doubtlessly 'romantic in the extreme', foreigners may find them of less interest.

Turning left/south at about km52.5 coming from Telavi, an asphalt road leads about 1km to three attractive, modern properties owned by the Villa Ikalto winery (m *790 102050; www.villaikalto.ge*). Immediately west of Ikalto is Atskhuri (km55), with the 10th–13th-century church of St George on a hill 2km south. The Khatoba Festival held here on 14 August retains pagan elements such as the sacrifice of sheep.

Where to stay and eat

Hotel Savineti m 790 102040. Just to the right of the Bazieri. Small but nicely presented rooms (but with huge leather sofas on the landing), with plenty of light & power points; the bar-restaurant offers good food & wine (of course) & there's a swimming pool. **$$$$**

Hotel Tamarioni m 790 102000. Similar to the Savineti, also with a good restaurant, a wine cellar & chacha distillery. **$$$$**

Guesthouse Bazieri m 790 102020. The first of the properties owned by Villa Ikalto winery on the road from Telavi. **$$$**

Akhmeta and around From the junction at km56/16, from where it's 9km north to Alaverdi, the main road continues for 16km to **Akhmeta**, a winemaking town of no particular importance (except as the birthplace of the theatre director Sandro Akhmetili) near the point where the Alazani River emerges from the hills. There are two ATMs at a roundabout where taxis wait, just south of the bus station; a few hundred metres west on Kazbegi there's a tiny rectangular basilica on the right that dates from the 6th century. A road follows the Alazani north into the **Pankisi Gorge**, home to Georgia's Kists, ethnic Chechens who settled here from the late 17th century to the early 19th century. The Kists are Muslim (with a Sufi slant) and are frequently accused, especially by Russia, of kidnapping and terrorism, but in fact this is really a very interesting and welcoming place to visit. It's much like the rest of Georgia but with ducks, turkeys and geese instead of pigs, and many women wearing headscarves; it's a great base for exploring into the mountains to the north.

From Akhmeta, marshrutkas and shared taxis (both charging GEL2) run via Duisi and Jokolo to Birkiani; from Ortachala in Tbilisi there are marshrutkas to Duisi at 07.30 and 14.20 (*returning 06.00 & 11.40; 3hrs; GEL10*), and others to Akhmeta at 10.00, 14.00, 17.00 and 19.00 (GEL8). The valley's main festival is Pankisoba in late July.

In **Jokolo**, you can visit the mosque and church, as well as a felt-making school and some tiny waterwheels; it's a 3km walk to Pankisi's main village, Duisi, where there's a grander mosque and a small museum at the southern end (300m south of km15/7; you'll need to get someone to call the curator). To the north, it's 5km, through increasingly wild scenery, to the **Batsara Reserve**, a unique forest of yew trees, up to 25m high, 1.2m in diameter and 2,000 years old. Trails lead up to the lovely Batana Lake and on in to Tusheti, while a jeep track continues past a summer-only hotel near the Chinese-built Khadori hydro-electric station to a waterfall at the intake to the power station.

Kvetera, a ruined town-fortress, lies hidden in the hills to the west of Akhmeta; 9km along the road to Tianeti, you should fork left on to the upper road, and left again after 2km. In another kilometre you'll find the fortress and its tiny jewel of an 11th-century church. Built of white tuff, with blue tiles, it has a most unusual semi-diamond-shaped ground plan, with four equal transepts and four smaller niches between them. Tianeti itself, on the upper Iori River, is a tranquil village set in the foothills of the Caucasus; it's surprisingly close to Tbilisi, which can be reached by a poor road to Gldani, in the northwestern suburbs.

Where to stay and eat

Nazy's Guesthouse Jokolo; e nazy@ nazysguesthouse.com; http://nazysguesthouse. com. To the right past the church (1888) from the shops, this is the best base in this area. Nazy speaks excellent English & is keen to give as much

help & information as you might require. Guides & horses can be provided for hiking & horseback expeditions into Tusheti. See www.pankisi.org for accommodation in other villages. There's also the Restaurant Pankisi ($$$). **$$$**

Alaverdi Turning right at the junction 2.5km west of Ikalto, it's 9km north through the vineyards to the great **Cathedral of St George** (⊕ *08.00–18.00 daily*) at Alaverdi, 20km from Telavi. From Akhmeta, it's 15km east from a junction off the Pankisi road to Kvemo Alvani, and then 3km south to Alaverdi. Founded by Joseph, another of the Syrian Fathers, the present church was built in the early 11th century, one of the largest medieval churches built in Georgia. Built of *shirmi*, the tuff (or travertine) stone ubiquitous in Kakheti and Armenia, it was damaged by the Mongols, by Shah Abbas in 1616 (with repairs in brick in the 15th century), and again by an earthquake in 1742, after which it was restored by Erekle II. It was surrounded with defensive walls in the early 18th century, with the massive gate-tower added in the following century. From the destruction of the Bagrat Cathedral in Kutaisi in 1691–2 until the construction of Tbilisi's Sameba Cathedral in 1995–2004, this was the highest church in Georgia, its dome rising 50m from the ground. It's a triconch church, but with an ambulatory to the west as well, the north and south apses being incorporated into a rectangular plan.

The frescoes date from the 11th to 13th centuries and the 15th century; they were whitewashed by the Russians in the 19th century, and gradually uncovered and restored from 1967. They include St George over the west door, the Virgin and Child over the altar, and others in the south transept. See also the single hand, carved in relief on a flagstone to the left inside the entrance; the story goes that a local prince was captured by the Turks, and before being killed cut off his hand, so that it could be taken home and buried in holy ground. This is also the burial place of Queen Ketevan the Martyr, who was tortured to death by Shah Abbas in 1624. To the northwest of the church are the ruins of the Persian governor's summer palace, built in 1615, including a low octagonal brick pavilion.

The Alaverdoba pilgrimage and folk festival lasts for two weeks from 14 September, the feast of the Exaltation of the Life-Giving Cross (relics of which were given by the Patriarch of Jerusalem to King Levan in the 16th century), and climaxes on 28 September, the feast of St Joseph of Alaverdi.

Marshrutkas continue to the village of Alaverdi, just north, and return after half an hour, making this an easy excursion from Telavi. Like several other Kakheti churches, Alaverdi was thoroughly renovated in 2010, with future plans to adapt the sacristy as a treasury to display the church's treasure of icons, vestments and manuscripts. It's also known for its very traditional **winery**, with a display plot of about 100 grape varieties right in front of the church. Across the road is an apparently non-smoking car park and the Matsoni House restaurant, specialising in natural local products such as matsoni, cheese and honey.

TUSHETI თუშეთი

The region of Tusheti was effectively autonomous as a tribal democracy until the end of the 17th century, and a road was not built here until 1978–82. It's similar in many ways to Svaneti, with traditions of hospitality coupled with building spectacular defensive towers; but, unlike Svaneti, there were never any reports of

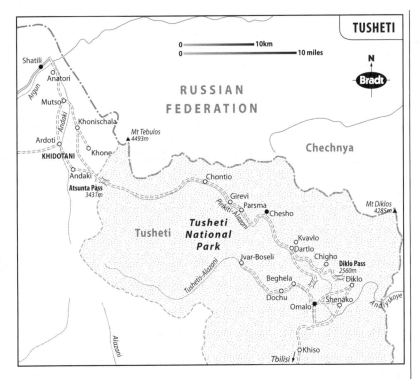

0 _____ 10km
0 _____ 10 miles

N

Bradt

Shatili
Anatori
Argun
Mutso
Andaki
Khonischala
Ardoti
KHIDOTANI
Khone
Mt Tebulos
▲4493m
Andaki
Atsunta Pass
3431m

RUSSIAN
FEDERATION

Chechnya

Chontio
Girevi
Pirikiti-Alazani
Parsma
●Chesho
Mt Diklos
4285m▲

Tusheti
*Tusheti
National
Park*

Kvavlo
Dartlo
Jvar-Boseli
Chigho
Diklo Pass
2560m
Beghela
Diklo
Dochu
Shenako
Omalo
Andiys-koye

Tushetis-Alazani

Alazani

Khiso
Tbilisi

robberies here. The scenery is almost as spectacular as in Svaneti, with peaks up to 4,500m, deep gorges and high waterfalls, and well-preserved pine forests of *Pinus kochiana*. Tusheti delicacies include *kotori*, a bread with a cheese and potato filling, the hard, dry *kalti* cheese and very salty *gudiskweli* cheese, made of sheep's milk in a bag (*guda*) of sheepskin, with the wool on the inside. There's also homemade beer and *zhipitauri* firewater (as in Khevsureti).

KVEMO ALVANI Just beyond Alaverdi, on the far bank of the Alazani, is Kvemo (Lower) Alvani, a village which in summer is very quiet but in winter acts as home to the bulk of the population of Tusheti, with only about 20 people remaining there on the far side of the Caucasus watershed. It's also the administrative centre for the Tusheti National Park (*www.tusheti.ge*), which comprises a total of 16,297ha in the Tushetis, Batcharis and Babaneuris reserves. The Babaneuris Reserve, just north of Kvemo Alvani, has yews about 1,000 years old, from 950m to 1,350m altitude. The Tushetis Reserve (also to the north) protects possibly unique virgin forests of pine (2,000–2,200m) and birch (2,300–2,600m). Although the national park is still relatively new, it has managed to support a number of guesthouses (see www.tusheti.ge). Tours are available from Tbilisi for around US$100 per day, as well as hiking and horse-trekking trips of various durations. Local specialists include Caucasus Trekking Company (m *595 629927 (Apr–Oct), 599 728162; France* ☎ *+331 6947 2397 (all yr), +336 3378 0441 (Nov–Mar);* e *caucasustrek@msn. com; www.caucasus-trek.com*) and Tusheti Tour (m *593 744090, 568 647945;* e *sualak2013@gmail.com; http://sualak2013.wordpress.com*).

One particularly interesting project is the development of **ski-touring and snow-shoeing**, as Tusheti is virtually abandoned in winter (m *577 907272; www.*

tusheti-winter.net); it's run by a German guide, Devi Asmadiredja, based in Birkiani in the Pankisi Gorge (e *deyazoye@googlemail.com; http://deviadventure. wordpress.com*).

The **Atingenoba Festival** is held in Tusheti 100 days after Easter, with horse races and human pyramids; men brew beer in a sacred place where no mature women are allowed.

OMALO A poor road runs north from Laliskuri (km51/78) to the 2,927m Koja (or Abanos, meaning hot baths) Pass, which is only passable between mid-June and mid-October. You'll pay US$60–70 for a jeep to Omalo (plus US$40–50 per day there), or GEL20 to ride on an old green ex-military truck which leaves Kvemo Alvani most days at about 08.00; you may also have to pay the same again for a rucksack, making a total of GEL80 for a return trip. The road runs through Pshaveli, the main settlement in Pshaveti or land of the Pshavs, relatives of the Tushetians and Khevsurs living on the south side of the Caucasus watershed. The poet Vazha Pshavela ('son of Pshaveti') was born here and returned in the 1880s to live as a peasant.

It takes 4–5 hours to cover the 72km from Laliskuri to Omalo in a jeep, perhaps twice as long in the truck, passing through Khiso and then Khakhabo, marked by abandoned towers (*the Guesthouse Kekhi is in Khakhabo; 3 dbls, 1 trpl, all en suite;* m *557 143907;* e *io.bakuridze@gmail.com; €20 HB*). In fact, Georgian hiking trips may use horses for almost the entire journey from Alvani, taking two days to reach Omalo, with a decent wild campsite halfway. Omalo is also the base of the OSCE (Organization for Security and Co-operation in Europe) monitors, ensuring that no Chechen fighters cross the border; Georgian frontier troops may check your passports.

The new town of Kvemo (Lower) Omalo, where the National Park Visitor Centre, airstrip, boarding school, clinic and seemingly half-built Soviet houses are located, is by the track in the valley of the Pirikiti Alazani; Zemo (Upper) Omalo, a cluster of fortified tower-houses, is high on the slope just to the north.

Horses can be rented by calling m 555 020171, 598 859945, 599 064030 or 595 515688. You can visit the small ethnographic museum in the 12th–13th-century fortress of Keselo between the upper and lower villages.

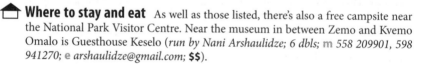 **Where to stay and eat** As well as those listed, there's also a free campsite near the National Park Visitor Centre. Near the museum in between Zemo and Kvemo Omalo is Guesthouse Keselo (*run by Nani Arshaulidze; 6 dbls;* m *558 209901, 598 941270;* e *arshaulidze@gmail.com;* **$$**).

Kvemo Omalo

Guesthouse Tusheti (6 dbls, 2 trpls; Vaja Shabalaidze) Near the road from Laliskuri; m 599 790092, 599 231132; e hoteltusheti@ yahoo.com **$$**

Tushuri Koshki (8 rooms; Nugzar Idoidze) m 599 110879, 599 272265; e nidoidze@yahoo. com **$$**

Mamuka Kindolauri (3 dbls, 1 trpl) m 593 323586, 599 313913, 593 531796 **$**

Zurab Mouravidze (1 dbl, 2 trpls) m 598 540545, 598 252123; e mouravidze@gmail.com **$**

Zemo Omalo

Guesthouse Lasharai (7 dbls, 2 trpls; Vefkhia Rainauli) m 568 861084, 555 645254; e guesthouselasharai@yahoo.com **$$$**

Guesthouse Shina (6 dbls, 2 trpls; Sergo Meltsaidze) m 595 262046, 597 970112; e hotelshina@gmail.com. **$$$**

Guesthouse Tower (3 dbls, 1 trpl; Nugzar Idoidze) m 593 769135, 599 110879; e nidoidze@ yahoo.com. **$$**

Kamsuri (6 dbls; Gela Bakhturidze) m 595 544111 **$$**

HIKING IN TUSHETI An attractive walk of about 2 hours back along the road south from Omalo leads to the village of **Khiso**, where there's a 12th-century fortress, and a similar distance to the northeast (crossing the Pirikiti Alazani by a suspension bridge) is **Shenako** (2,050m), where there's a spectacular 16th-century church, as well as a few guesthouses (page 276). From Shenako, it's a 15-minute walk to the abandoned village of Agiurta, dominated by a seven-storey tower. The people of Agiurta now live in Tbilisi but want to return home; there are plans to help them find a sustainable livelihood here. A mountain path leads east from Shenako across the border (closed) into Daghestan, and another leads north, further into the heart of Tusheti. It's an hour or so to **Diklo**, overshadowed by the 4,285m peak of Diklos, to the north. A 2km-path loops north to reach the fortress of Old Diklo, just east. You can walk up to the hilltop village of Dano or make side-trips to the Gometsri and Tsovati gorges, where there are 18th-century tombs in which plague victims are said to have voluntarily shut themselves up. There's also a path into Daghestan, in the Russian Federation. There's a guesthouse in Diklo (m 599 775372), and there are festivals here on 20 July and 10 August. The WWF is funding an ecotourism project in this area, providing alternative energy sources to boost tourism, and other sustainable sources of income, such as making honey and carpets using natural dyes and the wool of the aboriginal Tusheti mountain sheep.

From Diklo, a path continues westwards, at times only 50cm wide and hugging the edge of a vertiginous cliff, and then crosses the **Diklo** or **Sonekhi Pass** (2,560m) after 3 hours, before dropping slightly to **Chigho** (2,400m), known for its pagan festival of Lasharoba, when a ram is sacrificed 100 days after Easter, honouring the spirit of war. The path then follows the valley to the village of **Dartlo** (1,990m). This can also be reached by a direct path (13km; over a 3,000m pass) from Omalo, going northeast past the cemetery and the church of Tamar and her son Giorgi Lash, and hiking on for 4–5 hours, but the classic five-day hike to Khevsureti goes via Shenako and Diklo. The World Bank is funding a project here to restore (perhaps excessively) its 30-odd towers and houses with typical wooden balconies. There are also accommodation options (page 276), and jeep tours are run by Levan Patараia (m 599 681661).

Above Dartlo is **Kvavlo**, with a beautiful tower with a tetrahedral roof. There are more towers, and shrines to those drowned in the river, as the trail continues west up the Pirikiti Alazani into the mountains passing Chesho. Just up a side-valley to the north is **Parsma** (1,960m, with fine medieval towers and houses linked as a virtual fort); continue north to reach the village of Girevi, just 11km south of the Chechen border, where there's an army checkpoint.

Most hikers will return to Omalo, but it is possible to continue from Girevi by a long, tough trail to Khevsureti – allow a week from Omalo to Shatili. This follows the upper Pirikiti Alazani and then the Kvakhidistqali through Chontio and largely abandoned settlements such as Baso and Hegho, before the tough climb on scree to the **Atsunta Pass** (the highest in Georgia at 3,431m; closed early Oct–Mar), between Tebulos (4,493m) to the north and a peak of 3,839m to the south. This is an unpopulated region, but as you camp in alpine meadows you may come across the occasional shepherd. Descending into the Andaki Gorge and heading northwest through Ardoti, you'll eventually reach **Mutso**, the first Khevsur village, from where a rough track leads virtually to the border and then south to **Shatili** (page 170). You can also hike west from Omalo up the even remoter Tushetis Alazani Valley to villages such as Beghela, Dochu (where there is accommodation) and Jvar-Boseli, from where a pass crosses north into the Pirikiti Alazani east of Girevi.

Where to stay and eat

Shenako

Nino Sekhniashvili (6 rooms) m 558 639722, 593 173708 **$$$**

Erekle Bukvaidze (3 rooms) m 599 481812 **$$** inc meals

Irodi Bukvaidze (3 dbls, 1 trpl, 1 sgl) m 558 639722, 577 101876; e hotelshenaqo@ yahoo.com. **$$**

Nino Jijuridze m 858 279792 **$$** inc meals

Dartlo

Guesthouse Samtsikhe (11 rooms; Beso Elanidze) m 599 118993, 599 785302; e bes.el@ posta.ge. 8 dbls & 3 trpls with shared bathrooms. **$$**

Hotel Dartlo (13 rooms; Mariam Otiuridze) m 598 174966; www.dartlo.ge **$$$**

Dochu

Guesthouse Kruiskari (6 rooms; Usupi Torgvaidze) m 599 285647; e hotelkruiskari@ yahoo.com. 1 dbl with en suite, 2 trpls with shared bathroom. **$$**

EAST OF TELAVI – FROM GREMI TO KVARELI AND LAGODEKHI

NAPAREULI, GREMI AND NEKRESI Alvani lies on the road along the left/north bank of the Alazani, from Akhmeta to the Azerbaijani border. Heading east, it passes through **Napareuli** (km59/70), a village known for the Twins Wine Cellar (m *551 747474; www.cellar.ge*), the first modern qvevri winery, founded in 1994; they also have a hotel-restaurant and a wine museum. Just north from about km62, is the Lake Lopota Resort (m *591 700777, 591 149494; e lopotaresort@yahoo.com; www.lopota.ge; $$$$*), which started the trend of luxury resorts in the Kakhetian foothills and has tennis and mini golf facilities, bikes, pedalos, three swimming pools and of course fancy bars and restaurants.

After a junction from Telavi (11km south) it reaches **Gremi**; marshrutkas run from Telavi to Eniseli, immediately beyond Gremi, where the Château Eniseli-Bagrationi winery (*www.eniselibagrationi.ge*), founded in the 1880s, includes a six-room hotel. You can also stay at the Guesthouse Gremi (m *579 948895; $$*), or at the English-speaking Guesthouse Nona in Shilda, just east (*km80;* m *599 979838, 599 060059; $$*). Gremi is now little more than a pleasant village (known for its brandy), but there was a city here by the 6th century AD, and it was the capital of Kakheti from 1466 until 1616, when it was utterly destroyed by Shah Abbas. High on a rocky ledge at the west end of the village (with good steps leading up from the main road), a few crumbling ruins remain of the fort, built in 1565, and the palace and three-storey dwelling-tower, built of red brick on stone blocks. The dome church is in great condition; it was built in 1565, with paintings completed in 1577, and reconsecrated in 1989. Along with the tower at Ninotsminda, the **citadel of Gremi** is the best example of Georgian adaptation of Persian styles of architecture, such as patterned brickwork (ie: arches in relief). There's a museum (⊕ *11.00–18.00 Tue–Sun; GEL3*) by the church displaying ceramics, spear- and arrowheads and various implements; there's a shop and they'll lay on a tour to Nekresi for US$3 – it's worth paying for if only as a way to get the church opened and go up the tower, which gives great views to the Caucasus. The real museum (⊕ *10.00–17.00 Tue–Sun; GEL3*) is below the church to the west, by the main road (through an underpass from the car park/toilets), and displays ceramics from the 4th and 3rd millennia BC to the 14th century AD, bronze daggers from the 12th to 7th centuries BC, and has useful information in English on the area that was covered by the capital. Nearby are two small churches (just on the west side of the hill) and the foundations of a caravanserai and covered market, all built in the

15th and 16th centuries and being restored; there also a replica of a two-storey bathhouse that was across the road.

At km85.5, 9km east of Gremi, a rough road leads up into the hills to the left/ north to **Nekresi**, site of one of the oldest churches in Georgia, a little basilica dating from the third quarter of the 4th century. Inscriptions found here recently are claimed to date from the 1st to the 3rd centuries AD, making them the earliest examples of the Georgian alphabet. In the 6th century this monastery was the base of the Syrian Father Abibos, who was martyred by the Persians after pouring water on a Zoroastrian sacred fire; in the next century a three-church basilica, perhaps the finest example of the genre, was added (and painted in the 16th century), followed in the 8th and 9th centuries by a bishop's palace (with a tower added in the 16th century), and a cruciform church, by the present entrance. Frequently raided by the Lesghians, it was finally destroyed in the 18th century. From the end of the road you'll have to walk for 45 minutes to reach the monastery, a vertical kilometre above the valley. This is the only place in Georgia where pigs are still sacrificed, because a Persian army was driven away by rolling pigs' heads down the hill at them.

Kvareli (*Telephone code 352*) Continuing eastwards from Gremi for half an hour, you'll come to Kvareli, a small town (home of the Kindzmarauli and Khareba wineries), which has become an upmarket tourist spot since President Saakashvili bought a house here. Marshrutkas from Ortachala in Tbilisi come to Kvareli via Gurdjaani every 30 minutes (*08.00–18.00; GEL8*); from Telavi marshrutkas run roughly hourly (*09.30–17.30; GEL2*). From the highway junction (km92) the tree-lined Chavchavadze Avenue leads north for 2km, through the town to the marshrutka terminal on Gogebashvili; returning south for about 200m you'll see the Church of St John the Baptist to the right, with the **tourist office** hidden behind it at Rustaveli 8 (✆ *22 1340/50;* e *tickvareli@gmail.com;* ⏱ *10.00–18.00, summer until 19.00*). There's an ATM on the main square and another at Bank Republic opposite the Koté Marjanishvili museum.

🏠 **Where to stay and eat** In addition to the places listed, there are also guesthouses in town, such as Iva Kuprashvili (*Rustaveli 12*), Liana Baidashvili (*Leist 33A;* ✆ *22 0955;* m *593 758458*) and Salome Varamishvili (*Marjanishvili 53;* ✆ *22 0989;* m *593 173425*). There are few places to eat in town other than the hotels: the Konchis Zaodi, up against the fort walls behind the Château Kvareli, is an entertaining option.

In town

🏠 **Château Kvareli** (26 rooms) Kudigora 1; m 790 924090, 599 466595; www.chateaukvareli. ge. The best hotel in town, on the south side of the square near the fort. Above its huge lobby are comfortable rooms & there's a good restaurant; at the rear is a hostel with dorms (some en suite) with triple-decker bunks, deep new mattresses & a kitchen with hot plates but no pans or cutlery. **$$–$$$$**

🏠 **Hotel-Restoran Shua Kalakshi** Tsereteli 7; ✆ 22 1446; m 557 406633, 592 405061; e eka.elo@mail.ru **$$**

🏠 **Kavkasioni** Chavchavadze 32; ✆ 22 1751; m 598 383412; e todadze.e@mail.ru **$$**

Outside Kvareli

🏠 **Kvareli Lake Resort** (19 rooms) ✆ 322 30 3030; e welcome@kvarelilakeresort.ge; www. kvarelilakeresort.ge. To the east (7km along Davit Agmashenebelis from the centre), rooms here have panoramic views, although the food is not as good as at other hotels. **$$$$$**

🏠 **Royal Batoni Hotel** (31 rooms) m 595 996611, 595 996600; www.royalbatoni.ge. Part of the Ilia Lake complex, built in 2011 in the Duruji Gorge (known for its healthy populations of raptors), across the river just west of Kvareli but 7km by road (turning off the main road west at km87). This castle-like hotel is kitschy but comfortable, with a terrace & infinity pool overlooking the lake. Rooms have wonderful mountain views & stylish bathrooms with transparent walls (& curtains, thankfully). **$$$$$**

🏠 **Kvareli Eden Hotel & Wine Spa** David Agmashenebelis 78A; ☎ 322 97 0165; www. kvarelieden.ge. Nearer town (but still set in vineyards) this is a striking Mediterranean-style building with a luxurious (& very expensive)

spa, where you can soak in a copper tub filled with wine, in addition to the usual steam rooms, massages & aromatherapy; there's also a bowling alley. **$$$$**

🏠 **Ioseba's Dukani** Sadzmakaco. A restaurant which also has cheap rooms. On the way to the lake. **$**

What to see and do About 500m to the south on Chavchavadze, the remains of an 18th-century **fort** rise to the right beyond the Public Service Hall, which looks like a small glass tower with a couple of gigantic white bras draped over it; the square of walls, with seven towers, is intact, but inside there's only a football pitch, visible through a gate on the north side.

Opposite the church is a white building like a Corbusier chapel; built in 1978, this is the **house-museum of Ilia Chavchavadze** (1837–1907) (⊕ *10.00–17.00 except Mon; GEL0.50*), the editor of the popular newspaper *Iveria*, founder of critical realism in Georgian literature, and creator of Georgian theatre, translating Molière and Gogol and introducing the plays of Shakespeare. He also reformed the alphabet, and became a deputy in the Russian duma or parliament. As leader of the moderate reformist and nationalist tendency, he was officially declared a secular saint after his murder by either tsarist or Bolshevik agents – just who is disputed, and both seem to have had an interest in removing him. The Iliaoba Festival is held on 8 November on Ilias Gora, a hill with the country's largest statue of him, which is a popular picnic spot. In the garden behind the museum is the defensive tower in which he was born in 1837 while the family hid from an attack by Lesghian tribesmen – this is seen as deeply symbolic, as he spent his life defending Georgian culture. Beyond the tower is the 17th-century house in which he lived until the age of 11; most striking is the huge marani wine store with 40 qvevris, and two limewood wine presses, one for Saperavi grapes and one for Rkatsiteli.

Hidden next to the church across the road is the tourist office, and under it the National Bank's **Money Museum** (⊕ *09.00–13.00 & 14.00–18.00 Mon–Fri; free*). This exhibits Georgian coins dating as far back as the 6th century BC (from Vani), a stater issued by Alexander the Great in the 4th century BC, Roman denarii, Parthian coins, 8th-century Arabian coins minted in Tbilisi, 11th-century Bagratid coins from Georgia, irregularly shaped copper coins issued by Tamar, then more from 13th- to 18th-century Georgia, 16th-century Venetian gold ducats, and Austrian and Polish thalers. It ends with roubles issued by the Transcaucasian Federation and the USSR, coupons issued in 1993–94, and finally a colourful display of modern notes, from Europe, Iraq (Saddam), Iran (Khomeini), Israel, the Central Asian 'stans', Asia, the Antipodes, the US and (very nice) Madagascar.

Just to the right at Rustaveli 13 is the **house-museum** of the theatre director Koté Marjanishvili (1872–1933), which opens slightly erratically (⊕ *in theory 10.00–18.00 Tue–Sun; GEL3*); it displays his personal effects, photos and theatre posters and has a fine garden with sculptures.

The **Kindzmarauli Wine House** (signed in English) is at Chavchavadze 55 about 200m south of the main square (m *790 100061;* e *office@kindzmarauli.ge; www. kindzmaraulicorporation.ge;* ⊕ *09.00–18.00 daily*). Tastings are free, and you can buy wine from GEL10; its history dates back to the establishment of a royal castle and wine cellar here in 1533. The **Khareba Winery** (*www.winery-khareba.com*), across the river to the east (go back to the main road, turn left to cross the bridge, left on to the Lagodekhi road and at once left again) is famous for its 8km ex-military tunnel (at a constant 14°C), 3km of which is now in use for wine storage. They do good tours (GEL3), tastings in fluent English and you can eat at the Restaurant Saperavi, with good views but less good service.

Lagodekhi (*Telephone code 335*) From Kvareli you have the choice of returning by a direct road to km18, just west of Gurdjaani, or continuing for 41km to Lagodekhi, on the border with Azerbaijan; the junction is a few hundred metres to the east of the Kvareli junction (beyond the bridge). There should be a marshrutka at 10.00 from Kvareli to Lagodekhi, but after that there's virtually no public transport; you'll need to hitch between Akhalsopeli and Kabali at least, so it may be better to head 26km south to Gurdjaani and loop back via Tsnori from there. It's 41km from Tsnori up to Lagodekhi, crossing the Alazani Wetlands, the mainly marshy, seasonally flooded woods with good birdwatching. There are marshrutkas (*GEL7*) from Isani metro station in Tbilisi via Tsnori (*at least hourly 08.00–18.15*), as well as from Telavi (*GEL5*). These arrive on St Nino, just north of the main road.

Where to stay and eat There are good rooms at the **Visitor Centre Guesthouse** (*Vashlovani 177;* \ *254 22515;* **$$–$$$**) at the national park headquarters at the edge of the forest, or they can help you find rooms elsewhere. A few places to eat can be found along the main road, where there is also a small market and a couple of ATMs.

Hotels
Hotel Hereti (14 rooms) Kostava 15; \ 22 4988; m 591 111211, 593 280502. Head uphill from St Nino & take the 1st left for 1 block to the main square to find this basic hotel, which looks a bit dysfunctional from the outside but has tolerable rooms. **$$**

Hotel-Restaurant Lagodekhi (13 rooms) m 555 543802. Opposite the Hereti, this is more a restaurant than a hotel (GEL50 for 2). **$$**

Homestays
Kiwi House (6 rooms) Vashlovani 35; m 557 427819, 551 245072; e thekiwihouse. lagodekhi@gmail.com. Known in Georgian as Kivis Sakhli, there's nothing Antipodean here (despite the name); they just grow kiwi fruit where other Georgians have a grape vine. Has dbl & trpl rooms, some with mini-kitchen, & a garden with BBQ pit;

they're adding more rooms with a bar & terrace on top. **$$**

Guesthouse Vashlovani (6 rooms) Vashlovani 90; m 597 185467, 599 856657. Solid modern building with garden & good food. **$$**

Hotel Bio-Yard (10 rooms) Vashlovani 167 m 595 293945. Organic food & swimming pool. **$$**

Lago (5 rooms) Zakatala 53; m 899 349932. 4 blocks east from St Nino on the main road, just east of the centre. **$$**

Lile (11 rooms) David Agmashenebelis 93; \ 254 25988; m 599 580963. Friendly homestay. Head north from the square with the marshrutkas, go past the sports ground, keeping it on your left, & you will see it on the left after a 20min gentle uphill walk. Rates inc meals. **$$**

Robinson Crusoe Davit Agmashenebelis 107; m 599 398832. Recently renovated, with lavish food & homemade wine. **$$**

Around Lagodekhi Very strong tobacco is grown in the Lagodekhi area (as well as kiwi fruit and peanuts), but immediately to the north the mountains rise very steeply to the Caucasus watershed, and it's just a few kilometres to the wild and almost unknown **Lagodekhi National Park** (*www.apa.gov.ge*). The first national park in the Caucasus, it was founded in 1912 by a Polish general in the Tsarist army, on the basis of Prince Demidov's hunting reserve, with forests of chestnut and hornbeam, plus red and roe deer, wolves, bear, lynx, chamois and tur. Red deer numbers dropped from 750 in the 1980s to 150 in 2003 due to poaching, but are now on the increase again. Bearded vultures live here all year, and griffon and cinereous vultures are here from May to September, plus Egyptian vultures passing through on migration. It covers 17,932ha (from 400m to 3,500m), but borders the Zakatala Nature Reserve (in Azerbaijan) and the Tliarata Federal Sanctuary (in Daghestan), so the total protected area is considerable; entry is allowed only to the lowest part, but even a short walk from town soon takes you into fantastically unspoilt forest. The visitor centre (*Vashlovani 197;* m *577 101845;* e *gsulamanidze@ apa.gov.ge*) can provide detailed maps and there are plenty of information boards and waymarked trails, including a short loop for families with 12 information boards. The Ninoskhevi or Great Waterfall Trail (*8.5km; 4–6hrs*) leads up the Ninoskhevi Valley to the waterfall and back the same way, and likewise the Black Grouse Waterfall Trail (*9.5km; 4–5hrs*) leads up the Shromoskhevi Valley and back the same way, with 12 interpretative stations. There's also a 4–5-hour trail between Matsimi and Machis Tsikhe Castle on the Azerbaijan border, and a 3-day, 48km route to Shalvi Klde Lake on the Daghestan border that involves camping and can be done on horseback.

SOUTHEAST OF TELAVI

SIGHNAGHI (*Telephone code 355*) From the Lagodekhi border, the A302 heads south across the Alazani to the junction with the Telavi road 103km from Tbilisi, and 50km from Lagodekhi. The main attraction along this road is the walled city of Sighnaghi, which is more commonly reached from the Tbilisi direction (turning off at km94.5). High on the ridge looking out across the Alazani Valley towards the Caucasus, Sighnaghi was ringed by a 4.5km wall and 28 towers in 1772 by Erekle II (who settled Armenians here to make this a trading centre on the Silk Road). They surround a remarkably large area with a small town at its centre. With its cypress trees and fine 18th- and 19th-century buildings, it's reminiscent of an Italian hill town, featuring a sloping piazza with a large statue at its top end. This was more or less the first town to be identified by the Saakashvili government as a future tourism hotspot and underwent extensive renovation in 2007. Sighnaghi became just a little bit too pristine for its own good and, somehow, just a bit soulless, but it has weathered and mellowed a little since then. While it is undeniably attractive, especially at night when the town's balconies are beautifully illuminated, Sighnaghi does not as yet appear to have attracted the number of tourists that you might reasonably expect in such a self-consciously attractive honeypot. Branded as 'The City of Love', its wedding palace was to be open 24 hours a day to attract Georgian wedding parties as much as foreigners; this may not have worked, but some excellent hotels and restaurants are attracting reasonable numbers of foreign visitors. Efforts to boost tourism continue: a wine festival is held here in October and there are several other events staged throughout the year, such as a Pirosmani Day in May, book fairs, folk performances and even Georgian wrestling.

Getting there and around From Lagodekhi, the junction to Sighnaghi is on a hairpin bend at the east end of Anaga, at km110.5 (49.5km from the border). It's 6km of hairpins up to the town, with a lovely new surface; however, there's little traffic so if you're in a hurry it's better to get off the marshrutka in Tsnori (km117.5/42.5, where the famous gold lion, made in 2300–2000BC and now in the National Museum, was found in a kurgan or burial mound) and take a taxi (*GEL10*) or a shared taxi (*GEL3*), waiting at the junction about 300m west.

The direct road from km94.5 on the Tbilisi highway (by a petrol station and police checkpoint) passes a weird monument at km12/9 and, beyond Nukriani, a big monument of an ogre or ninja turtle with sword and torch, after which you soon have a view of Bodbe Church. Marshrutkas (*GEL6*) leave six times a day from Tbilisi's Samgori metro station (also calling at Isani) and take 90 minutes; the last return to Tbilisi is at 18.00, so a day trip from the capital is possible.

Taxis wait at the top and bottom of the piazza, while buses wait in a large yard (with a ticket kiosk and toilets) behind the police station, across the road from the

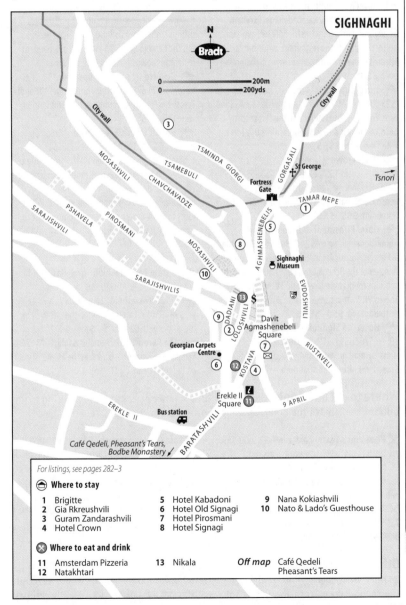

SIGHNAGHI

For listings, see pages 282–3

🛏 **Where to stay**

1	Brigitte	5	Hotel Kabadoni	9	Nana Kokiashvili
2	Gia Rkreushvili	6	Hotel Old Signagi	10	Nato & Lado's Guesthouse
3	Guram Zandarashvili	7	Hotel Pirosmani		
4	Hotel Crown	8	Hotel Signagi		

✖ **Where to eat and drink**

11	Amsterdam Pizzeria	13	Nikala	*Off map*	Café Qedeli
12	Natakhtari				Pheasant's Tears

tourist information centre. Departures are at 07.00, 09.00, 11.00, 13.00, 16.00 and 18.00 to Tbilisi, at 09.20 to Telavi and every 30 minutes from 09.45 to 16.45 and at 17.30 to Tsnori.

⌂ Where to stay
In addition to those below, there are a dozen or so more guesthouses in town. See map, page 281.

Hotels

⌂ **Hotel Kabadoni** (21 rooms) Tamar Mepe 1; ☎ 322 24 0400; www.kabadoni.ge. Excellent by any standards, from the friendly welcome in perfect English to the restaurant, wine-bar, 2 terraces & the spa with saunas, gym & swimming pool. **$$$$**

⌂ **Hotel Signagi** (14 rooms) Chavchavadze 1; ☎ 23 1002; m 595 960770; e hotelsignagi@yahoo.com. Formerly the Hotel Nugo, this has recently been taken over & renovated. Comfortable rooms with TV & bath. **$$$$**

⌂ **Hotel Crown** (12 rooms) Davit Agmashenebelis 10; ☎ 23 1393; m 551 355818, 599 477634; e shotanikvashvili@mail.com. All the rooms here have AC, bath, TV & minibar. There's also a bar & restaurant. **$$$–$$$$**

⌂ **Hotel Pirosmani** (18 rooms) Davit Agmashenebelis Sq 6; ☎ 24 3030; m 599 164104; e hotel_pirosmani@mail.ru; www.rcheuli.ge. Another of the Rcheuli Group boutique hotels, the spacious rooms here have bath, TV, AC & minibar. There's Wi-Fi, tours are available & there's a restaurant too. **$$$–$$$$**

⌂ **Hotel Old Signagi** (10 rooms) Dadiani 19; m 570 505551, 598 770101; e hotel-old-signagi@mail.ru; www.myhotels.ge/old-signagi. Sometimes also called Khalichebi or Carpets House, rooms here are decorated with carpets made in the workshop immediately up the hill, which the owner will give you a tour of (he also offers fishing & other tours); lights & Wi-Fi are weak but the heating is not. B/fast in the independent restaurant downstairs is not inc. **$$$**

⌂ **Brigitte** (13 rooms) Tamar Mepe 13; ☎ 23 8080; m 571 575785; http://brigitte.ge. A friendly & cosy hotel with swimming pool, restaurant & wine cellar. **$$**

⌂ **Nato & Lado's Guesthouse** (7 rooms) Pirosmani 5; m 599 212988, 595 338351; e natolado@gmail.com. Behind the green gate is this simple & welcoming guesthouse, run by Nato who speaks good English (but very quickly). You can sample their own wine & folk singing, & take tours to Davit-Gareja or to Nato's home village to sample their wine & chacha. **$**

Homestays

⌂ **Guram Zandarashvili** Tsminda Giorgi 11; ☎ 23 1029; m 599 750510. **$$**

⌂ **Nana Kokiashvili** Sarajishvili 2; ☎ 23 1829; m 599 795093. Entered through the gift shop on the corner with Dadiani. **$–$$**

⌂ **Gia Rkreushvili** Bebrebis Baghi; ☎ 23 1264. Speaks excellent English. Also at the Market shop on Bebrebis Baghi (☎ 31 156). **$**

✗ Where to eat and drink
There's a handful of other places to eat in addition to the options available at the hotels and guesthouses. See map, page 281.

✗ **Pheasant's Tears** Baratashvili 18; ☎ 23 1556; m 599 534484; www.pheasantstears.com; ⊙ 10.00–22.00 daily. The best place to eat in town, this winebar has wonderfully authentic, natural qvevri wines. **$$$**

✗ **Amsterdam Pizzeria** 9 April 15; m 595 755610. Below the tourist information centre, this does exactly what you'd hope. **$$**

✗ **Café Qedeli** Baratashvili 15; ☎ 23 1048; m 557 644355; e signagi@heim.ge. Supports a home for the disabled in Bodbe. **$$**

✗ **Natakhtari** Kostava 1; ☎ 31 449; ⊙ 10.00–22.00 daily. Traditional Georgian fare. **$**

✗ **Nikala** Loloshvili 4; ☎ 18 9256; ⊙ 09.00–22.00 daily. Serves all the Georgian favourites. **$**

Other practicalities
There's a **tourist information centre** at Kostava 10 (☎ 23 2414; e ticsignagi@gmail.com; ⊙ 10.00–18.00 daily, summer until 19.00) through the second door from the left of the wedding palace (an attractive 19th-century

building), on the east side of Davit Agmashenebelis Square, at the bottom of town. They have good maps of the town (not always available in English) and can book you a bed from about GEL20 without food, GEL25 with half-board. The **Zedashe Cultural Center** (e *zedashemusic@gmail.com; www.zedashe.com*) is not a building but an organisation running a fine choir and putting on concerts.

There's a Bank Republic **ATM** by the Hotel Kabadoni at the top of the main square and another further down; the **post office** (*Davit Agmashenebelis 9;* ⊕ *Mon–Fri 10.00–15.00*) is opposite the Hotel Pirosmani, and there's internet access at Kostava 13.

What to see and do To the right/east (facing the Hotel Signagi) is the **Sighnaghi Museum** (*www.museum.ge;* ⊕ *10.00–18.00 Tue–Sun, Nov–May until 17.00; GEL3*), which was renovated in 2007. In addition to archaeological and ethnographic displays that include Stone Age artefacts, bits of mastodons, chain mail, musical instruments and so on, there is also a permanent exhibition of paintings by Niko Pirosmanashvili, Georgia's most famous painter, who was born not so far away in the village of Mirzaani. At the top of the piazza you can fork right and head down the Tsnori road to the small **basilica of St George**, built in the 17th–18th centuries, with a bare interior and a separate, 12-sided, brick bell-tower set on the base of a defensive tower. There are three **house-museums** in Sighnaghi, commemorating obscure musicians. There's not a lot else to see, but it's a nice place in which to stroll through the backstreets; the most photogenic balconies are on Sarajishvili and Dadiani to the west of Bebrebis Baghi (the Old People's Garden, the triangular plaza southwest of the upper one). At the bottom of Bebrebis Baghi is the **Georgian Carpets Knitting by Old Methods Educational Experiment Centre** (⊕ *Apr–Oct 08.00–18.00 daily*), where you can watch weavers at work on hand looms, taking up to three months to produce a traditional carpet of cotton, silk and wool, with natural dyes such as apple roots and indigo. The best views of the Caucasus are from the very end of Tamar Mepis, to the northeast, and along Chavchavadze.

Guided **horseriding** is available at the excellent Living Roots Ranch (m *599 534484, 598 722848; www.travellivingroots.com; GEL35/1hr to GEL85/3hrs*) – take the Tbilisi road and follow the Bodbiskhevi/Zemo Machkhaani road, ie: go straight on where the main road takes a hairpin to the right.

AROUND SIGHNAGHI It's just 3km from here to the nunnery of **Bodbe** (also known as Ninotsminda), where St Nino, who converted Georgia to Christianity, is buried. Heading south beyond the bottom square and up Baratashvili, you'll soon fork left on the Tbilisi road, and again after about 1km (about 200m after a petrol station and km8/14); a taxi will charge about GEL5 return including a wait. You can take a marshrutka towards Tbilisi, but you'll be getting off after about 5 minutes, just beyond the petrol station, where an asphalt road leads down to the left. It's about 1km more through oak and pine woods to a junction on a bend; the nunnery is 300m to the right in a grove of cypress trees. Across the car park are the pretty decent Pilgrim Refectory and an outdoor café.

The rather tatty, 19th-century buildings were used as a hospital in the communist period and have only recently reopened as a nunnery. Below it stand the older three-storey bell-tower and the church, largely red brick in the western European style with a nave, aisles and chancel, though its core probably dates from the 8th–11th centuries. A church was first built in the 4th century, over the grave of St Nino, the illuminator of Georgia. Most of the kings of Kakheti were crowned here; it has attractive, slightly naïve frescoes, including Adam and Eve on the ceiling of the nave and a Last Judgement at the west end, plus a Baroque golden iconostasis. A big, new church in classic medieval Georgian style is being finished just below. Following signs past the gift shop and the nuns' tranquil cemetery, you can take steps a long way down the hill (allow 15 minutes to come back up) to a tiny chapel where you can witness locals queuing up to collect water from the holy spring that is said to have burst into life after Nino prayed at the spot.

If you turn left at the bend and then right, a good unmade track will take you down the escarpment to Tsnori, about an hour's pleasant walk (less pleasant uphill). Turning right onto the Sighnaghi–Tsnori road, you'll reach the main highway at km117/43, 500m west of the centre of Tsnori; alternatively you can make your way through some residential lanes to reach the main highway further west at about km116/44. There's a new supermarket facing the taxi rank and Tbilisi marshrutkas, and a busy market uphill from the highway at about km117.5, while the bus yard is below, in front of the former railway station.

From Tsnori a rough road continues east into the desert (dominated by wormwood, *Artemisia fragrans*) towards Azerbaijan, to the small town of **Dedoplis-Tskaro** (terminal of a freight-only rail branch). This passes through **Mirzaani**, the painter Pirosmani's home village, where you can visit the house-museum (⊕ *Tue–Sun 10.00–17.00; GEL3*) in his home. Pirosmani Memorial Day is on the third Saturday of October, when celebrations include a concert of Georgian folk music and dance, and a recreation of Pirosmani's painting of a supra, at the round table in the centre of the museum. Marshrutkas run hourly (*to 18.00; GEL7*) from Ortachala in Tbilisi to Rustaveli 37 in Dedoplis-Tskaro; there are two restaurants at Rustaveli 18 and 139. The Guesthouse Megzuri is at Megobroba 97 (m *599 19633; $$*), and there's another at the Vashlovani National Park headquarters at Baratashvili 5 (m *577 101849; $*), where you can also camp.

An even rougher track continues from Dedoplis-Tskaro a long way eastwards to the **Vashlovani National Park**, the driest part of Georgia (with just 300–500mm of rain per year) and where temperatures may be over 40°C in summer. There's very dry steppe and savannah flora (*Tulipa eichleri* is endemic to the banks of the Iori), with light forests of pistachio trees and *Paliurus* thorns, and three species of juniper, including the rare black juniper *Juniperus foetidissima*, and the endemic pear tree *Pirus sakhokiana*, with grassland dominated by *Bothriochloa ischaenum*. Cinereous vultures nest in low junipers, and Egyptian and griffon vultures and great imperial and steppe eagles are also seen here. Animals include wolves, bears, boars, lizards, tortoises, and the very rare striped hyenas and goitred gazelles; there are too many snakes for it to be safe in summer, although they concentrate on hunting hamsters; there are also fossils. The track from Dedoplis-Tskaro ends at a birdwatching spot in the Pantishara Gorge, where bee-eaters, rollers, swallows and bearded and griffon vultures can be seen. This is near the Mjniskhura visitors' village, where you can camp or sleep in a bungalow (*GEL40 for 2*) or dorm (*GEL25pp*); guides are available for GEL50 per day. To the south of Dedoplis-Tskaro, a rough track leads a long way south to the **Dalis-Mta Reservoir**, where there's good fishing and 134 species of birds; it's 8km further to the Kila-Kupra and Takhti–Tefa mud volcanoes, up to 4m in diameter. Northwards from Dedoplis-Tskaro, a yet rougher track leads past the Artsvisi Canyon to **Khornabuji**, a limestone pinnacle above the Alazani Valley, topped by the ruins of a fortress built by Queen Tamar and abandoned in the 17th century; it's not an easy climb up.

Also in Kakheti, though usually visited separately as a day trip from Tbilisi, is the Davit-Gareja complex of monasteries. In what is now virtual desert on the Azerbaijani border at 400–878m is a group of **cave monasteries** founded in the mid 6th century by St David (one of the 13 Holy Syrian Fathers), and his disciple Lukian, after his stay on Tbilisi's Holy Mountain. Over two dozen monasteries have been identified, but only a few are widely known or visited and just three are in use; the roads are still bad, and although cars can get here, it's best to have a 4x4. There's no way to get here other than by mountain bike, car or a trip organised by a tourist agency; it's about 70km, or under two hours, each way from Tbilisi. A day trip costs around GEL150 per person for two people, or about half that if you have your own car; if not you'll usually be accompanied by both a driver and a pretty knowledgeable guide. Tariel Tabashidze (\ *226 48 928;* m *899 648928;* e *tariel_ tabashidze@yahoo.com*), who speaks good German and some English, is a good driver-guide, and charges around US$50 per person (including fuel) to take three or possibly four passengers in a 4x4 Pajero, with about 3 hours at the monasteries. If you're thinking of moving from Tbilisi to a hotel in Sighnaghi or Telavi, ask about a transfer including the detour to Davit-Gareja, which makes a very cost-effective combination. A cheaper but fussier way to reach the monastery complex from Tbilisi is to first take a marshrutka to Gardabani or Sagarejo and then hire a taxi for the round trip from there. This does involve far more hanging around at bus stations, however. Don't be tempted by the daily bus to Udabno village, it's tiny and you won't find a taxi to get to the actual monasteries. There's no government involvement at all, with lots of graffiti, bad paths and no safety warnings; it's not at all easy for the elderly or less able to reach Udabno Monastery or enter the caves. Two hours is enough time to see the Lavra and Udabno monasteries.

HISTORY The area has been populated for at least four millennia, as shown by Bronze Age tombs and pottery; it was then a forested area, but iron smelting eventually led to deforestation in the first half of the 1st millennium BC, and thus climate change and desertification. When the monks arrived in the 6th century they had to construct channels and reservoirs for water, and their 9th-century frescoes show their close relationship with nature, notably an image of wild deer being milked, referring to the deer that gave the first monks sustenance. The monasteries were constructed from natural sandstone caves which were expanded by heating the rock with fire then pouring on water to split it; all have a church with a main nave and a lesser deacon's nave to the north, as well as cells, stores and other chambers. Above, a dozen of the monasteries built towers to send signals between them. The high point of the monastic community was from the 10th century to the coming of the Mongols in the 13th century, although most survived until the early 17th century, when Shah Abbas massacred 6,000 monks (all subsequently canonised) during the Easter Night procession. The monasteries were re-established, but declined and were abandoned in the 19th century, although three have now been re-established.

Their greatest crisis has come in the last 50 years, during which the Soviet army used the area as an artillery range, often aiming directly at the monasteries. From the late 1980s nationalists demanded an end to military training in the area, and it was finally halted in 1991. The military were keen to train here because of its resemblance to Afghanistan, but once that war had finished in 1989 they lost interest. In 1994 the first cultural and biological survey of the area was undertaken,

Kakheti DAVIT-GAREJA

10

and some water channels were reopened. Another monastery, abandoned in the 12th century, was rediscovered in 1995, with domes of a type otherwise unknown in Eastern Christendom, as were 10–12th-century frescoes and graffiti, which have given interesting information on the development of the Georgian alphabet. In mid 1995 the Georgian army resumed training in the area, and in 1996 artillery firing; this was suspended in 1997 after protests and legal action, which was seen as proof of the development of 'civil society' in Georgia. The army appealed to the Supreme Court, but the Church finally joined the battle against it, and the cultural (and touristic) value of the area was eventually preserved.

It's pretty much a lunar landscape in many places, but it's transformed from April to early June when the steppe flowers bloom; the dominant species is the bearded grass *Botriochloa ischaenum*, with other grasses such as *Festuca sulcata*, *Stipa capillata*, *S. lessingiana* and *S. pulcherrima*. There's a healthy population of snakes, lizards and rabbits, and a remarkable range of raptors, such as eagles, vultures, buzzards and owls, that prey on them. In addition there are wolves, bats in many of the caves, and there were goitred gazelles until relatively recently. May and June are the best time for flowers and birds, notably nesting vultures and displaying chukar, as well as huge tadpoles.

TOWARDS DAVIT-GAREJA The best way in is via the A302 (the Tbilisi–Telavi/ Sighnaghi road), turning off at km51, just east of the roundabout at the east end of Sagarejo. From here it takes a little over an hour to the main monastery at Davitis Lavra, crossing the railway and turning right (on asphalt) before km2, and crossing the Iori River at km8. Following signs to **Udabno**, the road climbs to a low col after 20 minutes, passing between two salty lakes (with poor grazing), and turns sharp right after another 10 minutes to skirt around Udabno village to the left. This is one of several villages in the area built for Svans moving from the mountains (there was a fresh influx in 1988 after a terrible avalanche in Ushguli); there's a basic lunch spot here which has accommodation in simple pod-like cabins.

The road on from Udabno is much rougher; you'll soon turn 90° left on to the unpaved road from Rustavi and Gardabani (with huge-motorway-scale signs), from where it's 5km to Davitis Lavra, passing dramatically eroded hills and the tower of Chichkhituri Monastery (founded in the 12th century) and then a seismological station (which records around 100 tremors each year), reaching the Lavra about 25 minutes from Udabno. You can also turn right towards Rustavi to visit the Monastery of St John the Baptist (page 287), about 7km from the junction.

It's also possible to come from the west via **Rustavi**, although the road is much worse. Established on virgin land immediately after World War II, this was Soviet Georgia's leading industrial centre, and its metallurgical plant was the republic's largest employer, closely followed by chemical and pharmaceutical works; these are mostly closed, with Georgia's first 'European-standard' prison (with closed cells) built instead. People moved here from all over the country, especially from mountain areas such as Svaneti, and its population is now in the region of 150,000, but the work conditions were so bad that workers retired at 45 or 50. It's worth noting that the town has no connection with the poet Rustaveli, who came from Meskheti (page 189).

There are a couple of adequate places to stay in Rustavi: the Hotel Rustavi (*60 rooms; Megobroba 32;* \ *341 22 2212;* m *599 192599; www.hotelrustavi.ge;* **$$**), a communist block in the centre; and the Grand Vejini (*57 rooms;* m *568 154949;* **$$$**), a modern business hotel to the north at the start of the bypass, which offers much better food.

It's also possible to take a marshrutka (*GEL2*) from Didube to Gardabani, the last town before the Azerbaijani border, just beyond Rustavi, from where a taxi will charge GEL50–60 to the monasteries and back. The road to Davit-Gareja starts by turning left in front of the immense administration block of the Rustavi metallurgical plant (far grander than the city hall, to show exactly where the true power used to lie), crossing the railway and turning right to pass through a post-industrial wasteland for a considerable distance. Turn left (on an unsigned asphalt road) just after a barrier gate when the biggish white village of Jandara comes into view ahead, and then turn right at the top of the rise (with the white wall of a collective farm on the left), onto a very rough track (also unsigned), which climbs past wrecked armoured personnel carriers onto the very scrubby dry steppe. The Monastery of John the Baptist is visible to the left once on the plateau, where the road becomes slightly smoother; to reach it fork left and soon left again to go down a valley, forking right (with an abandoned collective farm to the left) to park just below the monastery. Returning to the top of the valley and continuing over a ridge, keep to the right where the Sagarejo road joins from the left.

THE MAIN MONASTERIES Set into a cliff face, the **Monastery of John the Baptist** (Natlismcemli), 12km from the main Lavra, was founded in the 6th century, but the main church was completed and painted only in the 13th century (there's a portrait of Queen Tamar in the rear right-hand corner). The refectory, with its Persian-style vaulting, was added in the 17th century, and there's a 19th-century tomb. Above is a tower decorated with blue tiles; it clearly used to be taller, as the foot of a tile cross survives.

Arriving at the main **Lavra Monastery** (Davitis Lavra), park at the houses (there's a fairly horrid toilet in the field), and walk up past the Church Shop (selling icons and candles but no water or snacks). It was founded by St David in the 6th century and is now occupied by notoriously fundamentalist monks who take great exception to noise and especially to inappropriate clothing. Tourists are not allowed in the inner court or, of course, the monks' cells. Inside, go around to the right and

> **INTO AZERBAIJAN**
>
> The main road-crossing into Azerbaijan is at the Tsiteli Khidi (the Krasni Most or Red Bridge), south of Tbilisi. The bridge dates from the 17th century, but a new one was built in 1998, with EU funding. From here the road to Baku crosses largely featureless semi-desert; the railway runs just to the north, with trains taking almost twice as long as buses, about 15 hours from Tbilisi to Baku.
>
> The Lagodekhi crossing leads to a far more interesting route, through the foothills of the High Caucasus and passing the lovely historic town of Shekhi; local buses cross the border from Lagodekhi to Balakan, Zakatala, Qakh and even occasionally to Shekhi. There are also taxis, charging GEL4–6 for the 8km from Lagodekhi to the border and about 5 manat (US$5) for the 15km (lined with walnut trees) on to Balakan. From the far side of the border, marshrutkas run to Baku in about 6 hours (10 manat). There are also marshrutkas from Tbilisi (Ortachala) to Qakh two to four times a day (6 hrs).
>
> In either case you should get your Azerbaijani visa in advance (invitation or hotel booking required). And don't take the 'Azerbaijan Border – Good Luck' road sign too seriously.

down steps in the rock to the lower court: David and Lukian are buried here in the Church of the Transfiguration (Peristvaleba) or Rock Church (plain and with modern icons), near a spring known as the Tears of David. The diagonal lines of the rocks above the outer court and the cells are striking, and very photogenic; channels also lead water off the bare rocks outside the main doorway.

A bad path starts immediately above the Church Shop, reaching a viewpoint over the Lavra in a couple of minutes. This is the path to the **Udabno Monastery** (literally 'Desert'), constructed between the 8th and 10th centuries, on the far side of the ridge; this is in both religious and artistic terms the most important of the monasteries. The trail climbs to the left (alongside a railing) for about 10 minutes and then from a hairpin to the right for another 10 minutes to reach the ridge, with vast views of the desert in all directions. Heading down to the left you'll pass cave-churches with trees growing in their entrances; after No 37 (each has a crudely painted number) you should go up to the left to the refectory. The monks knelt at the stone table down the middle, with their food hidden from each other in hollows; the frescoes of Bible scenes were painted in the 13th and 14th centuries. Just a bit further on, the main church has superb frescoes from the late 10th and early 11th centuries, including the life of St David on the north wall (with a deer feeding on milk), the Virgin and Child in the apse, a Last Judgement on the east wall, and a Deesis in the east apse. The path then continues for 5 minutes along the cliff edge, pocked with cave chambers, before climbing back to a new chapel on the ridge just before a triangulation point, from which you can return to the left past the ruins of a 6th-century chapel, reaching the hairpin bend on the path in about 15 minutes. From the ridge you have superb views across the desert, deep into Azerbaijan, and there are amazing sunsets here.

The monastery with the best frescoes (painted 1212–13, including portraits of Tamar and her son Giorgi IV Lash) is **Bertubani**, which has been 2km inside Azerbaijan since the dying Soviet Union moved the border in 1991 to run across the Udabno ridge (813m; known in Azerbaijan as Keshishdag). Georgia is offering a land swap to regain control of Bertubani and Chichkhituri, but Azerbaijan is being bolshy.

From Lavra it's also possible to hike 11km to **Dodos Rq'a** (meaning 'the horn of Dodo', one of David's disciples), towards the Sagarejo road. Also one of the original 6th-century monasteries, to which monks have recently returned, this has 8th–9th-century frescoes with the oldest surviving traces of Georgian inscriptions.

11

Kvemo (Lower) Kartli
ქვემო ქართლი

Kvemo Kartli, or Lower Kartli, is the area to the southwest of Tbilisi, far smaller and less important than Shida (Inner) Kartli, but attractive and convenient for short trips from the capital. Its population is largely Azerbaijani, while there are also traces of German colonists, who settled in the area of Bolnisi (which they called Luxemburgi) in the 18th century and were deported to Central Asia at the start of World War II, after which they went to Germany; wine in this area is more Germanic in taste than the Georgian norm. The Azerbaijanis are hardworking farmers, and you'll see women in typically Islamic leggings selling apples, pomegranates, persimmons and sweetcorn by the roadside.

MARNEULI AND BOLNISI მარნეული, ბოლნისი

You're most likely to see this area on your way to or from Armenia; the traditional route to Yerevan was that built by Russian military engineers in 1834–75, but as this passes through Azerbaijan the main route is now via Sadakhlo. It's also possible to take the A304 via Bolnisi and Gyumri, which is in pretty poor condition towards the border. It's well worth stopping to see a group of churches south of Bolnisi, which are among the loveliest in the country. The A304 turns off the highway to Rustavi and Baku in the outskirts of Tbilisi and climbs on to the steppe, with an old fort to the right; from km11/86 it drops steeply to the village of Kumisi (where a Canadian firm is drilling for natural gas) and climbs again to Koda, start of the new road to Tsalka (page 293). These villages are both notable for their solid houses of grey tuff, far more typical of Armenia than of Georgia. At km36/70 you'll see the huge Algeti statue on a hill to the left/east; it's a war memorial, depicting a mother handing a sword to her two small sons. From here the road drops to **Marneuli**, not a tourist destination in any sense, but rather a thoroughly drab industrial town, although there is an ATM at Cholokashvili 3. Known as Borchali until 1947, it was also famous for its carpets. The population is 85% Azerbaijani, so you should make a point of stopping at the Mugham Azerbaijani restaurant on 26 May (↖ 790 105949, m 592 396600, 514 399797; e mugam.marneuli@mail.ru).

Passing the modern bus station and turning left at a roundabout by the Public Service Hall, the A310 passes the Marneuli military airbase (bombed by the Russians in 2008) and continues through Azeri-populated villages with gaudy mosques. After 29km it reaches the village of Sadakhlo and 4km further on the modern **border post**, with 24-hour duty-free shops and toilets. In addition to international services, there are local buses from Marneuli to Sadakhlo; taxis wait at the border, and charge GEL 45–50 to Tbilisi.

Forking right in Marneuli, the road heads southwest across a fertile valley, with a new railway parallel. At km59/59 (about 1¼ hours from Tbilisi) it reaches **Bolnisi**, a marginally more attractive town that stretches for 5km along the road, and may

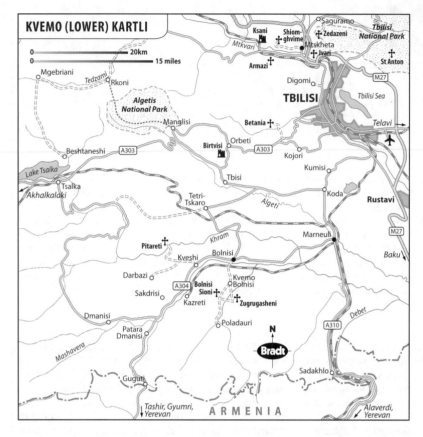

become slightly livelier with the arrival of an Australian–Georgian joint venture extracting gold from slag heaps at Soviet-era copper mines. Bolnisi was founded in 1818 by German colonists who called it Katharinenfeld; from 1921 to 1944 it was named Luxemburg after the German revolutionary Rosa Luxemburg, and since then it has been Bolnisi. There's a tourist office at Sulkhansaba 115 (e *ticbolnisi@ gmail.com;* ⊕ *10.00–18.00 daily, summer until 19.00*). The obvious place to stay (or eat) is the German-owned Hotel Deutsche Mühle at Sioni 4 (☎ *322 61 4750;* e *service@muehle-bolnisi.com; www.muehle-bolnisi.com;* **$$$$**); this beautifully restored watermill now offers both German and Georgian food, indoors or on the terrace. They can also organise local tours and give information on the area's German heritage. The Walkerhaus, a former German school, is also to be restored for the bicentenary of the Germans' arrival in Georgia in 2017, along with the church of Asureti (Elisabethtal), on the road from Koda to Manglisi. In Asureti you can ask for Manfred Tikhonov, who makes good red wine and has restored a typical Swabian half-timbered house.

BOLNISI SIONI AND ZUGRUGASHENI CHURCHES

The **church of Bolnisi Sioni**, 10km south of the town of Bolnisi, is an outstanding example of the earliest Georgian church architecture, and the only surviving example of the original type of three-aisled basilica (without transepts). It's striking for its simplicity and calm (set in a tranquil rose-planted churchyard), and for the lovely green tuff of its western façade (added in the 17th century). The turning to Sioni is just west of km62/56, at the west end of the town centre, marked by a defunct set of traffic lights. From here it's 7km to Sioni, an easy road to walk, although there are also marshrutkas, mainly at peak hours.

Walking down to the bridge you'll see a few typically German houses, solidly built of stone, and a former watermill (now a hotel – page 290) by the river. Ten minutes from the main road you'll pass the railway station and start to climb steadily to a pass 5km from Bolnisi; it's another 1km to the large village of Kvemo Bolnisi that sprawls (in a most un-Germanic way) across a fertile valley; its new mosque is one of the largest in Georgia. You need to fork right at the entrance to the village to bypass it; the church visible ahead on a hilltop is not Sioni but Zugrugasheni. With the village to your left, you'll pass a couple of small abandoned chapels of striking green tuff, below the bare limestone outcrops to the right. It takes 25 minutes on foot to reach the end of Kvemo Bolnisi, and then just ten more to reach the village of Sioni, where you'll find the wonderful Bolnisi Sioni church to the left.

Entering by the west door, you descend a flight of steps into the dark church; the only natural light comes from the door and from a few narrow lancet windows. It's a remarkably long church by Georgian standards, with a six-bay nave. The only frescoes are in the apse, and have faded with time; likewise the carved capitals in the nave have been damaged. The lintel over the north door (now replaced with a copy) gives the church's construction dates as AD478–93; this is the oldest inscription in the Georgian language found within Georgia itself (slightly older ones were found in Palestine). To the northeast a chapel added in the 8th century projects beyond the main apse; there's another, shorter, chapel on the church's southeastern corner. There are also the remains of ambulatories or external aisles along both sides of the church. The separate bell-tower or kolokolnaya, its steps swathed in vines, dates from 1678–88.

To reach the **church of Zugrugasheni**, 2km away on the far side of the valley, with a car you'll have to go via Kvemo Bolnisi, but on foot you can go there directly. Turn left from the Sioni church into the village, fork left after 5 minutes and then turn left down a muddy track; it takes 15 minutes to reach the bridge (just after the junction from Kvemo Bolnisi) and another ten to wind up to the church, strikingly set high on a hill with a high thin barrel dome to add to the effect. The nearest houses are at a farm further up the valley, so it's a nice spot to camp. Built in the 11th century and now disused, it's still a very impressive building, despite the metal sleeve and telegraph poles holding up one pillar. It has a two-bay nave and aisles, plus a separate deacon's nave to the north, and lateral chapels on either side of the apse. To the south a porch has been demolished. Externally there are fine carvings and high niches marking the position of the apses inside the east end. The barrel dome, with its ornamental platform bands, is typical of the 18th century in style.

A **mountain-bike route** designed by Czech consultants and named the Griffon Way (*www.facebook.com/griffonway*) comes here from Tbilisi, via Kojori, Kiketi, Ardisubani, Jorjashvili, Dagheti and Bolnisi; it continues (with extra loops and detours to fortresses and churches) to Samtsevrisi, Opreti and Shulaveri, on the main road south of Marneuli.

FROM BOLNISI TO DMANISI AND THE ARMENIAN BORDER Continuing along the main road towards Armenia, at Kveshi (km36/61) there's a turning west to Pitareti and Darbazi. It is about 8km from the junction to the River Khram and a taxi could be taken to reach this (they wait by the roadside at the junction), although it needs to be a 4x4 in order to cope with the rough track and the crossing of a ford. The **church of Pitareti** built by Tamar's son Giorgi IV in 1213–22 stands alone across the river, by a washed-out bridge. Crossing the river is not that straightforward. The washed-out bridge involves a descent of 3m down a strategically placed tree trunk to a small marshy island. Then, another branch of the Khram needs to be crossed by pushing across another tree trunk lying across the water. Finally, another small branch needs to be waded before jumping a stream to reach the other side. The church plan is cruciform, almost square, with only a porch to the south to spoil its regularity, with three virtually equal apses, a single-bay aisle, and a tall central drum; there are excellent carvings on the eastern façade. The church was surrounded in medieval times by a double wall, with a two-storey gate-tower added in 1696. At Darbazi, reached by turning left halfway to Pitareti, are the remains of a 12th–13th-century royal palace. Pitareti can also be reached by 4x4 or mountain bike from Tetri-Tskaro to the north, 59km from Tbilisi (reached by two marshrutkas per hour from Samgori metro); this was the centre of a Greek community, most of which has now emigrated. In Samshvilde, also on the Khram 4km south of Tetri-Tskaro, there's a cupola church built in AD759–77.

Just 1km further along the main road you'll pass the castle of Kveshi set on a rock to the west above the village of the same name. At km76/42, after passing through the village of Kianeti, a side road heads southeast for 3km to Kazreti, whose apartment blocks are soon very obvious; this is the terminus of the railway and the commercial centre for the upper Mashavera Valley. The main road gets worse, entering a limestone valley rather like a Derbyshire dale; at km88/30 it enters **Patara Dmanisi** (2¼ hours from Tbilisi), known for its cheese factory, sweetbriar jelly, walnuts, hazelnuts, and its mineral springs. Although Patara means 'Little', in fact this is the only village there is here; Didi ('Big') Dmanisi comprises the remains of a medieval fortified town, covering 13ha, on the hill above the village. In addition to the ruins of a palace and baths dating from the 13th and 14th centuries, there's a 6th-century three-nave basilica, with a narthex added by Giorgi IV in 1213–22, which was reopened in 1988. A skull of *Homo erectus* about 1.7 million years old and remains of *Homo sapiens* about 200,000 years old have been found at Dmanisi (pages 14 and 131), as well as Palaeolithic artefacts and the remains of extinct species of rhino, elephant, giraffe, ostrich, bear, sabre-toothed tiger, deer and cow. The site is managed by the Georgian National Museum, and there is a new visitor centre (✆ 322 99 9022; ⊕ *May–Oct 10.00–18.00 Tue–Sun; free*); homestays are also to be provided.

Nearby is **Sakdrisi**, where traces of gold mining almost 5,000 years ago were excavated in 2006; at the end of 2014 the government controversially gave RMG Gold permission to mine there, destroying the remains.

The road climbs through open beech forest, and then out on to the high plateau that characterises Armenia; the first **border post** is at km105/13 (3 hours from Tbilisi), just south of the tiny village of Guguti.

BETANIA AND MANGLISI

It's odd that in both Britain and Georgia, it's the A303 that goes west from the capital to the country's finest ancient monument, from London to Stonehenge and from Tbilisi to Vardzia. The Georgian A303 starts as Chavchavadze Avenue, passing Vake Park and the 'mountain resort suburb' of Tskhneti, before reaching the junction with the minor road from Freedom Square that winds up between Mtatsminda and Narikala as the Kojoris Gzatketsili or Kojori highway. This passes through **Kojori**, 16km from Tbilisi, which, at 1,280m, was a summer resort for the

Georgian nobility; it was also the birthplace of composer Aram Khachaturian, and in February 1921 the site of a last stand by Georgian troops, including the heroic pupils of the Cadet School, against the invading Red Army. Just to the southwest is a ruined 17th-century castle, and 1.5km to the northeast on a wooded spur of Mount Udzo is the Kabeni Church, much visited by barren women. This is a dome church built in the 9th century and altered in both the 12th and 18th centuries. Marshrutka 10 runs to Kojori once or twice an hour from Orbeliani Square in Tbilisi, making this a popular outing for picnicking and strolling.

A rough road turns right 22km from Tbilisi to the **monastery of Betania**, in the wooded Vere Valley, 10km north; its church is a masterpiece of Georgian architecture and is also famous for supposedly housing part of the Virgin Mary's robe. Set on a ridge, it's surrounded on three sides by trees, with only its high barrel dome reaching above. The monastery was founded in the 11th century, and the cruciform church was built in the 12th and 13th centuries; the frescoes were painted in 1207, and include one of just four portraits of Queen Tamar painted in her lifetime. Tourists have been robbed here, so don't go alone. Just to its west is the Darbazuli Church of St George the Triumphant (1196).

Continuing along the A303, at Orbeti there's a turning south to **Birtvisi**, site of a medieval fortress. This is just north of a minor road from Koda, on the main road to Armenia, to Manglisi, which was rebuilt (and launched by Saakashvili with great fanfare as the new Silk Road) and is now used by most of the relatively few marshrutkas that come this way.

The Birtvisi Canyon is described as a 'rock labyrinth' by the Sustainable Tourism Centre, who offer trips of one or two days' easy trekking and simple climbing, for US$50–100 each, depending on numbers (best from September to November). They also run mountain-biking trips across the Trialeti range, starting from Manglisi, the next major village along the main road; there's a lovely 11th-century church set in the trees here. From Manglisi, at 1,200m, the trail climbs north to 1,800m in the 6,822ha **Algetis National Park** (founded in 1965), and descends to Rkoni, 25km and 5–6 hours away; from here a road runs north to Ertatsminda and Kaspi (page 144). The reserve was founded in 1965 to protect the forests of spruce (*Picea orientalis*) and Caucasian silver fir (*Abies nordmanniana*) which cover 80% of its area, as well as over 1,000 plant species and over 80 bird species. There's no visitor centre but national park staff in Manglisi (*Kurorti 4;* m *577 101801, 577 907272;* e *gkavtaradze@apa.gov.ge*) are happy to help. Manglisi is reached by regular marshrutkas from Tbilisi, leaving Station Square hourly between 11.00 and 18.00 (*except at noon; GEL4*). There are two guesthouses, run by Givi Chokheli (*Stalin 38;* m *599 428444;* **$$**) and Akaki Gogichadze (*Gantiadi 1;* m *599 010111;* **$$**).

Further to the southwest the road reaches the Trialeti Plateau, passing to the southwest of several lakes. From the first large lake, Tsalka, a three-day trekking route leads north to the Tedzami Canyon and Rkoni. **Lake Tsalka** is the centre of Georgia's Greek population, still speaking Pontian Ancient Greek. This area was unpopulated as it was laid waste by every army invading from the south, but it is very fertile and ideal for raising cattle and growing potatoes; nevertheless, about a third of the population has emigrated in recent years, although Svans have come in to replace them. The A303 used to be a very bad road, and most traffic from Tbilisi to Akhalkalaki and Vardzia still goes via Borjomi. At Beshtasheni, 5km north of the highway at the east end of Lake Tsalka, there are Cyclopean fortified settlements dating from the 3rd and 2nd centuries BC, with massive stone walls 6m high.

Appendix 1

LANGUAGE

If you have any knowledge of Russian already, you might as well concentrate on that; most older people speak Russian, and there's no prejudice against it. You can study Georgian at summer schools organised by the Centre for Kartvelian (Georgian) Studies, Tbilisi State University, Chavchavadze 1, 380028 Tbilisi (✆ 322 29 0833), or at the International Centre for the Georgian Language, Gogebashvili 18 (✆ 322 98 3285; e rusiko@causcasus.net). A web-based introductory course in Georgian can be found at www.101languages.net/georgian.

There are three phrase books that are of use; my favourite is the *Curzon Dictionary and Phrasebook*, by Nicholas Awde and Thea Khitarishvili (Curzon, London, 1997), which uses a transliterated version of Georgian, easy for us but unintelligible to most Georgians. The *Hippocrene Concise Dictionary* by John J Torikashvili (Hippocrene, New York, 1992) uses Georgian and Latin script. *Georgian – A Learner's Grammar* by G Hewitt (Routledge, London, 1996) is for students rather than travellers.

THE GEORGIAN ALPHABET
This is only a rough guide, as there are many variants, especially in handwriting.

a	ა	k'	პ	t'	ტ	dż	დ
b	ბ	l	ლ	u	უ	ts	ჳ
g	გ	m	მ	ph	ფ	ch'	ჭ
d	დ	n	ნ	k	ქ	x	ხ
e	ე	o	ო	y/ġh	ღ	j	ჯ
v	ვ	p'	პ	q'	ყ	h	ჰ
z	ზ	zh	ჟ	sh	შ		
t	თ	r	რ	ch	ჩ		
i	ი	s	ს	ts	ც		

ESSENTIAL VOCABULARY
These words and phrases have been transliterated for English-speakers. You will also find transliterations for German-speakers, which can occasionally catch you out.

beautiful	*lamazi*	go	*tsadi*
bed	*sats'oli*	good	*kargia*
beer	*ludi*	goodbye	*nakhvamdis*
big	*didi*	good morning	*dila mush-wido-bisa*
bread	*puri*	grandfather	*papa*
breakfast	*sauzme*	grandmother	*bebia*
car	*mankana*	hello	*gamarjobat*
cheap	*ee-api*	help!	*mishwelet!*
cheers!	*gaumarjos!*	home	*sakhli*
	(response *gagimarjos*)	hot	*tskhela*
cheese	*qu-weli*	how are you?	*rogora khar?*
closed	*dak'et'ilia*	how many?	*ramdeni?*
cold	*tsiva*	how much?	*ra ghirs?*
come here	*modi ak*	included	*shedis*
expensive	*ds-weeri*	let's go	*tsa-vayd-et*
father	*mama*	mother	*deda*
fine	*kargad*	my name is …	*me mkvia …*
food	*satch'meli*	new	*akhali*
fruit	*khili*	no	*ara*

old	ds-weli	warm	tbili
open	ghia	water	ts'kali
please	inebet, tu sheidzleba	welcome	mober-zandit
room	otakhi	what is your name?	ra gkvia?
small	patara	when?	rodis?
sorry!	bodishit! map'at'iet!	where is?	sad aris?
thank you	madlobt	who, what, which?	romeli?
vegetables	bost'neuli	yes	diakh, ki, ho
very	dsarlian	you're welcome	arapris

NUMBERS

0	nuli	40	ormotsi
1	erti	50	ormots-da-ori
2	ori	60	samotsi
3	sami	70	samots-da-ti
4	otkhi	80	otkhmotsi
5	khuti	90	okhmots-da-ati
6	ekvsi	100	asi
7	shwidi	101	as-erti
8	rva	200	or-asi
9	tskhra	1,000	at-asi
10	ati	10,000	ati at-asi
11	tert-met'i	100,000	asi at-asi
12	tor-met'i	one million	milioni
13	tsa-met'i	once	ertkhel
14	totkh-met'i	twice	or-jer
15	tkhit-met'i	first	p'irveli
16	tekvs-met'i	second	meore
17	chwid-met'i	third	mesame
18	tvra-met'i	fourth	meotkhe
19	tskhra-met'i	fifth	mekhute
20	otsi	sixth	meekvse
21	ots-da-erti	tenth	meate
30	ots-de-ati	twentieth	meotse

DAYS AND TIME

Monday	orshabati	Friday	p'arask'evi
Tuesday	samshabati	Saturday	shabati
Wednesday	otkhshabati	Sunday	k'wira
Thursday	khutshabati		

today	dghes	now	akhla
tomorrow	khwal	hour	saati
the day after		minute	ts'uti
tomorrow	zeg	in the morning	dilit
yesterday	gushin	in the afternoon	nashuadghevs
What time is it?	romeli saati a?	in the evening	saghamos
It is … o'clock	… saati a		

GEOGRAPHICAL GLOSSARY

airport	aeroporti	museum	muzeumi
avenue	gamziri	mountain	mta
bridge	khidi	river	mdinare
bus station	avtobusebis sadguri	spring	tskaro
castle	tsikhe	square	moedani
church	eklesia	station	sadguri (also voksal)
gorge	khevi	street	kucha
hotel	sastumro	town	kalaki
inner	shida	train	mat'arebeli
lower	kvemo	upper	zemo
map	r'uka		

Appendix 2

BOOKS

Travellers' tales Herodotus and Strabo both wrote about Georgia in classical times.

Anderson, Tony *Bread and Ashes: A Journey through the Mountains of Georgia* Vintage, 2004. A rather episodic but very atmospheric and informative account of hiking through much of the Georgian Caucasus.

Bitov, Andrei *A Captive of the Caucasus* Weidenfeld & Nicholson/Harvill, 1993. Full of associative anecdotes, more a journey through the literary culture of Russia than through Georgia and Armenia.

Brook, Stephen *Claws of the Crab: Georgia and Armenia in Crisis* Sinclair Stevenson, 1992/Picador, 1993.

Bullough, Oliver *Let Our Fame Be Great: Journeys among the Defiant People of the Caucasus* Allen Lane, 2010.

Dumas, Alexandre the elder *Adventures in the Caucasus* (1859) Owen/Chiltern Books, 1962.

Farson, Daniel *A Dry Ship to the Mountains* Michael Joseph, 1994/Penguin, 1995. Following his father's footsteps (see following entry).

Farson, Negley *Caucasian Journey* Evans, 1951/Penguin, 1988.

Griffin, Nicholas *Caucasus: In the Wake of Warriors* Review, 2001. Published in the US as *Caucasus, A Journey to the Land between Christianity and Islam*, taking us through Georgia, Armenia and Azerbaijan on the trail of Shamil.

Keun, Odette *In the Land of the Golden Fleece* London, 1924.

Maclean, Fitzroy *Eastern Approaches* Cape, 1949/Penguin, 2004.

Maclean, Fitzroy *To Caucasus* Cape, 1976.

Marsden, Philip *The Spirit Wrestlers* HarperCollins, 1998. A beautifully written quest to find the surviving Doukhobors, a dissident Russian Orthodox sect, ending up in Javakheti.

Nansen, Fridthof *Through the Caucasus to the Volga* George Allen & Unwin, 1931.

Nasmyth, Peter *Georgia: A Rebel in the Caucasus* Cassell, 1992.

Nasmyth, Peter *Georgia, in the Mountains of Poetry* Curzon/Palgrave, 1998/RoutledgeCurzon, 2006. Nasmyth's are the best books on post-Soviet Georgia.

Pereira, Michael *Across the Caucasus* Geoffrey Bles, 1973.

Russell, Mary *Please Don't Call it Soviet Georgia* Serpent's Tail, 1991.

Severin, Tim *The Jason Voyage* Arrow, 1990.

Shaw, Peter *Hole: Kidnapped in Georgia* Accent Press, 2006. A gripping account of Shaw's 2000 kidnapping ordeal, which also offers insights into the social and political background.

Steavenson, Wendell *Stories I Stole* Atlantic Books/Grove Press, 2003. An evocative view of 1990s Georgia through the eyes of a young foreign correspondent.

Steinbeck, John *A Russian Journal* Viking, 1948/Penguin, 1999. Including 44 pages on Georgia, with photos by Robert Capa.

Thubron, Colin *Where Nights Are Longest* Atlantic Monthly Press, 1984.

History and politics

Allen, W E D *History of the Georgian People* Barnes & Noble, 1971.

Almond, Mark *Post-Communist Georgia: A Short History* CreateSpace Independent Publishing Platform, 2012. A pretty negative view of the first 20 years of Georgia's post-Soviet history.

Asmus, Ronald D *A Little War that Shook the World: Georgia, Russia, and the Future of the West* Palgrave Macmillan, 2009. An account of the five-day war of 2008 by an American diplomat who was involved at the time.

Aves, Jonathan *Paths to National Independence in Georgia 1987–90* School of Slavonic and East European Studies, 1991.

Aves, Jonathan *Post-Soviet Transcaucasia* Royal Institute of International Affairs Post-Soviet Business Forum, 1993.

Aves, Jonathan *Georgia: From Chaos to Stability* Royal Institute of International Affairs, Former Soviet South Project, 1996.

Awde, N (ed) *Ancient Peoples of the Caucasus: A Handbook* Curzon, 1999.

Braund, David *Georgia in Antiquity* Clarendon, 1994.

Chervonnaya, Svetlana *Conflict in the Caucasus – Georgia, Abkhazia and the Russian Shadow* Gothic Image Publications, Glastonbury, 1995.

Coppieters, Bruno and Legvold, Robert (eds) *Statehood and Security: Georgia after the Rose Revolution* American Academy Studies in Global Security, MIT Press, 2005.

Cornell, S E and Frederick Starr, S (eds) *The Guns of August 2008: Russia's War in Georgia* M E Sharpe, 2009.

Curtis, Glenn E (ed) *Armenia, Azerbaijan and Georgia* Bernan Lanham, Maryland, 1995.

de Waal, Thomas *The Caucasus: An Introduction* OUP USA, 2010. Written after the 2008 war, an interesting look at the American and Russian roles in the Rose Revolution and Saakashvili government.

Gahrton, Per *Georgia: Pawn in the New Great Game* Pluto Press, 2010.

Goldenberg, S *A Pride of Small Nations: The Caucasus and Post-Soviet Disorder* Zed Books, London, 1994.

Goltz, Thomas *Georgia Diary: A Chronicle of War and Political Chaos in the Post-Soviet Caucasus* M E Sharpe, 2006. An entertaining and perceptive account of journalistic travels across the Caucasus.

Jones, Stephen F 'Georgia: A Failed Democratic Transition', in *Nations & Politics in the Soviet Successor States* (ed) I Bremmer, Cambridge UP, 1993.

King, Charles *The Ghost of Freedom, A Modern History of the Caucasus* Oxford UP, 2009. Starting with the arrival of Russian imperialists at the end of the 18th century, this deftly picks through the complex strands leading to the modern nations of the Caucasus.

Kleveman, Lutz *The New Great Game* Atlantic Books, 2003. A compelling account of the politicking and arm-twisting involved in extracting oil and gas from Central Asia and the Caspian, and building pipelines across the Caucasus.

Kotkin, Stephen *Stalin Vol 1: Paradoxes of Power, 1878-1928* Penguin, 2014. The latest biography of Stalin, using new archive material to understand his formative years in the Caucasus.

Lang, D M *Last Years of the Georgian Monarchy 1658–1832* Columbia UP, 1957.

Lang, D M *Modern History of Soviet Georgia* Grove Press, 1962.

Lang, D M *The Georgians* Thames & Hudson, 1966.

Rayfield, Donald *Edge of Empires, A History of Georgia* Reaktion/Chicago UP, 2012. A wide-ranging examination of Georgia from the earliest civilisations to the Saakashvili era.

Sebag-Montefiore, Simon *Young Stalin* Weidenfeld & Nicholson, 2007. The prequel to the successful *Stalin: Court of the Red Tsar*. The story of his childhood in Georgia and the revolutionary exploits across the Caucasus that made him what he later became.

Shevardnadze, Eduard *The Future Belongs to Freedom* Sinclair Stevenson, 1991.

Skinner, Peter *Georgia – The Land Below the Caucasus* Mta Publications/Central Books, UK, 2014. A new history of Georgia from Hellenic times to the Soviet takeover of 1921 with 20 detailed maps and well-chosen photos.

Suny, Ronald *The Making of the Georgian Nation* IB Tauris, London 1989; 2nd edition Indiana UP, 1994.

van der Leeuw, Charles *Storm over the Caucasus* Curzon, 1998.

Waters, Chris (ed) *The State of Law in the South Caucasus* Euro-Asian Studies, Palgrave Macmillan 2005. Not just the law, but the way in which judicial, governmental, commercial and criminal interests are bound together in the Caucasus.

Wheatley, Jonathan *Georgia from National Awakening to Rose Revolution: Delayed Transition in the Former Soviet Union* Ashgate Publishing, 2005. A very academic approach to contemporary Georgian history.

Wright, J F R et al (eds) *Transcaucasian Boundaries* UCL Press, 1996.

The Royal Institute for International Affairs has published the following (distributed outside Britain by the Brookings Institute Press):

Coppieters, Bruno *Federalism and Conflict in the Caucasus* 2001.

Herzig, Edmund *The New Caucasus: Armenia, Azerbaijan and Georgia* 1999.

Lynch, Dov *Russian Peacekeeping Strategies in the CIS: The Cases of Moldova, Georgia and Tajikistan* 1999.

Lynch, Dov *The Conflict in Abkhazia* 1998.

MacFarlane, Neil *Western Engagement in the Caucasus and Central Asia* 1999.

Literature

Coffin, Lyn & Jokhadze, Gia *Georgian Poetry: Rustaveli To Galaktion* Slavica Publishers/ Indiana UP, 2013. An anthology of nine poets (some in both English and Georgian) from the 12th to the 20th century.

Karumidze, Zurab *Dagny*, or a *Love Feast* Dalkey Archive Press, 2014. A complicated and ambitious phantasmagoria of mysticism and eroticism via Stalin, Bach's Art of Fugue and much else, this tells the story of Edvard Munch's muse who died in a Tbilisi hotel in 1901.

Khantadze, Archil (transl.) *12 Short Stories - A key to the Georgian mentality* Shemetsneba, 2009. Folk tales, really, that offer humorous insights into the Georgian mind.

Khantadze, Jumber *The Amorous Detective and Other Stories* Shemetsneba 2012. Stories of Georgian life under communism that read a bit like oral history.

Lermontov, Mikhail *A Hero of Our Time* Penguin, 1977. Look out also for the Nabokov translation (1958).

Nicholson, Anthea *The Banner of the Passing Clouds* Granta, 2013. Odd insights into Georgian life under communism (from the 1950s) and during the civil war.

Pasternak, Boris *Letters to Georgian Friends* Penguin, 1971. Letters written by the author of Dr Zhivago in 1931–59, notably to the poets Titsian Tabidze and Paolo Iashvili, both to be killed in Stalin's purges.

Pushkin, Alexander *Journey to Arzrum* (ie: Erzurum) Ardis, 1974. Also included in *Tales of Belkin and other Prose Writings* Penguin, 1998.

Rustaveli, Shota, translated by R H Stevenson *Lord of the Panther Skin* SUNY Press, 1977.

Said, Kurban *Ali and Nino* Vintage, 2000. Set in Baku, an Azeri-Georgian *Romeo and Juliet* by a mystery author; full of romantic colour and period detail.

Wildlife guides

Flint, Vladimir *Field Guide to the Birds of Russia and the Adjacent Territories* Princeton UP, 1984. English, Russian and scientific names.

Gavashelishvili, Lexo et al *A Birdwatching Guide to Georgia* Buneba, 2005. Available through www.nhbs.com in Europe or Buteo Books in the Americas, an excellent guide to birding sites which covers flora and other wildlife.

Knystautas, A *Birds of Russia* Collins, 1993. Good photos, English and scientific (not Russian or Georgian) names.

Miscellaneous

Bender, Friedrich *Classic Climbs in the Caucasus* Diadem, London/Menasha Ridge, Birmingham, Alabama, 1992.

Elliott, Mark *Azerbaijan with Georgia* Trailblazer, 2nd edition 2001.

Gachechildze, Revaz *The New Georgia: Space, Society, Politics* UCL Press, 1995. A geography text.

Goldstein, Darra *The Georgian Feast* University of California Press, 1993.

Häberli, Katharina and Harker, Andrew *Under Eagles' Wings: Hikes, Bikes, Horseback and Skitours in Georgia* H & H Travelogue, 2005.

Holding, Deidre and Nicholas *Armenia with Nagorno Karabakh* 4th edition, Bradt Travel Guides, 2014.

Khutsishvili, Georgi *Tbilisi: A Guide* Progress, USSR, 1981.

Kolomiets, Yury and Solovyev, Aleksey *Trekking in the Caucasus* Cicerone, 1994.

Nasmyth, Peter *Walking in the Caucasus: Georgia* MTA Publications/IB Tauris, 2005.

Rayfield, Donald *The Literature of Georgia: A History* Clarendon, 1994 (revised 2010).

Rosen, Roger *Passport Guide to the Georgian Republic* 3rd edition, Odyssey, 1999.

Saldadze, Anna and Gigauri, David *Be My Guest – the Georgian recipe for cooking success* Sulakauri Publishing, 2013.

Salkeld, Audrey and Bermudez, Jose *On the Edge of Europe: Mountaineering in the Caucasus* The Mountaineers, 1994.

Salkeld, Audrey and Bermudez, Jose *The Forgotten Range of Europe: An Anthology of Exploration in the Caucasus* Teach Yourself, 1993.

Soltes, O. *National Treasures of Georgia* Philip Wilson, 2001.

Wright, John *Tbilisi: A Guide* W & M Press, Tbilisi, 2000. The best maps of Tbilisi, though with south at the top.

Curzon Press's Caucasus series is now published by Routledge Books (*2 Park Sq, Milton Park, Abingdon OX14 4RN, UK;* 020 7017 6000; *www.routledge.com/asianstudies*):

Baddeley, J F *The Russian Conquest of the Caucasus* (reprint).

Mgaloblishvili, Tamila (ed) *Ancient Christianity in the Caucasus.*

WEBSITES

www.amcham.ge and **www.yell.ge**. For business contacts.

www.bu.edu/iscip Academic material.

www.cenn.org The Caucasus Environmental NGO Network (CENN) website; for a round-up of environmental and NGO activities.

www.cia.gov/library/publications/the-world-factbook/geos/gg.html The CIA Factbook.

www.georgiatoday.ge The website of *Georgia Today.*

www.civil.ge Detailed news from Georgia, especially relating to civil society and NGOs.

www.eurasianet.org/resource/georgia General resource pages.

www.georgia.travel The Georgian government's useful tourism website.

http://georgia.usembassy.gov US government information (US embassy in Tbilisi).

www.georgien-news.de A new weekly news magazine, in German only.

http://geotourism.ge Georgian tourism news website.

http://groups.yahoo.com/group/caucasus To post queries on the Caucasus Discussion List.

www.messenger.com.ge The website of *The Messenger.*

www.rferl.org/reports/caucasus-report Radio Free Europe's weekly online newsletter with background analysis (see also *www.rferl.org/section/Georgia/155.*

www.sarke.com The website of the *Daily News* and *Weekly Economic Review.*

http://tbilisiguide.ge A useful online resource about Tbilisi.

http://usa.mfa.gov.ge The Georgian embassy in Washington.

Index

INDEX OF ADVERTISERS

Wanderlust
travel magazine